A Concise Bibliography for Students of English

ARTHUR G. KENNEDY AND
DONALD B. SANDS

Fourth Edition

λ

Eyn yslyk schal syk tor wyssheyt keren,
Dat quade to myden unde de dögede leren.
Dar umme is dyt boek ghedycht,
Dyt is de syn unde anders nicht.

. . . .

Wultu wetten der werlde stad,
So koep dyt boek, dat is rad!

6831–6842
Reinke de vos
Printed Lübeck 1498

A CONCISE BIBLIOGRAPHY FOR STUDENTS OF ENGLISH

FOURTH EDITION

ARTHUR G. KENNEDY
DONALD B. SANDS

STANFORD UNIVERSITY PRESS
STANFORD, CALIFORNIA

Stanford University Press
Stanford, California

Library of Congress Catalog Card Number: 60–8564

Printed in the United States of America
First published 1940
Fourth edition, 1960

PREFACE

The present edition represents a substantial revision of the third edition of 1954. Six modifications in particular may be noted. First, each work is entered only once, and not, as in previous editions, in all the various categories into which it might conceivably fall. Second, the number of categories has been increased approximately fourfold in an effort to make the mere presence of an entry within a particular category define the nature and scope of the entry itself. Third, bibliographies within works are mentioned if they seem likely to be of use to a research student in English. Fourth, whenever it seemed advisable to note whether a relatively significant work is printed with double or triple column pages, such notation has been made. Fifth, there has been a slight general reorganization away from late nineteenth-century titles toward those of the twentieth century, a shift perhaps most apparent in such categories as The New Criticism, Structural Linguistics, and Censorship and the Law.

Sixth, and perhaps most strikingly, the new edition is much longer. In the last decade English studies have become increasingly complex and diffuse, and innumerable twilight zones now connect what were once isolated academic spheres. The English scholar is no longer concerned solely with philology and historical study; he now makes use of psychology, sociology, religion, statistics, and other peripheral disciplines in ways that no teacher of the last generation would have thought seemly, or even remotely feasible. It is this complexity and diffusion, together with the enormous increase of titles for the years 1950–59, which explains the almost threefold expansion of the fourth edition overs its predecessors. Heretofore, it might also be noted, bibliographies for English scholars have listed only reference literature which bore significantly on humanistic and linguistic study. This literature the fourth edition has also listed; but it has added, with the help of specialists in areas unfamiliar to the editor, a series of studies and monographs in each of the major periods and fields of English literature. As a result, each category in the early chapters on literature offers a well-rounded reading list which in itself could stand as the basis for a specialized course given on the upper undergraduate or graduate level.

I am grateful to Boston College for making available to me the services of two graduate assistants for the preparation of this volume. Of the many kind, helpful, and forbearing librarians I consulted, I should like to single out as the most helpful of all Mr. Foster Palmer of the Widener Library at Harvard and Mr. John O'Loughlin of the Bapst Library of Boston College. I am indebted to

Miss Dorothy Conklin of the Serials Division of the Widener for allowing me to use the enormous serials file of the University in checking the terminal dates in Chapter VI. Finally, I would like to thank the following of my colleagues on the faculty of Boston College for reviewing sections in their particular fields: Leonard R. Casper, P. Albert Duhamel, Bernard P. Farragher, Albert M. Folkard, Leo J. Hines, Edward L. Hirsh, Richard E. Hughes, John L. Mahoney, John J. McAleer, Francis J. McDermott, and Maurice J. Quinlan.

DONALD B. SANDS

Boston, Massachusetts
August 1960

TABLE OF CONTENTS

CHAPTER I

THE PERIODS OF ENGLISH LITERATURE

1. Northup, Clark S. A Register of Bibliographies of the English Language and Literature. With contributions by Joseph Quincy Adams and Andrew Keogh. New Haven, Yale Univ. Press, 1925. 507 (double column) pp. —In the series Cornell Studies in English.

2. Van Patten, Nathan. An Index to Bibliographies and Bibliographical Contributions Relating to the Work of American and British Authors 1923–1932. Stanford Univ. Press, 1934. vii + 324 pp.

3. Mummendy, Richard. Language and Literature of the Anglo-Saxon Nations as Presented in German Doctoral Dissertations 1885–1950. Charlottesville, Bibliographical Society of the University of Virginia, 1954. xvi + 200 pp.

4. Répertoire bio-bibliographique de la Société des écrivains canadiens. Montréal, Éditions de la Société des écrivains canadiens, 1954. xix + 256 pp.

5. Miller, E[dmund] Morris. Australian Literature. A bibliography to 1938. Extended to 1950, edited with a historical outline and descriptive commentaries by Frederick T. Macartney. Rev. ed. Sydney, Angus and Robertson, 1956. ix + 503 (double column) pp.—Original ed. 1940.

6. Bateson, F[rederick] W., ed. The Cambridge Bibliography of English Literature. Vol. I: 600–1660; Vol. II: 1660–1800; Vol. III: 1800–1900; Vol. IV: Index. New York, Macmillan Co., 1941. 4 (double column page) vols.—Also *Volume V: Supplement A.D. 600–1900*, edited by George Watson, Cambridge Univ. Press, 1957, xiv + 710 (double column) pp.

7. Watson, Geo., ed. The Concise Cambridge Bibliography of English Literature 600–1950. Cambridge Univ. Press, 1958. xi + 272 pp.

8. Watters, Reginald Eyre. A Check List of Canadian Literature and Background Materials 1628–1950. Being a comprehensive list of the books which constitute Canadian literature written in English, together with a selective list of other books by Canadian authors which reveal the backgrounds of that literature. University of Toronto Press, 1959. xx + 789 pp.

---

9. Abstracts of English Studies. Boulder, University of Colorado, 1958–date. —Monthly. Coverage of over forty journals.

10. Bibliography of English Language and Literature. Cambridge, Eng., Bowes and Bowes for the Modern Humanities Research Association, 1921 (for 1920)–date.—Annual. Now somewhat behind, the 1957 volume covering the year 1948.

11. Dissertation Abstracts. Abstracts of dissertations and monographs in microfilm. Ann Arbor, Mich., University Microfilms, 1938–date.—Monthly. Formerly *Microfilm Abstracts.*

12. Progress of Medieval and Renaissance Studies in the United States of America. Boulder, Col., American Council of Learned Societies, Committee on Medieval Latin, Mediaeval Academy of America, 1923–date.—Two issues a year (since 1935).

13. Year's Work in English Studies. Oxford Univ. Press for the English Association, 1921 (for 1919/20)–date.—Annual.

---

§1. OUTLINES, ANNALS, AND LITERARY LEXICONS

17. Wheeler, Wm. A. Explanatory and Pronouncing Dictionary of the Noted Names of Fiction. Including also familiar pseudonyms, surnames bestowed on eminent men, and analogous proper appellations often referred to in literature and conversation. With an appendix by Charles G. Wheeler. 19th ed. Boston, Houghton Mifflin Co., 1889. xxxv + 440 (double column) pp.—Original ed. 1863; nineteenth ed. reprinted 1917.

18. Ryland, Frederick. Chronological Outlines of English Literature. London, Macmillan Co., 1890. xii + 351 pp.—Reprint 1914.

19. Allibone, S[amuel] Austin. A Critical Dictionary of English Literature and British and American Authors, Living and Deceased, from the Earliest Accounts to the Middle of the Nineteenth Century. Vol. I: A–J; Vol. II: K–S; Vol. III: T–Z. Philadelphia, Childs and Peterson [Vol. I] and J. B. Lippincott and Co. [Vols. II and III], 1858–71. 3 (double column page) vols.—Also John Foster Kirk, *A Supplement to Allibone's Critical Dictionary,* Philadelphia, J. B. Lippincott Co., 1891, 2 (double column page) vols.

20. Magnus, Laurie. A Dictionary of European Literature. Designed as a

companion to English studies. 2nd impression rev. with addenda. London, George Routledge and Sons, 1927. xii + 605 (double column) pp.—Original ed. 1926.

21. Young, John L. English from Piers Plowman to the Forsyte Saga. A chronological record with notes and a list of available editions. Introduction by R. Brimley Johnson. London, W. and G. Foyle, 1928. 75 + xxii pp.

22. Ghosh, J[yotish] C., and Withycombe, E[lizabeth] G. Annals of English Literature 1475–1925. The principal publications of each year together with an alphabetical index of authors with their works. Oxford, Clarendon Press, 1935. vi + 340 leaves.—The annals 1901–25 and the index by E. G. Withycombe.

23. Thrall, Wm. Flint, and Hibbard, Addison. A Handbook of Literature. With an outline of literary history English and American. New York, Odyssey Press, 1936. xi + 579 pp.—Revised ed. 1960.

24. Patrick, David, ed. Chambers's Cyclopaedia of English Literature. Vol. I: 7th–17th Century, revised by J. Liddell Geddie; Vol. II: 18th Century, revised by J. Liddell Geddie; Vol. III: 19th–20th Century, revised and expanded by J. Liddell Geddie and J. C. Smith. Revised ed. London, W. and R. Chambers Ltd., 1927–38. 3 (double column page) vols.—Original ed. 1844 in 2 vols.; another ed. 1901 in 3 vols. A series of short, signed biographies grouped under literary periods with each period introduced by a short essay.

25. Harvey, Paul. Oxford Companion to English Literature. 3rd ed. Oxford, Clarendon Press, 1946. viii + 932 (chiefly double column) pp.—Original ed. 1932; second ed. 1937; third ed. frequently reprinted, as in 1955. See also the *Concise Oxford Dictionary of English Literature*, edited by John Mulgan, Oxford Univ. Press, 1939, viii + 567 (double column) pp.

26. Watt, Homer A. and Wm. W. A Handbook of English Literature. New York, Barnes and Noble Inc., 1946. ix + 430 pp.—Number 258 in the series College Outlines and Everyday Handbooks.

27. Barnhart, Clarence L. The New Century Handbook of English Literature. With the assistance of William D. Halsey. New York, Appleton-Century-Crofts Inc., 1956. vii + 1167 (double column) pp.

28. Grebanier, Bernard D. N. English Literature. Vol. I: From the Beginnings to the End of the Eighteenth Century, Revised ed.; Vol. II: [To the Present]. Great Neck, N.Y., Barron's Educational Series Inc., 1948–58. 2 vols.—Original ed. vol. one 1948.

§2. BIOGRAPHICAL REFERENCE: WRITERS

[See also §212. Biographical Reference: General.]

32. Adams, Oscar F. A Dictionary of American Authors. 5th ed. rev. and enl. Boston, Houghton Mifflin Co., 1905. viii + 587 (double column) pp.—Original ed. 1897. A development of Adams's *Brief Handbook of American Authors,* Boston, Houghton Mifflin Co., 1884, x + 188 pp.

33. Williamson, Claude C. H. Writers of Three Centuries 1789–1914. Philadelphia, George W. Jacobs and Co., [1920]. 515 pp.

34. Adcock, A[rthur] St. John. Gods of Modern Grub Street. Impressions of contemporary authors. Thirty-two portraits by E. O. Hoppé. London, Sampson Low, Marston and Co., [1923]. vi + 327 pp.

35. Hamilton, Cosmo. People Worth Talking About. With caricatures by Conrado Massaguer. New York, Robert M. McBride and Co., 1933. xiv + 283 pp.

36. Colby, Elbridge. English Catholic Poets. Milwaukee, Wis., Bruce Publ'ing Co., 1936. xix + 208 pp.

37. Walbridge, Earle. Literary Characters Drawn from Life. "Romans à clef," "drames à clef," real people in poetry with some other literary diversions. New York, H. W. Wilson Co., 1936. 192 pp.—Also *Index and Key to Literary Characters Drawn from Life,* prepared by the class in Advanced Reference 1936–37 of the University of Illinois Library School, New York, H. W. Wilson Co., 1938, 32 (double column) pp.

38. Kunitz, Stanley J., and Haycraft, Howard. American Authors 1600–1900. A biographical dictionary of American literature complete in one volume with 1300 biographies and 400 portraits. New York, H. W. Wilson Co., 1938. vi + 846 (double column) pp.—Reprint 1949.

39. Romig, Walter. The Book of Catholic Authors. First series. Informal self-portraits of famous modern Catholic writers. . . . Detroit, Mich., Walter Romig and Co., 1942. viii + 9–302 pp.—Also *Second Series,* 1943, viii + 9–332 pp. *Third Series,* 1945, ix + 11–316 pp. *Fourth Series,* [1948], x + 11–330 pp. *Fifth Series,* [1957], 302 pp. Since the *Third Series,* published in Grosse Pointe, Mich.

40. MacCarthy, B[ridget] G. The Female Pen. Vol. I: Women Writers. Their contribution to the English novel 1621–1744; Vol. II: The Later Women Novelists 1744–1818. Cork, Ireland, Cork Univ. Press, 1944–47. 2 vols.

41. Phelps, Gilbert. Living Writers. Being critical studies broadcast in the B.B.C. Third Programme. London, Sylvan Press, 1947. 157 pp.

42. Noyce, Wilfred. Scholar Mountaineers. Pioneers of Parnassus. London, Dennis Dobson Ltd., 1950. 164 pp.—"A Short Bibliography," pp. 163–164.

43. Wallace, W[illiam] Stewart. A Dictionary of North American Authors Deceased before 1950. Toronto, Ryerson Press, 1951. ix + 525 (double column) pp.—A list of names giving where possible birth and death dates, places of birth and death, vocations, and references to full biographic treatment.

44. Hoehn, Matthew, ed. Catholic Authors. Contemporary biographical sketches 1930–47. Newark, N.J., St. Mary's Abbey, 1948. xvii + 812 pp. —Also *Catholic Authors, . . .* 1948–52, Newark, N.J., St. Mary's Abbey, 1952, xiv + 633 pp.

45. Kunitz, Stanley J., and Haycraft, Howard. British Authors before 1800. A biographical dictionary complete in one volume with 650 biographies and 220 portraits. New York, H. W. Wilson Co., 1952. vii + 584 (double column) pp.—Reprint 1956.

46. Kunitz, Stanley J., and Haycraft, Howard. British Authors of the Nineteenth Century. Complete in one volume with 1000 biographies and 350 portraits. New York, H. W. Wilson Co., 1936. [v] + 677 (double column) pp.—Reprint 1955.

47. Kunitz, Stanley J., and Haycraft, Howard. Twentieth Century Authors. A biographical dictionary of modern literature complete in one volume with 1850 biographies and 1700 portraits. New York, H. W. Wilson Co., 1942. vii + 1577 (double column) pp.—Reprint 1950. *First Supplement*, by Stanley J. Kunitz and Vineta Colby, New York, H. W. Wilson Co., 1955, vii + 1123 (double column) pp.

48. Breit, Harvey. The Writer Observed. Cleveland, World Publ'ing Co., 1956. 287 pp.—Biographical essays from *New York Times* interviews.

49. Browning, D[avid] C. Everyman's Dictionary of Literary Biography English and American. Compiled after John W. Cousin. London, J. M. Dent and Sons, 1958. x + 752 pp.—In the series Everyman's Reference Library. Earlier editions, as that of 1910, bear the title *A Short Biographical Dictionary of English Literature.*

50. Handley-Taylor, Geoffrey. The International Who's Who in Poetry. Vol. I: A to L; Vol. II: M to Z. London, Cranbrook Tower Press, 1958. 2 vols.

§3. BRITISH LITERATURE: HISTORICAL SURVEYS

54. Brink, Bernhard ten. History of English Literature. Vol. I: To Wyclif, translated by Horace M. Kennedy; Vol. II: Wyclif, Chaucer, Earliest Drama, Renaissance, translated by William Clark Robinson; Vol. III: From the Fourteenth Century to the Death of Surrey, translated by L. Dora Schmitz and edited by Alois Brandl. London, George Bell and Sons, 1895–96. 3 vols.—Original Ger. ed. 1887–93 in 2 vols.; frequent reprints of Eng. tr., as in 1926. There was a 2nd Ger. ed. 1899–1912 in 2 vols.
55. Gosse, Edmund. Modern English Literature. New York, D. Appleton and Co., 1897. vii + 416 pp.—In the series Literatures of the World. A treatment of English literature from Chaucer to Tennyson.
56. Körting, Gustav. Grundriss der Geschichte der englischen Literatur von ihren Anfängen bis zur Gegenwart. 5. Aufl. Münster, H. Schöningh, 1910. xv + 443 pp.—Volume I, no. 1, in the series Sammlung von Kompendien für das Studium und die Praxis. Original ed. 1887.
57. Mair, G[eorge] H. Modern English Literature. From Chaucer to the present day. New York, Henry Holt and Co., 1914. ix + 310 pp.—Number 27 in the series Home University Library of Modern Knowledge. A development of Mair's *English Literature,* Modern, New York, Henry Holt and Co., 1911, vii + 8–256 pp.
58. Jusserand, J[ean] J. A Literary History of the English People from the Origins to the Civil War. London, T. F. Unwin Ltd., 1925–26. 2 vols. (vol. 1 third ed.; vol. 2 second ed.)—Original ed. 1895–1909 in 3 vols.
59. Ward, A[dolphus] W., and Waller, A[lfred] R., eds. The Cambridge History of English Literature. Vol. I: From the Beginnings to the Cycles of Romance; Vol. II: The End of the Middle Ages; Vol. III: Renascence and Reformation; Vol. IV: Prose and Poetry from Sir Thomas North to Michael Drayton; Vol. V: The Drama to 1642, Part I; Vol. VI: The Drama to 1642, Part II; Vol. VII: Cavalier and Puritan; Vol. VIII: The Age of Dryden; Vol. IX: From Steele and Addison to Pope and Swift; Vol. X: The Rise of the Novel: Johnson and His Circle; Vol. XI: The Period of the French Revolution; Vol. XII: The Nineteenth Century, Part I; Vol. XIII: The Nineteenth Century, Part II; Vol. XIV: The Nineteenth Century, Part III; Vol. XV: General Index. Cambridge Univ. Press, 1908–27. 15 vols.—Extensive bibliographies at the end of each vol. except the last. A "cheap edition" in 15 vols. without bibliographies was issued by Cambridge in 1932.

60. Saintsbury, Geo. A Short History of English Literature. [Corrected ed.] New York, Macmillan Co., 1929. xix + 818 pp.—Original ed. 1898; corrected ed. reprinted 1937.

61. Legouis, Émile. A Short History of English Literature. Translated by V. F. Boyson and J. Coulson. Oxford, Clarendon Press, 1934. xvi + 404 pp.

62. Gosse, Edmund, and Garnett, Richard. English Literature. An illustrated record. Vols. I and II: From the Beginnings to the Age of Milton; Vols. III and IV: From Milton to the Age of Tennyson. New ed. Four volumes in two. With a supplementary chapter on the literature from 1892 to 1922 by John Erskine. New York, Macmillan Co., 1935. 2 vols.—Original ed. 1903 vol. I, 1904 vol. II, 1903 vol. III, and 1904 vol. IV.

63. Schirmer, W[alter] F. Geschichte der englischen Literatur von den Anfängen bis zur Gegenwart. Halle a. S., Max Niemeyer Verlag, 1937. 679 pp.—"Ausgewählte Bibliographie," pp. 591–653.

64. Sampson, Geo. The Concise Cambridge History of English Literature. Cambridge Univ. Press, 1941. xv + 1094 pp.

65. Legouis, Émile, and Cazamian, Louis. A History of English Literature. The Middle Ages and Renascence (650–1660), by Émile Legouis. Translated by Helen D. Ervine. Modern Times (1660–1947), by Louis Cazamian. Translated by W. D. MacInnes and the author. Preface by Arthur Quiller-Couch. London, J. M. Dent and Sons, 1947. xxi + 1401 pp.—Original Fr. ed. 1924; original Eng. ed. 1926 in 2 vols.; first one-volume Eng. ed. 1930; reprint of 1947 ed. 1957.

66. Craig, Hardin, ed. A History of English Literature. Old and Middle English Literature from the Beginnings to 1485, by George K. Anderson. The Literature of the English Renaissance 1485–1660, by Hardin Craig. The Literature of the Restoration and the Eighteenth Century 1660–1798, by Louis I. Bredvold. The Literature of the Nineteenth and the Early Twentieth Centuries 1798 to the First World War, by Joseph Warren Beach. New York, Oxford Univ. Press, 1950. xiii + 697 pp.

67. Praz, Mario. Cronache letterarie anglosassoni. Vol. I: Cronache inglesi; Vol. II: Cronache inglesi e americane. Rome, Edizioni di Storia e Letteratura, 1950–51. 2 vols.

68. Osgood, Chas. Grosvenor. The Voice of England. A history of English literature. With a chapter in postscript on English literature since 1910 by Thomas Riggs Jr. 2nd ed. New York, Harper and Bros., 1952. 671 pp. —Original ed. 1935.

69. Parry, Thos. A History of Welsh Literature. Translated from the Welsh by H. Idris Bell. Oxford Univ. Press, 1955. xii + 534 pp.—"Bibliographical Notes," pp. 499–501.

70. Ward, A[lfred] C. Illustrated History of English Literature. Illustrations collected by Elizabeth Williams. Vol. I: Chaucer to Shakespeare; Vol. II:

Ben Jonson to Samuel Johnson; Vol. III: Blake to Bernard Shaw. London, Longmans, Green and Co., 1953–55. 3 vols.

71. Compton-Rickett, Arthur. A History of English Literature. From earliest times to 1916. London, Thomas Nelson and Sons, 1956. xi + 702 (double column) pp.

§4. ENGLISH LITERATURE: CLASSICAL INFLUENCES

[See also §70. Aristotle.]

75. Lathrop, Henry B. Translations from the Classics into English from Caxton to Chapman 1477–1620. Madison, University of Wisconsin Press, 1933. 350 pp.—Number 35 in the series University of Wisconsin Studies in Language and Literature.

---

76. Cunliffe, John W. The Influence of Seneca on Elizabethan Tragedy. London, Macmillan and Co., 1893. iv + 155 pp.

77. Taylor, Henry Osborn. The Classical Heritage of the Middle Ages. New York, Columbia Univ. Press, 1901. xv + 400 pp.—In the series Columbia University Studies in Literature.

78. Canning, Albert S. G. British Writers on Classic Lands. A literary sketch. London, T. Fisher Unwin, 1907. 296 pp.

79. Collins, John C. Greek Influence on English Poetry. Edited with preface by Michael Macmillan. London, Isaac Pitman and Sons, 1910. xiv + 127 pp.

80. Gayley, Chas. M. The Classic Myths in English Literature and in Art. New ed. rev. and enl. Boston, Ginn and Co., 1911. xli + 597 pp.—Original ed. 1855; reprint of new ed. 1939.

81. Gordon, G[eorge] S., ed. English Literature and the Classics. Oxford Univ. Press, 1912. 252 pp.—Lectures by various persons on tragedy, platonism, Theophrastus, Greek romances, Ciceronianism, Virgil, Ovid, Satura, and Senecan tragedy.

82. Goldmark, Ruth I. Studies in the Influence of the Classics on English Literature. Preface by Ashley H. Thorndike. Biographical note by Felix Adler. New York, Columbia Univ. Press, 1918. xii + 106 pp.

83. Nitchie, Elizabeth. Virgil and the English Poets. New York, Columbia Univ. Press, 1919. ix + 251 pp.

84. Lucas, F[rank] L. Seneca and Elizabethan Tragedy. Cambridge Univ. Press, 1922. [viii] + 136 pp.

85. Whipple, T[homas] K. Martial and the English Epigram from Sir Thomas Wyatt to Ben Jonson. Berkeley, University of California Press, 1925. 279–414 pp.—Volume X, no. 4, in the series University of California Publications in Modern Philology. "Bibliography," pp. 407–411.

86. Murray, Gilbert. The Classical Tradition in Poetry. Cambridge, Mass., Harvard Univ. Press, 1927. xvii + 274 pp.—The Charles Eliot Norton Lectures.

87. Emperor, John Bernard. The Catullian Influence in English Lyric Poetry circa 1600–1650. Columbia, University of Missouri Press, 1928. 133 pp. —Volume III, no. 3, in the series University of Missouri Studies.

88. Bush, Douglas. Mythology and the Renaissance Tradition in English Poetry. Minneapolis, University of Minnesota Press, 1932. ix + 360 pp. —"A chronological conspectus of mythological poems . . . up to 1680," pp. 301–323, "Bibliography," pp. 327–344.

89. Bush, Douglas. Mythology and the Romantic Tradition in English Poetry. Cambridge, Mass., Harvard Univ. Press, 1937. xvi + 647 pp.—Volume XVIII in the series Harvard Studies in English. A chronological list of mythological poems 1681–1936, pp. 539–592. "Bibliography," pp. 595–627.

90. Baldwin, Chas. Sears. Renaissance Literary Theory and Practice. Classicism in the rhetoric and poetic of Italy, France, and England 1400–1600. Edited with introduction by Donald Lemen Clark. New York, Columbia Univ. Press, 1939. xiv + 251 pp.—Reprint Gloucester, Mass., Smith, 1959.

91. McPeek, James A. S. Catullus in Strange and Distant Britain. Cambridge, Mass., Harvard Univ. Press, 1939. xvii + 411 pp.—Volume XV in the series Harvard Studies in Comparative Literature.

92. Stern, Bernard H. The Rise of Romantic Hellenism in English Literature 1732–1786. Menasha, Wis., George Banta Publ'ing Co. for the author, 1940. x + 182 pp.

93. Thomson, J[ames] A. K. The Classical Background of English Literature. London, George Allen and Unwin Ltd., 1948. 272 pp.

94. Highet, Gilbert. The Classical Tradition. Greek and Roman influences on Western culture. New York, Oxford Univ. Press, 1949. xxxviii + 763 pp.

95. Thomson, J[ames] A. K. Classical Influences on English Poetry. London, George Allen and Unwin Ltd., 1951. 271 pp.—A treatment of the epic, didactic poetry, tragedy, comedy, the lyric, pastoral poetry, satire, and the epigram.

96. Norton, Dan S., and Rushton, Peters. Classical Myths in English Literature. With an introduction by Charles Grosvenor Osgood. New York, Rinehart and Co., 1952. xvii + 444 pp.

97. Palmer, Ralph Graham. Seneca's De Remediis Fortvitorum and the Elizabethans. An essay on the influence of Seneca's ethical thought in the sixteenth century. . . . Chicago, Institute of Elizabethan Studies, 1953. [ix] + 66 pp.—Number 1 in the series Institute of Elizabethan Studies.

98. Seznec, Jean. The Survival of the Pagan Gods. The mythological tradition and its place in Renaissance humanism and art. Translated from the French by Barbara F. Sessions. New York, Pantheon Books Inc., 1953. xvii + 376 pp.—Volume XXXVIII in the Bollingen Series.—Original Fr. ed. 1940. The Pantheon translation was revised by the author. "Bibliography," pp. 327–345.

99. Boughner, Daniel C. The Braggart in Renaissance Comedy. A study in comparative drama from Aristophanes to Shakespeare. Minneapolis, University of Minnesota Press, 1954. ix + 328 pp.—"Bibliographical Supplement," pp. 312–318.

100. Spencer, Terence. Fair Greece Sad Relic. Literary philhellenism from Shakespeare to Byron. London, Weidenfeld and Nicolson, 1954. xi + 312 pp.

§5. LATIN LITERATURE CHIEFLY MEDIEVAL: ANGLO-LATIN AND SOME GENERAL EUROPEAN TITLES

[For related materials in lyric poetry see also §45. Surveys: The Old and Middle English Periods.]

104. Franklin, Alfred. Dictionnaire des noms, surnoms, et pseudonymes latins de l'histoire littéraire du moyen âge 1100 à 1530. Paris, Libraire de Firmin-Didot, 1875. xi + 683 (double column) pp.

105. Little, A[ndrew] G. Initia operum Latinorum quae saeculis xiii, xiv, xv attribuntur secundum ordinem alphabeti disposita. Manchester, Eng., University Press, 1904. xv + 275 pp.—Number 2 in the Historical Series. Reprint New York, Burt Franklin, 1958, volume VII in the Burt Franklin Bibliographical Series.

106. Baxter, J[ames] H., Johnson, C[harles], and Willard, J[ames] F. An Index of British and Irish Latin Writers 400–1520. Nogent-le-Rotrou,

France, Impr. Daupeley-Gouverneur, 1932. 115 pp.—"Extrait du Bulletin Du Cange, tome VII, 1932 [pp. 110–219]."

107. Ogilvy, J[ack] D. A. Books Known to Anglo-Latin Writers from Aldhelm to Alcuin 670–804. Cambridge, Mass., Mediaeval Academy of America, 1936. xxi + 109 pp.—Number 2 in the series Studies and Documents of the Mediaeval Academy of America.

---

108. Symonds, John Addington. Wine, Women, and Song. Medieval Latin students' songs now first translated into English verse, with an essay. London, Chatto and Windus, 1884. xv + 208 pp.—Reprint 1925. Translations chiefly from the "Carmina Burana."

109. Manitius, Max. Geschichte der christlich-lateinischen Poesie bis zur Mitte des achten Jahrhunderts. Stuttgart, J. G. Cotta, 1891. ix + 518 pp.

110. Raby, F[rederic] J. E. A History of Christian-Latin Poetry from the Beginnings to the Close of the Middle Ages. Oxford, Clarendon Press, 1927. xii + 491 pp.—Bibliography, pp. 461–485. See also 118.

111. Allen, Philip S. The Romanesque Lyric. Studies in its background and development from Petronius to the Cambridge Songs 50–1050. With renderings into English verse by Howard M. Jones. Chapel Hill, University of North Carolina Press, 1928. xviii + 373 pp.

112. Waddell, Helen. Mediaeval Lyrics. London, Constable and Co., 1929. viii + 352 pp.—Texts in Latin and English.

113. Allen, Philip Schuyler. Medieval Latin Lyrics. University of Chicago Press, 1931. ix + 341 pp.

114. Manitius, Max. Geschichte der lateinischen Literatur des Mittelalters. München, Beck, 1911–31. 3 vols.—Volume IX in the series Handbücher der klassischen Altertumswissenschaft.

115. Mann, Wolfgang. Lateinische Dichtung in England vom Ausgang des Frühumanismus bis zum Regierungsantritt Elizabeths. Halle a. S., Max Niemeyer Verlag, 1939. 207 pp.—"Quellen," pp. 205–207.

116. Bradner, Leicester. Musae Anglicanae. A history of Anglo-Latin poetry 1500–1925. New York, Modern Language Association of America, 1940. xii + 383 pp.—Volume X in the Modern Language Association of America General Series, "Chronological List of Publications of Anglo-Latin Poetry," pp. 346–373.

117. Brittain, F[rederick]. The Medieval Latin and Romance Lyric to A.D. 1300. 2nd ed. Cambridge Univ. Press, 1951. xiii + 274 pp.—Original ed. 1937. Essentially an anthology, but with a full introduction, pp. 1–61, and a bibliography, pp. 255–259.

118. Raby, F[rederic] J. E. A History of Christian-Latin Poetry from the

Beginnings to the Close of the Middle Ages. 2nd ed. Oxford, Clarendon Press, 1953. xii + 494 pp.—Original ed. 1927. "Bibliography," pp. 461–489.

119. Browne, R[ichard] A. British Latin Selections A.D. 500–1400. With introduction, notes mainly linguistic and literary and vocabulary of mediaeval words and meanings. Oxford, Eng., Basil Blackwell, 1954. lxi + 144 pp.

120. Raby, F[rederic] J. E. A History of Secular Latin Poetry in the Middle Ages. 2nd ed. Oxford, Clarendon Press, 1957. 2 vols.—Original ed. 1934. "Bibliography," II, pp. 361–399.

121. Raby, F[rederic] J. E. Oxford Book of Medieval Latin Verse. Oxford Univ. Press, 1959. xix + 512 pp.

§6. BRITISH LITERATURE: ANGLO-NORMAN

125. Menger, Louis Emil. The Anglo-Norman Dialect. A manual of its phonology and morphology with illustrative specimens of the literature. New York, Columbia Univ. Press, 1904. xx + 167 pp.—In the series Columbia University Studies in Romance Philology and Literature.

126. Tanquerey, Frédéric Joseph. Recueil de lettres anglo-françaises 1265–1399. Paris, H. Champion, 1916. lx + 187 pp.

127. Vising, Johan. Anglo-Norman Language and Literature. Oxford Univ. Press, 1923. 111 pp.—Catalogue of works, pp. 41–78; bibliography, pp. 101–103.

128. Baker, A[lfred] J. Saints' Lives Written in Anglo-French. Their historical, social, and literary importance. Essays by Divers Hands, Being the transactions of the Royal Society of Literature, New Series, IV (1924), 119–156.

129. Studer, Paul, and Evans, Joan. Anglo-Norman Lapidaries. Paris, É. Champion, 1924. xx + 404 pp.

130. Walberg, E[manuel]. Quelques aspects de la littérature anglo-normande. Leçons faites à l'École des chartes. Paris, E. Droz, 1936. 143 pp.

131. West, C[onstance] B. Courtoisie in Anglo-Norman Literature. Oxford, Eng., Basil Blackwell, 1938. [vii] + 175 pp.—Number 3 in the series Medium Aevum Monographs. "Bibliography," pp. 170–175.

132. Ewert, Alfred, ed. Marie de France Lais. Oxford, Eng., Basil Blackwell, 1947. xxxi + 202 pp.—In the series Blackwell's French Texts. Bibliography, pp. xxvi–xxxi.

133. Legge, M[ary] Dominica. Anglo-Norman in the Cloisters. The influence of the orders upon Anglo-American literature. Edinburgh, University Press, 1950. vii + 147 pp.

134. Dean, Ruth J. A Fair Field Needing Folk. Anglo-Norman. PMLA, LXIX, 4 (Sept. 1954), 965–978.

135. Rychner, Jean, ed. Marie de France. Le lai de Lanval. Texte critique et édition diplomatique des quatre manuscrits français. Accompagné du texte du *Ianuals ljoth* et de sa traduction française avec une introduction et des notes par Paul Aebischer. Geneva, Librairie Droz, 1958.—In the series Textes littéraires français.

---

136. Publications of the Anglo-Norman Text Society. Oxford, Anglo-Norman Texts, Vol. I (1939)–Vol. XI (1953).

§7. BRITISH LITERATURE: OLD AND MIDDLE ENGLISH

[See also §37. Minor Prose: Hagiography, Homiletics, and Devotional Literature; §38. Minor Prose: Historiography Including Reprints of Early Annals and Chronicles; §44. The English Epic and Its Heroic and Classical Prototypes; §45. Surveys: The Old and Middle English Periods; §54. The Medieval, Tudor, and Jacobean Stage; §63. Drama: Medieval; §79. Medieval Periodicals; §105. Old English Readers; §106. Middle English Readers.]

140. Benham, Allen Rogers. English Literature from Widsith to the Death of Chaucer. A source book. New Haven, Yale Univ. Press, 1916. xxix + 634 pp.

141. Tucker, Lena Lucile, and Benham, Allen Rogers. A Bibliography of Fifteenth Century Literature. With special reference to the history of English culture. Seattle, University of Washington Press, 1928. 113–274 pp. —Volume II, no. 3, in the series University of Washington Publications in Language and Literature.

142. Heusinkveld, Arthur H., and Bashe, Edwin J. A Bibliographical Guide to Old English. A selective bibliography of the language, literature, and history of the Anglo-Saxons. Iowa City, University of Iowa, 1931. 153 pp.—Volume IV, no. 5, in the series University of Iowa Studies: Humanistic Studies.

143. Russell, Josiah Cox. Dictionary of Writers of Thirteenth Century England. London, Longmans, Green and Co., 1936. x + 210 (double column) pp.—Number 3 in the series Special Supplements to the Bulletin of the Institute of Historical Research.

144. Wells, John E. A Manual of the Writings in Middle English 1050–1400. New Haven, Yale Univ. Press, 1916. 941 pp.—Also *Supplements I* 1919, *II* 1923, *III* 1926, *IV* 1929, *V* 1932, *VI* 1935, *VII* 1938, *VIII* 1941, and *IX* 1951, the last prepared by Beatrice D. Brown, Eleanor K. Heningham, and Francis L. Utley.

145. Renwick, W[illiam] L., and Orton, Harold. The Beginnings of English Literature to Skelton. Editor's preface by Bonamy Dobrée. 2nd ed. London, Cresset Press, 1952. 450 pp.—Volume I in the series Introductions to English Literature. Original ed. 1939. "Students' Guide" [essentially a bibliography], pp. 125–442.

146. Bonser, Wilfred. An Anglo-Saxon and Celtic Bibliography 450–1087. Oxford, Eng., Basil Blackwell, 1957. xxxix + 574 (double column) pp.—Also a supplement with identical title page but with "Indices" added Oxford, Eng., Basil Blackwell, 1957, [v] + 123 (double column) pp.

---

147. Wülker, Richard. Grundriss zur Geschichte der angelsächsischen Litteratur. Mit einer Übersicht der angelsächsischen Sprachwissenschaft. Leipzig, Verlag von Veit und Comp., 1885. xii + 532 pp.

148. Brooke, Stopford A. English Literature. From the beginning to the Norman Conquest. London, Macmillan Co., 1898. ix + 340 pp.—Frequent reprints, as in 1926. "Bibliography," pp. 326–335.

149. Schofield, Wm. Henry. English Literature. From the Norman Conquest to Chaucer. New York, Macmillan Co., 1906. xiii + 500 pp.

150. Dale, Edmund. National Life and Character in the Mirror of Early English Literature. Cambridge Univ. Press, 1907. xiv + 337 pp.

151. Taylor, Rupert. The Political Prophecy in England. New York, Columbia Univ. Press, 1911. xx + 165 pp.—In the series Columbia University Studies in English.

152. Ker, Wm. P. Medieval English Literature. Oxford Univ. Press, 1912. 192 pp.—Number 43 in the series Home University Library of Modern Knowledge. Frequent reprints, as in 1955.

153. Snell, F[rederick] J. The Age of Alfred 664–1154. London, G. Bell and Sons, 1912. vii + 257 pp.

154. Leach, Henry Goddard. Angevin Britain and Scandinavia. Cambridge, Mass., Harvard Univ. Press, 1921. xi + 432 pp.—Volume VI in the series Harvard Studies in Comparative Literature.

155. Snell, F[rederick] J. The Fourteenth Century. Edinburgh, William Blackwood and Sons, 1923. xi + 428 pp.—Volume III in the series Periods of European Literature. A treatment of general European literature of the fourteenth century.

156. Thomas, P[ercy] G. English Literature before Chaucer. London, E. Arnold and Co., 1924. vii + 156 pp.

157. Patch, Howard R. The Goddess Fortuna in Medieval Literature. Cambridge, Mass., Harvard Univ. Press, 1927. xii + 215 pp.—"Bibliography," pp. 183–200.

158. Smith, G[eorge] Gregory. The Transition Period. Edinburgh, William Blackwood and Sons, 1927. xv + 422 pp.—Volume IV in the series Periods of European Literature. A treatment of fifteenth century literature.

159. Bennett, H[enry] S., ed. England from Chaucer to Caxton. New York, Harcourt, Brace and Co., 1928. xii + 246 pp.—Volume I in the series English Life in English Literature. An anthology of short literary pieces from the fifteenth century.

160. Hecht, Hans, and Schücking, Levin L. Die englische Literatur im Mittelalter. Wildpark-Potsdam, Athenaion, 1926–30. 190 pp. issued in 6 fascicles.

161. Schirmer, Walter F. Der englische Frühumanismus. Ein Beitrag zur englischen Literaturgeschichte des 15. Jahrhunderts. Leipzig, Bernhard Tauchnitz, 1931. 184 pp.

162. Baldwin, Chas. S. Three Medieval Centuries of Literature in England 1100–1400. Boston, Little, Brown and Co., 1932. ix + 274 pp.—See also Baldwin's earlier *An Introduction to English Medieval Literature*, London, Longmans, Green and Co., 1914, xii + 261 pp., reprint 1922.

163. Mohl, Ruth. The Three Estates in Medieval and Renaissance Literature. New York, Columbia Univ. Press, 1933. xi + 425 pp.

164. Wilson, R[ichard] M. Early Middle English Literature. London, Methuen and Co., 1939. ix + 309 pp.—Volume II in the series Methuen's Old English Library: C. Studies.

165. Utley, Francis L. The Crooked Rib. An analytical index to the argument about women in English and Scots literature to the end of the year 1568. Columbus, Ohio State Univ. Press, 1944. xii + 368 pp.—Number 10 in the series Contributions to Language and Literature of Ohio State University.

166. Chambers, Edmund K. English Literature at the Close of the Middle Ages. Oxford, Clarendon Press, 1945. 247 pp.—Volume II, pt. 2, in the series Oxford History of English Literature. Reprint 1957. "Bibliography," pp. 206–231.

167. Chaytor, H[enry] J. From Script to Print. An introduction to medieval literature. Cambridge Univ. Press, 1945. vii + 156 pp.

168. Coulton, G[eorge] G. Chaucer and His England. 7th ed. London, Methuen and Co., 1946. xviii + 321 pp.—Original ed. 1908.

169. Bennett, Henry S. Chaucer and the Fifteenth Century. [Corrected ed.] Oxford, Clarendon Press, 1948. vii + 326 pp.—Volume II, pt. 1, in the series Oxford History of English Literature. Original ed. 1947; corrected ed. reprinted 1954. "Chronological Tables and Bibliography," pp. 219–318.

170. Malone, Kemp, and Baugh, Albert C. The Middle Ages. The Old English Period to 1100, by Kemp Malone, and The Middle English Period 1100–1500, by Albert C. Baugh. New York, Appleton-Century-Crofts Inc., 1948. vi + 312 + x pp.—Volume I of *A Literary History of England,* edited by Albert C. Baugh.

171. Anderson, Geo. K. The Literature of the Anglo-Saxons. Princeton, N.J., University Press, 1949. ix + 431 pp.—Full bibliographies at the end of each of the fourteen chapters.

172. Kane, Geo. Middle English Literature. A critical study of the romances, the religious lyrics, Piers Plowman. London, Methuen and Co., 1951. xii + 252 pp.—In the series Methuen's Old English Library.

173. Wilson, R[ichard] M. The Lost Literature of Medieval England. London, Methuen and Co., 1952. xiv + 272 pp.—In the series Methuen's Old English Library.

174. Sisam, Kenneth. Studies in the History of Old English Literature. Oxford Univ. Press, 1953. vii + 314 pp.

175. Everett, Dorothy. Essays on Middle English Literature. Edited by Patricia Kean. Memoir by Mary Lascelles. Oxford Univ. Press, 1955. xi + 179 pp.—"Bibliography of Writings by Dorothy Everett," pp. 175–176.

176. Schlauch, Margaret. English Medieval Literature and Its Social Foundations. New York, Albert Daub and Co., 1956. xvii + 366 pp.—A treatment of medieval literature in Marxist terms.

177. Weiss, R[oberto]. Humanism in England during the Fifteenth Century. 2nd ed. Oxford, Eng., Basil Blackwell, 1957. xxiii + 202 pp.—Original ed. 1941. "Bibliography," pp. xiii–xxi.

178. Wallach, Luitpold. Alcuin and Charlemagne. Studies in Carolingian history and literature. Ithaca, N.Y., Cornell Univ. Press, 1959. x + 325 pp. —In the series Cornell Studies in Classical Philology.

§8. BRITISH LITERATURE: TUDOR AND RENAISSANCE

[See also §29. Fiction: From the Beginnings to *Circa* 1800; §39. Minor Prose: Travel and Descriptive Geography; §46. Surveys: The Tudor and Jacobean Periods; §54. The Medieval, Tudor, and Jacobean Stage; §64. Drama: Tudor and Jacobean.]

182. Hazlitt, W[illiam] Carew. Collections and Notes 1867–1876. London, Reeves and Turner, 1876. xi + 498 (double column) pp.—Also *Second Series of Bibliographical Collections and Notes on Early English Literature 1474–1700,* London, Bernard Quaritch, 1882, x + 717 (double column) pp. *Third and Final Series of Bibliographical Collections and Notes on Early English Literature 1474–1700,* London, Bernard Quaritch, 1887, xii + 315 (double column) pp. *Supplements to the Third and Final Series of Bibliographical Collections and Notes 1474–1700,* London, Bernard Quaritch, 1889, viii + 181 (double column) pp. Also G[eorge] J. Gray, *A General Index to Hazlitt's Handbook and His Bibliographical Collections,* edited by W. C. Hazlitt, London, Bernard Quaritch, 1893, 866 (double column) pp.

183. Scott, Mary Agusta. Elizabethan Translations from the Italian. [Revised ed.] Boston, Houghton Mifflin Co., 1916. lxxx + 558 pp.—Original ed. 1895–99 in *PMLA.* A list of 394 translations and 72 Italian and Latin publications.

184. Southern, A C. Elizabethan Recusant Prose 1559–1582. A historical and critical account of the books of the Catholic Refugees printed and published abroad and at secret presses in England together with an annotated bibliography of the same. With a foreword by H. O. Evennett. London, Sands and Co., [1950]. xxxv + 553 pp.—"Principal Sources and Works Consulted," pp. xxi–xxxv; "Bibliography," pp. 367–516.

185. Pinto, Vivian de S. The English Renaissance 1510–1688. With a chapter on literature and music by Bruce Pattison. Editor's preface by Bonamy Dobrée. 2nd ed. London, Cresset Press, 1951. 381 pp.—Volume II in the series Introductions to English Literature. Original ed. 1938. "Students' Guide to Reading," pp. 139–372.

186. Herford, Chas. H. Studies in the Literary Relations of England and Germany in the Sixteenth Century. Cambridge Univ. Press, 1886. xxx + 426 pp.

187. Saintsbury, Geo. A History of Elizabethan Literature. New York, Macmillan Co., 1887. xv + 471 pp.—Volume II in the series History of English Literature. Reprint 1921.

188. Underhill, John Garrett. Spanish Literature in the England of the Tudors. New York, Macmillan Co. for Columbia Univ. Press, 1899. x + 438 pp.—In the series Columbia Studies in Literature. Bibliographic materials, pp. 374–425.

189. Saintsbury, Geo. The Earlier Renaissance. Edinburgh, William Blackwood and Sons, 1901. xvi + 423 pp.—Volume V in the series Periods of European Literature.

190. Seccombe, Thos., and Allen, J[ohn] W. The Age of Shakespeare 1579–1631. With an introduction by Professor [John W.] Hales. Vol. I: Poetry and Prose; Vol. II: Drama. 2nd ed. London, George Bell and Sons, 1904. 2 vols.—In the series Handbooks of English Literature. Original ed. 1903.

191. Snell, F[rederick] J. The Age of Transition 1400–1580. Vol. I: The Poets; Vol. II: The Dramatists and Prose Writers. [Vol. II with an introduction by John W. Hales.] London, G. Bell and Sons, 1905. 2 vols.—In the series Handbooks of English Literature. Reprint 1920.

192. Swinburne, Algernon C. The Age of Shakespeare. New York, Harper and Bros., 1908. 302 pp.

193. Upham, Alfred H. The French Influence in English Literature from the Accession of Elizabeth to the Restoration. New York, Columbia Univ. Press, 1908. x + 560 pp.—Reprint 1911.

194. Lee, Sidney. The French Renaissance in England. An account of the literary relations of England and France in the sixteenth century. New York, Charles Scribner's Sons, 1910. xxiv + 494 pp.

195. Robertson, J[ohn] M. Elizabethan Literature. London, Williams and Norgate, 1914. 256 pp.—Number 89 in the series Home University Library of Modern Knowledge. "Bibliographical Note," pp. 253–254.

196. Greenlaw, Edwin. An Outline of the Literature of the English Renaissance. Chicago, Benjamin H. Sanborn, 1916. vi + 136 pp.

197. Bullen, A[rthur] H. Elizabethans. London, Chapman and Hall Ltd., 1924. xi + 226 pp.—A study *inter alios* of Drayton, Daniel, Chapman, Dekker, Breton, Campion, and Greville.

198. Camp, Chas. W. The Artisan in Elizabethan Literature. New York, Columbia Univ. Press, 1924. 170 pp.—In the series Columbia University Studies in English and Comparative Literature.

199. Thompson, Elbert N. S. Literary Bypaths of the Renaissance. New

Haven, Yale Univ. Press, 1924. vii + 189 pp.—A treatment of character and emblem books, war journals, familiar letters, courtesy books, and Joseph Hall as a representative man of letters.

200. Pompen, Aurelius, O.F.M. The English Versions of The Ship of Fools. A contribution to the history of the early French Renaissance in England. London, Longmans, Green and Co., 1925. xiv + 345 pp.

201. Schoell, Frank L. Études sur l'humanisme continental en Angleterre à la fin de la Renaissance. Avec une préface par Émile Legouis. Paris, Librairie ancienne Honoré Champion, 1926. vii + 270 pp.—Volume XXIX in the series Bibliothèque de la Revue de littérature comparée.

202. Schelling, Felix E. English Literature during the Lifetime of Shakespeare. Revised ed. New York, Henry Holt and Co., 1927. xv + 492 pp.—Original ed. 1910. "Bibliography," pp. 427–465.

203. Pearson, Lu E. Elizabethan Love Conventions. Berkeley, University of California Press, 1933. xi + 365 pp.—"Selected Bibliography," pp. 347–355.

204. Eliot, T[homas] S. Elizabethan Essays. London, Faber and Faber Ltd., 1934. 195 pp.—Number 24 in the series Faber Library.

205. Craig, Hardin. The Enchanted Glass. The Elizabethan mind in literature. New York, Oxford Univ. Press, 1936. xiii + 293 pp.

206. Dunn, Esther Cloudman. The Literature of Shakespeare's England. New York, Charles Scribner's Sons, 1936. ix + 326 pp.—Annotated reading list, pp. 311–320.

207. Mills, Laurens J. One Soul in Bodies Twain. Friendship in Tudor literature and drama. Bloomington, Ind., Principia Press, 1937. ix + 470 pp.

208. Harrison, G[eorge] B. The Elizabethan Journals. Being a record of those things most talked of during the years 1591–1603. Comprising an Elizabethan journal 1591–4; a second Elizabethan journal 1595–8; a last Elizabethan journal 1599–1603. Ann Arbor, University of Michigan Press, 1938. xv + 395 + 379 + 364 + [51] pp.—A revision and reprinting of three parts that appeared originally in 1928, 1931, and 1933. Reprint of one-volume version 1955.

209. Schücking, Levin L. The Baroque Character of the Elizabethan Hero. Oxford Univ. Press, 1938. 29 pp.—Number 25 in the series Annual Shakespeare Lectures. Reprint from *Proceedings of the British Academy*, Vol. XXIV.

210. Bush, Douglas. The Renaissance and English Humanism. University of Toronto Press, 1939. 139 pp.—The Alexander Lectures in English 1939. Reprint 1941.

211. Wilson, Elkin Calhoun. England's Eliza. Cambridge, Mass., Harvard

Univ. Press, 1939. xiv + 479 pp.—"A study of the idealization of Queen Elizabeth in the poetry of her age," p. vii.

212. Tillyard, E[ustace] M. W. The Elizabethan World Picture. London, Chatto and Windus, 1943. viii + 108 pp.—Frequent reprints, as in 1950.

213. Lewis, C[live] S. English Literature in the Sixteenth Century Excluding Drama. Oxford Univ. Press, 1944. vii + 696 pp.—Volume III in the series Oxford History of English Literature. The completion of the Clark Lectures, Trinity College, Cambridge, 1944. "Chronological Table," pp. 559–593; "Bibliography," pp. 594–685.

214. Wilson, F[rank] P. Elizabethan and Jacobean. Oxford Univ. Press, 1945. vii + 144 pp.

215. Brooke, [Charles] Tucker. The Renaissance 1500–1660. New York, Appleton-Century-Crofts Inc., 1948. xi + 315–696 + xv pp.—Volume II of *A Literary History of England,* edited by Albert C. Baugh.

216. McManaway, James G., Dawson, Giles E., and Willoughby, Edwin E., eds. Joseph Quincy Adams. Memorial studies. Washington, D.C., Folger Shakespeare Library, 1948. x + 808 pp.—"Bibliography 1904–46 of Joseph Quincy Adams," pp. 13–20.

217. Harris, Victor. All Coherence Gone. University of Chicago Press, 1949. x + 255 pp.—"Bibliography," pp. 234–250.

218. Babb, Lawrence. The Elizabethan Malady. A study of melancholia in English literature from 1580 to 1642. East Lansing, Michigan State College Press, 1951. xi + 206 pp.—In the series Studies in Language and Literature. "Bibliography," pp. 189–197.

219. Tillyard, E[ustace] M. W. The English Renaissance. Fact or fiction? Introduction by Don Cameron Allen. Baltimore, Johns Hopkins Press, 1952. xviii + 118 pp.—The Turnbull Memorial Lectures, Johns Hopkins University, 1950–51.

220. Carroll, Wm. Meredith. Animal Conventions in English Renaissance Non-Religious Prose 1550–1600. New York, Bookman Associates, 1954. 166 pp.—"Appendix. A list of the animals, birds, reptiles, and other creatures . . . ," pp. 91–120; "Bibliography," pp. 121–125. See also Thomas P. Harrison, *They Tell of Birds,* Chaucer, Spenser, Milton, Drayton; Austin, University of Texas Press, 1956, xviii + 159 pp.

221. Holden, Wm. P. Anti-Puritan Satire 1572–1642. New Haven, Yale Univ. Press, 1954. xii + 165 pp.—Volume CXXVI in the series Yale Studies in English. "Bibliography," pp. 155–158.

222. Rosenberg, Eleanor. Leicester. Patron of letters. New York, Columbia Univ. Press, 1955. xx + 395 pp.—"A Chronological List of Works Dedicated to the Earl of Leicester," pp. 355–362; "List of Sources Consulted," pp. 363–378.

223. Nicoll, Allardyce, ed. The Elizabethans. Cambridge Univ. Press, 1957. viii + 174 (double column) pp.—"In this book an attempt is made to allow the Elizabethans to give an image of their times in their own words and in their own pictures," p. vii.

224. Morris, Helen. Elizabethan Literature. Oxford Univ. Press, 1958. ix + 239 pp.—Number 233 in the series Home University Library of Modern Knowledge. "Bibliography," pp. 220–228.

225. Wind, Edgar. Pagan Mysteries in the Renaissance. London, Faber and Faber Ltd., 1958. 230 pp. + lxxvii plates.

§9. BRITISH LITERATURE: SHAKESPEARE BIBLIOGRAPHIES, HANDBOOKS, AND STUDIES

[See also §54. The Medieval, Tudor, and Jacobean Stage; §64. Drama: Tudor and Jacobean.]

229. Jaggard, Wm. Shakespeare Bibliography. A dictionary of every known issue of the writings of our national poet and of recorded opinion thereon in the English language. Stratford-on-Avon, Shakespeare Press, 1911. xxi + 729 pp.—Reprint New York, Frederick Ungar, 1958.

230. Ebisch, Walther, and Schücking, Levin L. A Shakespeare Bibliography. Oxford Univ. Press, 1931. xviii + 294 pp.

231. Ebisch, Walther, and Schücking, Levin L. Supplement for the Years 1930–1935 to a Shakespeare Bibliography. Oxford Univ. Press, 1937. [v] + 104 pp.

---

232. Bartlett, John. A New and Complete Concordance or Verbal Index to Words, Phrases, and Passages in the Dramatic Works of Shakespeare. With a supplementary concordance to the poems. London, Macmillan Co., 1894. [vii] + 1910 (double column) pp.

233. Schmidt, Alexander. Shakespeare-Lexicon. A complete dictionary of all the English words, phrases, and constructions in the works of the poet. Third ed. rev. and enl. by Gregor Sarrazin. Berlin, Georg Reimer, 1902. 2 (double column page) vols.—Original ed. 1874–75; second ed. 1886.

234. Stokes, Francis Griffin. A Dictionary of the Characters and Proper Names in the Works of Shakespeare with Notes on the Sources and Dates of the Plays and Poems. Boston, Houghton Mifflin Co., [1924]. xv + 360 (double column) pp.

235. Sugden, Edward H. A Topographical Dictionary to the Works of Shakespeare and His Fellow Dramatists. Manchester, Eng., University Press, 1925. xix + 580 (double column) pp.

236. Semper, I[sidore] J. A Shakespere Study Guide. New York, Century Co., 1931. xi + 204 pp.—In the series Century Catholic College Texts.

237. Stevenson, Burton. The Home Book of Shakespeare Quotations. Being also a concordance and a glossary of the unique words and phrases in the plays and poems. New York, Charles Scribner's Sons, 1937. xl + 1762 (double column) + 1763–2055 (triple column) pp.

238. Thomson, W[ilfrid] H. Shakespeare's Characters. A historical dictionary. Altrincham, Eng., John Sherratt and Son, 1951. 320 pp.

239. Partridge, Eric. Shakespeare's Bawdy. A literary and psychological essay and a comprehensive glossary. Revised ed. New York, E. P. Dutton and Co., 1955. ix + 226 pp.—Original ed. 1947.

---

240. Boas, F[rederick] S. Shakespeare and His Predecessors. New York, Charles Scribner's Sons, 1896. viii + 555 pp.—Frequent reprints, as in 1908.

241. Thorndike, Ashley H. Shakespeare's Theatre. New York, Macmillan Co., 1916. xiv + 472 pp.—Reprint 1940. "Bibliographical Notes," pp. 445–460.

242. Lee, Sidney, et al., eds. Shakespeare's England. An account of the life and manners of his age. Oxford Univ. Press, 1917. 2 vols.—Reprint 1926.

243. Odell, Geo. C. D. Shakespeare from Betterton to Irving. New York, Charles Scribner's Sons, 1920. 2 vols.

244. Chambers, E[dmund] K. William Shakespeare. A study of facts and problems. Oxford, Clarendon Press, 1930. 2 vols.—See Beatrice White, *An Index to "The Elizabethan Stage" and "William Shakespeare . . . ,"* Oxford Univ. Press for the Shakespeare Association, 1934, 161 pp.

245. Ralli, Augustus. A History of Shakespearean Criticism. Oxford Univ. Press, 1932. 2 vols.—Reprint New York, Humanities Press, 1959.

246. Clarkson, Paul S., and Warren, Clyde T. The Law of Property in Shakespeare and the Elizabethan Drama. Baltimore, Johns Hopkins Press, 1942. xxvii + 346 pp.

247. Greg, W[alter] W. The Editorial Problem in Shakespeare. 2nd ed. Ox-

ford Univ. Press, 1951. lv + 210 pp.—The Clark Lectures, Trinity College, Cambridge, 1939. Original ed. 1942.

248. Halliday, F[rank] E. A Shakespeare Companion 1550–1950. London, Gerald Duckworth and Co., 1952. xv + 742 pp. + xxxii pp. of illustrations.

249. Kökeritz, Helge. Shakespeare's Pronunciation. New Haven, Yale Univ. Press, 1953. xv + 516 pp.—A companion piece is the 33⅓ rpm microgroove record by Helge Kökeritz, "Shakespeare's Pronunciation," Columbia Records Inc., TV 19232 and TV 19233.

250. Greg, W[alter] W. The Shakespeare First Folio. Its bibliographical and textual history. Oxford Univ. Press, 1955. xvi + 496 pp.

---

251. Shakespeare Jahrbuch. Weimar, Herausgegeben im Auftrage der deutschen Shakespeare-Gesellschaft, 1865–date.—Annual.

252. Shakespeare Newsletter. New York, L. Marder, 1951–date.—Six issues a year. Abstracts. Reviews.

253. Shakespeare Quarterly. New York, Shakespeare Association of America Inc., 1950–date.—Reviews. Spring issue "Annual Shakespeare Bibliography"; winter issue "Current Theatre Notes."

254. Shakespeare Stage. London, Shakespeare Stage Society, 1953–date.—Quarterly. Reviews of plays.

255. Shakespeare Survey. An annual survey of Shakespearian study and production. Cambridge, Eng., 1948–date.—Issued under the sponsorship of the University of Birmingham, the Shakespeare Memorial Theatre, and the Shakespeare Birthplace Trust.

§10. BRITISH LITERATURE: SEVENTEENTH CENTURY

[See also §29. Fiction: From the Beginnings to *Circa* 1800; §34. Minor Prose: The Character; §36. Minor Prose: The Essay and Personal Letter; §47. Surveys: The Seventeenth Century; §55. The Stage of the Later Seventeenth and Eighteenth Centuries; §64. Drama: Tudor and Jacobean; §65. Drama: Restoration and Eighteenth Century.]

259. Catalogue of Original and Early Editions of Some of the Poetical and Prose Works of English Writers from Wither to Prior. With collations, notes, and more than two-hundred facsimiles of title-pages and frontispieces. New York, Grolier Club, 1905. 3 vols.

260. Crane, Ronald S., Bredvold, Louis I., Bond, Richmond P., Friedman, Arthur, and Landa, Louis A. English Literature 1660–1800. A bibliography of modern studies compiled for Philological Quarterly. Foreword by Louis A. Landa. Vol. I: 1926–1938; Vol. II: 1939–1950. Princeton, N.J., University Press, 1950–52. 2 vols.

---

261. Garnett, R[ichard]. The Age of Dryden. London, George Bell and Sons, 1895. vii + 292 pp.—In the series Handbooks of English Literature. Reprint 1907.

262. Wendell, Barrett. The Temper of the Seventeenth Century in English Literature. New York, Charles Scribner's Sons, 1904. ix + 360 pp.—The Clark Lectures, Trinity College, Cambridge, 1902–03.

263. Dowden, Edward. Puritan and Anglican. Studies in literature. 3rd ed. New York, Henry Holt and Co., 1910. xii + 341 pp.—Original ed. 1900; second ed. 1901.

264. Masterman, J[ohn] Howard B. The Age of Milton. With an introduction by J. Bass Mullinger. [7th ed.] London, George Bell and Sons, 1915. xxi + 254 pp.—In the series Handbooks of English Literature. Original ed. 1897; seventh ed. reprinted 1927.

265. Maar, Harko [G.] de. A History of Modern English Romanticism. Vol. I: Elizabethan and Modern Romanticism in the Eighteenth Century. Oxford Univ. Press, 1924. viii + 246 pp.—Concentration on Milton and his age. A companion volume did not appear.

266. Grierson, H[erbert] J. C. Cross Currents in English Literature of the Seventeenth Century. Or the word, the flesh, and the spirit, their actions and reactions. London, Chatto and Windus, 1929. xiv + 344 pp.—The Messenger Lectures, Cornell University, 1926–27. Reprint 1948.

267. Dobrée, Bonamy. Variety of Ways. Discussions on six authors. Oxford Univ. Press, 1932. viii + 118 pp.—A study of Dryden, George Savile, Bunyan, Congreve, Steele, and Mandeville.

268. Willey, Basil. The Seventeenth Century Background. Studies in the thought of the age in relation to poetry and religion. London, Chatto and Windus, 1934. viii + 315 pp.

269. Seventeenth Century Studies Presented to Sir Herbert Grierson. Preface by J. Dover Wilson. Oxford Univ. Press, 1938. xv + 415 pp.—"List of Sir Herbert Grierson's Publications," pp. 395–403.

270. Bush, Douglas. English Literature in the Earlier Seventeenth Century 1600–1660. Oxford Univ. Press, 1945. vi + 621 pp.—Volume V in the series Oxford History of English Literature. "Chronological Tables," pp. 406–439; "Bibliography," pp. 440–610.

271. Knights, L[ionel] C. Explorations. Essays in criticism mainly on the literature of the seventeenth century. London, Chatto and Windus, 1946. xii + 199 pp.—Reprint 1951.

272. Wilson, John H. The Court Wits of the Restoration. An introduction. Princeton, N.J., University Press, 1948. ix + 264 pp.

273. Wedgwood, C[icely] V. Seventeenth-Century English Literature. Oxford Univ. Press, 1950. 186 pp.—Number 218 in the series Home University Library of Modern Knowledge. "Bibliography," pp. 176–180.

274. Jones, Richard F., et al. The Seventeenth Century. Studies in the history of English thought and literature from Bacon to Pope. Stanford Univ. Press, 1951. viii + 392 pp.

275. Wiley, Margaret L. The Subtle Knot. Creative scepticism in seventeenth-century England. Cambridge, Mass., Harvard Univ. Press, 1952. 303 pp.

276. Marks, Emerson R. Relativist and Absolutist. The early neoclassical debate in England. New Brunswick, N.J., Rutgers Univ. Press, 1955. xiii + 171 pp.

277. Walton, Geoffrey. Metaphysical to Augustan. Studies in tone and sensibility in the seventeenth century. London, Bowes and Bowes Publ'ers, 1955. xii + 13–160 pp.

§11. BRITISH LITERATURE: EIGHTEENTH CENTURY

[See also §29. Fiction: From the Beginnings to *Circa* 1800; §48. Surveys: The Eighteenth Century; §55. The Stage of the Later Seventeenth and Eighteenth Centuries; §65. Drama: Restoration and Eighteenth Century.]

281. Williams, Iolo A. Seven XVIIIth Century Bibliographies. London, Dulau and Co., 1924. vii + 244 pp.—A bibliography of first editions of John Armstrong, William Shenstone, Mark Akenside, William Collins, Oliver Goldsmith, Charles Churchill, and Richard Brinsley Sheridan.

282. Tobin, James E. Eighteenth Century English Literature and Its Cultural Background. A bibliography. New York, Fordham Univ. Press, 1939.

ix + 190 pp.—Two parts: "Cultural and Critical Background" and "Bibliographies of Individual Authors."

283. Dyson, H[enry] v. D., and Butt, John. Augustans and Romantics 1689–1830. With chapters on art, economics, and philosophy by Geoffrey Webb, F. J. Fisher, and H. A. Hodges. Editor's preface by Bonamy Dobrée. 2nd ed. London, Cresset Press, 1950. 320 pp.—Volume III in the series Introductions to English Literature. Original ed. 1940. "Bibliography," pp. 156–312.

---

284. Dennis, John. The Age of Pope 1700–1744. London, George Bell and Sons, 1894. vii + 260 pp.—In the series Handbooks of English Literature. Frequent reprints, as in 1906.

285. Millar, John H. The Mid-Eighteenth Century. New York, Charles Scribner's Sons, 1902. xii + 387 pp.—Volume IX in the series Periods of European Literature.

286. Stephen, Leslie. English Literature and Society in the Eighteenth Century. London, Duckworth and Co., 1904. vi + 224 pp.—The Ford Lectures. Reprint 1931.

287. Seccombe, Thos. The Age of Johnson 1748–1798. 6th ed. London, G. Bell and Sons, 1913. xxxviii + 366 pp.—In the series Handbooks of English Literature. Original ed. 1899; sixth ed. reprinted 1926.

288. Tinker, Chauncey B. The Salon and English Letters. Chapters on the interrelation of literature and society in the age of Johnson. New York, Macmillan Co., 1915. ix + 290 pp.

289. Saintsbury, Geo. The Peace of the Augustans. A survey of eighteenth century literature as a place of rest and refreshment. London, G. Bell and Sons, 1916. x + 399 pp.

290. Tinker, Chauncey Brewster. Nature's Simple Plan. A phase of radical thought in the mid-eighteenth century. Princeton, N.J., University Press, 1922. vi + 117 pp.—The Louis Clark Vanuxem Foundation Lectures 1922.

291. Elton, Oliver. A Survey of English Literature 1730–1780. New York, Macmillan Co., 1928. 2 vols.

292. Whitney, Lois. Primitivism and the Idea of Progress in English Popular Literature of the Eighteenth Century. Foreword by Arthur O. Lovejoy. Baltimore, Johns Hopkins Press, 1934. xxi + 343 pp.

293. Green, F[rederick] C. Minuet. A critical survey of French and English literary ideas in the eighteenth century. New York, E. P. Dutton and Co., 1935. ix + 489 pp.

294. Monk, Samuel H. The Sublime. A study of critical theories in eighteenth-century England. New York, Modern Language Association of America, 1935. vii + 252 pp.—In the Modern Language Association of America General Series. "Bibliography," pp. 239–248.

295. Lovejoy, Arthur O. The Great Chain of Being. A study of the history of an idea. Cambridge, Mass., Harvard Univ. Press, 1936. xi + 382 pp.—The William James Lectures, Harvard University, 1933. A treatment of an idea which reaches its culmination in the eighteenth century.

296. Dobrée, Bonamy, ed. From Anne to Victoria. Essays by various hands. New York, Charles Scribner's Sons, 1937. x + 630 pp.

297. Watkins, W[alter] B. C. Perilous Balance. The tragic genius of Swift, Johnson, and Sterne. Princeton, N.J., University Press, 1939. ix + 172 pp.

298. Willey, Basil. The Eighteenth Century Background. Studies on the idea of nature in the thought of the period. London, Chatto and Windus, 1940. viii + 301 pp.

299. Essays on the Eighteenth Century. Presented to David Nichol Smith in honor of his seventieth birthday. Oxford Univ. Press, 1945. vii + 288 pp.—"List of the Writings of David Nichol Smith," pp. 274–283.

300. McKillop, Alan D. English Literature from Dryden to Burns. New York, Appleton-Century-Crofts Inc., 1948. xii + 445 pp.—In the series Appleton-Century Handbooks of Literature. Bibliography, pp. 419–425.

301. Sherburn, Geo. The Restoration and Eighteenth Century 1660–1789. New York, Appleton-Century-Crofts Inc., 1948. vii + 699–1108 + xvi pp.—Volume III of *A Literary History of England,* edited by Albert C. Baugh.

302. The Age of Johnson. Essays presented to Chauncey Brewster Tinker. Introduction by Wilmarth S. Lewis. New Haven, Yale Univ. Press, 1949. xi + 426 pp.

303. Bate, Walter Jackson. From Classic to Romantic. Premises of taste in eighteenth-century England. Cambridge, Mass., Harvard Univ. Press, 1949. ix + 197 pp.

304. Clifford, James L., and Landa, Louis A., eds. Pope and His Contemporaries. Essays presented to George Sherburn. Oxford Univ. Press, 1949. viii + 278 pp.—"List of the Writings of George Sherburn," pp. 260–262.

305. McCutcheon, Roger P. Eighteenth-Century English Literature. New York, Oxford Univ. Press, 1949. 192 pp.—Number 212 in the series Home University Library of Modern Knowledge. "Suggestions for Further Reading," pp. 173–175.

306. Butt, John. The Augustan Age. London, Hutchinson House, 1950. viii + 9–152 pp.—Number 43 in the series Hutchinson's University Library.

307. Chapman, R[obert] W. Johnsonian and Other Essays and Reviews. Oxford Univ. Press, 1953. 243 pp.

308. Churchill, R[eginald] C. English Literature of the Eighteenth Century. With a preface on the relations between literary history and literary criticism. London, University Tutorial Press, 1953. xxiii + 320 pp.

309. Moore, Cecil A. Backgrounds of English Literature 1700–1760. Minneapolis, University of Minnesota Press, 1953. xi + 254 pp.

310. Hipple, Walter J., Jr. The Beautiful, the Sublime, and the Picturesque in Eighteenth-Century British Aesthetic Theory. Carbondale, Southern Illinois Univ. Press, 1957. 390 pp.

311. Clifford, James L., ed. Eighteenth Century English Literature. Modern essays in criticism. New York, Oxford Univ. Press, 1959. xi + 351 pp. —Number 23 in the series Galaxy Books.

312. Nicolson, Marjorie Hope. Mountain Gloom and Mountain Glory. The development of the aesthetics of the infinite. Ithaca, N.Y., Cornell Univ. Press, 1959. 403 pp.

313. Dobrée, Bonamy. English Literature in the Early Eighteenth Century 1700–1740. Oxford, Clarendon Press, 1960. 701 pp.

§12. BRITISH LITERATURE: ROMANTIC

[See also §49. Surveys: The Romantic Period.]

317. Bernbaum, Ernest. Guide through the Romantic Movement. 2nd ed. New York, Ronald Press, 1949. xi + 351 pp.—Original ed. 1930. A companion volume to Bernbaum's *Anthology of Romanticism,* 3rd ed., New York, Ronald Press, 1948, xxviii + 1238 pp.

318. Nangle, Benjamin Christie. The Monthly Review. Second series 1790–1815. Indexes of contributors and articles. Oxford Univ. Press, 1955. xix + 268 pp.

---

319. DeQuincey, Thos. Recollections of the Lake Poets. Edited with an Introduction by Edward Sackville-West. London, John Lehmann Ltd., 1948. xvii + 19–328 pp.—Initial publication by DeQuincey in journals 1834–40.

320. Courthope, Wm. J. The Liberal Movement in English Literature. London, John Murray, 1885. xv + 240 pp.

321. Beers, Henry A. A History of English Romanticism in the Eighteenth Century. New York, Henry Holt and Co., 1898. vii + 455 pp.—Reprints 1926, 1929.

322. Herford, C[harles] H. The Age of Wordsworth. 3rd ed. London, G. Bell and Sons, 1899. xxix + 315 pp.—In the series Handbooks of English Literature. Original and 2nd eds. 1897; third ed. frequently reprinted, as in 1934. "Chronological Table," pp. 285–294.

323. Beers, Henry A. A History of English Romanticism in the Nineteenth Century. New York, Henry Holt and Co., 1901. ix + 424 pp.

324. Farley, Frank Edgar. Scandinavian Influences in the English Romantic Movement. Boston, Ginn and Co., 1903. viii + 250 pp.—Volume IX in the series Studies and Notes in Philology and Literature published under the direction of the Modern Language Departments of Harvard University.

325. Brandes, Geo. Naturalism in England. London, William Heinemann, 1905. viii + 366 pp.—Volume IV of Brandes's *Main Currents in Nineteenth Century Literature,* London, William Heinemann, 1901–05, 6 vols., originally published in Danish 1872–90. Reprint as *Naturalism in Nineteenth Century English Literature,* London, Russell and Russell Inc., 1957. A treatment of Romanticism and the English Romantic poets.

326. Elton, Oliver. A Survey of English Literature 1780–1830. New York, Longmans, Green and Co., 1912. 2 vols.

327. Pierce, Frederick E. Currents and Eddies in the English Romantic Generation. New Haven, Yale Univ. Press, 1918. 342 pp.

328. Babbitt, Irving. Rousseau and Romanticism. Boston, Houghton Mifflin Co., 1919. xxiii + 426 pp.—Reprint 1924. "Bibliography," pp. 399–419.

329. Robertson, J[ohn] G. Studies in the Genesis of Romantic Theory in the Eighteenth Century. Cambridge Univ. Press, 1923. vi + 298 pp.

330. Snyder, Edward D. The Celtic Revival in English Literature 1760–1800. Cambridge, Mass., Harvard Univ. Press, 1923. xi + 208 pp.

331. Maar, Harko G. de. Elizabethan Romance in the Eighteenth Century. Zalt-Bommel, Holland, Van de Garde and Co.'s Drukkerij, [1924]. 248 + iv pp.—Volume I of de Maar's *A History of Modern English Romanticism.*

332. Abercrombie, Lascelles. Romanticism. New York, Viking Press, 1927. 192 pp.

333. Railo, Eino. The Haunted Castle. A study of the elements of English romanticism. London, George Routledge and Sons, 1927. xix + 388 pp.

334. Fairchild, Hoxie N. The Noble Savage. A study in romantic naturalism. New York, Columbia Univ. Press, 1928. xi + 535 pp.

335. Blunden, Edmund. Nature in English Literature. London, Hogarth Press, 1929. 156 pp.—Number 9 in the Hogarth Lectures on Literature Series. Reprint 1949. A treatment of rural or rustic writers, as White, Duck, Bloomfield, Clare, and Hood.

336. Stockley, V[iolet]. German Literature as Known in England 1750–1830. London, George Routledge and Sons, 1929. xiv + 339 pp.—Bibliographies, pp. 305–334.

337. Fairchild, Hoxie N. The Romantic Quest. New York, Columbia Univ. Press, 1931. ix + 444 pp.

338. Marshall, Roderick. Italy in English Literature 1755–1815. Origins of the romantic interest in Italy. New York, Columbia Univ. Press, 1934. xiii + 432 pp.—Number 16 in the series Columbia University Studies in English and Comparative Literature.

339. Lucas, F[rank] L. The Decline and Fall of the Romantic Ideal. New York, Macmillan Co., 1937. [ix] + 280 pp.

340. Adams, M[artin] R. Studies in the Literary Backgrounds of English Radicalism. With special reference to the French Revolution. Lancaster, Penn., Franklin and Marshall College, 1947. vii + 330 pp.—Number 5 in the series Franklin and Marshall College Studies.

341. James, D[avid] G. The Romantic Comedy. Oxford Univ. Press, 1948. xi + 276 pp.

342. Bowra, C[ecil] M. The Romantic Imagination. Cambridge, Mass., Harvard Univ. Press, 1949. [xi] + 306 pp.

343. Willey, Basil. Nineteenth Century Studies. Coleridge to Matthew Arnold. New York, Columbia Univ. Press, 1949. v + 288 pp.

344. Brailsford, H[enry] N. Shelley, Godwin, and Their Circle. 2nd ed. Oxford Univ. Press, 1951. 189 pp.—Number 77 in the series Home University Library of Modern Knowledge. Original ed. 1913.

345. Praz, Mario. The Romantic Agony. Translated from the Italian by Angus Davidson. 2nd ed. Oxford Univ. Press, 1951. xix + 502 pp.—Original Eng. ed. 1933; original It. ed. 1930; second It. ed. 1942; third It. ed. 1948; second Eng. ed. reprinted New York, Meridian Books, 1956.

346. Abrams, M[eyer] H. The Mirror and the Lamp. Romantic theory and the critical tradition. New York, Oxford Univ. Press, 1953. xiii + 406 pp.—Bibliographical references, pp. 337–392.

347. Brand, C[harles] P. Italy and the English Romantics. The Italianate fashion in early nineteenth-century England. Cambridge Univ. Press, 1957. xi + 285 pp.—"Bibliography," pp. 255–259.

348. Clive, John. Scotch Reviewers. The Edinburgh Review 1802–1815. Cambridge, Mass., Harvard Univ. Press, 1957. 224 pp.—"Bibliography," pp. 198–210.

349. Houtchens, Carolyn W. and Lawrence H., eds. The English Romantic Poets and Essayists. A review of research and criticism. New York, Modern Language Association of America, 1957. [xii] + 363 pp.—Number 20 in the Revolving Fund Series of the Modern Language Association of America.

§13. BRITISH LITERATURE: VICTORIAN TO *CIRCA* 1900

[See also §30. Fiction: British and American in the Nineteenth Century; §50. Surveys: The Victorian Era; §56. The Victorian and the Modern English Stage; §66. Drama: Nineteenth Century and Modern British and American.]

353. Sadleir, Michael. Excursions in Victorian Bibliography. London, Chaundry and Cox, 1922. vii + 240 pp.

354. Ehrsam, Theodore G., Deily, Robt. H., and Smith, Robt. M. Bibliographies of Twelve Victorian Authors. New York, H. W. Wilson Co., 1936. 362 (double column) pp.—Bibliographies of Arnold, E. B. Browning, Clough, Fitzgerald, Hardy, Kipling, Morris, C. G. Rossetti, D. G. Rossetti, Stevenson, Swinburne, and Tennyson.—See also Joseph G. Fucilla, "Bibliographies of Twelve Victorian Authors: A Supplement," *Modern Philology*, XXXVII, 1 (August 1939), 89–96.

355. Templeman, Wm. D., ed. Bibliographies of Studies in Victorian Literature for the Thirteen Years 1932–1944. Urbana, University of Illinois Press, 1945. ix + 450 (double column) pp.

356. Batho, Edith C., and Dobrée, Bonamy. The Victorians and After 1830–1914. With a chapter on the economic background by Guy Chapman. Editor's preface by Bonamy Dobrée. 2nd ed. London, Cresset Press, 1950. 360 pp.—Volume IV in the series Introductions to English Literature. Original ed. 1938. "Biography and Autobiography," pp. 147–352.

357. Wright, Austin, ed. Bibliographies of Studies in Victorian Literature for the Ten Years 1945–1954. Urbana, University of Illinois Press, 1956. [vii] + 310 (double column) pp.—Photolithographic reproductions of the annual Victorian Bibliographies for the years 1945 through 1954 published in *Modern Philology*.

358. Morley, Henry. Of English Literature in the Reign of Victoria. With a glance at the past. Leipzig, Germany, Bernard Tauchnitz, 1881. xl facsimiles + xii + 416 pp.—Number 200 in the series Tauchnitz Editions. The Frontispiece contains facsimiles of the signatures of authors photographed from their correspondence with Baron Tauchnitz.

359. Dowden, Edward. Studies in Literature 1789–1877. 4th ed. London, Kegan Paul, Trench and Co., 1887. xii + 523 pp.—Original ed. 1878.

360. Saintsbury, Geo. A History of Nineteenth Century Literature 1780–1895. New York, Macmillan Co., 1896. xii + 477 pp.—In the series Macmillan's History of English Literature. Reprint 1904. See also Saintsbury's earlier *Corrected Impressions,* Essays on Victorian writers, New York, Dodd, Mead and Co., 1895, vi + 218 pp.

361. Walker, Hugh. The Age of Tennyson. London, G. Bell and Sons, 1897. x + 309 pp.—In the series Handbooks of English Literature. Frequent reprints, as in 1914.

362. Scudder, Vida D. Social Ideals in English Letters. Boston, Houghton Mifflin Co., 1898. 329 pp.

363. Brownell, W[illiam] C. Victorian Prose Masters. Thackeray, Carlyle, George Eliot, Matthew Arnold, Ruskin, George Meredith. New York, Charles Scribner's Sons, 1901. viii + 289 pp.

364. Harrison, Frederick. Studies in Early Victorian Literature. 4th ed. London, Edward Arnold, 1902. 224 pp.—Original ed. 1895.

365. Magnus, Laurie. English Literature in the Nineteenth Century. An essay in criticism. New York, G. P. Putnam's Sons, 1909. ix + 418 pp.

366. Walker, Hugh. The Literature of the Victorian Era. Cambridge Univ. Press, 1910. xxxvi + 1067 pp.—Reprint 1921. See also Hugh and Mrs. Hugh Walker's *Outlines of Victorian Literature,* Cambridge Univ. Press, 1913, viii + 224 pp.

367. Jackson, Holbrook. The Eighteen-Nineties. A review of art and ideas at the close of the nineteenth century. London, G. Richards, 1913. 304 pp.—Reprints New York, A. A. Knopf, 1922, and Harmondsworth, Eng., Penguin Books, 1939.

368. Kennedy, J[ohn] M. English Literature 1880–1905. Boston, Small, Maynard and Co., 1913. vi + 340 pp.

369. Chesterton, G[ilbert] K. The Victorian Age in Literature. Rev. ed. London, Williams and Norgate Ltd., 1914. vi + 7–256 pp.—Number 61 in the series Home University Library of Modern Knowledge. Original ed. 1913; second ed. frequently reprinted, as in 1928.

370. Hudson, Wm. H. A Short History of English Literature in the Nineteenth Century. London, G. Bell and Sons, 1918. 309 pp.

371. Elton, Oliver. A Survey of English Literature 1830–1880. New York, Macmillan Co., 1920. 2 vols.

372. Bald, Marjory A. Women-Writers of the Nineteenth Century. Cambridge Univ. Press, 1923. viii + 288 pp.

373. Broers, Bernarda C. Mysticism in the Neo-Romanticists. Amsterdam, Holland, Firma A. H. Kruyt, [1923]. viii + 233 pp.—A study *inter alios* of Morris, Patmore, Swinburne, and Thompson.

374. Saintsbury, Geo. The Late Nineteenth Century. Edinburgh, William Blackwood and Sons, 1923. xviii + 471 pp.—Volume XII in the series Periods of European Literature.

375. Williams, Stanley T. Studies in Victorian Literature. New York, E. P. Dutton and Co., 1923. ix + 299 pp.

376. Ellis, Stewart M. Mainly Victorian. London, Hutchinson and Co., [1924]. 402 pp.

377. Burdett, Osbert. The Beardsley Period. An essay in perspective. New York, Boni and Liveright, 1925. xi + 302 pp.

378. Knickerbocker, Wm. S. Creative Oxford. Its influence in Victorian literature. Syracuse, N.Y., University Press, 1925. ix + 224 pp.

379. Le Gallienne, Richard. The Romantic '90s. Garden City, N.Y., Doubleday, Page and Co., 1925. 271 pp.

380. Granville-Barker, Harley, ed. The Eighteen-Seventies. Essays by fellows of the Royal Society of Literature. New York, Macmillan Co., 1929. xiii + 290 pp.

381. Welby, T[homas] Earle. The Victorian Romantics 1850–70. The early work of Dante Gabriel Rossetti, William Morris, Burne-Jones, Swinburne, Simeon Solomon, and their associates. London, Gerald Howe Ltd., 1929. x + 161 pp.

382. De La Mare, Walter, ed. The Eighteen-Eighties. Essays by fellows of the Royal Society of Literature. Cambridge Univ. Press, 1930. xxviii + 271 pp.

383. Farmer, Albert J. Le mouvement esthétique et "décadent" en Angleterre 1873–1900. Paris, Librairie ancienne Honoré Champion, 1931. ix + 413 pp.—Volume LXXV in the series Bibliothèque de la Revue de littérature comparée.

384. Drinkwater, John, ed. The Eighteen-Sixties. Essays by fellows of the Royal Society of Literature. New York, Macmillan Co., 1932. x + 282 pp.

385. Winwar, Frances. Poor Splendid Wings. The Rossettis and their circle. Boston, Little, Brown and Co., 1933. xii + 413 pp.

386. Cunliffe, John W. Leaders of the Victorian Revolution. New York, D. Appleton-Century Co., 1934. viii + 343 pp.—A sociological treatment of Victorian literature.

387. Winwar, Frances. The Romantic Rebels. Boston, Little, Brown and Co., 1935. 507 pp.

388. Hicks, Granville. Figures of Transition. A study of British literature at the end of the nineteenth century. New York, Macmillan Co., 1939. xvii + 326 pp.—"Bibliography," pp. 317–322.

389. Davis, Herbert, DeVane, Wm. C., and Bald, R[obert] C., eds. Nineteenth-Century Studies. Dedicated by his colleagues . . . to Clark Sutherland Northup. Ithaca, N.Y., Cornell Univ. Press, 1940. ix + 303 pp.

390. Schilling, Bernard N. Human Dignity and the Great Victorians. New York, Columbia Univ. Press for Grinnell College, 1946. xiii + 246 pp.

391. Chew, Samuel C. The Nineteenth Century and After 1789–1939. New York, Appleton-Century-Crofts Inc., 1948. xii + 1111–1606 + xxix pp.—Volume IV of *A Literary History of England,* edited by Albert C. Baugh.

392. Essays Mainly on the Nineteenth Century. Presented to Sir Humphrey Milford. Introduction by G. F. J. C[umberlege]. Oxford Univ. Press, 1948. vii + 160 pp.

393. Jackson, Holbrook. Dreamers of Dreams. The rise and fall of nineteenth century idealism. London, Faber and Faber Ltd., 1948. 283 pp.

394. Cook, John D., and Stevenson, Lionel. English Literature of the Victorian Period. New York, Appleton-Century-Crofts Inc., 1949. xii + 438 pp.—In the series Appleton-Century Handbooks of Literature.

395. Hough, Graham. The Last Romantics. London, Gerald Duckworth and Co., 1949. xix + 284 pp.—A study *inter alios* of Morris, Pater, Rossetti, and Ruskin.

396. Baker, Joseph E., ed. The Reinterpretation of Victorian Literature. Princeton, N.J., University Press, 1950. ix + 236 pp.—Eleven critical essays published by the Victorian Literature Group of the Modern Language Association of America.

397. Shine, Hill, ed. Booker Memorial Studies. Eight essays on Victorian literature in memory of John Manning Booker 1881–1948. Chapel Hill, University of North Carolina Press, 1950. xiv + 183 pp.

398. Vines, Sherard. A Hundred Years of English Literature. London, Gerald Duckworth and Co., 1950. 316 pp.—"Table of Dates" [1830–1941], pp. 267–275; "Select Bibliography," pp. 276–306.

399. Buckley, Jerome H. The Victorian Temper. A study in literary culture. Cambridge, Mass., Harvard Univ. Press, 1951. xiii + 282 pp.

400. Churchill, R[eginald] C. English Literature of the Nineteenth Century. London, University Tutorial Press, 1951. vii + 270 pp.

401. Decker, Clarence R. The Victorian Conscience. New York, Twayne Publ'ers, 1952. 213 pp.—A study of men who opposed Victorian materialism.

402. Halloway, John. The Victorian Sage. Studies in argument. London, Macmillan Co., 1953. viii + 301 pp.—A study *inter alios* of Arnold, Carlyle, Disraeli, George Eliot, Hardy, and Newman.

403. LeRoy, Gaylord C. Perplexed Prophets. Six nineteenth-century British authors. Philadelphia, Temple Univ. Publications, 1953. vii + 205 pp.

404. Temple, Ruth Zabriskie. The Critic's Alchemy. A study of the introduction of French symbolism into England. New York, Twayne Publ'ers, 1953. 345 pp.—"Bibliography," pp. 304–321.

405. Angeli, Helen R. Pre-Raphaelite Twilight. The story of Charles Augustus Howell. London, Richards Press, 1954. xiii + 256 pp.

406. Thomson, Patricia. The Victorian Heroine. A changing ideal 1837–1873. Oxford Univ. Press, 1956. 178 pp.

407. Bentley, Eric. A Century of Hero-Worship. A study of the idea of heroism in Carlyle and Nietzsche with notes on Wagner, Spengler, Stephan George, and D. H. Lawrence. 2nd ed. Boston, Beacon Press, 1957. xii + 271 pp.—Original ed. 1944.

§14. BRITISH LITERATURE: TWENTIETH CENTURY

[See also §31. Fiction: Modern British and American; §51. Surveys: The Modern Era; §56. The Victorian and Modern British Stage; §66. Drama: Nineteenth Century and Modern British and American.]

411. Danielson, Henry. Bibliographies of Modern Authors. London, Bookman's Journal, 1921. xi + 211 pp.—Title pages and full descriptions of works by Beerbohm, Brooke, Crackanthorpe, De La Mare, Drinkwater, Dunsany, Flecker, Gissing, Ledwidge, MacKenzie, Masefield, Merrick, Middleton, Symons, and Walpole.

412. Manly, John Matthews, and Rickert, Edith. Contemporary British Literature. Outlines for study, indexes, bibliographies. Revised and enl. ed. New York, Harcourt, Brace and Co., 1928. 345 pp.—Original ed. 1921.

413. Bibliographies of Modern Authors. First, Second, and Third Series. London, Bookman's Journal, 1921–31. 3 vols.—The imprint varies; the Second Series has the imprint "John Castle." Titles listed are for late nineteenth and early twentieth century poets and novelists. There are occasional facsimile title pages.

414. Ullrich, Kurt. Who Wrote about Whom. A bibliography of books on contemporary British authors. Berlin, Germany, Arthur Collignon, 1932. 60 pp.—Coverage of authors productive c. 1920–30.

415. Millett, Fred B. Contemporary British Literature. A critical survey and 232 author-bibliographies. Third rev. and enl. ed. based on the 2nd rev. and enl. ed. by John M. Manly and Edith Rickert. New York, Harcourt, Brace and Co., 1935. xi + 556 pp.—Reprint 1948. "The Third Revised and Enlarged Edition . . . differs from its predecessors in purpose, scope, and method. It is virtually a new book," p. vii.

416. Daiches, David. The Present Age. After 1920. Editor's preface by Bonamy Dobrée. London, Cresset Press, 1958. x + 376 pp.—Volume V in the series Introductions to English Literature. "Bibliography," pp. 169–368. American edition under the title *The Present Age in British Literature,* Bloomington, Indiana Univ. Press, 1958. The replacement of Edwin Muir, *The Present Age from 1914,* London, Cresset Press, 1939, 309 pp.

---

417. Williams, Harold H. Modern English Writers. Being a study of imaginative literature 1890–1914. New York, Alfred A. Knopf, 1919. xxix + 504 pp.

418. Ervine, St. John G. Some Impressions of My Elders. New York, Macmillan Co., 1922. 305 pp.

419. Mais, S[tuart] P. B. Books and Their Writers. New York, Dodd, Mead and Co., 1920. 343 pp.

420. Cunliffe, J[ohn] W. English Literature during the Last Half Century. 2nd ed. rev. and enl. New York, Macmillan Co., 1923. viii + 357 pp. —Original ed. 1919.

421. Scott, Dixon. Men of Letters. With an introduction by Max Beerbohm. London, Hodder and Stoughton Ltd., 1923. xxi + 313 pp.

422. Priestley, J[ohn] B. Figures in Modern Literature. New York, Dodd, Mead and Co., 1924. 215 pp.

423. Lacon [pseud. of Edmund Henry Lacon Watson]. Lectures to Living Authors. Adorned with portraits of some of the various subjects. Boston, Houghton Mifflin Co., 1925. 231 pp.

424. Muir, Edwin. Transition. Essays on contemporary literature. New York, Viking Press, 1926. xi + 218 pp.—Studies in Robert Graves, Aldous Huxley, D. H. Lawrence, and Virginia Woolf.

425. Adcock, [Arthur] St. John. The Glory That Was Grub Street. Impressions of contemporary authors. New York, Frederick A. Stokes Co., [1928]. x + 340 pp.

426. Braybrooke, Patrick. Some Goddesses of the Pen. Philadelphia, J. B. Lippincott Co., 1928. 156 pp.

427. Dobrée, Bonamy. The Lamp and the Lute. Studies in six modern authors. Oxford Univ. Press, 1929. xvi + 133 pp.—Studies in Ibsen, Hardy, Kipling, Forster, Lawrence, and Eliot.

428. Braybrooke, Patrick. Some Victorian and Georgian Catholics. Their art and outlook. London, Burns, Oates and Washbourne Ltd., [1932]. xi + 202 pp.

429. Cunliffe, J[ohn] W. English Literature in the Twentieth Century. New York, Macmillan Co., 1933. 341 pp.

430. The Post Victorians. With an introduction by W[illiam] R. Inge. London, Ivor Nicholson and Watson Ltd., 1933. xi + 648 pp.

431. Swinnerton, Frank. The Georgian Scene. A literary panorama. New York, Farrar and Rinehart, 1934. x + 522 pp.

432. Maurois, André. Prophets and Poets. Translated by Hamish Miles. New York, Harper and Bros., 1935. xviii + 345 pp.—A study of Chesterton, Conrad, Huxley, Kipling, Lawrence, Mansfield, Shaw, Strachey, and Wells.

433. Elwin, Malcolm. Old Gods Falling. New York, Macmillan Co., 1939. 412 pp.

434. Van Doren, Carl and Mark. American and British Literature since 1890. Rev. and enl. ed. New York, D. Appleton-Century Co., 1939. xi + 350 pp.—Original ed. 1925. "Suggestions for Study," pp. 313–334.

435. Muir, Edwin. The Present Age from 1914. New York, Robert M. McBride and Co., 1940. 309 pp.—Volume V in the series Introductions to English Literature.

436. Ward, A[lfred] C. Twentieth-Century Literature 1901-1940. 7th ed. London, Methuen and Co., 1940. xi + 265 pp.—Original ed. 1928. Reprint of 7th ed. New York, Barnes and Noble, [1957], 248 pp.

437. Tindall, Wm. York. Forces in Modern British Literature 1885–1946. New York, Alfred A. Knopf Inc., 1947. xiii + 385 + xviii pp.—Reprint New York, Vintage Books, 1956.

438. Evans, B[enjamin] Ifor. English Literature between the Wars. 2nd ed. London, Methuen and Co., 1949. ix + 133 pp.—Original ed. 1948.

439. Fraser, G[eorge] S. Post-War Trends in English Literature. Tokyo, Hokuseido Press, [1950 ?]. 167 pp.

440. Routh, H[arold] V. English Literature and Ideas in the Twentieth Century. An inquiry into present difficulties and future prospects. 3rd ed. London, Methuen and Co., 1950. viii + 204 pp.—Original ed. 1946; second ed. 1948.

441. Collins, Arthur Simons. English Literature of the Twentieth Century. London, University Tutorial Press, 1951. vi + 376 pp.

442. Longaker, Mark, and Bolles, Edwin C. Contemporary English Literature. New York, Appleton-Century-Crofts Inc., 1953. xvii + 526 pp.

443. Johnstone, J[ohn] K. The Bloomsbury Group. A study of E. M. Forster, Lytton Strachey, Virginia Woolf, and their circle. London, Secker and Warburg, 1954. x + 383 pp.

444. Spender, Stephen. The Creative Element. A study of vision, despair, and orthodoxy among some modern writers. New York, British Book Center, 1954. 199 pp.

445. Eastwood, Wilfred, and Good, John Thompson. Signposts. A guide to modern English literature. Cambridge Univ. Press for the National Book League, 1960. 79 pp.

§15. IRISH LITERATURE: PROSE, DRAMA, AND VERSE

[For histories of the modern Irish stage see §56. The Victorian and the Modern British Stage.]

449. Brown, Stephen J., S.J. Ireland in Fiction. A guide to Irish novels, tales, romances, and folk-lore. New ed. Dublin, Maunsel and Co., 1919. xx + 362 pp.—Original ed. 1916.

---

450. Weygandt, Cornelius. Irish Plays and Playwrights. Boston, Houghton Mifflin Co., 1913. [ix] + 314 pp.

451. Boyd, Ernest. Ireland's Literary Renaissance. Rev. ed. New York, Alfred A. Knopf, 1922. 456 pp.—Original ed. 1916.

452. MacDonagh, Thos. Literature in Ireland. Studies Irish and Anglo-Irish. Dublin, Talbot Press, 1916. xxii + 248 pp.—Reprint 1919.

453. Boyd, Ernest A. Appreciations and Depreciations. Irish literary studies. Dublin, Talbot Press, 1917. 162 pp.

454. Morris, Lloyd R. The Celtic Dawn. A survey of the renascence in Ireland 1889–1916. New York, Macmillan Co., 1917. xix + 251 pp.

455. Law, Hugh Alexander. Anglo-Irish Literature. With a foreword by AE [i.e. George William Russell]. Dublin, Talbot Press, 1926. xviii + 302 pp.

456. Boyd, Ernest A. The Contemporary Drama of Ireland. Boston, Little, Brown and Co., 1928. 225 pp.

457. Malone, Andrew E. The Irish Drama. New York, Charles Scribner's Sons, 1929. 351 pp.

458. Seymour, St. John D. Anglo-Irish Literature 1200–1582. Cambridge Univ. Press, 1929. [ix] + 169 pp.

459. Gwynn, Stephen. Irish Literature and Drama in the English Language. A short history. London, Thomas Nelson and Sons, 1936. ix + 240 pp.

460. Ellis-Fermor, Una. The Irish Dramatic Movement. London, Methuen and Co., 1939. xvii + 233 pp.

461. Kelly, Blanche Mary. The Voice of the Irish. New York, Sheed and Ward Inc., 1952. xi + 340 pp.

462. Carney, James. Studies in Irish Literature and History. Dublin, Dublin Institute for Advanced Studies, 1955. xi + 412 pp.

463. Murphy, Gerard. Early Irish Lyrics. Eighth to twelfth century. Edited with translation, notes, and glossary. Oxford Univ. Press, 1956. xxii + 315 pp.

464. Knott, Eleanor. Irish Classical Poetry. Commonly called bardic poetry. Dublin, Colm O Lochlainn for the Cultural Relations Committee of Ireland, 1957. 82 pp.—Volume VI in the series Irish Life and Culture. A brief account of the origin of Irish verse.

§16. SCOTTISH LITERATURE: PROSE, DRAMA, AND VERSE

468. Horstmann, [Johann] C[arl]. Barbour's des schottischen Nationaldichters Legendensammlung nebst den Fragmenten seines Trojanerkrieges. Heilbronn, Verlag von Gebrüder Henninger, 1881–82. 2 vols.

469. Veitch, John. The Feeling for Nature in Scottish Poetry. Edinburgh, William Blackwood and Sons, 1887. 2 vols.

470. Eyre-Todd, Geo. Early Scottish Poetry. Thomas the Rhymer, John Barbour, Androw of Wyntown, Henry the Minstrel. London, Sands and Co., [1891]. [iv] + 220 pp.—In the Abbotsford Series of the Scottish Poets. An anthology.

471. Eyre-Todd, Geo., ed. Mediaeval Scottish Poetry. King James the First, Robert Henryson, William Dunbar, Gavin Douglas. London, Sands and Co., [1892]. viii + 269 pp.—In the Abbotsford Series of the Scottish Poets. An anthology.

472. Eyre-Todd, Geo. Scottish Poetry of the Sixteenth Century. Sir David Lyndsay, John Bellenden, King James the Fifth, Sir Richard Maitland, Alexander Scot, Alexander Montgomerie. London, Sands and Co., [1892]. viii + 269 pp.—In the Abbotsford Series of the Scottish Poets. An anthology.

473. Veitch, John. The History and Poetry of the Scottish Border. Their main features and relations. New and enl. ed. Edinburgh, William Blackwood and Sons, 1893. 2 vols.—Original ed. 1878.

474. Browne, Wm. Hand. Selections from the Early Scottish Poets. With introduction, notes, and glossary. Baltimore, Johns Hopkins Univ. Press, 1896. 240 pp.

475. Eyre-Todd, Geo. Scottish Poetry of the Eighteenth Century. Glasgow, William Hodge and Co., 1896. 2 vols.—In the Abbotsford Series of the Scottish Poets. An anthology.

476. Henderson, T[homas] F. Scottish Vernacular Literature. A succinct history. London, David Nutt, 1898. ix + 462 pp.

477. Graham, Henry G. Scottish Men of Letters in the Eighteenth Century. London, A. and C. Black, 1901. xii + 441 pp.

478. Smith, G[eorge] Gregory. Specimens of Middle Scots. With introduction, notes, and glossary. Edinburgh, William Blackwood and Sons, 1902. lxxvi + 374 pp.

479. Harvey, Wm. Scottish Chapbook Literature. Paisley, Scotland, Alexander Gardner, 1903. 153 pp.

480. Millar, J[ohn] H. A Literary History of Scotland. London, T. F. Unwin, 1903. xv + 703 pp.—Glossary, pp. 687–692; bibliography, pp. 685–686.

481. Douglas, Geo. Scottish Poetry. Drummond of Hawthornden to Fergusson. Glasgow, James Maclehose and Sons, 1911. x + 193 pp.

482. Millar, John Hepburn. Scottish Prose of the Seventeenth and Eighteenth Centuries. Glasgow, James Maclehose and Sons, 1912. xi + 273 pp.—A series of lectures delivered in the University of Glasgow 1912.

483. Watt, Lauchlan Maclean. Scottish Life and Poetry. London, James Nisbet and Co., 1912. viii + 509 pp.—"Bibliography," pp. 501–502.

484. Lawson, Robb. The Story of the Scots Stage. Paisley, Scotland, Alexander Gardner, 1917. [iv] + 303 pp.—"Bibliography," pp. 287–292.

485. Smith, G[eorge] Gregory. Scottish Literature. Character and influence. London, Macmillan Co., 1919. viii + 296 pp.

486. Schofield, Wm. Henry. Mythical Bards and the Life of William Wallace. Cambridge, Mass., Harvard Univ. Press, 1920. xiii + 381 pp.—Volume V in the series Harvard Studies in Comparative Literature.

487. Mill, Anna Jean. Mediaeval Plays in Scotland. Edinburgh, William Blackwood and Sons, 1927. vii + 8–356 pp.—Number 24 in the series Saint Andrews University Publications.

488. Craigie, Wm. The Northern Element in English Literature. University of Toronto Press, 1933. 135 pp.

489. Mackenzie, Agnes M. An Historical Survey of Scottish Literature to 1714. London, A. Maclehose and Co., 1933. viii + 252 pp.

490. Gray, M[argaret] M. Scottish Poetry. From Barbour to James VI. London, J. M. Dent and Sons, 1935. xxx + 385 pp.—An anthology.

491. Brie, Friedrich. Die nationale Literatur Schottlands von den Anfängen bis zur Renaissance. Halle a. S., Max Niemeyer Verlag, 1937. xiii + 371 pp.

492. Speirs, John. The Scots Literary Tradition. An essay in criticism. London, Chatto and Windus, 1940. viii + 191 pp.

493. Wood, H[enry] Harvey. Scottish Literature. London, Longmans, Green and Co. for the British Council, 1952. 72 pp.

494. Kinsley, James, ed. Scottish Poetry. A critical survey. London, Cassell and Co., 1955. ix + 330 pp.—Essays on all major historical eras of Scottish poetry.

495. Wittig, Kurt. The Scottish Tradition in Literature. Edinburgh, Oliver and Boyd Ltd., 1958. viii + 352 pp.—A complete history of Scottish literature.

496. Smith, Sydney Goodsir. Gavin Douglas. A selection from his poetry. Edinburgh, Oliver and Boyd for the Saltire Society, 1959. 100 pp.

§17. AMERICAN LITERATURE

500. Rusk, Ralph L. The Literature of the Middle Western Frontier. Vol. II: Bibliographies. New York, Columbia Univ. Press, 1926. vi + 419 pp.

501. Fullerton, B[radford] M. Selective Bibliography of American Literature 1775–1900. A brief estimate of the more important American authors and a description of their representative works. With an introduc-

tion by Carl Van Doren. New York, W. F. Payson, 1932. xiii + 327 pp. —Reprint New York, Dial Press, 1936.

502. Millett, Fred B. Contemporary American Authors. A critical survey and 219 bio-bibliographies. New York, Harcourt, Brace and Co., 1940. xiii + 716 pp.—Reprint 1944.

503. Burke, W[illiam] J., and Howe, Will D. American Authors and Books 1640–1940. New York, Gramercy Publ'ing Co., 1943. x + 858 (double column) pp.—An alphabetical list of authors with titles in chronological order after each author.

504. Spiller, Robt. E., Thorp, Willard, Johnson, Thos. H., and Canby, Henry Seidel. Literary History of the United States. Bibliography. Associates Howard Mumford Jones, Dixon Wecter, and Stanley T. Williams. New York, Macmillan Co., 1948. xxii + 817 pp.

505. Vail, R[obert] W. G. The Voice of the Old Frontier. Philadelphia, University of Pennsylvania Press, 1949. xii + 492 pp.—In the series Publications of the A.S.U. Rosenbach Fellowship in Bibliography. "A Bibliography of North American Frontier Literature 1542–1800," pp. 84–466.

506. Palmer, Philip Motley. German Works on America 1492–1800. Berkeley, University of California Press, 1952. 271–412 pp.—Volume XXXVI, no. 10, in the series University of California Publications in Modern Philology.

507. Leary, Lewis. Articles on American Literature 1900–1950. Durham, N.C., Duke Univ. Press, 1954. xv + 437 pp.

508. Blanck, Jacob. Bibliography of American Literature. Compiled . . . for the Bibliographic Society of America. Vol. I: Henry Adams to Donn Byrne; Vol. II: George W. Cable to Timothy Dwight. New Haven, Yale Univ. Press, 1955–57. 2 vols.

509. Woodress, James Leslie. Dissertations in American Literature 1891–1955. Durham, N.C., Duke Univ. Press, 1957. x + 100 pp.

510. Gohdes, Clarence. Bibliographical Guide to the Study of the Literature of the U.S.A. Durham, N.C., Duke Univ. Press, 1959. 102 pp.

§18. AMERICAN LITERATURE: HISTORICAL SURVEYS

514. Duyckinck, Evert A. and Geo. L. Cyclopaedia of American Literature. Embracing personal and critical notices of authors and selections from their writings. Edited by M. Laird Simonds. Philadelphia, William Rutter and Co., 1875. 2 vols.—Original ed. 1855.

515. Whitcomb, Selden L. Chronological Outlines of American Literature. With an introduction by Brander Matthews. New York, Macmillan and Co., 1893. x + 285 pp.

516. Stanton, Theodore. A Manual of American Literature. New York, G. P. Putnam's Sons, 1909. xiii + 493 pp.—Number 4000 in the series Tauchnitz Editions.

517. Miller, James McDonald. An Outline of American Literature. New York, Farrar and Rinehart Inc., 1934. viii + 386 pp.

518. Crawford, Bartholomew V., Kern, Alexander C., and Needleman, Morriss H. An Outline History of American Literature. New York, Barnes and Noble Inc., 1945. xv + 323 pp.—In the College Outline Series.

519. Hart, James D. Oxford Companion to American Literature. 3rd ed., rev. and enl. New York, Oxford Univ. Press, 1956. viii + 890 (double column) pp.—Original ed. 1941; second ed. 1948.

520. Richards, Robt. Fulton. Concise Dictionary of American Literature. New York, Philosophical Library, 1955. vii + 253 (double column) pp. —Reprint Ames, Iowa, Littlefield, Adams and Co., 1956, number 122 in the series Littlefield College Outlines.

521. Smith, Guy E. American Literature. A complete survey with plot summaries of major works. Dictionary of literary terms. Ames, Iowa, Littlefield, Adams and Co., 1957. xv + 283 pp.—Number 30 in the series Littlefield College Outlines.

---

522. Bates, Katherine Lee. American Literature. New York, Macmillan Co., 1897. ix + 325 + xii pp.

523. Wendell, Barrett. A Literary History of America. New York, Charles Scribner's Sons, 1900. xiii + 574 pp.—Reprint 1914.

524. Wendell, Barrett, and Greenough, Chester Noyes. A History of Literature in America. New York, Charles Scribner's Sons, 1904. xvii + 443 pp.—Reprint 1911.

525. Lawton, Wm. Cranston. Introduction to the Study of American Literature. New rev. ed. Yonkers-on-Hudson, N.Y., World Book Co., 1914. vii + 371 pp.—Original ed. 1902.

526. Kellner, Leon. American Literature. With a preface by Gustav Pollak. Translated from the German by Julia Franklin. Garden City, N.Y., Doubleday, Page and Co., 1915. xiv + 254 pp.—In the series American Books. Original Ger. ed. 1913.

527. Boynton, Percy H. A History of American Literature. Boston, Ginn and Co., 1919. v + 513 pp.

528. Trent, Wm. Peterfield, Erskine, John, Sherman, Stuart P., and Van Doren, Carl. The Cambridge History of American Literature. New York, G. P. Putnam's Sons, 1917–21. 4 vols.—Reprint 1933 in 3 vols. and 1943 and 1946 in one. Also by the same authors *A Short History of American Literature,* Based upon the Cambridge History of American Literature, New York, G. P. Putnam's Sons, 1922, v + 428 pp.

529. Leisy, Ernest Erwin. American Literature. An interpretative survey. New York, Thomas Y. Crowell Co., 1929. x + 299 pp.

530. Cairns, Wm. B. A History of American Literature. Rev. ed. New York, Oxford Univ. Press, 1930. ix + 569 pp.—Original ed. 1912.

531. Angoff, Chas. A Literary History of the American People. New York, A. A. Knopf, 1931. 2 vols.

532. Dickinson, Thos. H. The Making of American Literature. Being a near view of the procession of American writings and writing men from the earliest settlements up to our own times with some consideration of the way men and women lived, their vocations, opinions, and amusements. New York, Century Co., 1932. xii + 733 pp.

533. Knight, Grant C. American Literature and Culture. New York, Ray Long and Richard R. Smith Inc., 1932. ix + 523 pp.

534. Hicks, Granville. The Great Tradition. An interpretation of American literature since the Civil War. Rev. ed. New York, Macmillan Co., 1935. xv + 341 pp.—Original ed. 1933. Bibliography, pp. 331–336.

535. Taylor, Walter Fuller. A History of American Letters. With bibliographies by Harry Hartwick. Boston, American Book Co., 1936. xv + 678 pp.

536. Lewisohn, Ludwig. The Story of American Literature. New York, Random House, [1939]. xxxii + 652 pp.—In the series Modern Library of World's Best Books. Originally *Expression in America,* New York, Harper and Bros., 1932, to which the Random House ed. adds a section "Postscript – 1939."

537. Quinn, Arthur Hobson, ed. The Literature of the American People. An historical and critical survey. Part I: The Colonial and Revolutionary Period, by Kenneth B. Murdock; Part II: The Establishment of National Literature, by Arthur H. Quinn; Part III: The Later Nineteenth Century, by Clarence Gohdes; Part IV: The Twentieth Century, by George F.

Whicher. New York, Appleton-Century-Crofts Inc., 1951. xix + 1172 pp.

538. Spiller, Robt. E., Thorp, Willard, Johnson, Thos. H., and Canby, Henry S. Literary History of the United States. With associates Howard M. Jones, Dixon Wecter, and Stanley T. Williams. New York, Macmillan Co., 1948. 2 (continuously paged) vols. of text plus a volume of bibliography.—Revised ed. 1953 of the text only in 1 vol. (issued without a revision of the volume of bibliography).

539. Spiller, Robt. E. The Cycle of American Literature. An essay in historical criticism. New York, Macmillan Co., 1955. xvii + 318 pp.—Reprint New York, New American Library, 1957, xi + 240 pp., number MD188 in the series Mentor Books.

540. Brooks, Van Wyck, and Bettmann, Otto L. Our Literary Heritage. A pictorial history of the writer in America. New York, E. P. Dutton and Co., 1956. ix + 246 (double column) pp.

§19. AMERICAN LITERATURE: CRITICAL EXPOSITION AND EVALUATION

544. Holliday, Carl. A History of Southern Literature. New York, Neale Publ'ing Co., 1906. 406 pp.

545. Moses, Montrose J. The Literature of the South. New York, Thomas Y. Crowell and Co., 1910. xv + 511 pp.

546. Trent, W[illiam] P., and Erskine, John. Great American Writers. New York, Henry Holt and Co., 1912. 256 pp.—Number 48 in the series Home University Library of Modern Knowledge.

547. Perry, Bliss. The American Spirit in Literature. A chronicle of great interpreters. New Haven, Yale Univ. Press, 1918. 281 pp.—Reprint 1921.

548. Lawrence, D[avid] H. Studies in Classic American Literature. New York, Thomas Seltzer Inc., 1923. ix + 264 pp.—Reprints by various firms, as in 1933, 1951, 1955.

549. Rusk, Ralph L. The Literature of the Middle Western Frontier. New York, Columbia Univ. Press, 1925. 2 vols.

550. Dondore, Dorothy. The Prairie and the Making of Middle America. Four centuries of description. Cedar Rapids, Iowa, Torch Press, 1926. viii + 472 pp.

551. Hazard, Lucy L. The Frontier in American Literature. New York, Crowell Co., 1927. xx + 308 pp.

552. Parrington, Vernon Louis. Main Currents in American Thought. An interpretation of American literature from the beginnings to 1920. Vol. I: 1620–1800 The Colonial Mind; Vol. II: 1800–1860 The Romantic Revolution in America; Vol. III: The Beginnings of Critical Realism in America. New York, Harcourt, Brace and Co., 1927. 3 vols.—Reprint 1930 in one vol. (xvii + 413 + xxii + 493 + xxxix + 429 pp.).

553. Smith, C[harles] Alphonso. Southern Literary Studies. A collection of literary, biographical, and other sketches. With a biographical study by F. Stringfellow Barr. Chapel Hill, University of North Carolina Press, 1927. 192 pp.—"Bibliography of Negro Folk-Lore and Dialect," pp. 155–157; "Bibliography of C. Alphonso Smith," pp. 185–192.

554. Foerster, Norman, ed. The Reinterpretation of American Literature. Some contributions toward the understanding of its historical development. New York, Harcourt, Brace and Co., 1928. xv + 271 pp.

555. Macy, John, ed. American Writers on American Literature by Thirty-Seven Contemporary Writers. New York, Horace Liveright Inc., 1931. xxii + 3–539 pp.

556. Masson, Thos. L. Our American Humorists. New and enl. ed. New York, Dodd, Mead and Co., 1931. [xxi] + 448 pp.—Original ed. 1922.

557. Van Doren, Carl. What Is American Literature? New York, William Morrow and Co., 1935. 128 pp.—A development of Van Doren's *American Literature*, Los Angeles, U.S. Library Association, 1933, 92 pp.

558. Rahv, Philip, ed. Discovery of Europe. The story of American experience in the old world. With an introduction and comments. Boston, Houghton Mifflin Co., 1947. xix + 743 pp.

559. Blankenship, Russell. American Literature as an Expression of the National Mind. Rev. ed. New York, Henry Holt and Co., 1949. xx + 775 pp.—Original ed. 1931.

560. Horton, Rod W., and Edwards, Herbert W. Backgrounds of American Literary Thought. New York, Appleton-Century-Crofts Inc., 1952. xi + 425 pp.

561. Clark, Harry Hayden, ed. Transitions in American Literature. Durham, N.C., Duke Univ. Press, 1954. xv + 479 pp.

562. Wilson, Edmund. The Shock of Recognition. The development of literature in the United States recorded by the men who made it. 2nd ed. New York, Farrar, Straus and Cudahy, 1955. 1290 pp.—Original ed. 1943.

563. Walcutt, Chas. C. American Literary Naturalism, a Divided Stream. Minneapolis, University of Minnesota Press, 1956. xii + 332 pp.

564. Larrabee, Eric, ed. American Panorama. Essays by fifteen American critics on 350 books past and present which portray the U.S.A. in its many aspects. Foreword by John W. Gardner. New York Univ. Press, 1957. xxiv + 436 pp.

565. Spencer, Benjamin T. The Quest for Nationality. An American campaign. Syracuse, N.Y., University Press, 1957. xv + 389 pp.

566. Brooks, Van Wyck. The Dream of Arcadia. American writers and artists in Italy 1760–1915. New York, E. P. Dutton and Co., 1958. xiii + 272 pp.

567. Feidelson, Chas., Jr., and Brodtkorb, Paul, Jr., eds. Interpretations of American Literature. New York, Oxford Univ. Press, 1959. ii + 386 pp. —In the series Galaxy Books.

568. McNeir, Waldo F., and Levy, Leo B., eds. Studies in American Literature. Baton Rouge, Louisiana State Univ. Press, 1959. 192 pp.—Number 8 in the Louisiana State University Studies: Humanities Series.

§20. AMERICAN LITERATURE: FROM THE BEGINNINGS TO *CIRCA* 1900

[See also §30. Fiction: British and American in the Nineteenth Century; §50. Surveys: The Victorian Era; §57. The American Stage; §66. Drama: Nineteenth Century and Modern British and American.]

572. Tyler, Moses Coit. A History of American Literature 1607–1765. Vol. I: First Colonial Period 1607–1676; Vol. II: Second Colonial Period 1677–1765. New York, G. P. Putnam's Sons, 1878. 2 vols.—Reprint 1897 as *A History of American Literature during the Colonial Period;* reprint 1904 in 1 vol.; reprint in 1 vol. Ithaca, N.Y., Cornell Univ. Press, 1949, xxxiii + 551 pp., with a foreword by Howard Mumford Jones.

573. Richardson, Chas. F. American Literature 1607–1885. Part I: The Development of American Thought; Part II: American Poetry and Fiction. New York, G. P. Putnam's Sons, 1886–88. 2 vols.—Reprint 1902 in 1 vol. (xxi + 528 + [iv] + 462 pp.).

574. Tyler, Moses Coit. The Literary History of the American Revolution 1763–1783. New York, G. P. Putnam's Sons, 1897. 2 vols.—Reprint New York, Friedrich Ungar, [1957]. "Bibliography," II, pp. 429–483.

575. Trent, Wm. P. A History of American Literature 1607–1865. New York, D. Appleton and Co., 1903. x + 608 pp.

576. Vincent, Leon H. American Literary Masters. Boston, Houghton Mifflin Co., 1906. xiv + 518 pp.

577. Brownell, W[illiam] C. American Prose Masters. Cooper, Hawthorne, Emerson, Poe, Lowell, Henry James. New York, Charles Scribner's Sons, 1909. xlv + 345 pp.

578. Canby, Henry Seidel. Classic Americans. A study of eminent American writers from Irving to Whitman with an introductory survey of the colonial background of our national literature. New York, Harcourt, Brace and Co., 1931. xvii + 371 pp.

579. Phelps, Wm. L. Some Makers of American Literature. Boston, Marshall Jones Co., 1923. xi + 187 pp.—A study *inter alios* of Cooper and Hawthorne.

580. Pattee, Fred Lewis. The First Century of American Literature 1770–1870. New York, D. Appleton–Century Co., 1935. viii + 613 pp.—See also Pattee's *A History of American Literature since 1870,* New York, Century Co., 1915, 449 pp.

581. Brooks, Van Wyck. New England Indian Summer 1865–1915. New York, E. P. Dutton and Co., 1940. [xi] + 557 pp.—Volume IV of Brooks's *Makers and Finders,* A history of the writer in America 1800–1915.

582. Brooks, Van Wyck. The Flowering of New England 1815–1865. New and rev. ed. New York, E. P. Dutton and Co., 1940. [xi] + 550 pp.—Volume II of Brooks's *Makers and Finders,* A history of the writer in America 1800–1915. Original ed. 1936; new ed. frequently reprinted, as in 1952.

583. Brooks, Van Wyck. The World of Washington Irving. Philadelphia, Blakiston Co., 1944. [ix] + 495 pp.—Volume I of Brooks's *Makers and Finders,* A history of the writer in America 1800–1915. Reprint 1945.

584. Brooks, Van Wyck. The Times of Melville and Whitman. New York, E. P. Dutton and Co., 1947. ix + 489 pp.—Volume III of Brooks's *Makers and Finders,* A history of the writer in America 1800–1915. Reprint 1953.

585. Knight, Grant C. The Critical Period in American Literature. Chapel Hill, University of North Carolina Press, 1951. xiii + 208 pp.—A treatment of the period 1890 to 1900.

586. Brooks, Van Wyck. The Confident Years 1885–1915. New York, E. P. Dutton and Co., 1952. ix + 627 pp.—Volume V of Brooks's *Makers and Finders,* A history of the writer in America 1800–1915.

587. Stafford, John. The Literary Criticism of "Young America." A study in the relationship of politics and literature 1837–1850. Berkeley, University

of California Press, 1952. 154 pp.—Number 3 in the series University of California Publications: English Studies. "Bibliography," pp. 143–148.

588. Hubbell, Jay B. The South in American Literature 1607–1900. Durham, N.C., Duke Univ. Press, 1954. xix + 987 pp.

§21. AMERICAN LITERATURE: FROM *CIRCA* 1900 TO THE PRESENT DAY

[See also §31. Fiction: Modern British and American; §51. Surveys: The Modern Era; §57. The American Stage; §66. Drama: Nineteenth Century and Modern British and American.]

592. Jones, Howard Mumford. Guide to American Literature and Its Backgrounds since 1890. 2nd ed. Cambridge, Mass., Harvard Univ. Press, 1959. 192 pp.—Original ed. 1953.

---

593. Hansen, Harry. Midwest Portraits. A book of memories and friendships. New York, Harcourt, Brace and Co., 1923. 357 pp.—Studies *inter alios* of Sandburg, Sherwood Anderson, and E. L. Masters.

594. Overton, Grant. Authors of the Day. Studies in contemporary literature. New York, George H. Doran, 1924. viii + 9–390 pp.—A treatment of individual authors and poets. The chapters are taken from two earlier books by the same author: *When Winter Comes to Main Street,* New York, George H. Doran, 1922, x + 11–384 pp.; and *American Nights Entertainment,* New York, D. Appleton and Co., 1923, xi + 12–414 pp. See also Overton's *Cargoes for Crusoes,* New York, D. Appleton and Co., 1924, x + 11–416 pp.

595. Beach, Joseph Warren. The Outlook for American Prose. University of Chicago Press, 1926. vii + 285 pp.

596. Coblentz, Stanton A. The Literary Revolution. New York, Frank-Maurice Inc., 1927. 202 pp.

597. Pattee, Fred L. The New American Literature 1890–1930. New York, Century Co., 1930. ix + 507 pp.

598. Luccock, Halford E. American Mirror. Social, ethical, and religious aspects of American literature 1930–1940. New York, Macmillan Co., 1940. ix + 300 pp.

599. Kazin, Alfred. On Native Grounds. An interpretation of modern American prose literature. New York, Reynal and Hitchcock, 1942. xiii + 541 pp.

600. Straumann, Heinrich. American Literature in the Twentieth Century. London, Hutchinson House, 1951. 189 pp.—In the series Hutchinson's University Library.

601. Brodbeck, May, Gray, James, and Metzger, Walter. American Non-Fiction 1900–1950. Preface by William V. O'Connor and Frederick J. Hoffman. Chicago, Henry Regnery Co., 1952. ix + 198 pp.—In the series Twentieth-Century Literature in America.

602. Wilson, Edmund. The Shores of Light. A literary chronicle of the twenties and thirties. New York, Farrar, Straus and Young, 1952. xii + 814 pp.—Reprint in *A Literary Chronicle: 1920–1950,* Garden City, N.Y., Doubleday and Co., 1956, 442 pp., number 85 in the series Anchor Books.

603. Rubin, Louis D., Jr., and Jacobs, Robt. D., eds. Southern Renascence. The literature of the modern South. Baltimore, Johns Hopkins Press, 1953. xii + 450 pp.

604. Cowley, Malcolm. The Literary Situation. New York, Viking Press, 1954. xi + 259 pp.

605. Knight, Grant C. The Strenuous Age in American Literature. Chapel Hill, University of North Carolina Press, 1954. xiii + 270 pp.—A treatment of the years 1900 to 1910.

606. [(London) Times Literary Supplement.] American Writing Today. Its independence and vigor. Edited by A[llan] Angoff. New York Univ. Press, 1957. xx + 433 pp.—Texts which first appeared Sept. 17, 1954 in the *TLS*. See also "The American Imagination, Its strength and scope," *TLS* special no., Nov. 6, 1959.

607. Heiney, Donald. Recent American Literature. Great Neck, N.Y., Barron's Educational Series Inc., 1958. [xi] + 609 pp.—"Bibliography," pp. 574–601.

CHAPTER II

PROSE

§22. THE ART OF PROSE

[See also §69. Basic Principles of Criticism.]

611. Read, Herbert. English Prose Style. New York, Henry Holt and Co., 1928. xv + 229 pp.—Reprint Boston, Beacon Press, 1955 (reprint 1959), number 10 in the series Beacon Paperbacks.

612. Montague, C[harles] E. A Writer's Notes on His Trade. London, Chatto and Windus, 1930. 254 pp.—Reprint 1946.

613. Tempest, Norton R. The Rhythm of English Prose. A manual for students. Cambridge Univ. Press, 1930. viii + 138 pp.

614. Dobrée, Bonamy. Modern Prose Style. Oxford, Clarendon Press, 1934. vi + 252 pp.—Reprint 1946.

615. Richards, Ivor A. The Philosophy of Rhetoric. New York, Oxford Univ. Press, 1936. ix + 138 pp.—Number 3 in the series Mary Flexner Lectures on the Humanities.

616. De La Mare, Walter. Poetry in Prose. New York, Oxford Univ. Press, 1937. 85 pp.—The Warton Lecture on English Poetry, British Academy, 1935.

617. Baum, Paull F. The Other Harmony of Prose. An essay in English prose rhythm. Durham, N.C., Duke Univ. Press, 1952. 230 pp.

618. Weaver, Richard M. The Ethics of Rhetoric. Chicago, Henry Regnery Co., 1953. [vi] + 234 pp.—A treatment with a semantic emphasis.

619. Boulton, Marjorie. The Anatomy of Prose. London, Routledge and Kegan Paul Ltd., 1954. xii + 190 pp.

620. Sutherland, James. On English Prose. University of Toronto Press, 1957. ix + 123 pp.—The Alexander Lectures 1956–57.

621. Brooke-Rose, Christine. A Grammar of Metaphor. London, Secker and Warburg Ltd., 1958. xi + 343 pp.

§23. THE HISTORY OF ENGLISH PROSE

[See also §68. Criticism: Histories and Historical Studies.]

625. Dawson, W[illiam] J. The Makers of English Prose. New and rev. ed. New York, Fleming H. Revell Co., 1906. 308 pp.—Original ed. 1899.

626. Saintsbury, Geo. A History of English Prose Rhythm. London, Macmillan Co., 1912. xvi + 489 pp.—Reprint 1922.

627. Krapp, Geo. Philip. The Rise of English Literary Prose. New York, Oxford Univ. Press, 1915. xiii + 551 pp.

628. Chambers, R[aymond] W. On the Continuity of English Prose from Alfred to Moore and His School. An extract from the introduction to Nicholas Harpsfield's Life of Sir Thomas More edited by E. V. Hitchcock and R. W. Chambers. Oxford Univ. Press for the Early English Text Society, 1932. xlv–clxxiv pp.—Reprint 1950.

629. Crane, Wm. G. Wit and Rhetoric in the Renaissance. The formal basis of Elizabethan prose style. New York, Columbia Univ. Press, 1937. vii + 285 pp.—Number 129 in the series Columbia University Studies in English and Comparative Literature. "Bibliography," pp. 253–276.

630. Workman, Samuel K. Fifteenth Century Translation as an Influence on English Prose. Princeton, N.J., University Press, 1940. vii + 210 pp.—Number 18 in the series Princeton Studies in English.

631. Williamson, Geo. The Senecan Amble. A study in prose from Bacon to Collier. London, Faber and Faber Ltd., 1951. 377 pp.

632. Howell, Wilbur Samuel. Logic and Rhetoric in England 1500–1700. Princeton, N.J., University Press, 1956. ix + 411 pp.

633. Thomson, J[ames] A. K. Classical Influences on English Prose. London, George Allen and Unwin Ltd., 1956. xiii + 303 pp.

§24. FICTION

636. Griswold, Wm. M. A Descriptive List of Novels and Tales. Cambridge, Mass., W. M. Griswold, 1890–95. 2 vols. in 10 pts.

637. Dixon, Zella Allen. The Comprehensive Subject Index to Universal Prose Fiction. New York, Dodd, Mead and Co., 1897. ix + 421 pp.

638. Baker, Ernest A., and Packman, James. A Guide to the Best Fiction, English and American, Including Translations from Foreign Languages. New and enl. ed. London, Routledge, 1932. viii + 634 pp.—Original ed. 1903; new ed. 1913.

639. Block, Andrew. The English Novel 1740–1850. A catalogue including prose romances, short stories, and translations of foreign fiction. With an introduction by Ernest A. Baker. London, Grafton and Co., 1939. xi + 367 (double column) pp.

640. Lenrow, Elbert. Reader's Guide to Prose Fiction. An introductory essay, with bibliographies of 1500 novels selected, topically classified, and annotated for use in meeting the needs of individuals in general education. New York, D. Appleton–Century Co., 1940. xi + 371 (double column) pp.—In the series Progressive Education Association Publications.

641. Goodman, Roland A. Plot Outlines of a Hundred Famous Novels. New York, Barnes and Noble Inc., 1942. xvi + 421 pp.—Number 215 in the series Everyday Handbooks. Frequent reprints, as in 1959.

642. Kerr, Elizabeth Margaret. Bibliography of the Sequence Novel. Minneapolis, University of Minnesota Press, 1950. v + 126 pp.—Sequence novels in Continental languages as well as in English.

643. Cotton, G[erald] B., and Glencross, Alan. Fiction Index. A guide to over 10000 works of fiction including short story collections, anthologies, and omnibus volumes, most of which have been published, republished, or re-issued since the war, arranged under 2000 subject headings with numerous references and intended for use in public and circulating libraries, schools, and bookshops and by the general reader. London, Association of Assistant Librarians, 1953. 223 pp.

644. Gardner, Frank M. Sequels. Incorporating Aldred and Parker's Sequel Stories. 4th ed. London, Association of Assistant Librarians, 1955. 189 (double column) pp.—Original ed. 1922; second ed. 1928; third ed. 1947. Original title *A List of English and American Sequel Stories.*

645. Whiteman, Maxwell. A Century of Fiction by American Negroes 1853–1952. A descriptive bibliography. Philadelphia, Maurice Jacobs Inc., 1955. 64 pp.

646. Coan, Otis W., and Lillard, Richard G. America in Fiction. An annotated list of novels that interpret aspects of life in the United States. 4th ed. Stanford Univ. Press, 1956. viii + 200 pp.—First ed. 1941; second ed. 1945; third ed. 1949. List of works treating pioneering, farm and village life, industrial America, politics and institutions, religion, and minority ethnic groups.

647. Bell, Inglis, and Baird, Donald. The English Novel, 1578–1956. A checklist of twentieth-century criticisms. Denver, Col., Swallow Press, 1958. 169 pp.

648. Cook, Dorothy E., and Fidell, Estelle A. Fiction Catalogue 1950 Edition. A subject, author, and title list of 3400 works of fiction in the English language with annotations. New York, H. W. Wilson Co., 1951. x + 561 (double column) pp.—*Supplement 1951–1955,* by Estelle A. Fidell, New York, H. W. Wilson Co., 1956, viii + 233 (double column) pp. *Supplement 1956,* by Estelle A. Fidell, New York, H. W. Wilson Co., 1957, viii + 56 (double column) pp. *Supplement 1957,* by Estelle A. Fidell, New York, H. W. Wilson Co., 1958, viii + 47 (double column) pp.

---

§25. FICTION: CRITICAL EXPOSITION AND EVALUATION OF THE ENGLISH AND AMERICAN NOVEL AND ITS NOVELISTS

652. Burton, Richard. Masters of the English Novel. A study of principles and personalities. New York, Henry Holt and Co., 1909. ix + 357 pp.

653. Phelps, Wm. Lyon. Essays on Modern Novelists. New York, Macmillan Co., 1910. ix + 293 pp.—"List of Publications" [of B. Björnson, R. D. Blackmore, S. L. Clemens, W. De Morgan, W. D. Howells, R. Kipling, A. Ollivant, H. Sienkiewicz, R. L. Stevenson, H. Sudermann, and Mrs. Humphry Ward], by Andrew Keogh, pp. 261–293.

654. Scarborough, Dorothy. The Supernatural in Modern English Fiction. New York, G. P. Putnam's Sons, 1917. vii + 329 pp.

655. Sherman, Stuart P. On Contemporary Literature. New York, Henry Holt and Co., 1917. [vii] + 312 pp.—Reprint 1923. A study *inter alios* of Bennett, Dreiser, Moore, Twain, and Wells.

656. Whiteford, Robt. N. Motives in English Fiction. New York, G. P. Putnam's Sons, 1918. xi + 378 pp.

657. Hall, Ernest Jackson. The Satirical Element in the American Novel. Philadelphia, University of Pennsylvania, 1922. 89 pp.—"Chronological List of American Novels in Which the Satirical Element Is Significant," pp. 82–86.

658. Schelling, Felix E. Appraisements and Asperities as to Some Contemporary Writers. Philadelphia, J. B. Lippincott Co., 1922. 199 pp.—A collection of reviews published in the *Evening Public Ledger* of Philadelphia.

659. Follett, Wilson. The Modern Novel. A study of the purpose and the meaning of fiction. Rev. ed. New York, Alfred A. Knopf, 1923. xxxii + 338 pp.—Original ed. 1918.

660. Mansfield, Katherine. Novels and Novelties. Edited by J. Middleton Murry. New York, Alfred A. Knopf, 1930. 322 + v pp.

661. Braybrooke, Patrick. Some Catholic Novelists. Their art and outlook. London, Burns, Oates and Washbourne Ltd., 1931. xv + 232 pp.—See also Braybrooke's earlier *Philosophies in Modern Fiction,* London, C. W. Daniel Co., 1929, 86 pp.

662. Michaud, Régis. The American Novel Today. A social and psychological study. Boston, Little, Brown and Co., 1931. xi + 293 pp.

663. Beach, Joseph Warren. The Twentieth Century Novel. Studies in technique. New York, D. Appleton–Century Co., 1932. viii + 569 pp.

664. Linn, James W., and Taylor, Houghton W. A Foreword to Fiction. New York, D. Appleton-Century Co., 1935. vii + 202 pp.

665. Verschoyle, Derek, ed. The English Novelists. A survey of the novel by twenty contemporary novelists. London, Chatto and Windus, 1936. xii + 293 pp.

666. Muller, Herbert J. Modern Fiction. A study of values. New York, Funk and Wagnalls Co., 1937. xvi + 447 pp.

667. Daiches, David. The Novel and the Modern World. University of Chicago Press, 1939. x + 228 pp.—Reprint 1948.

668. Monroe, N[ellie] Elizabeth. The Novel and Society. A critical study of the modern novel. Chapel Hill, University of North Carolina Press, 1941. vi + 282 pp.

669. Fox, Ralph. The Novel and the People. 2nd ed. London, Cobbett Press Ltd., 1944. 172 pp.—Original ed. 1937; second ed. reprinted 1948.

670. Blair, Eric [pseud. George Orwell]. Critical Essays. London, Secker and Warburg, 1946. 169 pp.—American ed. title *Dickens, Dali, and Others.* A study *inter alios* of Wells, Kipling, Yeats, Dickens, Koestler, and Wodehouse.

671. Hinkley, Laura L. Ladies of Literature. Fanny Burney, Jane Austen, Charlotte and Emily Brontë, Elizabeth Barrett Browning, George Eliot. New York, Hastings House, 1946. 374 pp.

672. Pritchett, V[ictor] S. The Living Novel. London, Chatto and Windus, 1946. xi + 260 pp.—Reprint 1949.

673. Burgum, Edwin B. The Novel and the World's Dilemma. New York, Oxford Univ. Press, 1947. 352 pp.

674. Maugham, W[illiam] Somerset. Great Novelists and Their Novels. Essays on the ten greatest novels of the world and the men and women who

wrote them. Philadelphia, John C. Winston Co., 1948. vii + 245 pp.—Reprint as *The World's Ten Greatest Novels,* New York, Fawcett World Library, 1959, 240 pp., number D 276 in the series Crest Giants.

675. O'Connor, Wm. Van, ed. Forms of Modern Fiction. Essays collected in honor of Joseph Warren Beach. Minneapolis, University of Minnesota Press, 1948. [viii] + 305 pp.—Reprint Bloomington, Indiana Univ. Press, 1959, number 16 in the series Midland Books.

676. Savage, D[erek] S. The Withered Branch. Six studies in the modern novel. London, Eyre and Spottiswoode, 1950. 207 pp.—A study *inter alios* of Hemingway, Virginia Woolf, Aldous Huxley, and James Joyce.

677. Aldridge, John W., ed. Critiques and Essays on Modern Fiction 1920–1951. Representing the achievement of modern American and British critics. With a foreword by Mark Schorer. New York, Ronald Press Co., 1952. xx + 610 pp.—"Selected Bibliography of Criticism of Modern Fiction," by Robert Wooster Stallman, pp. 553–610.

678. Gardiner, Harold C., S.J., ed. Fifty Years of the American Novel. A Christian appraisal. New York, Charles Scribner's Sons, 1952. xv + 304 pp. Essays by Catholics on Wharton, Hemingway, Farrell, and other American authors.

679. Van Ghent, Dorothy. The English Novel. Form and function. New York, Rinehart and Co., 1953. xii + 473 pp.

680. Fiedler, Leslie A. An End to Innocence. Essays on culture and politics. Boston, Beacon Press, 1955. x + 214 pp.—In the Beacon Contemporary Affairs Series. Reprint 1957. Essays *inter alia* on American fiction.

681. O'Connor, Frank. The Mirror in the Roadway. A study of the modern novel. New York, Alfred A. Knopf, 1956. vii + 316 + vi pp.

682. O'Faolain, Sean. The Vanishing Hero. Studies in novelists of the twenties. Boston, Little, Brown and Co., 1956. xliii + 204 pp.—New copyright 1957.

683. Hicks, Granville, ed. The Living Novel. A symposium. New York, Macmillan Co., 1957. xiii + 230 pp.

684. Fuller, Edmund. Man in Modern Fiction. Some minority opinions on contemporary American writing. New York, Random House, 1958. xvii + 171 pp.

685. Rathburn, Robt. C., and Steinman, Martin, Jr., eds. From Jane Austen to Joseph Conrad. Essays collected in memory of James T. Hillhouse. Minneapolis, University of Minnesota Press, 1958. xii + 326 pp.

686. Shapiro, Chas., ed. Twelve Original Essays on Great American Novels. Detroit, Mich., Wayne State Univ. Press, 1958. xi + 289 pp.

687. Tillyard, E[ustace] M. W. The Epic Strain in the English Novel. London, Chatto and Windus Ltd., 1958. 208 pp.

688. Bewley, Marius. The Eccentric Design. Form in the classic American novel. New York, Columbia Univ. Press, 1959. 327 pp.

689. Kennedy, Margaret. The Outlaws on Parnassus. New York, Viking Press, 1960. 214 pp.

§26. FICTION: HISTORICAL SURVEYS OF ENGLISH AND AMERICAN FICTION

693. Tuckerman, Bayard. A History of English Prose Fiction. From Sir Thomas Malory to George Eliot. New York, G. P. Putnam's Sons, 1882. vii + 331 pp.—Reprint 1899.

694. Lanier, Sidney. The English Novel. A study in the development of personality. New York, Charles Scribner's Sons, 1883. xv + 302 pp.—Reprint 1908 as a "Revised Edition."

695. Dunlop, John Colin. History of Prose Fiction. A new ed., rev. with notes, appendices, and index by Henry Wilson. London, George Bell and Sons, 1888. 2 vols.—Original ed. 1814 in 3 vols.; new ed. reprinted 1906.

696. Cross, Wilbur L. The Development of the English Novel. New York, Macmillan Co., 1899. xvii + 329 pp.—Frequent reprints, as in 1911, 1920.

697. Dawson, W[illiam] J. The Makers of English Fiction. 2nd ed. New York, Fleming H. Revell Co., 1906. 316 pp.—Original ed. 1905.

698. Raleigh, Walter A. The English Novel. Being a short sketch of its history from the earliest times to the appearance of Waverley. 5th ed. New York, Charles Scribner's Sons, 1905. xii + 298 pp.—Original ed. 1894; fifth ed. reprinted 1935.

699. Jackson, Holbrook. Great English Novelists. London, Grant Richards, [1908]. 312 pp.

700. Williams, Harold H. Two Centuries of the English Novel. London, Smith, Elder and Co., 1911. ix + 430 pp.

701. Halliday, Carl. English Fiction from the Fifth to the Twentieth Century. New York, Century Co., 1912. xvi + 425 pp.

702. Saintsbury, Geo. The English Novel. London, J. M. Dent and Sons, 1913. vii + 319 pp.—In the series Channels of English Literature. Frequent reprints, as in 1931.

703. Phelps, Wm. Lyon. The Advance of the English Novel. 5th ed. New York, Dodd, Mead and Co., 1917. xi + 334 pp.—Original ed. 1915.

704. Stoddard, Francis H. The Evolution of the English Novel. New York, Macmillan Co., 1923. v + 235 pp.

705. Weygandt, Cornelius. A Century of the English Novel. Being a consideration of the place in English literature of the long story together with an estimate of its writers from the heyday of Scott to the death of Conrad. New York, Century Co., 1925. [ix] + 504 pp.

706. Ford, Ford M. The English Novel. From the earliest days to the death of Joseph Conrad. Philadelphia, J. B. Lippincott Co., 1928. 149 pp.—In the One Hour Series.

707. Knight, Grant C. The Novel in English. New York, Richard R. Smith Inc., 1931. viii + 395 pp.

708. Lovett, Robt. M., and Hughes, Helen S. The History of the Novel in England. Boston, Houghton Mifflin Co., 1932. viii + 495 pp.—"Bibliography," pp. 465–479.

709. Collins, Norman. The Facts of Fiction. New York, E. P. Dutton and Co., 1933. 312 pp.—Biographies of prominent English novelists from Fielding on.

710. Edgar, Pelham. The Art of the Novel from 1700 to the Present Time. New York, Macmillan Co., 1933. x + 493 pp.

711. Singh, Bhupal. A Survey of Anglo-Indian Fiction. Oxford Univ. Press, 1934. xi + 344 pp.

712. Quinn, Arthur Hobson. American Fiction. An historical and critical survey. New York, D. Appleton–Century Co., 1936. xxiii + 805 pp.—Bibliography, pp. 725–772.

713. Baker, Ernest A. The History of the English Novel. Vol. I: The Age of Romance from the Beginnings to the Renaissance; Vol. II: The Elizabethan Age and After; Vol. III: The Later Romances and the Establishment of Realism; Vol. IV: Intellectual Realism from Richardson to Sterne; Vol. V: The Novel of Sentiment and the Gothic Romance; Vol. VI: Edgeworth, Austen, Scott; Vol. VII: The Age of Dickens and Thackeray; Vol. VIII: From the Brontës to Meredith: Romanticism in the English Novel; Vol. IX: The Day before Yesterday; Vol. X: Yesterday. London, H. F. and G. Witherby Ltd., 1924–39. 10 vols.—Reprint New York, Barnes and Noble Inc., 1950.

714. Van Doren, Carl. The American Novel 1789–1939. Rev. and enl. ed. New York, Macmillan Co., 1940. vii + 406 pp.—Original ed. 1921.

715. Wagenknecht, Edward. Cavalcade of the English Novel from Elizabeth to George VI. New York, Henry Holt and Co., 1943. xxi + 646 pp.—"Selected Bibliography with Annotations," pp. 577–619.

716. McCullough, Bruce Welker. Representative English Novelists from Defoe to Conrad. New York, Harper and Bros., 1946. ix + 359 pp.—"Selected Reading List" [of novels only], pp. 349–352.

717. Snell, Geo. The Shapes of American Fiction 1798–1947. New York, E. P. Dutton and Co., 1947. 316 pp.

718. Cowie, Alexander. The Rise of the American Novel. New York, American Book Co., 1948. xiii + 877 pp.—"Bibliography," pp. 861–862.

719. Church, Richard. The Growth of the English Novel. London, Methuen and Co., 1951. ix + 220 pp.—In the series Home Study Books.

720. Neill, S Diana. A Short History of the English Novel. London, Jarrolds Publ'ers, 1951. 340 pp.—Bibliography, pp. 325–328.

721. Wagenknecht, Edward. Cavalcade of the American Novel. From the birth of the nation to the middle of the twentieth century. New York, Henry Holt and Co., 1952. xvi + 575 pp.

722. Kettle, Arnold. An Introduction to the English Novel. Vol. I: To George Eliot; Vol. II: Henry James to the Present Day. London, Hutchinson House, 1951–53. 2 vols.—In the series Hutchinson's University Library.

723. Allen, Walter. The English Novel. A short critical history. New York, E. P. Dutton and Co., 1954. xxiv + 454 pp.—Reprint New York, E. P. Dutton and Co., 1958, number 9 in the series Dutton Everyman Paperbacks.

724. Chase, Richard. The American Novel and Its Traditions. Garden City, N.Y., Doubleday and Co., 1957. xii + 266 pp.—Number 116 in the series Anchor Books.

§27. FICTION: TYPES OF THE ENGLISH AND AMERICAN NOVEL AND SOME OF ITS SUB-LITERARY SPECIES

727. Baker, Ernest A. A Guide to Historical Fiction. New ed. London, George Routledge and Sons, 1914. xv + 418 (single column) + 419–566 (triple column) pp.—Original ed. 1907 in 2 vols.

728. Nield, Jonathan. A Guide to the Best Historical Novels and Tales. 5th ed. London, Elkin, Mathews and Marrot, 1929. xxviii + 424 pp.—Original ed. 1902.

729. Miller, W[illiam] C. Dime Novel Authors 1860–1900. Grafton, Mass., R. F. Cummings, 1933. 25 pp.—A compilation of pen names, together with the real names of authors, and stock names.

730. Summers, Montague. A Gothic Bibliography. London, Fortune Press, [1941]. xx + 621 pp.

731. Bleiler, Everett. The Checklist of Fantastic Literature. A bibliography of fantasy, weird, and science fiction books published in the English language. Preface by Melvin Korshak. Chicago, Shasta Publishers, 1948. xix + 455 pp.

732. Leclaire, Lucien. A general Analytical Bibliography of the Regional Novelists of the British Isles 1800–1950. Clermont-Ferrand, France, Imp. De Bussac, [1954]. 399 pp.

733. Dikty, T[haddeus] E. Best Science Fiction and Novels. Ninth series.... Chicago, Advent Publ'ers, 1958. 258 pp.—Also T[haddeus] E. Dikty and E[verett] F. Bleiler, *Best Science Fiction Stories 1953–56,* Toronto, George J. McLeod, 1956, 4 vols. Also Dikty and Bleiler's *Best Science Fiction 1951–53,* London, Grayson and Grayson, 1953, 3 vols. Also Dikty and Bleiler's *Best Science Fiction Stories 1949–52,* Toronto, George J. McLeod, 1952, 4 vols. Title and imprint vary.

---

734. Rickett, Arthur. The Vagabond in Literature. London, J. M. Dent and Co., 1906. xvii + 207 pp.

735. Chandler, Frank Wadleigh. The Literature of Roguery. Boston, Houghton Mifflin Co., 1907. 2 vols.—In the series Types of English Literature. Reprint New York, Burt Franklin, 1958, number 9 in the Burt Franklin Bibliographic Series.

736. Matthews, Brander. The Historical Novel and Other Essays. New York, Charles Scribner's Sons, 1914. 321 pp.

737. Kaye, James R. Historical Fiction. Chronologically and historically related. Chicago, Snowdon Publ'ing Co., 1920. xii + 747 pp.

738. Birkhead, Edith. The Tale of Terror. A study of the Gothic romance. London, Constable and Co., 1921. xi + 241 pp.

739. Speare, Morris E. The Political Novel. Its development in England and in America. New York, Oxford Univ. Press, 1924. ix + 377 pp.

740. Pearson, Edmund. Dime Novels. Or following an old trail in popular fiction. Boston, Little, Brown and Co., 1929. x + 280 pp.

741. Thomson, H[enry] Douglas. Masters of Mystery. A study of the detective story. London, William Collins Sons, 1931. 288 pp.

742. Shepperson, Archibald B. The Novel in Motley. A history of the burlesque novel in English. Cambridge, Mass., Harvard Univ. Press, 1936. ix + 301 pp.—"Appendix. A list of burlesque and parody-burlesque novels that appeared between 1830 and 1900," pp. 249–280; "Bibliography," pp. 283–285.

743. Summers, Montague. The Gothic Quest. A history of the Gothic novel. London, Fortune Press, [1938]. vi + 7–443 pp.

744. Black, Frank G. The Epistolary Novel in the Late Eighteenth Century. A descriptive and bibliographical study. Eugene, University of Oregon Press, 1940. v + 184 pp.—Number 2 in the series University of Oregon Monographs, Studies in Literature and Philology.

745. Haycraft, Howard. Murder for Pleasure. The life and times of the detective story. New York, D. Appleton–Century Co., 1941. xix + 409 pp.—"Who's Who in Detection. Being a quick finding-list of the best-known sleuths of fiction," pp. 340–386.

746. Haycraft, Howard. The Art of the Mystery Story. New York, Simon and Schuster, 1946. ix + 546 pp.

747. Danny, Frederic, and Lee, Manfred B. [pseud. Ellery Queen]. Queen's Quorum. A history of the detective-crime short story as revealed by the 106 most important books published in this field since 1845. Boston, Little, Brown and Co., 1948. ix + 132 pp.—Reprint 1951.

748. Johannsen, Albert. The House of Beadle and Adams and Its Dime and Nickel Novels. The story of a vanished literature. With a foreword by John T. McIntyre. Norman, University of Oklahoma Press, 1950. 2 (double column page) vols.

749. Leisy, Ernest E. The American Historical Novel. Norman, University of Oklahoma Press, 1950. x + 280 pp.

750. Rodell, Marie F. Mystery Fiction. Theory and technique. Rev. ed. New York, Hermitage House, 1952. 230 pp.—In the series Professional Writers Library. Original ed. 1943.

751. Bretnor, Reginald, ed. Modern Science Fiction. Its meaning and its future. New York, Coward-McCann Inc., 1953. xii + 294 pp.—A treatment via individual essays of science fiction in its relationship to art, morality, and society.

752. Gerber, Richard. Utopian Fantasy. A study of English utopian fiction since the end of the nineteenth century. London, Routledge and Kegan Paul Ltd., 1955. xii + 162 pp.

753. Dalziel, Margaret. Popular Fiction a Hundred Years Ago. An unexplored tract of literary history. London, Cohen and West, 1957. vii + 188 pp.—"Cheap Periodicals of the Mid-Nineteenth Century," pp. 183–184.

754. Proctor, Mortimer R. The English University Novel. Berkeley, University of California Press, 1957. xi + 228 pp.

755. Taylor, W[illiam] A. Historical Fiction. Introduction by Alfred Duggan. Cambridge Univ. Press for the National Book League, 1957. 48 pp.—Number 11 in the series Reader's Guides: Second Series. Two hundred seventy-nine summaries of modern historical novels.

756. Green, Roger Lancelyn. Into Other Worlds. Space-flight in fiction, from Lucian to Lewis. London, Abelard-Schuman Ltd., 1958. 190 pp.—"Short Bibliography of Journeys into Other Worlds," pp. 187–190.

757. Murch, Alma E. The Development of the Detective Novel. New York, Philosophical Library, 1958. 272 pp.

758. Davinport, Basil, Heinlein, Robt. A., Kornbluth, C[yril] M., Bester, Alfred, and Bloch, Robt. The Science Fiction Novel. Imagination and social criticism. Chicago, Advent Publ'ers, 1959. 160 pp.

§28. FICTION: STUDIES IN THE ESSENCE, PURPOSE, FORM, AND TECHNIQUE OF THE NOVEL

762. Norris, Frank. The Responsibilities of the Novelist and Other Literary Essays. New York, Doubleday, Page and Co., 1903. 311 pp.

763. Horne, Chas. F. The Technique of the Novel. The elements of the art, their evolution, and present use. New York, Harper and Bros., 1908. x + 285 pp.

764. Bennett, Arnold. The Author's Craft. London, Hodder and Stoughton, 1914. 132 pp.

765. Lathrop, Henry B. The Art of the Novelist. New York, Dodd, Mead and Co., 1919. xi + 291 pp.

766. Anderson, Sherwood. The Modern Writer. San Francisco, Lantern Press, 1925. 44 pp.

767. Wharton, Edith. The Writing of Fiction. New York, Charles Scribner's Sons, 1925. 178 pp.

768. Forster, E[dward] M. Aspects of the Novel. New York, Harcourt, Brace and Co., 1927. 250 pp.—The Clark Lectures, Trinity College, Cambridge, spring 1927. Reprint New York, Harcourt, Brace and Co., 1954, number 19 in the series Harvest Books.

769. Ames, Van Meter. Aesthetics of the Novel. University of Chicago Press, 1928. ix + 221 pp.

770. Grabo, Carl H. The Technique of the Novel. New York, Charles Scribner's Sons, 1928. xx + 331 pp.

771. Muir, Edwin. The Structure of the Novel. London, Hogarth Press, 1928. 151 pp.—Number 6 in the series Hogarth Lectures on Literature. Reprint 1954.

772. Overton, Grant. The Philosophy of Fiction. New York, D. Appleton and Co., 1928. xiii + 367 pp.

773. Lubbock, Percy. The Craft of Fiction. Revised format. New York, Jonathan Cape and Harrison Smith, 1929. 277 pp.—Original ed. 1921; reprints of revised format ed. New York, Peter Smith, 1947, and New York, Viking Press, 1957, number 31 in the series Compass Books.

774. Roberts, Morris. Henry James's Criticism. Cambridge, Mass., Harvard Univ. Press, 1929. ix + 131 pp.—"Bibliography," pp. 123–125.

775. Beach, Joseph Warren. The Twentieth-Century Novel. Studies in technique. New York, Century Co., 1932. viii + 567 pp.

776. James, Henry. The Art of the Novel. Critical prefaces. With an introduction by Richard P. Blackmur. New York, Charles Scribner's Sons, 1934. xli + 348 pp.—Reprint 1950.

777. Mirrielees, Edith R. The Story Writer. Boston, Little, Brown and Co., 1939. 295 pp.

778. Brooks, Cleanth, Jr., and Warren, Robt. Penn, eds. Understanding Fiction. New York, F. S. Crofts and Co., 1943. xxv + 608 pp.—Frequent reprints, as in 1946.

779. Glasgow, Ellen. A Certain Measure. An interpretation of prose fiction. New York, Harcourt, Brace and Co., 1943. viii + 272 pp.—Bibliography, pp. 265–272.

780. Bentley, Phyllis E. Some Observations on the Art of Narrative. London, Home and Van Thal, 1946. 41 pp.—Also New York, Macmillan Co., 1947, 50 pp.

781. Liddell, Robt. A Treatise on the Novel. London, Jonathan Cape, 1947. 168 pp.—Reprints 1949, 1953.

782. Uzzell, Thos. H. The Technique of the Novel. A handbook on the craft of the long narrative. Chicago, J. B. Lippincott Co., 1947. vi + 300 pp.

783. Comfort, Alexander. The Novel and Our Time. Letchworth, Eng., Phoenix House, 1948. 80 pp.

784. James, Henry. The Art of Fiction and Other Essays. With an introduction by Morris Roberts. New York, Oxford Univ. Press, 1948. xxiv + 240 pp.

785. Ortega y Gasset, José. The Dehumanization of Art and Notes on the Novel. Translated by Helen Weyl. Princeton, N.J., University Press, 1948. 103 pp.—Spanish original 1925; reprint of Eng. translation New York, Smith, 1951.

786. Orvis, Mary Burchard. The Art of Writing Fiction. New York, Prentice-Hall Inc., 1948. vi + 248 pp.

787. Cather, Willa. On Writing. Critical studies on writing as an art. With a foreword by Stephen Tennant. New York, Alfred A. Knopf Inc., 1949. xxvi + 126 pp.

788. West, Ray B., Jr., and Stallman, R[obert] W., eds. The Art of Modern Fiction. New York, Rinehart and Co., 1949. x + 652 pp.

789. Brown, E[dward] K. Rhythm in the Novel. University of Toronto Press, 1950. xv + 118 pp.—The Alexander Lectures 1949–50.

790. De Voto, Bernard. The World of Fiction. Boston, Houghton Mifflin Co., 1950. xiii + 299 pp.

791. McHugh, Vincent. Primer of the Novel. New York, Random House, 1950. xv + 308 pp.

792. Schorer, Mark, ed. The Story. A critical anthology. New York, Prentice-Hall Inc., 1950. xi + 606 pp.—In the Prentice-Hall English Composition and Introduction to Literature Series.

793. Mendilow, A[dam] A. Time and the Novel. Introduction by J. Isaacs. London, Peter Nevill Ltd., 1952. x + 245 pp.

794. Gardiner, Harold C., S.J. Norms for the Novel. New York, America Press, 1953. 180 pp.

795. Humphrey, Robt. Stream of Consciousness in the Modern Novel. Berkeley, University of California Press, 1954. 127 pp.—Number 3 in the series Perspectives in Criticism.

796. Liddell, Robt. Some Principles of Fiction. Bloomington, Indiana Univ. Press, 1954. 162 pp.

797. Friedman, Melvin. Stream of Consciousness. A study in literary method. New Haven, Yale Univ. Press, 1955. xi + 279 pp.

798. Zabel, Morton D. Craft and Character. Texts, method, and vocation in modern fiction. New York, Viking Press, 1957. xv + 331 pp.

799. Cary, Joyce. Art and Reality. Ways of the creative process. New York, Harper and Bros., 1958. xv + 175 pp.—Volume XX in the series World Perspectives, whose purpose is explained (pp. ix–xiv) by Ruth Nanda Anshen.

800. Allcott, Miriam, ed. Novelists on the Novel. New York, Columbia Univ. Press, 1959. 336 pp.

801. Martin, Harold C., ed. Style in Prose Fiction. New York, Columbia Univ. Press, 1959. xi + 209 pp.—Issue for 1958 in the series English Institute Essays. "Bibliography," pp. 191–200.

§29. FICTION: FROM THE BEGINNINGS TO *CIRCA* 1800

805. Rolfe, Franklin P. On the Bibliography of Seventeenth Century Prose Fiction. PMLA, XIL, 4 (Dec. 1934), 1071–1086.

806. Mish, Chas. C. English Prose Fiction 1600–1700. A chronological check-list. Charlottesville, Bibliographical Society of the University of Virginia, 1952. v + 34 + iii + 21 + v + 87 pp.

807. O'Dell, Sterg. A Chronological List of Prose Fiction in English Printed in England and Other Countries 1475–1640. Cambridge, Mass., Technology Press of MIT, 1954. v + 147 pp.

---

808. Jusserand, J[ean] J. The English Novel in the Time of Shakespeare. Revised and enl. by the author. Translated from the French by Elizabeth Lee. London, T. Fisher Unwin, 1890. [iv] + 433 pp.—Original Fr. ed. 1887; frequent reprints of Eng. tr., as in 1903.

809. Warren, F[rederick] M. A History of the Novel Previous to the Seventeenth Century. New York, Henry Holt and Co., 1895. xii + 361 pp.

810. Dibelius, Wilhelm. Englische Romankunst. Die Technik des englischen Romans im achzehnten und zu Anfang des neunzehnten Jahrhunderts. Berlin, Mayer und Müller, 1910. 2 vols.—Volumes XCII and XCVIII in the series Palaestra. Bibliographies, I, pp. xiii–xv, and II, p. xi.

811. Morgan, Charlotte E. The Rise of the Novel of Manners. A study of English prose fiction between 1600 and 1740. New York, Columbia Univ. Press, 1911. ix + 430 pp.—In the series Columbia University Studies in English.

812. Wolff, Samuel Lee. The Greek Romances in Elizabethan Prose Fiction. New York, Columbia Univ. Press, 1912. ix + 529 pp.—In the series Columbia University Studies in Comparative Literature. "Bibliography," pp. 483–505.

813. Tieje, Arthur Jerrold. The Theory of Characterization in Prose Fiction Prior to 1740. Minneapolis, University of Minnesota Press, 1916. [iii] + 131 pp.—Number 5 in the series Studies in Language and Literature of the University of Minnesota. "Bibliography," pp. 115–131.

814. Lord Ernle [Rowland Edmund Prothero]. The Light Reading of Our Ancestors. Chapters in the growth of the English novel. New York, Brentano's Publ'ers, [1927]. ix + 326 pp.

815. Watson, Harold F. The Sailor in English Fiction and Drama 1550–1800. New York, Columbia Univ. Press, 1931. 241 pp.

816. Tompkins, J[oyce] M. S. The Popular Novel in England 1770–1800. London, Constable and Co., 1932. xi + 388 pp.

817. Utter, Robt. P., and Needham, Gwendolyn B. Pamela's Daughters. New York, Macmillan Co., 1936. xiii + 512 pp.

818. Wright, Walter F. Sensibility in English Prose Fiction 1760–1814. A reinterpretation. Urbana, University of Illinois Press, 1937. 158 pp.—Volume XXII, nos. 3–4, in the series Illinois Studies in Language and Literature.

819. Tarr, Sister Mary Muriel. Catholicism in Gothic Fiction. A study of the nature and function of Catholic materials in Gothic fiction in England 1762–1820. Washington, D.C., Catholic Univ. of America Press, 1946. vii + 141 pp.

820. Foster, James R. History of the Pre-Romantic Novel in England. New York, Modern Language Association of America, 1949. xi + 294 pp.—Volume XVII in the Modern Language Association of America Monograph Series. "Selected Bibliography," pp. 277–282.

821. Noyes, Robt. G. The Thespian Mirror. Shakespeare in the eighteenth century novel. Providence, R.I., Brown Univ. Press, 1953. v + 6–200 pp.

822. McKillop, Alan D. The Early Masters of English Fiction. Lawrence, University of Kansas Press, 1956. 233 pp.—A study of Defoe, Fielding, Richardson, Smollett, and Sterne.

823. Watt, Ian. The Rise of the Novel. Studies in Defoe, Richardson, and Fielding. Berkeley, University of California Press, 1957. 319 pp.—Reprint 1959.

§30. FICTION: BRITISH AND AMERICAN IN THE NINETEENTH CENTURY

827. Johnson, James G. Southern Fiction Prior to 1860. An attempt at a first-hand bibliography. Charlottesville, Va., Michie Co., 1909. vii + 126 pp.

828. Wegelin, Oscar. Early American Fiction 1774–1830. A compilation of the titles of works of fiction by writers born or residing in North America north of the Mexican border and printed previous to 1831. 3rd ed. corrected and enl. New York, Peter Smith, 1929. 37 pp.—Original ed. 1902; second ed. 1913.

829. Raddin, Geo. G., Jr. An Early New York Library of Fiction. With a checklist of the fiction in H. Caritat's Circulating Library, No. 1 City Hotel, Broadway, New York, 1804. New York, H. W. Wilson Co., 1940. 113 pp.

830. Wright, Lyle H. American Fiction 1774–1850. A contribution toward a bibliography. Rev. ed. San Marino, Calif., Henry E. Huntington Library and Art Gallery, 1948. xviii + 355 pp.—Original ed. 1939.

831. Sadleir, Michael. Nineteenth Century Fiction. A bibliographical record based on his own collection. London, Constable and Co., 1951. 2 vols., the first with double column pp.—Volume I author list; volume II series list.

832. Wright, Lyle H. American Fiction 1851–1875. A contribution toward a bibliography. San Marino, Calif., Henry E. Huntington Library and Art Gallery, 1957. xx + 413 pp.

---

833. Oliphant, James. Victorian Novelists. London, Blackie and Sons, 1899. 251 pp.

834. Melville, Lewis. Victorian Novelists. London, Archibald Constable and Co., 1906. 321 pp.

835. Loshe, Lillie D. The Early American Novel. New York, Columbia Univ. Press, 1907. vi + 131 pp.—In the series Columbia University Studies in English and Comparative Literature. Reprint 1930.

836. Underwood, John Curtis. Literature and Insurgency. Ten studies in racial evolution. Mark Twain, Henry James, William Dean Howells, Frank Norris, David Graham Phillips, Stewart Edward White, Winston Churchill, Edith Wharton, Gertrude Atherton, and Robert W. Chambers. New York, Mitchell Kennerley, 1914. xii + 480 pp.

837. Phillips, Walter C. Dickens, Reade, and Collins. Sensation novelists. A study in the conditions and theories of novel writing in Victorian England. New York, Columbia Univ. Press, 1919. xi + 230 pp.—In the

series Columbia University Studies in English and Comparative Literature.

838. Russell, Frances Theresa. Satire in the Victorian Novel. New York, Macmillan Co., 1920. xv + 335 pp.—"Bibliographical Note," pp. 317–327.

839. Ellis, S[tewart] M. Wilkie Collins, LeFanu, and Others. London, Constable and Co., 1931. 343 pp.—In the series Constable Lives. Reprint 1951.

840. Cecil, David. Early Victorian Novelists. Essays in revaluation. London, Constable and Co., 1934. [ix] + 332 pp.—A study of the Brontës, Dickens, Eliot, Gaskell, Thackeray, and Trollope.

841. Hartwick, Harry. The Foreground of American Fiction. Foreword by Harry Hayden Clark. New York, American Book Co., 1934. xvi + 447 pp.—A study *inter alios* of Crane, Dreiser, and Norris.

842. Rosa, Matthew W. The Silver-Fork School. Novels of fashion preceding Vanity Fair. New York, Columbia Univ. Press, 1936. x + 223 pp.—Number 123 in the series Columbia University Studies in English and Comparative Literature.

843. Brown, Herbert R. The Sentimental Novel in America 1789–1860. Durham, N.C., Duke Univ. Press, 1940. ix + 407 pp.—Reprint New York, Pageant Books Inc., 1959.

844. Taylor, Walter Fuller. The Economic Novel in America. Chapel Hill, University of North Carolina Press, 1942. xi + 378 pp.—A study of Bellamy, Garland, Howells, Norris, and Clemens.

845. Stebbins, Lucy P. A Victorian Album. Some lady novelists of the period. New York, Columbia Univ. Press, 1946. xi + 226 pp.

846. Baily, F[rancis] E. Six Great Victorian Novelists. London, MacDonald and Co., 1947. ix +10–199 pp.—A study of Dickens, Eliot, Meredith, Stevenson, Thackeray, and Trollope.

847. Åhnebrink, Lars. The Beginnings of Naturalism in American Fiction. A study of the works of Hamlin Garland, Stephen Crane, and Frank Norris with special reference to some European influences 1891–1903. Cambridge, Mass., Harvard Univ. Press, 1950. xi + 505 pp.—Volume IX in the series Essays and Studies on American Language and Literature of the American Institute in the University of Uppsala.

848. Leavis, F[rank] R. The Great Tradition. George Eliot, Henry James, Joseph Conrad. London, Chatto and Windus Ltd., 1948. [viii] + 266 pp.

849. Tillotson, Kathleen. Novels of the Eighteen-Forties. Oxford Univ. Press, 1954. xiv + 328 pp.

850. Praz, Mario. The Hero in Eclipse in Victorian Fiction. Translated from the Italian by Angus Davidson. Oxford Univ. Press, 1956. [viii] + 478 pp.—Original It. ed. 1952.

851. Davis, David Brion. Homicide in American Fiction 1798–1860. A study of social values. Ithaca, N.Y., Cornell Univ. Press, 1957. xviii + 346 pp.

852. Lively, Robt. A. Fiction Fights the Civil War. An unfinished chapter in the literary history of the American people. Chapel Hill, University of North Carolina Press, 1957. ix + 230 pp.

853. Stang, Richard. The Theory of the Novel in England 1850–1870. London, Routledge and Kegan Paul, 1959. xii + 251 pp.

§31. FICTION: MODERN BRITISH AND AMERICAN (I.E., FROM *CIRCA* 1900 TO THE PRESENT)

857. Follett, Helen T. and Wilson. Some Modern Novelists. Appreciations and estimates. New York, Henry Holt and Co., 1918. ix + 368 pp.—A study of Bennett, Conrad, Galsworthy, Gissing, Howells, James, Meredith, de Morgan, Phillpotts, Wells, and Wharton.

858. Gordon, Geo. The Men Who Make Our Novels. Modern American writers. New York, Moffat, Yard and Co., 1919. viii + 262 pp.

859. Van Doren, Carl. Contemporary American Novelists 1900–1920. New York, Macmillan Co., 1922. xiii + 176 pp.—Frequent reprints, as in 1936.

860. Cumberland, Gerald. Written in Friendship. A book of reminiscences. New York, Brentano's Publ'ers, 1924. 308 pp.—See also Cumberland's earlier *Set Down in Malice,* A book of reminiscences, New York, Brentano's, 1919, 286 pp. Both works treat authors of the twenties, some of whom are novelists.

861. Gould, Gerald. The English Novel of Today. London, John Castle, 1924. 224 pp.—Also New York, Dial Press, 1925.

862. Chevalley, Abel. The Modern English Novel. Translated from the French by Ben R. Redman. New York, Alfred A. Knopf, 1925. xi + 259 pp.—Original Fr. ed. 1921. "List of French Books on the English Novel and on English Novelists," pp. 255–259.

863. Drew, Elizabeth A. The Modern Novel. Some aspects of contemporary fiction. New York, Harcourt, Brace and Co., 1926. ix + 274 pp.

864. Myers, Walter L. The Later Realism. A study of characterization in the British novel. University of Chicago Press, 1927. ix + 173 pp.—"Bibliography," pp. 163–166.

865. Marble, Annie R. A Study of the Modern Novel British and American since 1900. New York, D. Appleton and Co., 1928. xi + 440 pp.

866. Michaud, Régis. The American Novel Today. A social and psychological study. Boston, Little, Brown and Co., 1928. xiii + 293 pp.

867. Whipple, Thos. K. Spokesmen. Modern Writers and American Life. New York, D. Appleton and Co., 1928. v + 276 pp.

868. Jameson, Storm. The Georgian Novel and Mr. Robinson. New York, William Morrow and Co., 1929. 75 pp.

869. Hatcher, Harlan. Creating the Modern American Novel. New York, Farrar and Rinehart Inc., 1935. x + 307 pp.

870. Cowley, Malcolm, ed. After the Genteel Tradition. American writers since 1910. New York, W. W. Norton and Co., 1937. 270 pp.—Reprint Gloucester, Mass., Peter Smith, 1959.

871. McCole, C[amille] John. Lucifer at Large. London, Longmans, Green and Co., 1937. vii + 337 pp.—A study *inter alios* of Anderson, Cabell, Dreiser, O'Hara, and Faulkner.

872. Boynton, Percy H. America in Contemporary Fiction. University of Chicago Press, 1940. ix + 274 pp.

873. Beach, Joseph Warren. American Fiction 1920–1940. John Dos Passos, Ernest Hemingway, William Faulkner, Thomas Wolfe, Erskine Caldwell, James T. Farrell, John P. Marquand, John Steinbeck. New York, Macmillan Co., 1941. x + 371 pp.

874. Wilson, Edmund. The Boys in the Back Room. Notes on California novelists. San Francisco, Colt Press, 1941. 72 pp.—A study of Cain, O'Hara, Saroyan, Storm, and Steinbeck.

875. Frierson, Wm. C. The English Novel in Transition 1885–1940. Norman, University of Oklahoma Press, 1942. xvi + 333 pp.

876. Geismar, Maxwell. Writers in Crisis. The American novel 1925–1940. Ring Lardner, Ernest Hemingway, John Dos Passos, William Faulkner, Thomas Wolfe, John Steinbeck. Boston, Houghton Mifflin Co., 1942. xi + 308 pp.

877. Gerould, Gordon Hall. The Patterns of English and American Fiction. A history. Boston, Little, Brown and Co., 1942. x + 526 pp.—"Bibliography," pp. 493–504.

878. Adams, J[ames] Donald. The Shape of Books to Come. New York, Viking Press, 1944. xvii + 202 pp.

879. Reed, Henry. The Novel since 1939. London, Longmans, Green and Co., 1946. 43 pp.—Number 4 in the series The Arts in Britain.

880. Gloster, Hugh M. Negro Voices in American Fiction. Chapel Hill, University of North Carolina Press, 1948. xiv + 295 pp.

881. Magny, Claude-Edmonde. L'Age du roman américain. Paris, Éditions du Seuil, 1948. 252 pp.—In the series Collection pierres vives.

882. Geismar, Maxwell. The Last of the Provincials. The American novel 1915–1925. H. L. Mencken, Sinclair Lewis, Willa Cather, Sherwood Anderson, F. Scott Fitzgerald. 2nd ed. Boston, Houghton Mifflin Co., 1949. xiii + 404 pp.—Original ed. 1947.

883. Aldridge, John W. After the Lost Generation. A critical study of the writers of two wars. New York, McGraw-Hill Co., 1951. xvii + 263 pp. —Reprint New York, Noonday Press, 1958.

884. Blake, Geo. Barrie and the Kailyard School. New York, Roy Publ'ers, 1951. 103 pp.

885. Hoffman, Frederick J. The Modern Novel in America 1900–1950. Chicago, Henry Regnery Co., 1951. viii + 216 pp.—In the series Twentieth-Century Literature in America. Reprint Chicago, Henry Regnery Co., 1956, number 6035 in the series Gateway Editions.

886. Warfel, Harry R. American Novelists of Today. New York, American Book Co., 1951. vii + 478 pp.

887. Geismar, Maxwell. Rebels and Ancestors. The American Novel 1890–1915. Frank Norris, Stephen Crane, Jack London, Ellen Glasgow, Theodore Dreiser. Boston, Houghton Mifflin Co., 1953. xii + 435 pp.

888. Gelfant, Blanche H. The American City Novel. Theodore Dreiser, Thomas Wolfe, Sherwood Anderson, Edith Wharton, John Dos Passos, James T. Farrell, Nelson Algren, Betty Smith, Leonard Bishop, Willard Motley, and others. Norman, University of Oklahoma Press, 1954. x + 289 pp.

889. Edel, Leon. The Psychological Novel 1900–1950. Philadelphia, J. B. Lippincott Co., 1955. 221 pp.

890. Lynn, Kenneth S. The Dream of Success. A study of the modern American imagination. Boston, Little, Brown and Co., 1955. 269 pp.—A study primarily of Dreiser, London, Phillips, and Norris.

891. Lewis, Richard W. B. The Picaresque Saint. Representative figures in contemporary fiction. Philadelphia, J. B. Lippincott Co., 1956. 317 pp. —New copyright 1958.

892. Rideout, Walter B. The Radical Novel in the United States 1900–1954. Some interrelations of literature and society. Cambridge, Mass., Harvard Univ. Press, 1956. xi + 339 pp.

893. Frohock, Wilbur M. The Novel of Violence in America. Dallas, Tex., Southern Methodist Univ. Press, 1950. 216 pp.

894. Geismar, Maxwell. American Modern. From rebellion to conformity. New York, Hill and Wang, 1958. xii + 265 pp.—A study of Algren,

Bellow, Cozzens, Dos Passos, Dreiser, Faulkner, Griffin, Hemingway, Hersey, Jones, Lewis, Mailer, Marquand, Salinger, Styron, Wolfe, and Wouk.

895. Maschler, Tom, ed. Declaration [by] Colin Wilson and Others. New York, E. P. Dutton and Co., 1958. 201 pp.—See also Maschler's earlier *Declaration [by] L. Anderson and Others,* London, MacGibbon and Kee, 1957, 202 pp.

896. Wasserstrom, Wm. Heiress of All the Ages. Sex and sentiment in the genteel tradition. Minneapolis, University of Minnesota Press, 1959. 157 pp.—A study of Henry James, W. D. Howells, and Edith Wharton, and minor writers of their period.

§32. FICTION: THE SHORT STORY

900. Hannigan, Francis J. The Standard Index of Short Stories 1900–1914. Boston, Small, Maynard and Co., 1918. [ix] + 334 (double column) pp.

901. Firkins, Ina Ten Eyck. Index to Short Stories. Second and enl. ed. New York, H. W. Wilson Co., 1923. xiv + 537 (double column) pp.—Original ed. 1915. *Supplement,* by Ina Ten Eyck Firkins, New York, H. W. Wilson Co., 1929, xiv + 332 (double column) pp. *Second Supplement,* by Ina Ten Eyck Firkins, New York, H. W. Wilson Co., 1936, x + 287 (double column) pp.

902. Thurston, Jarvis. Analyses of Short Fiction. A checklist. Perspective, A quarterly of literature and the arts, VI, 3 (Summer 1953), 126–170. —A bibliography of analytic (i.e., "nonextrinsic") studies of British and American short stories.

903. Cook, Dorothy E., and Monro, Isabel S. Short Story Index. An index to 60000 stories in 4320 collections. New York, H. W. Wilson Co., 1953. 1553 (double column) pp.—*Supplement 1950–1954,* by Dorothy E. Cook and Estelle A. Fidell, New York, H. W. Wilson Co., 1956, 394 (double column) pp.

---

904. Smith, C[harles] Alphonso. The American Short Story. Boston, Ginn and Co., 1912. iii + 50 pp.—Original printing in *Internationale Wochenschrift für Wissenschaft, Kunst und Technik,* December 10, 1910.

905. Lieberman, Elias. The American Short Story. A study of the influence of locality in its development. Foreword by Archibald L. Bonton. Ridgewood, N. J., Editor Co., 1912. xvi + 183 pp.

906. Canby, Henry S. The Short Story. New ed. New Haven, Yale Univ. Press, 1913. v + 77 pp.—Volume XII in the series Yale Studies in English. Original ed. 1902.

907. Grabo, Carl H. The Art of the Short Story. New York, Charles Scribner's Sons, 1913. x + 321 pp.

908. Baker, Harry T. The Contemporary Short Story. A practical manual. Boston, D. C. Heath and Co., 1916. ix + 271 pp.

909. Pattee, Fred Lewis. The Development of the American Short Story. An historical survey. New York, Harper and Bros., 1923. v + 388 pp.

910. Newman, Frances. The Short Story's Mutations from Petronius to Paul Morand. New York, B. W. Huebsch Inc., 1925. viii + 332 pp.

911. Williams, Blanche Colton. Our Short Story Writers. New York, Dodd, Mead and Co., 1929. 384 pp.—In the series Modern American Writers.

912. Bement, Douglas. Weaving the Short Story. New York, Richard R. Smith Inc., 1931. 285 pp.

913. O'Brien, Edward J. The Advance of the American Short Story. Revised ed. New York, Dodd, Mead and Co., 1931. 314 pp.—Original ed. 1923.

914. Bates, H[erbert] E. The Modern Short Story. London, Thomas Nelson and Sons, 1941. 231 pp.—Reprint Boston, Writer Inc., 1956.

915. O'Faolain, Sean. The Short Story. London, Collins, 1948. 320 pp.

916. Gordon, Caroline, and Tate, Allen, eds. The House of Fiction. An anthology of the short story with commentary. New York, Charles Scribner's Sons, 1950. x + 649 pp.

917. Welty, Eudora. Short Stories. New York, Harcourt, Brace and Co., 1950, 53 pp.

918. West, Ray B., Jr. The Short Story in America 1900–1950. Chicago, Henry Regnery Co., 1952. 147 pp.—Number 6037 in the series Gateway Editions.

§33. MINOR PROSE: BIOGRAPHY AND AUTOBIOGRAPHY INCLUDING DIARIES

922. O'Neill, Edward H. Biography by Americans 1658–1936. A subject bibliography. Philadelphia, University of Pennsylvania Press, 1939. x + 465 pp.

923. Matthews, Wm. American Diaries. An annotated bibliography of American diaries written prior to the year 1861. With the assistance of Roy Harvey Pearce. Berkeley, University of California Press, 1945. xiv + 383 pp.—Volume XVI in the series University of California Publications in English.

924. Matthews, Wm. British Autobiographies. An annotated bibliography of British autobiographies published or written before 1951. Berkeley, University of California Press, 1955. xiv + 376 (double column) pp.

---

925. Burr, Anna R. The Autobiography. A critical and comparative study. Boston, Houghton Mifflin Co., 1909. viii + 451 pp.

926. Dunn, Waldo H. English Biography. London, J. M. Dent and Sons, 1916. xxi + 323 pp.—In the series Channels of English Literature.

927. Thayer, Wm. R. The Art of Biography. New York, Charles Scribner's Sons, 1920. viii + 155 pp.

928. Ponsonby, Arthur. English Diaries. A review of English diaries from the sixteenth to the twentieth century with an introduction on diary writing. London, Methuen and Co., [1923]. xiii + 447 pp.—See also Ponsonby's *More English Diaries,* Further reviews of diaries from the sixteenth to the nineteenth century with an introduction on diary reading, London, Methuen and Co., 1927, viii + 250 pp.

929. Dobrée, Bonamy. Essays in Biography 1680–1726. Oxford Univ. Press, 1925. xi + 362 pp.—On Sir John Vanbrugh and Joseph Addison.

930. Ponsonby, Arthur. Scottish and Irish Diaries. From the sixteenth to the nineteenth century. . . . London, Methuen and Co., 1927. viii + 192 pp.

931. Nicholson, Harold. The Development of English Biography. New York, Harcourt, Brace and Co., 1928. 158 pp.—Number 4 in the Hogarth Lectures on Literature Series.

932. Maurois, André. Aspects of Biography. Translated by S. C. Roberts. Cambridge Univ. Press, 1929. x + 188 pp.—Originally six lectures delivered in English at Trinity College, Cambridge, 1928, and later revised into French.

933. Schütt, Marie. Die englische Biographie der Tudor-Zeit. Hamburg, W. de Gruyter und Co., 1930. 162 pp.—Number 1 in the series Britannica.

934. Stauffer, Donald A. English Biography before 1700. Cambridge, Mass., Harvard Univ. Press, 1930. xvii + 392 pp.—"Bibliography," pp. 287–379.

935. Longaker, Mark. English Biography in the Eighteenth Century. Philadelphia, University of Pennsylvania Press, 1931. ix + 519 pp.

936. O'Neill, Edward H. History of American Biography 1800–1935. Philadelphia, University of Pennsylvania Press, 1935. xi + 428 pp.

937. Britt, Albert. The Great Biographies. New York, McGraw-Hill Book Co., 1936. xi + 223 pp.

938. Bates, E[rnest] Stuart. Inside Out. An introduction to autobiography. Oxford, Eng., Basil Blackwell, 1936–37. 2 vols.—Bibliography, I, pp. 283–288, and II, pp. 331–339; "Index of Autobiographers," II, pp. 340–344.

939. Johnson, Edgar. One Mighty Torrent. The drama of biography. New York, Stackpole Sons, 1937. 595 pp.

940. Stauffer, Donald A. The Art of Biography in Eighteenth Century England. Princeton, N.J., University Press, 1941. xiv + 572 pp.—Also *Bibliographical Supplement*, Princeton, N.J., University Press, 1941, viii + 293 pp.

941. Misch, Georg. A History of Autobiography in Antiquity. Translated [with collaboration of the author from the 3rd Ger. ed.] by Ernest W. Dickes. London, Routledge and Kegan Paul, 1950. 2 vols.—In the series International Library of Sociology and Social Reconstruction. Original Ger. ed. 1907; second Ger. ed. 1931; third Ger. ed. 1949. Bibliography, I, pp. 339–352, and II, pp. 693–699.

942. Garraty, John A. The Nature of Biography. New York, Alfred A. Knopf, 1957. xiii + 289 + xiii pp.—"Essay on Sources," pp. 261–289.

§34. MINOR PROSE: THE CHARACTER

946. Murphy, Gwendolen. A Bibliography of English Character Books 1608–1700. Oxford Univ. Press, 1925. 179 pp.—Number 4 in the series Supplements to Transactions of the Bibliographical Society.

947. Greenough, Chester Noyes. A Bibliography of the Theophrastan Character in English with Several Portrait Characters. Prepared for publica-

tion by J. Milton French. Cambridge, Mass., Harvard Univ. Press, 1947. xii + 280 (double column) + 281–347 (triple column) pp.—Volume XVIII in the series Harvard Studies in Comparative Literature.

---

948. Van Laun, Henry. The Characters of Jean de la Bruyère. Newly rendered into English. With an introduction, a biographical memoir, and notes. London, John C. Nimmo, 1885. 492 pp.

949. Boyce, Benjamin. The Theophrastan Character in England to 1642. With the assistance of notes by Chester Noyes Greenough. Cambridge, Mass., Harvard Univ. Press, 1947. xi + 324 pp.

950. Boyce, Benjamin. The Polemic Character 1640–1661. A chapter in English literary history. Lincoln, University of Nebraska Press, 1955. xv + 160 pp.

§35. MINOR PROSE: COURTESY BOOKS

954. Noyes, Gertrude E. Bibliography of Courtesy and Conduct Books in Seventeenth-Century England. New Haven, published by the author, 1937. iv + 111 pp.

955. Heltzel, Virgil B. A Check List of Courtesy Books in the Newberry Library. Chicago, Newberry Library, 1942. ix + 161 pp.

§36. MINOR PROSE: THE ESSAY AND PERSONAL LETTER

959. Hansche, Maud B. The Formative Period of English Familiar Letter-Writers and Their Contribution to the English Essay. Philadelphia, University of Pennsylvania, 1902. 70 pp.—Bibliography, pp. 60–70.

960. Conway, Adeline M. The Essay in American Literature. New York University, 1914. 127 pp.—Number 3 in the series New York University Graduate School Studies.

961. MacDonald, W[ilbert] L. Beginnings of the English Essay. University of Toronto, 1914. 121 pp.—Number 3 in the series University of Toronto Studies: Third Series. Bibliography, pp. 119–122.

962. Walker, Hugh. The English Essay and Essayists. London, J. M. Dent and Sons, 1915. vii + 343 pp.—Reprint 1923.

963. Davis, Wm. H. English Essayists. A reader's handbook. Boston, Richard G. Badger, 1916. vi + 217 pp.

964. Wylie, Laura J. The English Essay. A study in literary development. Boston, Houghton Mifflin Co., 1916. 216 pp.

965. Eleanore, Sister M[ary]. The Literary Essay in English. Boston, Ginn and Co., 1923. ix + 260 pp.—"Reading List," pp. 249–253.

966. Farrington, Dora W. The Essay. How to study and write it. Richmond, Va., Johnson Publ'ing Co., 1924. xxii + 385 pp.

967. Marr, Geo. S. The Periodical Essays of the Eighteenth Century. With illustrative extracts from the rarer periodicals. New York, D. Appleton and Co., 1924. 264 pp.

968. Opdycke, John B. The Literature of Letters. Chicago, Lyons and Carnahan, 1925. 504 pp.

969. Thompson, Elbert N. S. The Seventeenth Century English Essay. Iowa City, University of Iowa, 1926. 149 pp.—Volume III, no. 3, in the series University of Iowa Humanistic Studies.

970. O'Leary, R[aphael] D. The Essay. New York, Thomas Y. Crowell Co., 1928. xvi + 230 pp.—Bibliographic materials, pp. 197–205.

971. Hornbeak, Katherine G. The Complete Letter-Writer in English 1568–1800. Northampton, Mass., Smith College, 1934. xii + 150 pp.—Volume XV, nos. 3 and 4, in the series Smith College Studies in Modern Languages.

972. Law, Marie H. The English Familiar Essay in the Early Nineteenth Century. Philadelphia, University of Pennsylvania Press, 1934. 238 pp.

973. Irving, Wm. Henry. The Providence of Wit in the English Letter Writers. Durham, N.C., Duke Univ. Press, 1955. [v] + 382 pp.

§37. MINOR PROSE: HAGIOGRAPHY, HOMILETICS, AND DEVOTIONAL LITERATURE

[See also §77. Religion and Literature; §88. Journals of Psychology and Religion; §221. Philosophy, Psychology, and Religion.]

977. Caplan, Harry. Mediaeval Artes Praedicandi. A handlist. Ithaca, N.Y., Cornell Univ. Press, 1934. 52 pp.—Volume XXIV in the series Cornell Studies in Classical Philology.

---

978. Horstmann, [Johann] Carl. Altenglische Legenden. Kindheit Jesu, Geburt Jesu, Barlaam und Josaphat, St. Patrik's Fegefeuer. Aus den verschiedenen MSS zum ersten Male herausgegeben. Paderborn, F. Schoningh, 1875. xliv + 240 pp.

979. Horstmann, [Johann] Carl. Sammlung altenglischer Legenden grössenteils zum ersten Male herausgegeben. Heilbronn, Gebrüder Henninger, 1878. 227 pp.—Also Horstmann's *Altenglische Legenden,* Neue Folge, Mit Einleitung und Ammerkungen, Heilbronn, Gebrüder Henninger, 1881, cxxviii + 536 pp.

980. Gerould, Gordon H. The North-English Homily Collection. A study of MS relations and of the sources of the tales. Lancaster, Penn., New Era Printing Co., 1902. 104 pp.—Bibliography, pp. 22–25.

981. Mosher, Joseph A. The Exemplum in Early Religious and Didactic Literature in England. New York, Columbia Univ. Press, 1911. xi + 150 pp. —In the series Columbia University Studies in English.

982. Gerould, Gordon H. Saints' Legends. Boston, Houghton Mifflin Co., 1916. ix + 393 pp.—In the series Types of English Literature. Bibliography, pp. 349–376.

983. Crane, T[homas] F. Mediaeval Sermon-Books and Stories. Proceedings of the American Philosophical Society, XXI, 114 (April 1883–Jan. 1884), 49–78.—Also Crane's continuation in *Proceedings of the American Philosophical Society,* LVI, 5 (1917), 369–402.

984. Plummer, Chas. Bethada náem nÉrenn. Lives of Irish saints edited from the original manuscripts with introduction, translations, notes, glossary, and indexes. Oxford, Clarendon Press, 1922. 2 vols.—Bibliography, I, pp. xli–xliv.

985. Owst, G[erald] R. Preaching in Medieval England. An introduction to sermon manuscripts of the period c. 1350–1450. Cambridge Univ. Press, 1926. xviii + 381 pp.—In the series Cambridge Studies in Medieval Life and Thought.

986. Richardson, Caroline F. English Preachers and Preaching 1640–70. New York, Macmillan Co., 1928. xii + 359 pp.

987. White, Helen C. English Devotional Literature [Prose] 1600–1640. Madison, University of Wisconsin Press, 1931. 307 pp.—Number 29 in the series University of Wisconsin Studies in Language and Literature.

988. Mitchell, W[illiam] Fraser. English Pulpit Oratory from Andrews to Tillotson. A study of its literary aspects. London, S.P.C.K., 1932. xii + 516 pp.—"Select Bibliography," pp. 403–473.

989. Owst, G[erald] R. Literature and Pulpit in Medieval England. A neglected chapter in the history of English letters and of the English people. Cambridge Univ. Press, 1933. xxiv + 616 pp.

990. Kapp, Rudolf. Heilige und Heiligenlegenden in England. Halle a. S., Max Niemeyer Verlag, 1934. xiii + 372 pp.—Volume I in the series Studien zum 16. und 17. Jahrhundert.

991. Rosenthal, Constance L. The Vitae Patrum in Old and Middle English Literature. Philadelphia, University of Pennslvania Press, 1936. 172 pp.

992. Pfander, Homer G. The Popular Sermon of the Medieval Friar in England. New York Univ. Press, 1937. 66 pp.

993. White, Helen C. The Tudor Books of Private Devotion. Madison, University of Wisconsin Press, 1951. [xii] + 284 pp.

994. Bethurum, Dorothy. The Homilies of Wulfstan. Oxford, Clarendon Press, 1957. xiii + 384 pp.—"Bibliography," pp. 106–112.

§38. MINOR PROSE: HISTORIOGRAPHY INCLUDING REPRINTS OF EARLY ANNALS AND CHRONICLES

[See Chapter XIV for general works on history.]

998. Ingram, James. The Saxon Chronicle. With an English translation and notes. . . . London, Longman, Hurst, Rees, Orme and Brown, 1823. xxxii + 463 pp.—Reprint of Ingram's translation *The Anglo-Saxon Chronicle,* London, J. M. Dent and Sons, 1912 (reprint 1938), viii + 301, number 624 in the series Everyman's Library.

999. Giles, J[ohn] A. Six Old English Chronicles. . . . Ethelwerd's Chronicle, Asser's Life of Alfred, Geoffrey of Monmouth's British History, Gildas, Nennius, and Richard of Cirencester. London, H. G. Bohn, 1848.

xx + 512 pp.—In the series Bohn's Antiquarian Library. Reprint as *Old English Chronicles* . . . , London, George Bell and Sons, 1901.

1000. Earle, John. Two of the Saxon Chronicles Parallel 787–1001 A.D. With supplementary extracts from the others. A revised text, edited, with introduction, critical notes, and a glossary . . . by Charles Plummer. Oxford, Clarendon Press, 1889. xv + 136 pp.—Original ed. 1865. Plummer's ed. issued 1892–99 in 2 vols. and reprinted 1927 in 1 vol.

1001. Rerum britannicarum medii aevi scriptores. Or chronicles and memorials of Great Britain and Ireland during the Middle Ages. London, published under the direction of the Master of the Rolls, 1858–1911. 99 vols.—About 250 individually bound parts. Often called the "Rolls Series."

1002. Kingsford, Chas. Lethbridge. English Historical Literature in the Fifteenth Century. With an appendix of chronicles and historical pieces hitherto for the most part unprinted. Oxford Univ. Press, 1913. xvi + 429 pp.

1003. Black, John B. The Art of History. A study of four great historians of the eighteenth century. London, Methuen and Co., 1926. viii + 188 pp.

1004. Poole, R[eginald] L. Chronicles and Annals. A brief outline of their origin and growth. Oxford, Clarendon Press, 1926. 79 pp.

1005. Peardon, Thos. P. The Transition in English Historical Writing 1760–1830. New York, Columbia Univ. Press, 1933. 340 pp.—Number 390 in the series Studies in History, Economics, and Public Law.

1006. Smith, A[lbert] H., ed. The Parker Chronicle 832–900. London, Methuen and Co., 1935. viii + 72 pp.—In the series Methuen's Old English Library. Reprint 1954. "Bibliography," pp. 53–55.

1007. Wright, C[yril] E. The Cultivation of Saga in Anglo-Saxon England. Edinburgh, Oliver and Boyd, 1939. xi + 310 pp.—A treatment of the orally preserved Old English tales which survive primarily in post-Conquest Latin chronicles.

1008. Thompson, James W. A History of Historical Writing. New York, Macmillan Co., 1942. 2 vols.

1009. Rositzke, Harry A. The Peterborough Chronicle. Translated with an introduction. New York, Columbia Univ. Press, 1951. 193 pp.—Number 94 in the series Records of Civilization, Sources and Studies. "Bibliography," pp. 175–178.

1010. Garmondsway, G[eorge] N. The Anglo-Saxon Chronicle. Translated with an introduction. [2nd ed.] London, J. M. Dent and Sons, [1955]. xlviii + 295 pp.—Number 624 in the series Everyman's Library. Original ed. 1953. "Select Bibliography," pp. xlv–xlviii.

1011. Clark, Cecily. The Peterborough Chronicle 1070–1154. Edited from MS. Bodley Laud Misc. 636 with introduction, commentary, and an appendix containing the interpolations. Oxford Univ. Press, 1958. lxx + 120 pp.—In the series Oxford English Monographs.

§39. MINOR PROSE: TRAVEL AND DESCRIPTIVE GEOGRAPHY

[See also §219. Maps and Mapmaking.]

1015. Gove, Philip Babcock. The Imaginary Voyage in Prose Fiction. A history of its criticism and a guide for its study, with an annotated check list of 215 imaginary voyages from 1700 to 1800. New York, Columbia Univ. Press, 1941. xi + 445 pp.—Number 152 in the series Columbia University Studies in English and Comparative Literature.

1016. Connolly, Francis X., and Tobin, James Edward. To an Unknown Country. Discovery and exploration in English literature. A reading list. New York, Cosmopolitan Science and Art Science Co., 1942. 56 pp.

1017. Cox, Edward G. A Reference Guide to the Literature of Travel. Vol. I: The Old World; Vol. II: The New World. Including voyages, geographical descriptions, adventures, shipwrecks, and expeditions; Vol. III: Great Britain. Including tours, descriptions, towns, histories and antiquities, surveys, ancient and present state, gardening, etc. Seattle, University of Washington Press, 1935–49. 3 vols.—Volumes IX, X, and XII in the series University of Washington Publications in Language and Literature.

1018. Guilford, E[verard] L. Travellers and Travelling in the Middle Ages. London, Sheldon Press, 1924. viii + 9–75 pp.—Number 38 in the series Texts for Students.

1019. Taylor, E[va] G. R. Tudor Geography 1485–1583. London, Methuen and Co., 1930. xi +290 pp.—"Catalogue of English Geographical or Kindred Work . . . to 1583," pp. 163–190; "Catalogue and Bibliography of Contemporary Libraries," pp. 193–243.

1020. Taylor, E[va] G. R. Late Tudor and Early Stuart Geography 1583–1650. A sequel to Tudor Geography 1485–1583. London, Methuen and

Co., 1934. xiii + 322 pp.—"Bibliography of English Geographical Literature 1583–1650," pp. 177–298.

1021. Cowley, Robt. R. The Voyagers and Elizabethan Drama. Boston, D. C. Heath and Co., 1938. xiv + 428 pp.—Volume VIII in the Modern Language Association of America Monograph Series.

1022. Cawley, Robt. Ralston. Unpathed Waters. Studies in the influence of the voyagers on Elizabethan literature. Princeton, N.J., University Press, 1940. x + 285 pp.—"Bibliography," pp. 257–275.

1023. Rowse, A[lfred] L. The Elizabethans and America. London, Macmillan Co., 1959. xiii + 222 pp.

CHAPTER III

POETRY

1027. Wegelin, Oscar. Early American Poetry. A compilation of the titles of volumes of verse and broadsides by writers born or residing in North America. . . . Vol. I: 1650–1799; Vol. II: 1800–1820. 2nd ed. New York, Peter Smith, 1930. 2 vols. in one (253 pp.).—Original ed. 1903–07.

1028. Case, Arthur E. A Bibliography of English Poetical Miscellanies 1521–1750. Oxford Univ. Press for the Bibliographical Society, 1935. xi + 386 pp.

1029. Bruncken, Herbert. Subject Index to Poetry. A guide for adult readers. Chicago, American Library Association, 1940. xx + 201 (double column) pp.

1030. [Granger, Edith.] Granger's Index to Poetry. Fourth ed. completely rev. and enl. indexing anthologies published through Dec. 31, 1950. Edited by Raymond J. Dixon. New York, Columbia Univ. Press, 1953. xxxvii + 1832 (double column) pp.—Original ed. 1904; second ed. 1918 and supplement 1929; third ed. 1940 and supplement 1945. Also *Supplement,* New York, Columbia Univ. Press, 1957, xvi + 458 (double column) pp.

§40. VERSIFICATION: HISTORIES AND HISTORICAL STUDIES

1034. Brink, Bernhard ten. The Language and Metre of Chaucer. Second ed. rev. by Friedrich Kluge. Translated by M. Bentinck Smith. London, Macmillan Co., 1901. xxxvi + 280 pp.—Original Ger. ed. 1884; second Ger. ed. 1899. There is a 3rd Ger. ed.: *Chaucers Sprache und Verskunst,* 3. Aufl. bearbeitet von Eduard Eckhart, Leipzig, C. H. Tauchnitz, 1920, xii + 243 pp.

1035. Omond, Thos. S. English Metrists in the Eighteenth and Nineteenth Centuries. Being a sketch of English prosodical criticism during the last two hundred years. Oxford Univ. Press, 1907. vii + 274 pp.

1036. Saintsbury, Geo. A History of English Prosody. From the twelfth century to the present day. Vol. I: From the Origins to Spenser; Vol. II: From Shakespeare to Crabbe; Vol. III: From Blake to Mr. Swinburne. London, Macmillan Co., 1906–10. 3 vols.

1037. Schipper, Jakob. A History of English Versification. Oxford, Clarendon Press, 1910. xix + 390 pp.—Original Ger. ed. 1895.

1038. Schelling, Felix E. The English Lyric. Boston, Houghton Mifflin Co., 1913. xi + 335 pp.

1039. Lilly, Marie Loretto. The Georgic. A contribution to the study of the Virgilian type of didactic poetry. Baltimore, Johns Hopkins Press, 1919. vii + 175 pp.—Number 6 in the Hesperia Supplementary Series: Studies in English Philology.

1040. Cohen, Helen L. Lyric Forms from France. Their history and their use. With an anthology of ballads, chants royal . . . in English verse. New York, Harcourt, Brace and Co., 1922. xxix + 527 pp.—See also Cohen's earlier *The Ballade,* New York, Columbia Univ. Press, 1915, xix + 397 pp.

1041. Quayle, Thos. Poetic Diction. A study of eighteenth century verse. London, Methuen and Co., 1924. vii + 212 pp.

1042. Parry, Milman. Whole Formulaic Verses in Greek and South-Slavic Heroic Song. Transactions of the American Philological Association, LXIV (1933), 179–197.—For application of Parry's theories to English verse see 1052.

1043. Empson, Wm. Some Versions of Pastoral. London, Chatto and Windus, 1935. [v] + 298 pp.—American ed. *English Pastoral Poetry,* New York, W. W. Norton, 1938.

1044. Oakden, J[ames] P. Alliterative Poetry in Middle English. [Vol. I:] The Dialectal and Metrical Survey; [Vol. II:] A Survey of Traditions. Manchester, Eng., University Press, 1930–35. 2 vols.—Volume II with the assistance of Elizabeth R. Innes.

1045. Willcock, Gladys D., and Walker, Alice, eds. The Arte of English Poesie by George Puttenham [1589]. Cambridge Univ. Press, 1936. cx + 358 pp.

1046. Shuster, Geo. N. The English Ode from Milton to Keats. New York, Columbia Univ. Press, 1940. vii + 314 pp.—Number 150 in the series Columbia University Studies in English and Comparative Literature.

1047. Pope, John C. The Rhythm of Beowulf. An interpretation of the normal and hypermetric verse-forms in Old English poetry. New Haven, Yale Univ. Press, 1942. x + 386 pp.

1048. Miles, Josephine. The Vocabulary of Poetry. Three studies. Berkeley, University of California Press, 1946. 426 pp.—Originally vol. XII, nos. 1–3, in the series University of California Publications in English. The three studies are: 1. Wordsworth and the vocabulary of emotion (1942, pp. 1–181); 2. Pathetic fallacy in the nineteenth century (1942, pp. 183–304); 3. Major adjectives in English poetry from Wyatt to Auden (1946, pp. 305–426).

1049. Miles, Josephine. The Primary Language of Poetry in the 1640's. Berkeley, University of California Press, 1948. 160 pp.—Volume XIX, no. 1, in the series University of California Publications in English.

1050. Miles, Josephine. The Primary Language of Poetry in the 1740's and 1840's. Berkeley, University of California Press, 1950. 161–382 pp.—Volume XIX, no. 2, in the series University of California Publications in English.

1051. Miles, Josephine. The Primary Language of Poetry in the 1940's. Berkeley, University of California Press, 1951. 383–542 pp.—Volume XIX, no. 3, in the series University of California Publications in English.

1052. Magoun, Francis Peabody, Jr. Oral Formulaic Character of Anglo-Saxon Narrative Poetry. Speculum, XXVIII, 3 (July 1953), 446–467. —See also Ronald A. Waldron, "Oral-Formulaic Technique and Middle English Alliterative Poetry," *Speculum,* XXXII, 4 (Oct. 1957), 792–804.

1053. Fussell, Paul, Jr. Theory of Prosody in Eighteenth-Century England. New London, Connecticut College, 1954. x + 170 pp.—Number 5 in the series Connecticut College Monographs.

1054. Southworth, James G. Verses of Cadence. An introduction to the prosody of Chaucer and his followers. Oxford, Eng., Basil Blackwell, 1954. 94 pp.

1055. Lehmann, Winifred P. The Development of Germanic Verse Form. Austin, University of Texas Press, 1956. xix + 217 pp.

1056. Bliss, Alan J. The Metre of Beowulf. Oxford, Eng., Basil Blackwell, 1958. 166 pp.

§41. VERSIFICATION: EXPOSITIONAL STUDIES OF RHYME, METER, AND FORM

1060. Wood, Clement. The Complete Rhyming Dictionary and Poet's Craft Book. Garden City, N.Y., Garden City Publ'ing Co., 1936. xii + 607 pp.

1061. Wood, Clement. Poet's Handbook. Cleveland, World Publ'ing Co., 1940. xvi + 466 pp.—Reprint 1946.

1062. Hartman, Dennis. Rhyming Dictionary. A dictionary of rhymes. Los Angeles, National High School Poetry Association, 1949. 224 pp.

1063. Whitfield, Jane Shaw. The Improved Rhyming Dictionary. Edited by Francis Stillman. New York, Thomas Y. Crowell Co., 1951. xx + 283 (double column) pp.—Reprint 1955.

1064. Walker, J[ohn]. The Rhyming Dictionary of the English Language. In which the whole language is arranged according to its terminations, with an index of allowable rhymes. Revised and enl. by Lawrence H. Dawson. London, Routledge and Kegan Paul, 1953. vii + 549 pp.—Original ed. 1775; frequent revisions.

1065. Deutsch, Babette. Poetry Handbook. A dictionary of terms. New York, Funk and Wagnalls Co., 1957. 177 pp.

1066. Johnson, Burges. New Rhyming Dictionary and Poet's Handbook. Rev. ed. New York, Harper and Bros., 1957. x + 464 pp.—Original ed. 1931.

1067. Lanier, Sidney. The Science of English Verse. New York, Charles Scribner's Sons, 1880. xv + 315 pp.—Frequent reprints, as in 1923.

1068. Symonds, John Addington. Blank Verse. New York, Charles Scribner's Sons, 1895. viii + 113 pp.

1069. Dabney, J[ulia] P. The Musical Basis of Verse. London, Longmans, Green and Co., 1901. xi + 269 pp.

1070. Mayor, Joseph B. Chapters on English Metre. 2nd ed. Cambridge Univ. Press, 1901. xvi + 308 pp.—Original ed. 1886.

1071. Liddell, Mark H. An Introduction to the Scientific Study of English Poetry. Being prolegomena to a science of English prosody. New York, Doubleday, Page and Co., 1902. xvi + 312 pp.

1072. Alden, Raymond MacDonald. English Verse. Specimens illustrating its principles and history. New York, Henry Holt and Co., 1903. xiv + 459 pp.

1073. Lewis, Charlton M. The Principles of English Verse. New York, Henry Holt and Co., 1906. iii + 143 pp.

1074. Matthews, Brander. A Study of Versification. Boston, Houghton Mifflin Co., 1911. ix + 275 pp.

1075. Crosland, T[homas] W. H. The English Sonnet. New York, Dodd, Mead and Co., [1917]. 276 pp.—Reprint London, Martin Secker Ltd., 1926, 224 pp., number 16 in the series New Adelphi Library.

1076. Andrews, C[larence] E. The Writing and Reading of Verse. New York, D. Appleton and Co., 1918. xiv + 331 pp.—Reprint 1925.

1077. Baum, Paull Franklin. The Principles of English Versification. Cambridge, Mass., Harvard Univ. Press, 1924. xi + 215 pp.—"Glossarial Index," pp. 209–215.

1078. Grew, Sydney. A Book of English Prosody. London, Grant Richards Ltd., 1924. xii + 238 pp.

1079. Sonnenschein, E[dward] A. What Is Rhythm? An essay . . . accompanied by an appendix on experimental syllable-measurement in which Stephen Jones and Eileen MacLeod have co-operated. Oxford, Eng., Basil Blackwell, 1925. viii + 228 pp.

1080. Felkin, F[rederick] W. The Craft of the Poet. An outline of English verse composition. New York, Henry Holt and Co., 1926. 70 pp.

1081. Young, Geo. An English Prosody on Inductive Lines. Cambridge Univ. Press, 1928. ix + 296 pp.

1082. Hamer, Enid. The Meters of English Poetry. New York, Macmillan Co., 1930. xi + 340 pp.—Reprint London, Methuen and Co., 1951. "List of Texts and Editions," pp. 327–334.

1083. Lanz, Henry. The Physical Basis of Rime. An essay on the aesthetics of sound. Stanford Univ. Press, 1931. xiv + 365 pp.

1084. Hamer, Enid. The English Sonnet. An anthology. London, Methuen and Co., 1936. lviii + 192 pp.

1085. Hillyer, Robt. First Principles of Verse. Rev. ed. Boston, Writer Inc., 1950. xi + 158 pp.—Original ed. 1938; revised ed. reprinted 1957.

1086. Bartlett, Phyllis. Poems in Process. New York, Oxford Univ. Press, 1951. ix + 267 pp.—The composition and revision of lyric poetry.

§42. HISTORICAL SURVEYS AND STUDIES

1090. Hamilton, Walter. The Poets Laureate of England. A history of the office of poet laureate, biographical notices of its holders, and a collection of the satires, epigrams, and lampoons directed against them. London, Elliot Stock, 1879. xxvii + 308 pp.

1091. Minto, Wm. Characteristics of English Poets. From Chaucer to Shirley. 2nd ed. Boston, Ginn and Co., 1885. xi + 382 pp.—Original ed. 1874; second ed. reprinted 1889.

1092. Onderdonk, James L. History of American Verse 1610–1897. Chicago, A. C. McClurg and Co., 1901. xii + 395 pp.

1093. MacKail, J[ohn] W. The Springs of Helicon. A study in the progress of English poetry from Chaucer to Milton. New York, Longmans, Green and Co., 1909. xvi + 204 pp.

1094. Courthope, Wm. J. A History of English Poetry. Vol. I: The Middle Ages; Vol. II: The Renaissance and the Reformation; Vol. III: The Intellectual Conflict of the Seventeenth Century; Vol. IV: Development and Decline of the Poetic Drama; Vol. V: The Constitutional Compromise of the Eighteenth Century; Vol. VI: The Romantic Movement. London, Macmillan Co., 1895–1910. 6 vols.—Reprint 1920–26.

1095. Reed, Edward B. English Lyrical Poetry from Its Origins to the Present Time. New Haven, Yale Univ. Press, 1912. vi + 616 pp.

1096. Cowl, R[ichard] P. The Theory of Poetry in England. Its development in doctrines and ideas from the sixteenth century to the nineteenth century. London, Macmillan Co., 1914. xiv + 319 pp.—Short critical dicta from Gascoigne to Arnold.

1097. Gray, W[illiam] Forbes. The Poets Laureate of England. Their history and their odes. London, Isaac Pitman and Sons, 1914. xi + 315 pp.

1098. Welby, T[homas] Earle. A Popular History of English Poetry. London, A. M. Philpot Ltd., 1924. ix + 282 pp.

1099. MacKail, J[ohn] W. Studies in English Poets. New York, Longmans, Green and Co., 1926. xii + 251 pp.—A study *inter alios* of Shakespeare, Pope, Young, Collins, Keats, Morris, Swinburne, and Tennyson.

1100. Kreymborg, Alfred. Our Singing Strength. An outline of American poetry 1620–1930. New York, Coward-McCann Inc., 1929. xiii + 643 pp.—Reprint as *A History of American Poetry*, Our singing strength, New York, Tudor Publ'ing Co., 1934.

1101. Harris, L[ancelot] S. The Nature of English Poetry. An elementary survey. Preface by Arthur Quiller-Couch. London, J. M. Dent and Sons, 1931. viii + 173 pp.

1102. Elton, Oliver. The English Muse. A sketch. London, G. Bell and Sons, 1933. xiv + 464 pp.—Reprint 1950. Essentially a history of English lyric poetry.

1103. Smith, Chard Powers. Annals of the Poets. Their origins, backgrounds, private lives, habits of composition, characters, and personal peculiarities. New York, Charles Scribner's Sons, 1935. xxv + 523 pp.

1104. Grierson, Herbert J. C., and Smith, J[ames] C. A Critical History of English Poetry. 2nd ed. London, Chatto and Windus, 1947. viii + 539 pp.—Original ed. 1944; second ed. reprinted 1950.

1105. Elvin, Lionel. Introduction to the Study of Literature. Volume One: Poetry. London, Sylvan Press, 1949. 224 pp.—In the series Sylvan Books on Modern Studies in association with Ruskin College, Oxford.

1106. Bateson, F[rederick] W. English Poetry. A critical introduction. London, Longmans, Green and Co., 1950. x + 272 pp.—See also Bateson's earlier *English Poetry and the English Language,* An experiment in literary history. Oxford Univ. Press, 1934, viii + 129 pp.

1107. Bush, Douglas. English Poetry. The main currents from Chaucer to the present. New York, Oxford Univ. Press, 1952. ix + 222 pp.

1108. Sells, A[rthur] Lytton. The Italian Influence in English Poetry from Chaucer to Southwell. Bloomington, Indiana Univ. Press, 1955. 346 pp.

1109. Miles, Josephine. Eras and Modes in English Poetry. Berkeley, University of California Press, 1957. xi + 233 pp.

1110. Untermeyer, Louis. Lives of the Poets. The story of one thousand years of English and American poetry. New York, Simon and Schuster, 1959. x + 758 pp.

§43. INTERPRETATIVE STUDIES BY INDIVIDUAL CRITICS

[See also §71. Anthologies of Critical Essays; §72. Essays by Individuals on Phases of Criticism; §73. The New Criticism.]

1114. Courthope, Wm. J. Life in Poetry: Law in Taste. London, Macmillan Co., 1901. 452 pp.—Two series of lectures delivered at Oxford 1895–1900.

1115. Bailey, John. Poets and Poetry. Being articles reprinted from the literary supplement of The Times. Oxford Univ. Press, 1911. 217 pp.

1116. Reed, Edward Bliss. English Lyrical Poetry. New Haven, Yale Univ. Press, 1912. 616 pp.

1117. Rhys, Ernest. Lyric Poetry. London, J. M. Dent and Sons, 1913. x + 374 pp.—In the series Channels of English Literature.

1118. Newbolt, Henry. A New Study of English Poetry. London, Constable and Co., 1917. vii + 306 pp.—Reprint 1919.

1119. Palmer, Geo. H. Formative Types in English Poetry. Boston, Houghton Mifflin Co., 1918. xi + 310 pp.—A study of Chaucer, Spenser, Herbert, Pope, Wordsworth, Tennyson, and Browning as "types."

1120. Lowes, John Livingston. Convention and Revolt in Poetry. Boston, Houghton Mifflin Co., 1919. ix + 346 pp.—Reprint 1924.

1121. Brooke, Stopford A. Naturalism in English Poetry. New York, E. P. Dutton and Co., 1920. ix + 289 pp.

1122. Johnson, R[eginald] Brimley, ed. Poetry and the Poets. London, Faber and Gwyer, [1920]. vii + 364 pp.—A collection of essays on the nature of poetry written by Sidney, Wordsworth, Coleridge, Shelley, and Arnold.

1123. Perry, Bliss. A Study of Poetry. Boston, Houghton Mifflin Co., 1920. ix + 396 pp.

1124. Brett-Smith, H[erbert] F. B., ed. Peacock's Four Ages of Poetry; Shelley's Defence of Poetry; Browning's Essay on Shelley. Boston, Houghton Mifflin Co., 1921. xxxiii + 112 pp.

1125. Graves, Robt. On English Poetry. Being an irregular approach to the psychology of this art, from evidence mainly subjective. London, William Heinemann, 1922. xi + 12–149 pp.

1126. Noyes, Alfred. Some Aspects of Modern Poetry. New York, Frederick A. Stokes Co., 1924. 349 pp.

1127. Drinkwater, John. The Muse in Council. Being essays on poets and poetry. Boston, Houghton Mifflin Co., 1925. x + 303 pp.

1128. Riding, Laura, and Graves, Robt. A Pamphlet against Anthologies. Garden City, N.Y., Doubleday, Doran and Co., 1928. 192 pp.

1129. Bradby, G[odfrey] F. About English Poetry. Oxford Univ. Press, 1929. 78 pp.

1130. Chilton, Eleanor C., and Agar, Herbert. The Garment of Praise. Garden City, N.Y., Doubleday, Doran and Co., 1929. vii + 401 pp.

1131. Elliott, G[eorge] R. The Cycle of Modern Poetry. A series of essays toward clearing our present poetic dilemma. Princeton, N.J., University Press, 1929. xv + 194 pp.—A study *inter alios* of Arnold, Browning, Byron, Milton, and Shelley.

1132. Williams, Chas. Poetry at Present. Oxford Univ. Press, 1930. xii + 216 pp.

1133. Garrod, H[eathcote] W. Poetry and the Criticism of Life. Cambridge, Mass., Harvard Univ. Press, 1931. viii + 168 pp.—The Charles Eliot Norton Lectures 1929–30. See also Garrod's earlier *The Profession of Poetry and Other Lectures,* Oxford Univ. Press, 1929, xii + 270 pp.

1134. Salomon, Louis B. The Devil Take Her. The rebellious lover in English poetry. Philadelphia, University of Pennsylvania Press, 1931. [iii] + 359 pp.—Bibliography of poetry with anti-courtly love themes, pp. 298–351.

1135. Wilkinson, Bonaro. The Poetic Way of Release. With an introduction by H. A. Overstreet. New York, Alfred A. Knopf Inc., 1931. xi + 386 + xiv pp.

1136. Strong, L[eonard] A. G. Common Sense about Poetry. New York, Alfred A. Knopf, 1932. viii + 139 pp.

1137. Williams, Chas. The English Poetic Mind. Oxford Univ. Press, 1932. viii + 214 pp.

1138. Eliot, T[homas] S. The Use of Poetry and the Use of Criticism. Studies in the relation of criticism to poetry in England. Cambridge, Mass., Harvard Univ. Press, 1933. viii + 149 pp.—The Charles Eliot Norton Lectures 1932–33. Reprint London, Faber and Faber Ltd., 1948.

1139. Gilkes, Martin. On Poetry. Birmingham, Eng., Cornish Bros., 1933. 32 pp.

1140. Housman, A[lfred] E. The Name and Nature of Poetry. New York, Macmillan Co., 1933. [v] + 50 pp.—The Leslie Stephen Lecture delivered at Cambridge, Eng., 9 May 1933.

1141. Bodkin, Maud. Archetypal Patterns in Poetry. Psychological studies of imagination. Oxford Univ. Press, 1934. xiv + 340 pp.—Reprints 1948, 1951.

1142. Selincourt, E[rnest] de. Oxford Lectures on Poetry. Oxford Univ. Press, 1934. 256 pp.

1143. Sparrow, John. Sense and Poetry. Essays on the place of meaning in contemporary verse. New Haven, Yale Univ. Press, 1934. xxiv + 156 pp.

1144. Deutsch, Babette. This Modern Poetry. New York, W. W. Norton and Co., 1935. 284 pp.

1145. Leavis, F[rank] R. Revaluation. Tradition and development in English poetry. London, Chatto and Windus, 1936. ix + 275 pp.—Reprint 1949.

1146. Imam, Syed Mehdi. The Poetry of the Invisible. An interpretation of the major English poets from Keats to Bridges. London, George Allen and Unwin Ltd., 1937. 231 pp.

1147. James, D[avid] G. Scepticism and Poetry. An essay on the poetic imagination. London, George Allen and Unwin Ltd., 1937. 275 pp.

1148. MacNeice, Louis. Modern Poetry. A personal essay. Oxford Univ. Press, 1938. 205 pp.

1149. Bailey, Ruth. A Dialogue on Modern Poetry. Oxford Univ. Press, 1939. 99 pp.

1150. Evans, B[enjamin] Ifor. Tradition and Romanticism. Studies in English poetry from Chaucer to W. B. Yeats. London, Methuen and Co., 1940. [ix] + 213 pp.

1151. Knight, G[eorge] Wilson. The Starlit Dome. Studies in the poetry of vision. Oxford Univ. Press, 1941. vii + 314 pp.

1152. Osgood, Chas. G. Poetry as a Means of Grace. Princeton, N.J., University Press, 1941. 131 pp.

1153. Coffin, Robt. P. T. The Substance That Is Poetry. New York, Macmillan Co., 1942. xiii + 167 pp.

1154. Day-Lewis, C[ecil]. A Hope for Poetry. Reprint with a postscript. 5th ed. Oxford, Eng., Basil Blackwell, 1942. 98 pp.—Original ed. 1934; postscript first added to the 3rd ed. 1936.

1155. Tillyard, E[ustace] M. W. Poetry Direct and Oblique. Rev. ed. London, Chatto and Windus, 1945. 116 pp.—Original ed. 1934; revised ed. reprinted 1948.

1156. Pottle, Frederick A. The Idiom of Poetry. Rev. ed. Ithaca, N.Y., Cornell Univ. Press, 1946. xvii + 234 pp.—Original ed. 1941.

1157. Reid, Forrest. The Milk of Paradise. Some thoughts on poetry. London, Faber and Faber, 1946. 80 pp.

1158. Stauffer, Donald A. The Nature of Poetry. New York, W. W. Norton and Co., 1946. 291 pp.—"Book List" [chiefly of works defining poetry], pp. 283–287.

1159. Watts, Nevile. The Vision Splendid. New York, Sheed and Ward Inc., 1946. ix + 165 pp.

1160. Brooks, Cleanth, Jr. The Well Wrought Urn. Studies in the structure of poetry. New York, Harcourt, Brace and Co., 1947. xi + 270 pp.

1161. Richmond, W[illiam] Kenneth. Poetry and the People. London, George Routledge and Sons, 1947. v + 247 pp.

1162. Tillyard, E[ustace] M. W. Five Poems 1470–1870. An elementary essay on the background of English literature. London, Chatto and Windus, 1948. viii + 128 pp.

1163. Every, Geo. Poetry and Personal Responsibility. An interim report on contemporary literature. London, SCM Press, 1949. 96 pp.—Number 14 in the series Viewpoints, Contemporary Issues of Thought and Life.

1164. Frankenberg, Lloyd. Pleasure Dome. On reading modern poetry. Boston, Houghton Mifflin Co., 1949. xii + 372 pp.

1165. Graves, Robt. The Common Asphodel. Collected essays on poetry—1922–1949. London, Hamish Hamilton Ltd., 1949. xi + 335 pp.

1166. Hamilton, G[eorge] Rostrevor. The Tell-Tale Article. A critical approach to modern poetry. London, William Heinemann Ltd., 1949. xii + 114 pp.

1167. Read, Herbert. Phases of English Poetry. New and rev. ed. London, Faber and Faber, 1950. 148 pp.—Original ed. 1928 no. 7 in the Hogarth Lectures in Literature Series.

1168. Vivante, Leone. English Poetry and Its Contribution to the Knowledge of a Creative Principle. Preface by T. S. Eliot. London, Faber and Faber, 1950. xv + 340 pp.

1169. Bodkin, Maud. Studies of Type-Images in Poetry, Religion, and Philosophy. Oxford Univ. Press, 1951. xii + 184 pp.

1170. Brower, Reuben Arthur. The Fields of Light. An experiment in critical reading. New York, Oxford Univ. Press, 1951. xii + 218 pp.

1171. Blackmur, Richard P. Language as Gesture. Essays in poetry. New York, Harcourt, Brace and Co., 1952. 440 pp.—Reprint London, George Allen and Unwin Ltd., 1954.

1172. Deutsch, Babette. Poetry in Our Time. New York, Columbia Univ. Press, 1952. xix + 411 pp.—Reprint 1956.

1173. Crane, R[onald] S. Language of Criticism and the Structure of Poetry. University of Toronto Press. 1953. xxi + 214 pp.—The Alexander Lectures 1951–52.

1174. Whalley, Geo. Poetic Process. London, Routledge and Kegan Paul Ltd., 1953. xxxix + 256 pp.

1175. Eliot, T[homas] S. The Three Voices of Poetry. New York, Cambridge Univ. Press, 1954. 39 pp.

1176. Davie, Donald. Articulate Energy. An inquiry into the syntax of English poetry. London, Routledge and Kegan Paul, 1955. vii + 173 pp.—See also Davie's earlier *Purity of Diction in English Verse,* New York, Oxford Univ. Press, 1953, viii + 211 pp.

1177. Groom, Bernard. The Diction of Poetry from Spenser to Bridges. University of Toronto Press, 1955. ix + 284 pp.

1178. Wain, John, ed. Interpretations. Essays on twelve English poems. London, Routledge and Kegan Paul, 1955. xv + 237 pp.

1179. Krieger, Murray. New Apologists for Poetry. Minneapolis, University of Minnesota Press, 1956. xiv + 225 pp.

1180. Schlauch, Margaret. Modern English and American Poetry. Techniques and ideologies. London, C. A. Watts and Co., 1956. xi + 200 pp.

1181. Unger, Leonard. The Man in the Name. Essays on the experience of poetry. Minneapolis, University of Minnesota Press, 1956. xi + 249 pp.

1182. Blackmur, Richard P. Form and Value in Modern Poetry. Garden City, N.Y., Doubleday and Co., 1957. 388 pp.

1183. Eliot, T[homas] S. On Poetry and Poets. London, Faber and Faber Ltd., 1957. 262 pp.

1184. Adams, Christopher. The Worst English Poets. With decorations by John R. Matthews. London, Allan Wingate, 1958. 128 pp.—See also D[ominic] B. Wyndham Lewis and Charles Lee, *The Stuffed Owl*, An anthology of bad verse, with eight cartoons from the works of Max Beerbohm, New York, Coward McCann Inc., 1930, xxxii + 236 pp. Both anthologies are classics in the left-handed evaluation of English poetry.

1185. Alvarez, Alfred. Stewards of Excellence. Studies in modern English and American poets. New York, Charles Scribner's Sons, 1958. 191 pp.

1186. Press, John. The Chequer'd Shade. Reflections on obscurity in poetry. Oxford Univ. Press, 1958. 229 pp.

§44. THE ENGLISH EPIC AND ITS HEROIC AND CLASSICAL PROTOTYPES

1190. Gurteen, S[tephen] Humphreys. The Epic and the Fall of Man. A comparative study of Caedmon, Dante, and Milton. New York, G. P. Putnam's Sons, 1896. xi + 449 pp.

1191. Clark, John. A History of Epic Poetry. Post-Virgilian. Edinburgh, Oliver and Boyd, 1900. xx + 329 pp.

1192. Hart, Wm. Morris. Ballad and Epic. A study in the development of the narrative art. Boston, Ginn and Co., 1907. vii + 315 pp.—Volume XI in the series Studies and Notes in Philology and Literature published under the direction of the Modern Language Departments of Harvard University.

1193. Bédier, Joseph. Les légendes épiques. Paris, H. Champion, 1908. 4 vols.

1194. Ker, W[illiam] P. Epic and Romance. 2nd ed. London, Macmillan Co., 1908. xxiv + 398 pp.—Original ed. 1896; second ed. reprinted New York, Dover Publications, 1957.

1195. Smithson, Geo. A. The Old English Christian Epic. A study in the plot technique of the Juliana, the Elene, the Andreas, and the Christ in comparison with the Beowulf and with the Latin literature of the Middle Ages. Berkeley, University of California Press, 1910. 303–400 pp.—Volume I, no. 4, in the series University of California Publications in Modern Philology.

1196. Chadwick, H[ector] Munro. The Heroic Age. Cambridge Univ. Press, 1912. xi + 474 pp.—Reprint 1926. A treatment of Greek and Teutonic Heroic epic.

1197. Dixon, W[illiam] Macneile. English Epic and Heroic Poetry. London, J. M. Dent and Sons, 1912. xi + 339 pp.

1198. Abercrombie, Lascelles. The Epic. New York, George H. Doran Co., [1914]. 96 pp.

1199. Brie, Friedrich. Englische Rokoko-Epik. Munich, Max Hueber Verlag, 1927. 110 pp.—A study of the "Rape of the Lock" tradition.

1200. Routh, H[arold] V. God, Man, and Epic Poetry. A study in comparative literature. Vol. I: Classical; Vol. II: Medieval. Cambridge Univ. Press, 1927. 2 vols.

1201. Lawrence, Wm. W. Beowulf and Epic Tradition. Cambridge, Mass., Harvard Univ. Press, 1928. xv + 349 pp.

1202. Haber, T[om] B. Beowulf and the Aeneid. A comparative study. Princeton, N.J., University Press, 1931. x + 145 pp.

1203. Murray, Gilbert. The Rise of the Greek Epic. Oxford Univ. Press, 1934. xxiv + 356 pp.—A course of lectures delivered at Harvard University.

1204. Swedenberg, H[ugh] T., Jr. The Theory of the Epic in England 1650–1800. Berkeley, University of California Press, 1944. xiv + 396 pp.—Volume XV in the series University of California Publications in English.

1205. Crosland, Jessie. The Old French Epic. Oxford, Eng., Basil Blackwell, 1951. ix + 304 pp.

1206. Whitelock, Dorothy. The Audience of Beowulf. Oxford Univ. Press, 1951. 111 pp.

1207. Bowra, C[ecil] M. Heroic Poetry. London, Macmillan Co., 1952. ix + 590 pp.

1208. Tillyard, E[ustace] M. W. The English Epic and Its Background. New York, Oxford Univ. Press, 1954. x + 548 pp.—See also Tillyard's earlier *The English Epic Tradition*, Oxford Univ. Press, 1936, 23 pp., number 26 in the series Warton Lectures on English Poetry.

1209. Gradon, P[amela] O. E. Cynewulf's Elene. London, Methuen and Co., 1958. x + 114 pp.—In the series Methuen's Old English Library. "Bibliography," pp. 76–80.

1210. Whitman, Cedric H. Homer and the Heroic Tradition. Cambridge, Mass., Harvard Univ. Press, 1958. xv + 365 pp.

1211. Brodeur, Arthur Gilchrist. The Art of Beowulf. Berkeley, University of California Press, 1959. ix + 283 pp.

1212. Chambers, R[aymond] W. Beowulf. An introduction to the study of the poem with a discussion of the stories of Offa and Finn. Third ed. with a supplement by C[harles] L. Wrenn. Cambridge Univ. Press, 1959. 628 pp.—Original ed. 1921; second ed. 1932.

§45. SURVEYS: THE OLD AND MIDDLE ENGLISH PERIODS

[See also §105. Old English Readers; §106. Middle English Readers.]
[Several anthologies are here listed because their introductions contain excellent Old and Middle English literary history. Also, a few titles not belonging to English literature are present; but these titles, dealing chiefly with courtly love and the Romance lyric, are indispensable to a knowledge of Middle English poetry.]

1216. Brown, Carleton. A Register of Middle English Religious and Didactic Verse. Part I: List of Manuscripts; Part II: Index of First Lines and Index of Subjects and Titles. Oxford Univ. Press for the Bibliographical Society, 1916–20. 2 vols.

1217. Brown, Carleton, and Robbins, Rossell Hope. The Index of Middle English Verse. New York, Columbia Univ. Press for the Index Society, 1943. xix + 785 pp.—A list alphabetically arranged of 4287 first lines of Middle English poems.

1218. Rowbotham, J[ohn] F. The Troubadours and Courts of Love. London, S. Sonnenschein and Co., 1895. xxiii + 324 pp.—In the Social England Series. "List of Authorities," pp. 315–317.

1219. Neilson, Wm. A. Origins and Sources of the Court of Love. Boston, Ginn and Co., 1899. vi + 284 pp.—Volume VI in the series Harvard Studies and Notes in Philology and Literature.

1220. Tucker, Samuel M. Verse Satire in England before the Renaissance. New York, Columbia Univ. Press, 1908. xi + 245 pp.—Volume III, no. 2, in the Columbia University Studies in English: Second Series.

1221. Tupper, Frederick J. The Riddles of the Exeter Book. Edited with introduction, notes, and glossary. Boston, Ginn and Co., 1910. cxi + 292 pp.—"Bibliography," pp. ci–cviii.

1222. Müller, Alexander. Mittelenglische geistliche und weltliche Lyrik des XIII. Jahrhunderts (Mit Ausschluss der politischen Lieder). Nach Motiven und Formen. Halle a. S., Verlag von Max Niemeyer, 1911. xi + 160 pp.—Volume XLIV in the series Studien zur englischen Philologie.

1223. Patterson, Frank A. The Middle English Penitential Lyric. A study and collection of early religious verse. New York, Columbia Univ. Press, 1911. 203 pp.

1224. Sandison, Helen E. The "Chanson d'aventure" in Middle English. Bryn Mawr, Penn., Bryn Mawr College, 1913. xii + 152 pp.—Volume XII in the Bryn Mawr College Monograph Series.

1225. Williams, Blanch C. Gnomic Poetry in Anglo-Saxon. New York, Columbia Univ. Press, 1914. xiv + 171 pp.—In the series Columbia University Studies in English and Comparative Literature.

1226. Chaytor, H[enry] J. The Troubadours and England. Cambridge Univ. Press, 1923. vii + 164 pp.

1227. Brown, Carleton. Religious Lyrics of the XIVth Century. Oxford, Clarendon Press, 1924. xxii + 358 pp.

1228. Audiau, Jean. Les troubadours et l'Angleterre. Contribution à l'étude des poètes anglais de l'amour au moyen-âge. (XIIIe et XIVe siècles). Nouv. éd., rev. et complétée. Paris, Librairie Philosophique J. Vim, 1927. 136 pp.—Original ed. 1920. "Bibliographie," pp. 9–15.

1229. Brown, Carleton. English Lyrics of the XIIIth Century. Oxford, Clarendon Press, 1932. xlii + 312 pp.

1230. Smith, A[lbert] H., ed. Three Northumbrian Poems. Caedmon's hymn, Bede's death song, and the Leiden riddle. London, Methuen and Co., 1933. x + 54 pp.—In the series Methuen's Old English Library.

1231. Tuve, Rosemond. Seasons and Months. Studies in a tradition of Middle English poetry. Paris, Librairie Universitaire, 1933. 232 pp.

1232. Bartlett, A[deline] C. The Larger Rhetorical Patterns in Anglo-Saxon Poetry. New York, Columbia Univ. Press, 1935. ix + 130 pp.—Number 122 in the series Columbia University Studies in English and Comparative Literature.

1233. Greene, Richard Leighton. The Early English Carols. Oxford Univ. Press, 1935. cxlv + 323 (double column) + 324–461 (single column) pp.

1234. Brown, Carleton. Religious Lyrics of the XVth Century. Oxford, Clarendon Press, 1939. xxxii + 394 pp.

1235. Kirby, Thos. A. Chaucer's Troilus. A study of courtly love. Baton Rouge, Louisiana State Univ. Press, 1940. xi + 337 pp.—Number 39 in the series Louisiana State University Studies. Reprint Gloucester, Mass., Peter Smith, 1958.

1236. Parry, John Jay. Andreas Cappelanus. The Art of Courtly Love. With introduction, translation, and notes. New York, Columbia Univ. Press, 1941. xi + 218 pp.—Number 33 in the series Records of Civilization: Sources and Studies. Bibliography, pp. 213–218.

1237. Kennedy, Chas. W. The Earliest English Poetry. A critical survey of the poetry written before the Norman Conquest with illustrative translations. Oxford Univ. Press, 1943. viii + 375 pp.—Reprint 1948. "Selected Bibliography," pp. 369–375. See also Kennedy's *An Anthology of Old English Poetry*, Translated into alliterative verse, New York, Oxford Univ. Press, 1960, xvi + 174 pp.

1238. Nykl, A[lois] R. Hispano-Arabic Poetry and Its Relations with the Old Provençal Troubadours. Baltimore, published by the author, 1946. xxvii + 416 pp.

1239. Denomy, Alexander, C. S. B. The Heresy of Courtly Love. Introduction by William Lane Keleher, S.J. New York, Declan X. McMullen Co., 1947. 92 pp.—The Boston College Candlemas Lectures on Christian Literature.

1240. Moore, Arthur K. The Secular Lyric in Middle English. Lexington, University of Kentucky Press, 1951. xi + 255 pp.

1241. The Anglo-Saxon Poetic Records. A collective edition. Vol. I: The Junius Manuscript, edited by George Philip Krapp; Vol. II: The Vercelli Book, edited by George Philip Krapp; Vol. III: The Exeter Book, edited by George Philip Krapp and Elliott Van Kirk Dobbie; Vol. IV: The Beowulf Manuscript: Beowulf and Judith, edited by Elliott Van Kirk Dobbie; Vol. V: The Paris Psalter and the Meters of Boethius, edited by George Philip Krapp; Vol. VI: The Anglo-Saxon Minor Poems, edited by Elliott Van Kirk Dobbie. New York, Columbia Univ. Press, 1931–53. 6 vols.—Extensive bibliographies arranged chronologically before each text. Vol I: 1931; Vol. II: 1932; Vol. III: 1936; Vol. IV: 1953; Vol. V: 1932; Vol. VI: 1942.

1242. Bell, H[arold] Idris. The Nature of Poetry as Conceived by the Welsh Bards. Oxford Univ. Press, 1955. 27 pp.—The Taylorian Lecture 1955.

1243. Robbins, Rossell Hope. Secular Lyrics of the XIVth and XVth Centuries. 2nd ed. Oxford, Clarendon Press, 1955. lv + 331 pp.—Original ed. 1952.

1244. Huppé, Bernard Felix. Doctrine and Poetry. Augustine's influence on Old English poetry. Albany, State Univ. of New York, 1959. vi + 248 pp.

1245. Robbins, Rossell Hope. Historical Poems of the XIVth and XVth Centuries. New York, Columbia Univ. Press, 1959. xlvii + 440 pp.

§46. SURVEYS: THE TUDOR AND JACOBEAN PERIODS

1249. Gosse, Edmund [W.]. The Jacobean Poets. London, John Murray, 1894. vii + 226 pp.—In the series University Extension Manuals. Reprint 1899.

1250. Erskine, John. The Elizabethan Lyric. New York, Macmillan Co., 1903. xvi + 344 pp.—In the series Columbia University Studies in English.

1251. Harrison, John Smith. Platonism in English Poetry of the Sixteenth and Seventeenth Centuries. New York, Columbia Univ. Press, 1903. xi + 235 pp.—In the series Columbia University Studies in Comparative Literature.

1252. Cruse, Amy. The Elizabethan Lyrists and Their Poetry. London, George G. Harrap, 1919. 147 pp.

1253. Berdan, John M. Early Tudor Poetry 1485–1547. Studies in Tudor literature. New York, Macmillan Co., 1920. xix + 564 pp.—Reprint 1931.

1254. Fellows, E[dmund] H. English Madrigal Verse 1588–1632. Edited from the original song books. 2nd ed. Oxford, Clarendon Press, 1929. xxiv + 644 pp.—Original ed. 1920; second ed. reprinted 1950. See also Fellows' *The English Madrigal Composers,* Oxford, Clarendon Press, 1921, 364 pp.

1255. Scott, Janet G. [Mrs. Janet Girvan Espiner]. Les sonnets élisabéthains. Les sources et l'apport personnel. Paris, H. Champion, 1929. 343 pp.—Volume LX in the series Bibliothèque de la Revue de littérature comparée.. "Chronologie," pp. 229–302; "Liste de sources," pp. 303–332.

1256. John, Lisle C. The Elizabethan Sonnet Sequences. Studies in conventional conceits. New York, Columbia Univ. Press, 1938. x + 278 pp.—Number 133 in the series Columbia University Studies in English and Comparative Literature.

1257. Rubel, Veré L. Poetic Diction in the English Renaissance. From Skelton through Spenser. New York, Modern Language Association of America, 1941. xiv + 312 pp.—Volume XII in the Modern Language Association of America Revolving Fund Series.

1258. Tuve, Rosemond. Elizabethan and Metaphysical Imagery. Renaissance poetic and twentieth-century critics. University of Chicago Press, 1947. xiv + 442 pp.—"Bibliography," pp. 429–434.

1259. Zocca, Louis R. Elizabethan Narrative Poetry. New Brunswick, N.J., Rutgers Univ. Press, 1950. xii + 306 pp.—"Bibliography," pp. 289–296.

1260. Ing, Catherine. Elizabethan Lyrics. A Study in the development of English metres and their relation to poetic effect. London, Chatto and Windus, 1951. 252 pp.—"Select Bibliography," pp. 237–243.

1261. Danby, John F. Poets on Fortune's Hill. Studies in Sidney, Shakespeare, Beaumont, and Fletcher. London, Faber and Faber, 1952. 212 pp.

1262. Smith, Hallett. Elizabethan Poetry. A study in conventions, meanings, and expression. Cambridge, Mass., Harvard Univ. Press, 1952. xii + 355 pp.

1263. Evans, Maurice. English Poetry in the Sixteenth Century. London, Hutchinson and Co., 1955. 183 pp.—In the series Hutchinson's University Library.

1264. Lever, J[ulius] W. The Elizabethan Love Sonnet. London, Methuen and Co., 1956. ix + 282 pp.

1265. Valency, Maurice. In Praise of Love. An introduction to the love-poetry of the Renaissance. New York, Macmillan Co., 1958. xi + 319 pp.—"Selective Bibliography," pp. 273–285.

§47. SURVEYS: THE SEVENTEENTH CENTURY

1268. Spencer, Theodore, and Van Doren, Mark. Studies in Metaphysical Poetry. Two essays and a bibliography. New York, Columbia Univ. Press, 1939. [vii] + 88 pp.—"A Bibliography of Studies in Metaphysical Poetry 1912–1938," by Theodore Spencer with the assistance of Evelyn Orr, pp. 31–83.

1269. Shafer, Robt. The English Ode to 1660. An essay in literary history. Princeton, N.J., University Press, 1918. vi + 167 pp.

1270. Havens, Raymond D. The Influence of Milton on English Poetry. Cambridge, Mass., Harvard Univ. Press, 1922. xii + 722 pp.

1271. Eliot, T[homas] S. Homage to John Dryden. Three essays on poetry of the seventeenth century. London, Hogarth Press, 1924. 46 pp.

1272. Williamson, Geo. The Donne Tradition. A study in English poetry from Donne to the death of Cowley. Cambridge, Mass., Harvard Univ. Press, 1930. xi + 264 pp.—Reprint New York, Noonday Press, 1958. "Bibliography," pp. 258–264.

1273. West, Albert H. L'influence française dans la poésie burlesque en Angleterre entre 1660 et 1700. Paris, Librairie ancienne Honoré Champion, 1931. 219 pp.—Volume LXXIV in the series Bibliothèque de la Revue de littérature comparée.

1274. Friederich, Werner P. Spiritualismus und Sensualismus in der englischen Barocklyrik. Vienna, Wilhelm Braumüller, 1932. viii + 304 pp.—Vol. LVII in the series Wiener Beiträge zur englischen Philologie.

1275. Leishman, J[ames] B. The Metaphysical Poets. Donne, Herbert, Vaughan, Traherne. Oxford Univ. Press, 1934. [vii] + 232 pp.

1276. Jonas, Leah. The Divine Science. The aesthetic of some representative seventeenth-century English poets. New York, Columbia Univ. Press, 1940. xii + 292 pp.—Number 151 in the series Columbia University Studies in English and Comparative Literature.

1277. Sharp, Robt. Lathrop. From Donne to Dryden. The revolt against metaphysical poetry. Chapel Hill, University of North Carolina Press, 1940. xiii + 221 pp.

1278. Freeman, Rosemary. English Emblem Books. London, Chatto and Windus, 1948. xiv + 256 pp.—"Bibliography of Emblem Books to 1700," pp. 229–240.

1279. Husain, Itrat. The Mystical Elements in the Metaphysical Poets of the Seventeenth Century. Foreword by Evelyn Underhill. Edinburgh, Oliver and Boyd, 1948. 351 pp.

1280. Mahood, M[olly] M. Poetry and Humanism. London, Jonathan Cape, 1950. 335 pp.—A study chiefly of Donne, Vaughan, and Milton.

1281. Nicolson, Marjorie Hope. The Breaking of the Circle. Studies in the effect of the "New Science" upon seventeenth century poetry. Evanston, Ill., Northwestern Univ. Press, 1950. xxii + 193 pp.

1282. Wallerstein, Ruth. Studies in Seventeenth-Century Poetic. Madison, University of Wisconsin Press, 1950. x + 421 pp.

1283. Bowden, Wm. R. The English Dramatic Lyric 1603–42. A study in Stuart dramatic technique. New Haven, Yale Univ. Press, 1951. xii + 219 pp.—Volume CXVIII in the series Yale Studies in English. "Bibliography," pp. 211–219.

1284. Bennett, Joan. Four Metaphysical Poets. Donne, Herbert, Vaughan, Crashaw. 2nd ed. Cambridge Univ. Press, 1953. ix + 127 pp.—Original ed. 1934; second ed. reprinted with corrections 1957.

1285. Mourgues, Odette de. Metaphysical, Baroque, and Précieux Poetry. Oxford Univ. Press, 1953. viii + 184 pp.

1286. Cruttwell, Patrick. The Shakespearean Moment and Its Place in the Poetry of the Seventeenth Century. New York, Columbia Univ. Press, 1954. [vii] + 262 pp.

1287. Esch, Arno. Englische religiöse Lyrik des 17. Jahrhunderts. Studien zu Donne, Herbert, Crashaw, Vaughan. Tübingen, Max Niemeyer Verlag, 1955. xi + 225 pp.—Volume V in the Buchreihe der Anglia, Zeitschrift für englische Philologie.

1288. Duncan, Joseph E. The Revival of Metaphysical Poetry. The history of a style, 1800 to the present. Minneapolis, University of Minnesota Press, 1959. 227 pp.

§48. SURVEYS: THE EIGHTEENTH CENTURY

1292. Osborne, Edna. Oriental Diction and Theme in English Verse 1740–1840. Lawrence, University of Kansas, 1916. 142 pp.—Volume II, no. 1, in the series University of Kansas Humanities Studies.

1293. Doughty, Oswald. Forgotten Lyrics of the Eighteenth Century. London, H. F. and G. Witherby, 1924. 212 pp.—See also Doughty's earlier *English Lyric in the Age of Reason,* London, Daniel O'Connor, 1922, xvi + 461 pp.

1294. Bragg, Marion K. The Formal Eclogue in Eighteenth Century England. Orono, University of Maine, 1926. xi + 147 pp.—Number 6 in the University of Maine Studies: Second Series.

1295. Bond, Richmond P. English Burlesque Poetry 1700–1750. Cambridge, Mass., Harvard Univ. Press, 1932. xiii + 483 pp.—"Register of Burlesque Poems," pp. 233–453; "Bibliography," pp. 455–460.

1296. Durling, Dwight L. Georgic Tradition in English Poetry. New York, Columbia Univ. Press, 1935. xii + 259 pp.—Number 121 in the series Columbia University Studies in English and Comparative Literature. "Translations of Didactic Poetry into English to 1850," pp. 219–223.

1297. Whelan, Sister M[ary] Kevin, S.S.J. Enthusiasm in English Poetry of the Eighteenth Century 1700–1771. Washington, D.C., Catholic Univ. of America, 1935. viii + 169 pp.

1298. Aubin, Robt. Arnold. Topographical Poetry in Eighteenth Century England. New York, Modern Language Association of America, 1936. xiii + 419 pp.—Volume VI in the Modern Language Association of America Revolving Fund Series.

1299. Smith, David Nichol. Some Observations on Eighteenth Century Poetry. University of Toronto Press, 1937. 81 pp.

1300. Nicolson, Marjorie Hope. Newton Demands the Muse. Newton's Opticks and the eighteenth century poets. Princeton, N.J., University Press, 1946. xi + 178 pp.—Number 2 in the History of Ideas Series.

1301. Fitzgerald, Margaret Mary. First Follow Nature. Primitivism in English poetry 1725–1750. New York, Columbia Univ. Press, 1947. xi + 270 pp.

1302. Wasserman, Earl R. Elizabethan Poetry in the Eighteenth Century. Urbana, University of Illinois Press, 1947. 291 pp.—Volume XXXII, nos. 2 and 3, in the series Illinois Studies in Language and Literature.

1303. Brown, Wallace Cable. The Triumph of Form. A study of the later masters of the heroic couplet. Chapel Hill, University of North Carolina Press, 1948. ix + 212 pp.—A study *inter alios* of Gay, Churchill, Young, and Cowper.

1304. Sutherland, James. A Preface to Eighteenth Century Poetry. Oxford Univ. Press, 1948. viii + 175 pp.

1305. Tillotson, Geoffrey. The Manner of Proceeding in Certain Eighteenth- and Early Nineteenth-Century Poems. Oxford Univ. Press, 1948. 30 pp. —Number 39 in the series Warton Lectures on English Poetry.

1306. Arthos, John. The Language of Natural Description in Eighteenth Century Poetry. Ann Arbor, University of Michigan Press, 1949. xiv + 463 pp.—Volume XXIV in the University of Michigan Publications: Language and Literature Series.

1307. Congleton, J[ames] E. Theories of Pastoral Poetry in England 1684–1798. Gainesville, University of Florida Press, 1952. 355 pp.—Bibliography, pp. 343–350.

1308. Jack, Ian. Augustan Satire. Intention and idiom in English poetry 1660–1750. Oxford Univ. Press, 1952. x + 164 pp.

1309. Unwin, Rayner. The Rural Muse. Studies in the peasant poetry of England. London, George Allen and Unwin Ltd., 1954. 202 pp.—A study *inter alios* of James Thompson, Stephen Duck, and Robert Bloomfield.

1310. Chapin, Chester F. Personification in Eighteenth-Century English Poetry. New York, Columbia Univ. Press, 1955. x + 175 pp.

1311. Hagstrum, Jean H. The Sister Arts. The tradition of literary pictorialism and English poetry from Dryden to Gray. University of Chicago Press, 1958. xxii + 337 pp. + xxxii plates.

§49. SURVEYS: THE ROMANTIC PERIOD

1315. Hancock, Albert Elmer. The French Revolution and the English Poets. A study in historical criticism. New York, Henry Holt and Co., 1899. xvi + 197 pp.

1316. Brandes, Geo. Naturalism in England. London, William Heinemann, 1905. viii + 366 pp.—Volume IV of Brandes's *Main Currents in Nineteenth Century Literature*, London, William Heinemann, 1901–1905, 6 vols. Reprint as *Naturalism in Nineteenth Century English Literature*, London, Russell and Russell Inc., 1957. A treatment of the English Romantic poets.

1317. Brooke, Stopford A. Studies in Poetry. New York, G. P. Putnam's Sons, 1907. 253 pp.—A study *inter alios* of Blake, Keats, and Shelley.

1318. Symonds, Arthur. The Romantic Movement in English Poetry. New York, E. P. Dutton and Co., 1909. xi + 344 pp.

1319. Gingerich, Solomon F. Essays in the Romantic Poets. New York, Macmillan Co., 1924. 276 pp.—Reprint 1929.

1320. Powell, A[nnie] E. The Romantic Theory of Poetry. An examination in the light of Croce's aesthetic. London, Edward Arnold and Co., 1926. viii + 263 pp.

1321. Chapman, J[ohn] A. Papers on Shelley, Wordsworth, and Others. Oxford Univ. Press, 1929. 171 pp.

1322. Draper, John W. The Funeral Elegy and the Rise of English Romanticism. New York Univ. Press, 1929. xvi + 358 pp.

1323. Grierson, H[erbert] J. C. Lyric Poetry of the Nineteenth Century. New York, Harcourt, Brace and Co., 1929. 159 pp.—Number 6 in the Hogarth Lectures on Literature Series. A study chiefly of Blake, Wordsworth, Coleridge, Scott, and Byron.

1324. Sickels, Eleanor M. The Gloomy Egoist. Moods and themes of melancholy from Gray to Keats. New York, Columbia Univ. Press, 1932. x + 456 pp.

1325. Sherwood, Margaret. Undercurrents of Influence in English Romantic Poetry. Cambridge, Mass., Harvard Univ. Press, 1934. xi + 365 pp.—"Bibliography," pp. 357–359.

1326. Hungerford, Edward B. Shores of Darkness. New York, Columbia Univ. Press, 1941. 314 pp.—A study *inter alios* of Shelley and Keats.

1327. Larrabee, Stephen A. English Bards and Grecian Marbles. The relationship between sculpture and poetry especially in the Romantic period. New York, Columbia Univ. Press, 1943. xiii + 312 pp.

1328. Gugler, Ilse. Das Problem der fragmentischen Dichtung in der englischen Romantik. Bern, Verlag A. Franke, 1944. 89 pp.—Volume XV in the series Schweizer anglistische Arbeiten.

1329. Elwin, Malcolm. The First Romantics. London, MacDonald and Co., 1947. xii + 13–304 pp.—"Bibliography," pp. 292–295. A study of Wordsworth, Coleridge, and Southey.

1330. Selincourt, Ernest de. Wordsworthian and Other Studies. Preface by Helen Darbishire. Oxford Univ. Press, 1947. 206 pp.

1331. Heath-Stubbs, John. The Darkling Plain. A study of the later fortunes of Romanticism in English poetry from George Darley to W. B. Yeats. London, Eyre and Spottiswoode Ltd., 1950. xvii + 18–221 pp.

1332. Raysor, Thos. M. The English Romantic Poets. A review of research. New York, Modern Language Association of America, 1950. [viii] + 241 pp.—Number 16 in the Revolving Fund Series of the Modern Language Association of America.

1333. Hough, Graham. The Romantic Poets. London, Hutchinson House, 1953. vii + 9–200 pp.—In the series Hutchinson's University Library.

1334. Read, Herbert. The True Voice of Feeling. Studies in English Romantic poetry. London, Faber and Faber, 1953. 382 pp.

1335. Wain, John, ed. Contemporary Reviews of Romantic Poetry. Foreword by Vivian de Sola Pinto. London, George G. Harrap, 1953. 240 pp.—In the series Life, Literature, and Thought Library.

1336. Gérard, Albert. L'idée romantique de la poésie en Angleterre. Études sur la théorie de la poésie chez Coleridge, Wordsworth, Keats, et Shelley. Paris, Société d'édition "Les Belles Lettres," 1955. 416 pp.—Number 136 in the series Bibliothèque de la faculté de philosophie et lettres de l'université de Liége. "Bibliographie," pp. 379–404.

1337. Thorpe, Clarence, Baker, Carlos, and Weaver, Bennett, eds. The Major English Romantic Poets. A symposium in reappraisal. Carbondale, Southern Illinois Univ. Press, 1957. xvii + 269 pp.

1338. Perkins, David. The Quest for Permanence. The symbolism of Wordsworth, Shelley, and Keats. Cambridge, Mass., Harvard Univ. Press, 1959. viii + 301 pp.

1339. Wasserman, Earl R. The Subtler Language. Critical readings of neoclassic and romantic poems. Baltimore, Johns Hopkins Press, 1959. 361 pp.

§50. SURVEYS: THE VICTORIAN ERA

1343. Faverty, Frederic E. The Victorian Poets. A guide to research. Cambridge, Mass., Harvard Univ. Press, 1956. [x] + 292 pp.

1344. Stedman, Edmund Clarence. Poets of America. Boston, Houghton Mifflin Co., 1885. xvii + 516 pp.

1345. Lawton, Wm. Cranston. The New England Poets. A study of Emerson, Hawthorne, Longfellow, Whittier, Lowell, Holmes. New York, Macmillan Co., 1898. xvi + 265 pp.

1346. Archer, Wm. Poets of the Younger Generation. London, John Lane, 1902. viii + 565 pp.

1347. Hoyt, Arthur S. The Spiritual Message of Modern English Poetry. New York, Macmillan Co., 1924. xi + 290 pp.—A study of Arnold, Browning, and Tennyson.

1348. Grierson, H[erbert] J. C. Lyric Poetry from Blake to Hardy. London, Hogarth Press, 1928. 159 pp.—Number 5 in the series Hogarth Lectures on Literature. Reprint 1950.

1349. Stevenson, Lionel. Darwin among the Poets. University of Chicago Press, 1932. vii + 357 pp.—A study chiefly of Browning, Hardy, Meredith, and Tennyson.

1350. Evans, Benjamin I. English Poetry in the Later Nineteenth Century. London, Methuen and Co., 1933. xxv + 404 pp.

1351. Beach, Joseph Warren. The Concept of Nature in Nineteenth Century Poetry. New York, Macmillan Co., 1936. xii + 618 pp.

1352. Weygandt, Cornelius. The Time of Tennyson. English Victorian poetry as it affected America. New York, D. Appleton–Century Co., 1936. x + 349 pp.

1353. Lucas, F[rank] L. Ten Victorian Poets. [New ed.] Cambridge Univ. Press, 1940. xx + 199 pp.—Original ed. 1930. A study of Tennyson, Browning, Arnold, Clough, Patmore, D. G. and Christina Rossetti, Morris, Swinburne, and Hardy.

1354. Warren, Alba H., Jr. English Poetic Theory 1825–1865. Princeton, N.J., University Press, 1950. vii + 243 pp.—Number 29 in the series Princeton Studies in English. "Bibliography," pp. 229–235.

1355. Johnson, E[dward] D. H. The Alien Vision of Victorian Poetry. Sources of the poetic imagination in Tennyson, Browning, and Arnold. Princeton, N. J., University Press, 1952. xvi + 224 pp.—Number 34 in the series Princeton Studies in English.

1356. Foakes, R[eginald] A. The Romantic Assertion. A study in the language of nineteenth century poetry. New Haven, Yale Univ. Press, 1958. 186 pp.

§51. SURVEYS: THE MODERN ERA

1361. Irish, Wynot R. The Modern American Muse. A complete bibliography of American verse 1900–1925. Syracuse, N.Y., University Press, 1950. xii + 259 pp.

1362. Rittenhouse, Jessie B. The Younger American Poets. Boston, Little, Brown and Co., 1904. xvii + 352 pp.

1363. Dawson, W[illiam] J. The Makers of English Poetry. 2nd ed. New York, Fleming H. Revell Co., 1906. 404 pp.—Original ed. 1902 *The Makers of Modern Poetry.*

1364. Jack, A[dolphus] A. Poetry and Prose. Being essays in modern English poetry. London, Constable and Co., 1912. ix + 278 pp.

1365. Sturgeon, Mary C. Studies of Contemporary Poets. London, Harrap and Co., 1916. 330 pp.

1366. Lowell, Amy. Tendencies in Modern American Poetry. Boston, Houghton Mifflin Co., 1917. xiii + 2–349 pp.—Frequent reprints, as in 1928.

1367. Phelps, Wm. L. The Advance of English Poetry in the Twentieth Century. New York, Dodd, Mead and Co., 1917. xv + 343 pp.

1368. Cook, Howard Willard. Our Poets of Today. 3rd rev. ed. New York, Moffat, Yard and Co., 1923. x + 421 pp.—Original ed. 1918.

1369. Untermeyer, Louis. American Poetry since 1900. New York, Henry Holt and Co., 1923. x + 405 pp.—Reprint 1934. See also Untermeyer's earlier *The New Era in American Poetry,* New York, Henry Holt and Co., 1919, xi + 364 pp.

1370. Davison, Edward. Some Modern Poets and Other Critical Essays. New York, Harper and Bros., 1928. 255 pp.—A study *inter alios* of AE, James Stephens, John Masefield, and W. B. Yeats.

1371. Wood, Clement. Hunters of Heaven. The American soul as revealed by its poetry. New York, Frederick A. Stokes Co., 1929. [xv] + 351 pp.—See also Wood's earlier *Poets of America,* New York, E. P. Dutton and Co., 1925, xiii + 392 pp.

1372. Hughes, Glenn. Imagism and the Imagists. A study in modern poetry. Stanford Univ. Press, 1931. xiii + 283 pp.—Reprint New York, Humanities Press, 1959. A study of Aldington, H.D., Fletcher, Flint, Lawrence, Lowell, and Pound. "Bibliography," pp. 253–267.

1373. Bullough, Geoffrey. The Trend of Modern Poetry. Edinburgh, Oliver and Boyd, 1934. vii + 181 pp.

1374. Palmer, Herbert. Post Victorian Poetry. London, J. M. Dent and Sons, 1938. xiii + 378 pp.

1375. Daiches, David. Poetry and the Modern World. A study of poetry in England between 1900 and 1939. University of Chicago Press, 1940. x + 247 pp.—Reprint 1948.

1376. Southworth, James G. Sowing the Spring. Studies in British poets from Hopkins to MacNeice. Oxford, Eng., Basil Blackwell, 1940. 178 pp.

1377. Church, Richard. Eight for Immortality. London, J. M. Dent and Sons, 1941. ix + 113 pp.—Studies of eight British and American poets.

1378. Gregory, Horace, and Zaturenska, Marya. A History of American Poetry 1900–1940. New York, Harcourt, Brace and Co., 1942. xi + 524 pp.—Reprint 1946.

1379. Gilkes, Martin. A Key to Modern English Poetry. 2nd ed. London, Blackie and Son, 1945. vi + 178 pp.—Original ed. 1937; second ed. reprinted 1948.

1380. Spender, Stephen. Poetry since 1939. London, Longmans, Green and Co., 1946. viii + 70 pp.

1381. Stanford, Derek. The Freedom of Poetry. Studies in contemporary verse. London, Falcon Press, 1947. 251 pp.—A study of Sidney Keyes, David Gascoyne, Alex Comfort, Lawrence Durrell, Nicholas Moore, Norman Nicholson, Wrey Gardiner, Kathleen Raine, Ruthven Todd, and Anne Ridler.

1382. Winters, Yvor. In Defense of Reason. Primitivism and decadence. A study of American experimental poetry. New York, Swallow Press, 1947. viii + 611 pp.—See also Winters' earlier *Primitivism and Decadence,* A study of American experimental poetry, New York, Arrow Editions, 1937, xiii + 146 pp.

1383. Leavis, F[rank] R. New Bearings in English Poetry. A study of the contemporary situation. 2nd ed. London, Chatto and Windus, 1950. 238 pp.—Original ed. 1932.

1384. Bogan, Louise. Achievement in American Poetry. Chicago, Henry Regnery Co., 1951. 157 pp.

1385. Pinto, Vivian de S. Crisis in English Poetry 1880–1940. London, Hutchinson House, 1951. 228 pp.—In the series Hutchinson's University Library.

1386. Durrell, Lawrence. Key to Modern Poetry. London, Peter Nevill Ltd., 1952. xii + 209 pp.—American ed. *A Key to Modern British Poetry,* Norman, University of Oklahoma Press, 1952.

1387. Isaacs, J[acob]. The Background of Modern Poetry. New York, E. P. Dutton and Co., 1952. 94 pp.—Reprint New York, E. P. Dutton and Co., 1958, [x] + 116 pp., number 17 in the series Dutton Everyman Paperbacks. Lectures given in the BBC Third Programme 1948–51.

1388. Quinn, Sister M[ary] Bernetta. The Metamorphic Tradition in Modern Poetry. Essays on the work of Ezra Pound, Wallace Stevens, William Carlos Williams, T. S. Eliot, Hart Crane, Randall Jarrell, and William Butler Yeats. New Brunswick, N.J., Rutgers Univ. Press, 1955. 263 pp.—"Bibliography," pp. 237–263.

1389. Bayley, John. The Romantic Survival. London, Constable and Co., 1957. vii + 231 pp.—A study chiefly of Yeats, Auden, and Dylan Thomas.

1390. Kermode, Frank. Romantic Image. London, Routledge and Kegan Paul Ltd., 1957. xi + 171 pp.

1391. Blunden, Edmund. War Poets 1914–1918. London, Longmans, 1958. 43 pp.

CHAPTER IV

STAGE AND DRAMA

[In this chapter, works on the stage, §§52–59, precede those on the drama, §§60–66; but wherever possible, a category on the stage should be consulted along with its corresponding category on the drama, since the distinction between the two major groups is sometimes quite tenuous.]

[See also §85. Theater and Drama Periodicals.]

§52. CRITICAL AND EXPOSITORY WRITING ON THE STAGE

1395. Craig, Edward G. On the Art of the Theatre. Chicago, Browne's Bookstore, [1911]. xix + 296 pp.

1396. Nathan, Geo. J. The Popular Theatre. New York, Alfred A. Knopf, 1918. 236 pp.

1397. Nathan, Geo. J. The Critic and the Drama. New York, Alfred A. Knopf, 1922. 152 pp.

1398. Ervine, St. John. The Organized Theatre. A plea in civics. New York, Macmillan Co., 1924. 213 pp.

1399. Seldes, Gilbert. The Seven Lively Arts. New York, Harper and Bros., 1924. x + 398 pp.—Reprint New York, Sagamore Press, 1957, 306 pp.

1400. Drinkwater, John. The Art of Theatre-Going. Boston, Houghton Mifflin Co., 1927. xiv + 217 pp.

1401. Brown, John Mason. The Modern Theatre in Revolt. New York, W. W. Norton and Co., 1929. xii + 89 pp.—In the series The New Arts. "Selected Bibliography," pp. 87–89.

1402. Mitchell, Roy. Creative Theatre. New York, John Day Co., 1929. xx + 256 pp.

1403. Beerbohm, Max. Around Theatres. New York, Alfred A. Knopf, 1930. 2 vols. Reprint one vol., New York, Simon and Schuster, 1954, xvi + 583 pp.—Original ed. London, William Heinemann, 1924.

1404. Stevens, Thos. Wood. Theatre. From Athens to Broadway. New York, D. Appleton Co., 1932. xii + 264 pp.

1405. Brown, John M. The Art of Playgoing. New York, W. W. Norton and Co., 1936. 204 pp.

1406. Nathan, Geo. J. The Morning after the First Night. New York, Alfred A. Knopf, 1938. ix + 282 pp.

1407. Hamilton, Clayton. The Theory of the Theatre and Other Principles of Dramatic Criticism. With a foreword by Burns Mantle. New York, Henry Holt and Co., 1939. xviii + 481 pp.

1408. McCleery, Albert, and Glick, Carl. Curtains Going Up. New York, Pitman Publ'ing Corp., 1939. ix + 407 pp.

1409. Brown, John M. Broadway in Review. New York, W. W. Norton and Co., 1940. 295 pp.

1410. Gorelik, Mordecai. New Theatres for Old. [New York], Samuel French, 1940. 553 pp.—Frequent reprints, as in 1955.

1411. Nathan, Geo. J. Encyclopaedia of the Theatre. New York, Alfred A. Knopf, 1940. ix + 449 pp.

1412. Nathan, Geo. J. The Entertainment of a Nation. Or three sheets in the wind. New York, Alfred A. Knopf, 1942. 290 pp.

1413. Granville-Barker, Harley. The Use of the Drama. Princeton, N.J., University Press, 1945. vi + 91 pp.

1414. Bentley, Eric. The Playwright as Thinker. A study of drama in modern times. New York, Reynal and Hitchcock, 1946. x + 382 pp.

1415. Seldes, Gilbert. The Great Audience. New York, Viking Press, 1950. viii + 299 pp.

1416. Barrault, Jean-Louis. Reflections on the Theatre. Translated by Barbara Wall. London, Rockliff Publ'ing Co., 1951. xi + 185 pp.—Original French ed. 1949.

1417. Bentley, Eric. In Search of Theater. New York, Alfred A. Knopf, 1953. xxiii + 411 + ix pp.

1418. Whiting, Frank M. An Introduction to the Theatre. New York, Harper and Bros., 1954. xvi + 315 pp.

1419. Gard, Robt. Grassroots Theater. A search for regional arts in America. With a foreword by David H. Stevens. Madison, University of Wisconsin Press, 1955. xiii + 263 pp.

1420. Hunningher, B[enjamin]. The Origin of the Theater. An essay. Amsterdam, Holland, Em. Querido, 1955. 141 pp.

1421. Gassner, John. Form and Idea in Modern Theatre. New York, Dryden Press, 1956. xiv + 290 pp.

1422. Seldes, Gilbert. The Public Arts. New York, Simon and Schuster, 1956. 303 pp.

1423. Kerr, Walter. Pieces of Eight. New York, Simon and Schuster, 1957. viii + 245 pp.

1424. Busfield, Roger M., Jr. The Playwright's Art. Stage, radio, television, motion pictures. New York, Harper and Bros., 1958. xi + 260 pp.—Bibliography, pp. 245–254. An attempt to approach drama from the playwright's point of view.

1425. Joseph, Bertram L. The Tragic Actor. London, G. Routledge and Sons, 1959. xv + 415 pp.

§53. STAGE SURVEYS CHIEFLY HISTORICAL

1429. Lowe, Robt. W. A Bibliographical Account of English Theatrical Literature from the Earliest Times to the Present Day. New York, J. W. Bouton, 1888. xii + 384 pp.

1430. Gamble, Wm. B. The Development of Scenic Art and Stage Machinery. A list of references in the New York Public Library. New York, New York Public Library, 1928. 231 pp.

1431. Baker, Henry Barton. English Actors from Shakespeare to Macready. New York, Henry Holt and Co., 1879. 2 vols.

1432. Pascoe, Chas. Eyre. The Dramatic List. A record of the principal performances of living actors and actresses of the British stage. With criticisms from contemporary journals. Boston, Roberts Bros., 1879. v + 358 (double column) pp.

1433. Doran, [John]. Annals of the English Stage from Thomas Betterton to Edmund Kean. Edited and rev. by Robert W. Lowe. London, John C. Nimmo, 1888. 3 vols.—Original ed. 1865 in 2 vols. Reprint Philadelphia, D. McKay, 1890, 2 vols., with a memoir of Dr. Doran and an introduction and conclusion by R. H. Stoddard. Often listed under the title *Their Majesties' Servants,* Annals of the English stage. . . .

1434. Adams, W[illiam] Davenport. A Dictionary of the Drama. A guide to the plays, playwrights, players, and playhouses of the United Kingdom, and America, from the earliest times to the present. Vol. I: A–G. London, Chatto and Windus, 1904. viii + 627 (double column) pp.—No more published.

1435. Nungezer, Edwin. A Dictionary of Actors and Other Persons Associated with the Public Representation of Plays in England before 1642. New Haven, Yale Univ. Press, 1929. vii + 438 pp.

1436. Gilder, Rosamond, and Freedley, Geo. Theatre Collections in Libraries and Museums. An international handbook. New York, Theatre Arts Inc., 1936. [vii] + 182 pp.

1437. MacMillan, Dougald. Drury Lane Calendar 1746–1776. Compiled from the playbills and edited with an introduction. Oxford, Clarendon Press, 1938. xxxiv + 364 pp.

1438. Sobel, Bernard, ed. The Theatre Handbook and Digest of Plays. Preface by George Freedley. [Rev. ed.] New York, Crown Publ'ers, 1950. xvi + 19–897 pp.—Original ed. 1940. Bibliography, by George Freedley, pp. 867–889.

1439. Hartnoll, Phyllis. The Oxford Companion to the Theatre. Second ed. with illustrated supplement. Oxford Univ. Press, 1957. xi + 888 (double column) + 32 (double column) pp. + lxiv plates.—Original ed. 1951. "Bibliography," pp. 856–888.

1440. Baker, Daniel E. Biographia dramatica. Or a companion to the playhouse . . . of British and Irish dramatic writers. . . . Originally compiled to the year 1764 . . . , continued thence to 1782 by Isaac Reed and brought down to . . . 1811 . . . by Stephen Jones. London, Longman, Hurst, et al., 1812. 3 vols. with Vol. I in two individually bound parts.

1441. Sharp, R[obert] Farquharson. A Short History of the English Stage from Its Beginnings to the Summer of the Year 1908. London, Walter Scott Publ'ing Co., 1909. 355 pp.

1442. Mantzius, Karl. A History of Theatrical Art in Ancient and Modern Times. With an introduction by William Archer. Authorized translation by Louise von Cossel. Vol. I: The Earliest Times; Vol. II: Middle Ages and Renaissance; Vol. III: The Shakespearean Period in England; Vol. IV: Molière and His Times; Vol. V: Great Actors of the Eighteenth Century; Vol. VI: Classicism and Romanticism. London, Duckworth and Co., 1903–21. 6 vols.—Original Danish ed. 1901. Reprint New York, Peter Smith, 1937.

1443. Thaler, Alwin. Shakespere to Sheridan. A book about the theatre of yesterday and today. Cambridge, Mass., Harvard Univ. Press, 1922. xviii + 339 pp.

1444. Hughes, Glenn. The Story of the Theatre. A short history of theatrical art from its beginnings to the present day. New York, Samuel French, 1928. ix + 422 pp.

1445. Simonson, Lee. The Stage Is Set. New York, Harcourt, Brace and Co., 1932. xvii + 585 pp.—Reprint New York, Dover Publications, 1946. "A Critical Bibliography," pp. 533–546.

1446. Nicoll, Allardyce. The English Theatre. A short history. London, Thomas Nelson and Sons, 1936. xi + 252 pp.—Reprint 1938.

1447. Stockwell, La Tourette. Dublin Theatres and Theatre Customs 1637–1820. Kingsport, Tenn., Kingsport Press, 1938. xvii + 406 pp.—"Selected Bibliography," pp. 379–397.

1448. Cheney, Sheldon. The Theatre. Three thousand years of drama, acting, and stagecraft. Rev. and enl. ed. New York, Longmans, Green and Co., 1952. xiv + 592 pp.—Original ed. 1929.

1449. Macqueen-Pope, W[alter J.]. Ladies First. The story of woman's conquest of the British stage. London, W. H. Allen and Co., 1952. xiv + 384 pp.

1450. Clark, Wm. S. The Early Irish Stage. The beginnings to 1720. Oxford, Clarendon Press, 1955. x + 227 pp.

1451. Freedley, Geo., and Reeves, John A. A History of the Theatre. Newly revised with a supplementary section by George Freedley. New York, Crown Publ'ers, 1955. xvi + 784 pp.—Original ed. 1941.

1452. Bridges-Adams, Wm. The Irresistible Theatre. [A history of the English stage from the Conquest to the Commonwealth.] Cleveland, World Publ'ing Co., 1957. xiv + 446 pp.

1453. Nicoll, Allardyce. Development of the Theatre. 4th ed. London, Harrap, 1958. 318 pp.—Original ed. 1927; second ed. 1937; third ed. 1948.

§54. THE MEDIEVAL, TUDOR, AND JACOBEAN STAGE

[See also §9. British Literature: Shakespeare Bibliographies, Handbooks, and Studies.]

1457. Fleay, Frederick Gard. A Chronicle History of the London Stage 1559–1642. London, Reeves and Turner, 1890. x + 424 pp.

1458. Ordish, T[homas] Fairman. Early London Theatres. [In the Fields.] London, Elliot Stock, 1894. xvi + 298 pp.

1459. Chambers, E[dmund] K. The Mediaeval Stage. Oxford Univ. Press, 1903. 2 vols.—"List of Authorities," I, pp. xiii–xlii.

1460. Murray, John T. English Dramatic Companies 1558–1642. Vol. I: London Companies; Vol. II: Provincial Companies. Boston, Houghton Mifflin Co., 1910. 2 vols.

1461. Spencer, M[atthew] Lyle. Corpus Christi Pageants in England. New York, Baker and Taylor Co., 1911. [xi] + 276 pp.

1462. Adams, Joseph Quincy. Shakespearean Playhouses. A history of English theatres from the beginnings to the Restoration. Boston, Houghton Mifflin Co., 1917. xiv + 473 pp.—Bibliography, pp. 433–456.

1463. Campbell, Lily B. Scenes and Machines on the English Stage during the Renaissance. A classical revival. Cambridge Univ. Press, 1923. x + 302 pp.

1464. Chambers, Edmund K. The Elizabethan Stage [1558–1616]. Oxford, Clarendon Press, 1923. 4 vols.—See Beatrice White, *An Index to "The Elizabethan Stage" and "William Shakespeare, A Study of Facts and problems," by Sir Edmund Chambers,* Oxford Univ. Press for the Shakespeare Association, 1934, 161 pp.

1465. Hillebrand, Harold N. The Child Actors. A chapter in Elizabethan stage history. Urbana, University of Illinois Press, 1926. 171–355 pp.—Volume XI, no. 2, in the series University of Illinois Studies in Language and Literature.

1466. Steele, Mary S. Plays and Masques at Court during the Reigns of Elizabeth, James, and Charles. New Haven, Yale Univ. Press, 1926. xiii + 300 pp.—In the series Cornell Studies in English.

1467. Baldwin, Thos. W. The Organization and Personnel of the Shakespearean Company. Princeton, N.J., University Press, 1927. xii + 464 pp.

1468. Lawrence, Wm. J. The Physical Conditions of the Elizabethan Public Playhouse. Cambridge, Mass., Harvard Univ. Press, 1927. viii + 129 pp.

1469. Greg, W[alter] W. Dramatic Documents from the Elizabethan Playhouses. Stage plots, actors' parts, prompt books. Oxford Univ. Press, 1931. xiii + 378 pp.

1470. Lea, Katherine. The Italian Popular Comedy. A study in the commedia dell'arte 1560–1620 with special reference to the English stage. Oxford, Clarendon Press, 1934. 2 vols.—"Bibliography," II, pp. 675–684.

1471. Lawrence, Wm. J. Old Theatre Days and Ways. London, George G. Harrap and Co., 1935. 256 pp.

1472. Lawrence, Wm. J. Those Nut-Cracking Elizabethans. Studies of the early theatre and drama. London, Argonaut Press, 1935. xi + 212 pp.

1473. Sharpe, Robt. B. The Real War of the Theatres. Shakespeare's fellows in rivalry with the Admiral's Men 1594–1603. Boston, D. C. Heath and Co., 1935. viii + 260 pp.—Volume V in the Monograph Series of the Modern Language Association of America.

1474. Nicoll, Allardyce. Stuart Masques and the Renaissance Stage. New York, Harcourt, Brace and Co., 1938. 224 pp.

1475. Reynolds, Geo. F. The Staging of Elizabethan Plays at the Red Bull Theater 1605–1625. New York, Modern Language Association of America, 1940. 203 pp.

1476. Adams, John C. The Globe Playhouse. Its design and equipment. Cambridge, Mass., Harvard Univ. Press, 1942. x + 420 pp.

1477. Gardiner, Harold C., S.J. Mysteries' End. An investigation of the last days of the medieval religious stage. New Haven, Yale Univ. Press, 1946. xv + 142 pp.—Volume CIII in the series Yale Studies in English.

1478. Hyde, Mary C. Playwriting for Elizabethans. New York, Columbia Univ. Press, 1949. xiii + 258 pp.—Number 167 in the series Columbia University Studies in English and Comparative Literature.

1479. Joseph, Bertram L. Elizabethan Acting. Oxford Univ. Press, 1951. 156 pp.

1480. Venezky, Alice S. Pageantry on the Shakespearean Stage. New York, Twayne Publ'ers, 1951. 242 pp.

1481. Hosking, G[eorge] L. The Life and Times of Edward Alleyn, Actor, Master of the King's Bears, Founder of the College of God's Gift at Dulwich. With a foreword by Lord Gorell. London, Jonathan Cape, 1952. 285 pp.—"Sources," pp. 275–278.

1482. Reed, Robt. R., Jr. Bedlam on the Jacobean Stage. Cambridge, Mass., Harvard Univ. Press, 1952. ix + 190 pp.

1483. Hodges, C[yril] Walter. The Globe Restored. A study of the Elizabethan theatre. London, Ernest Benn Ltd., 1953. xiii + 14–199 pp.

1484. Sanvic, Romain. Le théâtre élisabéthain. Brussels, Office de Publicité, 1955. 137 pp.—Number 114 in the series Collections Lebèque et Nationale.

1485. Bentley, Gerald E. The Jacobean and Caroline Stage. Vols. I and II: Dramatic Companies and Players; Vols. III, IV, and V: Plays and Playwrights. Oxford, Clarendon Press, 1941–56. 5 vols.

1486. Southern, Richard. The Medieval Theatre in the Round. A study of the staging of The Castle of Perseverance and related matters. London, Faber and Faber Ltd., 1957. xviii + 240 pp.

1487. Craik, T[homas] W. The Tudor Interlude. Stage, costume, and acting. Leicester, Eng., University Press, 1958. xiii + 158 pp.

1488. Wickham, Glynne. Early English Stages 1300 to 1660. Volume One: 1300 to 1576. London, Routledge and Kegan Paul, 1959. xliv + 428 pp.—"List of MSS," pp. 401–404; "List of Printed Books," pp. 405–413.

§55. THE STAGE OF THE LATER SEVENTEENTH AND THE EIGHTEENTH CENTURIES

1492. [Genest, John.] Some Account of the English Stage from the Restoration in 1660 to 1830. Bath, Eng., H. E. Carrington for Thomas Rodd, 1832. 10 vols.

1493. Fitzgerald, Percy. A New History of the English Stage from the Restoration to the Liberty of the Theatres. . . . London, Tinsley Bros., 1882. 2 vols.

1494. Armstrong, Cecil Ferard. A Century of Great Actors 1750–1850. London, Mills and Boon Ltd., 1912. [vii] + 412 pp.—"Books Consulted," pp. 411–412.

1495. Sprague, Arthur C. Beaumont and Fletcher on the Restoration Stage. Cambridge, Mass., Harvard Univ. Press, 1926. xx + 299 pp.

1496. Lawrence, Wm. J. Pre-Restoration Stage Studies. Cambridge, Mass., Harvard Univ. Press, 1927. ix + 435 pp.

1497. Hotson, [John] Leslie. The Commonwealth and Restoration Stage. Cambridge, Mass., Harvard Univ. Press, 1928. xiii + 424 pp.

1498. Melville, Lewis. Stage Favorites of the Eighteenth Century. Garden City, N.Y., Doubleday, Doran and Co., 1928. 288 pp.

1499. Melville, Lewis. More Stage Favorites of the Eighteenth Century. London, Hutchinson and Co., 1929. 286 pp.

1500. Gray, Chas. H. Theatrical Criticism in London to 1795. New York, Columbia Univ. Press, 1931. vi + 333 pp.

1501. Boswell, Eleanore. [Eleanore Boswell Murrie.] The Restoration Court Stage 1660–1702. With a particular account of the production of Calisto. Cambridge, Mass., Harvard Univ. Press, 1932. xviii + 370 pp.—"A Calendar of Plays to Be Acted at Court," pp. 278–293.

1502. Summers, Montague. The Restoration Theatre. London, Kegan Paul, Trench, Trubner and Co., 1934. xxi + 352 pp.

1503. Summers, Montague. The Playhouse of Pepys. New York, Macmillan Co., 1935. xv + 485 pp.

1504. Kelly, John A. German Visitors to English Theaters in the Eighteenth Century. Princeton, N.J., University Press, 1936. 178 pp.

1505. Smith, Dane F. The Critics in the Audience of the London Theatres from Buckingham to Sheridan. A study of Neoclassicism in the playhouse 1671–1779. Albuquerque, University of New Mexico Press, 1953. 192 pp.—Number 12 in the series University of New Mexico Publications in Language and Literature.

1506. Lynch, James J. Box, Pit, and Gallery. Stage and society in Johnson's London. Berkeley, University of California Press, 1953. xii + 362 pp.

1507. Pedicord, Harry W. The Theatrical Public in the Time of Garrick. New York, Columbia Univ. Press, 1954. xiii + 267 pp.

1508. Goldstein, Malcolm. Pope and the Augustan Stage. Stanford Univ. Press, 1958. viii + 139 pp.—Number 17 in the series Stanford Studies in Language and Literature. Bibliographical notes, pp. 120–132.

1509. Wilson, John H. All the King's Ladies. Actresses of the Restoration. University of Chicago Press, 1958. ix + 260 pp.

§56. THE VICTORIAN AND THE MODERN BRITISH STAGE

1513. Filon, Augustin. The English Stage. Being an account of the Victorian drama. Translated from the French by Frederic Whyte with an introduction by Henry A. Jones. London, John Milne, 1897. 319 pp.

1514. Borsa, Mario. The English Stage of To-Day. Translated from the original Italian and edited with a prefatory note by Selwyn Brinton. London, John Lane, 1908. xi + 317 pp.

1515. Beerbohm, Max. Around Theatres. London, William Heinemann, 1924. 2 vols.—A collection of 153 articles written from 1898 to 1910. See 1403.

1516. Vernon, Frank. The Twentieth-Century Theatre. With an introduction by John Drinkwater. London, George G. Harrap and Co., 1924. v + 159 pp.

1517. Carter, Huntley. The New Spirit in the European Theatre 1914–1924. A comparative study of the changes effected by the War and Revolution. London, Ernest Benn Ltd., 1925. xi + 292 pp.

1518. Disher, M[aurice] Willson. Clowns and Pantomimes. Boston, Houghton Mifflin Co., 1925. xx + 344 pp.

1519. Sherson, Erroll. London's Lost Theatres of the Nineteenth Century. With notes on plays and players seen there. With a foreword by Mrs. Kendal. . . . London, Bodley Head Ltd., 1925. 392 pp.

1520. Watson, Ernest Bradlee. Sheridan to Robertson. A study of the nineteenth century London stage. Foreword by George P. Baker. Cambridge, Mass., Harvard Univ. Press, 1926. xiv + 485 pp.—"Bibliography," pp. 449–455.

1521. Shaw, Geo. B. Our Theatres in the Nineties. Criticism contributed week by week to the Saturday Review from January 1895 to May 1898. New York, William H. Wise and Co., 1931. 3 vols.

1522. Mason, A[lfred] E. W. Sir George Alexander and the St. James' Theatre. London, Macmillan and Co., 1935. x + 247 pp.

1523. Wilson, A[lbert] E. King Panto. The story of pantomime. New York, E. P. Dutton and Co., 1935. 262 pp.

1524. Duggan, G[eorge] C. The Stage Irishman. A history of the Irish play and stage characters from the earliest times. Dublin, Talbot Press, 1937. 331 pp.—"Chronological List of Plays," pp. 318–320.

1525. Short, Ernest, and Compton-Rickett, Arthur. Ring up the Curtain. Being a pageant of English entertainment covering half a century. London, Herbert Jenkins Ltd., 1938. 319 pp.

1526. Robinson, Lennox, ed. The Irish Theatre. London, Macmillan Co., 1939. xiii + 229 pp.—Lectures delivered during the Abbey Theatre Festival held in Dublin, August 1938.

1527. Kavanagh, Peter. The Irish Theatre. Being a history of the drama in Ireland from the earliest period up to the present day. Tralee, Ireland, Kerryman Ltd., 1946. 489 pp.

1528. Short, Ernest. Fifty Years of Vaudeville. London, Eyre and Spottiswoode, 1946. ix + 271 pp.

1529. Macqueen-Pope, W[alter J.] Carriages at Eleven. The story of the Edwardian theatre. London, Hutchinson and Co., 1948. 232 pp.

1530. Macqueen-Pope, W[alter J.] Haymarket. Theatre of perfection. London, W. H. Allen, 1948. 394 pp.

1531. Williamson, Audrey. Old Vic Drama. A twelve years' study of plays and players. Foreword by Dame Sybil Thorndike. London, Rockliff Publ'ing Corp., 1948. xvii + 228 pp.—Reprint 1953.

1532. Kavanagh, Peter. The Story of the Abbey Theatre. From its origins in 1899 to the present. New York, Devin-Adair Co., 1950. xi + 243 pp.

1533. Pearson, Hesketh. The Last Actor-Managers. London, Methuen and Co., 1950. xii + 84 pp.

1534. Rice, Chas. The London Theatre in the Eighteen-Thirties. Edited by Arthur Cobby Sprague and Bertram Shuttleworth. London, Society for Theatre Research, 1950. x + 86 pp.

1535. Hudson, Lynton. The English Stage 1850–1950. London, George G. Harrap and Co., 1951. 223 pp.

1536. Robinson, Lennox. Ireland's Abbey Theatre. A history 1899–1951. London, Sidgwick and Jackson Ltd., 1951. xiv + 224 pp.

1537. Trewin, J[ohn] C. The Theatre since 1900. London, Andrew Dakers Ltd., 1951. x + 11–339 pp.—In the series Twentieth Century Histories.

1538. Williamson, Audrey. Theatre of Two Decades. London, Rockliff Publishing Corp., 1951. xv + 391 pp.—A treatment of the London stage.

1539. Wilson, A[lbert] E. Edwardian Theatre. London, Arthur Baker Ltd., 1951. 256 pp.

1540. Rowell, Geo. The Victorian Theatre. A survey. Oxford Univ. Press, 1956. xiii + 203 pp.—"Play-List 1792–1914," pp. 151–157; "A Bibliography of the English Theatre 1792–1914," pp. 159–189.

§57. THE AMERICAN STAGE

1544. Seilhamer, Geo. O. History of the American Theater [1749–1797]. Philadelphia, Globe Printing House, 1888–91. 3 vols.

1545. Brown, T[homas] Allston. History of the New York Stage from 1732 to 1901. New York, Dodd, Mead and Co., 1903. 3 vols.

1546. Ryan, Kate. Old Boston Museum Days. Boston, Little, Brown and Co., 1915. xii + 264 pp.

1547. Hornblow, Arthur. A History of the Theatre in America from Its Beginnings to the Present Time. Philadelphia, J. B. Lippincott Co., 1919. 2 vols.

1548. Nathan, Geo. J. The World in Falseface. New York, Alfred A. Knopf, 1923. xxix + 326 pp.

1549. Sayler, Oliver M. Our American Theatre. New York, Brentano's Pub-l'ers, 1923. xiv + 399 pp.

1550. Crawford, Mary C. The Romance of the American Theatre. New York, Halcyon House, 1925. xiv + 508 pp.—Reprint 1940.

1551. Coad, Oval Sumner, and Mims, Edwin, Jr. The American Stage. New Haven, Yale Univ. Press, 1929. 362 pp.—Volume XIV in the series Pageant of America.

1552. Macgowan, Kenneth. Footlights across America. Towards a national theater. New York, Harcourt, Brace and Co., 1929. xviii + 398 pp.

1553. Brown, John M. Upstage. The American theatre in performance. New York, W. W. Norton and Co., 1930. xi + 276 pp.

1554. Wittke, Carl. Tambo and Bones. A history of the American minstrel stage. Durham, N.C., Duke Univ. Press, 1930. ix + 269 pp.

1555. Moses, Montrose J., and Brown, John Mason, eds. The American Theatre as Seen by Its Critics 1752–1934. New York, W. W. Norton and Co., 1934. 391 pp.

1556. Nathan, Geo. J. The Theatre of the Moment. A journalistic commentary. New York, Alfred A. Knopf, 1936. viii + 310 pp.

1557. Brown, John M. Two on the Aisle. Ten years of the American theatre in performance. New York, W. W. Norton and Co., 1938. ix + 321 pp.

1558. Gilbert, Douglas. American Vaudeville. Its life and times. New York, McGraw-Hill Book Co., 1940. x + 428 pp.

1559. MacMinn, Geo. R. The Theater of the Golden Era in California. Caldwell, Idaho, Caxton Printers, 1941. 529 pp.

1560. Odell, G[eorge] C. D. Annals of the New York Stage. New York, Columbia Univ. Press, 1927–45. 15 vols.

1561. Graham, Philip. Showboats. The history of an American institution. Austin, University of Texas Press, 1951. x + 224 pp.

1562. Hughes, Glenn. A History of the American Theatre 1700–1950. New York, Samuel French, 1951. ix + 562 pp.

1563. Morris, Lloyd. Curtain Time. The story of the American theater. New York, Random House, 1953. xvi + 381 pp.

1564. Nathan, Geo. J. The Theatre of the Fifties. New York, Alfred A. Knopf, 1953. 298 + viii pp.

1565. Gassner, John. The Theatre in Our Times. A survey of the men, materials, and movements in the modern theatre. New York, Crown Publ'ers, [1954]. xiv + 609 pp.

1566. Blum, Daniel. A Pictorial History of the American Theatre 1900–1956. New York, Greenberg Publ'er, 1956. 320 pp.—Original ed. 1950 with coverage 1900–1950.

1567. Hewitt, Barnard. Theatre U. S. A. 1668 to 1957. New York, McGraw-Hill Book Co., 1959. xi + 528 pp.

§58. ACTING AND PLAY PRODUCTION

1571. Archer, Wm. Play-Making. A manual of craftsmanship. New York, Dodd, Mead and Co., 1912. x + 419 pp.—Frequent reprints, as in 1928.

1572. Baker, Geo. Pierce. Dramatic Technique. Boston, Houghton Mifflin Co., 1919. vii + 531 pp.

1573. Macgowan, Kenneth. The Theatre of Tomorrow. New York, Boni and Liveright Publ'ers, 1921. 302 pp.

1574. Andrews, Harry L., and Weirick, Bruce. Acting and Play Production. A manual for classes, dramatic clubs, and little theatres. New York, Longmans, Green and Co., 1925. xi + 292 pp.

1575. Pichel, Irving. Modern Theatres. New York, Harcourt, Brace and Co., 1925. xi + 102 pp.

1576. Crafton, Allen, and Royer, Jessica. The Process of Play Production. A book for the nonprofessional theatre worker. New York, F. S. Crofts and Co., 1926. x + 314 pp.

1577. Dolman, John, Jr. The Art of Play Production. New York, Harper and Bros., 1928. xv + 466 pp.

1578. Lawson, John H. Theory and Technique of Playwriting. New York, G. P. Putnam's Sons, 1936. xiv + 315 pp.

1579. Brown, Gilmor, and Garwood, Alice. General Principles of Play Direction. London, Samuel French Ltd., 1937. 190 pp.

1580. Schonberger, Emanuel D. Play Production for Amateurs. New York, Thomas Nelson and Sons, 1938. xiii + 241 pp.

1581. Heffner, Hubert C., Selden, Samuel, and Sellman, Hunton D. Modern Theatre Practice. A handbook for nonprofessionals. With an appendix on costume and makeup by Fairfax Proudfit Walkup. 2nd ed. New York, F. S. Crofts Inc., 1939. xviii + 425 pp.—Original ed. 1935; second ed. reprinted 1946. Bibliography, pp. 402–417.

1582. Dean, Alex. Fundamentals of Play Directing. New York, Farrar and Rinehart, 1941. xxi + 428 pp.

1583. Crafton, Allen, and Royer, Jessica. The Complete Acted Play from Script to Final Curtain. New York, F. S. Crofts and Co., 1943. xiv + 385 pp.

1584. Davis, Eugene C. Amateur Theater Handbook. A complete guide to successful play production. New York, Greenberg Pub'ler, 1945. xvii + 237 pp.

1585. Cole, Toby, and Chinoy, Helen Krich, eds. Directing the Play. A source book of stagecraft. Indianapolis, Bobbs-Merrill Co., 1953. 341 pp.—"Bibliography," pp. 323–334.

1586. Cornberg, Sol, and Gebauer, Emanuel L. A Stage Crew Handbook. Drawings by Jack Forman. Rev. ed. New York, Harper and Bros., 1957. xi + 291 pp.—Original ed. 1941.

1587. Melvill, Harald. Magic of Make-Up. Drawings by the author. New York, Citadel Press, 1957. x + 85 pp.

1588. Young, John W. The Community Theatre and How It Works. New York, Harper and Bros., 1957. xi + 166 pp.

1589. Young, John Wray. Directing the Play. From selection to opening night. New York, Harper and Bros., 1958. xv + 171 pp.

§59. DRAMATIC DICTION AND DELIVERY AND THE ART OF SPEECH

[See also §94. Periodicals Devoted to Speech, Speeches, and Debating.]

1593. Thonssen, Lester, and Fatherson, Elizabeth. Bibliography of Speech Education. With the assistance of Dorothea Thonssen. New York, H. W. Wilson Co., 1939. 800 (double column) pp.

1594. Sutton, Roberta Briggs. Speech Index. An index to 64 collections of world-famous orations and speeches for various occasions. New York, H. W. Wilson Co., 1935. 272 (double column) pp.—Supplement Roberta Briggs Sutton, *Speech Index 1935–1955*, New Brunswick, N.J., Scarecrow Press, 1956, 448 pp.

1595. Dobrée, Bonamy. Histriophone. A dialogue on dramatic diction. London, Hogarth Press, 1925. 40 pp.

1596. Avery, Elizabeth, Dorsey, Jane, and Sickels, Vera A. First Principles of Speech Training. New York, D. Appleton and Co., 1930. xxxviii + 518 pp.

1597. Parrish, Wayland M. Reading Aloud. A technique in the interpretation of literature. New York, Nelson and Sons, 1932. 401 pp.

1598. O'Neill, James M., and Weaver, Andrew T. The Elements of Speech. Rev. ed. New York, Longmans, Green and Co., 1933. x + 534 pp.—Original ed. 1926. Bibliography, pp. 513–517.

1599. Vizetelly, Frank H. How to Speak English Effectively. A guide to the art of correct enunciation. . . . New York, Funk and Wagnalls Co., 1933. xxviii + 29–260 pp.

1600. Holmes, F[rank] Lincoln D. A Handbook of Voice and Diction. New York, F. S. Crofts and Co., 1935. viii + 279 pp.—Reprint 1940.

1601. Woolbert, Chas. H., and Nelson, Severina E. The Art of Interpretative Speech. Rev. ed. New York, F. S. Crofts and Co., 1934. xi + 541 pp.—Original ed. 1927.

1602. Brigance, Wm. N. Speech Composition. New York, F. S. Crofts and Co., 1937. ix + 385 pp.—A development of Brigance's *The Spoken Word,* F. S. Crofts and Co., 1927, x + 329 pp.

1603. Winans, James A. Speech-Making. . . . With a chapter on voice and speech by Charles K. Thomas. New York, D. Appleton-Century Co., 1938. viii + 488 pp.

1604. Tresidder, Argus J. Reading to Others. Chicago, Scott, Foresman and Co., 1940. xiii + 529 pp.

1605. Anderson, Virgil A. Training the Speaking Voice. New York, Oxford Univ. Press, 1942. xx + 387 pp.—Reprint 1947. "Bibliography," pp. 373–376.

1606. Monroe, Alan H. Principles and Types of Speech. 3rd ed. Chicago, Scott, Foresman and Co., 1943. xiv + 658 pp.—Original ed. 1935; second ed. 1939; third ed. reprinted 1949.

1607. Sarett, Lew, and Foster, Wm. Trufant. Basic Principles of Speech. Rev. ed. Boston, Houghton Mifflin Co., 1946. 604 pp.—Original ed. 1936.

1608. Soper, Paul L. Basic Public Speaking. 2nd ed. New York, Oxford Univ. Press, 1956. 394 pp.—Original ed. 1949.

1609. Langbaum, Robt. The Poetry of Experience. The dramatic monologue in modern literary tradition. London, Chatto and Windus, 1957. 246 pp.

§60. PLAY INDEXES: MODERN

1613. Silk, Agnes K., and Fanning, Clara E. Index to Dramatic Readings. Boston, F. W. Faxon Co., 1925. 303 (double column) pp.—Number 31 in the Useful Reference Series.

1614. Plays. A guide to the works in the library of the National Operatic and Dramatic Association. Issued by authority of the Council. London, Noda Ltd., 1929. 167 pp.—A list of modern stage plays, including musicals, with synopses and some pertinent data for each.

1615. Smith, Milton. Guide to Play Selection. A descriptive index of full-length and short plays for production by schools, colleges, and little theaters. New York, D. Appleton-Century Co., 1934. x + 174 pp.

1616. Firkins, Ina Ten Eyck. Index to Plays 1800–1926. New York, H. W. Wilson Co., 1927. 307 (double column) pp.—Also *Supplement,* by Ina Ten Eyck Firkins, New York, H. W. Wilson Co., 1935, ix + 140 (double column) pp.

1617. Thompson, Ruth Gibbons. Index to Full Length Plays 1926 to 1944. Boston, F. W. Faxon Co., 1946. ix + 306 pp.

1618. Index to the Best Plays Series 1899–1950. Foreword by Lydia Sears Mantle. New York, Dodd, Mead and Co., 1950. xii + 147 (double column) pp.—An index to *Best Plays 1899–1909* (published 1944) and *Best Plays 1909–1919* (published 1933) and the annual *Burns Mantle Best Plays* 1926–date.

1619. [Drury, Francis K. W.] Drury's Guide. Best plays. Washington, D.C., Scarecrow Press, 1953. 367 pp.—"This guide to plays includes more than 1200 plays available in English which have been successful . . . ," p. [7]. Brief summaries of each play.

1620. West, Dorothy Herbert, and Peake, Dorothy Margaret. Play Index 1949–1952. An index to 2616 plays in 1138 volumes. New York, H. W. Wilson Co., 1953. 239 (double column) pp.

1621. The Player's Library. The catalogue of the library of the British Drama League. With an introduction by Frederick S. Boas. London, Faber and Faber Ltd. for the British Drama League, 1950. xvi + 1115 pp.—*First Supplement,* Prefatory note by Frederick S. Boas, London, Faber and Faber, 1951, 128 pp. *Second Supplement,* Prefatory note by Frederick S. Boas, London, Faber and Faber, 1954, 256 pp. *Third Supplement,* Prefatory note by Frederick S. Boas, London, Faber and Faber, 1956, 256 pp.

1622. Shipley, Joseph T. Guide to Great Plays. Washington, D.C., Public Affairs Press, 1956. xii + 867 pp.

1623. Thompson, Ruth Gibbons. Index to Full Length Plays 1895–1925. Boston, F. W. Faxon Co., 1956. xi + 172 pp.—Number 85 in the Useful Reference Series.

1624. Ottemiller, John H. Index to Plays in Collections. An author and title index to plays appearing in collections published between 1900 and 1956. 3rd ed. New York, Scarecrow Press, 1957. v + 6–496 pp.—Original ed. 1943; second ed. 1951.

1625. Ireland, Norma Olin. An Index to Skits and Stunts. Boston, F. W. Faxon Co., 1958. xxix + 348 pp.—Number 88 in the Useful Reference Series.

1626. Logasa, Hannah, and Ver Nooy, Winifred. An Index to One-Act Plays, Boston, F. W. Faxon Co., 1924. 327 pp.—Number 30 in the Useful Reference Series. *Supplement 1924–1931,* by Hannah Logasa and Winifred Ver Nooy, Boston, F. W. Faxon Co., 1932, 432 pp., number 46 in the Useful Reference Series. *Second Supplement 1932–1940,* by Hannah Logasa and Winifred Ver Nooy, Boston, F. W. Faxon Co., 1941, 556 pp., number 68 in the Useful Reference Series. *An Index to One-Act Plays for Stage and Radio* [altered title], Third supplement 1941–1948, by Hanna Logasa, Boston, F. W. Faxon Co., 1950, 318 pp., number 78 in the Useful Reference Series. *An Index to One-Act Plays for Stage, Radio, and Television* [altered title], Fourth supplement 1948–1957, Boston, F. W. Faxon Co., 1958, 245 pp., number 87 in the Useful Reference Series.

1627. Ireland, Norma Olin. An Index to Monologs and Dialogs. Rev. and enl. ed. Boston, F. W. Faxon Co., 1949. xxiii + 171 pp.—Number 77 in the Useful Reference Series. Original ed. 1939 by Norma O. and David E. Ireland. Also *Supplement,* by Norma O. Ireland, Boston, F. W. Faxon Co., 1959, 133 pp., number 89 in the Useful Reference Series.

§61. DRAMA: HISTORICAL LISTS AND HANDBOOKS

[A bibliography devoted to a particular period is placed before the category dealing with the period.]

1631. Hazlitt, W[illiam] Carew. A Manual for the Collector and Amateur of Old English Plays. Edited from the material formed by Kirkman, Langbaine, Downes, Oldys, and Halliwell-Phillipps, with extensive additions and corrections. London, Pickering and Chatto, 1892. viii + 284 pp.

1632. Wegelin, Oscar. Early American Plays 1714–1830. A compilation of the titles of plays and dramatic poems written by authors born in or residing in North America previous to 1830. 2nd ed. New York, Literary Collector Press, 1905. 94 pp.—Original ed. 1900.

1633. Clarence, Reginald [pseud. for H. J. Eldredge]. The Stage Cyclopaedia. A bibliography of plays. An alphabetical list of plays and other stage pieces of which any record can be found since the commencement of the English stage, together with descriptions, authors' names, dates and places of production, and other useful information, comprising in all nearly 50000 plays and extending over a period of upwards of 500 years. London, The Stage, 1909. 503 (double column) pp.

1634. Hill, Frank Pierce. American Plays Printed 1714–1830. A bibliographical record. Stanford Univ. Press, 1934. xii + 152 pp.

1635. MacMillan, Dougald. Catalogue of Larpent Plays in the Huntington Library. San Marino, Calif., Henry E. Huntington Library and Art Gallery, 1939. xv + 442 pp.—English play titles 1737 to 1824.

1636. Harbage, Alfred. Annals of English Drama 975–1700. An analytical record of all plays, extant or lost, chronologically arranged and indexed .... Philadelphia, University of Pennsylvania Press, 1940. vii + 264 pp.

1637. Nicoll, Allardyce. A History of English Drama 1660–1900. Vol. VI: A Short-Title Alphabetical Catalogue of Plays Produced or Printed in England from 1660 to 1900. Cambridge Univ. Press, 1959. xii + 565 pp.

1638. Greg, W[alter] W. A Bibliography of the English Printed Drama to the Restoration. Oxford Univ. Press for the Bibliographical Society, 1939–60. 4 vols.—Number 24 in the series Illustrated Monographs Issued by the Bibliographical Society.

§62. DRAMA: HISTORIES, SURVEYS, AND CRITICISM

[See also §70. Aristotle.]

1642. Leach, H[oward] S. A Union List of Collections of English Drama in American Libraries. Princeton, N.J., University Library, 1916. 12 pp.

1643. Coleman, Edward Davidson. Bible in English Drama. An annotated list of plays including translations from other languages. New York, New York Public Library, 1931. iv + 212 pp.

1644. Baker, Blanch M. Theatre and Allied Arts. A guide to books dealing with the history, criticism, and technic of the drama and theatre and related arts and crafts. Rev. ed. New York, H. W. Wilson Co., 1952. xiv + 536 (double column) pp.—Original ed. 1933.

1645. Drama Index. Boston, F. W. Faxon Co., 1910–52. 40 vols.—Part II of the *Annual Magazine Subject Index* 1907–52.

1646. Vowles, Richard B. Dramatic Theory. A bibliography. New York, New York Public Library, 1956. 59 (double column) pp.—"Reprinted from the Bulletin of the New York Public Library of August–November 1955," p. 4.

1647. Walbridge, Earle F. Drames à clef. A list of plays with characters based on real people. With an introduction by John Mason Brown. New York, New York Public Library, 1956. 47 pp.

1648. Scott, Clement W. The Drama of Today and Yesterday. London, Macmillan Co., 1899. 2 vols.

1649. Ward, Adolphus Wm. A History of English Dramatic Literature to the Death of Queen Anne. New and rev. ed. London, Macmillan Co., 1899. 3 vols.—Original ed. 1875 in 2 vols.

1650. Thorndike, Ashley H. Tragedy. Boston, Houghton Mifflin Co., 1908. vii + 390 pp.—In the series Types of English Literature.

1651. Schelling, Felix E. English Drama. New York, E. P. Dutton and Co., 1914. 341 pp.—In the series Channels of English Literature.

1652. Wynne, Arnold. The Growth of English Drama. Oxford Univ. Press, 1914. 281 pp.

1653. Whitmore, Chas. Edward. The Supernatural in Tragedy. Cambridge, Mass., Harvard Univ. Press, 1915. viii + 370 pp.—"Bibliography," pp. 361–363.

1654. Creizenach, Wilhelm. Geschichte des neueren Dramas. Vol. I: Mittelalter und Frührenaissance (1893); Vols. II and III: Renaissance und Reformation (1901–03); Vols. IV and V: Das englische Drama im Zeitalter Shakespeares (1909–16). Halle a. S., Max Niemeyer, 1893–1916. 5 vols.—See no. 1725.

1655. Brawley, Benjamin. A Short History of the English Drama. New York, Harcourt, Brace and Co., 1921. ix + 260 pp.

1656. Archer, Wm. The Old Drama and the New. An essay in revaluation. Boston, Small, Maynard and Co., 1923. viii + 396 pp.

1657. Greig, J[ohn] Y. T. The Psychology of Laughter and Comedy. London, George Allen and Unwin Ltd., 1923. 304 pp.—"Bibliography," pp. 280–298.

1658. Balmforth, Ramsden. Ethical and Religious Value of the Drama. London, G. Allen and Unwin Ltd., 1925. 250 pp.

1659. Montague, C[harles] E. Dramatic Values. 3rd ed. London, Chatto and Windus, 1925. xi + 274 pp.—Number 76 in the series Phoenix Library. Original ed. 1910; second ed. 1911; third ed. reprinted 1931.

1660. Priestley, J[ohn] B. The English Comic Characters. New York, Dodd, Mead and Co., 1925. 276 pp.—Reprint London, John Lane, 1937, in the series Bodley Head Library.

1661. Balmforth, Ramsden. The Problem-Play and Its Influence on Modern Thought and Life. New York, Henry Holt and Co., 1928. 155 pp.

1662. Thorndike, Ashley H. English Comedy. New York, Macmillan Co., 1929. vii + 635 pp.

1663. Eaton, Walter Prichard. The Drama in English. New York, Charles Scribner's Sons, 1930. xv + 365 pp.—"Bibliography," pp. 345–356.

1664. Granville-Barker, Harley. On Dramatic Method. London, Sidgwick and Jackson Ltd., 1931. [vii] + 192 pp.—The Clark Lectures 1930. A treatment specifically of blank verse, Shakespeare, Wycherly, Dryden, and dramatic form.

1665. Nicoll, Allardyce. The Theory of Drama. New York, Thomas Y. Crowell Co., [1931]. 262 pp.—Reprint 1937. "Suggestions for Reading," pp. 245–256. A development of Nicoll's *Introduction to Dramatic Theory*, London, G. G. Harrap, 1923, 217 pp.

1666. Craig, Hardin, ed. Essays in Dramatic Literature. The Parrott Presentation Volume. By pupils of Professor Thomas Marc Parrott of Princeton University, published in his honor. Princeton, N.J., University Press, 1935. [vii] + 470 pp.

1667. Perry, Henry Ten Eyck. Masters of Dramatic Comedy and Their Social Themes. Cambridge, Mass., Harvard Univ. Press, 1939. xxii + 428 pp.—"A Selected Bibliography of Works in English Relating to the Subject of This Book," pp. 409–417.

1668. Gassner, John. Masters of the Drama. New York, Random House Inc., 1940. xvii + 804 pp.—"Bibliography," pp. 739–763.

1669. [Seyler, Athene, and Haggard, Stephen.] The Craft of Comedy. Correspondence. Note by Athene Seyler. 2nd ed. London, Frederick Muller Ltd., 1944. 86 pp.—Original ed. 1943.

1670. Clark, Barrett H., ed. European Theories of the Drama with a Supplement on the American Drama. An anthology of dramatic theory and criticism from Aristotle to the present day, in a series of selected texts, with commentaries, biographies, and bibliographies. Rev. ed. New York, Crown Publ'ers, 1947. xvi + 576 (double column) pp.—Original ed. 1918.

1671. Clark, Barrett H., and Freedley, Geo., eds. A History of Modern Drama. New York, D. Appleton–Century Co., 1947. xiii + 832 pp.

1672. Nicoll, Allardyce. British Drama. An historical survey from the beginnings to the present time. 4th ed. London, George G. Harrap, 1947. vii + 533 pp.—Original ed. 1925; second ed. 1927; third ed. 1932.

1673. Prior, Moody E. The Language of Tragedy. New York, Columbia Univ. Press, 1947. ix + 411 pp.

1674. Potts, L[eonard] J. Comedy. London, Hutchinson's Univ. Library, [1948]. 174 pp.—Number 41 in the series Hutchinson's University Library.

1675. Nicoll, Allardyce. British Drama. An historical survey from the beginning to the present day. 4th ed. London, George G. Harrap and Co., [1949]. vii + 532 pp.—Original ed. 1925.

1676. Nicoll, Allardyce. World Drama. From Aeschylus to Anouilh. London, George G. Harrap and Co., 1949. [iv] + 1000 pp.

1677. Eliot, T[homas] S. Poetry and Drama. London, Faber and Faber Ltd., 1951. 35 pp.—The Theodore Spencer Memorial Lecture.

1678. Littlewood, S[amuel] R. The Art of Dramatic Criticism. With a foreword by Sir Barry Jackson. London, Isaac Pitman and Sons, 1952. x + 182 pp.

1679. Herrick, Marvin T. Tragicomedy. Its origin and development in Italy, France, and England. Urbana, University of Illinois Press, 1955. vii + 331 pp.—Volume XXXIX in the series Illinois Studies in Language and Literature.

1680. Muller, Herbert J. The Spirit of Tragedy. New York, Alfred A. Knopf Inc., 1956. xiv + 335 + viii pp.

1681. Trewin, J[ohn] C. Verse Drama since 1800. Cambridge Univ. Press for the National Book League, 1956. 27 pp.—Number 8 in the series Reader's Guides, Second Series.

1682. West, Rebecca. The Court and the Castle. Some treatments of a recurrent theme. New Haven, Yale Univ. Press, 1957. 319 pp.

1683. Nicoll, Allardyce. A History of English Drama 1600–1900. Vol. I: Restoration Drama 1660–1700 (4th ed. 1952; 1st ed. 1923); Vol. II: Early Eighteenth Century Drama [1700–1750] (3rd ed. 1952; 1st ed. 1925); Vol. III: Late Eighteenth Century Drama 1750–1800 (2nd ed. 1952; 1st ed. 1927); Vol. IV: Early Nineteenth Century Drama 1800–1850 (2nd ed. 1955; 1st ed. 1930); Vol. V: Late Nineteenth Century Drama 1850–1900 (2nd ed. 1959; 1st ed. 1946); Vol. VI: A Short-Title Alphabetical Catalogue of Plays (1959). Cambridge Univ. Press, 1952–59. 6 vols.

§63. DRAMA: MEDIEVAL

1686. Stratman, Carl J., C.S.V. Bibliography of Medieval Drama. Foreword by John Webster Spargo. Berkeley, University of California Press, 1954. x + 423 pp.

1687. Bates, Katherine L. The English Religious Drama. New York, Macmillan Co., 1893. [vii] + 254 pp.—Reprint 1921.

1688. Cushman, L[ysander] W. The Devil and the Vice in the English Dramatic Literature before Shakespeare. Halle a. S., Germany, Max Niemeyer, 1900. xv + 148 pp.—Volume VI in the series Studien zur englischen Philologie. "Bibliography," pp. 146–148.

1689. Tunison, Joseph S. Dramatic Traditions of the Dark Ages. University of Chicago Press, 1907. xviii + 350 pp.

1690. Thompson, E[lbert] N. S. The English Moral Plays. New Haven, Yale Univ. Press, 1910. 291–413 pp.—Volume XIV in the series Transactions of the Connecticut Academy of Arts and Sciences. Bibliographies, pp. 404–413.

1691. Wallace, Chas. Wm. The Evolution of the English Drama up to Shakespeare. With a history of the first Blackfriars Theatre. A survey .... Berlin, G. Reimer, 1912. xxi + 246 pp.—Volume IV in the series Schriften der deutschen Shakespeare-Gesellschaft.

1692. Mackenzie, W[illiam] Roy. The English Moralities from the Point of View of Allegory. Boston, Ginn and Co., 1914. xv + 278 pp.—Volume II in the series Harvard Studies in English. "List of Authorities and Editions," pp. 271–273.

1693. Kretzmann, Paul Edward. The Liturgical Element in the Earliest Forms of the Medieval Drama. With special reference to the English and German plays. Minneapolis, University of Minnesota, 1916. vii + 170 pp.—Number 4 in the series University of Minnesota Studies in Language and Literature. "Bibliography," pp. 165–170.

1694. Adams, Joseph Quincy. Chief Pre-Shakespearean Dramas. A selection of plays illustrating the history of English drama from its origin down to Shakespeare. Boston, Houghton Mifflin Co., 1924. vii + 712 (double column) pp.

1695. Moore, John B. The Comic and the Realistic in English Drama. University of Chicago Press, 1925. viii + 231 pp.

1696. Carey, Millicent. The Wakefield Group in the Towneley Cycle. A study to determine the conventional and original elements in four plays commonly ascribed to the Wakefield author. A dissertation. Baltimore, Johns Hopkins University, 1926. [vi] + 251 pp.—"Bibliography," pp. 245–251.

1697. Pollard, Alfred W. English Miracle Plays, Moralities, and Interludes. Specimens of the pre-Elizabethan drama. 8th ed. rev. Oxford, Clarendon Press, 1927. lxxii + 250 pp.—Original ed. 1890.

1698. Young, Karl. The Drama of the Medieval Church. New York, Oxford Univ. Press, 1933. 2 vols.—Reprint 1951. "List of Books," II, pp. 544–562.

1699. Farnham, Willard. The Medieval Heritage of Elizabethan Tragedy. Berkeley, University of California Press, 1936. xiv + 487 pp.

1700. Rossiter, A[rthur] P. English Drama from Early Times to the Elizabethans. Its background, origins, and development. London, Hutchinson and Co., 1950. 176 pp.—Reprint 1958.

1701. Williams, Arnold. The Characterization of Pilate in the Towneley Plays. East Lansing, Michigan State College Press, 1950. xiii + 112 pp.—"Bibliography," pp. 103–108.

1702. Craig, Hardin. English Religious Drama of the Middle Ages. Oxford Univ. Press, 1955. vii + 421 pp.—"Bibliography," pp. 390–401.

1703. Salter, F[rederick] M. Medieval Drama in Chester. University of Toronto Press, 1955. xi + 138 pp.—The Alexander Lectures 1953–54.

1704. Cawley, A[rthur] C. The Wakefield Pageants in the Towneley Cycle. Manchester, Eng., University Press, 1958. xxxix + 187 pp.—In the series Old and Middle English Texts. An edition with a full "Introduction," pp. xi–xxxiii, and "Select Bibliography," pp. xxxiv–xxxviii.

§64. DRAMA: TUDOR AND JACOBEAN

[See also §9. British Literature: Shakespeare Bibliographies, Handbooks, and Studies.]

1708. Fleay, Frederick Gard. A Biographical Chronicle of the English Drama 1559–1642. London, Reeves and Turner, 1891. 2 vols.

1709. Greg, Walter W. A List of English Plays Written before 1643 and Printed before 1700. London, Blades, East and Blades, 1900. xi + 158 pp.—Number 5 in the series Publications of the Bibliographical Society. See also Greg's *A List of Masques, Pageants Supplementary to a List of English Plays*, London, Blades, East and Blades, 1902, xi + 35 + cxxxi pp., number 6 in the series Publications of the Bibliographical Society.

1710. Steele, Mary S. Plays and Masques at Court during the Reigns of Elizabeth, James, and Charles. New Haven, Yale Univ. Press, 1926. xiii + 300 pp.

1711. Albright, Evelyn M. Dramatic Publications in England 1580–1640. New York, Modern Language Association of America, 1927. vi + 442 pp.—Number 2 in the series Modern Language Association Monographs.

1712. Sibley, Gertrude M. The Lost Plays and Masques 1500–1642. Ithaca, N.Y., Cornell Univ. Press, 1933. xiii + 205 pp.—Volume XIX in the series Cornell Studies in English.

1713. Carpenter, Frederic Ives. Metaphor and Simile in the Minor Elizabethan Drama. A dissertation . . . . University of Chicago Press, 1895. xvi + 217 pp.

1714. Symonds, John Addington. Shakespere's Predecessors in the Elizabethan Drama. New ed. London, Smith, Elder and Co., 1900. xix + 551 pp.—Original ed. 1884.

1715. Schelling, Felix E. The English Chronicle Play. A study in the popular historical literature envisioning Shakespeare. New York, Macmillan Co., 1902. xi + 310 pp.—"A List of Plays on English Historical Subjects," pp. 278–286.

1716. Boas, Frederick S. Shakespeare and the Universities and Other Studies in Elizabethan Drama. New York, D. Appleton and Co., 1903. vii + 272 pp.

1717. Greg, Walter W. Pastoral Poetry and Pastoral Drama. A literary inquiry, with special reference to the Pre-Restoration stage in England. London, A. H. Bullen, 1906. xii + 464 pp.

1718. Schelling, Felix E. Elizabethan Drama 1558–1642. A history of the drama in England from the accession of Queen Elizabeth to the closing of the theaters, to which is prefixed a résumé of the earlier drama from its beginnings. London, Archibald Constable and Co., 1908. 2 vols.—"Bibliographical Essay," II, pp. 433–537; "A List of Plays and Like Productions Written, Acted, or Published in England between the Years 1558 and 1642," II, pp. 538–624.

1719. Ristine, Frank H. English Tragicomedy. Its origin and history. New York, Columbia Univ. Press, 1910. xv + 247 pp.—In the series Columbia University Studies in English.

1720. Brooke, C[harles] F. Tucker. The Tudor Drama. A history of English national drama to the retirement of Shakespeare. Boston, Houghton Mifflin Co., 1911. xiii + 461 pp.

1721. Wallace, Chas. W. The Evolution of the English Drama up to Shakespeare. Berlin, G. Reimer, 1912. xxi + 246 pp.—Volume IV in the series Schriften der deutschen Shakespeare-Gesellschaft.

1722. Boas, Frederick S. University Drama in the Tudor Age. Oxford Univ. Press, 1914. xi + 414 pp.

1723. Boyer, Clarence V. The Villain as Hero in Elizabethan Tragedy. London, George Routledge and Sons, 1914. xii + 264 pp.

1724. Freeburg, Victor O. Disguise Plots in Elizabethan Drama. New York, Columbia Univ. Press, 1915. ix + 241 pp.

1725. Creizenach, Wilhelm. The English Drama in the Age of Shakespeare. Translated from the German by Cécile Hugon. London, Sidgwick and Jackson Ltd., 1916. xv + 454 pp.—Original Ger. ed. 1904. "The present volume corresponds to Books I–VIII of the fourth volume of Geschichte des neueren Dramas," LC card. See no. 1654.

1726. Symonds, Arthur. Studies in the Elizabethan Drama. New York, E. P. Dutton and Co., 1919. 261 pp.

1727. Spens, Janet. Elizabethan Drama. London, Methuen and Co., 1922. ix + 148 pp.

1728. Harrison, G[eorge] B. Shakespeare's Fellows. London, Bodley Head Ltd., 1923. 207 pp.—A study *inter alios* of Greene, Dekker, and Marlowe.

1729. Sykes, H[enry] Dugdale. Sidelights on Elizabethan Drama. A series of studies dealing with the authorship of sixteenth and seventeenth century plays. Oxford Univ. Press, 1924. 231 pp.

1730. Cardozo, Jacob L. The Contemporary Jew in the Elizabethan Drama. Amsterdam, Holland, H. J. Paris, 1925. xvi + 335 pp.—Bibliography, pp. 331–335. See also Montagu F. Modder, *The Jew in the Literature of England to the End of the Nineteenth Century*, Philadelphia, Jewish Publication Society of America, 1939, xvii + 435 pp., reprint 1944.

1731. Schelling, Felix E. Elizabethan Playwrights. A short history of the English drama from medieval times to the closing of the theaters in 1642. New York, Harper and Bros., 1925. xv + 335 pp.—"A List of Books (more especially of those published since 1908)," pp. 289–302; "A Chronological List of Important Dates," pp. 303–315.

1732. Reed, A[rthur] W. Early Tudor Drama. Medwall, the Rastells, Heywood, and the More circle. London, Methuen and Co., 1926. xv + 246 pp.

1733. Baskerville, Chas. Read. The Elizabethan Jig and Related Song Drama. University of Chicago Press, 1929. x + 642 pp.

1734. Motter, T[homas] H. Vail. The School Drama in England. London, Longmans, Green and Co., 1929. xiii + 325 pp.

1735. Spek, C[ornelis] van der. The Church and the Churchman in English Dramatic Literature before 1642. Amsterdam, Holland, H. J. Paris, 1930. 188 pp.—"List of Plays," pp. 177–184.

1736. Lindabury, Richard V. A Study of Patriotism in the Elizabethan Drama. Princeton, N.J., University Press, 1931. ix + 218 pp.

1737. Boas, Frederick S. An Introduction to Tudor Drama. Oxford Univ. Press, 1933. viii + 176 pp.

1738. Bradbrook, M[uriel] C. Themes and Conventions of Elizabethan Tragedy. Cambridge Univ. Press, 1935. viii + 275 pp.—Reprint 1952.

1739. Linthicum, M[arie] Channing. Costume in the Drama of Shakespeare and His Contemporaries. Oxford, Clarendon Press, 1936. viii + 307 pp.

1740. Sisson, C[harles] J. Lost Plays of Shakespeare's Age. Cambridge Univ. Press, 1936. xi + 221 pp.

1741. Spencer, Theodore. Death and Elizabethan Tragedy. A study of convention and opinion in the Elizabethan drama. Cambridge, Mass., Harvard Univ. Press, 1936. xiii + 288 pp.

1742. Harrison, G[eorge] B. The Story of Elizabethan Drama. Cambridge Univ. Press, 1924. 134 pp.—Reprint 1937.

1743. Knights, L[ionel] C. Drama and Society in the Age of Jonson. London, Chatto and Windus, 1937. xvii + 347 pp.—Reprint 1951. "Bibliography," pp. 333–339.

1744. Withington, Robt. Excursions in English Drama. New York, D. Appleton–Century Co., 1937. xix + 264 pp.—A treatment of Elizabethan drama with essays on the Vice and related matters.

1745. Baker, Howard. Induction to Tragedy. A study in a development of form in Gorboduc, the Spanish Tragedy, and Titus Andronicus. Baton Rouge, Louisiana State Univ. Press, 1939. [ix] + 247 pp.

1746. Bernard, J[ules] E. The Prosody of the Tudor Interlude. New Haven, Yale Univ. Press, 1939. xi + 225 pp.

1747. West, Robt. H. The Invisible World. A study of pneumatology in Elizabethan Drama. Athens, University of Georgia Press, 1939. xvii + 275 pp.

1748. Bowers, Fredson Thayer. Elizabethan Revenge Tragedy 1587–1642. Princeton, N.J., University Press, 1940. ix + 288 pp.

1749. Wells, Henry W. Elizabethan and Jacobean Playwrights. New York, Columbia Univ. Press, 1939. xiv + 327 pp.—"Biographical and Bibliographical Notes," pp. 279–315. Also Wells's pamphlet supplement

A Chronological List of Extant Plays Produced in or about London 1581–1642, New York, Columbia Univ. Press, 1940, [ii] + 17 pp.

1750. Adams, Henry H. English Domestic or Homiletic Tragedy 1575 to 1642. New York, Columbia Univ. Press, 1943. x + 228 pp.—Number 159 in the series Columbia University Studies in English and Comparative Literature. Bibliography, pp. 207–220.

1751. Parrott, Thos. Marc, and Ball, Robt. Hamilton. A Short View of Elizabethan Drama. Together with some account of its principal playwrights and the conditions under which it was produced. New York, Charles Scribner's Sons, 1943. vii + 311 pp.—"Bibliography," pp. 295–303.

1752. Boas, Frederick S. An Introduction to Stuart Drama. Oxford Univ. Press, 1946. viii + 443 pp.

1753. Ellis-Fermor, Una. The Jacobean Drama. An interpretation. 2nd ed. London, Methuen and Co., 1947. xvi + 340 pp.—Original ed. 1936.

1754. Boas, Frederick S. Queen Elizabeth in Drama, and Related Studies. London, George Allen and Unwin Ltd., 1950. 212 pp.

1755. James, D[avid] G. The Dream of Learning. An essay on The Advancement of Learning, Hamlet, and King Lear. Oxford Univ. Press, 1951. [vii] + 126 pp.

1756. Doran, Madeleine. Endeavors of Art. A study of form in Elizabethan drama. Madison, University of Wisconsin Press, 1954. xv + 482 pp.

1757. Gagen, Jean Elizabeth. The New Woman. Her emergence in English drama 1600–1730. New York, Twayne Publ'ers, 1954. 193 pp.

1758. Bradbrook, M[uriel] C. The Growth and Structure of Elizabethan Comedy. London, Chatto and Windus Ltd., 1955. ix + 246 pp.—"Chronological Table of Plays," pp. 207–210.

1759. Eliot, T[homas] S. Essays on Elizabethan Drama. New York, Harcourt, Brace and Co., 1956. x + 178 pp.—Number 18 in the series Harvest Books.

1760. Harrison, G[eorge] B. Elizabethan Plays and Players. London, G. Routledge and Sons, 1940. viii + 306 pp.

1761. Barber, C[harles] L. The Idea of Honour in the English Drama 1591–1700. Göteborg, Sweden, Elanders Boktryckeri Aktiebolag, 1957. 367 pp.—Volume VI in the series Gothenburg Studies in English.

1762. Ribner, Irving. The English History Play in the Age of Shakespeare. Princeton, N.J., University Press, 1957. xii + 354 pp.

1763. Jewkes, Wilfred T. Act Division in Elizabethan and Jacobean Plays 1583–1616. Hamden, Conn., Shoe String Press, 1958. x + 374 pp.—"Bibliography," pp. 353–372.

1764. Bennett, Josephine W., Cargill, Oscar, and Hall, Vernon, Jr., eds. Studies in the English Renaissance Drama. London, Peter Owen and Vision Press, 1959. 368 pp.

1765. Campbell, Lily B. Divine Poetry and Drama in Sixteenth-Century England. Berkeley, University of California Press, 1959. 267 pp.

§65. DRAMA: RESTORATION AND EIGHTEENTH CENTURY

1769. Summers, Montague. A Bibliography of the Restoration Drama. London, Fortune Press, [1934]. 143 pp.—An attempt to list all plays, acted and unacted, printed and unprinted, between 1660 and 1700.

1770. Paine, Clarence S. The Comedy of Manners 1660–1700. A reference guide to the comedy of the Restoration. Boston, Faxon Co., 1941. 51 pp.—Number 36 in the series Bulletin of Bibliography Pamphlets.

1771. Woodward, Gertrude L., and McManaway, James G. A Check List of English Plays 1641–1700. Chicago, Newberry Library, 1945. [x] + 155 pp.—Also *Supplement,* by Fredson Bowers, Charlottesville, Bibliographical Society of the University of Virginia, 1949, 22 pp.

1772. Chase, Lewis Nathaniel. The English Heroic Play. A critical description of the rhymed tragedy of the Restoration. New York, Columbia Univ. Press, 1903. xii + 250 pp.—In the series Columbia University Studies in Comparative Literature. "List of Plays in Heroic Verse," pp. 232–244.

1773. Marks, Jeannette. English Pastoral Drama from the Restoration to the Date of the Publication of the "Lyrical Ballads" 1660–1798. London, Methuen and Co., 1908. xiii + 228 pp.

1774. Miles, D[udley] H. The Influence of Molière on Restoration Comedy. New York, Columbia Univ. Press, 1910. xi + 272 pp.—In the series Columbia University Studies in Comparative Literature. Bibliography, pp. 243–268.

1775. Palmer, John [L.]. The Comedy of Manners. London, George Bell and Sons, 1913. vii + 308 pp.

1776. Nettleton, Geo. Henry. English Drama of the Restoration and Eighteenth Century 1642–1780. New York, Macmillan Co., 1914. xv + 366 pp.—Reprint 1921. "Biographical Notes," pp. 315–340.

1777. Bernbaum, Ernest. The Drama of Sensibility. A sketch of the history of English sentimental comedy and domestic tragedy 1696–1780. Boston, Ginn and Co., 1915. ix + 288 pp.—Volume III in the series Harvard Studies in English. Reprint 1925.

1778. Dobrée, Bonamy. Restoration Comedy 1660–1720. [Rev. ed.] Oxford, Clarendon Press, 1925. 189 pp.—Original ed. 1924. "A Short List of Plays and a Brief Bibliography," pp. 174–178.

1779. Perry, Henry Ten Eyck. The Comic Spirit in Restoration Drama. Studies in the comedy of Etherege, Wycherley, Congreve, Vanbrugh, and Farquhar. New Haven, Yale Univ. Press, 1925. xii + 148 pp.

1780. Lynch, Kathleen. The Social Mode of Restoration Comedy. New York, Macmillan Co., 1926. xi + 242 pp.—Volume III in the series University of Michigan Publications in Language and Literature. "Bibliography," pp. 219–230.

1781. Elwin, Malcolm. The Playgoer's Handbook to Restoration Drama. London, J. Cape, 1928. 260 pp.

1782. Dobrée, Bonamy. Restoration Tragedy 1660–1720. Oxford, Clarendon Press, 1929. 189 pp.—Reprint 1954. "A Brief Bibliography," pp. 183–186.

1783. Bastiaenen, Johannes A. The Moral Tone of Jacobean and Caroline Drama. Amsterdam, Holland, H. J. Paris, 1930. 198 pp.

1784. Deane, Cecil V. Dramatic Theory and the Rhymed Heroic Play. Oxford Univ. Press, 1931. vi + 235 pp.

1785. Green, Clarence C. The Neo-Classic Theory of Tragedy in England during the Eighteenth Century. Cambridge, Mass., Harvard Univ. Press, 1934. ix + 245 pp.—Volume XI in the series Harvard Studies in English.

1786. Harbage, Alfred. Cavalier Drama. An historical and critical supplement to the study of the Elizabethan and Restoration stage. New York, Modern Language Association of America, 1936. ix + 302 pp.—In the Modern Language Association of America General Series. "A List, Chronologically Arranged, of All Plays of the Caroline, Commonwealth, and Early Restoration Periods," pp. 259–285.

1787. Smith, Dane Farnsworth. Plays about the Theatre in England from The Rehearsal in 1671 to the Licensing Act in 1737. Or the self-conscious stage and its burlesque and satirical reflections in the age of criticism. Oxford Univ. Press, 1936. xxiii + 287 pp.—"The Principal Plays about the Theatre in England 1671 to 1737/8," pp. 247–250; "Bibliography," pp. 251–258.

1788. Wilcox, John. The Relation of Molière to Restoration Comedy. New York, Columbia Univ. Press, 1938. ix + 240 pp.

1789. Wiley, Autrey Nell. Rare Prologues and Epilogues 1642–1700. London, George Allen and Unwin Ltd., 1940. xlv + 358 pp.

1790. Alleman, Gellert S. Matrimonial Law and the Materials of Restoration Comedy. Wallingford, Penn., published by the author, 1942. vii + 155 pp.

1791. Evans, Bertrand. Gothic Drama from Walpole to Shelley. Berkeley, University of California Press, 1947. viii + 257 pp.—Volume XVIII in the series University of California Publications in English.

1792. Mignon, Elisabeth. Crabbed Age and Youth. The old men and women in the Restoration comedy of manners. Durham, N.C., Duke Univ. Press, 1947. ix + 194 pp.

1793. Krutch, Joseph W. Comedy and Conscience after the Restoration. Second printing with a new preface, additional bibliographical material, and an index. New York, Columbia Univ. Press, 1949. xi + 300 pp.—Original printing 1924.

1794. Fujimura, Thos. H. The Restoration Comedy of Wit. Princeton, N.J., University Press, 1952. ix + 232 pp.—"Bibliography," pp. 204–219.

1795. Boas, Frederick S. An Introduction to Eighteenth-Century Drama 1700–1780. Oxford Univ. Press, 1953. x + 365 pp.

1796. Hughes, Leo. A Century of English Farce. Princeton, N.J., University Press, 1956. vii + 307 pp.—"Bibliography," pp. 286–291.

1797. Sherbo, Arthur. Sentimental Drama. East Lansing, Michigan State Univ. Press, 1957. viii + 181 pp.

1798. Holland, Norman N. The First Modern Comedies. The significance of Etherege, Wycherley, and Congreve. Cambridge, Mass., Harvard Univ. Press, 1959. [vii] + 274 pp.

1799. Loftis, John. Comedy and Society from Congreve to Fielding. Stanford Univ. Press, 1959. xiii + 154 pp.—Volume XIX in the series Stanford Studies in Language and Literature.

§66. DRAMA: NINETEENTH CENTURY AND MODERN BRITISH AND AMERICAN

1803. Davis, Mary W., et al. Dramatic Compositions Copyrighted in the United States 1870–1916. Washington, D.C., Government Printing Office, 1918. 2 vols.

1804. Cant, Monica. A Bibliography of English Drama from 1890 to 1920. Library Association Record, XXIV (1922), 41–57.

1805. MacNamara, Brinsley, ed. Abbey Plays 1899–1948. Including the productions of the Irish Literary Theatre. Dublin, Colm O Lochlainn, [1949]. 84 pp.

1806. Burton, Richard. The New American Drama. New York, Thomas Y. Crowell Co., 1913. viii + 277 pp.

1807. Chandler, Frank Wadleigh. Aspects of Modern Drama. New York, Macmillan Co., 1914. ix + 494 pp.—"Representative Modern Plays and Their English Translations," pp. 423–445; "Critical Aids for the Study of Modern Drama," pp. 446–479.

1808. Dickinson, Thos. H. Playwrights of the New American Theater. New York, Macmillan Co., 1925. vi + 331 pp.

1809. Moses, Montrose J. The American Dramatist. New rev. ed. Boston, Little, Brown and Co., 1925. xix + 474 pp.—Original ed. 1911; revised ed. 1917. "Bibliography of the American Dramatist," pp. 379–394.

1810. Cunliffe, John W. Modern English Playwrights. A short history of the English drama from 1825. New York, Harper and Bros., 1927. xi + 260 pp.

1811. Nicoll, Allardyce. A History of Early Nineteenth Century Drama 1800–1850. Cambridge Univ. Press, 1930. 2 vols.—See also Arnold Biella, "Additions and Corrections to the Bibliography of 19th Century British Drama," *Philological Quarterly*, XXI, 3 (July 1942), 298–322, and James Edward Tobin, "More English Plays 1800–1850," *Philological Quarterly*, XXIII, 4 (Oct. 1944), 320–332.

1812. Dickinson, Thos. H. The Contemporary Drama of England. [New ed.] Boston, Little, Brown and Co., 1931. 355 pp.—Original ed. 1917.

1813. Thouless, Priscilla. Modern Poetic Drama. Oxford, Eng., Basil Blackwell, 1934. 204 pp.—Bibliography, pp. 202–204.

1814. Quinn, Arthur Hobson. A History of the American Drama from the Civil War to the Present Day. New York, F. S. Crofts and Co., 1936. 2 vols. in one. The text of the 2 vol. ed. of 1927 plus the chapter "The New Decade 1927–1936." "General Bibliography and List of American Plays 1860–1936," II, pp. 303–402.

1815. Reynolds, Ernest. Early Victorian Drama 1830–1870. Cambridge, Eng., Heffer, 1936. vii + 163 pp.

1816. Clark, Barrett H. A Study of the Modern Drama. A handbook for the study and appreciation of typical plays, European, English, and American, of the last three-quarters of a century. Rev. ed. New York, D. Appleton-Century Co., 1938. xv + 534 pp.—Original ed. 1925. "Bibliographies," pp. 433–487.

1817. Mantle, Burns. Contemporary American Playwrights. New York, Dodd, Mead and Co., 1938. x + 357 pp.—See also Burns's *American Playwrights of Today*, New York, Dodd, Mead and Co., 1929, xiii + 324 pp.

1818. Hartman, John G. The Development of American Social Comedy from 1787 to 1936. New York, Stechert and Co., 1939. v + 151 pp.

1819. Tolles, Winton. Tom Taylor and the Victorian Drama. New York, Columbia Univ. Press, 1940. vii + 299 pp.—Number 148 in the series Columbia University Studies in English and Comparative Literature. "General Bibliography," pp. 282–286.

1820. Quinn, Arthur H. A History of the American Drama from the Beginning to the Civil War. 2nd ed. New York, F. S. Crofts and Co., 1943. xvii + 530 pp.—Original ed. 1923; second ed. reprinted 1951. "A List of American Plays," pp. 423–497; "Bibliography," pp. 393–421.

1821. Nicoll, Allardyce. A History of Late Nineteenth Century Drama 1850–1900. Cambridge Univ. Press, 1946. 2 vols.—Reprint 1949.

1822. Gagey, Edmond M. Revolution in American Drama. New York, Columbia Univ. Press, 1947. ix + 315 pp.

1823. Reynolds, Ernest. Modern English Drama. A survey of the theatre from 1900. With a foreword by Allardyce Nicoll. London, George G. Harrap, 1949. 243 pp.—American ed. Norman, University of Oklahoma Press, 1951.

1824. Downer, Alan S. Fifty Years of American Drama 1900–1950. Chicago, Henry Regnery Co., 1951. 158 pp.

1825. Lumley, Frederick. Trends in Twentieth Century Drama. A survey since Ibsen and Shaw. Fair Lawn, N.J., Essential Books Inc., 1956. xii + 275 pp.

1826. Krutch, Joseph Wood. The American Drama since 1918. An informal history. Rev. ed. New York, George Braziller Inc., 1957. xii + 3–344 pp.—Original ed. 1939.

1827. Melchinger, Siegfried. Drama zwischen Shaw und Brecht. Ein Leitfaden durch das zeitgenössische Schauspiel. Bremen, Carl Schünemann Verlag, 1957. 312 pp.

CHAPTER V

CRITICISM AND INTERPRETATION

[See also §22. The Art of Prose; §28. Fiction: Studies in the Essence, Purpose, Form, and Technique of the Novel; §43. Interpretative Studies (of poetry) by Individual Critics; §52. Critical and Expository Writing on the Stage; §62. Drama: Histories, Surveys, and Criticism; §82. Humanistic Periodicals; §83. Belletristic Periodicals; §84. Reviews; §86. Journals of Criticism.]

§67. TERMINOLOGY

1832. Elton, Wm. A Glossary of the New Criticism. Chicago, Modern Poetry Association, 1949. 48 pp.

1833. Duffy, C[harles], and Pettit, H[enry]. Dictionary of Literary Terms. Denver, Col., University of Denver Press, 1951. iii + 111 pp.

1834. Fechter, Paul. Kleines Wörterbuch für literarische Gespräche. Gütersloh, C. Bertelsmann Verlag, 1952. 348 pp.—Brief essays on literary words.

1835. Shipley, Joseph T., ed. Dictionary of World Literature. Criticism, forms, technique. New rev. ed. New York, Philosophical Library, 1953. xii + 453 (double column) pp.—Original ed. 1943.

1836. A Glossary of Literary Terms. Revised by M[eyer] H. Abrams. New York, Rinehart and Co., 1957. v + 105 pp.—In the series Rinehart English Pamphlets. Original ed. 1941 by Dan S. Norton and Peters Rushton.

1837. Barnet, Sylvan, Berman, Morton, and Burto, Wm. The Study of Literature. A handbook of critical essays and terms. Boston, Little, Brown and Co., 1960. xi + 368 pp.—"Dictionary of Literary Terms," pp. 261–354.

§68. CRITICISM: HISTORIES AND HISTORICAL STUDIES

1841. Draper, John W. Eighteenth Century English Aesthetics. A bibliography. Heidelberg, Carl Winter, 1931. 140 pp.—Number 71 in the series

Anglistische Forschungen. See also William D. Templeman, "Contributions to the Bibliography of Eighteenth-Century Aesthetics," *Modern Philology,* XXX, 3 (Feb. 1933), 309–316.

1842. Hammond, Wm. A. A Bibliography of Aesthetics and of the Philosophy of the Fine Arts from 1900 to 1932. . . . Rev. and enl. ed. New York, Longmans, Green and Co., 1934. x + 205 pp.—Original ed. 1933.

1843. Ebisch, Walther, and Schücking, Levin Ludwig. Bibliographie zur Geschichte des literarischen Geschmacks in England. Anglia, Zeitschrift für englische Philologie, LXIII, 1/2 (Jan. 1939), 1–64.

1844. Arms, Geo., and Kunitz, Joseph M. Poetry Explication. A checklist of interpretations since 1925 of British and American poems past and present. New York, Swallow Press and William Morrow and Co., 1950. 188 pp.

1845. Sears, Lorenzo. The History of Oratory from the Age of Pericles to the Present Time. Chicago, S. C. Griggs and Co., 1896. 440 pp.

1846. Spingarn, Joel Elias. A History of Literary Criticism in the Renaissance. With special reference to the influence of Italy in the formation and development of modern classicism. 2nd ed. New York, Columbia Univ. Press, 1908. xii + 350 pp.—In the series Columbia University Studies in Literature. Original ed. 1899; second ed. frequently reprinted, as in 1938.

1847. Klein, David. Literary Criticism from the Elizabethan Dramatists. Repertory and synthesis. With an introductory note by J. E. Spingarn. New York, Sturgis and Walton Co., 1910. xviii + 257 pp.

1848. Saintsbury, Geo. A History of English Criticism. Being the English chapters of A History of Criticism and Literary Taste in Europe, revised, adapted, and supplemented. Edinburgh, William Blackwood and Sons, 1911. xv + 551 pp.—Reprint 1955.

1849. Clark, Donald L. Rhetoric and Poetry in the Renaissance. A study of rhetorical terms in English Renaissance literary criticism. New York, Columbia Univ. Press, 1922. x + 166 pp.

1850. Baldwin, Chas. Sears. Ancient Rhetoric and Poetic. Interpreted from representative works. New York, Macmillan Co., 1924. xiv + 261 pp.

1851. Faral, Edmond. Les arts poétiques du XIIe et du XIIIe siècle. Recherches et documents sur la technique littéraire du moyen âge. Paris, É. Champion, 1924. xvi + 384 pp.

1852. Clark, A[lexander] F. B. Boileau and the French Classical Critics in England 1660–1830. Paris, É. Champion, 1925. xviii + 534 pp.—Volume XIX in the series Bibliothèque de la Revue de littérature comparée. "Bibliography," pp. 505–522.

1853. Baldwin, Chas. Sears. Medieval Rhetoric and Poetic (to 1400). Interpreted from representative works. New York, Macmillan Co., 1928. xvii + 321 pp.

1854. Foerster, Norman. American Criticism. A study in literary theory from Poe to the present. Boston, Houghton Mifflin Co., 1928. xvi + 273 pp.—A study *inter alios* of Poe, Emerson, Lowell, and Whitman.

1855. Roberts, W[illiam] Rhys. Greek Rhetoric and Literary Criticism. New York, Longmans, Green and Co., 1928. vii + 164 pp.—In the series Our Debt to Greece and Rome. "Bibliography," pp. 163–164.

1856. Saintsbury, Geo. A History of Criticism and Literary Taste in Europe from the Earliest Texts to the Present Day. 4th and 5th ed. Vol. I: Classical and Mediaeval Criticism; Vol. II: From the Renaissance to the Decline of Eighteenth Century Orthodoxy; Vol. III: Modern Criticism. Edinburgh, William Blackwood and Sons, 1922–29. 3 vols.—Original ed. 1900–04.

1857. Bosker, Aisso. Literary Criticism in the Age of Johnson. Groningen, Holland, J. B. Wolters, 1930. xi + 294 pp.—Bibliography, pp. 273–284.

1858. Vines, Sherard. The Course of English Classicism. New York, Harcourt, Brace and Co., 1930. 160 pp.—Number 12 in the Hogarth Lectures on Literature Series.

1859. DeMille, Geo. E. Literary Criticism in America. A preliminary survey. New York, Dial Press, 1931. xii + 288 pp.

1860. Thomas, P[ercy] G. Aspects of Literary Theory and Practice 1550–1870. London, Heath Cranton Ltd., 1931. viii + 9–210 pp.

1861. Atkins, J[ohn] W. H. Literary Criticism in Antiquity. A sketch of its development. Cambridge Univ. Press, 1934. 2 vols.

1862. Allen, Beverley S. Tides in English Taste 1619–1800. A background for the study of literature. Cambridge, Mass., Harvard Univ. Press, 1937. 2 vols.

1863. Glunz, H[ans] H. Die Literarästhetic des europäischen Mittelalters. Wolfram, Rosenroman, Chaucer, Dante. Bochum-Langendreer, H. Pöppinghaus, 1937. xvi + 608 pp. + xiv plates.—Volume II in the series Das Abendland: Forschungen zur Geschichte europäischen Geisteslebens.

1864. Gilbert, Katherine Everett, and Kuhn, Helmut. A History of Esthetics. New York, Macmillan Co., 1939. xxi + 582 pp.

1865. Atkins, J[ohn] W. H. English Literary Criticism. The medieval phase. New York, Macmillan Co., 1943. ix + 211 pp.—Reprint London, Methuen and Co., 1952. "Summary of Medieval Poetic (Geoffrey of Vinsauf)," pp. 200–203.

1866. Atkins, J[ohn] W. H. English Literary Criticism. Seventeenth and eighteenth centuries. London, Methuen and Co., 1951. xi + 383 pp.

1867. Atkins, J[ohn] W. H. English Literary Criticism. The Renascence. 2nd ed. London, Methuen and Co., 1951. xi + 371 pp.—Original ed. 1947.

1868. Glicksberg C[harles] I. American Literary Criticism 1900–1950. New York, Hendricks House, 1951. x + 574 pp.

1869. Tillotson, Geoffrey. Criticism and the Nineteenth Century. London, Athlone Press, 1951. xi + 283 pp.

1870. Clarke, Martin Lowther. Rhetoric at Rome. A historical survey. London, Cohen and West, [1953]. 203 pp.

1871. Stovall, Floyd, ed. The Development of American Literary Criticism. Chapel Hill, University of North Carolina Press, 1955. ix + 262 pp. —"Selected Reading List," pp. 247–253.

1872. Wellek, René. A History of Modern Criticism 1750–1950. Vol. I: The Later Eighteenth Century; Vol. II: The Romantic Age. New Haven, Yale Univ. Press, 1955. 2 vols.

1873. Pritchard, John P. Criticism in America. An account of the development of critical techniques from the early period of the Republic to the middle years of the twentieth century. Norman, University of Oklahoma Press, 1956. x + 325 pp.

1874. Wimsatt, Wm. K., Jr., and Brooks, Cleanth, Jr. Literary Criticism. A short history. New York, Alfred A. Knopf, 1957. xviii + 755 + xxii pp.—A history of criticism from Classical to modern times.

§69. BASIC PRINCIPLES OF CRITICISM

1879. Santayana, Geo. The Sense of Beauty. Being the outlines of aesthetic theory. New York, Charles Scribner's Sons, 1896. ix + 275 pp.— Reprints 1902, 1936, 1955.

1880. Robertson, John Mackinnon. New Essays towards a Critical Method. London, John Lane, 1897. xi + 379 pp.—See also Robertson's earlier *Essays towards a Critical Method,* London, T. Fisher Unwin, 1889, vii + 287 pp.

1881. Gayley, Chas. M., and Scott, F[red] N. Introduction to the Methods and Materials of Literary Criticism. The bases in aesthetics and poetics. Boston, Ginn and Co., 1899. xii + 587 pp.

1882. Winchester, C[aleb] T. Some Principles of Literary Criticism. New York, Macmillan Co., 1899. xiii + 352 pp.—Frequent reprints, as in 1941.

1883. Bosanquet, Bernard. A History of Aesthetic. 2nd ed. London, Swan Sonnenschein and Co., 1904. xxiii + 502 pp.—In the series Library of Philosophy. Original ed. 1892. "Bibliography," pp. 495–498. Reprint New York, Meridian Library, 1957, number 8 in the series Meridian Books.

1884. Spingarn, Joel E. Creative Criticism. Essays on the unity of genius and taste. New York, Harcourt, Brace and Co., 1911. 138 pp.—See no. 1988 for further publication history.

1885. Worsfold, W[illiam] Basil. The Principles of Criticism. An introduction to the study of literature. New ed. New York, Longmans, Green and Co., 1912. viii + 256 pp.—Original ed. 1902.

1886. Gayley, Chas. M., and Kurtz, B[enjamin] P. Methods and Materials of Literary Criticism. Lyric, epic, and allied forms of poetry. . . . Boston, Ginn and Co., [1920]. xi + 911 pp.—In the series Semicentennial Publications of the University of California. "Bibliography of Poetry," pp. 785–846.

1887. Nitchie, Elizabeth. The Criticism of Literature. New York, Macmillan Co., 1928. xii + 397 pp.—"References," pp. 341–377.

1888. Cazamian, Louis. Criticism in the Making. New York, Macmillan Co., 1929. xi + 196 pp.

1889. Buck, Philo M. Literary Criticism. A study of values in literature. New York, Harper and Bros., 1930. xi + 432 pp.

1890. Brightfield, Myron F. The Issue in Literary Criticism. Berkeley, University of California Press, 1932. xiii + 316 pp.

1891. Guérard, Albert L. Art for Art's Sake. Boston, Lothrop, Lee and Shepard Co., 1936. xxxii + 349 pp.

1892. Torossian, Aram. A Guide to Aesthetics. Stanford Univ. Press, 1937. vii + 343 pp.—Bibliography, pp. 313–323.

1893. Baker, Herschel. The Dignity of Man. Studies in the persistence of an idea. Cambridge, Mass., Harvard Univ. Press, 1947. xii + 365 pp.—"Bibliography," pp. 337–357.

1894. Farrell, James T. Literature and Morality. New York, Vanguard Press, [1947]. xv + 304 pp.

1895. Carritt, Edgar F. The Theory of Beauty. 5th ed. London, Methuen and Co., 1949. viii + 344 pp.—Original ed. 1914.

1896. Eliot, T[homas] S. Notes towards the Definition of Culture. New York, Harcourt, Brace and Co., 1949. 128 pp.

1897. Shumaker, Wayne. Elements of Critical Theory. Berkeley, University of California Press, 1952. x + 131 pp.

1898. Goodman, Paul. The Structure of Literature. University of Chicago Press, 1954. vii + 282 pp.—"Glossary," pp. 267–277.

1899. Frye, Northrop. Anatomy of Criticism. Four essays. Princeton, N.J., University Press, 1957. x + 383 pp.—Glossary of [non-Aristotelian] critical terms, pp. 365–367.

1900. Levin, Harry. Contexts of Criticism. Cambridge, Mass., Harvard Univ. Press, 1957. xiii + 294 pp.—Number 22 in the series Harvard Studies in Comparative Literature.

1901. Beardsley, Monroe C. Aesthetics. Problems in the philosophy of criticism. New York, Harcourt, Brace and Co., 1958. xi + 614 pp.

§70. ARISTOTLE AND OTHER ANCIENT AUTHORITIES

[See also §4. English Literature: Classical Influences.]

1905. Cooper, Lane, and Gudeman, Alfred. A Bibliography of The Poetics of Aristotle. New Haven, Yale Univ. Press, 1928. xi + 193 pp.—Volume XI in the series Cornell Studies in English.

1906. Orgon, Troy Wilson. An Index to Aristotle in English Translation. Princeton, N.J., University Press, 1949. vi + 181 pp.

1907. Butcher, S[amuel] H., ed. Aristotle's Theory of Poetry and Fine Art. With a critical text and translation of The Poetics. 4th ed. London, Macmillan Co., 1907. xl + 421 pp.—Original ed. 1895; second ed. 1898; third ed. 1902. Reprint of the 4th ed. New York, Dover Publications, 1951.

1908. Butcher, S[amuel] H., ed. The Poetics of Aristotle. With critical notes and a translation. 4th ed. London, Macmillan Co., 1907. xxviii + 111 pp.—Original ed. 1895; second ed. 1898; third ed. 1902; fourth ed. reprinted 1936.

1909. Bywater, Ingram, ed. Aristotle on the Art of Poetry. A revised text with a critical introduction, translation, and commentary. Oxford Univ. Press, 1909. xlvii + 387 pp.

1910. Jebb, Richard Claverhouse. The Rhetoric of Aristotle. A translation. Edited with an introduction and with supplementary notes by John Edwin Sandys. Cambridge Univ. Press, 1909. xxviii + 207 pp.

1911. Cooper, Lane. An Aristotelian Theory of Comedy. With an adaptation of The Poetics and a Translation of the Tractatus Coislinianus. New York, Harcourt, Brace and Co., 1922. xxi + 323 pp.—Bibliography, pp. xv + xxi.

1912. Cooper, Lane. The Poetics of Aristotle. Its meaning and influence. Boston, Marshall Jones Co., [1923]. x + 157 pp.—In the series Our Debt to Greece and Rome. Bibliography, pp. 154–157.

1913. Lucas, F[rank] L. Tragedy in Relation to Aristotle's Poetics. New York, Harcourt, Brace and Co., 1928. 160 pp.—Number 2 in the Hogarth Lectures on Literature Series.

1914. Cooper, Lane. Aristotelian Papers. Revised and reprinted. Ithaca, N.Y., Cornell Univ. Press, 1939. x + 237 pp.

1915. Pritchard, John Paul. Return to the Fountains. Some classical sources of American criticism. Durham, N.C., Duke Univ. Press, 1942. xiii + 271 pp.—"Bibliography and Notes," pp. 207–261.

1916. Longinus. Longinus on the Sublime. An English translation by Benedict Einarson. . . . And Sir Joshua Reynolds' Discourses on Art. With an Introduction by Elder Olson. Chicago, Packard and Co., 1945. xxi + 345 pp.—In the series University Classics.

1917. Herrick, Marvin T. The Fusion of Horatian and Aristotelian Literary Criticism 1531–1555. Urbana, University of Illinois Press, 1946. viii + 117 pp.—Volume XXXII, no. 1, in the series Illinois Studies in Language and Literature. Bibliography, pp. 110–113.

1918. House, Humphry. Aristotle's Poetics. A course of eight lectures. Revised with a preface by Colin Hardie. London, Rupert Hart-Davis, 1956. 128 pp.—"Bibliography," pp. 127–128.

1919. Else, Gerald Frank. Aristotle's Poetics. The argument. Cambridge, Mass., Harvard Univ. Press, 1957. xvi + 670 pp.—Annotations.

1920. Holland, L[aura] Virginia. Counterpoint. Kenneth Burke and Aristotle's theories of rhetoric. New York, Philosophical Library, 1959. 128 pp.

§71. ANTHOLOGIES OF CRITICAL ESSAYS

1924. Cook, Albert S., ed. The Art of Poetry. The poetical treatises of Horace, Vida, and Boileau with the translations by Howes, Pitt, and Soame. Edited with introduction and notes. New York, G. E. Stechert and Co., 1892. lix + 303 pp.—Reprint 1926.

1925. Moulton, Chas. Wells, ed. The Library of Literary Criticism of English and American Authors. Vol. I: 680–1638; Vol. II: 1639–1729; Vol. III: 1730–1784; Vol. IV: 1785–1824; Vol. V: 1825–1854; Vol. VI: 1855–1874; Vol. VII: 1875–1890; Vol. VIII: 1891–1904. Buffalo, N.Y., Moulton Publ'ing Co., 1901–05. 8 (double column page) vols. —Reprint New York, Peter Smith, 1935.

1926. Saintsbury, Geo., ed. Loci Critici. Passages illustrative of critical theory and practice from Aristotle downwards. Boston, Ginn and Co., 1903. xi + 439 pp.

1927. Smith, G[eorge] G., ed. Elizabethan Critical Essays. Edited with an introduction. Oxford, Clarendon Press, 1904. 2 vols.

1928. Spingarn, Joel E., ed. Critical Essays of the Seventeenth Century. Vol. I: 1605–1650; Vol. II: 1650–1685; Vol. III: 1685–1700. Oxford, Clarendon Press, 1908–09. 3 vols.

1929. Jones, Edmund D., ed. English Critical Essays. Nineteenth century. Oxford Univ. Press, 1916. viii + 610 pp.—Volume CCVI in the series World's Classics. Frequent reprints, as in 1934.

1930. Criticism in America. Its functions and status. New York, Harcourt, Brace and Co., [1924]. 330 pp.—Essays by Irving Babbitt, Van Wyck Brooks, William C. Brownell, Ernest Boyd, T. S. Eliot, Henry L. Mencken, Stuart P. Sherman, Joel E. Spingarn, and George E. Woodberry.

1931. Mordell, Albert, ed. Notorious Literary Attacks. New York, Boni and Liveright, 1926. xlvii + 255 pp.

1932. Foerster, Norman, ed. Humanism and America. Essays on the outlook of modern civilization. New York, Farrar and Rinehart, 1930. xx + 294 pp.

1933. Gilbert, Allan H., ed. Literary Criticism. Plato to Dryden. New York, American Book Co., 1940. xii + 704 pp.—A collection of excerpts from key passages of English and Continental critics.

1934. Allen, Gay W., and Clark, Harry H., eds. Literary Criticism. Pope to Croce. New York, American Book Co., 1941. xii + 659 pp.

1935. Blackmur, R[ichard] P., Croce, Benedetto, Peyre, Henri M., Ransom, John C., Read, Herbert, and Tate, Allen. Lectures in Criticism. Introduction by Huntington Cairns. New York, Pantheon Books Inc., 1949. x + 209 pp.—Volume XVI in the Bollingen Series.

1936. Stallman, Robt. Wooster, ed. Critiques and Essays in Criticism 1920–1948. Representing the achievement of modern British and American critics. With a foreword by Cleanth Brooks. New York, Ronald Press Co., 1949. xxii + 571 pp.—"Bibliography," pp. 519–571.

1937. Levin, Harry, ed. Perspectives of Criticism. Cambridge, Mass., Harvard Univ. Press, 1950. xvii + 248 pp.—Number 20 in the series Harvard Studies in Comparative Literature.

1938. Stallman, Robt. W., ed. The Critic's Notebook. Minneapolis, University of Minnesota Press, 1950. xv + 303 pp.

1939. Bate, Walter Jackson, ed. Criticism. The major texts. New ed. New York, Harcourt, Brace and Co., 1955. xii + 610 pp.—Original ed. 1952.

1940. West, Ray B., Jr., ed. Essays in Modern Literary Criticism. New York, Rinehart and Co., 1952. xi + 611 pp.

1941. Rahv, Philip, ed. Literature in America. An anthology of literary criticism. New York, Meridian Books, 1957. 452 pp.—Number 11 in the series Meridian Books.

1942. Howe, Irving, ed. Modern Literary Criticism. An anthology. Boston, Beacon Press, 1958. 438 pp.

1943. Schorer, Mark, Miles, Josephine, and McKenzie, Gordon, eds. Criticism. The foundations of modern literary judgment. Rev. ed. New York, Harcourt, Brace and Co., 1958. 553 pp.—Original ed. 1948.

1944. Beaver, Harold, ed. American Critical Essays. Twentieth century. Oxford Univ. Press, 1959. 364 pp.

§72. ESSAYS BY INDIVIDUALS ON PHASES OF CRITICISM

1948. Babbitt, Irving. The New Laokoon. An essay on the confusion of the arts. Boston, Houghton Mifflin Co., 1910. xiv + 259 pp.—Frequent reprints, as in 1926.

1949. Waugh, Arthur. Tradition and Change. Studies in contemporary literature. New York, E. P. Dutton and Co., 1919. viii + 303 pp.

1950. Woolf, Virginia. The Common Reader. London, L. and V. Woolf, 1925. 305 pp.

1951. Raleigh, Walter. On Writing and Writers. Being extracts from his note-books. Selected and edited by George Gordon. London, Edward Arnold and Co., 1926. 221 pp.

1952. Read, Herbert. Reason and Romanticism. Essays in literary criticism. London, Faber and Gwyer Ltd., 1926. vii + 229 pp.

1953. Ralli, Augustus. Critiques. London, Longmans, Green and Co., 1927. 205 pp.

1954. Quiller-Couch, Arthur. Studies in Literature. First Series 1918. Second Series 1922. Third Series 1930. New York, G. P. Putnam's Sons, 1918–30. 3 vols.

1955. Wilson, Edmund. Axel's Castle. A study in the imaginative literature of 1870–1930. New York, Charles Scribner's Sons, 1931. 319 pp.—Reprint New York, Charles Scribner's Sons, [195–], in the (paperback) series Student's Editions.

1956. Eliot, T[homas] S. Selected Essays 1917–1932. London, Faber and Faber Ltd., 1932. 454 pp.

1957. Woolf, Virginia. The Second Common Reader. New York, Harcourt, Brace and Co., 1932. viii + 295 pp.

1958. Grierson, H[erbert] J. C. The Background of English Literature Classical and Romantic. And other collected essays and addresses. 2nd ed. London, Chatto and Windus, 1934. ix + 290 pp.—Original ed. 1925; second ed. reprinted 1950.

1959. Guérard, Albert L. Literature and Society. Boston, Lothrop, Lee and Shepard Co., 1935. xii + 451 pp.

1960. More, Paul Elmer. Selected Shelburne Essays. New York, Oxford Univ. Press, 1935. xiii + 297 pp.—Volume CCCCXXXIV in the series World's Classics.

1961. Farrell, James T. A Note on Literary Criticism. New York, Vanguard Press, 1936. 221 pp.—Studies in impressionism, humanism, propaganda, and left-wing literature.

1962. Read, Herbert. Art and Society. New York, Macmillan Co., 1937. xix + 282 pp.

1963. Zabel, Morton D. Literary Opinions in America. Essays illustrating the status, methods, and problems of criticism in the United States since the War. New York, Harper and Bros., 1937. 691 pp.

1964. Lewis, C[live] S. Rehabilitations and Other Essays. Oxford Univ. Press, 1939. ix + 197 pp.—Studies of Shelley, Dryden, Eliot, Morris, and high and low brows.

1965. Grierson, H[erbert] J. C. Essays and Addresses. London, Chatto and Windus, 1940. x + 275 pp.

1966. Wilson, Edmund. The Wound and the Bow. Seven studies in literature. Boston, Houghton Mifflin Co., 1941. 295 pp.—Reprint 1947.

1967. Dixon, W[illiam] Macneile. An Apology for the Arts. London, Edward Arnold and Co., 1944. 215 pp.—Reprints 1945, 1947.

1968. Eliot, T[homas] S. What Is a Classic? London, Faber and Faber, 1945. 32 pp.—An address delivered before the Virgil Society on the 16th of October 1944.

1969. Slochower, Harry. No Voice Is Wholly Lost. Writers and thinkers in war and peace. New York, Creative Age Press, 1945. xix + 404 pp.—"Critical Bibliography" [i.e. bibliography of literary criticism], pp. 383–396. A treatment of "aspects of alienation in our war epoch."

1970. Clark, Arthur M. Studies in Literary Modes. Edinburgh, Oliver and Boyd, 1946. vii + 218 pp.—Studies in the historical novel, satire, rhetoric, and rhyme.

1971. Connolly, Cyril. Enemies of Promise. Rev. ed. Boston, Little, Brown and Co., 1948. xii + 265 pp.—Original ed. 1939.

1972. Lovejoy, Arthur O. Essays in the History of Ideas. Baltimore, Johns Hopkins Press, 1948. xvii + 359 pp.—"Bibliography of the Published Writings of Arthur O. Lovejoy 1898–1948," pp. 339–344.

1973. Wilson, Edmund. The Triple Thinkers. Twelve essays on literary subjects. New York, Oxford Univ. Press, 1948. x + 270 pp.—Original ed. *The Triple Thinkers,* Ten essays on literature, New York, Harcourt, Brace and Co., 1938, [vii] + 289 pp.

1974. Auden, W[ystan] H. The Enchafèd Flood. Or the romantic iconography of the sea. New York, Random House, 1950. 154 pp.

1975. Ellis, Havelock. From Marlow to Shaw. The studies 1876–1936 in English Literature. Edited with a foreword by John Gawsworth. With a prefatory letter from Thomas Hardy. London, Williams and Norgate Ltd., 1950. 320 pp.

1976. Jameson, Storm. The Writer's Situation and Other Essays. London, Macmillan Co., 1950. vi + 200 pp.

1977. Lehman, John. The Open Night. London, Longmans, Green and Co., 1952. ix + 128 pp.

1978. Dobrée, Bonamy. The Broken Cistern. London, Cohen and West Ltd., 1954. ix + 158 pp.—The Clark Lectures 1952–53.

1979. Ker, Wm. P. On Modern Literature. Lectures and addresses. Edited by Terence Spencer and James Sutherland. Oxford Univ. Press, 1955. xviii + 282 pp.

1980. Daiches, David. Critical Approaches to Literature. Englewood Cliffs, N.J., Prentice-Hall Inc., 1956. xi + 404 pp.

1981. James, Henry. Literary Reviews and Essays on American, English, and French Literature. Edited by Albert Mordell. New York, Twayne Publ'ers, 1957. 409 pp.—Also New York, Grove Press, 1957, number 116 in the series Evergreen Books.

1982. Read, Herbert. The Tenth Muse. Essays in criticism. London, Routledge and Kegan Paul, 1957. xi + 331 pp.—Reprint New York, Grove Press, 1958, number 153 in the series Evergreen Books.

1983. Russell, Bertrand. Understanding History and Other Essays. New York, Philosophical Library, 1957. 122 pp.

1984. Senior, John. The Way Down and Out. The occult in symbolist literature. Ithaca, N.Y., Cornell Univ. Press, 1959. xxvi + 217 pp.

§73. THE NEW CRITICISM: ITS FORESHADOWING, ITS BASIC VOICES, ITS EXTENSIONS

[A category on the New Criticism seems necessary, but what titles should be included few would agree on. What follows is simply a list of titles frequently cited in course calendars and reading lists devoted to the basic dogma of the school. Many of the works of Cleanth Brooks, John Crowe Ransom, Allen Tate, and Robert Penn Warren, whatever category they may appear in here, can also be considered New Critical. Whether T. S. Eliot and I. A. Richards should be included now seems debatable. William Van O'Connor's article (no. 2003) is an excellent detached history of the school.]

1988. Spingarn, J[oel] E. The New Criticism. A lecture delivered at Columbia University March 9, 1910. New York, Columbia Univ. Press, 1911. v + 35 pp.—Reprint in Spingarn's *Creative Criticism*, Essays on the unity of genius and taste, New York, Henry Holt and Co., 1917, 138 pp., of which a "new and enl. ed." appeared New York, Harcourt, Brace and Co., 1931, viii + 221 pp.

1989. Eliot, T[homas] S. The Sacred Wood. Essays on poetry and criticism. London, Methuen and Co., 1920. xviii + 155 pp.—Frequent reprints, as in 1948.

1990. Calverton, Victor F. The Newer Spirit. A sociological criticism of literature. New York, Boni and Liveright, 1925. xvi + 284 pp.

1991. Richards, I[vor] A. Principles of Literary Criticism. 2nd ed. New York, Harcourt, Brace and Co., 1926. vi + 290 pp.—Original ed. 1924; second ed. often reprinted, as in 1938.

1992. Eliot, T[homas] S. For Lancelot Andrewes. Essays on style and order. London, Faber and Gwyer, 1928. xii + 13–143 pp.

1993. Richards, Ivor A. Practical Criticism. A study of literary judgment. London, Routledge and Kegan Paul, 1929. xiii + 375 pp.—Frequent reprints, as in 1948.

1994. Burke, Kenneth. Counter-Statement. New York, Harcourt, Brace and Co., 1931. xiii + 268 pp.

1995. Leavis, F[rank] R. For Continuity. Cambridge, Eng., Minority Press, 1933. 219 pp.

1996. Dewey, John. Art as Experience. New York, Minton, Balch and Co., 1934. viii + 355 pp.

1997. Eliot, T[homas] S. After Strange Gods. A primer of modern heresy. New York, Harcourt, Brace and Co., 1934. 72 pp.—The Page-Barbour Lectures at the University of Virginia 1933.

1998. Blackmur, R[ichard] P. The Double Agent. Essays in craft and elucidation. New York, Arrow Editions, 1935. [v] + 302 pp.

1999. Ransom, John Crowe. The World's Body. New York, Charles Scribner's Sons, 1938. xvii + 350 pp.

2000. Brooks, Cleanth. Modern Poetry and the Tradition. Chapel Hill, University of North Carolina Press, 1939. xiii + 253 pp.—"A Selected Bibliography of Modern Criticism," p. 245.

2001. Blackmur, Richard P. The Expense of Greatness. New York, Arrow Editions, 1940. 305 pp.

2002. Burke, Kenneth. The Philosophy of Literary Form. Baton Rouge, Louisiana State University Press, 1941. xvii + 455 pp.

2003. Ransom, John Crowe. The New Criticism. Norfolk, Conn., New Directions, 1941. xiii + 339 pp.—See also William V. O'Connor, "A Short View of the New Criticism," *College English,* XI, 2 (Nov. 1949), 63–71.

2004. Eliot, T[homas] S. Points of View. London, Faber and Faber Ltd., 1942. 158 pp.

2005. Burke, Kenneth. A Grammar of Motives. New York, Prentice-Hall Inc., 1945. xxiii + 530 pp.

2006. Empson, Wm. Seven Types of Ambiguity. 2nd ed. Norfolk, Conn., New Directions, 1947. xv + 258 pp.—Original ed. 1930; second ed. reprinted 1949. Reprint New York, Meridian Books Inc., 1955, xix + 298 pp., number 11 in the series Meridian Books, with "Note for the Third Edition," pp. xviii–xix.

2007. Hyman, Stanley E. The Armed Vision. A study in the methods of modern literary criticism. New York, Alfred A. Knopf, 1948. xv + 417 + xxii pp.—Reprint New York, Vintage Books, 1955, xiii + 402 + xxvii, number K20 in the series Vintage Books, with the note "Revised Edition, Abridged by the Author."

2008. Tate, Allen. On the Limits of Poetry. Selected essays 1928–1948. New York, Swallow Press and William Morrow and Co., 1948. xviii + 379 pp.

2009. Burke, Kenneth. A Rhetoric of Motives. New York, Prentice-Hall Inc., 1950. xv + 340 pp.

2010. Ransom, John C., ed. The Kenyon Critics. Studies in modern literature from The Kenyon Review. Cleveland, World Publ'ing Co., 1951. x + 342 pp.

2011. Trilling, Lionel. The Liberal Imagination. New York, Viking Press, 1951. xvi + 303 pp.

2012. Crane, R[onald] S., ed. Critics and Criticism Ancient and Modern. By R. S. Crane, W. R. Keast, Richard McKeon, Norman MacLean, Elder Olson, Bernard Weinberg. University of Chicago Press, 1952. v + 649 pp.—An anthology of criticism by critics of the "Chicago School." Abridged ed. University of Chicago Press, 1957, vii + 276 pp., number 15 in the series Phoenix Books.

2013. Leavis, F[rank] R. The Common Pursuit. London, Chatto and Windus, 1952. viii + 9–307 pp.

2014. O'Connor, Wm. V. An Age of Criticism. Chicago, Henry Regnery Co., 1952. ix + 182 pp.

2015. Tate, Allen. The Forlorn Demon. Didactic and critical essays. Chicago, Henry Regnery Co., 1953. xi + 180 pp.

2016. Hulme, T[homas] E. Speculations. Essays on humanism and the philosophy of art. Edited by Herbert Read with a foreword by Jacob Epstein. 2nd ed. London, George Routledge and Co., 1954. xvi + 271 pp. —Original ed. 1924. Also *Further Speculations,* edited by S. Hynes, Minneapolis, University of Minnesota Press, 1955, xxxi + 226 pp.

2017. Wheelwright, Philip. The Burning Fountain. A study in the language of symbolism. Bloomington, University of Indiana Press, 1954. 406 pp.

2018. Wimsatt, W[illiam] K., Jr. The Verbal Icon. Studies in the meaning of poetry. And two preliminary essays written in collaboration with Monroe C. Beardsley. Lexington, University of Kentucky Press, 1954. xviii + 299 pp.

2019. Blackmur, R[ichard] P. The Lion and the Honeycomb. New York, Harcourt, Brace and Co., 1955. viii + 309 pp.—A study chiefly of the artist and his nature.

2020. Richards, I[vor] A. Speculative Instruments. University of Chicago Press, 1955. xii + 216 pp.

2021. Tindall, Wm. York. The Literary Symbol. New York, Columbia Univ. Press, 1955. ix + 278 pp.—Reprint, Bloomington, Indiana Univ. Press, 1955, number 7 in the series Midland Books.

2022. Trilling, Lionel. The Opposing Self. Nine essays in criticism. New York, Viking Press, 1955. xv + 232 pp.—Reprint, New York, Viking Press, 1959, number 49 in the series Compass Books.

2023. Rahv, Philip. Image and Idea. Twenty essays on literary themes. New York, New Directions, 1957. x + 241 pp.

2024. Nott, Kathleen. The Emperor's Clothes. London, William Heinemann Ltd., 1958. 328 pp.—American reprint Bloomington, Indiana Univ. Press, 1958, number 9 in the series Midland Books. An antidote to prevailing critical orthodoxy.

2025. Cowan, Louise. The Fugitive Group. A literary history. Baton Rouge, Louisiana State Univ. Press, 1959. 288 pp.—A study of Curry, Davidson, Moore, Ransom, Tate, and Warren.

2026. MacCaffrey, Isabel Gamble. Paradise Lost as Myth. Cambridge, Mass., Harvard Univ. Press, 1959. [x] + 229 pp.

§74. PRINCIPLES OF REVIEWING

[See also §87. Periodicals That Are Primarily Review Organs.]

2030. Mallory, Herbert S., ed. Backgrounds of Book Reviewing. Ann Arbor, Mich., George Wahr Publ'er, 1923. xvi + 533 pp.

2031. Wells, Henry. The Judgment of Literature. Introduction by Philip N. Youtz. New York, W. W. Norton Co., 1928. x + 11–95 pp.—In the series An Outline of Aesthetics.

2032. Swinnerton, Frank. The Reviewing and Criticism of Books. With a foreword by Martin Dent. London, J. M. Dent and Sons, 1939. 43 pp. —The Ninth Dent Memorial Lecture.

2033. Greene, Theodore M. The Arts and the Art of Criticism. Princeton, N.J., University Press, 1940. xxx + 690 pp.—A treatment which includes also music.

2034. Peyre, Henri. Writers and Their Critics. A study of misunderstanding. Ithaca, N.Y., Cornell Univ. Press, 1944. xii + 340 pp.

2035. Drewry, John E. Book Reviewing. Boston, Writer Inc., 1945. ix + 228 pp.

2036. Gardiner, Harold C., S.J. Tenets for Readers and Reviewers. Rev. and enl. ed. New York, America Press, [1948]. 48 pp.—Original ed. 1944.

2037. Merritt, LeRoy C., Boaz, Martha, and Tisdel, Kenneth S. Reviews in Library Book Selection. Foreword by Maurice F. Tauber. Detroit, Mich., Wayne State Univ. Press, 1958. xv + 188 pp.—Number 3 in the series Wayne State University Studies: Humanities.

§75. THE AUTHOR-PATRON-PUBLISHER-AUDIENCE RELATIONSHIP

[See also §96. Library and Publisher Periodicals.]

2041. Putnam, Geo. Haven. Authors and Their Public in Ancient Times. A sketch of literary conditions and of the relations with the public of literary producers, from the earliest times to the invention of printing. New York, G. P. Putnam's Sons, 1893. xvii + 309 pp.

2042. Collins, A[rthur] S. Authorship in the Days of Johnson. Being a study of the relations between author, patron, publisher, and public 1726–1784. London, R. Holden and Co., 1927. 278 pp.

2043. Collins, A[rthur] S. The Profession of Letters. A study of the relation of author to patron, publisher, and public. 1780–1832. London, G. Routledge and Sons, 1928. 279 pp.—"Bibliography of Books Used," pp. 270–273.

2044. Kellett, Ernest E. The Whirligig of Taste. London, Hogarth Press, 1929. 160 pp.—Number 8 in the series Hogarth Lectures on Literature.

2045. Cruse, Amy. The Englishman and His Books in the Early Nineteenth Century. New York, Thomas Y. Crowell Co., [1930]. 301 pp.

2046. Kellett, Ernest E. Fashion in Literature. A study of changing taste. London, George Routledge and Sons, 1931. 369 pp.

2047. Cruse, Amy. The Victorians and Their Reading. Boston, Houghton Mifflin Co., 1935. 444 pp.

2048. Cruse, Amy. After the Victorians. London, George Allen and Unwin Ltd., 1938. 264 pp.—A history of the reading audience 1887–1914.

2049. Link, Henry C., and Hopf, Harry Arthur. People and Books. A study of reading and book-buying habits. New York, Book Industry Committee, 1946. 167 pp.

2050. Mott, Frank Luther. Golden Multitudes. The story of best sellers in the United States. New York, Macmillan Co., 1947. xiii + 357 pp.

2051. Hart, James D. The Popular Book. A history of America's literary taste. New York, Oxford Univ. Press, 1950. 351 pp.

2052. Hackett, Alice Payne. Sixty Years of Best Sellers 1895–1955. New York, R. R. Bowker Co., 1956. xi + 260 pp.

2053. Altick, Richard D. The English Common Reader. A social history of the mass reading public 1800–1900. University of Chicago Press, 1957. ix + 430 pp.—"Chronology of the Mass Reading Public 1774–1900," pp. 379–380; "Best Sellers," pp. 381–390; "Periodical and Newspaper Circulation," pp. 391–396; "Bibliography," pp. 397–409.

§76. SATIRE AND IRONY AND ITS BACKGROUND

2057. Meredith, Geo. An Essay on Comedy and the Uses of the Comic Spirit. 2nd ed. Westminster, Eng., A. Constable and Co., 1898. 105 pp.—Original ed. 1877 in the April issue of the *New Quarterly Magazine*. Edition by Lane Cooper, New York, Charles Scribner's Sons, 1918, ix + 326 pp.; Cooper ed. reprinted Ithaca, N.Y., Cornell Univ. Press, 1956.

2058. Alden, Raymond Macdonald. The Rise of Formal Satire in England under Classical Influence. Philadelphia, University of Pennsylvania Press, 1899. vii + 264 pp.—Volume VII, no. 2, in the Publications of the University of Pennsylvania Series in Philology. Bibliography, pp. 247–249.

2059. Walker, Hugh. English Satire and Satirists. London, J. M. Dent and Sons, 1925. x + 325 pp.—In the series Channels of English Literature.

2060. Turner, F[rancis] McD. C. The elements of Irony in English Literature. An essay. Cambridge Univ. Press, 1926. vii + 109.

2061. Thomson, J[ames] A. K. Irony. An historical introduction. Cambridge, Mass., Harvard Univ. Press, 1927. [vii] + 242 pp.

2062. Jancke, Rudolf. Das Wesen der Ironie. Eine Strukturanalyse ihrer Erscheinungsformen. Leipzig, J. A. Barth, 1929. vi + 111 pp.

2063. Wolfe, Humbert. Notes on English Verse Satire. New York, Harcourt, Brace and Co., 1929. 158 pp.—Number 10 in the series Hogarth Lectures on Literature.

2064. Kitchin, Geo. A Survey of Burlesque and Parody in English. Edinburgh, Oliver and Boyd, 1931. xxiii + 337 pp.

2065. Duff, J[ohn] Wight. Roman Satire. Its outlook on social life. Berkeley, University of California Press, 1936. [ix] + 205 pp.—Volume XII in the series Sather Classical Lectures.

2066. Birney, Earle. English Irony before Chaucer. University of Toronto Quarterly, VI, 4 (July 1937), 538–557.

2067. Worcester, David. The Art of Satire. Cambridge, Mass., Harvard Univ. Press, 1940. ix + 191 pp.

2068. Sedgewick, Garnett Gladwin. Of Irony Especially in Drama. University of Toronto Press, 1935. ix + 127 pp.—The Alexander Lectures 1934. Reprint 1948.

2069. Thompson, Alan Reynolds. The Dry Mock. A study of irony in drama. Berkeley, University of California Press, 1948. ix + 278 pp.

2070. Knox, Edmund Valpy. The Mechanism of Satire. Cambridge Univ. Press, 1951. 31 pp.—The Leslie Stephen Lecture 1951.

2071. Clinton-Baddeley, Victor Clinton. The Burlesque Tradition in the English Theatre after 1660. London, Methuen and Co., [1952]. xvi + 152 pp.

2072. Holden, Wm. P. Anti-Puritan Satire 1572–1642. New Haven, Yale Univ. Press, 1954. xii + 165 pp.—Volume CXXVI in the series Yale Studies in English. Bibliography, pp. 155–158.

2073. Leyburn, Ellen Douglas. Satiric Allegory: Mirror of Man. New Haven, Yale Univ. Press, 1956. vii + 142 pp.—Volume CXXX in the series Yale Studies in English.

2074. Peter, John. Complaint and Satire in Early English Literature. Oxford, Clarendon Press, 1956. [ix] + 323 pp.

2075. Sypher, Wylie, ed. Comedy. An essay on comedy by George Meredith. Laughter [by] Henri Bergson. Introduction and appendix The Meanings of Comedy by Wylie Sypher. Garden City, N.Y., Doubleday and Co., 1956. xvi + 260 pp.

2076. Hopkins, Kenneth. Portraits in Satire. London, Barrie Books, 1958. xii + 290 pp.—A treatment of satire in English verse.

2077. Sutherland, James. English Satire. Cambridge Univ. Press, 1958. [ix] + 174 pp.—The Clark Lecture 1956.

2078. Sharpe, Robt. Boies. Irony in the Drama. An essay in impersonation, shock, and catharsis. Chapel Hill, University of North Carolina Press, [1959]. xv + 222 pp.

§77. RELIGION AND LITERATURE

[See also §88. Journals of Psychology and Religion.]

2082. Brooke, Stopford A. Theology in the English Poets. Cowper, Coleridge, Wordsworth, and Burns. London, Henry S. King, 1874. ix + 339 pp.—Reprint London, J. M. Dent and Co., 1915, in the series Everyman's Library.

2083. Frothingham, Octavius Brooks. Transcendentalism in New England. A history. New York, G. P. Putnam's Sons, 1876. ix + 395 pp.—Reprint New York, Harper and Bros., 1959, xxix + 386 pp.

2084. Church, R[ichard] W. The Oxford Movement. Twelve years 1833–1845. 3rd ed. London, Macmillan Co., 1892. xv + 416 pp.—Original ed. 1891; third ed. reprinted 1932.

2085. Scudder, Vida D. The Life of the Spirit in Modern English Poets. Boston, Houghton Mifflin Co., 1895. v + 349 pp.

2086. Goddard, Harold Clarke. Studies in New England Transcendentalism. New York, Columbia Univ. Press, 1908. 217 pp.—Volume II, no. 3, in the 2nd series Columbia University Studies in English. Reprint New York, Hillary House, 1959.

2087. Chapman, Edward M. English Literature in Account with Religion 1800–1900. Boston, Houghton Mifflin Co., 1910. xiii + 578 pp.

2088. Fisher, Lizette A. The Mystic Vision in the Grail Legend and in the Divine Comedy. New York, Columbia Univ. Press, 1917. xi + 148 pp.—In the series Columbia University Studies in English and Comparative Literature.

2089. Robinson, Gertrude. In a Mediaeval Library. A study in pre-Reformation religious literature. London, Sands and Co., 1918. x + 243 pp.

2090. Osmond, Percy H. The Mystical Poets of the English Church. London, S.P.C.K., 1919. xi + 436 pp.

2091. Spurgeon, Caroline F. E. Mysticism in English Literature. 2nd ed. Cambridge Univ. Press, 1922. 168 pp.—In the series Cambridge Manuals of Science and Literature. Original ed. 1913; second ed. reprinted 1927.

2092. Kerr, Hugh Thompson. The Gospel in Modern Poetry. New York, Fleming H. Revell Co., 1926. 187 pp.

2093. Atkins, Gaius G. Reinspecting Victorian Religion. A back to normal critique. New York, Macmillan Co., 1928. 151 pp.—The Samuel Harris Lectures on Literature, Bangor Theological Seminary, 1928.

2094. Bloor, Robt. Henry Underwood. Christianity and the Religious Drama. Boston, American Unitarian Association, 1928. 64 pp.—In the series Essex Hall Lectures.

2095. Schuster, Geo. N. The Catholic Spirit in Modern English Literature. New York, Macmillan Co., 1928. xiii + 365 pp.

2096. Cargill, Oscar. Drama and Liturgy. New York, Columbia Univ. Press, 1930. ix + 151 pp.—In the series Columbia University Studies in English and Comparative Literature.

2097. Schneider, Herbert W. The Puritan Mind. New York, Henry Holt and Co., 1930. 3–301 pp.—Volume I in Studies in Religion and Culture: American Religion Series.

2098. Macaulay, Rose. Some Religious Elements in English Literature. New York, Harcourt, Brace and Co., 1931. 160 pp.—Number 14 in the series Hogarth Lectures on Literature.

2099. Horning, Sister Mary Eulogia. Evidences of Romantic Treatment of Religious Elements in Late Eighteenth-Century Minor Poetry 1771–1800. Washington, D.C., Catholic Univ. of America, 1932. ix + 103 pp.

2100. Os, A[rnold] B. van. Religious Visions. The development of the eschatological elements in mediaeval English religious literature. Amsterdam, Holland, H. J. Paris, 1932. 286 pp.

2101. Knight, G[eorge] Wilson. The Christian Renaissance. With interpretations of Dante, Shakespeare, and Goethe and a note on T. S. Eliot. Toronto, Macmillan Co., 1933. x + 374 pp.

2102. White, Helen C. The Metaphysical Poets. A study in religious experience. New York, Macmillan Co., 1936. xi + 444 pp.

2103. Haller, Wm. The Rise of Puritanism. Or the way to the New Jerusalem as set forth in pulpit and press from Thomas Cartwright to John Lilburne and John Milton 1570–1643. New York, Columbia Univ. Press, 1938. ix + 464 pp.—"Bibliographical Notes," pp. 405–440. Reprint

New York, Harper and Bros., 1957, xi + 464 pp., number 22 in the series Harper Torchbooks.

2104. Eliot, T[homas] S. The Idea of a Christian Society. London, Faber and Faber Ltd., 1939. 99 pp.—"Three lectures . . . with some revision and division . . . delivered in March 1939 at . . . Corpus Christi College, Cambridge," Preface.

2105. Collins, Joseph B., S.S. Christian Mysticism in the Elizabethan Age. With its background in mystical methodology. Baltimore, Johns Hopkins Press, 1940. xv + 251 pp.

2106. Wilder, Amos N. The Spiritual Aspects of the New Poetry. New York, Harper and Bros., 1940. xxiv + 262 pp.—"Orientation and Reading Guide," pp. 235–249.

2107. McLachlan, H[erbert]. The Religious Opinions of Milton, Locke, and Newton. Manchester, Eng., University Press, 1941. vii + 221 pp.—Number 276 in the series Publications of the University of Manchester: Theological Series VI.

2108. Plumb, Harry Grant. Restoration Puritanism. A study of the growth of English liberty. Chapel Hill, University of North Carolina Press, 1943. ix + 129 pp.—"Selected Bibliography," pp. 103–123.

2109. Doughty, W[illiam] L. Studies in Religious Poetry of the Seventeenth Century. London, Epworth Press, 1946. xiv + 200 pp.

2110. Hutton, Edward. Catholicism and English Literature. 2nd ed. London, Frederick Muller Ltd., 1948. 223 pp.—Original ed. 1942.

2111. Ruggiero, Guido de. Existentialism. Disintegration of man's soul. Introduction by Rayner Heppenstall. New York, Social Sciences Publ'ers, 1948. 96 pp.

2112. Murdock, Kenneth B. Literature and Theology in Colonial New England. Cambridge, Mass., Harvard Univ. Press, 1949. xi + 235 pp.

2113. Brown, W[inifred] E. M. The Polished Shaft. Studies in the purpose and influence of the Christian writer in the eighteenth century. London, S.P.C.K., 1950. viii + 132 pp.

2114. Cragg, G[erald] R. From Puritanism to the Age of Reason. A study of changes in religious thought within the Church of England 1660 to 1700. Cambridge Univ. Press, 1950. vii + 247 pp.—"Bibliography," pp. 231–242.

2115. Woodhouse, A[rthur] S. P., ed. Puritanism and Liberty. Being the Army Debates (1647–9) from the Clarke Manuscripts with supplementary documents. Foreword by A. D. Lindsay. 2nd ed. London, J. M. Dent and Sons, 1950. 506 pp.—Original ed. 1938.

2116. Ralli, Augustus. Poetry and Faith. London, Bodley Head Ltd., 1951. 160 pp.

2117. Baker, Herschel. The Wars of Truth. Studies in the decay of Christian humanism in the earlier seventeenth century. Cambridge, Mass., Harvard Univ. Press, 1952. xi + 390 pp.—"Bibliography," pp. 367–376.

2118. Wilder, Amos N. Modern Poetry and the Christian Tradition. A study in the relation of Christianity to culture. New York, Charles Scribner's Sons, 1952. xviii + 287 pp.—Number 16 in the Bross Library.

2119. Watkin, E[dward] I. Poets and Mystics. London, Sheed and Ward, 1953. ix + 318 pp.

2120. Martz, Louis L. The Poetry of Meditation. A study in English religious literature of the seventeenth century. New Haven, Yale Univ. Press, 1954. xv + 375 pp.—Volume CXXV in the series Yale Studies in English. "Bibliography," pp. 357–366.

2121. Ross, Malcolm MacKenzie. Poetry and Dogma. The transfiguration of eucharistic symbols in seventeenth century English poetry. New Brunswick, N.J., Rutgers Univ. Press, 1954. xiii + 256 pp.

2122. Stromberg, Roland. Religious Liberalism in Eighteenth Century England. Oxford Univ. Press, 1954. 192 pp.

2123. Simpson, Alan. Puritanism in Old and New England. University of Chicago Press, 1955. 125 pp.

2124. MacIver, R[obert] M., ed. Great Moral Dilemmas in Literature Past and Present. New York, Institute for Religious and Social Studies, 1956. viii + 189 pp.

2125. Fairchild, Hoxie Neale. Religious Trends in English Poetry. Vol. I: 1700–1740 Protestantism and the Cult of Sentiment; Vol. II: 1740–1780 Religious Sentimentalism in the Age of Johnson; Vol. III: 1780–1830 Romantic Faith; Vol. IV: 1830–1880 Christianity and Romanticism in the Victorian Era. New York, Columbia Univ. Press, 1939–57. 4 vols.

2126. Rupp, Gordon. Six Makers of English Religion 1500–1700. London, Hodder and Stoughton, 1957. xii + 13–127 pp.—A treatment of Tyndale, Cranmer, Foxe, Milton, Bunyan, and Watts.

2127. Scott, Nathan A., Jr., ed. The Tragic Vision and the Christian Faith. New York, Association Press, 1957. xxii + 23–346 pp.—In the series Haddam House Books.

2128. Scott, Nathan A., Jr. Modern Literature and the Religious Frontier. New York, Harper and Bros., 1958. xv + 138 pp.

2129. Wilder, Amos N. Theology and Modern Literature. Cambridge, Mass., Harvard Univ. Press, 1958. x + 145 pp.—The William Belden Noble Lectures 1956.

2130. Stewart, Randall. American Literature and Christian Doctrine. Baton Rouge, Louisiana State Univ. Press, 1959. 176 pp.

§78. SCIENCE, PSYCHOLOGY, AND LITERATURE

[See also §88. Journals of Psychology and Religion.]

2134. Mordell, Albert. The Erotic Motive in Literature. New York, Boni and Liveright, 1919. 250 pp.

2135. Whitehead, Alfred North. Science and the Modern World. New York, Macmillan Co., 1925. xii + 304 pp.—The Lowell Lectures 1925. Frequent reprints, as in 1948.

2136. Richards, I[vor] A. Science and Poetry. New York, W. W. Norton and Co., 1926. 96 pp.—Volume II in the New Science Series.

2137. Eastman, Max. The Literary Mind. Its place in an age of science. New York, Charles Scribner's Sons, 1935. xi + 343 pp.

2138. Johnson, Francis R. Astronomical Thought in Renaissance England. A study of English scientific writings from 1500 to 1645. Baltimore, Johns Hopkins Press, 1937. xv + 355 pp.—See also Francis R. Johnson and Sanford V. Larkey, "Science," *Modern Language Quarterly*, II, 3 (Sept. 1941), 363–401, for a survey of the state of scholarship in the field of Renaissance science.

2139. Basler, Roy P. Sex, Symbolism, and Psychology in Literature. New Brunswick, N.J., Rutgers Univ. Press, 1948. 226 pp.

2140. Bonaparte, Marie. The Life and Works of Edgar Allan Poe. A psychoanalytic interpretation. Foreword by Sigmund Freud. Translated by John Rodker. London, Imago Publ'ing Co., 1949. xi + 749 pp.—Original Fr. ed. 1933 in 2 vols.; reprint of Eng. tr. 1952.

2141. Jones, Ernest. Hamlet and Oedipus. New York, W. W. Norton and Co., 1949. 166 pp.—Reprint Garden City, N.Y., Doubleday and Co., [195–], 194 pp., number 31 in the series Anchor Books.

2142. Wormhoudt, Arthur. The Demon Lover. A psychoanalytical approach to literature. Introduction by Edmund Bergler. New York, Exposition Press, 1949. 150 pp.—A treatment *inter alios* of Byron, Keats, and Shelley.

2143. Bergler, Edmund. The Writer and Psychoanalysis. Garden City, N.Y., Doubleday and Co., 1950. xvii + 265 pp.

2144. Bush, Douglas. Science and English Poetry. A historical sketch 1590–1950. New York, Oxford Univ. Press, 1950. ix + 166 pp.—The Patten Lectures, Indiana University.

2145. Lucas, F[rank] L. Literature and Psychology. London, Cassell and Co., 1951. 340 pp.

2146. Werblowsky, Raphael Jehudah Zwi. Lucifer and Prometheus. A study of Milton's Satan. With an introduction by C. G. Jung. London, Routledge and Kegan Paul, 1952. xix + 120 pp.

2147. Evans, B[enjamin] I. Literature and Science. London, George Allen and Unwin Ltd., 1954. 114 pp.

2148. Hoffman, Frederick J. Freudianism and the Literary Mind. 2nd ed. Baton Rouge, Louisiana State Univ. Press, 1957. viii + 350 pp.—Original ed. 1945.

2149. Fiedler, Leslie A. Love and Death in the American Novel. New York, Criterion Books, 1960. 603 pp.

2150. Fraiberg, Louis. Psychoanalysis and American Literary Criticism. Detroit, Wayne State Univ. Press, 1960. xi + 263 pp.—Bibliographical notes, pp. 241–258.

CHAPTER VI

PERIODICALS AND SERIES

[For bibliographies and finding lists see Chapter XI: Journalistic Art, Periodical and Newspaper Bibliographies, and Publication Rights.]

§79. MEDIEVAL PERIODICALS

2154. Mediaevalia. Collana di studi e di testi latini e greci medievali. Bologna, Istituto di filologia classica, 1951–date.—Quarterly.

2155. Mediaeval Studies. Toronto, Pontifical Institute of Mediaeval Studies, 1939–date.—Quarterly. Abbr.: *MS.*

2156. Medium Aevum. Journal of the Society for the Study of Mediaeval Languages. Oxford, Eng., Basil Blackwell, 1932–date.—Irregular issues. Reviews. Abbr.: *MAE.*

2157. Moyen âge. Revue d'histoire et de philologie. Brussels, Belgium, 1888–date.—Irregular issues. Reviews. Abbr.: *MA.*

2158. Revue du moyen âge latin. Études, textes, chronique, bibliographie. Strasbourg, Université de Strasbourg, Centre national de la recherche scientifique, 1945–date.—Quarterly. Abstracts. Reviews. Abbr.: *RMAL.*

2159. Speculum. A journal of mediaeval studies. Cambridge, Mass., Mediaeval Academy of America, 1925–date.—Quarterly. Reviews. "Bibliography of Periodical Literature" and "Books Received" in each issue.

§80. SCHOLARLY JOURNALS

2163. American Journal of Philology. Baltimore, Johns Hopkins Press, 1880–date.—Quarterly. Reviews. Now exclusively devoted to classical antiquity, but early issues contain articles in the field of English philology. Abbr.: *AJP.*

2164. American Literature. A journal of literary history, criticism, and bibliography. Durham, N.C., Duke Univ. Press, 1929–date.—Quarterly.

Reviews. Published with the cooperation of the American Literature Group of the Modern Language Association. Current bibliography in each issue. Abbr.: *AL.*

2165. American Notes and Queries. A medium of intercommunication for literary men, general readers, etc. Philadelphia, Vol. I (1888)—Vol. IX (1892). Appearance irregular.—Successors *Searcher,* An American Notes and Queries, Philadelphia, No. 1 (1895)—No. 23 (1896); *American Notes and Queries,* A journal for the curious, New York 1941–1950.

2166. Anglia. Zeitschrift für englische Philologie. Tübingen, Max Niemeyer Verlag, 1877–date.—Quarterly. Reviews.

2167. Archiv für das Studium der neueren Sprachen. Mit Literaturblatt und Bibliographie. Braunschweig, Georg Westermann Verlag, 1846–date.—Quarterly. Reviews. Occasional articles on English literature. Often called "Herrig's Archiv." Abbr.: *Archiv.*

2168. Beiträge zur Geschichte der deutschen Sprache und Literatur. Halle a. S., Max Niemeyer Verlag, 1888–date.—Irregular issues. Occasional articles on English literature. Abbr.: *BGDSL.*

2169. Boston University Graduate Journal. A review of current graduate and research activities. Boston Univ. Graduate School, 1952–date.—Monthly September through June.

2170. E L H. A journal of English literary history. Baltimore, Johns Hopkins University, Tudor and Stuart Club, 1934–date.—Quarterly. March issue 1936–49 "The Romantic Movement, A selective and critical bibliography." Abbr.: *ELH.*

2171. English. Literature, criticism, teaching. Oxford Univ. Press for the English Association, 1906–date.—Three issues a year. Reviews.

2172. English Studies. A journal of English letters and philology. Amsterdam, Swets en Zeitlinger, 1919–date.—One issue every two months. Reviews. Abbr.: *ES.*

2173. Essays and Studies by Members of the English Association. Oxford Univ. Press, 1910–date.—Annual. Abbr.: *E&S.*

2174. Essays by Divers Hands. Being the transactions of the Royal Society of Literature of the United Kingdom. Oxford Univ. Press, 1921–date.—Annual. Abbr.: *EDH.*

2175. Études anglaises. Grande-Bretagne, États-Unis. Paris, Librairie Marcel Didier, 1937–date.—Quarterly. Reviews. Title 1924–35 *Revue anglo-américaine.* Abbr.: *EA.*

2176. Journal of English and Germanic Philology. Devoted to the English, German, and Scandinavian languages and literatures. Urbana, University of Illinois, 1887–date.—Quarterly. Reviews. Former title *Journal of Germanic Philology.* Abbr.: *JEGP.*

2177. Leuvense Bijdragen. Tijdschrift voor moderne philologie. The Hague, Martinus Nijhoff, 1896–date.—Quarterly. Abstracts. Reviews. Occasional articles on English literature. Abbr.: *LB.*

2178. Modern Language Notes. Baltimore, Johns Hopkins Press, 1886–date. —Monthly November through June. Reviews. Brief articles in a modern language on English, American, Romance, or Germanic literary or linguistic subjects. Abbr.: *MLN*.

2179. Modern Language Quarterly. Seattle, University of Washington, 1940. —Reviews. June issue "Bibliography of Critical Arthurian Literature." Abbr.: *MLQ*.

2180. Modern Language Review. A quarterly journal devoted to the study of medieval and modern literature and philology. Cambridge Univ. Press for the Modern Humanities Research Association, 1905–date.— Reviews. Title 1897–1904 (7 vols.) *Modern Language Quarterly*. Abbr.: *MLR*.

2181. Modern Philology. A journal devoted to research in medieval and modern literature. University of Chicago Press, 1903–date.—Quarterly. Reviews. Victorian bibliography. Abbr.: *MP*.

2182. Monatshefte. A journal devoted to the study of German language and literature. Madison, Wis., Modern Language Association of the Central West and South: German Section, 1899–date.—Eight issues a year. Reviews. Occasional articles on English literature in German or English.

2183. Neophilologus. Groningen, Holland, J. B. Wolters, 1916–date.—Quarterly. Abstracts. Reviews. Articles in various languages. Abbr.: *Neophil.*

2184. Neuphilologische Mitteilungen. Helsinki, Société néophilologique de Helsinki, 1899–date.—Eight issues a year. Reviews. Occasional articles on English literature in various languages. Abbr.: *NM*.

2185. Neuphilologische Zeitschrift. Berlin, Pädagogischer Verlag, 1949–date. —One issue every two months. Reviews. Articles in English as well as German.

2186. Notes and Queries. For readers and writers, collectors and librarians. Oxford Univ. Press, 1849–date.—Two issues a month. Reviews. Abbr.: *N&Q*.

2187. Philological Quarterly. A journal devoted to scholarly investigation of the classical and modern languages and literatures. Iowa City, State Univ. of Iowa, 1922–date.—April issue "The Romantic Movement, A selective and critical bibliography"; July issue "English Literature 1660–1800, A current bibliography." Abbr.: *PQ*.

2188. Publications of the Modern Language Association of America. New York, Modern Language Association of America, 1884–date.—Six issues a year, one being a directory of members and one other a bibliography of scholarly works which appeared in the year immediately preceding. Abbr.: *PMLA*.

2189. Review of English Studies. A quarterly journal of English literature and the English language. Oxford Univ. Press, 1925–date.—Reviews. Abbr.: *RES.*

2190. Scandinavian Studies. Menasha, Wis., Society for the Advancement of Scandinavian Study, 1911–date.—Quarterly. Reviews. Occasional articles on English literature. Abbr.: *SS.*

2191. SEL. Studies in English Literature 1500–1900. Houston, Tex., Rice University, 1961–date.—Quarterly. Winter: English Renaissance; summer: Restoration and Eighteenth Century; spring: Elizabethan and Jacobean drama; autumn: Romantic and Victorian. Abbr.: *SEL.*

2192. Studies in Philology. Chapel Hill, University of North Carolina Press, 1906–date.—Quarterly. April issue "Literature of the Renaissance," a bibliography; that for 1958 (published 1959) runs pp. 227–452. Abbr.: *SP.*

2193. Wisconsin Studies in Contemporary Literature. Madison, University of Wisconsin, 1960–date.—Three issues a year.

2194. Zeitschrift für Anglistik und Amerikanistik. Berlin, Deutscher Verlag der Wissenschaften, 1953–date.—Quarterly. Reviews. Abbr.: *ZAA.*

2195. Zeitschrift für deutsche Philologie. Berlin, Erich Schmidt Verlag, 1869–date.—Irregular issues. Reviews. Occasional articles on English literature. Abbr.: *ZDP.*

2196. Zeitschrift für deutsches Altertum und deutsche Literatur. Wiesbaden, Franz Steiner Verlag, 1841–date.—Quarterly. Reviews. Occasional articles on English literature. Abbr.: *ZDA.*

§81. JOURNALS OF GERMANIC, ROMANCE, CELTIC, AND SLAVIC SCHOLARSHIP

[See also preceding section.]

2200. Bulletin. Board of Celtic Studies, University of Wales. Cardiff, University Press, 1921–date.—Irregular issues. Abstracts. Articles in English and Welsh. Abbr.: *BBCS.*

2201. Classical Philology. Devoted to research in the languages, literatures, history, and life of classical antiquity. University of Chicago Press, 1906–date.—Quarterly. Reviews. Abbr.: *CP.*

2202. Éigse. A journal of Irish studies. Dublin, National University of Ireland, 1939–date.—Irregular issues. Reviews.

2203. Études germaniques. Journal de la Société des études germaniques. Lyons, Édition IAC, 1946–date.—Quarterly. Reviews. Occasional articles on English literary subjects. Abbr.: *EG*.

2204. Journal of Celtic Studies. Philadelphia, Temple University, 1949–date. —Two issues a year.

2205. Modern Languages. London, Modern Language Association, 1905–date. Three issues a year. Reviews. Abbr.: *ML*.

2206. Ogam. Journal of the Amis de la tradition celtique. Rennes, France, 1948–date.—Six issues a year. Reviews.

2207. Revue de littérature comparée. Paris, Librairie Marcel Didier, 1921–date.—Quarterly. Reviews. Abbr.: *RLC*.

2208. Romance Philology. Berkeley, University of California Press, 1947–date.—Quarterly. Reviews. Articles in various languages. Abbr.: *RPh*.

2209. Romania. Revue trimestrielle consacrée à l'étude des langues et des littératures romanes. Paris, Mario Roques, 1872–date.—Quarterly. Abstracts. Reviews. Abbr.: *Rom*.

2210. Romanic Review. New York, Columbia University, Department of Romance Languages, 1910–date.—Quarterly. Reviews. Abbr.: *RR*.

2211. Romanische Forschungen. Vierteljahrschrift für romanische Sprachen und Literaturen. Frankfurt a. M., Verlag Vittorio Klostermann, 1883–date.—Quarterly. Reviews. Abbr.: *RF*.

2212. Slavonic and East European Review. University of London, School of Slavonic and East European Studies, 1922–date.—Two issues a year. Reviews. Abbr.: *SEER*.

2213. Studia Neophilologica. A journal of Germanic and Romanic philology. Uppsala, Sweden, A.-B. Lundequistska Bokhandeln, 1928–date.—Two issues a year. Reviews. Abbr.: *SN*.

2214. Symposium. A journal devoted to modern foreign languages and literatures. Syracuse, N.Y., Syracuse University, Department of Romance Languages, 1946–date.—Two issues a year. Articles in various languages. Abbr.: *Sym*.

2215. Yale French Studies. New Haven, Yale Univ. Press, 1949–date.—Two issues a year. Abbr.: *YFS*.

§82. HUMANISTIC PERIODICALS

2220. American Quarterly. Philadelphia, University of Pennsylvania, Committee on American Civilization, 1949–date.—Reviews. Emphasis on American culture, but not exclusively. Abbr.: *AQ.*

2221. American Scholar. Journal of Phi Beta Kappa. Williamsburg, Va., Phi Beta Kappa Hall, 1932–date.—Quarterly. Reviews. Abbr.: *ASch.*

2222. Boston University Studies in English. Boston, Department of English, Graduate School, Boston University, 1955–date.—Quarterly. Abbr.: *BUSE.*

2223. Comparative Literature. Eugene, University of Oregon, 1949–date.—Quarterly. Reviews. Articles in English, French, Spanish, Italian, and German. Abbr.: *CL.*

2224. Dartmouth Quarterly. Hanover, N.H., Dartmouth College, 1947–date.

2225. Durham University Journal. Durham, Eng., Durham College Office, 1876–date.—Three issues a year. Reviews. Abbr.: *DUJ.*

2226. Emory University Quarterly. Atlanta, Ga., Emory University, 1945–date.—Reviews. Emphasis primarily on Southern literature. Abbr.: *EUQ.*

2227. English Institute Essays. New York, Columbia Univ. Press, 1939–date. —Annual. Former title *English Institute Annual* 1939–42; no issues 1943–45; publication under present name 1945–date. Each volume is usually a study of a basic phase of English literature: "Motive and Method in the Cantos of Ezra Pound" 1953; "English Stage Comedy" 1954; "Society and Self in the Novel" 1955; "Sound and Poetry" 1956; "Literature and Belief" 1957; "Style in Prose Fiction" 1958. Abbr.: *EIE.*

2228. Euphorion. Zeitschrift für Literaturgeschichte. Heidelberg, Carl Winter, 1894–date.—Quarterly. Reviews. Occasional articles on English literature. Abbr.: *Euph.*

2229. Hermathena. A series of papers on literature, science, and philosophy by members of Trinity College, Dublin. Dublin, Hodges, Figgis and Co., 1873–date.—Irregular issues. Reviews.

2230. Humanist. Yellow Springs, Ohio, American Humanist Association, 1941–date.—Two issues a month. Reviews.

2231. Journal of the History of Ideas. A quarterly devoted to cultural and intellectual history. New York, City College, Journal of the History of Ideas Inc., 1940–date.—Reviews. Abbr.: *JHI.*

2232. Main Currents in Modern Thought. A cooperative journal to promote the free association of those working toward the integration of all knowledge through the study of the whole of things. New York, Main Currents in Modern Thought, 1943–date.—Five issues a year. Reviews.

2233. Pacific Spectator. A journal of interpretation. Stanford, Calif., Pacific Coast Committee for the Humanities of the American Council of Learned Societies, 1947–1956.—Quarterly.

2234. Queen's Quarterly. A Canadian review. Kingston, Queen's University, 1893–date.—Reviews. Abbr.: *QQ*.

2235. Renascence. A critical journal of letters. Milwaukee, Wis., Marquette Univ. Press, 1948–date.—Quarterly. Reviews. Emphasis on works deriving from the Oxford Movement or of especial spiritual import written since the Oxford Movement. Abbr.: *Ren.*

2236. A Review of English Literature. London, Longmans, Green and Co., 1960–date.—Quarterly. One review in each issue. Occasional concentration in one issue on one theme or author.

2237. Rivista di Letterature Moderne e Comparate. Florence, 1946–date.—Quarterly. Reviews. Articles in various languages. Abbr.: *RLMC.*

2238. South Atlantic Bulletin. Chapel Hill, N.C., South Atlantic Modern Language Association, 1935–date.—Quarterly. Abbr.: *SAB.*

2239. South Atlantic Quarterly. Durham, N.C., Duke Univ. Press, 1902–date. —Reviews. Abbr.: *SAQ.*

2240. Southwestern Journal. Langston, Okla., Langston University, 1944–date.—Quarterly. Reviews.

2241. Texas Studies in Literature and Language. A journal of the humanities. Austin, University of Texas, 1959–date.—Quarterly. Reviews.

2242. Thought. Fordham University quarterly. New York, Fordham University, 1926–date.—Reviews.

2243. Transactions. Royal Society of Canada / Société royale du Canada. Sections I and II: Literature, history, archaeology, sociology, political economy, and allied subjects. Ottawa, Royal Society of Canada / Société royale du Canada, 1882–date.—Irregular issues. Abbr.: *PTRSC* [for *Proceedings and Transactions* . . .].

2244. University of Toronto Quarterly. A Canadian journal of the humanities. University of Toronto Press, 1930–date.—Reviews. July issue "Letters in Canada," a survey of the year's poetry, fiction, social studies, criticism, biography, belles lettres, and other humanistic writing whether in English or French. Abbr.: *UTQ.*

2245. Yearbook of Comparative and General Literature. Chapel Hill, University of North Carolina Studies in Comparative Literature, 1952–date.—Annual bibliography. Published in collaboration with the Comparative Literature Committee of the National Council of Teachers of English and the Comparative Literature Section of the Modern Language Association of America. Abbr.: *YCGL.*

§83. BELLETRISTIC PERIODICALS

2249. Accent. A quarterly of new literature. Urbana, University of Illinois, Department of English, 1940–date.—A "little magazine."

2250. Anglo-American Journal. Rochester, N.Y., University of Rochester, 1959–date. Quarterly.—A publication designed to fill the gap left by the discontinuance of *Scrutiny*.

2251. Arizona Quarterly. A journal of literature, history, folklore. Tucson, University of Arizona, 1945–date.—Reviews. A "little magazine." Abbr.: *ArQ*.

2252. Atlantic Monthly. Boston, Atlantic Monthly Co., 1857–date.—Monthly. Reviews. Double-thick issues in April, November, and December. Abbr.: *Atlantic*.

2253. Audience. A review of literature and the arts. Cambridge, Mass, 1957–date.—Quarterly. A "little magazine."

2254. Beloit Poetry Journal. Beloit, Wis., English Department, Beloit College, 1950–date.—Two issues a year. A "little magazine."

2255. Botteghe Oscure. Rome, 1948–date.—Two issues a year.

2256. Colorado Quarterly. Boulder, University of Colorado, 1952–date.—A "little magazine." Abbr.: *ColQ*.

2257. Cornhill Magazine. London, John Murray, 1860–date.—Quarterly, although prior to 1939 monthly. Reviews only in older issues. Abbr.: *CM*.

2258. Cresset. A review of literature, the arts, and current affairs. Valparaiso, Ind., Valparaiso Univ. Press, 1937–date.—Monthly September through July. Reviews.

2259. Dissent. A quarterly of socialist opinion. New York, Dissent Publ'ing Association, 1954–date.—Reviews. Occasional explications of modern literature.

2260. Dublin Magazine. A quarterly review of literature, science, and art. Dublin, 1923–1958.—Reviews. Abbr.: *DM*.

2261. Encounter. Literature, arts, current affairs. London, Panton House, 1953–date.—Monthly. Reviews.

2262. Epoch. A quarterly of contemporary literature. Ithaca, N.Y., Cornell University, Epoch Associates, 1948–date.—Occasional criticism. A "little magazine."

2263. Folio. A magazine of Indiana writing. Bloomington, Indiana University, 1936–date.—Three issues a year.

2264. Harper's Magazine. New York, Harper and Bros., 1850–date.—Monthly. Reviews. Occasional supplements (as one on American writing October 1959 and another on medicine summer 1960). Abbr.: *Harper's.*

2265. Harvard Advocate. Cambridge, Mass., Harvard Advocate, 1866–date.—Six issues a year.

2266. Horizon. A review of literature and art. London, 1949–50.—Quarterly.

2267. Interim. Pocatello, Idaho State College, 1944–date.—Irregular issues. Reviews. A "little magazine."

2268. Invitation to Learning. Discussions of great books and significant ideas. New York, 1951–date.—Quarterly. Reviews.

2269. Manchester Guardian Weekly. Manchester, Eng., Manchester Guardian and Evening News Ltd., 1920–date.—Reviews.

2270. New Mexico Quarterly. Albuquerque, University of New Mexico, 1931–date.—Reviews. A "little magazine." Abbr.: *NMQ.*

2271. New Republic. A journal of opinion. New York, Editorial Publications Inc., 1914–date.—Weekly. Reviews. Abbr.: *NR.*

2272. New Statesman and Nation. The week-end review. London, New Statesman and Nation Ltd., 1913–date.—Weekly. Reviews.

2273. New York Times Magazine. New York, New York Times Co., 1896–date.—Weekly.

2274. New Yorker. New York, New Yorker Magazine Inc., 1925–date.—Weekly. Reviews. Abbr.: *NY.*

2275. Perspective. A quarterly of literature and the arts. St. Louis, Mo., Washington University, 1947–date.—A "little magazine." Abbr.: *Per.*

2276. Poet Lore. World literature and the drama. Boston, Poet Lore Inc., 1889–date.—Quarterly. Reviews.

2277. Poetry and Drama Magazine. City Island, N.Y., Volume VIII (1956)–date.—Two issues a year. Volumes I–VII *Poetry Book Magazine.* A "little magazine."

2278. Prairie Schooner. Lincoln, University of Nebraska Press, 1927–date.—Quarterly. For the peculiar distinctions of this journal see Paul R. Stewart, *The Prairie Schooner Story*, Lincoln, University of Nebraska Press, 1955. A "little magazine." Abbr.: *PrS.*

2279. Shenandoah. Lexington, Va., Washington and Lee University, 1950–date.—Three issues a year. Reviews. A "little magazine." Abbr.: *Shen.*

2280. Sinn und Form. Beiträge zur Literatur. Potsdam, Rütten und Loening, 1949–date.—Quarterly. Abbr.: *SuF.*

2281. Trace. A chronicle of living literature, comprising annual directories of (English language) poetry and small literary magazines appearing throughout the world. London, Villiers Publications, 1952–date.—Three issues a year. "Each issue offers the Chronicle, a running-supplement to The International Guide to Literary and Art Periodicals, with up-to-date information on presses and magazines throughout the world," t.p. statement (Mar.–Apr. 1960).

§84. REVIEWS

2286. Antioch Review. Yellow Springs, Ohio, Antioch Press, 1941–date.—Quarterly. Reviews. Abbr.: *AR.*

2287. Black Mountain Review. Black Mountain, N.C., Black Mountain College, 1954–date.—Quarterly. Reviews.

2288. Bucknell Review. A scholarly journal of letters, arts, and science. Lewisburg, Penn., Bucknell University, 1956–date.—Quarterly. Abbr.: *BuR.*

2289. Chicago Review. University of Chicago, 1946–date.—Quarterly. Reviews. A "little magazine." Abbr.: *ChiR.*

2290. Colorado Review. A periodical of creative literature. Fort Collins, Col., 1956/57–date.—Quarterly. A "little magazine."

2291. Dalhousie Review. A Canadian quarterly of literature and opinion. Halifax, Nova Scotia, Dalhousie University, Review Publishing Co., 1921–date.—Reviews. Abbr.: *DR.*

2292. Dublin Review. London, Dublin Review, 1836–date.—Quarterly. Reviews. Abbr.: *DubR.*

2293. Evergreen Review. New York, Grove Press, 1957–date.—Quarterly. Abbr.: *EvR.*

2294. Hudson Review. New York, Hudson Review Inc., 1948–date.—Quarterly. Reviews. Abbr.: *HudR.*

2295. Kenyon Review. Gambier, Ohio, Kenyon College, 1939–date.—Quarterly. Abbr.: *KR.*

2296. Literary Review. Teaneck, N.J., Fairleigh Dickinson University, 1957–date.—Quarterly. A "little magazine." Abbr.: *LitR.*

2297. Northwest Review. Eugene, University of Oregon, Erb Memorial Student Union, 1957–date.—Three issues a year. Reviews. A "little magazine."

2298. Paris Review. Paris, La Table Ronde, 1953–date.—Quarterly. A "little magazine." Abbr.: *ParR.*

2299. Partisan Review. New York, Foundation for Cultural Projects Inc., 1934–date.—Originally one issue every two months; quarterly since 1944. Reviews. Abbr.: *PR.*

2300. Quarterly Review. London, John Murray, 1809–date.—Reviews. Abbr.: *QR.*

2301. Quarterly Review of Literature. Annandale-on-Hudson, N.Y., Bard College, 1943–date.—Usually three issues a year. A "little magazine." Abbr.: *QRL.*

2302. Sewanee Review. America's oldest literary quarterly. Sewanee, Tenn., University of the South, 1892–date.—Reviews. Abbr.: *SR.*

2303. Southwest Review. Dallas, Tex., Southern Methodist Univ. Press, 1915–date.—Quarterly. Emphasis chiefly on contemporary American literature. A "little magazine."

2304. Vassar Review. Poughkeepsie, N.Y., Vassar College, 1949–date.—Quarterly.

2305. Virginia Quarterly Review. A national journal of literature and discussion. Charlottesville, University of Virginia, 1925–date.—Reviews. Abbr.: *VQR.*

2306. Western Humanities Review. Salt Lake City, University of Utah, 1947–date.—Quarterly. Reviews. Former title *Utah Humanities Review.* Emphasis on the West as material for and in literature. A "little magazine." Abbr.: *WHR.*

2307. Western Review. A literary quarterly. Iowa City, State Univ. of Iowa, 1937–date.—Reviews. A "little magazine." Abbr.: *WR.*

2308. Yale Review. New Haven, Yale Univ. Press, 1892–date.—Quarterly. Reviews. Abbr.: *YR.*

§85. THEATER AND DRAMA PERIODICALS

2312. Billboard. Cincinnati, Billboard Publ'ing Co., 1894–date.—Weekly. Reviews.

2313. Drama. The quarterly theatre review. London, British Drama League, 1919–date.—Reviews.

2314. Drama Critique. A critical review of theatre arts and literature. Detroit, Mercy College, National Catholic Theatre Conference, 1958–date.—Three issues a year. Reviews.

2315. Dramatics. An educational magazine for directors, teachers, and students of dramatic arts. Cincinnati, National Thespian Society, 1929–date.—Eight issues a year. Orientation toward the secondary school.

2316. Educational Theatre Journal. Journal of the American Educational Theatre Association. Austin, University of Texas, Department of the Drama, 1949–date.—Quarterly. Reviews. Abbr.: *ETJ.*

2317. OSU Theatre Collection Bulletin. Devoted to research in theatre history. Columbus, Ohio State University, 1954–date.—Annual. Reviews.

2318. Stage. Theatre, variety, cabaret, television. London, Carson and Comerford Ltd., 1880–date.—Weekly. Reviews.

2319. Theatre Arts. A magazine for the world theatre. New York, National Theatre Arts Council, 1916–date.—Monthly. Reviews. Abbr.: *TAr.*

2320. Variety. Films, radio, video, music, stage. New York, Variety Inc., 1905–date.—Weekly. Reviews.

2321. World Theatre. Brussels, International Theatre Institute and Unesco, 1949–date.—Quarterly.

§86. JOURNALS OF CRITICISM

2325. Criticism. A quarterly for literature and the arts. Detroit, Mich., Wayne State Univ. Press, 1959–date.

2326. Critique. Studies in modern fiction. Minneapolis, Minn., 1956–date.—Three issues a year. Successor to *Faulkner Studies*, Denver, Col., Faulkner Society, 1952–56, quarterly.

2327. Essays in Criticism. A journal of literary criticism. Oxford, Eng., Basil Blackwell, 1951–date.—Quarterly. Abbr.: *EIC.*

2328. Explicator. Columbia, Vogue Press for the University of South Carolina, 1942–date.—Nine issues a year. Occasional reviews. Abbr.: *Expl.*

2329. Journal of Aesthetics and Art Criticism. Cleveland, Ohio, Western Reserve Univ. Press, American Society for Aesthetics, 1941–date.—Quarterly. Abbr.: *JAAC.*

2330. Modern Fiction Studies. A critical quarterly. Lafayette, Ind., Purdue University, Modern Fiction Club, 1955–date.—Brief staff-written reviews. Abbr.: *MFS.*

2331. Twentieth Century Literature. A scholarly and critical journal. Denver, Col., Swallow Press, 1955–date.—Quarterly. Abstracts. Numerous bibliographies, as of the works of W. H. Auden, Hart Crane, H. L. Mencken, and Yvor Winters, and précis of articles falling in the period of the present century. Abbr.: *TCL.*

§87. PERIODICALS THAT ARE PRIMARILY REVIEW ORGANS

2335. Best Sellers. Review of current popular fiction and nonfiction. Scranton, Pa., University of Scranton Library, 1942–date.—Two issues a month. Catholic point of view.

2336. Booklist. A guide to current books. Chicago, American Library Association, 1905–date.—Two issues a month September through July and single issue in August.

2337. Book-Review Digest. New York, H. W. Wilson Co., 1905–date.—Monthly except July and February with six-month cumulation in August and annual cumulation in February. Five-year cumulations 1926, 1931, 1936, 1941, 1946, 1951, and 1956. Abbr.: *BRD.*

2338. Books. London, National Book League, 1929–date.—Monthly.

2339. Books Abroad. An international literary quarterly. Norman, University of Oklahoma, 1927–date.—Brief reviews of recent works from all Western European nations. Abbr.: *BA.*

2340. British Book News. A guide to books published in the Commonwealth and Empire. London, National Book League for the British Council, 1940–date.—Monthly.

2341. The Critic. A Catholic review of books and the arts. Chicago, Thomas More Association, 1943–date.—Eight issues a year. Former title *Books on Trial.*

2342. New York Herald Tribune Book Review. New York, New York Herald Tribune Inc., 1924–date.—Weekly.

2343. New York Times Book Review. New York, New York Times Co., 1896–date.—Weekly. Abbr.: *NYTBR*.

2344. Saturday Review. New York, Saturday Review Associates Inc., 1924–date.—Weekly. Former title *Saturday Review of Literature*. Abbr.: *SatR*.

2345. Subscription Books Bulletin. Chicago, American Library Association, 1930–56.—Quarterly. Merged with *Booklist*, September 1, 1956.

2346. Times Literary Supplement. London, Times Publ'ing Co., 1902–date.—Weekly. Abbr.: *TLS*.

2347. Virginia Kirkus Service. Bulletin. New York, Virginia Kirkus, 1933–date.—Two issues a month.

§88. JOURNALS OF PSYCHOLOGY AND RELIGION

2351. America. National Catholic weekly review. New York, America Press, 1909–date.—Reviews.

2352. American Imago. A psychoanalytic journal for the arts and sciences. South Dennis, Mass., 1939–date.—Quarterly. Abbr.: *AI*.

2353. Catholic World. New York, Missionary Society of St. Paul the Apostle, 1865–date.—Monthly. Reviews. Abbr.: *CathW*.

2354. Christian Century. Chicago, Christian Century Foundation, 1884–date.—Weekly.

2355. Commonweal. New York, Commonweal Publ'ing Co., 1924–date.—Weekly. Reviews. Abbr.: *Cweal*.

2356. Hibbert Journal. A quarterly review of religion, theology, and philosophy. London, Hibbert Journal, 1902–date.—Reviews. Abbr.: *HJ*.

2357. Journal of Biblical Literature. Philadelphia, Society of Biblical Literature and Exegesis, 1881–date.—Quarterly. Reviews. Abbr.: *JBL*.

2358. Literature and Psychology. The quarterly newsletter of General Topics Ten of the Modern Language Association. New York, Literature and Psychology, 1951–date.—Quarterly, but from 1951 to 1954 five issues a year. Reviews. Abbr.: *L&P*.

2359. Modern Schoolman. A quarterly journal of philosophy. St. Louis, Mo., St. Louis University, 1925–date.—Abbr.: *MSch.*

2360. Psychological Issues. New York, International Universities Press, 1959–date.—Four monographs a year issued at irregular intervals.

2361. Recusant History. A journal of research in post-Reformation Catholic history in the British Isles. Bangor Regis, Eng., Arundel Press for the Catholic Record Society, 1951–date.—Three issues a year. Former title *Biographical Studies of English Catholics.*

2362. Review of Religion. New York, Columbia Univ. Press, 1936–date.—Two issues a year. Reviews. Abbr.: *RRel.*

2363. Revue d'histoire ecclésiastique. Louvain, Université catholique de Louvain, 1900–date.—Quarterly. Comprehensive annual bibliography of scholarly publications, especially rich in the medieval field. Abbr.: *RHE.*

2364. Vigiliae Christianae. A review of early Christian life and language. Amsterdam, North Holland Publ'ing Co., 1947–date.—Quarterly. Reviews. Articles in French, Latin, and English.

§89. PERIODICALS DEVOTED TO ONE LITERARY FIGURE OR ONE LITERARY PERIOD

2369. Baker Street Journal. An irregular quarterly of Sherlockiana. New York, Baker Street Irregulars, 1946–date.—Occasional reviews. Old Series 1946–1949; New Series 1951–date. Abbr.: *BSJ.*

2370. Dickensian. A magazine for Dickens lovers. London, Dickens Fellowship, 1905–date.—Three issues (Jan., May, Sept.) a year.

2371. Emerson Society Quarterly. Hartford, Conn., Emerson Society, 1955–date.—Reviews. Studies, in addition to those on Emerson, on Thoreau, Hawthorne, Whitman, and other prominent men of the period. Abbr.: *ESQ.*

2372. English Fiction in Transition 1880–1920. West Lafayette, Ind., Purdue University, 1957–date.—Two or three issues a year. The newsletter of the Conference on English Fiction in Transition of the Modern Language Association. Abbr.: *EFT.*

2373. Johnsonian News Letter. New York, Columbia University, 1959–date.—Quarterly.

2374. Keats-Shelley Journal. Keats, Shelley, Byron, Hunt, and their circle. New York, Keats-Shelley Association of America Inc., 1952–date.—Annual. Reviews. Abbr.: *KSJ*.

2375. Kipling Journal. London, Kipling Society, 1927–date.—Quarterly. Occasional reviews.

2376. Melville Society Newsletter. Greeley, Colorado State College, Melville Society, 1945–date.—Quarterly.

2377. Nineteenth-Century Fiction. Berkeley, University of California Press, 1945–date.—Quarterly. Reviews. Abbr.: *NCF*.

2378. Renaissance News. A quarterly newsletter. Hanover, N.H., Dartmouth College Library for the American Council of Learned Societies, 1947–date.—Reviews. Abbr.: *RN*.

2379. Seventeenth Century News. Including Neo-Latin News. New Brunswick, N.J., Rutgers University, 1942–date.—Quarterly. A journal of abstracts. Abbr.: *SCN*.

2380. Shavian. Journal of the Shaw Society. London, Shaw Society, 1946–date.—Monthly. Title 1946–52 *Shaw Society Bulletin*.

2381. Twainian. About the life and writings of Mark Twain. Perry, Mo., Mark Twain Research Foundation, 1939–date.—One issue every two months. Reviews.

2382. Victorian Studies. Bloomington, Indiana University, 1958–date.—Quarterly. Reviews. June issue "Victorian Bibliography." Abbr.: *VS*.

2383. Walt Whitman Newsletter. New York Univ. Press, 1955–date.—Quarterly. Reviews. "Whitman, A current bibliography" in each issue. Abbr.: *WWN*.

§90. LINGUISTICS PERIODICALS

2387. Acta philologica scandinavica. Tidsskrift for nordisk sprogforskning. Copenhagen, Einar Munksgaard for Rask-Ørsted Fondet, 1926–date.—Quarterly. Abbr.: *APS*.

2388. American Speech. A quarterly of linguistic usage. New York, Columbia Univ. Press, 1925–date.—Reviews. Annual bibliographies. Abbr.: *AS*.

2389. Anthropos. Revue internationale d'ethnologie et de linguistique. Freiburg, Switzerland, P. Fritz Borneman, 1906–date.—Quarterly. Reviews. Articles in French, German, and English.

2390. Archivum linguisticum. A review of comparative philology and general linguistics. Glasgow, Messrs. Jackson, Son and Co., 1949–date.—Two issues a year. Reviews. Articles in various languages. Abbr.: *ArL.*

2391. Arkiv för nordisk filologi. Lund, Sweden, C. W. K. Gleerup, 1883–date.—Irregular issues. Reviews. Annual bibliographies. Abbr.: *ANF.*

2392. British Esperantist. London, British Esperanto Association Inc., 1905–date.—Two issues a month. Reviews.

2393. Canadian Linguistic Association Journal. Edmonton, University of Alberta, 1954–date.—Two issues a year. Articles in English and French on the languages of Canada, including Amerindian languages. Abbr.: *JCLA.*

2394. General Linguistics. Lexington, University of Kentucky, Department of Modern Foreign Languages, 1955–date.—Two issues a year. Abbr.: *GL.*

2395. Indogermanische Forschungen. Zeitschrift für Indogermanistik und allgemeine Sprachwissenschaft. Berlin, Walter de Gruyter und Co., 1891–date.—Quarterly. Reviews. Abbr.: *IF.*

2396. International Journal of American Linguistics. Bloomington, Indiana University, 1917–date.—Quarterly. Reviews. Emphasis on descriptive linguistics and American Indian languages. Abbr.: *IJAL.*

2397. International Language Review. A clearing house for facts, theories, and fancies on the history, science, and bibliography of the international language movement. Denver, Col., 1955–date.—Quarterly. Reviews.

2398. Language. Journal of the Linguistic Society of America. Baltimore, Linguistic Society of America, 1925–date.—Quarterly. Reviews. Emphasis on American structural linguistics. Also supplementary publication *Language Dissertations*, 1927–date, irregular issues.

2399. Lingua. International review of general linguistics. Haarlem, Holland, J. H. Gottmer, 1947–date.—Quarterly. Reviews. Articles in English and French.

2400. Maître phonétique. Paris, Association phonétique internationale, 1889–date.—Two issues a year. Reviews. Abbr.: *MPhon.*

2401. Orbis. Bulletin international de documentation linguistique. Louvain, Centre international de dialectologie général près l'université catholique de Louvain, 1952–date.—Two issues a year.

2402. Publications of the American Dialect Society. University, University of Alabama Press for the Society, 1944–date.—Often two issues a year. Successor to *Dialect Notes*, 1890–1939 (6 vols.). Abbr.: *PADS.*

2403. Ricerche Linguistische. Rome, Città Universitaria Istituto di Glottologia, Facoltà di Lettere, 1950–date.—Two issues a year. Reviews.

2404. Société de linguistique de Paris Bulletin. Paris, Librairie C. Klincksieck, 1869–date.—Quarterly. Abstracts. Reviews.

2405. Studia Linguistica. Revue de linguistique générale et comparée. Lund, Sweden, C. W. K. Gleerup, 1947–date.—Three issues a year. Reviews. Abbr.: *SL.*

2406. Studies in Linguistics. Washington, D.C., Edith Crowell Trager, 1942–date.—Quarterly. Reviews.

2407. Word. Journal of the Linguistic Circle of New York. New York, Linguistic Circle of New York, 1945–date.—Three issues a year. Reviews. Articles in English and occasionally French.

2408. Word Study. Springfield, Mass., G. and C. Merriam Co., 1925–date.—Irregular issues. Short articles on words and word groups of a quasi-scholarly nature. Abbr.: *WSt.*

2409. Zeitschrift für Phonetik und allgemeine Sprachwissenschaft. Berlin, Akademie-Verlag, 1947–date.—Six issues a year. Reviews. Abbr.: *ZPAS.*

2410. Zeitschrift für vergleichende Sprachforschung auf dem Gebiete der indogermanischen Sprachen. Göttingen, Vandenhoeck und Ruprecht, 1852–date.—Irregular issues. Abbr.: *ZVS.*

§91. PERIODICALS DEVOTED TO TEACHING OF ENGLISH AND FOREIGN LANGUAGES

2414. College English. Journal of the National Council of Teachers of English. University of Chicago Press, 1939–date.—Monthly October through May. Reviews. Abbr.: *CE.*

2415. Englische Studien. Organ für englische Philologie unter Mitberücksichtigung des englischen Unterrichts auf höheren Schulen. Leipzig, Reisland, 1877–1944.—Quarterly. Reviews.

2416. English Journal. University of Chicago Press for the National Council of Teachers of English, 1912–date.—Monthly September through May. Reviews. Abbr.: *EJ.*

2417. Illinois English Bulletin. Urbana, Illinois Association of Teachers of English, 1913–date.—Monthly October through May.

2418. Language Learning. A journal of applied linguistics. Ann Arbor, Mich., Language Learning, 1948–date.—Quarterly. Reviews. Language problems as seen from the point of view of the descriptive linguist. Abbr.: *LL.*

2419. Modern Language Forum. Los Angeles, University of California, 1915–date.—Quarterly. Reviews. Occasional reference to English literature. Abbr.: *MLF.*

2420. Modern Language Journal. St. Louis, Mo., National Federation of Modern Language Teachers Associations, 1916–date.—Monthly October through May. Reviews. Abbr.: *MLJ.*

2421. Neuere Sprachen. Zeitschrift für Forschung und Unterricht auf dem Fachgebiet der modernen Fremdsprachen. Frankfurt a. M., Verlag Moritz Diesterweg, 1893–date.—Ten issues a year. Reviews. Abbr.: *NS.*

2422. Zeitschrift für neusprachlichen Unterricht. Berlin, Weidmannsche Verlagsbuchhandlung, 1902–date.—Quarterly. Former title *Zeitschrift für französischen und englischen Unterricht.*

§92. PERIODICALS DEVOTED TO THE STUDY OF NAMES

2426. Beiträge zur Namenforschung. Heidelberg, Carl Winter Universitätsverlag, 1950–date.—Three issues a year. Reviews. Abbr.: *BN.*

2427. Names. Journal of the American Name Society. Berkeley, Calif., American Name Society, 1953–date.—Quarterly. Reviews.

2428. Revue internationale d'onomastique. Paris, 1947–date.—Quarterly. Title 1947–48 *Onomastica.* Articles in various languages.

2429. Zeitschrift für Namenforschung. Munich, 1925–date.—Quarterly.

§93. PERIODICALS DEVOTED TO SEMANTICS

2433. Etc. A review of general semantics. Chicago, International Society for General Semantics, 1943–date.—Quarterly. Reviews. Originally an organ for Korzybskian general semantics. Abbr.: *ETC.*

2434. General Semantics Bulletin. Lakeville, Conn., Institute of General Semantics, 1950–date.—Irregular issues. Reviews. Abbr.: *GSB.*

2435. Journal of Communication. Devoted to communication in human relations. East Lansing, Michigan State College, Communication Skills Department, National Society for the Study of Communication, 1951–date. —Quarterly. Reviews.

§94. PERIODICALS DEVOTED TO SPEECH, SPEECHES, AND DEBATING

2439. Intercollegiate Debates. Yearbook of college debating. New York, Noble and Noble, 1919–date.

2440. Quarterly Journal of Speech. Iowa City, Iowa, Speech Association of America, 1915–date.—Reviews. Abbr.: *QJS.*

2441. Speech Monographs. Iowa City, Iowa, Speech Association of America, 1934–date.—Quarterly. Abbr.: *SM.*

2442. University Debaters' Annual. Constructive and rebuttal speeches delivered in debates of American colleges and universities. New York, H. W. Wilson Co., 1914–date.

2443. Vital Speeches of the Day. New York, City News Publ'ing Co., 1934–date.—Two issues a month.

§95. PERIODICALS DEVOTED CHIEFLY TO BIBLIOGRAPHIC DESCRIPTION AND HISTORICAL BIBLIOGRAPHY

2447. Bodleian Library Record. Oxford, Eng., Bodleian Library, 1938–date. —Three issues a year. Reviews. Abbr.: *BLR.*

2448. Bulletin of the New York Public Library. New York, New York Public Library, 1897–date.—Monthly. Reviews. Occasional bibliographies on special subjects. Abbr.: *BNYPL.*

2449. Colby Library Quarterly. Waterville, Me., Colby College Library, 1943–date.—Abbr.: *CLQ.*

2450. Gutenberg-Jahrbuch. Mainz, Gutenberg-Gesellschaft, 1926–date.—Annual. Abbr.: *GJ.*

2451. Harvard Library Bulletin. Cambridge, Mass., Harvard Univ. Library, 1947–date.—Three issues a year. Abbr.: *HLB.*

2452. Huntington Library Quarterly. A journal for the history and interpretation of English and American civilization. San Marino, Calif., Henry E. Huntington Library and Art Gallery, 1937–date.—Occasional emphasis on the English Renaissance. Abbr.: *HLQ.*

2453. John Rylands Library Bulletin. Manchester, Eng., University Press, 1903–date.—Two issues a year. Abbr.: *BJRL.*

2454. Library. Transactions of the Bibliographical Society. Oxford Univ. Press, 1893–date.—Quarterly. Reviews.

2455. Library Chronicle. Philadelphia, Friends of the University of Pennsylvania Library, 1933–date.—Two issues a year. Emphasis on bibliographical scholarship. Abbr.: *LCUP.*

2456. Newberry Library Bulletin. Chicago, Newberry Library, 1952–date.—Irregular issues. Abbr.: *NLB.*

2457. New Colophon. A book collector's quarterly. New York, Duschnes Crawford Inc., 1948–date.—Title (1928–40) *Colophon,* A quarterly for bookmen, New York, Pynson Printers.

2458. Papers of the Bibliographical Society of America. New York, Bibliographical Society of America, 1906–date.—Quarterly. Reviews. Abbr.: *PBSA.*

2459. Princeton University Library Chronicle. Princeton, N.J., University Library, 1939–date.—Quarterly. Abbr.: *PULC.*

2460. Studies in Bibliography. Papers of the Bibliographical Society of Virginia. Charlottesville, Bibliographical Society of Virginia, 1949–date.—Annual. Each issue contains a checklist of bibliographical scholarship. Abbr.: *SB.*

2461. University of Rochester Library Bulletin. Rochester, N.Y., University of Rochester, 1945–date.—Three issues a year. Abbr.: *URLB.*

2462. Yale University Library Gazette. New Haven, Yale Univ. Library, 1926–date.—Quarterly. Abbr.: *YULG.*

§96. LIBRARY AND PUBLISHER PERIODICALS

2467. American Documentation. A quarterly review of ideas, techniques, problems, and achievements in documentation. Cleveland, Ohio, Western Reserve University, School of Library Science, 1950–date.—Often contains articles on semantics and linguistic analysis.

2468. American Library Annual and Book Trade Almanac. New York, R. R. Bowker Co., 1955–date.—Sponsorship Council of National Library Associations and the Library Journal. Former title *American Library Annual.*

2469. American Library Association Bulletin. Chicago, American Library Association, 1907–date.—Monthly September through June and single issue for the months July and August. Abbr.: *BALA.*

2470. Books from the U. S. A. News of current U.S. books and book publishing. New York, R. R. Bowker Co., 1956–date.—Monthly. Reviews.

2471. Books to Come. New York, R. R. Bowker Co., 1959–date.—Six issues a year. Classified by subject with author-title index. Former title *Bowker's Advance Reference Source Reporting Service.*

2472. BPR. American book publishing record. New York, R. R. Bowker Co., 1960–date.—Monthly. Entries arranged by subject according to the Dewey Decimal Classification and indexed by author and by title as catalogued by the Library of Congress and annotated by *Publishers' Weekly.* Abbr.: *BPR.*

2473. Library Journal. New York, R. R. Bowker Co., 1876–date.—Two issues a month September through June and monthly July and August. Reviews. Abbr.: *LJ.*

2474. Library Quarterly. A journal of investigation and discussion in the field of library science. University of Chicago, 1930–date.—Reviews. Abbr.: *LQ.*

2475. Library Resources and Technical Services. Chicago, American Library Association, Resources and Technical Services Division, 1957–date.—Quarterly. Reviews.

2476. Library Science Abstracts. London, Library Association, 1950–date.—Quarterly.

2477. Onoma. Bulletin d'information et de bibliographie / Bibliographical and information bulletin. Louvain, International Centre of Onomastics, 1950–date.—Quarterly.

2478. Penrose Annual. Review of the graphic arts. London, 1895–date.

2479. Publishers' Circular and Booksellers' Record. London, Publishers Circular Ltd., 1837–date.—Weekly.

2480. Publishers' Weekly. The American book trade journal. New York, R. R. Bowker Co., 1872–date.—Weekly. Reviews. Abbr.: *PW*.

2481. Wilson Library Bulletin. New York, H. W. Wilson Co., 1914–date.—Monthly September through June. Reviews. Abbr.: *WLB*.

2482. Zentralblatt für Bibliothekswesen. Leipzig, Otto Harrassowitz, 1884–date.—Two issues a month. Reviews.

§97. PERIODICALS DEVOTED TO FOLKLORE

2486. Badger Folklore. Madison, Wis., Badger State Folklore Society, 1948–date.—Irregular issues. Reviews.

2487. Delaware Folklore Bulletin. Journal of the Delaware Folklore Society. Newark, University of Delaware, Institute of Delaware History and Culture, 1951–date.—Irregular issues.

2488. FF Communications. [Folklore Fellows' Communications.] Helsinki, Folklore Fellows, 1910–date.—Two to four issues a year (Vol. LXXV 1958). Articles in French, German, and English covering any subject of world folklore.

2489. Folk-Lore. A quarterly journal of myth, tradition, institutions, and customs. London, Folk-Lore Society, 1890–date.—Reviews. Incorporating the titles *Folk-Lore Record* (1879–82), *Folk-Lore Journal* (1883–89), and *Archaeological Review* (1888–90).

2490. Journal of American Folklore. Bloomington, Indiana University, American Folklore Society, 1888–date.—Quarterly. Reviews. An April supplement contains membership lists, reports, and an annual folklore bibliography. Abbr.: *JAF*.

2491. Journal of the Gypsy Lore Society. Leicester, Eng., Gypsy Lore Society, 1888–date.—Quarterly. Reviews. Abbr.: *JGLS*.

2492. Kentucky Folklore Record. Bowling Green, Western Kentucky State College, Kentucky Folklore Society, 1955–date.—Quarterly. Reviews. Abbr.: *KFR.*

2493. Keystone Folklore Quarterly. Lewisburg, Bucknell University, Pennsylvania Folklore Society, 1956–date.—Reviews.

2494. Midwest Folklore. Bloomington, Indiana University, 1951–date.—Quarterly. Reviews. Abbr.: *MF.*

2495. New York Folklore Quarterly. Cooperstown, New York Folklore Society, 1945–date.—Reviews. Abbr.: *NYFQ.*

2496. North Carolina Folklore. Journal of the North Carolina Folklore Society. Chapel Hill, University of North Carolina Folklore Council, 1953–date.—Quarterly.

2497. Revue de folklore français. Paris, Société du folklore français, 1930–date.—Quarterly. Reviews.

2498. Southern Folklore Quarterly. Journal of the Southeastern Folklore Society. Gainesville, University of Florida, 1937–date.—Reviews. March issue annual folklore bibliography. Abbr.: *SFQ.*

2499. Tennessee Folklore Society Bulletin. Cookeville, Tennessee Polytechnic Institute, 1935–date.—Quarterly. Reviews. Abbr.: *TFSB.*

2500. Volkskunde. Driemaandelijks tijdscrift voor de studie van het volksleven. Officiel organ van de Volkskunde-Commissie der Koninklijke Nederlandse Akademie van Wetenscappen. Amsterdam, Volkskunde-Commissie, 1888–date.—Quarterly. Reviews.

2501. West Virginia Folklore. Fairmont, Fairmont State College, West Virginia Folklore Society, 1950–date.—Quarterly.

2502. Western Folklore. Journal of the California Folklore Society. Berkeley, University of California Press, 1942–date.—Quarterly. Reviews. Title 1942–46 *California Folklore Quarterly.* Occasional special issues, as "Los Pastores Number" 1957 and "Utah Number" 1959. Abbr.: *WF.*

2503. Zeitschrift für Volkskunde. Stuttgart, W. Kohlhammer Verlag, 1891–date.—Irregular issues. Reviews. Title varies.

§98. HISTORICAL PERIODICALS

2507. American Historical Review. Richmond, Va., American Historical Association, 1895–date.—Quarterly. Reviews.

2508. American Slavic and East European Review. New York, Columbia Univ. Press for the American Association for the Advancement of Slavic Studies, 1941–date.—Quarterly. Reviews. Abbr.: *ASEER.*

2509. Atlanta Historical Bulletin. Atlanta, Ga., Atlanta Historical Society, 1927–date.—Irregular issues.

2510. English Historical Review. London, Longmans, Green and Co., 1886–date.—Quarterly. Reviews. Abbr.: *EHR.*

2511. Essex Institute. Historical collections. Salem, Mass., Essex Institute, 1859–date.—Quarterly. Reviews. Abbr.: *EIHC.*

2512. General Magazine and Historical Chronicle. Philadelphia, University of Pennsylvania, General Alumni Society, 1895–date.—Quarterly. Reviews.

2513. Historische Zeitschrift. Munich, 1859–date.—Three issues a year. Reviews. Abbr.: *HZ.*

2514. History. London, George Philip and Son for the Historical Association, 1912–date.—Quarterly. Reviews.

2515. Indiana Magazine of History. Bloomington, Indiana University and Indiana Historical Society, 1905–date.—Quarterly. Reviews. Abbr.: *IMH.*

2516. Isis. International review devoted to the history of science and its cultural influences. Cambridge, Mass., Widener Library, History of Science Society, 1913–date.—Quarterly. Reviews.

2517. Journal of Modern History. University of Chicago Press, 1929–date.—Quarterly. Reviews. Abbr.: *JMH.*

2518. Journal of Negro History. Washington, D.C., Association for the Study of Negro Life and History Inc., 1916–date.—Quarterly. Reviews. Abbr.: *JNH.*

2519. New England Quarterly. A historical review of New England life and letters. Brunswick, Me., Bowdoin College, Hubbard Hall, 1928–date.—Reviews. Annual bibliography "Articles on the History of New England in Periodical Publications." Abbr.: *NEQ.*

2520. Proceedings of the American Antiquarian Society. Worcester, Mass., American Antiquarian Society, 1812–date.—Two issues a year. Abbr.: *PAAS.*

2521. Revue historique. Paris, Presses universitaires de France, 1876–date.—Quarterly. Reviews. Abbr.: *RH.*

2522. Scottish Historical Review. Edinburgh, Thomas Nelson and Sons, 1903–date.—Two issues a year. Reviews.

2523. William and Mary Quarterly. A magazine of early American history. Williamsburg, Va., Institute of Early American History and Culture, 1892–date.—Reviews. Abbr.: *WMQ.*

[The student of literature should be well aware of State and city historical society publications, for invariably, at one time or another, they publish valuable material on a local literary figure. A selection of titles follows; they represent the more substantial and established journals. Complete data on them can be found in Ulrich's *Periodicals Directory* and in the *Union List of Serials*: Arkansas Historical Quarterly; Canadian Historical Review; Connecticut Historical Society Bulletin; Delaware History; Florida Historical Quarterly; General Magazine and Historical Chronicle (Pennsylvania); Journal of Southern History; Louisiana Historical Quarterly; Maryland Historical Magazine; Michigan History; Minnesota History; Mississippi Valley Historical Review; Nebraska History Magazine; New Jersey Historical Society Proceedings; New York Historical Society Quarterly; North Carolina Historical Review; Ohio Historical Quarterly; Pacific Historical Review; Register of the Kentucky Historical Society; Southwestern Historical Quarterly; Utah Historical Quarterly; Vermont History; Virginia Magazine of History and Biography; Westchester (New York) Historian; Western Pennsylvania Historical Magazine; Wisconsin Magazine of History.]

§99. BI-RACIAL AND BI-NATIONAL PERIODICALS

2527. American German Review. Philadelphia, Carl Schurz Memorial Foundation Inc., 1934–date.—Two issues a month. Reviews. Abbr.: *AGR.*

2528. American Hebrew. For better understanding between Christians and Jews. New York, 1879–date.—Weekly. Reviews.

2529. American Oxonian. Philadelphia, Association of American Rhodes Scholars, 1914–date.—Three issues a year. Reviews. Abbr.: *AO.*

2530. American-Scandinavian Review. New York, American-Scandinavian Foundation, 1913–date.—Quarterly. Reviews. Abbr.: *ASR.*

2531. American Swedish Monthly. New York, Swedish Chamber of Commerce of the U.S.A., 1907–date.—Reviews.

2532. Anglo-Welsh Review. Pembroke Dock, Wales, Pembroke Dock Press, 1950–date.—Two issues a year. Former title *Dock Leaves.* A national review in English of Welsh arts and letters.

2533. Commentary. Incorporating Jewish Record. Significant thought and opinion on Jewish affairs and contemporary issues. New York, American Jewish Committee, 1945–date.—Monthly. Reviews. Abbr.: *Com.*

2534. French American Review. Washington, D.C., Institut français de Washington, 1948–date.—Quarterly. Reviews.

2535. Jewish Quarterly Review. Philadelphia, Dropsie College for Hebrew and Cognate Learning, 1888–date.—Reviews.

2536. Jewish Social Studies. Devoted to contemporary and historical aspects of Jewish life. New York, Conference on Jewish Social Studies, 1939–date.—Quarterly. Reviews. Abbr.: *JSS.*

§100. PUBLISHER, ACADEMIC, AND SOCIETY SERIES

[See also §145. Learned Societies.]

2540. Scudder, Samuel Hubbard. Catalogue of the Scientific Serials of All Countries Including the Transactions of Learned Societies . . . 1633–1876. Cambridge, Mass., Harvard College Library, 1879. xii + 358 pp. —Number 1 in the series Special Publications of the Library of Harvard University.

2541. Catalogue of Publications in the Humanities by American Learned Societies. Washington, D.C., American Council of Learned Societies, 1932. 72 pp.

2542. Baer, Eleanora A. Titles in Series Published Prior to January 1953. A handbook for librarians and students. Washington, D.C., Scarecrow Press, 1953. xix + 856 (double column) pp.—Supplement *Titles in Series* . . . Vol. II: Books published prior to January 1957, New York, Scarecrow Press, 1957, xxx + 859–1167 (double column) pp.

2543. Mullins, E[dward] L. C. Texts and Calendars. An analytical guide to serial publications. London, Royal Historical Society, 1958. xi + 674 pp.—Number 7 in the series Royal Society Guides and Handbooks.

2544. Aberystwyth Studies. Aberystwyth, Wales. Vol. I (1912)–Vol. XIV (1936).

2545. American Folklore Society Memoirs. Philadelphia, American Folk-Lore Society Inc. Vol. I (1894)–Vol. XLVII (1956).

2546. Anglistische Arbeiten. Heidelberg, Carl Winter Universitätsbuchhandlung. Vol. I (1912)–Vol. IV (1913).

2547. Anglistische Forschungen. Heidelberg. Vol. I (1901)–Vol. XC (1957).

2548. Augustan Reprint Society Publications. Los Angeles, Augustan Reprint Society. Vol. I (1946)–Vol. LX (1956).—Abbr.: *ARS.*

2549. Aus Schriftum und Sprache der Angelsachsen. Leipzig. Vol. I (1934)–Vol. VI (1936).

2550. Ballad Society Publications. London, Ballad Society. 1868–97 (38 vols.).

2551. Beiträge zur englischen Philologie. Leipzig. Vol. I (1919)–Vol. XXXII (1938).

2552. Beiträge zur Erforschung der Sprache und Kultur Englands und Nordamerikas. Giessen, Englisches Seminar der Universität Giessen. Vol. I (1923)–Vol. VI (1930).

2553. Bollingen Series. New York, Pantheon Books Inc. Vol. I (1943)–Vol. LX (1956). Abbr.: *BS.*

2554. Bonner Studien zur englischen Philologie. Bonn. Vol. I (1909)–Vol. XXXIV (1938).—Successor to *Bonner Beiträge zur Anglistik,* Vol. I (1898)–Vol. XXV (1908).

2555. Boston College. Humanities and Language. Chestnut Hill, Mass., Boston College. 1947–1948 (3 vols.).

2556. Breslauer Beiträge zur Literaturgeschichte. Stuttgart. Vol. I (1904)–Vol. L (1919).

2557. Britannica et America. Hamburg, Seminar für englische Sprache und Kultur an der hamburgischen Universität. Vol. I (1956)–Vol. II (1957).—Successor to *Britannica,* Vol. I (1930)–Vol. XX (1941).

2558. Columbia University Studies in English and Comparative Literature. New York, Columbia Univ. Press. 1912–55 (168 issues).—Successor to *Columbia University Studies in English,* First Series Vol. I (1900)–Vol. III (1904); Second Series Vol. I (1907)–Vol. XIX (1912); and *Columbia University Studies in Comparative Literature,* 1899–15 (12 vols.).

2559. Comparative Literature Studies. Cardiff, Wales, Priory Press. Vol. I (1940)–Vol. XXIV (1946).

2560. Connecticut College Monographs. New London, Connecticut College for Women. Vol. I (1941)–Vol. IV (1950).

2561. Contributions in Languages and Literatures. Columbus, Ohio State University. Vol. I (1918)–Vol. XV (1955).

2562. Cornell Studies in English. Ithaca, N.Y., Cornell University. Vol. I (1917)–Vol. XL (1955).—Abbr.: *CSE.*

2563. Early English Manuscripts in Facsimile. Copenhagen, Rosenkilde and Bagger. Vol. I (1951)–Vol. VI (1956).

2564. Early English Text Society. Original Series. London, Early English Text Society. Vol. I (1864)–Vol. CCXXXIII (1956).—Original founders Frederick James Furnivall, Richard Morris, Walter W. Skeat, et al. The *New England Dictionary* utilized the Society's publications. See also *Extra Series,* Vol. I (1867)–Vol. CXXVI (1935), which presented texts already printed but not in accurate or obtainable editions. Abbr.: *EETS:OS/ES.*

2565. Elizabethan Bibliographies. Gainesville, Fla., Scholars' Facsimiles and Reprints. Vol. I (1937)–Vol. XLI (1950).

2566. English Association Pamphlets. Oxford Univ. Press. Vol. I (1907)–Vol. XCIII (1935).

2567. English Dialect Society. Publications. London, Dialect Society. 1873–96 (32 vols.).

2568. English Monographs. Chicago, National Council of Teachers of English. Vol. I (1932)–Vol. XVIII (1951).

2569. English Place-Name Society. Publications. Cambridge Univ. Press. Vol. I (1924)–Vol. XXVI (1956).

2570. Essays and Studies on American Language and Literature. Uppsala, Sweden, University of Uppsala, Universitet Amerikanska Seminariet. Vol. I (1945)–Vol. XI (1954).

2571. Facsimile Text Society Series. New York, Columbia Univ. Press. 1930–42 (56 issues).—Abbr.: *FTS.*

2572. Folk-Lore Society Publications. London, William Glaisher Ltd. Vol. I (1878)–Vol. CXII (1946).

2573. Forschungen zur englischen Philologie. Jena. Vol. I (1930)–Vol. VIII (1939).—Also *Jenaer germanistische Forschungen,* Vol. I (1923)–Vol. XXXV (1939).

2574. Greifswalder Beiträge zur Literatur und Stilforschung. Greifswald. Vol. I (1932)–Vol. XXIV (1939).

2575. Hakluyt Society Publications. London, British Museum. First Series Vol. I (1847)–Vol. C (1899); Second Series Vols. I/II (1899)–Vol. CVII (1954); Extra Series Vol. I/XII (1903–1905)–Vol. XXIV (1955).

2576. Harvard Studies and Notes in Philology and Literature. Cambridge, Mass., Harvard Univ. Press. Vol. I (1892)–Vol. XX (1938).

2577. Harvard Studies in Comparative Literature. Cambridge, Mass., Harvard Univ. Press. Vol. I (1910)–Vol. XXI (1954).—Abbr.: *HSCL.*

2578. Harvard Studies in English. Cambridge, Mass., Harvard Univ. Press. Vol. I (1913)–Vol. XXI (1939).

2579. Harvard University. Keats Memorial Studies. Cambridge, Mass., Harvard Univ. Press. Vol. I (1946).

2580. Harvard University. William James Lectures. Cambridge, Mass., Harvard Univ. Press. 1933–57 (7 issues).

2581. Hesperia. Ergänzungsreihe: Schriften zur englischen Philologie. Baltimore, Johns Hopkins Press. Vol. I (1912)–Vol. XXII (1947).

2582. Indiana University Publications. Folklore Series. Bloomington, University of Indiana. Vol. I (1940)–Vol. VI (1952).—Abbr.: *IUPFS.*

2583. Indiana University Publications. Humanistic Series. Bloomington, University of Indiana. Vol. I (1939)–Vol. XXXVII (1956).—Successor to *Indiana University Studies,* Vol. I (1910)–Vol. XXV (1939). Abbr.: *IUPHS.*

2584. Iowa Humanistic Studies. Iowa City, University of Iowa. Vol. I (1907)–Vol. VIII (1946).—Volumes I to III called *Iowa Studies in Language and Literature.*

2585. Kieler Studien zur englischen Philologie. Heidelberg. First Series Vol. I (1901)–Vol. V (1904); Second Series Vol. I (1905)–Vol. VII (1915).

2586. Kölner anglistische Arbeiten. Leipzig, Tauchnitz. Vol. I (1927)–Vol. XXXVIII (1940).

2587. Lebendige Sprache. Experimental-phonetische Untersuchungen. Berlin, Walther de Gruyter. Vol. I (1938)–Vol. XIII (1942).

2588. Leeds Studies in English and Kindred Languages. Leeds, Eng., University of Leeds for members of the School of English Language. Vol. I (1932)–Vol. VI (1937).

2589. Linguistic Society of America. Language Monographs. Austin, Texas, Linguistic Society of America. Vol. I (1925)–Vol. XXV (1950).—Also *Special Publications,* 1930–58 (c. 10 issues). Also *Language Dissertations,* Vol. I (1927)–Vol. LI (1955).

2590. London Mediaeval Studies. London, University College. Vol. I (1937)–Vol. II (1938).—Abbr.: *LMS.*

2591. London University. Warburg Institute Studies. University of London. Vol. I (1939)–Vol. XX (1952).

2592. Louisiana State University. Humanities Series. Baton Rouge, Louisiana State Univ. Press. Vol. I (1952)–Vol. V (1955).

2593. Lund Studies in English. Lund, Sweden, University of Lund. Vol. I (1933)–Vol. VII (1938).—Abbr.: *LSE.*

2594. Maine University Studies. Orono, Me., University Press. Original Series Vol. I (1900)–Vol. VII (1907); Second Series Vol. I (1924)–Vol. LXXIII (1958).

2595. Malone Society Reprints. Oxford Univ. Press. 1907–57 (c. 95 reprints).

2596. Marburger Studien zur englischen Philologie. Marburg, Elwert. Vol. I (1901)–Vol. XIII (1911).

2597. Mediaeval Academy of America Monographs. Cambridge, Mass., Mediaeval Academy of America. Vol. I (1928)–Vol. LXII (1955).

2598. Medieval Library. London, Chatto and Windus. Vol. I (1908)–Vol. XXVI (1926).

2599. Medium Aevum Monographs. London, Society for the Study of Mediaeval Language and Literature. Vol. I (1936)–Vol. V (1950).

2600. Memoires de la Société néo-philologique à Helsingfors. Helsinki, Neuphilologischer Verein. Vol. I (1893)–Vol. XIX (1956).

2601. Missouri University Bulletin. Literature Series. Columbia, University of Missouri. Vol. I (1917)–Vol. II (1917).—Successor to *University of Missouri Studies*, Literature and Linguistic Series, Vol. I (1909)–Vol. II (1911).

2602. Modern Language Association of America Monographs. New York, Modern Language Association of America. Vol. I (1926)–Vol. XIX (1954).

2603. Modern Language Association of America Revolving Fund Series. New York, Modern Language Association of America. Vol. I (1925)–Vol. XVIII (1955).

2604. Modern Language Studies. Oxford, Eng., Basil Blackwell. Vol. I (1945)–Vol. XX (1957).

2605. Münchener Beiträge zur romanischen und englischen Philologie. Leipzig, Deichert Verlag. Vol. I (1890)–Vol. LIV (1912).

2606. Münsterer anglistische Studien. Emsdette, H. und J. Lechte. Vol. I (1937)–Vol. III (1939?).

2607. Nebraska University Studies. New Series. Lincoln, University of Nebraska. Vol. I (1946)–Vol. XX (1958).—Successor to *Studies in the Humanities*, Vol. I (1941)–Vol. IV (1945), and *Studies in Language, Literature, and Criticism*, Vol. I (1916)–Vol. X (1940).

2608. Neudrucke frühenglischer Grammatiken. Halle a. S., Max Niemeyer Verlag. Vol. I (1905)–Vol. VIII (1913).

2609. Neue anglistische Arbeiten. Cöthen, Otto Schulze. Vol. I (1918)–Vol. VII (1926).

2610. Neue deutsche Forschungen. Abteilung: Englische Philologie. Berlin, Junker und Dünnhaupt. Vol. I (1935)–Vol. VIII (1940).

2611. New Shakespeare Society Publications. London, Trübner and Co. 1874–1908 (46 vols.).

2612. Northwestern University Studies in the Humanities. Evanston, Ill., Northwestern Univ. Press. Vol. I (1937)–Vol. XXXII (1956).

2613. Our Debt to Greece and Rome. New York, Longmans, Green and Co. Vol. I (1925)–Vol. XXXIX (1933).

2614. Oxford English Monographs. Oxford Univ. Press. Vol. I (1940)–Vol. III (1952).

2615. Oxford Historical and Literary Studies. Oxford Univ. Press. Vol. I (1913)–Vol. XII (1921).

2616. Palaestra. Untersuchungen und Texte aus der deutschen und englischen Philologie. Berlin. Vol. I (1898)–Vol. CCXXI (1941).

2617. Percy Society Publications. London, C. Richards for the Society. 1840–52 (30 vols.).—Abbr.: *PSP.*

2618. Princeton Studies in English. Princeton, N.J., University Press. Vol. I (1929)–Vol. XXXIV (1955).—Abbr.: *PSE.*

2619. Publications of the Pontifical Institute of Mediaeval Studies. Studies and Texts. Toronto, Pontifical Institute of Mediaeval Studies. Vol. I (1955)–Vol. IV (1958).

2620. Quellen und Forschungen zur Sprach- und Kulturgeschichte der germanischen Völker. Berlin. Vol. I (1874)–Vol. CXXIV (1918).

2621. Rostocker Studien. Rostock, Hinstorff. Vol. I (1937)–Vol. IX (1941).

2622. Roxburgh Club Publications. London, Roxburgh Club. Vol. [I] (1814)–Vol. [CCI] (1956).

2623. St. Andrews University Publications. Oxford Univ. Press. Vol. I (1901)–Vol. LVI (1956).

2624. Scandinavian Classics. New York, American Scandinavian Society. Vol. I (1914)–Vol. XXXIV (1930).

2625. Schweizer anglistische Arbeiten. Bonn. Vol. I (1936)–Vol. VII (1938).

2626. Scottish Text Society Publications. Edinburgh, William Blackwood and Sons for the Scottish Text Society. First Series 1884–1914 (64 vols.); Second Series 1911–30 (26 vols.); Third Series 1930–55 (23 vols.).—Abbr.: *STSP.*

2627. Smith College. Studies in Modern Languages. Northampton, Mass., Smith College. Original Series Vol. I (1920)–Vol. XXII (1944); New Series Vol. I (1950).

2628. Societas scientiarum fennica. Commentationes humanarum literarum. Helsinki. Vol. I (1922)–Vol. XXIII (1958).

2629. Society for Pure English. Tracts. Oxford Univ. Press. Vol. I (1919)–Vol. LXVI (1948).—Abbr.: *SPE Tracts.*

2630. Sprache und Kultur der germanischen und romanischen Völker. A: Anglistische Reihe. Breslau. Vol. I (1930)–Vol. XXXVI (1940).

2631. Stanford University Publications. University Series. Language and Literature. Stanford, Calif., Stanford University Press. Vol. I (1920)–Vol. XXI (1960). Vols. XIV ff. known as Stanford Studies in Language and Literature. Abbr.: *SUPUSLL/SSLL.*

2632. Stockholm Studies in English. Stockholm, Almqvist ok Wiksell. Vol. I (1937)–Vol. II (1955).

2633. Studien zur englischen Philologie. Halle a. S., Max Niemeyer Verlag. Vol. I (1897)–Vol. XCVI (1939).

2634. Studier i Modern Språkvetenskap. Stockholm, Nyfilologiska Sällskapet. Vol. I (1898)–Vol. XIX (1956).

2635. Studies in English by Members of the English Seminar. Prague, Charles University. Vol. I (1924)–Vol. V (1934).

2636. Studies in English Philology. Budapest, Angol filologiai tanulmányok. Vol. I (1936)–Vol. II (1937).

2637. Studies in Language and Literature. Research Publications of the University of Minnesota. Minneapolis, University of Minnesota. Vol. I (1914)–Vol. IX (1926).

2638. Texas Folk-Lore Society. Publications. Dallas, Texas, Southern Methodist University. Vol. I (1916)–Vol. XXVII (1956).—Abbr.: *PTFS.*

2639. Transactions of the Philological Society. London, Philological Society. 1911/14–1958 (34 vols.).—Abbr.: *TPS.*

2640. University of Kansas Bulletin. Humanistic Studies. Lawrence, University of Kansas. Vol. I (1912)–Vol. XXXII (1955).

2641. University of California Publications. English Studies. Berkeley, University of California. Vol. I (1950)–Vol. XIV (1956).—Successor to *Publications in English,* Vol. I (1929)–Vol. XIX (1951).

2642. University of California. Publications in Linguistics. Berkeley, University of California. Vol. I (1943)–Vol. XV (1958).

2643. University of California. Publications in Modern Philology. Berkeley, University of California. Vol. I (1909)–Vol. LI (1959).

2644. University of Colorado Studies. Series B: Studies in Humanities. Boulder, University of Colorado. Vol. I (1939)–Vol. IV (1945).

2645. University of Illinois. Studies in Language and Literature. Urbana, University of Illinois. Vol. I (1915)–Vol. XLII (1956).

2646. University of Michigan. Contributions in Modern Philology. Ann Arbor, University of Michigan. Vol. I (1947)–Vol. XXIV (1958).—See also *University of Michigan Publications: Linguistics*, Ann Arbor, University of Michigan, Vol. I (1945)–Vol. IV (1948).

2647. University of Michigan Publications. Language and Literature. Ann Arbor, University of Michigan. Vol. I (1925)–Vol. XXVI (1953).

2648. University of New Mexico. Publications in Language and Literature. Albuquerque, University of New Mexico. Vol. I (1949)–Vol. XII (1953).—Successor to *Bulletin*, Language Series, 1934–42.

2649. University of Oregon Monographs. Studies in Literature and Philology. Eugene, University of Oregon. Vol. I (1939)–Vol. VI (1952).

2650. University of Texas. Studies in English. Austin, University of Texas. Vol. I (1911)–Vol. XVII (1937).—Also *University of Texas Bulletin: Humanistic Series*, Austin, University of Texas, Vol. I (1904)–Vol. XVII (1914).

2651. University of Virginia Studies. Charlottesville, University of Virginia. Vol. I (1941)–Vol. [V] (1951).

2652. University of Washington. Publications in Language and Literature. Seattle, University of Washington. Vol. I (1920)–Vol. XIV (1959).—Successor to *Publications in English*, Vol. I (1911)–Vol. IV (1918).

2653. University of Wisconsin. Studies in Language and Literature. Madison, University of Wisconsin. Vol. I (1918)–Vol. XXXVIII (1936).—Successor to *University of Wisconsin Bulletin*, Philology and Literature Series, Vol. I (1901)–Vol. VI (1916).

2654. Washington University Studies. St. Louis, Mo., Washington University. Original Series Vol. I (1913)–Vol. XIII (1926); New Series Vol. I (1927)–Vol. XXIV (1953).

2655. Wiener Beiträge zur englischen Philologie. Vienna. Vol. I (1895)–Vol. LXVI (1958).

2656. Writers and Their Work. A bibliographical series of supplements to British Book News. London, Longmans, Green and Co. for the British Council and the National Book League, 1950–date.—Irregular issues, now apparently monthly. Each issue consists of the literary biography of a prominent English writer.

2657. Würzburger Beiträge zur englischen Literaturgeschichte. Heidelberg, Carl Winter Universitätsbuchhandlung. Vol. I (1911)–Vol. V (1933).

2658. Wyclif Society Publications. London, Wyclif Society. 1882–1907 (20 vols.).

2659. Yale Studies in English. New Haven, Yale Univ. Press. Vol. I (1898)–Vol. CXXXII (1956).—Abbr.: *YSE*.

CHAPTER VII

ENGLISH LANGUAGE: PERIODS

2663. [Best, Richard, ed.] Bibliography of Irish Philology and of Printed Irish Literature. Preface by T. W. Lyster. Dublin, printed under authority of His Majesty's Stationery Office by Browne and Nolan, 1913. xii + 307 pp.—Chiefly Old Irish language and literature.

2664. Kennedy, Arthur G. A Bibliography of Writings on the English Language from the Beginning of Printing to the End of 1922. Cambridge, Mass., Harvard Univ. Press; New Haven, Yale Univ. Press, 1927. xvii + 470 (double column) + 471–517 (triple column) pp.

2665. Best, R[ichard] I. Bibliography of Irish Philology and Manuscript Literature. Publications 1913–1941. Dublin, Dublin Institute for Advanced Studies, 1942. x + 254 pp.

---

§101. SURVEYS OF THE ENGLISH LANGUAGE CHIEFLY HISTORICAL

2669. Emerson, Oliver F. The History of the English Language. London, Macmillan and Co., 1894. xii + 415 pp.—Reprint 1926.

2670. Toller, T[homas] N. Outlines of the History of the English Language. Cambridge Univ. Press, 1900. xiv + 284 pp.—Reprint 1927.

2671. Bradley, Henry. The Making of English. London, Macmillan Co., 1904. viii + 245 pp.—Frequent reprints, as in 1948.

2672. Krapp, Geo. P. Modern English. Its growth and present use. New York, Charles Scribner's Sons, 1909. xi + 357 pp.

2673. Smith, Logan P. The English Language. Oxford Univ. Press, 1912. v + 169 pp.—Number 45 in the series Home University Library of Modern Knowledge. Reset version 1944 reprinted 1948.

2674. Einenkel, Eugen. Geschichte der englischen Sprache. Historische Syntax. 3. Aufl. Strassburg, K. J. Trübner, 1916. xviii + 222 pp.—Volume

VI in the series [Hermann Paul's] Grundriss der germanischen Philologie. Original ed. 1891; second ed. 1901.

2675. Wyld, Henry C. A Short History of English. With a bibliography of recent books on the subject and lists of texts and editions. 3rd ed. London, John Murray, 1927. vii + 294 pp.—Original ed. 1914; second ed. 1923; third ed. reprinted 1949. Bibliography, pp. 1–13.

2676. McKnight, Geo. H. Modern English in the Making. With the assistance of Bert Emsley. New York, D. Appleton and Co., 1928. xii + 590 pp.

2677. Kennedy, Arthur G. Current English. A study of present-day usages and tendencies, including pronunciation, spelling, grammatical practice, word coining, and the shifting of meanings. Boston, Ginn and Co., 1935. viii + 737 pp.

2678. Wyld, Henry Cecil. A History of Modern Colloquial English. 3rd ed. Oxford, Eng., Basil Blackwell, 1936. xviii + 433 pp.—Original ed. 1920; second ed. 1921; third ed. reprinted 1953.

2679. Jespersen, Otto. Growth and Structure of the English Language. 9th ed. London, Macmillan Co., 1938. iv + 244 pp.—Original ed. 1905. Reprints Oxford, Eng., Basil Blackwell, 1948; Garden City, N.Y., Doubleday and Co., 1955, number 46 in the series Anchor Books.

2680. Mossé, Fernand. Esquisse d'une histoire de la langue anglaise. Lyon, IAC, 1947. xv + 268 pp.—Volume II in the series Collection des langues du monde.

2681. Bryant, Margaret M. Modern English and Its Heritage. New York, Macmillan Co., 1948. xii + 407 pp.

2682. Partridge, Eric. English. A course for human beings. London, Winchester Publ'ions Ltd., 1949. xv + 192 + 174 + 173 pp.

2683. Jacobsson, Bengt. Inversion in English with Special Reference to the Early Modern English Period. Uppsala, Sweden, Almqvist ok Wiksells Boktryckeri, 1951. 233 pp.—"Bibliography," pp. 218–220.

2684. Partridge, Eric, and Clark, John W. British and American English since 1900. With contributions on English in Canada, South Africa, Australia, New Zealand, and India. New York, Philosophical Library, 1951. x + 341 pp.

2685. Gokak, V[inayak] K. The Poetic Approach to Language. With special reference to the history of English. Oxford Univ. Press, 1952. xii + 247 pp.

2686. Weekley, Ernest. The English Language. With a chapter on the history of American English by John W. Clark. Rev. ed. New York, British Book Centre, 1952. 138 pp.—Original ed. 1928.

2687. Jones, Richard F. The Triumph of the English Language. A survey of opinions concerning the vernacular from the introduction of printing to the Restoration. Stanford Univ. Press, 1953. xii + 340 pp.

2688. Robertson, Stuart. The Development of Modern English. Revised by Frederic G. Cassidy. 2nd ed. New York, Prentice-Hall Inc., 1954. 469 pp.—Original ed. 1934; revised and enl. ed. 1938.

2689. Vallins, G[eorge] H. The Pattern of English. London, André Deutsch, 1956. 188 pp.—Reprint Harmondsworth, Eng., Penguin Books Ltd., 1957, xi + 168 pp., number A398 in the series Pelican Books.

2690. Baugh, Albert C. A History of the English Language. 2nd ed. New York, Appleton-Century-Crofts, 1957. xiii + 506 pp.—Original ed. 1935.

2691. Brook, G[eorge] L. A History of the English Language. Fair Lawn, N.J., Essential Books, 1958. 224 pp.—In the series The Language Library.

§102. ENGLISH LANGUAGE GRAMMARS

2695. Maetzner, Edward. An English Grammar, Methodical, Analytical, and Historical. With a treatise on orthography, prosody, inflections, and syntax of the English tongue. Translated by Clair J. Grece. London, John Murray, 1874. 3 vols.—Original Ger. ed. 1860–65 in 2 vols.

2696. Sweet, Henry. A Short Historical English Grammar. Oxford, Clarendon Press, 1892. xii + 264 pp.

2697. Sweet, Henry. A New English Grammar, Logical and Historical. Vol. I: Introduction, Chronology, and Accidence; Vol. II: Syntax. Oxford, Clarendon Press, 1891–98. 2 vols.

2698. Poutsma, H[endrik]. A Grammar of Late Modern English. Groningen, P. Noordhoff, 1926–29. 2 parts in 5 vols. (Part I: 1928–29, 2nd ed.; Part II: 1926.)—Original ed. of Part I 1914.

2699. Kruisinga, E[tsko]. A Handbook of Present-Day English. Part I: English Sounds; Part II: English Accidence and Syntax. Part I: Utrecht, Kemink en zoon, 1925, 4th ed.; Part II: Groningen, P. Noordhoff, 1931–32, 5th ed. Part I: 1 vol.; Part II: 3 vols.—Original ed. 1909.

2700. Onions, C[harles] T. An Advanced English Syntax. Based on the principles and requirements of the Grammatical Society. 6th ed. London, Kegan Paul, Trench, Trubner and Co., 1932. vii + 166 pp.—Original ed. 1904.

2701. Jespersen, Otto. Essentials of English Grammar. New York, Henry Holt and Co., 1933. 387 pp.

2702. Curme, Geo. O. A Grammar of the English Language. Vol. II: Parts of Speech and Accidence; Vol. III: Syntax. Boston, D. C. Heath and Co., 1931–35. 2 vols.—Volume I did not appear.

2703. Jespersen, Otto. A Modern English Grammar on Historical Principles. Vol. I: Sounds and Spellings; Vol. II: Syntax, 1st pt.; Vol. III: Syntax, 2nd pt.; Vol. IV: Syntax, Time and Tense, 3rd pt.; Vol. V: Syntax, 4th pt.; Vol. VI: Morphology; Vol. VII: Syntax (completed by Niels Haislund). Heidelberg, Carl Winter, 1909–49. 7 vols.—The publishing history of this work is complex. It belongs to Carl Winter's series Germanische Bibliothek : I. Sammlung germanischer Elementar und Handbücher : I. Reihe : Grammatiken; but volumes V through VII were issued without series title and with the imprint Copenhagen, Einar Munksgaard in the years 1940–49. There was a fourth ed. of Vol. I in 1928 and a fourth ed. of Vol. II, 1st pt., in 1936.

2704. Jordan, John C. A Grammar for Heretics. New York, Rinehart and Co., 1949. x + 158 pp.

2705. Brunner, Karl. Die englische Sprache. Ihre geschichliche Entwicklung. Erster Band : Allgemeines. Lautgeschichte. Zweiter Band : Die Flexionsformen, ihre Verwendung. Das Englische ausserhalb Europas. Halle a. d. Saale, Max Niemeyer Verlag, 1950–51. 2 vols.—Number 6 in the series Sammlung kurzer Grammatiken germanischer Dialekte.

2706. Moore, Samuel. Historical Outlines of English Sounds and Inflections. Revised by Albert H. Marckwardt. Ann Arbor, Mich., George Wahr, 1951. vii + 179 pp.—Reprint 1957. A development of Samuel Moore, *Historical Outlines of English Phonology and Morphology (Middle English and Modern English)*, 2nd ed., Ann Arbor, Mich., George Wahr, 1929, viii + 153 pp.; original ed. 1925.

2707. Zandvoort, R[einard] W. A Handbook of English Grammar. 5th ed. Groningen, Holland, J. B. Wolters, 1953. 392 pp.—Original ed. 1945.

2708. Sledd, James. A Short Introduction to English Grammar. Chicago, Scott, Foresman and Co., 1959. [vi] + 346 pp.

§103. OLD ENGLISH GRAMMARS

2712. Wardale, E[dith] E. An Old English Grammar. New York, E. P. Dutton and Co., [1922]. ix + 131 pp.

2713. Wright, Joseph and Elizabeth M. An Elementary Old English Grammar. Oxford Univ. Press, 1923. vii + 192 pp.—Reprint 1930.

2714. Wright, Joseph and Elizabeth M. Old English Grammar. 3rd ed. Oxford Univ. Press, 1925. xv + 372 pp.—Original ed. 1908; second ed. 1913; third ed. reprinted 1934.

2715. Anderson, Marjorie, and Williams, Blanch C. Old English Handbook. Boston, Houghton Mifflin Co., 1935. vii + 503 pp.

2716. Andrew, Samuel O. Syntax and Style in Old English. Cambridge Univ. Press, 1940. 112 pp.

2717. Sievers, Eduard, and Brunner, Karl. Abriss der altenglischen (angelsächsischen) Grammatik. 12th ed. Halle a. d. Saale, Max Niemeyer Verlag, 1950. viii + 90 pp.—Number 2 in the series Sammlung kurzer Grammatiken germanischer Dialekte. Original ed. 1895.

2718. [Sievers, Eduard.] Altenglische Grammatik. Nach der angelsächsischen Grammatik von Eduard Sievers neuarbeitet von Karl Brunner. Halle a. S., Max Niemeyer, 1951. xi + 468 pp.—Number 3 in the series Sammlung kurzer Grammatiken germanischer Dialekte. Original ed. 1942.

2719. Quirk, Randolph, and Wrenn, C[harles] L. An Old English Grammar. London, Methuen and Co., 1955. x + 166 pp.—In the series Methuen's Old English Library.

2720. Campbell, A[listair]. Old English Grammar. Oxford Univ. Press, 1959. xvi + 423 pp.

§104. MIDDLE ENGLISH GRAMMARS

2724. Jordan, Richard. Handbuch der mittelenglischen Grammatik. I. Teil: Lautlehre. 2. verb. Aufl. von H. Ch. Matthes. Heidelberg, Carl Winter, 1934. xiv + 294 pp.—Original ed. 1925. No second volume published.

2725. Roseborough, Margaret M. An Outline of Middle English Grammar. New York, Macmillan Co., 1938. x + 112 pp.

2726. Brunner, Karl. Abriss der mittelenglischen Grammatik. 3rd ed. Tübingen, Max Niemeyer Verlag, 1953. 113 pp.—Number 6 in the series Sammlung kurzer Grammatiken germanischer Dialekte. Original ed. 1938; second ed. 1948.

§105. OLD ENGLISH READERS

[See also §7. British Literature: Old and Middle English; §45. Surveys: The Old and Middle English Periods.]

2730. Sweet, Henry. A Second Anglo-Saxon Reader. Archaic and dialectal. Oxford, Clarendon Press, 1887. iv + 214 pp.—In the Clarendon Press Series.

2731. Cook, Albert S. A First Book in Old English. Grammar, reader, notes, and vocabulary. 3rd ed. Boston, Ginn and Co., 1921. xiv + 330 pp.—Original ed. 1894; second ed. 1900.

2732. Krapp, Geo. P., and Kennedy, Arthur G. An Anglo-Saxon Reader. New York, Henry Holt and Co., 1929. cxiv + 359 pp.

2733. Flom, Geo. T. Introductory Old English Grammar and Reader. Boston, D. C. Heath and Co., 1930. xiv + 413 pp.

2734. Turk, Milton H. An Anglo-Saxon Reader. With a chapter on word formation by Francis P. Magoun Jr. Rev. ed. New York, Charles Scribner's Sons, 1931. x + 419 pp.—Original ed. 1927.

2735. [Bright, James W.] Bright's Anglo-Saxon Reader. Revised and enl. by James R. Hulbert. New York, Henry Holt and Co., 1935. cxxxii + 395 pp.—Original ed. 1891; fourth and last before the Bright-Hulbert version 1917; frequent reprints of the 1935 ed., as in 1953. Translation of the Bright-Hulbert texts Francis P. Magoun, Jr., and James A. Walker, *An Old-English Anthology*, Dubuque, Iowa, William C. Brown Co., 1950, x + 108 pp.

2736. Wyatt, A[lfred] J. The Threshold of Anglo-Saxon. 2nd ed. Cambridge Univ. Press, 1935. xiv + 126 pp.—Original ed. 1926.

2737. Setzler, Edwin B., Edwin L., and Hubert H. The Jefferson Anglo-Saxon Grammar and Reader. New York, Macmillan Co., 1938. xiv + 198 pp.

2738. Moore, Samuel, and Knott, Thos. A. The Elements of Old English. Elementary grammar, reference grammar, and reading selections. 9th ed. Ann Arbor, Mich., George Wahr, 1942. viii + 339 pp.—Original ed. 1919.

2739. Mossé, Fernand. Manuel de l'anglais du moyen âge des origines au XIVᵉ siècle. I: Vieil-Anglais. Tome premier: Grammaire et textes; Tome second: Notes et glossaire. Deuxième édition. Paris, Aubier, 1950. 2 (continuously paged) vols., 345 + 347–552 pp.—Volume VIII, pt. 1, in the series Bibliothèque de philologie germanique. Original ed. 1945. "Bibliographie," I, pp. 13–17.

2740. [Sweet, Henry.] Sweet's Anglo-Saxon Primer. Edited by Norman Davis. 9th ed. Oxford, Clarendon Press, 1953. vi + 129 pp.—Original ed. 1882.

2741. Brook, G[eorge] L. An Introduction to Old English. Manchester, Eng., University Press, 1955. xi + 138 pp.

2742. Lehnert, Martin. Poetry and Prose of the Anglo-Saxons. A textbook with introductions, translations, bibliography, and an Old English etymological dictionary. Berlin, VEB Deutscher Verlag der Wissenschaften, 1955–56. 2 vols.

2743. Lehnert, Martin. Altenglisches Elementarbuch. Einführung, Grammatik, Texte mit Übersetzung und Wörterbuch. 4th ed. Berlin, W. de Gruyter, 1959. 178 pp.—Number 1125 in the series Sammlung Göschen. Original ed. 1939.

2744. [Sweet, Henry.] Sweet's Anglo-Saxon Reader in Prose and Verse. Revised throughout by C. T. Onions. 14th ed. Oxford, Clarendon Press, 1959. viii + 312 pp.—Original ed. 1876.

§106. MIDDLE ENGLISH READERS

[See also §7. British Literature: Old and Middle English; §45. Surveys: The Old and Middle English Periods.]

2748. Sweet, Henry. First Middle English Primer. Extracts from the Ancren Riwle and Ormulum with grammar and glossary. Oxford, Clarendon Press, 1891. vii + 100 pp.—In the Clarendon Press Series. Original ed. 1884; second ed. reprinted 1909. See also Sweet's *Second Middle English Primer*, Extracts from Chaucer with grammar and glossary, 2nd ed., Oxford, Clarendon Press, 1905, vi + 115 pp., in the Clarendon Press Series, original ed. 1891, second ed. reprinted 1948.

2749. MacLean, Geo. E. An Old and Middle English Reader. On the basis of Professor Julius Zupitza's Alt- und Mittelenglische Übungsbuch. With introduction, notes, and glossary. New York, Macmillan Co., 1911. lxxiv + 295 pp.

2750. Cook, Albert S. A Literary Middle English Reader. Boston, Ginn and Co., 1915. xxviii + 554 pp.

2751. Emerson, Oliver F. A Middle English Reader. Edited, with grammatical introduction, notes, and glossary. New and rev. ed. London, Macmillan Co., 1915. cxxvii + 478 pp.—Original ed. 1905; second ed. reprinted 1950.

2752. Sisam, Kenneth. Fourteenth Century Verse and Prose. Oxford, Clarendon Press, 1921. xlvii + 292 + [vi] pp.—Bound in between text and index *A Middle English Vocabulary*, by J. R. R. Tolkien, 1922, [162] (double column) pp. Frequent reprints, as in 1956.

2753. Brandl, Alois, and Zippel, Otto. Middle English Literature. 2nd ed. New York, Chelsea Publ'ing Co., 1947. viii + 423 pp.—Reprint with English title page but with ME glosses in German and English of *Mittelenglische Sprach- und Literaturproben*, 2nd ed., Berlin, Weidmann, 1927, whose original ed. was 1915.

2754. Wardale, E[dith] E. An Introduction to Middle English. London, Kegan Paul, Trench, Trubner and Co., 1937. x + 130 pp.

2755. Mossé, Fernand. Manuel de l'anglais du moyen âge des origines au XIVe siècle. II: Moyen-Anglais. Tome premier: Grammaire et textes; Tome second: Notes et glossaire. Paris, Aubier, 1949. 2 vols.—Volume XII, pt. 2, in the series Bibliothèque de philologie germanique. "Bibliographie," II, pp. 11–16. Translation by J. A. Walker, *A Handbook of Middle English*, Foreword by Kemp Malone, Baltimore, Johns Hopkins Press, 1952, xxiv + 495 pp.

2756. Kaiser, Rolf. Medieval English. An Old English and Middle English Anthology. 3rd ed. West Berlin, Germany, published by the author, 1958. xxix + 592 pp.—Original ed. 1954; second ed. 1955.

§107. OLD ENGLISH DICTIONARIES AND GLOSSARIES

2760. Wright, Thos. Anglo-Saxon and Old English Vocabularies. Edited and collated by Richard P. Wülcker. 2nd ed. Vol. I: Vocabularies; Vol. II:

Indices. London, Trübner and Co., 1884. 2 vols.—Original ed. 1857–73 in 2 vols.

2761. Sweet, Henry. The Student's Dictionary of Anglo-Saxon. New York, Macmillan Co., 1897. xvi + 217 (double column) pp.

2762. Grein, C[hristian] W. M. Sprachschatz der angelsächsischen Dichter. Unter Mitwirkung von F. Holthausen, neu herausgegeben von J. J. Köhler. Heidelberg, Carl Winter, 1912. vi + 897 (double column) pp. —Volume IV in the series Germanische Bibliothek. Original ed. 1861–64 in 2 vols.

2763. Bosworth, Joseph. An Anglo-Saxon Dictionary. Edited and enl. by T[homas] Northcote Toller. Oxford, Clarendon Press, 1882–98. xiv + 1302 (double column) pp.—Also *Supplement,* by T. Northcote Toller, Oxford, Clarendon Press, 1908–21, 768 (double column) pp. Reprint of *Dictionary* and *Supplement* 1955.

2764. Hall, John R. Clark. A Concise Anglo-Saxon Dictionary. 3rd ed. rev. and enl. Cambridge Univ. Press, 1931. xv + 437 (double column) pp. —Original ed. 1894; second ed. 1916.

2765. Holthausen, Ferdinand. Altenglisches etymologisches Wörterbuch. Heidelberg, Carl Winter Universitätsbuchhandlung, 1934. xxviii + 428 pp.—Volume VII in the series Germanische Bibliothek, I. Sammlung germanischer Elementar- und Handbücher, IV. Reihe : Wörterbücher.

2766. Meritt, Herbert D. Fact and Lore about Old English Words. Stanford Univ. Press, 1954. xiv + 226 pp.

§108. MIDDLE AND EARLY ENGLISH DICTIONARIES

2770. Stratmann, Francis H. A Middle-English Dictionary. Containing words used by English writers from the twelfth to the fifteenth century. A new ed., rearranged, rev. and enl. by Henry Bradley. Oxford, Clarendon Press, 1891. xxiii + 708 (double column) pp.—Original ed. 1867; second ed. 1873; third ed. 1878 and supplement 1881.

2771. Mersand, Joseph. Chaucer's Romance Vocabulary. 2nd ed. New York, Comet Press, 1939. xiii + 179 pp.—Original ed. 1937.

2772. Kurath, Hans, and Kuhn, Sherman M., eds. Middle English Dictionary. Ann Arbor, University of Michigan Press, 1952–date. Double column page fascicules.—Coverage (1959) through the letter *f*. "Bibliography," by Margaret S. Ogden, Charles E. Palmer, and Richard L. McKelvey.

§109. HISTORICAL AND ETYMOLOGICAL DICTIONARIES

2776. Nares, Robt. A Glossary or Collection of Words, Phrases, Names, and Allusions to Customs, Proverbs . . . in the Works of English Authors Particularly Shakespeare and His Contemporaries. A new ed. . . . by James O. Halliwell and Thomas Wright. Vol. I: A–J; Vol. II: K–Z. London, John Russell Smith, 1859. 2 vols.—Original ed. 1822. New ed. reprint London, Gibbings and Co., 1901.

2777. Latham, Robt. Gordon. A Dictionary of the English Language. Founded on that of Dr. Samuel Johnson as edited by the Rev. H. J. Todd. With numerous emendations and additions. London, Longmans, Green and Co., et. al., 1866–70. 2 (triple column page) vols. issued in four separately bound parts.

2778. Skeat, Walter W. An Etymological Dictionary of the English Language. New ed. rev. and enl. Oxford, Clarendon Press, [1909]. xliv + 780 (double column) pp.—Original ed. 1879–82; second ed. 1883; third ed. 1897; fourth ed. reprinted 1946, 1956. Also *A Concise Etymological Dictionary of the English Language*, new and corrected impression, Oxford Univ. Press, 1911, xvi + 664 (double column) pp., original ed. 1882, second ed. reprinted 1936.

2779. Century Dictionary and Cyclopedia. With a new atlas of the world. A work of general reference in all departments of knowledge. Rev. and enl. ed. New York, Century Co., [1911]. 12 (chiefly triple column) pp.—Original ed. 1889–91 in 6 vols. The original was prepared under the direction of William D. Whitney; the revision was prepared by Benjamin E. Smith. Volume XI: *The Century Cyclopedia of Names* and Volume XII: *The Century Atlas of the World* were prepared under the direction of Benjamin E. Smith.

2780. Weekley, Ernest. An Etymological Dictionary of Modern English. New York, E. P. Dutton and Co., 1921. xx + 1659 (double column) pp.—Also *A Concise Etymological Dictionary of Modern English*, revised ed., New York, E. P. Dutton and Co., 1952, xv + 480 (double column) pp., original ed. 1921.

2781. Halliwell, James Orchard. A Dictionary of Archaic and Provincial Words, Obsolete Phrases, Proverbs, and Ancient Customs, from the Fourteenth Century. Two volumes in one. 7th ed. London, George Routledge and Sons, 1924. xxxvi + 960 (double column) pp.—Original ed. 1847. An "Eleventh Edition," identical to the above, except for being bound in two volumes, was issued London, Reeves and Turner, 1889.

2782. Murray, James A. H., Bradley, Henry, Craigie, W[illiam] A., and Onions, C[harles] T., eds. The Oxford English Dictionary. Being a corrected re-issue with an introduction, supplement, and bibliography of A New English Dictionary on Historical Principles Founded Mainly on the Materials Collected by the Philological Society. Oxford Univ. Press, 1933. 12 (triple column page) vols. plus a supplement vol. without vol. no. and with the title *Supplement and Bibliography.*—Original ed. 1884–1928 in 10 vols. Abbr.: *OED* or *NED.*

2783. Shipley, Joseph T. Dictionary of Word Origins. 2nd ed. New York, Philosophical Library, 1945. x + 430 (double column) pp.—Original ed. also 1945.

2784. Holthausen, Ferdinand. Etymologisches Wörterbuch der englischen Sprache. 3rd ed. Göttingen, Vandenhoeck und Ruprecht, 1949. vii + 226 pp.—Original ed. 1917; second ed. 1927.

2785. Little, Wm., Fowler, H[enry] W., and Coulson, J[ohn], eds. The Shorter Oxford English Dictionary on Historical Principles. Revised and edited by C. T. Onions. Third ed., rev. with addenda. Oxford Univ. Press, 1955. xxii + 2515 (triple column) pp.—Original ed. 1933; second ed. 1936.

2786. Wedeck, Harry E. Short Dictionary of Classical Word Origins. Introduction by Eric Partridge. New York, Philosophical Library, 1957. [xi] + 85 pp.—In the series Midcentury Reference Library.

2787. Partridge, Eric. Origins. A short etymological dictionary of modern English. London, Routledge and Kegan Paul, 1958. xix + 970 (double column) pp.

§110. AMERICAN ENGLISH

2791. Tucker, Gilbert M. American English. New York, Alfred A. Knopf, 1921. 375 pp.—"Bibliography," pp. 332–345.

2792. Krapp, Geo. Philip. The English Language in America. New York, Century Co. for the Modern Language Association of America, 1925. 2 vols.—"Bibliography," II, pp. 273–284.

2793. Fries, Chas. C. American English Grammar. The grammatical structure of present-day American English with especial reference to social differences or class dialects. New York, D. Appleton-Century Co., 1940. ix + 313 pp.—Number 10 in the series English Monographs of the National Council of Teachers of English.

2794. Wild, J[acob] Henry. Glimpses of the American Language and Civilization. Bern, Switzerland, A. Francke AG, 1945. 130 pp.

2795. Mallery, Richard D. Our American Language. Garden City, N.Y., Garden City Publ'ing Co., 1947. xii + 276 pp.

2796. Mencken, H[enry] L. The American Language. An inquiry into the development of English in the United States. 4th ed. New York, A. A. Knopf, 1936. xi + 769 + xxiv pp.—First ed. 1919; second ed. 1921; third ed. 1923; fourth ed. reprinted 1941, 1947. *Supplement I* (1945) xv + 739 + xxxv pp. *Supplement II* (1948) xiii + 890 + xliii pp.

2797. Faden, I B. How America Speaks and Writes. A dictionary of American idioms with a Swedish vocabulary. In collaboration with Ebba Dalin and Karin Pontoppidan-Sjövall. Introduction by Margaret Schlauch. Stockholm, Hugo Gebers Förlag, 1949. 363 pp.

2798. Galinsky, Hans. Die Sprache des Amerikaners. Eine Einführung in die Hauptunterscheide zwischen amerikanischen und britischen Englisch der Gegenwart. Band I: Das Klangbild, die Schreibung; Band II: Wortschatz und Wortbildung; Syntax und Flexion. Heidelberg, F. H. Kerle Verlag, 1951–52. 2 vols.

2799. Myers, L[ouis] M. American English. A twentieth century grammar. New York, Prentice-Hall Inc., 1952. xii + 237 pp.—In the series Prentice-Hall English Composition and Introduction to Literature.

2800. Pyles, Thos. Words and Ways of American English. New York, Random House, 1952. ix + 310 pp.

2801. Lloyd, Donald J., and Warfel, Harry R. American English in Its Cultural Setting. New York, Alfred A. Knopf, 1956. xvi + 554 + xviii pp.

2802. Marckwardt, Albert H. American English. New York, Oxford Univ. Press, 1958. xi + 194 pp.

§111. DICTIONARIES OF AMERICAN ENGLISH

2806. Bartlett, John R. Dictionary of Americanisms. A glossary of words and phrases regarded as peculiar to the United States. 4th ed. Boston, Little, Brown and Co., 1877. xlvi + 813 pp.—Original ed. 1848; fourth ed. reprinted 1896.

2807. Farmer, John S. Americanisms Old and New. A dictionary of words, phrases, and colloquialisms peculiar to the United States, British America, the West Indies. . . . London, privately printed by T. Poulter and Sons, 1889. xx + 564 pp.

2808. Thornton, Richard H. An American Glossary. Being an attempt to illustrate certain Americanisms upon historical principles. Vol. I: A–L; Vol. II: M–Z. Philadelphia, J. B. Lippincott Co., 1912. 2 (continuously paged) vols.—[*Supplement*] Volume III, edited by Louise Hanley, a biographical sketch of Richard Hopwood Thornton, foreword by William A. Craigie, introductory note by Percy W. Long, Madison, Wis., American Dialect Society, 1939, xiv + 452 pp. Volume III was originally published in *Dialect Notes*, 1931–39, and provided with drop-folio pagination.

2809. Craigie, Wm. A., Hulbert, James R., et al. A Dictionary of American English on Historical Principles. University of Chicago Press, 1936–44. 4 (chiefly double column page, continuously paged) vols.—Reprint 1960. "Bibliography," pp. 2529–2552.

2810. Mathews, Mitford M. A Dictionary of Americanisms on Historical Principles. University of Chicago Press, 1951. 2 (chiefly double column page, continuously paged) vols.—Reprint in one volume 1956, xvi + 1946 (chiefly double column) pp. "Bibliography," II, pp. 1913–1946.

CHAPTER VIII

ENGLISH LANGUAGE: SPECIAL SUBJECTS

[See also §90. Linguistics Periodicals.]

2814. Linguistic Bibliography. Utrecht, Spectrum Publ'ers, 1949 (for 1939–47)-date.—Annual. Published by the Permanent International Committee of Linguistics with a grant from the United Nations Educational, Scientific, and Cultural Organization.

2815. Year's Work in Modern Language Studies by a Number of Scholars. Oxford Univ. Press for the Modern Humanities Research Association, 1931 (for 1930)-date.—Annual. Abbr.: *YWMLS*.

---

§112. HANDBOOKS

2819. Meillet, A[ntoine], and Cohen, Marcel, eds. Les langues du monde. Nouvelle édition. Paris, Centre national de la recherche scientifique, 1952. xlii + 1296 pp. + Atlas des langues du monde (21 cartes).—Original ed. 1924.

2820. Ostermann, Georg F. von. Manual of Foreign Languages. For the use of librarians, bibliographers, research workers, editors, translators, and printers. 4th ed. New York, Central Book Co., 1952. [xv] + 414 pp.—Third ed. Georg F. von Ostermann and A[ugustus] E. Giegengack, *Manual of Foreign Languages*, For the use of printers and translators, Washington, D.C., Government Printing Office, 1936, ix + 347 pp. The work is a series of summaries of the salient features of some one hundred languages and in its second ed. 1935 was issued as a "Supplement to [the] Style Manual of the United States Government Printing Office."

2821. Newald, Richard, and Ristow, Brigitte. Sachwörterbuch zur deutschen Philologie. Lahr, Baden, Verlag Moritz Schauenburg, 1954. 144 pp.

2822. Pei, Mario A., and Gaynor, Frank. A Dictionary of Linguistics. New York, Philosophical Library, 1954. [viii] + 238 pp.—In the series Midcentury Reference Library.

2823. Bower, Wm. W. International Manual of Linguists and Translators. New York, Scarecrow Press, 1959. xvii + 18–451 pp.

§113. LEXICOGRAPHY

2827. Collison, Robt. L. Dictionaries of Foreign Languages. A bibliographical guide to the general and technical dictionaries of the chief foreign languages with historical and explanatory notes and references. New York, Hafner Publ'ing Co., 1955. xix + 210 pp.—"General Bibliography," pp. 191–192.

2828. Foreign Language-English Dictionaries. Vol. I: Special Subject Dictionaries with Emphasis on Science and Technology; Vol. II: General Language Dictionaries. Washington, D.C., Library of Congress, 1955. 2 vols.—"Miss Gladys R. Carpenter of this Division [i.e., General Reference and Bibliography Division] is responsible for the major part of the work," p. iv of the Introduction by Henry J. Dubester.

2829. Zaunmüller, Wolfram. Bibliographisches Handbuch der Sprachwörterbücher. Ein internationales Verzeichnis von 5600 Wörterbüchern der Jahre 1460–1958 für mehr als 500 Sprachen und Dialekte. An annotated bibliography of language dictionaries. Stuttgart, Anton Hiersemann, 1958. xvi + 496 numbered columns.

2830. Mason, Geo. A Supplement to Johnson's English Dictionary. Of which the palpable errors are attempted to be rectified and its material omissions supplied. London, printed by C. Roworth for John White, Leigh and Sotheby's, and T. Payne, 1801. Unpaginated (*circa* 200 double column pp.).

2831. Richardson, Chas. Illustrations of English Philology. Consisting of I. A critical examination of Dr. Johnson's Dictionary; II. Remarks on Mr. Dugdale Stewart's essay On the Tendency of Some Late Philological Speculations. London, Gale and Fenner, 1815. 292 pp.

2832. Mathews, M[itford] M. A Survey of English Dictionaries. Oxford Univ. Press, 1933. 123 pp.

2833. Noyes, Gertrude E. The Development of Cant Lexicography in England. Studies in Philology, XXXVIII (1941), 462–479.

2834. Starnes, DeWitt T., and Noyes, Gertrude E. The English Dictionary from Cawdrey to Johnson 1604–1755. Chapel Hill, University of North Carolina Press, 1946. x + 299 pp.

2835. Mathews, M[itford] M. Problems Encountered in the Preparation of a Dictionary of American Words and Meanings. English Institute Essays (New York, Columbia Univ. Press, 1947), pp. 76–96.

2836. Chapman, R[obert] W. Lexicography. Oxford Univ. Press, 1948. 34 pp.—The James Bryce memorial lecture 1948.

2837. Smalley, Vera E. The Sources of A Dictionary of the French and English Tongues by Randle Cotgrave (London, 1611). A study in Renaissance lexicography. Baltimore, Johns Hopkins Press, 1948. 252 pp.—Extra Volume XXV in the series Johns Hopkins Studies in Romance Literatures and Languages.

2838. Noyes, Gertrude E. The Beginning of the Study of Synonyms in England. PMLA, LXVI, 6 (Dec. 1951), 951–970.

2839. Hulbert, James R. Dictionaries British and American. London, André Deutsch, 1955. 107 pp.—In the series The Language Library.

2840. Sledd, James H., and Kolb, Gwin J. Dr. Johnson's Dictionary. University of Chicago Press, 1955. 255 pp.

2841. Starnes, DeWitt T., and Talbert, Ernest W. Classical Myth and Legend in Renaissance Dictionaries. A study of Renaissance dictionaries in their relation to the classical learning of contemporary English writers. Chapel Hill, University of North Carolina Press, 1955. ix + 517 pp.

§114. STUDIES IN WORD ORIGINS, SEMANTIC SHIFTS, MORPHOLOGIC CHANGE, AND SYNTAX

2845. Palmer, A[bram] Smythe. Folk-Etymology. A dictionary of verbal corruptions or words perverted in form or meaning by false derivation or mistaken analogy. London, George Bell and Sons, 1882. xxviii + 664 (double column) pp.

2846. Skeat, Walter W. Principles of English Etymology. First Series: The Native Element; Second Series: The Foreign Element. Oxford, Clarendon Press, 1887–91. 2 vols.

2847. Greenough, James B., and Kittredge, Geo. L. Words and Their Ways in English Speech. New York, Macmillan Co., 1901. x + 431 pp.—Reprint 1929.

2848. Skeat, W[alter] W. Notes on English Etymology. Chiefly reprinted from the transactions of the Philological Society. Oxford, Clarendon Press, 1901. xxii + 479 pp.—Studies of words of Mexican, Peruvian, West Indian, and Brazilian origin and of Anglo-French words.

2849. Efvergren, Carl. Names of Places in a Transferred Sense in English. Cambridge, Eng., W. Heffer and Sons, 1909. xi + 123 pp.

2850. Lounsbury, Thos. R. English Spelling and Spelling Reform. New York, Harper and Bros., 1909. xiv + 357 pp.

2851. Weekley, Ernest. The Romance of Words. 4th ed. New York, E. P. Dutton and Co., 1922. xii + 225 pp.—Original ed. 1912; fourth ed. frequently reprinted, as in 1934. A treatment *inter alia* of semantics, metaphor, folk etymology, doublets, and place and family names.

2852. McKnight, Geo. H. English Words and Their Background. New York, D. Appleton and Co., 1923. x + 449 pp.

2853. Hargrave, Basil. Origins and Meanings of Popular Phrases and Names. Rev. ed. London, T. Werner Laurie Ltd., 1925. vi + 350 pp.—Original ed. 1911; revised ed. frequently reprinted, as in 1948.

2854. Johnson, Edwin Lee. Latin Words of Common English. Boston, D. C. Heath and Co., 1931. viii + 327 pp.

2855. Smock, John C. The Greek Element in English Words. Edited by Percy W. Long. New York, Macmillan Co., 1931. xiv + 267 (double column) + vi + 356 (double column) pp.

2856. Smith, Logan Pearsall. Words and Idioms. Studies in the English language. 4th ed. London, Constable and Co., 1933. xi + 300 pp.—Original ed. 1925. A treatment *inter alia* of English sea terms, English in foreign languages, popular and standard speech, and current idioms.

2857. Serjeantson, Mary S. A History of Foreign Words in English. London, Kegan Paul, Trench, Trubner and Co., 1935. ix + 354 pp.

2858. Holt, Alfred H. Phrase Origins. A study of familiar expressions. New York, Thomas Y. Crowell Co., 1936. viii + 328 pp.

2859. Carr, Chas T. Nominal Compounds in Germanic. Oxford Univ. Press, 1939. xxxvi + 497 pp.—Number 41 in the series St. Andrews University Publications.

2860. Williams, Edna R. The Conflict of Homonyms in English. New Haven, Yale Univ. Press, 1944. vii + 130 pp.

2861. Hixson, Jerome C., and Colodny, I[sidor]. Word Ways. A study of our living language. New York, American Book Co., 1946. vi + 338 pp.—Original ed. 1939.

2862. Weekley, Ernest. Words Ancient and Modern. London, John Murray, 1946. viii + 214 pp.

2863. Partridge, Eric. Words at War: Words at Peace. Essays on language in general and particular words. London, Frederick Muller Ltd., 1948. ix + 176 pp.

2864. Vallins, G[eorge] H. The Making and Meaning of Words. A companion to the dictionary. London, Adam and Charles Black, 1949. vii + 216 pp.

2865. Funk, Chas. Earle. Thereby Hangs a Tale. Stories of curious word origins. New York, Harper and Bros., 1950. xiii + 303 pp.

2866. Funk, Wilfred. Word Origins and Their Romantic Stories. New York, Wilfred Funk Publ'ers, 1950. ix + 432 pp.

2867. Partridge, Eric. Here, There, and Everywhere. Essays upon language. 2nd ed. London, Hamish Hamilton, 1950. 188 pp.—Original ed. also 1950.

2868. Partridge, Eric. Name into Word. Proper names that have become common property. 2nd ed. New York, Macmillan Co., 1950. xv + 648 pp.—Original ed. 1949.

2869. Empson, Wm. The Structure of Complex Words. Norfolk, Conn., New Directions, [1951]. [ix] + 450 pp.

2870. Hatcher, Anna G. Modern English Word-Formation and Neo-Latin. A study of the origins of English (French, Italian, German) copulative compounds. Baltimore, Johns Hopkins Press, 1951. ix + 226 pp.

2871. Prins, A[nton] A. French Influence in English Phrasing. Leiden, Holland, Universitaire Pers, 1952. vii + 320 pp.—"Bibliography," pp. 307–320.

2872. Brown, Ivor. Words in Our Time. London, Jonathan Cape, 1958. 127 pp.

2873. Funk, Chas. Earle and Chas. Earle, Jr. Horsefeathers and Other Curious Words. Illustrations by Tom Funk. New York, Harper and Bros., 1958. xv + 240 pp.

2874. Ross, Alan S. C. Etymology. With especial reference to English. Fair Lawn, N.J., Essential Books, 1958. 169 pp.—In the series The Language Library.

§115. BASIC ENGLISH

2878. Ogden, C[harles] K. The System of Basic English. New York, Harcourt, Brace and Co., 1934. ix + 320 pp.

2879. Neurath, Otto. Basic by Isotype. London, Kegan Paul, Trench, Trubner and Co., 1937. 130 pp.—Number 86 in the Psyche Miniatures: General Series. Instruction by the use of pictures.

2880. Ogden, C[harles] K. The General Basic English Dictionary. Giving more than 40000 senses of over 20000 words in basic English. New York, W. W. Norton and Co., 1942. x + 441 pp.

2881. Richards, I[vor] A. Basic English and Its Uses. New York, W. W. Norton and Co., 1943. 143 pp.

2882. Ogden, C[harles] K. Basic English. A general introduction with rules and grammar. 9th ed. London, Kegan Paul, Trench, Trubner and Co., 1944. 184 pp.—Number 29 in the Psyche Miniatures: General Series. Original ed. 1930.

2883. Haber, Tom B. Handbook of Basic English. Introduction by Norman Angell. New York, D. Appleton-Century Co., 1945. xvii + 141 pp.

2884. Richards, I[vor] A., and Gibson, Christine. Learning Basic English. A practical handbook for English-speaking people. New York, W. W. Norton and Co., 1945. 116 pp.

§116. PRONUNCIATION MANUALS

2888. Mackey, Mary Stuart, and Goodwin, Maryette. The Pronunciation of Ten Thousand Proper Names. New ed. New York, Dodd, Mead and Co., 1922. xiii + 329 pp.—Original ed. 1901; new ed. reprinted 1938.

2889. Palmer, H[arold] E., Martin, J[ames] Victor, and Blanford, F[rancis] G. A Dictionary of English Pronunciation with American Variants.

(In phonetic transcription.) Cambridge, Eng., W. Heffer and Sons, 1926. xlix + 436 pp.

2890. Vizetelly, Frank H. A Desk Book of Twenty-Five Thousand Words Frequently Mispronounced. 4th ed. New York, Grosset and Dunlap, 1929. xxxvi + 906 pp.—Original ed. 1917.

2891. Larsen, Thorleif, and Walker, Francis C. Pronunciation. A practical guide to American standards. Oxford Univ. Press, 1930. viii + 198 pp.

2892. Colby, Frank O. The American Pronouncing Dictionary of Troublesome Words. New York, Thomas Y. Crowell Co., 1950. [xi] + 399 (chiefly double column) pp.

2893. Sweet, Fred A., and Williams, Maud D. Twenty Thousand Words Often Mispronounced. A complete handbook. . . . New York, G. P. Putnam's Sons, 1937. xvii + 791 pp.—Original ed. 1889.

2894. Greet, W[illiam] Cabell. War Words. Recommended pronunciations. New York, Columbia Univ. Press, 1943. 137 pp.

2895. Kenyon, John S., and Knott, Thos. A. A Pronouncing Dictionary of American English. Springfield, Mass., G. and C. Merriam Co., 1944. lii + 484 (double column) pp.—Reprint 1953.

2896. Opdycke, John B. Don't Say It. A cyclopedia of English use and abuse. 3rd ed. New York, Funk and Wagnalls, 1944. vii + 850 pp.—Original ed. 1939; second ed. 1943.

2897. Greet, W[illiam] Cabell. World Words. Recommended pronunciations. 2nd ed. New York, Columbia Univ. Press, 1948. lv + 608 pp.—Original ed. 1944.

2898. Needleman, Morriss H. A Manual of Pronunciation. New York, Barnes and Noble Inc., 1949. cxxiii + 323 pp.

2899. Bender, James F. NBC Handbook of Pronunciation. Foreword by Pat Kelly. 2nd ed. New York, Thomas Y. Crowell Co., 1951. xii + 372 pp. —Original ed. 1943.

2900. Jones, Daniel. Everyman's English Pronouncing Dictionary. Containing 58000 words in International Phonetic Transcription. 11th ed. New York, E. P. Dutton and Co., 1956. xlv + 538 pp.—In the series Everyman's Reference Library. Original ed. 1917.

§117. PHONOLOGY AND PHONETICS

2904. Sweet, Henry. A History of English Sounds from the Earliest Period. With full word-lists. Oxford, Clarendon Press, 1888. xv + 409 pp.—Original printing in *Transactions of the Philological Society* 1873–74.

2905. Krapp, Geo. P. The Pronunciation of Standard English in America. New York, Oxford Univ. Press, 1919. xv + 235 pp.

2906. Dewey, Godfrey. Relativ [sic] Frequency of English Speech Sounds. Introduction by C. H. Grandgent. Cambridge, Mass., Harvard Univ. Press, 1923. xii + 187 pp.

2907. Aiken, Janet Rankin. Why English Sounds Change. New York, Ronald Press Co., 1929. vii + 146 pp.

2908. Ward, Ida C. The Phonetics of English. Cambridge, Eng., W. Heffer and Sons, 1929. xi + 176 pp.—"Bibliography," pp. 169–170.

2909. Fuhrken, G[eorg] E. Standard English Speech. A compendium of English phonetics for foreign students. Cambridge Univ. Press, 1932. viii + 121 pp.—"Bibliography," pp. 115–116.

2910. Davies, Constance. English Pronunciation from the Fifteenth to the Eighteenth Century. A handbook to the study of historical grammar. London, J. M. Dent and Sons, 1934. xvi + 167 pp.

2911. Saxe, Joseph. Bernard Shaw's Phonetics. A comparative study of cockney sound-changes. Copenhagen, Denmark, Levin og Munksgaard, 1936. 86 pp.

2912. Palmer, H[arold] E., and Blanford, F[rancis] G. A Grammar of Spoken English on a Strictly Phonetic Basis. 2nd ed. Cambridge, Eng., W. Heffer and Sons, 1939. xxxviii + 298 pp.—Original ed. 1924.

2913. Curry, Robt. O. L. The Mechanism of the Human Voice. Foreword by Douglas Guthrie. New York, Longmans, Green and Co., 1940. ix + 205 pp.—"Bibliography and Selected References," pp. 194–202.

2914. Kruisinga, E[tsko]. An Introduction to the Study of English Sounds. 7th ed. Groningen, P. Noordhoff, 1940. 218 pp.—Original ed. 1914.

2915. Kantner, Claude E., and West, Robt. Phonetics. An introduction to the principles of phonetic science from the point of view of English speech. [Enlarged ed.] New York, Harper and Bros., 1941. xxxii + 418 pp.—Original ed. 1933.

2916. Kruisinga, E[tsko]. The Phonetic Structure of English Words. Bern, Switzerland, A. Francke AG, [1943]. vii + 179 pp.

2917. Pike, Kenneth L. Phonetics. A critical analysis of phonetic theory and a technic for the practical description of sounds. Ann Arbor, University of Michigan Press, 1943. ix + 182 pp.—Volume XXI in the series University of Michigan Publications in Language and Literature. Lithoprint with corrections 1944.

2918. Pike, Kenneth L. The Intonation of American English. Ann Arbor, University of Michigan Press, 1945. xi + 200 pp.—Number 1 in the series University of Michigan Publications in Linguistics. Frequent reprints, as in 1956.

2919. Joos, Martin. Acoustic Phonetics. Baltimore, Linguistic Society of America, 1948. 136 pp.—Number 23 in the series Language Monographs.

2920. Heffner, Roe-Merrill S. General Phonetics. With a foreword by W. F. Twaddell. Madison, University of Wisconsin Press, 1949. xvii + 253 pp.

2921. Jones, Daniel. The Pronunciation of English. 3rd ed. Cambridge Univ. Press, 1950. xx + 206 pp.—Original ed. 1909.

2922. Kenyon, John S. American Pronunciation. 10th ed. Ann Arbor, Mich., George Wahr, 1950. x + 265 pp.—Original ed. 1924. "Bibliographical Note," pp. 1–2.

2923. Martinet, André. Phonology as Functional Phonetics. Oxford Univ. Press, 1950. 40 pp.—Number 15 in the series Publications of the Philological Society. Reprint Oxford, Eng., Basil Blackwell, 1955. Three lectures delivered before the University of London 1946.

2924. Orr, John. Words and Sounds in English and French. Oxford, Eng., Basil Blackwell, 1953. viii + 279 pp.—In the series Modern Language Studies.

2925. Horn, Wilhelm, and Lehnert, Martin. Laut und Leben. Englische Lautgeschichte der neueren Zeit (1400–1950). Berlin, Deutscher Verlag der Wissenschaften, 1954. 2 vols.

2926. Lindblad, Karl-Erik. Noah Webster's Pronunciation and Modern New England Speech. A comparison. Uppsala, Sweden, A.-B. Lundequistska Bokhandeln, 1954. 90 pp.—Number 11 in the series Essays and Studies on American Language and Literature. "Bibliography," pp. 86–90.

2927. Hockett, Chas. Francis. A Manual of Phonology. Baltimore, Waverly Press, 1955. 246 pp.—Memoir 11 of the International Journal of American Linguistics. Indiana University Publications in Anthropology and Linguistics.

2928. Jones, Daniel. An Outline of English Phonetics. 8th ed. New York, E. P. Dutton and Co., 1956. xx + 378 pp.—Original ed. 1918.

2929. Dobson, E[ric] J. English Pronunciation 1500–1700. Vol. I: Survey of the Sources; Vol. II: Phonology. Oxford, Clarendon Press, 1957. 2 (continuously paged) vols.

2930. Wise, Claude Merton. Applied Phonetics. Englewood Cliffs, N.J., Prentice-Hall, 1957. xii + 546 pp.

2931. Schubiger, Maria. English Intonation. Its form and function. Tübingen, Germany, Max Niemeyer Verlag, 1958. iv + 112 pp.—A development of Maria Schubiger, *The Role of Intonation in Spoken English*, St. Gall, Switzerland, Fehr, 1935, vi + 74 pp.

2932. Thomas, Chas. K. An Introduction to the Phonetics of American English. 2nd ed. New York, Ronald Press, 1958. x + 273 pp.—Original ed. 1947.

2933. Carrell, James, and Tiffany, Wm. R. Phonetics. Theory and application to speech improvement. New York, McGraw-Hill Book Co., 1960. 361 pp.

§118. DIALECT STUDIES

2937. Axon, Wm. E. A. English Dialect Words of the Eighteenth Century as Shown in the Universal Etymological Dictionary of Nathaniel Bailey. London, Trübner and Co. for the English Dialect Society, 1883. xx + 213 pp.

2938. Joyce, P[atrick] W. English as We Speak It in Ireland. London, Longmans, Green and Co., 1910. xi + 356 pp.—"Vocabulary and Index," pp. 209–352.

2939. Skeat, Walter W. English Dialects from the Eighth Century to the Present Day. Cambridge Univ. Press, 1911. ix + 139 pp.

2940. Wright, Elizabeth Mary. Rustic Speech and Folk-Lore. Oxford Univ. Press, 1913. xx + 342 pp.

2941. Mackenzie, Barbara Alida. The Early London Dialect. Contributions to the history of the dialect of London during the Middle English period. Oxford Univ. Press, 1928. 152 pp.—"Bibliography," pp. 9–19.

2942. Matthews, Wm. Cockney Past and Present. A short history of the dialect of London. London, George Routledge and Sons, 1938. xv + 245 pp.—"Bibliography," pp. 233–235.

2943. Kurath, Hans. Linguistic Atlas of New England. With the collaboration of Miles L. Hanley, Bernard Bloch, Guy S. Lowman Jr., and Marcus L. Hansen. Vol. I: Maps 1–242; Vol. II: Maps 243–491; Vol. III: Maps 492–734. Providence, R.I., Brown University, 1939–43. 3 vols., each in 2 pts.—Also Hans Kurath, *Handbook of the Linguistic Geography of*

New England, With the collaboration of Marcus L. Hansen, Julia Bloch, and Bernard Bloch, Providence, R.I., Brown University, 1939, xii + 240 pp., "Bibliography of Linguistic Geography," pp. 54–61, "Bibliography of New England History," pp. 105–121.

2944. Baker, Sidney J. The Australian Language. An examination of the English language and English speech as used in Australia from convict days to the present with special reference to the growth of indigenous idiom and its use by Australian writers. Sidney, Angus and Robertson Ltd., 1945. xii + 425 pp.

2945. Herman, Lewis and Marguerite Shalett. Manual of American Dialects for Radio, Screen, and Television. Chicago, Ziff-Davis Publ'ing Co., 1947. xv + 326 pp.—Reprint as *American Dialects*, A manual for actors, directors, and writers, New York, Theatre Arts Books, 1959, 328 pp.

2946. Kurath, Hans. A Word Geography of the Eastern United States. Ann Arbor, University of Michigan Press, 1949. x + 88 (double column) pp. + 163 figures.—Number 1 in the series Studies in American English. A treatment of materials collected since 1931 for a linguistic atlas of the Eastern States.

2947. Hubbell, Allan F. The Pronunciation of English in New York City. Consonants and vowels. New York, King's Crown Press, 1950. 169 pp.

2948. Atwood, E[lmer] Bagby. A Survey of Verb Forms in the Eastern United States. Ann Arbor, University of Michigan Press, 1953. 53 pp. —Number 2 in the series Studies in American English. The text contains 31 maps.

2949. Haugen, Einar. The Norwegian Language in America. A study in bilingual behavior. Philadelphia, University of Pennsylvania Press, 1953. 2 vols.

2950. Randolph, Vance, and Wilson, Geo. P. Down in the Holler. A gallery of Ozark folk speech. Norman, University of Oklahoma Press, 1953. ix + 320 pp.—"Bibliography," pp. 303–314.

2951. Reed, Carroll E., and Seifert, Lester W. A Linguistic Atlas of Pennsylvania German. Marburg a. d. Lahn, Germany, Becker, 1954. 6 pp. + 90 maps.

2952. Hall, Robt A., Jr. Hands Off Pidgin English! Foreword by R. W. Robson. Sidney, Austral., Pacific Publications, 1955. 142 pp.

2953. Eliason, Norman E. Tarheel Talk. An historical study of the English language in North Carolina to 1860. Chapel Hill, University of North Carolina Press, 1956. x + 324 pp.

§119. DICTIONARIES OF THE DIALECTS OF ENGLISH

2957. Murray, James A. H. The Dialect of the Southern Counties of Scotland. Its pronunciation, grammar, and historical relations. With an appendix on the present limits of the Gaelic and Lowland Scotch, and the dialectical divisions of the Lowland tongue and a linguistic map of Scotland. London, Asher and Co. for the Philological Society, 1873. vii + 251 pp.

2958. Whitworth, Geo. Clifford. An Anglo-Indian Dictionary. A glossary of Indian terms used in English and of such English or other non-Indian terms as have obtained special meanings in India. London, Kegan Paul, Trench and Co., 1885. xvi + 351 (double column) pp.

2959. Jamieson, John. An Etymological Dictionary of the Scottish Language. . . . To which is prefixed a dissertation on the origin of the Scottish language. New ed., rev. and collated by John Longmuir and David Donaldson. Paisley, Alexander Gardner, 1879–82. 4 (double column page) vols.—Original ed. 1808 in 2 vols.; abridged ed. 1818; second ed. 1840–41. Also *Supplement to Jamieson's Scottish Dictionary with Memoir and Introduction*, by David Donaldson, Paisley, Alexander Gardner, 1887, x + 328 (chiefly double column) pp.

2960. Mackay, Chas. A Dictionary of Lowland Scotch. With an introductory chapter on the poetry, humor, and literary history of the Scottish language. Boston, Ticknor and Co., 1888. xxxii + 398 (double column) pp.

2961. Morris, Edward E. Austral English. A dictionary of Australian words, phrases, and usages. With those aboriginal Australian and Maori words which have become incorporated in the language and the commoner scientific words that have had their origin in Australasia. London, Macmillan Co., 1898. xxiv + 525 (double column) pp.

2962. Yule, Henry, and Burnell, Arthur Coke. Hobson-Jobson. A glossary of colloquial Anglo-Indian words and phrases, and of kindred terms, etymological, historical, geographical, and discursive. New ed. edited by William Crooke. London, J. Murray, 1903. xlviii + 1021 (double column) + xlviii + 263 (double column) pp. See also 2959 above.

2963. Wright, Joseph. The English Dialect Dictionary. Being the complete vocabulary of all dialect words still in use, or known to have been in use during the last two hundred years. Founded on the publications of the English Dialect Society and on a large amount of material never before printed. London, Henry Frowde, 1898–1905. 6 (double column page) vols.—Volume VI contains "Supplement," 179 pp.; "Bibliography," 62 pp.; "The English Dialect Grammar," x + 187 pp.

2964. [Jamieson, John.] Jamieson's Dictionary of the Scottish Language. Abridged by J[ohn] Johnstone and rev. and enl. by Dr. [John] Longmuir. With supplement, to which is prefixed an introduction by W. M. Metcalfe. Paisley, Alexander Gardner, 1912. lxi + 635 (double column + xlviii + 263 (double column) pp. See also 2959 above.

2965. Pettman, Chas. Africanderisms. A glossary of South African colloquial words and phrases and of place and other names. London, Longmans, Green and Co., 1913. xviii + 579 pp.

2966. Marwick, Hugh. The Orkney Norn. Oxford Univ. Press, 1929. lii + 232 (chiefly double column) pp.

2967. Jakobsen, Jakob. An Etymological Dictionary of the Norn Language in Shetland. London, David Nutt, 1928–32. 2 (double column page, consecutively paged) vols.

2968. Wentworth, Harold. American Dialect Dictionary. New York, Thomas Y. Crowell Co., 1944. xv + 747 (double column) pp.—"American Printed Sources Quoted in the American Dialect Dictionary," pp. 737–747.

2969. Herman, Lewis Helmar and Marguerite Shalett. Manual of American Dialects for Radio, Stage, Screen, and Television. Foreword by Vincent Price. Chicago, Ziff-Davis Publ'ing Co., 1947. xvii + 326 pp.—"Bibliography," pp. 321–326.

2970. Turner, Lorenzo D. Africanisms in the Gullah Dialect. University of Chicago Press, 1949. xi + 317 pp.—"Bibliography," pp. 293–299.

2971. Grant, Wm., and [since Vol. III] Murison, David D., eds. The Scottish National Dictionary. Designed partly on regional lines and partly on historical principles, and containing all the Scottish words known to be in use or to have been in use since c. 1700. Edinburgh, Scottish National Dictionary Association, [1931]–date.—Ten double column page volumes are planned; volume V, pt. 2, was issued 1958.

2972. Craigie, Wm. A., ed. A Dictionary of the Older Scottish Tongue. From the twelfth century to the end of the seventeenth. University of Chicago Press, 1937–date. xviii parts to "—LAW" to date (c. 150 double column pp. per part).—A. J. Aitken, ed., since issue of Part XVII.

§120. STUDIES IN SLANG AND SLANG DICTIONARIES

2976. Burke, W[illiam] J. The Literature of Slang. With an introductory note by Eric Partridge. New York, New York Public Library, 1939. vii + 180 (double column) pp.

2977. Bauman, Heinrich. Londonismen. Slang und Cant. Alphabetisch geordnete Sammlung der eigenartigen Ausdrucksweisen der Londoner Volkssprache sowie der üblichsten Gauner-, Matrosen-, Sport- und Zunft-Ausdrücke. Berlin, Langenscheidtsche Verlags-Buchhandlung, 1887. cviii + 239 (double column) pp.

2978. Maitland, James. The American Slang Dictionary. Embodying all American and English slang phrases in current use, with their derivation and philology. Chicago, R. J. Kittredge and Co. for the author, 1891. 308 pp.

2979. Barrère, Albert, and Leland, Chas. G. A Dictionary of Slang, Jargon, and Cant. Embracing English, American, and Anglo-Indian slang, pidgin English, Gypsies' jargon, and other irregular phraseology. 2nd ed. London, George Bell and Sons, 1897. 2 vols.—Original ed. 1889–90.

2980. The Slang Dictionary. Etymological, historical, and anecdotal. New ed. London, Chatto and Windus, 1903. vii + 382 pp.—Original ed. 1873.

2981. Farmer, John S., and Henley, W[illiam] E. Slang and Its Analogues, Past and Present. A dictionary, historical and comparative, of the heterodox speech of all classes of society for more than 300 years. London, privately printed, 1890–1904. 7 (double column page) vols.

2982. Farmer, John S., and Henley, W[illiam] E. A Dictionary of Slang and Colloquial English. Abridged from the seven-volume work, entitled Slang and Its Analogues. London, George Routledge and Sons, [1905]. viii + 534 (double column) pp.—Reprint New York, Dutton, 1929.

2983. Ware, J[ames] Redding. Passing English of the Victorian Era. A dictionary of heterodox English, slang and phrase. London, George Routledge and Sons, [1909]. viii + 271 (double column) pp.—In the series Routledge's Standard Reference Library.

2984. Fraser, Edward, and Gibbons, John. Soldier and Sailor Words and Phrases. Including slang of the trenches and the air force; British and American war-words and service terms and expressions in everyday use; nicknames, sobriquets, and titles of regiments, with their origins; the battle-honors of the Great War awarded to the British Army. New York, E. P. Dutton and Co., 1925. vii + 372 pp.

2985. Lyell, Thos. R. G. Slang, Phrase, and Idiom in Colloquial English and Their Use. Tokyo, Hokuseido Press, 1931. xxxii + 764 + 54 pp.

2986. Partridge, Eric, ed. A Classical Dictionary of the Vulgar Tongue by Captain Francis Grose [1796, 3rd ed.]. Edited with a biographical and critical sketch and an extensive commentary. London, Scholartis Press, 1931. xi + 396 pp. plus 4 pp. of corrigenda and consideranda.

2987. Baker, Sidney J. New Zealand Slang. A dictionary of colloquialisms. Christchurch, N.Z., Whitcombe and Tombs Ltd., [1941]. 114 pp.

2988. Philipson, Uno. Political Slang 1750–1850. Lund, Sweden, C. W. K. Gleerup, 1941. xvi + 314 pp.—Volume IX in the series Lund Studies in English.

2989. Hunt, J[ohn] L., and Pringle, A[lan] G. Service Slang. With a foreword by Air-Marshal Sir T. L. Leigh-Mallory. London, Faber and Faber Ltd., 1943. 72 pp.

2990. Johnson, Burges. The Lost Art of Profanity. Foreword by H. L. Mencken. Drawings by Orson Lowell. Indianapolis, Bobbs-Merrill Co., 1948. 223 pp.

2991. Granville, Wilfred. Sea Slang of the Twentieth Century. Royal Navy, Merchant Navy, yachtsmen, fishermen, bargemen, canalmen, miscellaneous. Introduction and etymologies by Eric Partridge. London, Winchester Publ'ions Ltd., 1949. xiv + 15–271 pp.

2992. Monteleone, Vincent J. Criminal Slang. The vernacular of the underworld lingo. Rev. ed. Boston, Christopher Publ'ing House, 1949. 292 pp.—Original ed. 1945.

2993. Partridge, Eric. A Dictionary of Slang and Unconventional English. Colloquialisms and catch-phrases, solecisms and catachreses, nicknames, vulgarisms, and such Americanisms as have been naturalized. 3rd ed. London, Routledge and Kegan Paul Ltd., 1949. xvi + 1230 (double column) pp.—Original ed. 1937; second ed. 1938.

2994. Goldin, Hyman, O'Leary, Frank, and Lipsius, Morris. Dictionary of American Underworld Lingo. New York, Twayne Publ'ers, 1950. 327 (chiefly double column) pp.

2995. Partridge, Eric. Slang To-Day and Yesterday. With a short historical sketch and vocabularies of English, American, and Australian slang. 3rd ed. New York, Macmillan Co., 1950. ix + 476 pp.—Original ed. 1933; second ed. 1935.

2996. Tempest, Paul. Lag's Lexicon. A comprehensive dictionary and encyclopaedia of the English prison of today. London, Routledge and Kegan Paul Ltd., 1950. viii + 234 pp.

2997. Berrey, Lester V., and Van Den Bark, Melvin. The American Thesaurus of Slang. A complete reference book of colloquial speech. Foreword by Louise Pound. 2nd ed. Foreword to second ed. by Louise Pound. New York, Thomas Y. Crowell Co., 1953. xxxv + 902 (double column) + 903–1272 (quadruple column) pp.—Original ed. 1942; second ed. reprinted 1956.

2998. Weingarten, Joseph A. An American Dictionary of Slang and Colloquial Speech. New York, published by the author, 1954. 390 pp.

2999. Freeman, Wm. A Concise Dictionary of English Slang. London, English Universities Press Ltd., 1955. xi +12–268 pp.

3000. Maurer, David W. Whiz Mob. A correlation of the technical argot of pickpockets with their behavior pattern. Gainesville, Fla., American Dialect Society, 1955. 199 pp.—Number 24 in the series Publications of the American Dialect Society.

3001. Wentworth, Harold, and Flexner, Stuart Berg. Dictionary of American Slang. New York, Thomas Y. Crowell Co., 1960. 669 pp.

§121. PLACE NAMES

[See also §92. Periodicals Devoted to the Study of Names.]

3004. Sealock, Richard B., and Seely, Pauline A. Bibliography of Place Name Literature. United States, Canada, Alaska, and Newfoundland. Chicago, American Library Association, 1948. [x] + 331 pp.—Supplement for the years 1946–51, *Names*, VI, 1 (March 1958), 26–50; for the years 1952–54, *Names*, III, 2 (June 1955), 102–116; for the years 1955–59, *Names*, VII, 4 (Dec. 1959), 203–232.

3005. Catalog of Publications. United States Board of Geographic Names. Washington, D.C., Department of the Interior, 1951. 21 pp.

3006. Gannett, Henry. The Origin of Certain Place Names in the United States. 2nd ed. Washington, D.C., Government Printing Office, 1905. 334 pp.—Original ed. 1902; second ed. reprint *American Names*, A guide to the origin of place names in the United States, Washington, D.C., Public Affairs Press, [1947].

3007. Mawer, A[llen], and Stenton, F[rank] M., eds. Introduction to the Survey of English Place-Names. Cambridge Univ. Press, 1924. 2 vols. —Volume I, parts 1 and 2, in the series Publications of the English Place-Name Society. Part 2 bears the title *The Chief Elements Used in English Place-Names.*

3008. Sixth Report of the United States Geographic Board 1890–1932. Washington, D.C., Government Printing Office, 1933. ix + 76 (single column) + 77–834 (double column) pp.

3009. Johnston, James B. Place-Names of Scotland. 3rd ed. London, John Murray, 1934. xvi + 335 pp.—Original ed. 1892; second ed. 1903.

3010. Ramsay, Robt. L., Read, Allen Walker, and Leech, Esther Gladys. Introduction to a Survey of Missouri Place-Names. Columbia, University of Missouri Press, 1934. 124 pp.—Volume IX, no. 1, in the series University of Missouri Studies.

3011. Holt, Alfred H. American Place Names. New York, Thomas Y. Crowell Co., 1938. 222 pp.—"Bibliography," pp. 221–222.

3012. Ekwall, Eilert. The Concise Oxford Dictionary of English Place-Names. 2nd ed. Oxford, Clarendon Press, 1939. xlviii + 524 (double column) pp.—Original ed. 1936.

3013. The Origin of Massachusetts Place Names of the State, Counties, Cities, and Towns. Compiled by workers of the Writers' Project of the WPA. . . . New York, Harian Publications, 1941. vi + 55 pp.—"Bibliography," pp. 54–55.

3014. Dyson, Taylor. Place Names and Surnames. Their origin and meaning. With special reference to the West Riding of Yorkshire. Huddersfield, Eng., Alfred Jubb and Sons, 1944. vii + 216 pp.

3015. Kenny, Hamill. West Virginia Place Names. Their origin and meaning including the nomenclature of the streams and mountains. Piedmont, W.Va., Place Name Press, 1945. xii + 768 pp.—"Bibliography," pp. 699–720.

3016. Alexander, Gerard L. Nicknames of American Cities, Towns, and Villages Past and Present. New York, Special Libraries Association, 1951. xiv + 74 pp.

3017. McMullen, Edwin Wallace, Jr. English Topographic Terms in Florida 1563–1874. Gainesville, University of Florida Press, 1953. 227 (double column) pp.

3018. Gardiner, Alan. The Theory of Proper Names. A controversial essay. Oxford Univ. Press, 1954. 67 pp.

3019. Chadbourne, Ava Harriet. Maine Place Names and the Peopling of Its Towns. Portland, Me., Bond Wheelwright Co., 1955. 530 pp.

3020. Shankle, Geo. E. American Nicknames. Their origin and significance. 2nd ed. New York, H. W. Wilson Co., 1955. vii + 524 (double column) pp.—Original ed. 1937. Coverage not exclusively on place names.

3021. Smith, A[lbert] H. English Place-Name Elements. Part I: Introduction, the Elements Á–IW, Maps; Part II: The Elements Jafn–Ytri, Index, and Maps. Cambridge Univ. Press, 1956. 2 vols.—Volumes XXV and XXVI in the series Publications of the English Place-Name Society.

3022. Stewart, Geo. R. Names on the Land. A historical account of place-naming in the United States. Rev. and enl. ed. Boston, Houghton Mifflin Co., 1958. xiii + 511 pp.—Original ed. 1945.

3023. Paff, Wm. J. The Geographical and Ethnic Names in the Thithriks Saga. Cambridge, Mass., Harvard Univ. Press, 1959. vi + 238 pp.—Volume II in the series Harvard Germanic Studies. Bibliography, pp. 233–238. Valuable for Old English toponymy.

3024. Barnes, Will C. Arizona Place Names. Revised and enl. by Byrd H. Granger. Illustrated by Anne Merriman Peck. Tucson, University of Arizona Press, 1960. xx + 519 (double column) pp.—"Bibliography," pp. 403–407.

§122. PERSONAL NAMES

[See also §92. Periodicals Devoted to the Study of Names.]

3028. Smith, Elsdon C. Personal Names. New York, New York Public Library, 1952. 226 (double column) pp.—A categorized, annotated bibliography reprinted from the *Bulletin of the New York Public Library* of 1950–51.

3029. Lower, Mark Anthony. A Dictionary of the Family Names of the United Kingdom. London, John Russell Smith, 1860. xxxix + 443 (double column) pp.

3030. Lower, Mark Anthony. English Surnames. An essay on family nomenclature, historical, etymological, and humorous, with several illustrative appendices. 4th ed. enl. London, John Russell Smith, 1875. 2 vols.—Original ed. 1842; second ed. 1843; third ed. 1849.

3031. Yonge, Charlotte M. History of Christian Names. London, Macmillan Co., 1878. 2 vols.—A survey of most of the common Western European Christian names.

3032. Bardsley, Chas. W. Curiosities of Puritan Nomenclature. New York, R. Worthington, 1880. xii + 252 pp.—A treatment of Old Testament and evangelically oriented Christian names. The "New Edition," printed London, Chatto and Windus, 1897, is apparently identical to the original ed. of 1880.

3033. Long, Harry Alfred. Personal and Family Names. A popular monograph on the origin and history of the nomenclature of the present and former times. London, Hamilton, Adams and Co., 1883. 362 pp.

3034. Frey, Albert R. Sobriquets and Nicknames. Boston, Ticknor and Co., 1887. iii + 482 (chiefly double column) pp.

3035. MacBain, Alexander. Personal Names and Surnames of the Town of Inverness. Inverness, Northern Counties Printing and Publ'ing Co., 1895. xi + 105 pp.

3036. Searle, Wm. Geo. Onomasticon Anglo-Saxonicum. A list of Anglo-Saxon proper names from the time of Beda to that of King John. Cambridge Univ. Press, 1897. lix + 601 (chiefly double column) pp.—"Bibliography and Abbreviations," pp. xxxii–lvii.

3037. Bardsley, Chas. Wareing. A Dictionary of English and Welsh Surnames. With special American instances. Revised for the press by his widow. Preface by the Lord Bishop of Carlisle. Oxford Univ. Press, 1901. xvi + 837 (triple column) pp.—Left unfinished at Bardsley's death in 1898.

3038. Bardsley, Chas. Wareing. English Surnames. Their sources and significations. 7th ed. London, Chatto and Windus, 1901. xxvii + 612 pp.—Original ed. 1873.

3039. Barber, Henry. British Family Names. Their origin and meaning. With lists of Scandinavian, Frisian, Anglo-Saxon, and Norman names. 2nd ed. London, Elliot Stock, 1902. xii + 286 pp.—Original ed. 1894.

3040. Baring-Gould, S[abine]. Family Names and Their Story. Philadelphia, J. B. Lippincott Co., 1910. xii + 13–432 pp.

3041. Björkman, Erik. Nordische Personennamen in England in Alt- und Frühmittel-Englischer Zeit. Ein Beitrag zur englischen Namenkunde. Halle a. S., Max Niemeyer, 1910. xv + 217 pp.—Volume XXXVII in the series Studien zur englischen Philologie. "Quellen- und Literaturverzeichnis," pp. 213–217.

3042. Hitching, F K. and S. References to English Surnames in 1601. An index giving about 19650 references to surnames contained in the printed registers of 778 English parishes during the first year of the seventeenth century. Walton-on-Thames, Eng., Charles A. Bernau, 1910. lxx pp.—Also *References to English Surnames in 1602*, London, Charles A. Bernau, 1911, xcv pp.

3043. Weekley, Ernest. The Romance of Names. 2nd ed. London, John Murray, 1914. xvi + 250 pp.—Original ed. also 1914.

3044. Forssner, Thorvald. Continental-Germanic Personal Names in England in Old and Middle English Times. Uppsala, Sweden, K. W. Appelbergs Boktryckeri, 1916. lxiii + 290 pp.

3045. Weekley, Ernest. Surnames. London, John Murray, 1916. xxii + 364 pp.

3046. Harrison, Henry. Surnames of the United Kingdom. A concise etymological dictionary. With the assistance of Gytha Pulling Harrison. London, Vol. I: Eaton Press, 1912; Vol. II: Morland Press, 1918. 2 (double column page) vols.

3047. Redin, Mats. Studies on Uncompounded Personal Names in Old English. Inaugural dissertation. Uppsala, Sweden, Edv. Berlings Boktryckeri, 1919. xlv + 196 pp.—Reprint from the *Uppsala Universitets Årsskrift* 1919.

3048. MacGiolla-Domhnaigh, Padraig. Some Anglicised Surnames in Ireland. Dublin, Gael Co-operative Society Ltd., 1923. 64 pp.—A list of English names anglicised from Gaelic originals.

3049. Wouffle, Patrick. Irish Names and Surnames. Collected and edited with explanatory and historical notes. Dublin, M. H. Gill and Sons, 1923. xlvii + 696 pp.—A list of names with explanations of origins and with the use of Irish letters.

3050. Eno, Joel N. Verified Origin of Irish Gaelic Clan-Names and Family Names Abundant in America. New York, American Historical Society Inc., 1927. 415–435 (chiefly double column) pp.—Separately bound section of Vol. XXI, no. 3, of *The America Illustrated.*

3051. Bowman, Wm. Dodgson. The Story of Surnames. London, George Routledge and Sons, 1931. vii + 280 pp.

3052. Ewen, C[ecil] L'Estrange. A History of Surnames of the British Isles. A concise account of their origin, evolution, etymology, and legal status. London, Kegan Paul, Trench, Trubner and Co., 1931. xx + 508 pp.—"Short Bibliography," pp. 429–436.

3053. Weidenhan, Joseph L., S.T.L. Baptismal Names. Embodying the various baptismal names used in America, England, Scotland, and Ireland together with their synonyms, their variants. . . . 4th ed. Baltimore, Kenmore Productions, 1931. 347 (double column) pp.—Original ed. 1931. List of saints' names and feast days.

3054. Weekley, Ernest. Words and Names. London, John Murray, 1932. viii + 200 pp.

3055. Longhead, Flora Haines. Dictionary of Given Names with Their Origins and Meanings. Glendale, Calif., Arthur H. Clark Co., 1933. 384 pp.

3056. Norden, Eduard. Alt-Germanen. Völker- und namengeschichtliche Untersuchungen. Leipzig, B. G. Teubner, 1934. xv + 325 pp.

3057. Fransson, Gustav. Middle English Surnames of Occupation 1100–1350. With an excursus on toponymical surnames. Lund, Sweden, C. W. K. Gleerup, 1935. 217 pp.—Volume III in the series Lund Studies in English.

3058. Kneen, J[ohn] J. The Personal Names of the Isle of Man. Oxford Univ. Press, 1937. lx + 295 pp.—An alphabetical list.

3059. Dellquest, Augustus Wilfrid. These Names of Ours. A book of surnames. New York, Thomas Y. Crowell Co., 1938. xxiii + 296 pp.—A semi-popular list with explanations of origin.

3060. Ewen, C[ecil] L'Estrange. A Guide to the Origin of British Surnames. London, John Gifford Ltd., 1938. 206 pp.

3061. Partridge, Eric. Name This Child. A dictionary of English (and American) Christian names. 2nd ed. London, Methuen and Co., 1938. ix + 233 pp.—Original ed. 1936.

3062. Attwater, Donald. Names and Name-Days. London, Burns, Oates and Washbourne Ltd., 1939. xv + 124 pp.

3063. Weekley, Ernest. Jack and Jill. A study in our Christian names. London, John Murray, 1939. xii + 193 pp.

3064. Woolf, Henry Bosley. The Old Germanic Principles of Name-Giving. Baltimore, Johns Hopkins Press, 1939. xii + 299 pp.—"Bibliography," pp. 265–271.

3065. Hutson, Arthur E. British Personal Names in the Historia Regum Britanniae. Berkeley, University of California Press, 1940. [iii] + 160 pp.—Volume V, no. 1, in the series University of California Publications in English.

3066. Löfvenberg, Mattias. Studies in Middle English Local Surnames. Lund, Sweden, C. W. K. Gleerup, 1942. xlviii + 255 pp.—Volume XI in the series Lund Studies in English.

3067. Withycombe, E[lizabeth] G. The Oxford Dictionary of English Christian Names. Oxford, Clarendon Press, 1945. xxxviii + 142 (double column) pp.—Reprint 1947.

3068. Black, Geo. F. The Surnames of Scotland. Their origin, meaning, and history. New York, New York Public Library, 1946. lxxii + 838 (double column) pp.—"List of Principal Works Referred To," pp. lix–

lxxi. Reprint from the *Bulletin of the New York Public Library* August 1943–September 1946.

3069. Wells, Evelyn. A Treasury of Names. New York, Essential Books, 1946. 326 (chiefly double column) pp.—A semi-popular treatment.

3070. Stewart, Geo. R. Men's Names in Plymouth and Massachusetts in the Seventeenth Century. Berkeley, University of California Press, 1948. 109–137 pp.—Volume VII, no. 2, in the series University of California Publications in English.

3071. Smith, Elsdon C. The Story of Our Names. New York, Harper and Bros., 1950. vi + 296 pp.

3072. Davies, Trefor Rendall. A Book of Welsh Names. London, Sheppard Press, 1952. xiv + 72 pp.

3073. Smith, Elsdon C. Dictionary of American Family Names. New York, Harper and Bros., 1956. xxxiv + 244 pp.

3074. Reaney, P[ercy] H. A Dictionary of British Surnames. London, Routledge and Kegan Paul, 1958. lix + 366 (double column) pp.

3075. Smith, Elsdon C. Literature on Personal Names in English. Names. Journal of the American Name Society. Vol. II (1954)–date.—An annual bibliography.

§123. INTRODUCTIONS TO LANGUAGE STUDY

[For works dealing with the history of language study and teaching see §148. Scholarship: Historical Studies *passim.*]

3079. Wyld, Henry Cecil. The Historical Study of the Mother Tongue. An introduction to philological method. London, John Murray, 1906. xi + 412 pp.—Reprint 1926. "List of Authors Referred To," pp. 409–412.

3080. Paul Hermann. Prinzipien der Sprachgeschichte. 5. Aufl. Halle a. S., Max Niemeyer, 1920. xv + 428 pp.—Original ed. 1880; second ed. 1886; third ed. 1898; fourth ed. 1909; fifth ed. reprinted 1937. Second ed. translated by H[erbert] A. Strong as *Principles of the History of Language*, New York, Macmillan and Co., 1889, xlviii + 512 pp. A re-edited and adapted ed. of Strong's translation was issued by Herbert A. Strong, Willem S. Logeman, and Benjamin Ide Wheeler, *Introduction to the Study of the History of Language*, London, Longmans, Green and Co., 1891, xi + 435 pp.

3081. Sapir, Edward. Language. An introduction to the study of speech. New York, Harcourt, Brace and Co., 1921. vii + 258 pp.—Reprint New York, Harcourt, Brace and Co., 1955, number 7 in the series Harvest Books.

3082. Jespersen, Otto. Language. Its nature, development, and origin. London, George Allen and Unwin Ltd., 1922. 448 pp.—Frequent reprints, as in 1949.

3083. Kent, Roland G. Language and Philology. Boston, Marshall Jones Co., 1923. vii + 174 pp.—In the series Our Debt to Greece and Rome.

3084. Gardiner, Alan. The Theory of Speech and Language. 2nd ed. Oxford Univ. Press, 1951. xii + 348 pp.—Original ed. 1932.

3085. Graff, Willem L. Language and Languages. An introduction to linguistics. New York, D. Appleton and Co., 1932. xlvi + 487 pp.—"Glossary," pp. xxxi–xlvi.

3086. Zipf, Geo. Kingsley. The Psycho-Biology of Language. An introduction to dynamic philology. Boston, Houghton Mifflin Co., 1935. xi + 336 pp.

3087. Goldberg, Isaac. The Wonder of Words. An introduction to language for everyman. New York, D. Appleton-Century Co., 1938. xiv + 485 pp.

3088. Gray, Louis H. Foundations of Language. New York, Macmillan Co., 1939. xv + 530 pp.

3089. Bodmer, Frederick. The Loom of Language. Edited by Lancelot Hogben. New York, W. W. Norton and Co., 1944. x + 692 pp.

3090. Sturtevant, Edgar H. An Introduction to Linguistic Science. New Haven, Yale Univ. Press, 1947. 173 pp.—See also Sturtevant's earlier *Linguistic Change,* An introduction to the historical study of language, University of Chicago Press, 1917, x + 185 pp.

3091. Partridge, Eric. The World of Words. An introduction to language in general and to English and American in particular. 3rd ed. London, Hamish Hamilton, 1948. x + 201 pp.—Original ed. 1938; second ed. 1939.

3092. Hall, Robert A., Jr. Leave Your Language Alone! Ithaca, N.Y., Linguistica, 1950. xi + 254 pp.

3093. Estrich, Robt. M., and Sperber, Hans. Three Keys to Language. New York, Rinehart and Co., 1952. xi + 358 pp.

3094. Laird, Charlton. The Miracle of Language. Cleveland, World Publ'ing Co., 1953. xii + 308 pp.

3095. Whatmough, Joshua. Language. New York, St. Martin's Press, 1956. 270 pp.

3096. Anshen, Ruth Nanda, ed. Language. An enquiry into its meaning and function. New York, Harper and Bros., 1957. xviii + 366 pp.—Volume VIII in the Science of Culture Series.

3097. Dean, Leonard F., and Wilson, Kenneth G., eds. Essays on Language and Usage. New York, Oxford Univ. Press, 1959. viii + 335 pp.

§124. CULTURAL, SOCIAL, PSYCHOLOGICAL, AND STATISTICAL STUDIES

3101. Jespersen, Otto. Progress in Language. With special reference to English. London, S. Sonnenschein and Co., 1894. xii + 370 pp.

3102. Guérard, Albert Léon. A Short History of the International Language Movement. New York, Boni and Liveright, [1921]. 268 pp.

3103. Jespersen, Otto. The Philosophy of Grammar. New York, Henry Holt and Co., 1924. 359 pp.—Reprint 1929.

3104. Jespersen, Otto. Mankind, Nation, and Individual from a Linguistic Point of View. Oslo, Norway, H. Aschehong og Co., 1925. 222 pp.—Volume IV in the series Instituttet for Sammenlignende Kulturforskning-Forelesninger. Reprint London, G. Allen and Unwin Ltd., 1946.

3105. DeWitt, M[arguerite] E. Our Oral Word as Social and Economic Factor. With a comprehensive group of Old World euphonetigraphs. Editor's note by Walter Ripman. London, J. M. Dent and Sons, 1928. xxv + 329 pp.

3106. Bryant, Margaret M. English in the Law Courts. The part that articles, prepositions, and conjunctions play in legal decisions. New York, Columbia Univ. Press, 1930. x + 312 pp.

3107. Vossler, Karl. The Spirit of Language in Civilization. Translated by Oscar Oeser. London, Routledge and Kegan Paul Ltd., 1932. vii + 247 pp.—In the series International Library of Psychology, Philosophy, and Scientific Method. Original Ger. ed. 1925; English translation reprinted 1951.

3108. Spier, Leslie, Hallowell, A[lfred] Irving, and Newman, Stanley S., eds. Language, Culture, and Personality. Essays in memory of Edward Sapir. Menasha, Wis., published by the Sapir Publ'ion Fund, 1941. x + 298 pp.

3109. Pollock, Thos. Clark. The Nature of Literature. Its relation to science, language, and human experience. Princeton, N.J., University Press, 1942. xxiv + 218 pp.

3110. Yule, G[eorge] Udny. The Statistical Study of Literary Vocabulary. Cambridge Univ. Press, 1944. viii + 306 pp.

3111. Sapir, Edward. Selected Writings in Language, Culture, and Personality. Berkeley, University of California Press, 1949. xv + 617 pp.—Edward Sapir Bibliography, pp. 601–617.

3112. Grove, Victor. The Language Bar. London, Routledge and Kegan Paul Ltd., 1950. v + 160 pp.—A treatment of the linguistic problems that face a native speaker of English.

3113. Duncan, Hugh Dalziel. Language and Literature in Society. A sociological essay on theory and method in the interpretation of linguistic symbols. With a bibliographical guide to the sociology of literature. University of Chicago Press, 1953. xv + 262 pp.—Bibliography, pp. 141–214.

3114. Entwistle, Wm. J. Aspects of Language. Editor's preface by L. R. Palmer. London, Faber and Faber Ltd., [1953]. xi + 370 pp.

3115. Weinreich, Uriel. Languages in Contact. Findings and problems. With a preface by André Martinet. New York, Linguistic Circle of New York, 1953. xii + 148 pp.—Number 1 in the series Publications of the Linguistic Circle of New York. Bibliography, pp. 123–146.

3116. Hoijer, Harry, ed. Language in Culture. Conference on the interrelations of language and other aspects of culture. Foreword by Robert Redfield and Milton Singer. University of Chicago Press, 1954. xi + 286 pp.—Also publication as no. 79 in the series Memoirs of the American Anthropological Association.

3117. Bram, Joseph. Language and Society. Garden City, N.Y., Doubleday and Co., 1955. 66 pp.—Number 8 in the series Doubleday Short Studies in Sociology.

3118. Siertsema, B[ertha]. A Study of Glossematics. Critical survey of its fundamental concepts. The Hague, Martinus Nijhoff, 1955. xi + 240 pp.

3119. Harris, Robt. T., and Jarrett, James L. Language and Informal Logic. New York, Longmans, Green and Co., 1956. xi + 274 pp.

3120. Herdan, G[ustav]. Language as Choice and Chance. Groningen, Holland, Erven P. Noordhoff Ltd., 1956. xiii + 356 pp.

3121. Pei, Mario. Language for Everybody. What it is and how to master it. New York, Devin-Adair Co., 1956. xii + 340 pp.

3122. Révész, Géza. The Origins and Prehistory of Language. Translated from the German by J. Butler. New York, Philosophical Library, 1956. 226 pp.—Original Ger. ed. 1946.

3123. Jacob, Henry. A Planned Auxiliary Language. New York, Dover, 1957. 166 pp.

3124. Skinner, Burrhus Frederic. Verbal Behavior. New York, Appleton-Century-Crofts, [1957]. x + 478 pp.

3125. Brown, Roger W. Words and Things. Glencoe, Ill., Free Press, [1958]. xvi + 398 pp.

3126. Henle, Paul, ed. Language, Thought, and Culture. Ann Arbor, University of Michigan Press, 1958. 273 pp.

3127. Reiss, Samuel. Language and Psychology. New York, Philosophical Library, 1959. [ix] + 299 pp.

3128. Robson, Ernest M. The Orchestra of Language. New York, Thomas Yoseloff, 1959. 206 pp.—"Bibliography," pp. 199–200.

§125. LANGUAGE TEACHING

[See also §91. Periodicals Devoted to Teaching of English and Foreign Languages.]

3132. Lado, Robt. Annotated Bibliography for Teachers of English as a Foreign Language. Washington, D.C., Government Printing Office, 1955. vii + 224 pp.—Bulletin 1955, no. 3, in the series issued by the U.S. Department of Health, Education, and Welfare.

3133. Jespersen, Otto. How to Teach a Foreign Language. Translated from the Danish by Sophia Yhlen-Olsen Bertelsen. 2nd ed. London, S. Sonnenschein and Co., 1908. 194 pp.—Original ed. 1904; second ed. reprinted 1923. "Select List of Books," pp. 193–194.

3134. Fries, Chas. C. The Teaching of the English Language. New York, Nelson and Sons, 1927. 187 pp.

3135. Huse, H[oward] R. The Psychology of Foreign Language Study. Chapel Hill, University of North Carolina Press, 1931. viii + 231 pp.—"Bibliography," pp. 214–226.

3136. Matthew, Robt. John. Language and Area Studies in the Armed Services. Their future significance. Washington, D.C., American Council on

Education, 1947. xix + 211 pp.—"For the Commission on Implications of Armed Services Educational Programs." Bibliography, pp. 188–211.

3137. Gray, Wm. S. On Their Own in Reading. How to give children independence in attacking new words. With editorial collaboration of Dorothy Horton. Chicago, Scott, Foresman and Co., 1948. xv + 268 pp.

3138. Abercrombie, David. Problems and Principles. Studies in the teaching of English as a second language. London, Longmans, Green and Co., 1956. vi + 96 pp.

§126. SEMANTICS

[See also §93. Periodicals Devoted to Semantics.]

3142. Collin, Carl S. R. A Bibliographical Guide to Sematology. Lund, Sweden, Lindstedt, 1914. 46 pp.

3143. Bréal, Michel. Semantics. Studies in the science of meaning. Translated by Mrs. Henry Crust. New York, Henry Holt and Co., 1900. lxvi + 341 pp.—Original Fr. ed. 1887.

3144. Stern, Gustaf. Meaning and Change of Meaning. With special reference to the English language. Göteborg, Sweden, Elanders Boktryckeri, 1931. xiii + 456 pp.—Volume XXXVIII, no. 1, in the series Göteborgs Högskolas Årsskrift.

3145. Bachmann, Armin. Zur psychologischen Theorie des sprachlichen Bedeutungswandels. München, C. H. Beck, 1935. 68 pp.—Number 15 in the series Arbeiten zur Entwicklungspsychologie. "Literaturverzeichnis," pp. 66–68.

3146. Chase, Stuart. The Tyranny of Words. New York, Harcourt, Brace and Co., 1938. xiv + 396 pp.—"Selected Bibliography," pp. 385–386.

3147. Walpole, Hugh R. Semantics. The nature of words and their meanings. Introduction by I. A. Richards. New York, W. W. Norton and Co., 1941. 264 pp.

3148. Morris, Chas. [W.] Signs, Language, and Behavior. New York, Prentice-Hall Inc., 1946. xii + 365 pp.—Bibliography, pp. 311–343.

3149. Hayakawa, S[amuel] I. Language in Thought and Action. In consultation with Basil H. Pillard. New York, Harcourt, Brace and Co., 1949. x + 307 + xii–xxxvi pp.—Original ed. 1939 entitled *Language in Action.*

3150. Reiss, Samuel. The Rise of Words and Their Meanings. New York, Philosophical Library, 1950. [ix] + 301 pp.

3151. Flew, Antony, ed. Essays on Logic and Language. Oxford, Eng., Basil Blackwell, 1951. vii + 206 pp.—Also Flew's *Logic and Language*, Second series, Oxford, Eng., Basil Blackwell, 1953, 242 pp.

3152. Kronasser, Heinz. Handbuch der Semasiologie. Kurze Einführung in die Geschichte, Problematik und Terminologie der Bedeutungslehre. Heidelberg, Carl Winter Verlag, 1952. 204 pp.

3153. Linsky, Leonard, ed. Semantics and the Philosophy of Language. A collection of readings. Urbana, University of Illinois Press, 1952. ix + 289 pp.—"Bibliography," pp. 287–289.

3154. Chase, Stuart. Power of Words. In collaboration with Marion Tyler Chase. New York, Harcourt, Brace and Co., 1954. 308 pp.

3155. Spang-Hanssen, Henning. Recent Theories on the Nature of the Language Sign. Copenhagen, Nordisk Sprog- og Kulturforlag, 1954. 142 pp.—Number 9 in the series Travaux du Cercle linguistique de Copenhague.

3156. Guiraud, Pierre. La sémantique. Paris, Presses universitaires de France, 1955. 118 pp.

3157. Ullmann, Stephen. The Principles of Semantics. 2nd ed. New York, Philosophical Library, 1957. 346 pp.—Number 84 in the series Glasgow University Publications. Original ed. 1951.

3158. Korzybski, Alfred H. Science and Sanity. An introduction to non-Aristotelian systems and general semantics. Fourth ed. with new preface by Russell Meyers. Lakeville, Conn., International Non-Aristotelian Library Publ'ing Co., 1958. 806 pp.—Original ed. 1933; second ed. 1941; third ed. 1948.

3159. Ogden, C[harles] K., and Richards, I[vor] A. The Meaning of Meaning. A study of the influence of language upon thought and of the science of symbolism. With supplementary essays by B. Malinowski and F. G. Crookshank. 8th ed. New York, Harcourt, Brace and Co., 1958. xxii + 263 pp.—In the series International Library of Psychology, Philosophy, and Scientific Method. Original ed. 1923.

§127. STRUCTURAL LINGUISTICS

3163. Bloomfield, Leonard. Language. New York, Henry Holt and Co., 1933. ix + 564 pp.—Reprint 1954. "Bibliography," pp. 524–545.

3164. Bloch, Bernard, and Trager, Geo. L. Outline of Linguistic Analysis. Baltimore, Linguistic Society of America, 1942. 82 pp.—In the series Special Publications of the Linguistic Society of America. "Reading List," pp. 80–82.

3165. Pike, Kenneth L. Phonemics. A technique for reducing languages to writing. Ann Arbor, University of Michigan Press, 1947. xvi + 254 pp.—Number 3 in the series University of Michigan Publications in Linguistics.

3166. Pittman, Dean. Practical Linguistics. Foreword by J. M. Cowan. Cleveland, Mid-Missions, 1948. xiii + 229 pp.—"Reading Lists," pp. 196–200; "Glossary," pp. 216–219.

3167. Nida, Eugene A. Morphology. The descriptive analysis of words. 2nd ed. Ann Arbor, University of Michigan Press, 1949. xvi + 342 pp.—Number 2 in the series University of Michigan Publications in Linguistics. Original ed. 1944; second ed. reprinted 1957.

3168. Trager, Geo. L. The Field of Linguistics. Norman, Okla., Battenburg Press, 1949. 8 pp.—Number 1 in the series Studies in Linguistics: Occasional Papers.

3169. Goodman, Nelson. The Structure of Appearance. Cambridge, Mass., Harvard Univ. Press, 1951. xv + 315 pp.

3170. Harris, Zellig Sabbettai. Methods in Structural Linguistics. University of Chicago Press, [1951]. xv + 384 pp.

3171. Trager, Geo. L., and Smith, H[enry] L. An Outline of English Structure. Norman, Okla., Battenburg Press, 1951. 92 pp.—Number 3 in the series Studies in Linguistics: Occasional Papers.

3172. Cohen, A[ntonie]. The Phonemes of English. A phonemic study of the vowels and consonants of standard English. The Hague, Martinus Nijhoff, 1952. 127 pp.—"Bibliography," pp. 108–113.

3173. Fries, Chas. C. The Structure of English. An introduction to the construction of English sentences. New York, Harcourt, Brace and Co., 1952. ix + 304 pp.

3174. Hjelmslev, Louis. Prolegomena to a Theory of Language. Translated by F. J. Whitfield. Baltimore, Waverly Press, 1953. 92 pp.—Memoir 7 of the International Journal of American Linguistics. Indiana University Publications in Anthropology and Linguistics. Original Danish ed. 1943.

3175. Martinet, André, and Weinreich, Uriel. Linguistics Today. New York, Linguistic Circle of New York, 1954. 280 pp.—Number 2 in the series Publications of the Linguistic Circle of New York.

3176. Gleason, Henry A., Jr. An Introduction to Descriptive Linguistics. New York, Henry Holt and Co., 1956. ix + 389 pp.—"Selected Bibliography," pp. 373–378. Also supplement *Workbook in Descriptive Linguistics*, New York, Henry Holt and Co., 1955, 88 pp.

3177. Jakobson, Roman, and Halle, Morris. Fundamentals of Language. The Hague, Mouton and Co., 1956. ix + 87 pp.—Number 1 in the series Janua linguarum: studia memoriae Nicolai van Wijk dedicata. "Selected List of Studies in General Phonology," pp. 85–87.

3178. Smith, Henry Lee, Jr. Linguistic Science and the Teaching of English. Cambridge, Mass., Harvard Univ. Press, 1956. 61 pp.

3179. Whitehall, Harold. Structural Essentials of English. New York, Harcourt, Brace and Co., 1956. 154 pp.

3180. Whorf, Benjamin Lee. Language, Thought, and Reality. Selected writings. Edited with an introduction by John B. Carroll. Foreword by Stuart Chase. Cambridge, Mass., Technology Press, 1956. xi + 278 pp.

3181. Chomsky, Noam. Syntactic Structures. The Hague, Mouton and Co., 1957. 116 pp.—Number 4 in the series Janua linguarum: studia memoriae Nicolai van Wijk dedicata. "Bibliography," pp. 115–116.

3182. Greenberg, Joseph H. Essays in Linguistics. University of Chicago Press, 1957. vii + 108 pp.

3183. Joos, Martin, ed. Readings in Linguistics. The development of descriptive linguistics in America since 1925. Washington, D.C., American Council of Learned Societies, 1957. viii + 421 (double column) pp.

3184. Allen, Harold B., ed. Readings in Applied English Linguistics. New York, Appleton-Century-Crofts, 1958. xiii + 428 pp.

3185. Francis, W[inthrop] Nelson. The Structure of American English. With a chapter on American dialects by Raven I. McDavid, Jr. New York, Ronald Press, 1958. vii + 614 pp.—"Glossary," pp. 589–597; "General Bibliography," pp. 598–602.

3186. Hill, Archibald A. Introduction to Linguistic Structure. From sound to sentence in English. New York, Harcourt, Brace and Co., 1958. xi + 496 pp.

3187. Hockett, Chas. F. A Course in Modern Linguistics. New York, Macmillan Co., 1958. xi + 621 pp.—"Bibliography," pp. 599–605.

3188. Nida, Eugene Albert. A Synopsis of English Syntax. Norman, University of Oklahoma Press, 1960. lxviii + 233 pp.—Number 4 in the Linguistics Series of the Summer Institute of Linguistics of the University of Oklahoma.

§128. MISCELLANEOUS GLOSSARIES

3192. Swainson, Chas. The Folk Lore and Provincial Names of British Birds. London, Elliot Stock, 1886. viii + 243 pp.—Volume XVII in the series Publications of the Folk-Lore Society.

3193. Farmer, John S. The Public School Word-Book. A contribution to a historical glossary of words, phrases, and turns of expression obsolete and in present use peculiar to our great public schools together with some that have been or are modish at the Universities. London, privately issued for subscribers only by Hirschfeld Bros., 1900. viii + 243 pp.

3194. Swann, H[arry] Kirke. A Dictionary of English and Folk-Names of British Birds. London, Witherby and Co., 1913. xii + 266 pp.

3195. Bentley, Harold W. A Dictionary of Spanish Terms in English. With special reference to the American Southwest. New York, Columbia Univ. Press, 1932. xi + 243 pp.—In the series Columbia University Studies in English and Comparative Literature.

3196. Adams, Ramon F. Cowboy Lingo. Boston, Houghton Mifflin Co., 1936. x + 257 pp.

3197. Garber, Max B. A Modern Military Dictionary. Ten thousand terms, ancient and modern, American and foreign. Washington, D.C., published by the author, 1936. 332 pp.

3198. Bense, J[ohan] F. A Dictionary of the Low Dutch Element in the English Vocabulary. The Hague, Martinus Nijhoff, 1939. xxxii + 663 (double column) pp.

3199. Colby, Elbridge. Army Talk. A familiar dictionary of soldier speech. Princeton, N.J., University Press, 1942. xiii + 232 pp.

3200. Colcord, Joanna Carver. Sea Language Comes Ashore. Illustrated by Larry. New York, Cornell Maritime Press, 1945. ix + 213 pp.

3201. Irving, John. Royal Navalese. A glossary of forecastle and quarterdeck words and phrases. London, Edward Arnold and Co., 1946. 196 pp.

3202. Taylor, A[nna] Marjorie. The Language of World War II. Abbreviations, captions, quotations, slogans, titles, and other terms and phrases. Rev. and enl. ed. New York, H. W. Wilson Co., 1948. [ix] + 265 pp.—Original ed. 1944.

3203. Buck, Carl Darling. A Dictionary of Selected Synonyms in the Principal Indo-European Languages. A contribution to the history of ideas. University of Chicago Press, 1949. xix + 1515 (double column) pp.

3204. Berg, Paul C. A Dictionary of New Words in English. London, George Allen and Unwin Ltd., 1953. 176 (chiefly double column) pp.

3205. Reifer, Mary. Dictionary of New Words. With an introduction by Eric Partridge. New York, Philosophical Library, 1955. xi + 234 (double column) pp.—In the series Midcentury Reference Library.

3206. Adams, Ramon F. Western Words. A dictionary of the range, cow camp, and trail. Norman, University of Oklahoma Press, 1944. xiv + 182 (double column) pp.—Reprint 1956.

3207. Manning, T[homas] D., and Walker, [Charles] F. British Warship Names. With a foreword by Admiral of the Fleet Earl Mountbatten of Burma. London, Putnam, 1959. 498 pp.

CHAPTER IX

FOLKLORE AND FORMS OF POPULAR LITERATURE

[See also §97. Periodicals Devoted to Folklore; §100. Publisher, Academic, and Society Series *passim.*]

3211. Lesser, Alex. Bibliography of American Folklore 1915–1928. Journal of American Folklore, XLI (1928), 1–60.

3212. Volkskundliche Bibliographie. Herausgegeben von Paul Geiger, mit Unterstützung von Eduard von Hoffmann-Krayer. Im Auftrage des Verbandes deutscher Vereine für Volkskunde. Berlin, Walther de Gruyter, 1919 (for 1917)–1933 (for 1928). 8 vols.

3213. Haywood, Chas. A Bibliography of North American Folklore and Folksong. New York, Greenberg Publ'er, 1951. xxxi + 1292 (double column) pp.

---

§129. MANUALS

3217. Gomme, Alice Bertha. The Traditional Games of England, Scotland, and Ireland. With tunes, singing-rhymes, and methods of playing according to the variants extant and recorded in different parts of the kingdom. Vol. I: Accroshay—Nuts in May; Vol. II: Oats and Beans—Would You Know. London, David Nutt, 1898. 2 vols.

3218. Strutt, Joseph. The Sports and Pastimes of the People of England from the earliest period. . . . New ed. . . . by J. Charles Cox. . . . London, Methuen and Co., 1903. lv + 322 pp.—Strutt's original ed. 1801.

3219. Hazlitt, W[illiam] Carew. Faiths and Folklore. A dictionary of national beliefs, superstitions, and popular customs, past and current, with their classical and foreign analogues, described and illustrated. Forming a new edition of The Popular Antiquities of Great Britain by Brand and Ellis . . . now first alphabetically arranged. London, Reeves and

Turner, 1905. 2 (double column page, continuously paged) vols.—A development of John Brand and Henry Ellis, *Observations on the Popular Antiquities of Great Britain*, London, G. Bell and Sons, 1900–02, 3 vols. Brand's original ed. 1777.

3220. Hoops, Johannes, ed. Reallexikon der germanischen Altertumskunde. Strassburg, K. J. Trübner, 1911–19. 4 (double column page) vols.

3221. Nourry, Émile D. [pseud. Paul Saintyves.] Manuel de folklore. Lettre-préface de S. Charléty. Paris, Librairie Émile Nourry, 1936. vii + 215 pp.

3222. ÓSúilleabháin, Seán. A Handbook of Irish Folklore. Introductory note by Séamus ÓDuilearga. Dublin, Educational Co. for the Folklore of Ireland Society, 1942. xxxi + 699 pp.

3223. Gennep, Arnold van. Manuel de folklore français contemporain. Paris, Éditions Auguste Picard, Vol. I: 1943, Vol. II: 1946, Vol. III: 1937, Vol. IV: 1938. 4 vols.

3224. Leach, Maria, and Fried, Jerome, eds. Funk and Wagnalls Standard Dictionary of Folklore. Vol. I: A–I; Vol. II: J–Z. New York, Funk and Wagnalls Co., 1949–50. 2 (double column page, continuously paged) vols.

3225. Erich, Oswald A., and Beitl, Richard. Wörterbuch der deutschen Volkskunde. Zweite Auflage, neu bearbeitet von Richard Beitl. Stuttgart, Alfred Kröner Verlag, 1955. x + 919 (double column) pp.—Volume CXXVII in the series Kröners Taschenausgaben. Original ed. 1936.

3226. Tallman, Marjorie. Dictionary of American Folklore. New York, Philosophical Library, 1960. 324 pp.

§130. STUDIES

3230. Gomme, Geo. Lawrence. The Handbook of Folklore. London, David Nutt, 1890. vii + 183 pp.—Volume XX [1887] in the series Publications of the Folk-Lore Society.

3231. Cox, Marian Roalfe. An Introduction to Folk-Lore. New and enl. ed. London, David Nutt, 1897. xv + 344 pp.—Original ed. 1895. "Bibliography of Folk-lore," pp. 322–344.

3232. Walsh, Wm. S. Curiosities of Popular Customs and of Rites, Ceremonies, Observances, and Miscellaneous Antiquities. Philadelphia, J. B. Lippincott Co., 1900. 1018 pp.

3233. Wood-Martin, W[illiam] G. Traces of the Elder Faiths of Ireland. A folklore sketch. A handbook of Irish pre-Christian traditions. London, Longmans, Green and Co., 1902. 2 vols.—Bibliography, II, pp. 329–416.

3234. Gomme, Geo. Laurence. Folklore as an Historical Science. London, Methuen and Co., 1908. xvi + 371 pp.

3235. Burne, Charlotte Sophia. The Handbook of Folklore. New ed., rev. and enl. London, Sidgwick and Jackson Ltd., 1914. x + 364 pp.—Volume LXXIII [1913] in the series Publications of the Folk-Lore Society. "Authorities Cited," pp. 356–364.

3236. Marett, R[obert] R. Psychology and Folk-Lore. London, Methuen and Co., 1920. ix + 275 pp.

3237. Meller, Walter Clifford. The Boy Bishop and Other Essays on Forgotten Customs and Beliefs of the Past. London, G. Bell and Sons, 1923. ix + 157 pp.

3238. Wright, A[rthur] R. English Folklore. New York, Robert M. McBride and Co., [1931]. 122 pp.

3239. Chambers, E[dmund] K. The English Folk-Play. Oxford Univ. Press, 1933. vii + 248 pp.

3240. Thompson, C[harles] J. S. The Mystic Mandrake. London, Rider and Co., 1934. 253 pp.

3241. MacKenzie, Donald A. Scottish Folk-Lore and Folk Life. Studies in race, culture, and tradition. London, Blackie and Son, 1935. ix + 310 pp.

3242. Dontenville, Henri. La mythologie française. Paris, Payot, 1948. 227 pp.

3243. Evans, Emyr E. Irish Folk Ways. New York, Devin-Adair Co., 1957. xvi + 324 pp.

3244. Sagendorph, Robb. The Old Farmer's Almanac Sampler. New York, Ives Washburn Inc., 1957. viii + 306 pp.

§131. WITCHCRAFT AND DEMONOLOGY

3248. Murray, Margaret Alice. The Witch-Cult in Western Europe. A study in anthropology. Oxford Univ. Press, 1921. 303 pp.

3249. Summers, Montague. The History of Witchcraft and Demonology. London, Kegan Paul, Trench, Trubner and Co., 1926. xv + 353 pp.—"Bibliography," pp. 315–346.

3250. Ewen, C[ecil] L'Estrange, ed. Witch Hunting and Witch Trials. The indictments for witchcraft from the records of 1373 assizes held for the Home Circuit A.D. 1559–1736. London, Kegan Paul, Trench, Trubner and Co., 1929. xiii + 345 pp.

3251. Kittredge, Geo. Lyman. Witchcraft in Old and New England. Cambridge, Mass., Harvard Univ. Press, 1929. ix + 641 pp.

3252. Summers, Montague, ed. Demonolatry by Nicolas Remy, Privy Councillor to the Most Serene Duke of Lorraine and Public Advocate to His Duchy. In three books. Translated by E. A. Ashwin. London, John Rodker, 1930. xliii + 188 (double column) pp.

3253. Ewen, C[ecil] L'Estrange. Witchcraft and Demonianism. A concise account derived from sworn depositions and confessions obtained in the courts of England and Wales. London, Heath Cranton Ltd., 1933. 495 pp.

3254. Lea, Henry Chas. Materials toward a History of Witchcraft. With an introduction by George Lincoln Burr. Edited by Arthur C. Howland. Philadelphia, University of Pennsylvania, 1939. 3 vols.—Reprint, New York, Thomas Yoseloff Inc., [1957], 3 vols. (1548 pp.)

3255. Bernheimer, Richard. Wild Men in the Middle Ages. A study in art, sentiment, and demonology. Cambridge, Mass., Harvard Univ. Press, 1952. xiii + 224 pp.—Bibliographical notes, pp. 189–216.

3256. Robbins, Rossell Hope. The Encyclopedia of Witchcraft and Demonology. New York, Crown Publ'ers, 1959. 571 (chiefly double column) pp.—"Select Bibliography," pp. 561–571 (triple column).

§132. MYTHOLOGY AND MYTH: HANDBOOKS

3260. [Bulfinch, Thos.] Bulfinch's Mythology. The age of fable. The age of chivalry. Legends of Charlemagne. New York, Thomas Y. Crowell Co., [1947]. xviii + 957 pp.—Original ed. 1855.

3261. Grimm, Jacob. Teutonic Mythology. Translated from the 4th ed. with notes and appendix by James Steven Stallybrass. London, George Bell and Sons, 1882–83. 3 vols.—Original Ger. ed. 1835; fourth Ger. ed. 1875–78.

3262. Munch, Peter Andreas. Norse Mythology. Legends of gods and heroes. In the revision of Magnus Olsen. Translated from the Norwegian by Sigurd Bernhard Hustvedt. New York, American-Scandinavian Foundation, 1926. xix + 392 pp.—"Bibliography," pp. 279–280. Original Norwegian ed. 1880, the English translation being from the 3rd Norwegian ed. 1922.

3263. Gray, Louis Herbert, and Moore, George Foot, eds. Mythology of All Races. Boston, Marshall Jones Co., 1916–32. 13 vols.

3264. Grimal, Pierre. Dictionnaire de la mythologie grecque et romaine. Préface de Charles Picard. Paris, Presses Universitaires de France, 1951. xxxi + 577 (double column) pp.—Full bibliographical references to classical sources at the foot of each page.

3265. Brett, Henry. English Myths and Traditions. London, B. T. Batsford Ltd., 1952. ix + 148 pp.

3266. Sykes, Egerton. Everyman's Dictionary of Non-Classical Mythology. New ed. London, J. M. Dent and Sons, 1952. xviii + 269 pp.—In the series Everyman's Reference Library. "Bibliography," pp. xvi–xvii.

3267. Branston, Brian. Gods of the North. New York, Vanguard Press, 1955. 318 pp.

3268. Branston, Brian. The Last Gods of England. London, Thames and Hudson, [1957]. 194 pp.

3269. Rose, H[erbert] J. Gods and Heroes of the Greeks. London, Methuen and Co., 1957. 202 pp.

3270. Rose, H[erbert] J. A Handbook of Greek Mythology. Including its extension to Rome. 6th ed. London, Methuen and Co., 1958. ix + 363 pp.—Original ed. 1928. "Bibliography," pp. 335–339.

3271. Hunger, Herbert. Lexikon der griechischen und römischen Mythologie, mit Hinweisen auf das Fortwirken antiker Stoffe und Motive in der bildenden Kunst, Literatur und Musik des Abendlandes bis zur Gegenwart. Fünfte, erweiterte und ergänzte Aufl. Vienna, Verlag Brüder Hollinek, 1959. xii + 387 pp.—Original ed. 1953.

3272. Larousse Encyclopedia of Mythology. With an introduction by Robert Graves. Translated by Richard Aldington and Delano Ames. New York, Prometheus Press, 1959. x + 500 (double column) pp.—French original *Larousse mythologie générale,* edited by Félix Guirand, Paris, Larousse, 1935, vii + 448 pp.

§133. MYTHOLOGY AND MYTH: STUDIES

3276. Lang, Andrew. Myth, Ritual, and Religion. London, Longmans, Green and Co., 1887. 2 vols.

3277. Weston, Jessie L. From Ritual to Romance. New York, Macmillan Co., 1920. xv + 202 pp.—Reprint New York, Peter Smith, 1941.

3278. Frazer, James G. The Golden Bough. A study in magic and religion. 3rd ed. London, Macmillan Co., 1907–15. 12 vols. in 11.—Original ed. 1890 in 2 vols.; second ed. 1900 in 3 vols. Also *Aftermath*, A Supplement to the Golden Bough, London, Macmillan Co., 1936, xx + 494 pp. One-volume abridged ed. *The Golden Bough*, New York, Macmillan Co., 1956, xvi + 864 pp. Also *The New Golden Bough*, A new abridgement of the classic work edited and with notes and foreword by Theodor H. Gaster, New York, Criterion Books, 1959, xxx + 738 pp.

3279. Lord Raglan. [Fitz Roy Richard Somerset.] The Hero. A study in tradition, myth, and drama. London, Methuen and Co., 1936. xi + 311 pp.—Reprint London, Watts, 1949, x + 310 pp., number 133 in the series Thinker's Library.

3280. Spence, Lewis. Myth and Ritual in Dance, Game, and Rhyme. London, Watts and Co., 1947. x + 202 pp.—"References," pp. 194–199.

3281. Campbell, Joseph. The Hero with a Thousand Faces. New York, Pantheon Books, 1949. xxiii + 416 pp.—Number 17 in the Bollingen Series.

3282. Chase, Richard. Quest for Myth. Baton Rouge, Louisiana State Univ. Press, 1949. xi + 150 pp.—Bibliographical notes, pp. 133–148. A treatment of literature as myth.

3283. Patch, Howard R. The Other World. According to descriptions in medieval literature. Cambridge, Mass., Harvard Univ. Press, 1950. 386 pp.

3284. Graves, Robt. The White Goddess. A historical grammar of poetic myth. [3rd ed. amended and enl.] London, Faber and Faber, 1952. 496 pp.—Original ed. 1948; second ed. also 1948.

3285. Murphy, Gerard. Saga and Myth in Ancient Ireland. Dublin, Colm O Lochlainn for the Cultural Relations Committee of Ireland, 1955. 63 pp.—Volume X in the series Irish Life and Culture.

3286. Sebeok, Thos. A., ed. Myth. A symposium. Philadelphia, American Folklore Society, 1955. 110 pp.—Number 5 in the Bibliographical and Special Series of the American Folklore Society. A treatment of myth as it relates to ritual, semantics, symbolism, and other similar areas of study.

3287. Rank, Otto. The Myth of the Birth of the Hero and Other Writings. Edited by Philip Freund. New York, Vintage Books, 1959. xiv + 315 pp.—Original German ed. 1909.

§134. CALENDAR CUSTOMS

3291. Hazeltine, Mary Emogene. Anniversaries and Holidays. A calendar of days and how to observe them. Chicago, American Library Association, 1928. xx + 288 (double column) pp.

3292. Wright, A[rthur] R. British Calendar Customs. England. Edited by J. E. Lones. With a preface by S. H. Hooke. London, William Glaisher Ltd. for the Folk-Lore Society, 1936–40. 3 vols.—Volumes XCVII, CII, and CVI in the series Publications of the Folk-Lore Society.

3293. Banks, M[ary] Macleod. British Calendar Customs. Scotland. With a preface by J. A. MacCulloch. London, William Glaisher Ltd. for the Folk-Lore Society, 1937–41. 3 vols.—Volumes C, CIV, and CVIII in the series Publications of the Folk-Lore Society.

3294. Douglas, Geo. Wm. The American Book of Days. A compendium of information about holidays, festivals, notable anniversaries, and Christian and Jewish holy days. . . . Revised by Helen Douglas Compton. New York, H. W. Wilson Co., 1948. xxii + 697 pp.—Original ed. 1937.

3295. Meyer, Robt., Jr. Festivals U.S.A. Illustrated by Lee Owens. New York, Ives Washburn Inc., 1950. 438 pp.—Arrangement by State with alphabetic subject list for each State.

3296. Hunt, Cecil. British Customs and Ceremonies. When, where, and why. London, Ernest Benn Ltd., 1954. 208 pp.

3297. Coates, Helen R. The American Festival Guide. A handbook of more than 200 colonial, homesteading, Western, Spanish, folk, rodeo, sports, cultural, and other festivals and celebrations in the United States and Canada with a calendar and a gazetteer of festivals for ready reference. New York, Exposition Press, 1956. x + 299 pp.

3298. Harper, Howard V. Days and Customs of All Faiths. New York, Fleet Publ'ing Corp., 1957. xiv + 17–399 pp.

3299. Weiser, Francis X. Handbooks of Christian Feasts and Customs. The year of the Lord in liturgy and folklore. New York, Harcourt, Brace and Co., 1958. xviii + 366 pp.

§135. SUPERSTITIONS AND POPULAR BELIEFS

3303. Black, Geo. Wm. Folk-Medicine. A chapter in the history of culture. London, Elliot Stock, 1883. ii + 227 pp.—Volume XII in the series Publications of the Folk-Lore Society.

3304. Bergen, Fanny D. Current Superstitions. Collected from the oral tradition of English-speaking folk. With notes and an introduction by William Wells Newell. Boston, Houghton Mifflin Co. for the American Folk-Lore Society, 1896. x + 161 pp.

3305. Bergen, Fanny D. Animal and Plant Lore. Collected from the oral tradition of English-speaking folk. With an introduction by Joseph Y. Bergen. Boston, Houghton Mifflin Co. for the American Folk-Lore Society, 1899. x + 180 pp.

3306. Latham, Minor W. The Elizabethan Fairies. The fairies of folklore and the fairies of Shakespeare. New York, Columbia Univ. Press, 1930. ix + 313 pp.

3307. Hoffmann-Krayer, E[duard] von, and Bächtold-Stäubli, Hanns, eds. Handwörterbuch des deutschen Aberglaubens. Berlin, Walther de Gruyter, 1927–42. 10 (double column page) vols.

3308. Radford, E[dwin] and M[ona] A. Encyclopaedia of Superstitions. With a foreword by Sir John Hammerton. London, Rider and Co., [1947]. ix + 11–269 (double column) pp.—Also New York, Philosophical Library, 1949. "Bibliography," pp. 265–269.

3309. Ackermann, A[lfred] S. E. Popular Fallacies. A book of common errors explained and corrected with copious references to authorities. With an introduction by Richard Gregory. 4th ed. London, Old Westminster Press, 1950. xv + 843 pp.—Original ed. 1907; second ed. 1909; third ed. 1923.

3310. Grattan, J[ohn] H. G., and Singer, Chas. Anglo-Saxon Magic and Medicine. Illustrated specially from the semi-pagan 'Lacnunga.' Oxford Univ. Press for the Wellcome Historical Medical Museum, 1952. xii + 234 pp. + iv plates.

3311. Thorndike, Lynn. A History of Magic and Experimental Science. New York, Macmillan Co., 1923–58. 8 vols.—Volumes III to VIII have the imprint Columbia University Press.

3312. Briggs, K[atherine] M. The Anatomy of Puck. An examination of fairy beliefs among Shakespeare's contemporaries and successors. London, Routledge and Kegan Paul, 1959. xi + 284 pp.—"List of Books and Authorities Cited or Quoted," pp. 262–276.

§136. ANTHOLOGIES: POPULAR

3316. Rhŷs, John. Celtic Folklore. Welsh and Manx. Oxford Univ. Press, 1901. 2 vols.

3317. Judges, A[rthur] V., ed. The Elizabethan Underworld. A collection of Tudor and early Stuart tracts and ballads telling of the lives and misdoings of vagabonds, thieves, rogues, and cozeners, and giving some account of the operation of the criminal law. London, George Routledge and Sons, 1930. lxiv + 543 pp.—"Glossary," pp. 522–532.

3318. Botkin, B[enjamin] A., ed. A Treasury of American Folklore. Stories, ballads, and traditions of the people. With a foreword by Carl Sandburg. New York, Crown Publ'ers, 1944. xxviii + 932 pp.

3319. Botkin, B[enjamin] A., ed. A Treasury of New England Folklore. Stories, ballads, and traditions of the Yankee people. New York, Crown Publ'ers, 1947. xxvi + 934 pp.

3320. Botkin, B[enjamin] A., ed. A Treasury of Southern Folklore. Stories, ballads, traditions, and folkways of the people of the South. With a foreword by Douglas Southall Freeman. New York, Crown Publ'ers, 1949. xxiv + 776 pp.

3321. Botkin, B[enjamin] A., ed. A Treasury of Western Folklore. Foreword by Bernard De Voto. New York, Crown Publ'ers, 1951. xxvi + 806 pp.

3322. Botkin, B[enjamin] A., and Harlow, Alvin F., eds. A Treasury of Railroad Folklore. The stories, tall tales, traditions, ballads and songs of the American railroad man. New York, Crown Publ'ers, 1953. xiv + 530 pp.

3323. Botkin, Benjamin A., ed. Sidewalks of America. Folklore, legends, sagas, traditions, customs, songs, stories, and sayings of city folk. Indianapolis, Bobbs-Merrill Co., 1954. xxii + 605 pp.

3324. Colum, Padraic, ed. A Treasury of Irish Folklore. The stories, traditions, legends, humor, wisdom, ballads, and songs of the Irish people. New York, Crown Publ'ers, 1954. xx + 620 pp.

3325. Botkin, B[enjamin] A., ed. A Treasury of Mississippi River Folklore. Stories, ballads, traditions, and folkways of the Mid-American river country. Foreword by Carl Carmer. New York, Crown Publ'ers, 1955. xx + 620 pp.

3326. Hughes, Langston, and Bontemps, Arna, eds. The Book of Negro Folklore. New York, Dodd, Mead and Co., 1958. xxxi + 624 pp.

§137. CHILDREN'S LITERATURE

3330. Brewton, John E. and Sara W. Index to Children's Poetry. A title, subject, author, and first line index to poetry in collections for children and youth. New York, H. W. Wilson Co., 1942. xxxii + 965 (double column) pp.—*Supplement*, New York, H. W. Wilson Co., 1954, xxii + 405 (double column) pp.

3331. St. John, Judith. The Osborne Collection of Early Children's Books 1566–1910. With an introduction by Edgar Osborne. Toronto Public Library, 1958. xxiv + 561 pp.

3332. Bett, Henry. Nursery Rhymes and Tales. Their origin and history. London, Methuen and Co., 1924. ix + 130 pp.

3333. Montgomerie, Norah and Wm. Scottish Nursery Rhymes. Illustrated by T. Ritchie. London, Hogarth Press, 1946. 151 pp.

3334. Berry, Erick, and Best, Herbert. Writing for Children. New York, Viking Press, 1947. x + 202 pp.

3335. Jordan, Alice M. From Rollo to Tom Sawyer and Other Papers. Decorations by Nora S. Unwin. Boston, Horn Book Inc., 1948. 160 pp.—A history of American children's literature.

3336. Kiefer, Monica. American Children through Their Books 1700–1835. Foreword by Dorothy C. Fisher. Philadelphia, John C. Winston Co., 1948. 248 pp.

3337. Opie, Iona and Peter. Oxford Dictionary of Nursery Rhymes. Oxford Univ. Press, 1951. xxvii + 467 pp.

3338. Adams, Bess P. About Books and Children. Historical survey of children's literature. New York, Henry Holt and Co., 1953. xvi + 573 pp.

3339. Meigs, Cornelia, Eaton, Anne, Nesbitt, Elizabeth, and Viguers, Ruth H. A Critical History of Children's Literature. A survey of children's books in English from earliest times to the present, prepared in four parts under the editorship of Cornelia Meigs. New York, Macmillan Co., 1953. xxiv + 624 pp.

3340. Muir, Percy [H.] English Children's Books 1600 to 1900. New York, Frederick A. Praeger Inc., 1954. 256 pp.

3341. Opie, Iona and Peter. Oxford Nursery Rhyme Book. Oxford, Clarendon Press, 1955. xi + 223 pp.

3342. Targ, Wm., ed. Bibliophile in the Nursery. A bookman's treasury of collectors' lore on old and rare children's books. Cleveland, World Publ'ing Co., 1957. 505 pp.

3343. Opie, Iona and Peter. The Lore and Language of Schoolchildren. Oxford Univ. Press, 1960. 417 pp.

§138. PROVERBS: COLLECTIONS AND STUDIES

[See also §157. Collections of Quotations, Anecdotes, and Epigrams.]

3347. Stephens, T[homas] A. Proverb Literature. A bibliography of works relating to proverbs. Edited by Wilfred Bonser. London, William Glaisher Ltd. for the Folk-Lore Society, 1930. xx + 496 pp.—Volume LXXXIX [1927–28] in the series Publications of the Folk-Lore Society.

3348. Taylor, Archer. An Introductory Bibliography for the Study of Proverbs. Modern Philology, XXX, 2 (Nov. 1932), 195–210.

3349. Moll, Otto E. Sprichwörterbibliographie. Frankfurt a. M., Vittorio Klostermann, 1958. xvi + 573 (double column) + 574–630 (triple column) pp.

3350. T[hiselton], W[illiam] M. National Anecdotes Interspersed with Historical Facts. English proverbial sayings and maxims. . . . London, C. Cradock and W. Joy, 1812. xii + 264 pp.

3351. Henderson, Andrew. Scottish Proverbs. With an introductory essay by W. Motherwell. Edinburgh, Oliver and Boyd, 1832. lxxxviii + 254 pp.

3352. Denham, M[ichael] A. A Collection of Proverbs and Popular Sayings Relating to the Seasons, the Weather, and Agricultural Pursuits. London, Percy Society, 1846. iv + 73 pp.

3353. Fitzgerald, Edward. Polonius. A collection of wise saws and modern instances. London, William Pickering, 1852. xvi + xclv pp.—Reprint Portland, Me., Thomas B. Mosher, 1901.

3354. Bohn, Henry G. A Polyglot of Foreign Proverbs. Comprising French, Italian, German, Dutch, Spanish, Portuguese, and Danish with English translations. London, Henry G. Bohn, 1857. iv + 579 pp.

3355. Hislop, Alexander. The Proverbs of Scotland. With explanatory and illustrative notes and a glossary. New ed. Edinburgh, Alexander Hislop and Co., 1868. xii + 13–367 pp.—Original ed. 1862.

3356. Henderson, Alfred. Latin Proverbs and Quotations. With translations and parallel passages and a copious English index. London, Sampson Low, Son, and Marston, 1869. vii + 505 pp.

3357. Reinsberg-Düringsfeld, Ida and Otto von. Sprichwörter der germanischen und romanischen Sprachen. Leipzig, Verlag von Hermann Fries, 1872–75. 2 (double column page) vols.

3358. Christy, Robt. Proverbs, Maxims, and Phrases of All Ages. Classified subjectively and arranged alphabetically. New York, G. P. Putnam's Sons, 1889. 2 vols.

3359. Vaughan, Henry Halford. Welsh Proverbs with English Translations. London, Kegan Paul, Trench and Co., 1889. vi + 378 pp.

3360. Cheviot, Andrew. Proverbs, Proverbial Expressions, and Popular Rhymes of Scotland. London, Alexander Gardner, 1896. xii + 434 pp.

3361. Hulme, F[rederick] Edward. Proverb Lore. Many sayings wise and otherwise, on many subjects, gleaned from many sources. London, Elliot Stock, 1902. vii + 269 pp.

3362. Hazlitt, W[illiam] Carew. English Proverbs and Proverbial Phrases. Collected from the most authentic sources alphabetically arranged and annotated. Rev. ed. London, Reeves and Turner, 1907. xxxii + 580 pp. —Original ed. 1869.

3363. Lipperheide, Franz von. Spruchwörterbuch. Sammlung deutscher und fremder Sinnsprüche. . . . Berlin, Verlag von Franz Lipperheide, 1907. viii + 1069 (double column) pp.

3364. Skeat, Walter W. Early English Proverbs. Chiefly of the thirteenth and fourteenth centuries. Oxford Univ. Press, 1910. xxiv + 147 pp.

3365. Marvin, Dwight Edwards. Curiosities in Proverbs. A collection of unusual adages, maxims, aphorisms, phrases, and other popular dicta from many lands. New York, G. P. Putnam's Sons, 1916. xi + 428 pp.

3366. Marvin, Dwight Edwards. The Antiquity of Proverbs. Fifty familiar proverbs and folk sayings with annotations and lists of connected forms, found in all parts of the world. New York, G. P. Putnam's Sons, 1922. xv + 329 pp.—"Authorities Consulted," pp. ix–xiii.

3367. Seiler, Friedrich. Deutsche Sprichwörterkunde. München, C. H. Beck'sche Verlagsbuchhandlung, 1922. x + 457 pp.—Volume IV, pt. 3, in the series Handbücher des deutschen Unterrichts an höheren Schulen.

3368. Tilley, Morris P. Elizabethan Proverb Lore in Lyly's Euphues and in Pettie's Petite Pallace. With parallels from Shakespeare. New York, Macmillan Co., 1926. x + 461 pp.—Volume II in the series University of Michigan Publications: Language and Literature.

3369. Apperson, G[eorge] L. English Proverbs and Proverbial Phrases. A historical dictionary. London, J. M. Dent and Sons, 1929. x + 721 (double column) pp.

3370. Taylor, Archer. The Proverb. Cambridge, Mass., Harvard Univ. Press, 1931. xi + 223 pp.

3371. Whiting, Bartlett Jere. Chaucer's Use of Proverbs. Cambridge, Mass., Harvard Univ. Press, 1934. xii + 297 pp.—Volume XI in the series Harvard Studies in Comparative Literature.

3372. Margadant, S[teven] W. F. Twintigduizend Citaten, Aphorismen en Spreekworden. The Hague, H. P. Leopolds Uitgeversmij, 1935. 741 (double column) pp.—Reprint 1952.

3373. Frank, Grace, and Miner, Dorothy. Proverbs in Rimes. Text and illustrations of the fifteenth century from a French manuscript in the Walters Art Gallery, Baltimore. Baltimore, Johns Hopkins Press, 1937. ix + 119 pp. + clxxxii plates.

3374. Champion, Selwyn Gurney. Racial Proverbs. A selection of the world's proverbs arranged linguistically with authoritative introductions to the proverbs of twenty-seven countries and races. London, George Routledge and Sons, 1938. cxxix + 767 (double column) pp.—"Authorities Consulted," pp. cix–cxxix.

3375. Whiting, Bartlett Jere. Proverbs in the Earlier English Drama. With illustrations from contemporary French plays. Cambridge, Mass., Harvard Univ. Press, 1938. xx + 505 pp.—Volume XIV in the series Harvard Studies in Comparative Literature.

3376. Davidoff, Henry. A World Treasury of Proverbs from Twenty-Five Languages. New York, Random House, 1946. xi + 526 pp.

3377. Singer, Samuel. Sprichwörter des Mittelalters. Teil I: Von den Anfängen bis ins 12. Jahrhundert; Teil II: Das 13. Jahrhundert; Teil III: Das 13. und 14. Jahrhundert. Bern, Verlag Herbert Lang und Cie, 1944–47. 3 vols.—Bibliographies, I, pp. 188–198; II, pp. 195–203; III, pp. 157–162.

3378. MacGregor, Forbes. Scots Proverbs and Rhymes. Edinburgh, Moray Press, 1948. 48 pp.

3379. Smith, Wm. Geo. The Oxford Dictionary of English Proverbs. With an introduction by Janet E. Heseltine. Second ed. revised throughout by Paul Harvey. Oxford Univ. Press, 1948. xxxii + 740 (double column) pp.—Original ed. 1935.

3380. Stevenson, Burton. The Home Book of Proverbs, Maxims, and Familiar Phrases. New York, Macmillan Co., 1948. viii + 2957 (double column) pp.

3381. Tilley, Morris P. A Dictionary of the Proverbs in England in the Sixteenth and Seventeenth Centuries. A collection of the proverbs found in English literature and the dictionaries of the period. Ann Arbor, University of Michigan Press, 1950. 854 (double column) pp.

3382. Nicolson, Alexander. Gaelic Proverbs. Collected and translated into English with equivalents from other European languages. Reprinted with index by Malcolm MacInnes. Glasgow, Caledonian Press, 1951. xxxvi + 470 pp.—Reprint of Nicolson's *A Collection of Gaelic Proverbs and Familiar Phrases Based on MacIntosh's Collection*, 2nd ed., 1882.

3383. Whiting, Bartlett J. Proverbs and Proverbial Sayings from Scottish Writings before 1600. Medieval Studies, XI (1949), 123–205; XIII (1951), 87–164.

3384. Kremer, Edmund. German Proverbs and Proverbial Phrases with Their English Counterparts. Stanford Univ. Press, 1955. ix + 116 pp.—"Bibliography," p. 116.

3385. Anderson, M L., ed. The James Carmichaell Collection of Proverbs in Scots. From the original manuscript in the Edinburgh University Library. Edinburgh, University Press, 1957. vii + 149 pp.

3386. Taylor, Archer, and Whiting, B[artlett] J. A Dictionary of American Proverbs and Proverbial Phrases 1820–1880. Cambridge, Mass., Harvard Univ. Press, 1958. xxiii + 418 (double column) pp.—"Bibliography," pp. xiii–xxii.

3387. Collins, V[ere] H. A Book of English Proverbs. With origins and explanations. London, Longmans, 1959. 144 pp.

§139. FOLK TALES, FAIRY TALES, TRADITIONAL ANECDOTES, AND FABLIAUX: STUDIES AND ANTHOLOGIES

3391. Aarne, Antti. The Types of the Folk-Tale. A classification and bibliography. Translated and enl. by Stith Thompson. Helsinki, Suomalainen tiedeakatemia, 1928. 279 pp.—Number 74 in the series F. F. Communications. Original ed. 1910 in German.

3392. Bolte, Johannes, and Polívka, Georg. Ammerkungen zu den Kinder- und Hausmärchen der Brüder Grimm. Leipzig, T. Weicher, 1913–32. 5 vols.—A reliable edition (of many reliable editions) of the *Märchen* collected by Jakob Ludwig Karl and Wilhelm Karl Grimm is *Kinder- und Hausmärchen* . . . ,14. Aufl., Berlin, W. Hertz, 1876, xx + 704 pp. See also their legend collection: *Deutsche Sagen*, 3 Aufl., Berlin, Nicolaische Verlagsbuchhandlung, 1891, 2 vols. in 1.

3393. Bolte, Johannes, et al. Handwörterbuch des deutschen Märchens. Berlin, W. de Gruyter, 1930–40, 2 vols.—*A* to *Gyges* only.

3394. Cross, Tom Peete. Motif-Index of Early Irish Literature. Bloomington, Indiana Univ. Press, 1952. xx + 537 pp.—Number 7 in the Indiana University Publications Folklore Series.

3395. Eastman, Mary H. Index to Fairy Tales, Myths, and Legends. 2nd ed. Boston, F. W. Faxon Co., 1926. ix + 610 pp.—Number 28 in the Useful Reference Series. Original ed. 1915. *Supplement*, Boston, F. W. Faxon Co., 1937, xi + 566 pp., number 61 in the Useful Reference Series. *Second Supplement*, Boston, F. W. Faxon Co., 1952, vii + 370 pp., number 82 in the Useful Reference Series.

3396. Thompson, Stith. Motif-Index of Folk-Literature. A classification of narrative elements in folktales, ballads, myths, fables, mediaeval romances, exempla, fabliaux, jest-books, and local legends. Vol. I: A–C; Vol. II: D–E; Vol. III: F–H; Vol. IV: J–K; Vol. V: L–Z; Vol. VI: Index. Rev. and enl. ed. Bloomington, Indiana Univ. Press, 1955–58. —Original ed. 1932–36 as vols. XIX–XXIII in the series Indiana University Studies and also as nos. 106–109 and 116–117 in the series FF Communications.

3397. Littlejohn, F[lavius] J. Legends of Michigan and the Old North West. Or a cluster of unpublished waifs gleaned along the uncertain misty line dividing traditional from historic times. Allegan, Mich., Northwest Bible and Publ'ing Co., 1875. 572 pp.—Reprint with a foreword by John C. Pahl, Ann Arbor, Mich., Edwards Bros., 1956.

3398. Schreiber, Lady Charlotte Elizabeth Guest. The Mabinogion. Medieval Welsh romances. With notes by Alfred Nutt. New York, New Amsterdam Book Co., 1902. xiii + 363 pp.—Frequent reprints of Schreiber's translation, as London, J. M. Dent and Sons, [1927], number 97 in the series Everyman's Library, which prints an introduction by R. Williams, the translator's notes of the Red Book of Hergest, and a translation of the Tale of Taliesin.

3399. Gerould, Gordon Hall. The Grateful Dead. The history of a folk story. London, David Nutt, 1908. x + 177 pp.—Volume LX [1907] in the series Publications of the Folk-Lore Society.

3400. MacDougall, James, collector. Folk Tales and Fairy Lore in Gaelic and English. Collected from oral tradition. Edited with introduction and notes by George Calder. Edinburgh, John Grant, 1910. xv + 328 pp.—Gaelic verso, English translation recto.

3401. Campbell, J[ohn] F., collector. The Celtic Dragon Myth. With the Geste of Fraoch and the Dragon. Translated with introduction by George Henderson. Edinburgh, John Grant, 1911. li + 172 pp.

3402. Bédier, Joseph. Les fabliaux. Études de littérature populaire et d'histoire littéraire du moyen âge. Quatrième édition revue et corrigée. Paris, Librairie Ancienne Édouard Champion, 1925. viii + 499 pp.—Original ed. 1893. List of fabliaux, pp. 436–441; "Notes bibliographiques," pp. 442–476.

3403. Bellows, Henry Adams. The Poetic Edda. Translated from the Icelandic with an introduction and notes. Two volumes in one. New York, American-Scandinavian Foundation, 1926. xxix + 583 pp.—Volumes XXI and XXII in the series Scandinavian Classics.

3404. Brodeur, Arthur Gilchrist. The Prose Edda by Snorri Sturluson. Translated from the Icelandic with an introduction. New York, American-Scandinavian Foundation, 1929. xxii + 266 pp.—Volume V in the series Scandinavian Classics.

3405. Lee, F[rank] H., ed. Folk Tales of All Nations. New York, Tudor Publ'ing Co., 1930. xxi + 947 pp.

3406. Bryan, W[illiam] F., Dempster, G[ermaine] C., et al., eds. Sources and Analogues of Chaucer's Canterbury Tales. University of Chicago Press, 1941. xvi + 765 pp.—Reprint New York, Humanities Press, 1958.

3407. Fuller, Edmund, ed. Thesaurus of Anecdotes. A new classified collection of the best anecdotes from ancient times to the present day. New York, Crown Publ'ers, 1942. 489 pp.

3408. Blair, Walter. Tall Tale America. A legendary history of our humorous heroes. New York, Coward-McCann Inc., 1944. ix + 262 pp.—Bibliographical notes, pp. 257–262.

3409. Carpenter, Rhys. Folk Tale, Fiction, and Saga in the Homeric Epics. Berkeley, University of California Press, 1946. 198 pp.—The Sather Classical Lectures. Reprint 1956.

3410. Thompson, Stith. The Folktale. New York, Dryden Press, 1946. x + 510 pp.

3411. Clough, Ben C., ed. The American Imagination at Work. Tall tales and folk tales. New York, Alfred A. Knopf, 1947. xix + 707 pp.—"Bibliography," pp. 701–707.

3412. Rugoff, Milton, ed. A Harvest of World Folk Tales. New York, Viking Press, 1949. xviii + 734 pp.

3413. Brett, Henry. English Legends. 2nd ed. London, B. T. Batsford Ltd., 1952. viii + 150 pp.—Original ed. 1952.

3414. Parry-Jones, D[aniel]. Welsh Legends and Fairy Lore. London, B. T. Batsford Ltd., 1953. ix + 181 pp.—"Bibliography," pp. 177–181.

3415. Leyen, Friedrich von der. Die Welt der Märchen. Düsseldorf, Eugen Diederichs Verlag, 1953–54. 2 vols.

3416. O'Faolain, Eileen. Irish Sagas and Folk-Tales. Oxford Univ. Press, 1954. ix + 245 pp.—In the series Oxford Myths and Legends.

3417. Campbell, J[ames] J. Legends of Ireland. London, B. T. Batsford Ltd., 1955. x + 210 pp.

3418. Jones, Gwyn. Welsh Legends and Folk-Tales. Oxford Univ. Press, 1955. [xv] + 230 pp.—In the series Oxford Myths and Legends.

3419. Jones, Thos., ed. Brut y Tywysogyon. Or the Chronicle of the Princes. Red Book of Hergest Version. Critical text and translation with introduction and notes. Cardiff, University of Wales Press, 1955. lxiv + 389 pp.—Number 16 in the Board of Celtic Studies: University of Wales History and Law Series.

3420. Tidwell, James N., ed. A Treasury of American Folk Humor. A rare confection of laughter, tall tales, jests, and other gems of merriment of the American people. New York, Crown Publ'ers, 1956. xx + 620 pp.

3421. Beit, Hedwig von. Symbolik des Märchens. [Vol. I:] Versuch einer Deutung; [Vol. II:] Gegensatz und Erneuerung im Märchen; [Vol. III:] Registerband. Bern, A. Francke AG, 1952–57. 3 vols., 792 (single column) + 647 (single column) + 267 (double column) pp.—"Bibliographie," [III], pp. 30–42.

3422. Botkin, Benjamin A., ed. A Treasury of American Anecdotes. Sly, salty, shaggy stories of heroes and hellions, beguilers and buffoons, spellbinders and scapegoats, gagsters and gossips, from the grassroots and sidewalks of America. New York, Random House, 1957. 321 pp.

3423. Nykrog, Per. Les fabliaux. Étude d'histoire littéraire et de stylistique médiévale. Copenhagen, Einar Munksgaard, 1957. lv + 339 pp.—"Bibliographie," pp. 292–308; "Inventaire alphabétique des fabliaux," pp. 309–325.

3424. Christiansen, Reidar Th. Studies in Irish and Scandinavian Folktales. Copenhagen, Rosenkilde and Bagger for the Irish Folklore Commission, 1959. vii + 249 pp.—Bibliographical notes, pp. 237–249. A study *inter alia* of ghosts, giants, dragons, and the devil.

§140. ROMANCE MATERIALS

[See also §29. Fiction: From the Beginnings to *Circa* 1800; §38. Minor Prose: Historiography Including Reprints of Early Annals and Chronicles.]

3428. Billings, Anna Hunt. A Guide to the Middle English Metrical Romances Dealing with English and Germanic Legends and with the Cycles of Charlemagne and of Arthur. New York, Henry Holt and Co., 1901. xxiv + 232 pp.—Volume IX in the series Yale Studies in English.

3429. Ward, H[enry] L. D. Catalogue of Romances in the Department of Manuscripts in the British Museum. Notice by E. Maunde Thompson. London, printed by order of the Trustees, 1883–93. 2 vols.—Also a third volume with a notice by G. F. Warner compiled by J[ohn] A. Herbert, London, printed by order of the Trustees, 1910, xii + 720 pp.

3430. Esdaile, Arundell. A List of English Tales and Prose Romances Printed before 1740. Part I: 1475–1642; Part II: 1643–1729. London, Blades, East and Blades for the Bibliographic Society, 1912. xxxvii + 329 pp.

3431. Spence, Lewis. A Dictionary of Medieval Romance and Romance Writers. London, George Routledge and Sons, 1913. vi + 395 (double column) pp.

3432. Saintsbury, Geo. The Flourishing of Romance and the Rise of Allegory. New York, Charles Scribner's Sons, 1897. xvii + 429 pp.—Volume II in the series Periods of European Literature.

3433. Weston, Jessie L. The Romance Cycle of Charlemagne and His Peers. London, David Nutt, 1901. 46 pp.—Number 10 in the series Popular Studies in Mythology, Romance, and Folklore. "Bibliographical Appendix," pp. 42–46.

3434. Deutschbein, Max. Studien zur Sagengeschichte Englands. Coethen, Otto Schultze, 1906. xii + 264 pp.

3435. Thoms, Wm. J., ed. Early English Prose Romances. New ed., rev. and enl. London, George Routledge and Sons, [1906]. ix + 10–958 pp.—Volume XI in the series Library of Early Novelists. Original ed. Henry Morley, ed., *Early Prose Romances*, London, Routledge, 1889, 446 pp., number 4 in the series Carisbrooke Library.

3436. Bury, J[ohn] B. Romances of Chivalry on Greek Soil. Oxford, Clarendon Press, 1911. 24 pp.—The Romanes Lecture 1911.

3437. Crane, Ronald S. The Vogue of the Mediaeval Chivalric Romance during the English Renaissance. Menasha, Wis., George Banta Co., 1919. 53 pp.

3438. Barrow, Sarah F. The Medieval Society Romances. New York, Columbia Univ. Press, 1924. 141 pp.—In the series Columbia University Studies in English and Comparative Literature.

3439. Lawrence, Wm. W. Medieval Story and the Beginnings of the Social Ideals of English-Speaking People. 2nd ed. New York, Columbia Univ. Press, 1926. xiv + 236 pp.—Original ed. 1911; second ed. reprinted 1931.

3440. French, Walter H., and Hale, Chas. B., eds. Middle English Metrical Romances. New York, Prentice-Hall Inc., 1930. x + 1041 pp.

3441. Taylor, Albert B. An Introduction to Medieval Romance. London, Heath Cranton Ltd., 1930. ix + 268 pp.

3442. Todd, F[rederic] A. Some Ancient Novels. Leucippe and Clitophon, Daphnis and Chloe, The Satiricon, The Golden Ass. Oxford Univ. Press, 1940. vii + 144 pp.

3443. Gist, Margaret A. Love and War in the Middle English Romances. Philadelphia, University of Pennsylvania Press, 1947. ix + 214 pp.

3444. Owings, Marvin A. The Arts in Middle English Romances. New York, Bookman Associates, 1952. 204 pp.

3445. Potter, K[enneth] R. William of Malmesbury. The Historia Novella. Translated from the Latin with introduction and notes. London, Thomas Nelson and Sons, 1955. xlv + 77 pp. Latin verso + 77 pp. English recto + 78–84 (regular) pp.—In the series Medieval Texts.

3446. Hibbard, Laura A. [Laura Alandis Loomis.] Mediaeval Romance in England. A study of the sources and analogues of the non-cyclic metrical romances. New ed., with additional bibliography by the author. New York, Burt Franklin, 1959. viii + 342 pp.—Number 17 in the Burt Franklin Bibliographical Series. Original ed. 1924.

§141. ARTHURIAN MATERIALS

[See also §29. Fiction: From the Beginnings to *Circa* 1800; §38. Minor Prose: Historiography Including Reprints of Early Annals and Chronicles.]

3450. Harding, Jane D. The Arthurian Legend. A check list of books in the Newberry Library. Introduction by George B. Utley. Chicago, Newberry Library, 1933. 120 pp.—Also *Supplement*, by Jane D. Harding, Chicago, Newberry Library, 1938, iv + 90 pp.

3451. Parry, John J. A Bibliography of Critical Arthurian Literature. Vol. I: 1922–29; Vol. II: 1930–35, with Margaret Schlauch. New York, Modern Language Association of America, 1931–36. 2 vols.

3452. Parry, John J., and Schlauch, Margaret. A Bibliography of Critical Arthurian Literature for the Year 1936–39. Modern Language Quarterly, I, 2 (June 1940), 129–174.—Now annual. To 1954 by John J. Parry; to 1955 by John J. Parry and Paul A. Brown; to date by Paul A. Brown.

3453. Ackerman, Robt. W. An Index of the Arthurian Names in Middle English. Stanford Univ. Press, 1952. xxv + 250 pp.—Volume X in the series Stanford University Publications in Language and Literature.

3454. Rhŷs, John. Studies in the Arthurian Legend. Oxford Univ. Press, 1891. viii + 411 pp.

3455. Sommer, H[einrich] Oscar. Le morte darthur. The original edition of William Caxton . . . with an introduction and glossary. With an essay on Malory's prose style by Andrew Lang. London, David Nutt, 1889–91. 3 vols.

3456. Gurteen, S[tephen] Humphreys. The Arthurian Epic. A comparative study of the Cambrian, Breton, and Anglo-Norman versions of the story and Tennyson's Idylls of the King. New York, G. P. Putnam's Sons, 1895. ix + 437 pp.

3457. Newell, Wm. Wells. King Arthur and the Table Round. Tales chiefly after the Old French of Crestien of Troyes with an account of Arthurian romance and notes. Boston, Houghton Mifflin Co., 1897. 2 vols.—Reprint 1905.

3458. Fletcher, Robt. Huntington. The Arthurian Material in the Chronicles, Especially Those of Great Britain and France. Boston, Ginn and Co. for Harvard University, 1906. ix + 313 pp.—Volume X in the series Harvard Notes and Studies in Philology. Reprint New York, Burt Franklin, 1958, number 10 in the Burt Franklin Bibliographical Series.

3459. Maynadier, Howard. The Arthur of the English Poets. Boston, Houghton Mifflin Co., 1907. ix + 454 pp.

3460. Evans, Sebastian. The High History of the Holy Graal. London, J. M. Dent and Sons, 1910. xx + 379 pp.—Number 445 in the series Everyman's Library. Reprint 1929. A translation of the first volume of the Old French "Perceval le Gallois ou le conte du Graal."

3461. Sommer, H[einrich] O. The Vulgate Version of the Arthurian Romances. Edited from manuscripts in the British Museum. Washington, D.C., Carnegie Institution, 1909–16. 8 vols.—"Index of Names and Places," vol. VIII.

3462. Entwistle, Wm. J. The Arthurian Legend in the Literatures of the Spanish Peninsula. London, J. M. Dent and Sons, 1925. vii + 271 pp.

3463. Van Der Ven-Ten Bensel, Elise Francisca Wilhelmina Maria. The Character of King Arthur in English Literature. Amsterdam, Holland, H. J. Paris, 1925. 219 pp.—"Bibliography," pp. 208–215.

3464. Loomis, Roger S. Celtic Myth and Arthurian Romance. New York, Columbia Univ. Press, 1926. xii + 371 pp.

3465. Chambers, E[dmund] K. Arthur of Britain. London, Sidgwick and Jackson Ltd., 1927. vii + 299 pp.—Bibliography, pp. 283–294.

3466. Bruce, James D. The Evolution of Arthurian Romance from the Beginnings down to the Year 1300. Second ed. with a supplement by Alfons Hilka. Göttingen, Vandenhoeck und Ruprecht, 1928. 2 vols.—Volumes VIII and IX in the series Hesperia: Ergänzungsreihe. Original ed. 1923. Reprint Gloucester, Mass., Peter Smith, 1958. "A Select Bibliography," II, pp. 380–412; "Bibliographischer Nachtrag," by Alfons Hilka, II, pp. 445–460.

3467. Jaffrey, Robt. King Arthur and the Holy Grail. An examination of the early literature pertaining to the legends of King Arthur and the Holy Grail, together with a brief review of the theories relating to the latter. . . . New York, G. P. Putnam's Sons, 1928. v + 248 pp.

3468. Jones, Robt. Ellis. The Historia Regum Britanniae of Geoffrey of Monmouth. With contributions to the study of its place in early British history by Acton Griscom. Together with a literal translation of the Welsh Manuscript No. LXI of Jesus College, Oxford. London, Longmans, Green and Co., 1929. xiii + 672 pp.—"Selected Bibliography," pp. 601–626.

3469. Brinkley, Roberta F. Arthurian Legend in the Seventeenth Century. Baltimore, Johns Hopkins Press, 1932. xi + 228 pp.—Volume III in the series Johns Hopkins Monographs in Literary History.

3470. Lewis, Chas. B. Classical Mythology and Arthurian Romance. A study of the sources of Chrestien de Troyes' Yvain and other Arthurian romances. Oxford Univ. Press, 1932. xviii + 332 pp.—Number 32 in the series St. Andrews University Publications. Bibliography, pp. 306–320.

3471. Millican, Chas. Bowie. Spenser and the Table Round. A study in the contemporaneous background for Spenser's use of the Arthurian legend. Cambridge, Mass., Harvard Univ. Press, 1932. xv + 237 pp.—Volume VIII in the series Harvard Studies in Comparative Literature.

3472. Parry, John Jay, ed. Brut y Brenhinedd. Cotton Cleopatra version. Cambridge, Mass., Mediaeval Academy of America, 1937. xviii + 243 pp. + vi plates.—An edition of a Welsh translation of Geoffrey of Monmouth's *Historia Regum Britanniae* with its English translation.

3473. Reid, Margaret J. C. The Arthurian Legend. Comparison of treatment in modern and medieval literature. A study in the literary value of myth and legend. Edinburgh, Oliver and Boyd, [1938]. viii + 277 pp.

3474. Brodeur, Arthur G. Arthur, Dux Bellorum. Berkeley, University of California Press, 1939. 237–283 pp.—Volume III, no. 7, in the series University of California Publications in English.

3475. Newstead, Helaine. Bran the Blessed in Arthurian Romance. New York, Columbia Univ. Press, 1939. 222 pp.—Number 141 in the series Columbia University Studies in English and Comparative Literature.

3476. Brown, Arthur C. L. The Origin of the Grail Legend. Cambridge, Mass., Harvard Univ. Press, 1943. ix + 476 pp.

3477. Jones, Ernest. Geoffrey of Monmouth 1640–1800. Berkeley, University of California Press, 1944. 357–442 pp.—Volume V, no. 3, in the series University of California Publications in English. "Bibliography," pp. 431–439.

3478. Vinaver, Eugène, ed. The Works of Sir Thomas Malory. Oxford Univ. Press, 1947. 3 (continuously paged) vols., 1742 pp.—"Bibliography," III, pp. 1647–1658.

3479. Tatlock, J[ohn] S. P. The Legendary History of Britain. Geoffrey of Monmouth's Historia Regum Britanniae and Its Early Vernacular Versions. Berkeley, University of California Press, 1950. xi + 545 pp.

3480. Starr, Nathan Comfort. King Arthur Today. The Arthurian legend in English and American literature 1901–1953. Gainesville, University of Florida Press, 1954. xvii + 218 pp.

3481. Loomis, Roger Sherman. Wales and the Arthurian Legend. Cardiff, University of Wales, 1956. ix + 231 pp.

3482. Loomis, Roger Sherman, ed. Arthurian Literature in the Middle Ages. Oxford, Clarendon Press, 1959. 574 pp.

3483. Paton, Lucy Allen. Studies in the Fairy Mythology of Arthurian Romance. Second ed. with bibliography, additional material, and notes by Roger Sherman Loomis. New York, Burt Franklin, 1959. 335 pp. —Number 18 in the Burt Franklin Bibliographical Series. Original ed. 1903.

3484. Schoepperle, Gertrude. [Mrs. Gertrude Loomis.] Tristan and Isolt. A study of the sources of the romance. New ed., with a classified bibliography and a survey of Tristan scholarship by Roger S. Loomis. New York, Burt Franklin, 1959. 2 vols.—Original ed. 1913.

3485. Bulletin bibliographique de la Société arthurienne / Bibliographical Bulletin of the International Arthurian Society. Paris, 1949–date.—Annual.

§142. BALLAD AND FOLKSONG STUDIES

[See also Chapter III: Poetry *passim*, especially §42. Historical Surveys and Studies.]

3492. Catalogue of English and American Chap-Books and Broadside Ballads in Harvard College Library. Cambridge, Mass., Library of Harvard University, 1905. xi + 171 pp.—Number 56 in the series Bibliographical Contributions of the Library of Harvard University.

3493. List of Works in the New York Public Library Relating to Folk Songs, Folk Music, Ballads, etc. New York Public Library Bulletin, XI, 5 (May 1907), pp. 183–226 (double column).

3494. Gummere, Francis B. The Popular Ballad. Boston, Houghton Mifflin Co., 1907. xv + 360 pp.

3495. Ker, W[illiam] P. On the History of the Ballads 1100–1500. London, Henry Frowde, 1910. 26 pp.—Also in Proceedings of the British Academy 1909–10, Vol. IV, London 1912, pp. 179–205.

3496. Henderson, Thos. F. The Ballad in Literature. Cambridge Univ. Press, 1912. ix + 128 pp.

3497. Bryant, Frank Egbert. A History of English Balladry and Other Studies. Boston, Richard G. Badger, 1913. 443 pp.

3498. Hustvedt, Sigurd Bernhard. Ballad Criticism in Scandinavia and Great Britain during the Eighteenth Century. New York, American-Scandinavian Foundation, 1916. xi + 335 pp.—Volume II in the series Scandinavian Monographs.

3499. Mackenzie, W[illiam] Roy. The Quest of the Ballad. Princeton, N.J., University Press, 1919. xiii + 247 pp.

3500. Pound, Louise. Poetic Origins of the Ballad. New York, Macmillan Co., 1921. x + 247 pp.

3501. Odum, Howard W., and Johnson, Guy B. The Negro and His Songs. A study of typical Negro songs in the South. Chapel Hill, University of North Carolina Press, 1925. xi + 306 pp.—"Select Bibliography of Negro Folk Songs," pp. 297–300.

3502. Graves, Robt. The English Ballad. A short critical survey. London, E. Benn Ltd., 1927. 139 pp.—"Ballads," pp. 37–139.

3503. Wimberly, Lowry Chas. Death and Burial Lore in the English and Scottish Popular Ballads. Lincoln, [University of Nebraska], 1927. 138 pp.—Number 8 in the series University of Nebraska Studies in Language, Literature, and Criticism. Bibliography, pp. 135–138.

3504. Wimberly, Lowry Chas. Folklore in the English and Scottish Ballads. University of Chicago Press, 1928. xiii + 466 pp.

3505. Hustvedt, Sigurd Bernhard. Ballad Books and Ballad Men. Raids and rescues in Britain, America, and the Scandinavian North since 1800. Cambridge, Mass., Harvard Univ. Press, 1930. xi + 376 pp.—"Bibliography," pp. 339–357.

3506. Gerould, Gordon H. The Ballad of Tradition. Oxford, Clarendon Press, 1932. viii + 311 pp.—"Selected Bibliography," pp. 297–304.

3507. Schmidt, Wolfgang. Die Entwicklung der englisch-schottischen Volksballaden. Anglia, LVII, 1 (Jan. 1933), 1–77; and LVII, 2 (April 1933), 113–207.

3508. Hendren, J[oseph] W. A Study of Ballad Rhythm. With special reference to ballad music. Princeton, N.J., University Press, 1936. xii + 177 pp.—Number 14 in the series Princeton Studies in English. "Bibliography," pp. 176–177.

3509. Thomas, Jean. The Singin' Fiddler of Lost Hope Hollow. New York, E. P. Dutton and Co., 1938. 242 pp.—A study of a Kentucky minstrel.

3510. Lomax, John A. Adventures of a Ballad Hunter. New York, Macmillan Co., 1947. xiii + 302 pp.

3511. Coffin, Tristram P. The British Traditional Ballad in North America. Philadelphia, American Folklore Society, 1950. xvi + 188 pp.—Volume II in the Publications of the American Folklore Society Bibliographical Series. Bibliography, pp. 173–181.

3512. Hodgart, M[atthew] J. C. The Ballads. London, Hutchinson House, 1950. 184 pp.—Number 38 in the series Hutchinson's University Library.

3513. Wells, Evelyn Kendrick. The Ballad Tree. A study of British and American ballads, their folklore, verse, and music, together with sixty traditional ballads and their tunes. New York, Ronald Press Co., 1950. ix + 370 pp.—"Bibliography," pp. 353–360.

3514. Sharp, Cecil James. English Folk Song. Some conclusions. Revised by Maud Karpeles. With an appreciation by Ralph Vaughan Williams. 3rd ed. London, Methuen and Co., 1954. xxi + 143 pp.—Original ed. 1907.

3515. Laws, G[eorge] Malcolm. American Balladry from British Broadsides. A guide for students and collectors of traditional song. Philadelphia, American Folklore Society, 1957. xiii + 315 pp.—Volume VIII in the Publications of the American Folklore Society Bibliographical and Special Series. "Selected Bibliography," pp. 302–309.

3516. Wilgus, D[onald] K. Anglo-American Folksong Scholarship since 1898. New Brunswick, N.J., Rutgers Univ. Press, 1959. xx + 466 pp.

§143. OLD WORLD SONGS AND BALLADS

3520. Rollins, Hyder E. An Analytical Index to the Ballad-Entries [1557–1709] in the Registers of the Company of Stationers of London. Studies in Philology, XXI, 1 (Jan. 1924), 1–324.

3521. Hustvedt, S[igurd] B. A Melodic Index of Child's Ballad Tunes. Los Angeles, University of California Press, 1936. 51–78 pp.—Volume I, no. 2, in the series Publications of the University of California at Los Angeles in Language and Literature.

3522. Dean-Smith, Margaret. A Guide to English Folk-Song Collections 1822–1952. With an index to their contents, historical annotations, and an introduction. Foreword by Gerald Abraham. Liverpool, University

Press, 1954. 120 (chiefly double column) pp.—See also Dean-Smith's earlier *An Index to English Songs Contributed to the Journal of the Folklore Society 1899–1931 and Its Continuation, the Journal of the English Folk Dance and Song Society, to 1950,* London, English Folk Dance and Song Society, 1951, xvi + 66 pp.

3523. Aytoun, Wm. Edmondstoune, ed. The Ballads of Scotland. Edinburgh, William Blackwood and Sons, 1858. 2 vols.

3524. Hazlitt, W[illiam] Carew. Remains of the Early Popular Poetry of England. Collected and edited with introduction and notes. London, John Russell Smith, 1864–66. 4 vols.

3525. Percy, Thomas. [Bishop of Dromore.] Reliques of Ancient English Poetry. Consisting of old heroic ballads, songs, and other pieces of our earlier poets together with some few of later date. Edited with a general introduction, additional prefaces, notes, glossary, etc. by Henry B. Wheatley. London, Bickers and Son, 1876–77. 3 vols.—Original ed. London, printed for J. Dodsley, 1765. Wheatley's ed. repeatedly reprinted, as London, George Allen and Unwin Ltd., 1927.

3526. MacQuoid, Gilbert S., ed. Jacobite Songs and Ballads Selected. With notes, genealogical table of the Stuarts, introduction, glossary, etc. London, Walter Scott Publ'ing Co., 1887. xxiv + 534 pp.

3527. Ashton, John, ed. Modern Street Ballads. London, Chatto and Windus, 1888. xvi + 405 pp.

3528. Ford, Robt., ed. A Budget of Auld Scots Ballads. Comprising some rare and curious blads [sic] of verse together with the pick and wale of the more popular of the ancient ballads of Scotland. Boston, Joseph George Cupples Bookseller, [1889]. viii + 296 pp.

3529. Buchan, Peter, ed. Gleanings of Scarce Old Ballads with Explanatory Notes. Aberdeen, D. Wyllie and Son, 1891. 216 pp.—Reprint of a collection of street ballads Buchan printed in 1825.

3530. Child, Francis J., ed. The English and Scottish Popular Ballads. Boston, Houghton Mifflin Co., 1882–98. 5 vols. in 10 parts.—Reprint New York, Folklore Press, in Association with Pageant Book Co., 1956, 5 vols., with vols. I–II and vols. III–IV bound together. Abridged version with the same number of ballads but without the scholarly apparatus of the original: Helen Child Sargent and George Lyman Kittredge, eds., *English and Scottish Popular Ballads,* Edited from the Collections of F. J. Child, Boston, Houghton Mifflin Co., 1905, xxxii + 729 pp.

3531. The Roxburghe Ballads. Hertford, Eng., S. Austin and Sons for the Ballad Society, 1871–99. 9 vols.

3532. Clark, Andrew, ed. The Shirburn Ballads 1585–1616. Edited from the MS. Oxford Univ. Press, 1907. viii + 380 pp.—A collection of 89 ballads of a sensational nature printed originally between 1585 and 1616.

3533. Quiller-Couch, Arthur T., ed. Oxford Book of Ballads. Oxford, Clarendon Press, 1910. xxiii + 871 pp.—Reprint 1920.

3534. Rollins, Hyder E., ed. Old English Ballads 1553–1625. Chiefly from MSS. Cambridge Univ. Press, 1920. xxxi + 423 pp.

3535. Rollins, Hyder E. Cavalier and Puritan. Ballads and broadsides illustrating the period of the Great Rebellion 1640–1660. Edited with introduction and notes. New York Univ. Press, 1923. xv + 532 pp.

3536. Bliss, Douglas Percy, ed. Border Ballads. Foreword by Herbert J. C. Grierson. Oxford Univ. Press, 1925. xv + 111 pp.

3537. Rollins, Hyder E., ed. The Pack of Autolycus or Strange and Terrible News. Of ghosts, apparitions, monstrous births, showers of wheat, judgments of God, and other prodigious and fearful happenings as told in broadside ballads of the years 1624–1693. Cambridge, Mass., Harvard Univ. Press, 1927. xvii + 270 pp.

3538. Wilson, James. Old Scotch Songs and Poems. Phonetically spelt and translated. Foreword by Robert Bruce. Oxford Univ. Press, 1927. 463 pp.

3539. Borrow, Geo., and Johnson, R[eginald] Brimley, eds. Ballads of All Nations. A selection. New York, Alfred A. Knopf, 1928. xxiii + 342 pp.

3540. Draper, John W., ed. A Century of British Elegies. Being ninety English and ten Scotch broadsides illustrating the biography and manners of the seventeenth century photographically reproduced and edited with an introduction and notes. London, Ingpen and Grant, 1928. xviii + 229 pp.

3541. Rollins, Hyder E., ed. The Pepys Ballads. Cambridge, Mass., Harvard Univ. Press, 1929–32. 8 vols.—See also Rollins's earlier *A Pepysian Garland*, Black-letter broadside ballads of the years 1595–1639 chiefly from the collection of Samuel Pepys, Cambridge Univ. Press, 1922, xxxi + 491 pp.

3542. Olrik, Axel. A Book of Danish Ballads. Selected and with an introduction. Translated by E. M. Smith-Dampier. Princeton, N.J., University Press, 1939. x + 339 pp.—Original Danish ed. 1899–1909.

3543. Beattie, Wm., ed. Border Ballads. Harmondsworth, Eng., Penguin Books Ltd., 1952. 247 pp.—Number D20 in the series Pelican Books.

3544. Christophersen, Paul, ed. The Ballad of Sir Aldingar. Its origins and analogues. Oxford Univ. Press, 1952. x + 258 pp.—"Bibliography," pp. 237–249.

3545. Gray, Alexander. Four-and-Forty. A selection of Danish ballads presented in Scots. Edinburgh Univ. Press, 1954. xxi + 184 pp.

3546. Leach, MacEdward. The Ballad Book. New York, Harper and Bros., 1955. xiv + 842 pp.

3547. Pinto, Vivian DeSola, and Rodway, Allan Edwin, eds. The Common Muse. An anthology of popular British ballad poetry fifteenth–twentieth century. London, Chatto and Windus Ltd., 1957. xi + 403 pp.—Street ballads.

3548. Reeves, James, ed. The Idiom of the People. English traditional verse edited with an introduction and notes from the manuscripts of Cecil J. Sharp. London, Heinemann Ltd., 1958. xii + 244 pp.—Street ballads.

§144. NEW WORLD SONGS AND BALLADS

3551. [Ford, Worthington Chauncey.] Broadsides, Ballads, Etc., Printed in Massachusetts 1639–1800. Boston, Massachusetts Historical Society, 1922. xvi + 483 pp.

3552. Henry, Mellinger Edward. Bibliography for the Study of American Folk-Songs. With many titles of folk-songs . . . from other lands. [London, Mitre Press, 1937.] 142 pp.

3553. Library of Congress Music Division. Check-List of Recorded Songs in the English Language in the Archive of American Folk Song to July 1940. Washington, D.C., Library of Congress, 1942. 2 vols.

3554. Davis, Arthur Kyle, Jr. Folk-Songs of Virginia. A descriptive index and classification of material collected under the auspices of the Virginia Folklore Society. Durham, N.C., Duke Univ. Press, 1949. lxiii + 389 pp.

3555. Campbell, Olive Dame, and Sharp, Cecil, eds. English Folk Songs from the Southern Appalachians. Comprising 122 songs and ballads and 323 tunes. With introduction and notes. New York, G. P. Putnam's Sons, 1917. xxix + 341 pp.—Scores.

3556. Pound, Louise, ed. American Ballads and Songs. New York, Charles Scribner's Sons, 1922. xxxvi + 266 pp.—In the series Modern Student's Library American Division.

3557. Talley, Thos. W. Negro Folk Rhymes. Wise and otherwise. With a study. Introduction by Walter Clyde Curry. New York, Macmillan Co., 1922. xiii + 347 pp.—Occasional scores.

3558. Gray, Roland Palmer, ed. Songs and Ballads of the Maine Lumberjacks with Other Songs from Maine. Cambridge, Mass., Harvard Univ. Press, 1924. xxi + 191 pp.

3559. Cox, John Harrington, ed. Folk-Songs of the South. Collected under the auspices of the West Virginia Folk-Lore Society. Cambridge, Mass., Harvard Univ. Press, 1925. xxxii + 545 pp.—"Folk Tunes" [scores], edited by Lydia I. Hinkel, pp. 519–532.

3560. Odum, Howard W., and Johnson, Guy B., eds. Negro Workaday Songs. Chapel Hill, University of North Carolina Press, 1926. xv + 278 pp.—In the University of North Carolina Social Study Series. "Selected Bibliography," pp. 265–270.

3561. Rickaby, Franz, ed. Ballads and Songs of the Shanty-Boy. Cambridge, Mass., Harvard Univ. Press, 1926. xli + 244 pp.—"Glossary," pp. 233–238. Occasional scores. Lumberman songs from Michigan, Wisconsin, and Minnesota c. 1870–1900.

3562. Eckstorm, Fannie Hardy, and Smyth, Mary Winslow, eds. Minstrelsy of Maine. Folk-songs and ballads of the woods and coast. Boston, Houghton Mifflin Co., 1927. xvi + 390 pp.—"List of Books on American Folk Song," pp. xi–xii.

3563. Finger, Chas. J. Frontier Ballads. New York, Doubleday, Page and Co., 1927. [xiii] + 181 pp.

3564. Sandburg, Carl. The American Songbag. New York, Harcourt, Brace and Co., 1927. xxiii + 495 pp.—Scores.

3565. Mackenzie, W[illiam] Roy, ed. Ballads and Sea Songs from Nova Scotia. Cambridge, Mass., Harvard Univ. Press, 1928. xxxix + 421 pp.

3566. Smith, Reed, ed. South Carolina Ballads. With a study of the traditional ballad to-day. Cambridge, Mass., Harvard Univ. Press, 1928. xi + 174 pp.—Occasional scores.

3567. White, Newman I. American Negro Folk-Songs. Cambridge, Mass., Harvard Univ. Press, 1928. xi + 501 pp.—"Bibliography," pp. 469–480.

3568. Barry, Phillips, Eckstorm, Fannie Hardy, and Smyth, Mary Winslow, eds. British Ballads from Maine. The development of popular songs with texts and airs. Versions of ballads included in Professor F. J. Child's collection. New Haven, Yale Univ. Press, 1929. xli + 535 pp.—"Bibliography," pp. 497–502. Occasional scores.

3569. Davis, Arthur Kyle, ed. Traditional Ballads of Virginia. Collected under the auspices of the Virginia Folk-Lore Society. Cambridge, Mass., Harvard Univ. Press, 1929. xviii + 634 pp.—Occasional scores.

3570. Larkin, Margaret, ed. Singing Cowboy. A book of Western songs. Arranged for piano by Helen Black. New York, Alfred A. Knopf, 1931. xx + 196 pp.

3571. Creighton, Helen, ed. Songs and Ballads from Nova Scotia. Toronto, J. M. Dent and Sons, 1932. xxii + 334 pp.—Scores.

3572. Flanders, Helen Hartness, and Brown, Geo., eds. Vermont Folk-Songs and Ballads. 2nd ed. Brattleboro, Vt., Stephen Daye Press, 1932. 256 pp.—Original ed. 1931. Scores.

3573. Karpeles, Maud, ed. English Folk Songs from the Southern Appalachians. Collected by Cecil J. Sharp. Comprising two hundred and seventy-three songs and ballads with nine hundred and sixty-eight tunes. Including thirty-nine tunes contributed by Olive Dame Campbell. Oxford Univ. Press, 1932. 2 vols.—"Bibliography," II, pp. 402–405. Scores.

3574. Greenleaf, Elisabeth Bristol, ed. Ballads and Sea Songs of Newfoundland. Music recorded in the field by Grace Yarrow Mansfield. Cambridge, Mass., Harvard Univ. Press, 1933. xliv + 395 pp.—Scores.

3575. Henry, Mellinger Edward, ed. Songs Sung in the Southern Appalachians. Many of them illustrating ballads in the making. London, Mitre Press, [1933]. xxvii + 253 pp.

3576. Jackson, Geo. Pullen. White Spirituals in the Southern Uplands. The story of the fasola folk, their songs, singings, and "buckwheat notes." Chapel Hill, University of North Carolina Press, 1933. xv + 444 pp.—"Bibliography," pp. 434–436. A discussion of Southern folk music with occasional words and scores.

3577. Lomax, John A. and Alan, eds. American Ballads and Folk Songs. New York, Macmillan Co., 1934. 625 pp.

3578. Hudson, Arthur Palmer, ed. Folksongs of Mississippi and Their Background. Chapel Hill, University of North Carolina Press, 1936. xii + 321 pp.—"Bibliography," pp. 305–311.

3579. Scarborough, Dorothy, ed. A Song Catcher in Southern Mountains. American folk-songs of British ancestry. New York, Columbia Univ. Press, 1937. xvii + 476 pp.—"Modal Aspects" [scores], by Elna Sherman, pp. 379–457.

3580. Henry, Mellinger Edward, ed. Folk-Songs from the Southern Highlands. New York, J. J. Augustin Publ'er, 1938. xv + 460 pp.—Scores.

3581. Neeser, Robt. W. American Naval Songs and Ballads. New Haven, Yale Univ. Press, 1938. xviii + 372 pp.

3582. Barry, Phillips, ed. The Maine Woods Songster. Cambridge, Mass., Powell Printing Co., 1939. 102 pp.—Scores.

3583. Gardner, Emelyn Elizabeth, and Chickering, Geraldine Jencks, eds. Ballads and Songs of Southern Michigan. Ann Arbor, University of Michigan Press, 1939. xx + 501 pp.—"Bibliography," pp. 491–494. Occasional scores.

3584. Gibbon, John Murray, ed. New World Ballads. Toronto, Ryerson Press, 1939. xv + 177 pp.—Scores. A semi-popular collection of Anglo-Canadian songs.

3585. Linscott, Eloise Hubbard, ed. Folk Songs of Old New England. With an introduction by James M. Carpenter. New York, Macmillan Co., 1939. xxiii + 337 pp.—"References," pp. 319–337. Scores.

3586. American Negro Songs and Spirituals. A comprehensive collection of 230 folk songs, religious and secular, with a foreword by John W. Work. New York, Crown Publ'ers, 1940. ix + 259 pp.—Scores.

3587. Belden, H[enry] M., ed. Ballads and Songs Collected by the Missouri Folk-Lore Society. Columbia, University of Missouri, 1940. xix + 530 pp.—Volume XV, no. 1, in the series University of Missouri Studies. Occasional scores.

3588. Ford, Ira W., ed. Traditional Music of America. New York, E. P. Dutton and Co., 1940. 480 pp.—A collection of scores for folk-songs and folk-dances.

3589. Thompson, Harold W. Body, Books, and Britches. Philadelphia, J. B. Lippincott Co., 1940. 530 pp.—New York State folklore. Numerous folksong texts throughout the work.

3590. Beck, Earl Clifton, ed. Songs of the Michigan Lumberjacks. Ann Arbor, University of Michigan Press, 1941. xi + 296 pp.—"Bibliography," pp. 291–292. Occasional scores.

3591. Carmer, Carl, ed. America Sings. Stories and songs of our country's growing. New York, Alfred A. Knopf, 1942. 243 pp.—Occasional scores. Orientation toward younger people, but not without value for the folklorist.

3592. Wheeler, Mary, ed. Steamboatin' Days. Folk songs of the river packet era. Baton Rouge, Louisiana State Univ. Press, 1944. xiii + 121 pp.

3593. Ewen, David, ed. Songs of America. A cavalcade of popular songs. Edited with commentaries. Arrangements by Mischa and Wesley Portnoff. Chicago, Ziff-Davis Publ'ing Co., 1947. [iv] + 246 pp.—A treatment of the less rural and traditional popular song.

3594. Beck, Earl Clifton, ed. Lore of the Lumber Camps. Ann Arbor, University of Michigan Press, 1948. xii + 348 pp.—"Bibliography," pp. 343–344. Transcriptions of folksongs.

3595. Arnold, Byron, ed. Folksongs of Alabama. University, University of Alabama Press, 1950. xiii + 193 pp.—Scores.

3596. Creighton, Helen, and Senior, Doreen H., eds. Traditional Songs from Nova Scotia. Toronto, Ryerson Press, 1950. xvi + 284 pp.—Scores.

3597. Morris, Alton C., ed. Folksongs of Florida. Collected and edited. Musical transcriptions by Leonhard Deutsch. Gainesville, University of Florida Press, 1950. xvii + 464 pp.—"Bibliography," pp. 451–457.

3598. Randolph, Vance, ed. Ozark Folksongs. Vol. I: British Ballads and Songs; Vol. II: Songs of the South and West; Vol. III: Humorous and Play-Party Songs; Vol. IV: Religious Songs and Other Songs. Columbia, State Historical Society of Missouri, 1946–50. 4 vols.

3599. Fisher, Miles Mark. Negro Slave Songs in the United States. With a foreword by Ray Allen Billington. Ithaca, N.Y., Cornell Univ. Press for the American Historical Association, 1953. xv + 223 pp.—"Bibliography," pp. 193–213.

3600. Flanders, Helen Hartness, and Olney, Marguerite, eds. Ballads Migrant in New England. With an introduction by Robert Frost. New York, Farrar, Straus and Young, 1953. xiv + 248 pp.

3601. Greenway, John. American Folksongs of Protest. Philadelphia, University of Pennsylvania Press, 1953. x + 348 pp.—"Bibliography," pp. 329–338.

3602. White, Newman Ivey, Belden, Henry M., et al., eds. The Frank C. Brown Collection of North Carolina Folklore. . . . Vol. I: Games and Rhymes, Beliefs and Customs, Riddles, Proverbs, Speech, Tales and Legends; Vol. II: Folk Ballads from North Carolina; Vol. III: Folk Songs from North Carolina; Vol. IV: The Music of the Ballads. Durham, N.C., Duke Univ. Press, 1952–57. 4 vols.; 3 more in preparation.

3603. Thompson, Harold W., ed. A Pioneer Songster. Texts from the Stevens-Douglas Manuscript of Western New York 1841–1856. With the assistance of Edith E. Cutting. Ithaca, N.Y., Cornell Univ. Press, 1958. xxii + 203 pp.—"Bibliography," pp. 193–198.

CHAPTER X

METHODS, STYLE, AND BASIC TEXTS FOR RESEARCH AND WRITING

§145. LEARNED SOCIETIES

[For the publications of learned societies see §100. Publisher, Academic, and Society Series.]

3607. Griffin, Appleton P. C. Bibliography of American Historical Societies. 2nd ed. Washington, D.C., Government Printing Office, 1907. 1374 pp. —Volume II in the series Annual Reports of the American Historical Association. Original ed. 1895.

3608. Handbook of Learned Societies and Institutions. Edited by J. David Thompson. Washington, D.C., Carnegie Institution, 1908. viii + 592 pp.—Number 39 in the series Publications of the Carnegie Institution.

3609. Steeves, Harrison Ross. Learned Societies and English Literary Scholarship in Great Britain and the United States. New York, Columbia Univ. Press, 1913. xiv + 245 pp.—In the series Columbia University Studies in English and Comparative Literature. "Bibliography," pp. 218–230.

3610. Müller, Johannes G. T. Die wissenschaftlichen Vereine und Gesellschaften Deutschlands im neunzehnten Jahrhundert. Bibliographie ihrer Veröffentlichungen. Vol. I: Seit ihrer Begründung bis auf die Gegenwart; Vol. II: Fortgeführt bis 1914. Vol. I: Berlin, A. Asher und Co., 1883; Vol. II: Berlin, Behrend und Co., 1917. 2 vols.

3611. Scientific and Learned Societies of Great Britain. A handbook compiled from official sources. 58th ed. London, Allen and Unwin, 1956. 211 pp. —Original ed. 1884.

§146. BIBLIOGRAPHIC MANUALS FOR STUDENTS: ENGLISH, FRENCH, AND GERMAN

[For major bibliographies see Chapter XIII: General Bibliographical Guides.]

3615. McKerrow, R[onald] B. Information for Students. London, Sidgwick and Jackson Ltd., 1927. 16 pp.—A list *inter alia* of periodicals, learned societies, and hours and regulations of some libraries together with information on obtaining photographs of MSS.

3616. Esdaile, Arundell. The Sources of English Literature. A bibliographical guide for students. Corrected reprint. Cambridge Univ. Press, 1929. vii + 131 pp.—The Sanders Lectures 1926. Original ed. 1928.

3617. Cowling, Geo. H. An English Bibliography. Being a short list of books recommended to students of English language and literature. Melbourne, Austral., University Press, 1931. [vi] + 49 pp.

3618. Brebner, J[ohn] Bartlet, and Neff, Emery. A Bibliography of English Literature and History. With a syllabus for a coordinated course. New York, Columbia Univ. Press, 1932. 20 pp.

3619. Loewenthal, Fritz. Bibliographisches Handbuch zur deutschen Philologie. Halle a. S., Max Niemeyer Verlag, 1932. xii + 217 pp.—A list of over 2079 items, many of which are useful to the student of Old and Middle English.

3620. Greenberg, Emil. A Guide to Research Sources in English and American Literature. New York Univ. Press, 1942. 110 pp.

3621. A Tutorial Bibliography of English Literature. Selected and compiled by members of the Tutorial Board and of the Department of English in the faculty of Arts and Sciences of Harvard University. Cambridge, Mass., Harvard University, 1948. 45 pp.—Reprint 1953.

3622. Cross, Tom Peete. Bibliographical Guide to English Studies. 10th ed. University of Chicago Press, 1951. xii + 81 pp.—Original ed. 1919; tenth ed. reprinted 1956.

3623. Schmidt, Karlernst. Anglistische Bücherkunde. Eine Auswahlbibliographie. Tübingen, Max Niemeyer Verlag, 1953. iv + 60 pp.

3624. Esdaile, Arundell. The Student's Manual of Bibliography. Revised by Roy Stokes. 3rd ed. London, George Allen and Unwin, 1954. 392 pp.—Number 1 in the Library Association Series of Library Manuals. Original ed. 1931; second ed. 1932.

3625. Malcles, Louise-Noëlle. Cours de bibliographie à l'intention des étudiants de l'université et des candidats aux examens de bibliothécaire. Geneva, Librairie E. Droz, 1954. xii + 350 pp.

3626. Spargo, John Webster. A Bibliographical Manual for Students of the Language and Literature of England and the United States. A short-title list. 3rd ed. New York, Hendricks House, 1956. x + 251 pp. printed and numbered recto + 252–285 regular pp.—Original ed. 1939; second ed. 1941. On pp. 253–269 "The Province of English Philology" by Albert Stanburrough Cook, an essay reprinted from *PMLA*, XII (1897). 1352 items.

3627. Russell, Harold G., Shove, Raymond H., and Moen, Blanche E. The Use of Books and Libraries. 9th ed. Oxford Univ. Press, 1958. v + 93 pp.—Original ed. 1933.

3628. Altick, Richard D., and Wright, Andrew. Selective Bibliography for the Study of English and American Literature. New York, Macmillan Co., [1960]. xii + 138 pp. (11 to 109 printed recto only).—Glossary, pp. 111–124.

§147. SCHOLARSHIP: METHODOLOGY

[See also §69. Basic Principles of Criticism.]

3632. Posnett, Hutcheson Macaulay. Comparative Literature. New York, D. Appleton and Co., 1886. x + 402 pp.—Volume LIX in the International Scientific Series.

3633. Körting, Gustav [Karl Otto]. Encyklopaedie und Methodologie der englischen Philologie. Heilbronn, Verlag von Gebr. Henninger, 1888. xx + 464 pp.

3634. Elster, Ernst. Principien der Literaturwissenschaft. Halle a. S., Max Niemeyer, 1897–1911. 2 vols.—"Das vorliegende Werk steckt sich insofern enge Grenzen, als es sich in vielen Partieen auf die neuhochdeutsche Literatur beschränkt," Einleitung.

3635. Morize, André. Problems and Methods of Literary History. With special reference to modern French literature. A guide for graduate students. Boston, Ginn and Co., 1922. x + 314 pp.

3636. Greg, W[alter] W. The Calculus of Variants. An essay on textual criticism. Oxford, Clarendon Press, 1927. vi + 63 pp.

3637. Rickert, Edith. New Methods for the Study of Literature. University of Chicago Press, 1927. xiii + 275 pp.

3638. Foerster, Norman, McGalliard, John C., Wellek, René, Warren, Austin, and Schramm, Wilbur L. Literary Scholarship. Its aims and methods. Chapel Hill, University of North Carolina Press, 1941. xi + 269 pp.

3639. Wilson, Louis Round, Lowell, Mildred Hawksworth, and Reed, Sarah Rebecca. The Library in College Instruction. A syllabus on the improvement of college instruction through library use. New York, H. W. Wilson Co., 1951. 347 pp.

3640. Sanders, Chauncey. An Introduction to Research in English Literary History. With a chapter on research in folklore by Stith Thompson. New York, Macmillan Co., 1952. vi + 423 pp.—Reprint 1957. Bibliographical notes and bibliographies, pp. 317–406.

3641. Wellek, René, and Warren, Austin. Theory of Literature. 2nd ed. New York, Harcourt, Brace and Co., 1955. x + 403 pp.—Original ed. 1949. Reprint New York, Harcourt, Brace and Co., 1956, xii + 368 pp., number 22 in the series Harvest Books. "Bibliography," pp. 347–387.

3642. Barzun, Jacques, and Graff, Henry F. The Modern Researcher. New York, Harcourt, Brace and Co., 1957. xiii + 386 pp.—Bibliography, pp. 356–367.

3643. Willoughby, Edwin Eliott. The Uses of Bibliography to the Students of Literature and History. Hamden, Conn., Shoe String Press, 1957. 105 pp.

3644. Lyon, Harvey T. Keats' Well-Read Urn. An introduction to literary method. New York, Henry Holt and Co., 1958. ix + 118 pp.

3645. Maas, Paul. Textual Criticism. Translated from the German by Barbara Flower. Oxford Univ. Press, 1958. [ix] + 59 pp.—A treatment primarily of classical models but with analyses of techniques applicable to modern English MSS.

3646. Bowers, Fredson. Textual and Literary Criticism. Cambridge Univ. Press, 1959. x + 186 pp.

3647. Dearing, Vinton A. A Manual of Textual Analysis. Berkeley, University of California Press, 1959. xi + 108 pp.

3648. Walsh, Wm. The Use of Imagination. Educational thought and the literary mind. London, Chatto and Windus Ltd., 1959. 252 pp.

3649. Stevenson, Noel C. Search and Research. The researcher's handbook. A guide to official records and library sources for investigators, historians, genealogists, lawyers, and librarians. Salt Lake City, Utah, Deseret Book Co., 1959. 364 pp.—Original ed. 1951.

3650. Wolfle, Dael, ed. Symposium on Basic Research. Preface by Warren Weaver. Washington, D.C., American Association for the Advancement of Science, 1959. xx + 308 pp.—Number 56 in the series Publications of the American Association for the Advancement of Science.

§148. SCHOLARSHIP: HISTORICAL STUDIES

3654. Loliée, Frédéric. A Short History of Comparative Literature from the Earliest Times to the Present Day. Translated by M. Douglas Power. London, Hodder and Stoughton, 1906. xii + 381 pp.—Original Fr. ed. 1903.

3655. Babbitt, Irving. Literature and the American College. Essays in defense of the humanities. Boston, Houghton Mifflin Co., 1908. ix + 263 pp.—Reprint Chicago, Henry Regnery Co., 1956, xvi + 177 pp., number 6041 in the series Gateway Editions.

3656. Sheavyn, Phoebe. The Literary Profession in the Elizabethan Age. Manchester, Eng., University Press, 1909. xii + 222 pp.—Number 1 in the Publications of the University of Manchester English Series.

3657. O'Leary, John G. English Literary History and Bibliography. A thesis accepted for the diploma of the Library Association. Foreword by R. A. Peddie. London, Grafton and Co., 1928. xii + 192 pp.

3658. Paull, H[arry] M. Literary Ethics. A study in the growth of the literary conscience. London, Thornton Butterworth Ltd., 1928. 358 pp.

3659. Firth, Chas. Modern Languages at Oxford 1724–1929. Oxford Univ. Press, 1929. 151 pp.

3660. Matthiessen, F[rancis] O. Translation. An Elizabethan art. Cambridge, Mass., Harvard Univ. Press, 1931. ix + 232 pp.

3661. Pedersen, Holger. Linguistic Science in the Nineteenth Century. Methods and results. Translated from the Danish by John Webster Spargo. Cambridge, Mass., Harvard Univ. Press, 1931. xi + 360 pp.—Original Danish ed. 1924.

3662. White, Harold Ogden. Plagiarism and Imitation during the English Renaissance. A study in critical distinctions. Cambridge, Mass., Harvard Univ. Press, 1935. xi + 209 pp.—Volume XII in the series Harvard Studies in English.

3663. Chadwick, H[ector] Munro. The Study of Anglo-Saxon. Second ed. edited and enl. by Nora K. Chadwick. Cambridge, Eng., W. Heffer and Sons, 1955. xiii + 99 pp.—Original ed. 1941. "Bibliography," pp. 88–92.

3664. Wellek, René. The Rise of English Literary History. Chapel Hill, University of North Carolina Press, 1941. xi + 275 pp.

3665. Clarke, Martin Lowther. Greek Studies in England 1700–1830. Cambridge Univ. Press, 1945. vi + 256 pp.

3666. Altick, Richard D. The Scholar Adventurers. New York, Macmillan Co., 1950. ix + 338 pp.—Reprint 1960.

3667. Douglas, David C. English Scholars 1660–1730. 2nd ed. London, Eyre and Spottiswoode, [1951]. 291 pp.—Original ed. 1939.

3668. Robins, R[obert] H. Ancient and Medieval Grammatical Theory in Europe. With particular reference to modern linguistic doctrine. London, Bell, 1951. vii + 104 pp.

3669. Carroll, John B. The Study of Languages. A survey of linguistics and related disciplines in America. Cambridge, Mass., Harvard Univ. Press, 1953. xiii + 289 pp.

3670. Ernest, Earnest. Academic Procession. An informal history of the American college 1636 to 1953. Indianapolis, Bobbs-Merrill Co., 1953. 368 pp.

3671. Curti, Merle, ed. American Scholarship in the Twentieth Century. Cambridge, Mass., Harvard Univ. Press, 1953. xi + 252 pp.—Essays by various hands on sociological, historical, literary, classical, and philosophical scholarship.

3672. Costello, Wm. T., S.J. The Scholastic Curriculum at Early Seventeenth Century Cambridge. Cambridge, Mass., Harvard Univ. Press, 1958. ix + 221 pp.—"Bibliography," pp. 151–168.

3673. Leary, Lewis, ed. Contemporary Literary Scholarship. A critical review. New York, Appleton-Century-Crofts Inc., 1958. x + 474 pp.

3674. Skard, Sigmund. American Studies in Europe. Philadelphia, University of Pennsylvania Press, 1958. 2 vols.

3675. Whitelock, Dorothy. Changing Currents in Anglo-Saxon Studies. An inaugural lecture. Cambridge Univ. Press, 1958. 31 pp.

3676. Brower, Reuben A., ed. On Translation. Cambridge, Mass., Harvard Univ. Press, 1959. xii + 297 pp.—Number 23 in the series Harvard Studies in Comparative Literature. "Bibliography 46 B.C.–1958," by Bayard Quincy Morgan, pp. 271–293.

§149. DESCRIPTIVE BIBLIOGRAPHY

[See also §95. Periodicals Devoted Chiefly to Bibliographic Description and Historical Bibliography.]

3680. Child, James B. Sixteenth Century Books. A bibliography of literature describing books printed between 1501 and 1601. Chicago, John Crerar Library for the author, 1925. 82 pp.—Also *Papers of the Bibliographical Society of America*, XVII, 2 (1923), 72–152.

3681. Cole, Geo. W. An Index to Bibliographical Papers Published by the Bibliographic Society and the Library Association, London, 1877–1932. University of Chicago Press for the Bibliographical Society of America, 1933. ix + 262 pp.

3682. Selective Check Lists of Bibliographical Scholarship 1949–1955. Charlottesville, Bibliographical Society of the University of Virginia, 1957. viii + 192 (double column) pp.—Seven annual lists, each in two parts—Part I: Incunabula and Early Renaissance; Part II: Later Renaissance to the Present.

3683. Peddie, Robt. A. Fifteenth-Century Books. A guide to their identification. With a list of the Latin names of towns and an extensive bibliography of the subject. London, Grafton and Co., 1913. 89 pp.

3684. McKerrow, Ronald B. An Introduction to Bibliography for Literary Students. Second impression with corrections. Oxford, Clarendon Press, 1928. xv + 359 pp.—Original impression 1927; second impression reprinted 1949. "A Short List of Some Books of Especial Utility to Students," pp. xiv–xvi. An enlargement of McKerrow's "Notes on Bibliographical Evidence for Literary Students and Editors of English Works of the Sixteenth and Seventeenth Centuries," originally printed 1913 in *Transactions of the Bibliographical Society*, of which a number of copies were issued in pamphlet form.

3685. Van Hoesen, Henry B., and Walter, Frank K. Bibliography, Practical, Enumerative, Historical. An introductory manual. New York, Charles Scribner's Sons, 1928. xvi + 519 pp.

3686. Schneider, [Edmund] Georg. Handbuch der Bibliographie. Vierte, gänzlich veränderte und stark vermehrte Auflage. Leipzig, Verlag Karl W. Hiersemann, 1930. ix + 674 pp.—Original ed. 1923; second ed. 1924; third ed. 1926. The third ed. was translated by Ralph Robert Shaw as *Theory and History of Bibliography*, New York, Columbia Univ. Press, 1934, xiv + 306 pp., number 1 in the series Columbia University Studies in Library Service.

3687. Haebler, Konrad. The Study of Incunabula. Translated from the German by Lucy E. Osborne. With a foreword by Alfred W. Pollard. New York, Grolier Club, 1933. xvi + 241 pp.—Original Ger. ed. 1925. Haebler's revisions of 1932 incorporated in the Eng. ed. of 1933.

3688. Besterman, Theodore. The Beginnings of Systematic Bibliography. Oxford Univ. Press, 1935. xi + 81 pp.—"List of Bibliographies Printed to the End of the Sixteenth Century," pp. 59–74.

3689. Goldschmidt, Ernst P. Medieval Texts and Their First Appearance in Print. Oxford Univ. Press, 1943. 143 pp.—Number 16 in the series Supplements to the Bibliographical Society's Transactions.

3690. Bowers, Fredson. Principles of Bibliographic Description. Princeton, N.J., University Press, 1949. xvii + 505 pp.

3691. Bühler, Curt F., McManaway, James G., and Wroth, Lawrence C. Standards of Bibliographic Description. Philadelphia, University of Pennsylvania Press, 1949. viii + 120 pp.—In the series Publications of the A. S. W. Rosenbach Fellowship in Bibliography.

3692. Bowers, Fredson. Purposes of Descriptive Bibliography, with Some Remarks on Methods. Library, Fifth Series, VIII, 1 (March 1953), 1–22.

3693. Jayne, Sears. Library Catalogues of the English Renaissance. Berkeley, University of California Press, 1956. ix + 225 pp.—"Previous Lists of English Renaissance Catalogues," pp. 189–191.

3694. Schottenloher, Karl. Das alte Buch. 3rd ed. Braunschweig, Klinkhardt und Biermann, 1956. 467 pp.—Volume XIV in the series Bibliothek für Kunst- und Antiquitäten-Freunde. Original ed. 1919; second ed. 1921. "Literatur," pp. 403–426.

3695. Taylor, Archer. Book Catalogues. Their varieties and uses. Chicago, Newberry Library, 1957. xii + 284 pp.—Bibliography, pp. 267–270.

3696. Linder, LeRoy Harold. The Rise of Current Complete National Bibliography. New York, Scarecrow Press, 1959. 290 pp.

§150. OLD RECORDS AND DOCUMENTS AND THEIR ABBREVIATIONS

3700. Thoyts, E[mma] E. [Mrs. Emma E. Cope.] How to Decipher and Study Old Documents. Being a guide to the reading of ancient manuscripts. The key to the family deed chest. With an introduction by C. Trice Martin. London, Elliot Stock, 1893. xvi + 143 pp.

3701. Rye, Walter. Records and Record Searching. 2nd ed. London, George Allen, 1897. viii + 253 pp.—Original ed. 1888.

3702. Martin, Chas. Trice. The Record Interpreter. A collection of abbreviations, Latin words, and names used in English historical manuscripts and records. 2nd ed. London, Stevens and Sons, 1910. xv + 464 (double column) pp.—Original ed. 1892.

3703. Lindsay, Wallace M. Notae Latinae. An account of abbreviations in Latin MSS of the early Minuscule Period *ca.* 700–850. Cambridge Univ. Press, 1915. xxiv + 500 pp.

3704. Graesse, Johan G. T. Orbis Latinus. Oder Verzeichnis der wichtigsten lateinischen Orts- und Ländernamen. Neu bearbeitet von Friederich Benedict. 3rd ed. Berlin, R. C. Schmidt und Co., 1922. 384 pp.—Original ed. 1861; second ed. 1909.

3705. Cappelli, Adriano. Lexicon abbreviaturarum. Dizionario di abbreviature latine ed italiane. . . . 3rd ed. Milan, U. Hoepli, 1929. lxxiii + 531 pp. + ix facsimiles.—Original ed. 1899; second ed. 1912. "Bibliographia," pp. 517–531.

3706. Peddie, Robt. A. Place-Names in Imprints. An index to the Latin and other forms used on title-pages. London, Grafton and Co., 1932. viii + 62 pp.

3707. Galbraith, Vivian H. An Introduction to the Use of the Public Records. Oxford Univ. Press, 1934. 112 pp.—Reprint 1935.

3708. Christopher, H[enry] G. T. Paleography and Archives. A manual for the librarian, archivist, and student. Introduction by J. D. Stewart. London, Grafton and Co., 1938. xv + 216 pp.—Bibliography, pp. 182–200.

§151. MANUSCRIPT HANDS AND MANUSCRIPT STUDY

3712. Wattenbach, Wilhelm. Das Schriftwesen im Mittelalter. 3rd ed. Leipzig, S. Hirzel, 1896. vi + 670 pp.—Original ed. 1871; second ed. 1875.

3713. Johnston, Harold W. Latin Manuscripts. An elementary introduction to the use of critical editions for high school and college classes. Chicago, Scott, Foresman and Co., 1897. 135 pp.—In the series Inter-Collegiate Latin Series.

3714. Keller, Wolfgang. Angelsächsische Palaeographie. Die Schrift der Angelsachsen mit besonderer Rücksicht auf die Denkmäler in der Volkssprache. Berlin, Mayer und Müller, 1906. 2 vols.—Volume XLIII in the series Palaestra. "Bibliographie," I, pp. 1–6.

3715. Thompson, Edward M. An Introduction to Greek and Latin Paleography. Oxford, Clarendon Press, 1912. xvi + 600 pp.—A development of Thompson's *Handbook of Greek and Latin Paleography*, 3rd ed., London, Kegan Paul, Trench, Trübner and Co., 1906. xiv + 361 pp.

3716. Wright, Andrew. Court-Hand Restored. Or the student's assistant in reading old deeds, charters, records, etc. Tenth ed. by Charles J. Martin. London, Stevens and Sons, 1912. xx pp. + xxx plates + 103 pp.—Original ed. 1776.

3717. Loew, E[lias] A. [On LC card: Lowe.] The Beneventan Script. A history of the South Italian minuscule. Oxford Univ. Press, 1914. xx + 384 pp.

3718. Jenkinson, Hilary. Palaeography and the Practical Study of Court Hand. Cambridge Univ. Press, 1915. 37 pp. + xiii facsimiles.

3719. Johnson, Chas., and Jenkinson, Hilary. English Court Hand A.D. 1066–1500. Illustrated chiefly from the Public Records. Oxford Univ. Press, 1915. Part I: Text xviii + 251 pp.; Part II: xliv plates.

3720. Sinks, Perry Wayland. The Reign of the Manuscript. Boston, Richard G. Badger, 1917. 176 pp.

3721. Madan, Falconer. Books in Manuscript. A short introduction to their study and use. With a chapter on records. 2nd ed. London, Kegan Paul, Trench, Trübner and Co., 1920. xv + 208 pp.—Original ed. 1893; second ed. reprinted 1927.

3722. Jenkinson, Hilary. Elizabethan Handwriting. A preliminary sketch. The Library, Fourth Series, III, 1 (June 1, 1922), 1–34.

3723. Jenkinson, Hilary. The Later Court Hands in England from the Fifteenth to the Seventeenth Century. Illustrated from the common paper of the Scriveners' Company of London, the English writing masters, and the public records. Cambridge Univ. Press, 1927. ix + 199 pp. + xlix plates.

3724. Degering, Hermann. Die Schrift. Atlas der Schriftformen des Abendlandes vom Altertum bis zum Ausgang des 18. Jahrhunderts. Berlin, E. Wasmuth AG, 1929. xxxvi + ccxl plates on 120 leaves.—English ed. *Lettering* . . . , From antiquity to the end of the 18th century, London, E. Benn, 1929.

3725. Löffler, Karl. Einführung in die Handschriftenkunde. Leipzig, K. W. Hiersemann, 1929. xii + 214 pp.

3726. Tannenbaum, Samuel A. The Handwriting of the Renaissance. New York, Columbia Univ. Press, 1930. xii + 210 pp. + xiv facsimiles.

3727. Heal, Ambrose. The English Writing-Masters and Their Copybooks 1570–1800. A biographical dictionary and a bibliography. With an introduction on the development of handwriting by Stanley Morison. Cambridge Univ. Press, 1931. xl + 225 pp. + lxxxi facsimiles.

3728. Greg, W[alter] W. English Literary Autographs 1550–1656. Selected for reproduction and edited. In collaboration with J. P. Gilson, Hilary Jenkinson, R. B. McKerrow, A. W. Pollard. Oxford Univ. Press, 1925–32. 278 pp. + cx plates.—Issued in fascicules. Limited number.

3729. Ullman, B[erthold] L. Ancient Writing and Its Influence. New York, Longmans, Green and Co., 1932. vii + 234 pp.—In the series Our Debt to Greece and Rome. "Bibliography," pp. 231–234. A treatment of alphabets, MSS, and scribal style.

3730. Haselden, Reginald B. Scientific Aids for the Study of Manuscripts. Oxford Univ. Press for the Bibliographical Society, 1935. x + 108 pp. —Number 10 in the series Supplements to the Transactions of the Bibliographical Society.

3731. Judge, Cyril B. Specimens of Sixteenth-Century English Handwriting. Cambridge, Mass., Harvard Univ. Press, 1935. 18 pp. + xxiv facsimiles. —"Selected Bibliography," pp. 14–16.

3732. Benjamin, Mary A. Autographs. A key to collecting. New York, R. R. Bowker Co., 1946. xviii + 305 pp. + xxxv facsimiles.

3733. Dain, A[lphonse]. Les manuscrits. Paris, Société d'édition "Les Belles-Lettres," 1949. 181 pp.—In the series Collection d'études anciennes.

3734. Diringer, David. The Hand Produced Book. New York, Philosophical Library, 1953. xii + 13–603 pp.

3735. Denholm-Young, N[oël]. Handwriting in England and Wales. Cardiff, University of Wales Press, 1954. xi + 102 pp. + xxxi plates.—A history of scribal practices.

3736. Devreesse, Robt. Introduction à l'étude des manuscrits Grecs. Paris, Librairie C. Klincksieck, 1954. ix + 347 pp.

3737. Grieve, Hilda E. P. Examples of English Handwriting 1150–1750. With transcripts and translations. Essex, Eng., Essex Education Committee, 1954. ii + 33 pp.—Number 21 in the series Essex Record Office Publications.

3738. Hector, L[eonard] C. The Handwriting of English Documents. London, Edward Arnold Ltd., [1958]. 126 pp.

§152. READING: TECHNIQUES AND VALUES

3742. LeGallienne, Richard. How to Get the Best out of Books. New York, Baker and Taylor Co., 1904. 171 pp.

3743. Kerfoot, J[ohn] B. How to Read. Boston, Houghton Mifflin Co., 1916. 297 pp.

3744. Quiller-Couch, Arthur. On the Art of Reading. New York, G. P. Putnam's Sons, 1920. ix + 250 pp.

3745. Gerould, Gordon Hall. How to Read Fiction. Oxford Univ. Press, 1937. 153 pp.

3746. Edge, Sigrid. Books for Self-Education. Chicago, American Library Association, 1938. 95 pp.

3747. Adler, Mortimer J. How to Read a Book. The art of getting a liberal education. New York, Simon and Schuster Inc., 1940. ix + 398 pp.

3748. Richards, I[vor] A. How to Read a Page. A course in efficient reading with an introduction to a hundred great words. New York, W. W. Norton and Co., 1942. 246 pp.

3749. Allen, Walter. Reading a Novel. London, Phoenix House Ltd., 1949. 58 pp.

3750. Belgion, Montgomery. Reading for Profit. [New ed.] London, Cresset Press, 1951. 313 pp.—Original ed. Harmondsworth, Eng., Penguin Books Inc., 1945, number A151 in the series Pelican Books.

3751. Center, Stella S. The Art of Book Reading. New York, Charles Scribner's Sons, 1952. xxii + 298 pp.

3752. Aggertt, Otis J., and Bowen, Elbert R. Communicative Reading. New York, Macmillan Co., 1956. xiv + 480 pp.

3753. Cecil, David. The Fine Art of Reading and Other Literary Studies. Indianapolis, Bobbs-Merrill Co., 1957. 282 pp.—Essays chiefly on English fiction.

3754. Gordon, Caroline. [Mrs. Caroline Gordon Tate.] How to Read a Novel. New York, Viking Press, 1957. 247 pp.

§153. DICTIONARIES: COLLEGIATE AND LARGER WORKS NOT BASED PRIMARILY ON HISTORICAL PRINCIPLES

[See also §107. Old English Dictionaries and Glossaries; §108. Middle and Early English Dictionaries; §109. Historical and Etymological Dictionaries; §111. Dictionaries of American English; §119. Dictionaries of the Dialects of English; §120. Studies in Slang and Slang Dictionaries.]

3758. Cawdrey, Robt. A Table Alphabeticall. Conteyning and teaching the true writing and understanding of hard usual English words borrowed from the Hebrew, Greeke, Latine or French, etc. London, J. R. for Edmund Weaver, 1604. [130] pp.—Reproduction Number 11 in the series Photographic Facsimiles of the Modern Language Association of America [Oxford 1923].

3759. Johnson, Samuel. A Dictionary of the English Language. London, W. Strahan, 1755. 2 vols. in folio.

3760. Webster, Noah. American Dictionary of the English Language. New York, S. Converse, 1828. 2 vols.

3761. Wyld, Henry Cecil. The Universal Dictionary of the English Language. A new and original compilation giving all pronunciations in simplified and in more exact phonetic notations, extensive etymologies, definitions, the latest accepted words in scientific, technical, and general use, with copious illustrative phrases, and colloquialisms. New York, E. P. Dutton and Co., 1932. xx + 1431 (triple column) pp.

3762. New Standard Dictionary of the English Language. Edited by Isaac K. Funk, et al. New York, Funk and Wagnalls Co., 1932. xxxviii + 2814 (triple column) pp.

3763. Webster's New International Dictionary of the English Language. Second ed. unabridged edited by William A. Neilson, Thomas A. Knott, Paul W. Carhart, et al. Springfield, Mass., G. and C. Merriam Co., 1934. cxxxvi + 3194 (triple column) pp.—Original ed. 1909; second ed. frequently reissued with minor changes and additions, as in 1959.

3764. Macmillan's Modern Dictionary. Rev. ed. Including a glossary of aeronautical terms. Edited by Bruce Overton. New York, Macmillan Co., 1943. xiii + 1494 (double column) pp.—Original ed. 1938; revised ed. reprinted 1945.

3765. American College Dictionary. Text ed. Edited by Clarence L. Barnhart. New York, Harper and Bros., 1948. xl + 1432 (double column) pp.

3766. Webster's New Collegiate Dictionary. Based on Webster's New International Dictionary Second Edition. Edited by John B. Bethel, et al. Springfield, Mass., G. and C. Merriam Co., 1951. xxii + 1174 (double column) pp.—Reprinted approximately every two years with minor modifications.

3767. Swan's Anglo-American Dictionary. Edited by George Ryley Scott. New York, Library Publ'ers, 1952. 1514 (double column) pp.

3768. Webster's New World Dictionary of the American Language. College ed. Edited by Joseph H. Friend, David B. Guralnik, Harold E. Whitehall, et al. Cleveland, World Publ'ing Co., 1953. xxxvi + 1724 (double column) pp.—Frequent reprints, as in 1958.

3769. Concise Oxford Dictionary of Current English. Edited by H[enry] W. and F[rancis] G. Fowler. Fourth ed. rev. by E. McIntosh. Oxford, Clarendon Press, 1954. xvi + 1536 (double column) pp.—Original ed. 1911; second ed. 1929; third ed. 1934.

3770. Thorndike-Barnhart Comprehensive Desk Dictionary. Edited by Clarence L. Barnhart. Garden City, N.Y., Doubleday and Co., 1958. xiii + 896 (double column) pp.

§154. STYLE: IDIOMS AND IDIOMATIC USAGE

[See also §22. The Art of Prose; §69. Basic Principles of Criticism.]

3774. Hyamson, Albert M. A Dictionary of English Phrases, Phraseological Allusions, Catchwords, Stereotyped Modes of Speech and Metaphors, Nicknames, Sobriquets, Derivations from Personal Names. . . . London, George Routledge and Sons, 1922. xvi + 365 (double column) pp.

3775. Krapp, Geo. P. A Comprehensive Guide to Good English. Chicago, Rand, McNally and Co., 1927. xxxviii + 688 pp.

3776. Leonard, Sterling A. The Doctrine of Correctness in English Usage 1700–1800. Madison, University of Wisconsin Press, 1929. 361 pp.—

Number 25 in the series University of Wisconsin Studies in Language and Literature. "Bibliographies," pp. 309–326.

3777. Leonard, Sterling A. Current English Usage. Chicago, Inland Press, 1932. xxii + 232 pp.—Number 1 in the series English Monographs of the National Council of Teachers of English.

3778. Herbert, A[lan] P. What a Word! Garden City, N.Y., Doubleday, Doran and Co., 1936. xii + 286 pp.

3779. Fowler, H[enry] W. A Dictionary of Modern English Usage. Last corrected ed. Oxford, Clarendon Press, 1937. viii + 742 (double column) pp.—Original ed. 1926; corrected ed. frequently reprinted, as in 1958.

3780. Marckwardt, Albert H., and Walcott, Fred G. Facts about Current English Usage. Including a discussion of current usage in grammar from Current English Usage by Sterling A. Leonard. New York, D. Appleton-Century Co., 1938. viii + 144 pp.—Number 7 in the series English Monographs of the National Council of Teachers of English.

3781. Horwill, H[erbert] W. An Anglo-American Interpreter. A vocabulary and phrase book. Oxford Univ. Press, 1939. 91 (double column) pp.—American locutions in the left column and their English equivalents in the right.

3782. McKerrow, R[onald] B. Form and Matter in the Publication of Research. Review of English Studies, XVI (1940), 116–121.—Reprint *PMLA*, LXV, 3B (April 1950), 3–8.

3783. Horwill, H[erbert] W. A Dictionary of Modern American Usage. 2nd ed. Oxford Univ. Press, 1944. xxxii + 360 (double column) pp.—Original ed. 1935.

3784. Opdycke, John B. Say What You Mean. Everyman's guide to diction and grammar. New York, Funk and Wagnalls Co., 1944. xx + 681 pp.

3785. Swann, Robt., and Sidgwick, Frank. The Making of Prose. A guide for writers. London, Sidgwick and Jackson, 1949. xii + 208 pp.

3786. Henderson, B[ernard] L. K. A Dictionary of English Idioms. Part I: Verbal Idioms; Part II: Colloquial Phrases [with G. O. E. Henderson]. London, James Blackwood and Co., 1939–50. 2 vols.—Reprint 1947 of vol. I.

3787. Partridge, Eric. A Dictionary of Clichés. With an introductory essay. 4th ed. London, George Routledge and Sons, 1950. ix + 259 pp.—Original ed. 1940; fourth ed. reprinted 1954.

3788. Weston, W[illiam] J. A Manual of Good English. London, George Newnes Ltd., 1950. 318 pp.

3789. Whitten, Wilfred, and Whitaker, Frank. Good and Bad English. A guide to speaking and writing. [4th ed.] London, George Newnes Ltd., 1950. xiv + 361 pp.—Original ed. 1939.

3790. Freeman, Wm. A Concise Dictionary of English Idioms. London, English Universities Press, 1951. ix + 10–300 pp.

3791. Vigilans [i.e., Eric Partridge]. Chamber of Horrors. A glossary of official jargon both English and American. With an introduction by Eric Partridge. New York, British Book Centre Inc., 1952. 140 pp.—In the series Language Library.

3792. Whitford, Harold C., and Dixon, Robt. J. Handbook of American Idioms and Idiomatic Usage. New York, Regents Publ'ing Co., 1953. [iv] + 155 (double column) pp.—An explanation of some 4500 idioms current in American English.

3793. Flesch, Rudolf. How to Make Sense. New York, Harper and Bros., 1954. xii + 202 pp.

3794. Gowers, Ernest. The Complete Plain Words. London, Her Majesty's Stationery Office, 1954. vi + 209 pp.—"This book is in the main a reconstruction of . . . two previous books, Plain Words [1948] and ABC of Plain Words [1951]," p. iii. Publication in the U.S. by Knopf under the title *Plain Words, Their ABC*. "Bibliography," pp. 200–201.

3795. Whitford, Robt. C., and Foster, James R. Concise Dictionary of American Grammar and Usage. New York, Philosophical Library, 1955. viii + 168 pp.

3796. Collins, V[ere] H. A Book of English Idioms with Explanations. 2nd ed. London, Longmans, Green and Co., 1957. xiii + 258 pp.—Original ed. 1956. A list of colloquial and literary metaphorical expressions.

3797. Evans, Bergen and Cornelia. A Dictionary of Contemporary American Usage. New York, Random House, 1957. viii + 567 (double column) pp.

3798. Nicholson, Margaret. A Dictionary of American-English Usage. Based on Fowler's Modern English Usage. New York, Oxford Univ. Press, 1957. xii + 671 (double column) pp.

3799. Partridge, Eric. Usage and Abusage. A guide to good English. New [5th] ed. London, H. Hamilton, 1957. 390 (double column) pp.—Original ed. 1942. Also *The Concise Usage and Abusage,* A modern guide to good English, New York, Philosophical Library, 1954, ix + 219 (double column) pp.

3800. Bernstein, Theodore M. Watch Your Language. A lively, informal guide to better writing, emanating from the News Room of the New York Times. Preface by Jacques Barzun. Great Neck, N.Y., Channel Press, 1958. xi + 276 pp.

3801. Taintor, Sarah Augusta, and Munro, Kate M. The Secretary's Handbook. A manual of correct usage. 8th ed. New York, Macmillan Co., 1958. xvi + 559 pp.—Original ed. 1929.

3802. Perrin, Porter G. Writer's Guide and Index to English. Third ed. rev. with the assistance of Karl W. Dykema. Chicago, Scott, Foresman and Co., 1959. xvi + 816 pp.—Original ed. 1942; second ed. 1950.

3803. Strunk, Wm., Jr. The Elements of Style. With revisions, an introduction, and a new chapter on writing by E. B. White. New York, Macmillan Co., 1959. xiv + 71 pp.—Original ed. 1936.

§155. STYLE: MECHANICS AND THE TECHNICAL RULES OF DISSERTATION WRITING

3807. Pugh, Griffith Thompson. Guide to Research Writing. Boston, Houghton Mifflin Co., 1948. 62 pp.—Reprint 1955.

3808. Skillin, Marjorie E., Gay, Robt. M., et al. Words into Type. A guide in the preparation of manuscripts for writers, editors, proofreaders, and printers. New York, Appleton-Century-Crofts Inc., 1948. xx + 585 pp.

3809. A Manual of Style. Containing typographical and other rules for authors, printers, and publishers, recommended by the University of Chicago Press, together with specimens of type. 11th ed. University of Chicago Press, 1949. x + 498 pp.—Original ed. 1906.

3810. Summey, Geo., Jr. American Punctuation. New York, Ronald Press Co., 1949. vii + 182 pp.

3811. Author's Guide for Preparing Manuscript and Handling Proof. New York, John Wiley and Sons, 1950. xi + 80 pp.—A development of *The Manuscript*, A guide for its preparation . . . , Third ed. prepared under the supervision of Samuel E. Norris, New York, J. Wiley and Sons, 1941, xv + 75 pp.

3812. Silver, Henry M. Putting it on Paper. PMLA, LXV, 3 (April 1950), 9–20.

3813. Ball, Alice Morton. The Compounding and Hyphenation of English Words. New York, Funk and Wagnalls Co., 1951. ix + 246 (chiefly triple column) pp.—See also Ball's prose exposition *Compounding in the English Language*, A complete review of variant authorities with a rational system for general use and a comprehensive alphabetic list of compound words, New York, H. W. Wilson Co., 1939, x + 226 pp.

3814. Johnson, Ellen. The Research Report. A guide for the beginner. New York, Ronald Press, 1951. vi + 141 pp.

3815. Hook, Lucyle, and Garver, Mary Virginia. The Research Paper. Gathering library material; organizing and preparing the manuscript. 2nd ed. New York, Prentice-Hall, Inc., 1952. ix + 85 pp.—In the Prentice-Hall Series in English Composition. Original ed. 1944; second ed. reprinted 1958.

3816. Partridge, Eric, and Clark, John W. You Have a Point There. A guide to punctuation and its allies. London, Hamish Hamilton, 1953. x + 230 pp.

3817. Campbell, Wm. Giles. Form and Style in Thesis Writing. Boston, Houghton Mifflin Co., 1954. vi + 114 pp.

3818. Parker, Wm. R. The MLA Style Sheet. Revised ed. New York, Modern Language Association of America, 1954. 31 pp.—Original ed. 1951; revised ed. frequently reprinted, as in 1958.

3819. Turabian, Kate L. A Manual for Writers of Dissertations. Revised ed. University of Chicago Press, 1955. 82 pp.—Original ed. 1937. Reprint of rev. ed. *A Manual for Writers of Term Papers, Theses, and Dissertations*, University of Chicago Press, 1960, vii + 110 pp., number 46 in the series Phoenix Books.

3820. Thompson, Denys. The English Language Paper. A handbook for candidates. London, Chatto and Windus, 1956. 288 pp.

3821. Style Manual. United States Government Printing Office. Issued by the Public Printer under Authority of Section 51 of an Act of Congress approved January 12, 1895. Revised ed. January 1959. Washington, D.C., Government Printing Office, 1959. viii + 496 pp.—The *Manual* has undergone almost yearly revision since 1911.

§156. SYNONYMIES AND THESAURI

3825. Fennell, C[harles] A. M. The Stanford Dictionary of Anglicised Words and Phrases. Cambridge Univ. Press, 1892. xvi + 826 (double column) pp.

3826. Hugon, Paul D. Morrow's Word-Finder. A living guide to modern usage, spelling, synonyms, pronunciation, grammar, word origins, and authorship, all in one alphabetical order. New York, William Morrow and Co., 1927. xi + 420 pp.

3827. Mawson, C[hristopher] O. Sylvester. The Dictionary Companion. Garden City, N.Y.,Doubleday, Doran and Co., 1932. xii + 479 pp.—Reprint 1934.

3828. [Allen, F(rederick) Sturges.] Allen's Synonyms and Antonyms. Revised and enl. by T. H. Vail Motter. New York, Harper and Bros., 1938. x + 427 pp.—Original ed. 1920.

3829. [Roget, Peter Mark.] The Roget Dictionary of Synonyms and Antonyms. Being a presentation of Roget's Thesaurus . . . in a modernized, more complete, and more convenient form together with briefer synonymies for the busy writer, the whole comprised in one alphabetical arrangement. Edited by C[hristopher] O. Sylvester Mawson. New York, G. P. Putnam's Sons, 1940. xi + 600 (double column) pp.—Mawson's original ed. of Roget 1913. Roget's original: *Thesaurus of English Words and Phrases*, Classified and arranged to facilitate the expression of ideas and assist in literary composition, London, Longman, Brown, Green and Longmans, 1852, xxxiii + 418 pp.

3830. Webster's Dictionary of Synonyms. A dictionary of discriminated synonyms with antonyms and analogous and contrasted words. Springfield, Mass., G. and C. Merriam Co., 1942. xxxiv + 907 (double column) pp. —Most of the introduction and text was written by Rose F. Egan, cf. p. vi.

3831. [Crabb, Geo.] Crabb's English Synonyms. Revised and enl. by the addition of modern terms and definitions arranged alphabetically with complete cross references throughout with an introduction by John H. Finley. New York, Grosset and Dunlap, 1945. [xiii] + 717 (double column) pp.—Original ed. 1817; repeated reissues by various companies. A series of synonym clusters with explanations of the differences between the partial synonyms within each cluster.

3832. Rodale, J[erome] I. The Word Finder. Garden City, N.Y., Garden City Books, 1947. xxxii + 1317 pp.—Reprint 1954.

3833. [Laird, Charlton.] Laird's Promptory. A dictionary of synonyms and antonyms and specific equivalents. New York, Henry Holt and Co., 1948. 957 (double column) pp.

3834. [Opdycke, John Baker.] The Opdycke Lexicon of Word Selection. New York, Funk and Wagnalls Co., 1950. xix + 492 pp.

3835. [Roget, Peter Mark.] Everyman's Thesaurus of English Words and Phrases. Revised from Peter Roget. Edited by D[avid] C. Browning. London, J. M. Dent and Sons, 1952. ix + 320 (chiefly double column) + 321–557 (triple column) + 558–572 (single column) pp.—In the series Everyman's Reference Library.

3836. Hogan, Homer. Dictionary of American Synonyms. New York, Philosophical Library, 1956. ix + 388 pp.

3837. Newmark, Maxim. Dictionary of Foreign Words. Compiled from English sources and containing foreign words, mottos, proverbs, place names, titles, allusions, and abbreviations . . . together with English equivalents and definitions and a supplement in Greek orthography. New York, Philosophical Library, 1957. 245 (double column) pp.

3838. Lewis, Norman. The Comprehensive Word Guide. Introduction by Clarence Barnhart. Garden City, N.Y., Doubleday and Co., 1958. xxiii + 912 pp.

3839. [March, Francis Andrew, and March, Francis A., Jr.] March's Thesaurus-Dictionary. Introduction by Clarence L. Barnhart. Issued under the editorial supervision of Norman Cousins. New supplement by R. A. Goodwin. Garden City, N.Y., Hanover House, 1958. viii + 1240 pp.—Original ed. Philadelphia, Historical Publishing Co., 1902; fourth ed. 1925.

§157. COLLECTIONS OF QUOTATIONS, ANECDOTES, AND EPIGRAMS

[See also §138. Proverbs: Collections and Studies; §139. Folk Tales, Fairy Tales, Traditional Anecdotes, and Fabliaux: Studies and Anthologies.]

3843. Riley, H[enry] T. Dictionary of Latin Quotations, Proverbs, Maxims, and Mottos, Classical and Mediaeval. Including law terms and phrases with a selection of Greek quotations. London, Henry G. Bohn, 1859. vi + 556 pp.

3844. Allibone, S[amuel] Austin. Prose Quotations from Socrates to Macaulay. . . . Philadelphia, J. B. Lippincott and Co., 1876. xii + 13–764 (double column) pp.

3845. Harbottle, Thos. B. Dictionary of Quotations. Classical. With authors' and subjects' indexes. London, Swan Sonnenschein and Co., 1897. 648 pp.—Reprint New York, Frederick Ungar Publ'ing Co., [195–], 678 pp.

3846. Harbottle, Thos. B., and Dalbiac, Philip H. Dictionary of Quotations. French and Italian. With authors' and subjects' indexes. London, Swan Sonnenschein and Co., 1901. 565 pp.

3847. King, W[illiam] Francis H. Classical and Foreign Quotations. A polyglot manual of historical and literary sayings. . . . 3rd ed. rev. and rewritten. London, J. Whiting and Sons, 1904. lxviii + 412 pp.—Original ed. 1887; second ed. 1889; third ed. reprinted New York, Frederick Ungar Publ'ing Co., 1958.

3848. Dalbiac, Lilian. Dictionary of Quotations. German. London, Swan Sonnenschein and Co., 1906. vi + 485 pp.

3849. Harbottle, T[homas] B., and Hume, Martin. Dictionary of Quotations. Spanish. With subject and authors' index. London, Swan Sonnenschein and Co., 1907. vii + 462 pp.

3850. Field, Claud. A Dictionary of Oriental Quotations. Arabic and Persian. London, Swan Sonnenschein and Co., 1911. 351 pp.

3851. Smyth, Mary W. Biblical Quotations in Middle English Literature before 1350. New York, Henry Holt and Co., 1911. lxxii + 303 pp.—Volume XLI in the series Yale Studies in English.

3852. Wilstach, Frank J. A Dictionary of Similes. New ed. Boston, Little, Brown and Co., 1924. liv + 578 pp.—Original ed. 1916; second ed. reprinted 1930.

3853. Mencken, Henry L. A New Dictionary of Quotations on Historical Principles from Ancient and Modern Sources. New York, A. A. Knopf, 1942. xii + 1347 pp.

3854. Fuller, Edmund, ed. Thesaurus of Epigrams. A new classified collection of witty remarks, bon mots, and toasts. New York, Crown Publ'ers, 1943. x + 11–382 pp.

3855. Berrey, Lester V. A Treasury of Biblical Quotations. Garden City, N.Y., Doubleday and Co., 1948. xiii + 240 (double column) pp.

3856. Esar, Evan. The Dictionary of Humorous Quotations. Garden City, N.Y., Doubleday and Co., 1949. 228 (single column) + 229–270 (double column) pp.

3857. Jones, Hugh Percy. Dictionary of Foreign Phrases and Classical Quotations. Comprising 14000 idioms, proverbs, maxims, mottoes, technical words and terms, and press allusions from the works of the great writers. . . . Edinburgh, John Grant Booksellers, 1949. xx + 532 (double column) pp.

3858. Stevenson, Burton. The Home Book of Bible Quotations. New York, Harper and Bros., 1949. xxv + 516 (double column) + 517–645 (triple column) pp.

3859. Browning, D[avid] C. Everyman's Dictionary of Quotations and Proverbs. London, J. M. Dent and Sons, 1951. x + 766 pp.—In the series Everyman's Reference Library.

3860. Woods, Ralph L. The Businessman's Book of Quotations. New York, McGraw-Hill Book Co., 1951. xxiii + 303 pp.

3861. Büchmann, Georg. Geflügelte Worte. Der klassische Zitatenschatz. Moderne Volksausgabe vollständig neu bearbeitet und bis zur Gegenwart ergänzt mit einem Anhang "Sprichwörtliche Redewendungen." Herausgeben von Roger Diener und Josef Falkenberg. Berlin, Verlag Praktisches Wissen, 1952. 444 pp.—Original ed. 1864.

3862. Ichikawa, Sanki, Nishikawa, Masami, and Shimizu, Mamoru. The Kenkyusha Dictionary of English Quotations with Examples of Their Use by Modern Authors. Tokyo, Kenkyusha Ltd., 1952. l + 968 (double column) pp.

3863. Hamilton, Robt. M. Canadian Quotations and Phrases Literary and Historical. With an introduction by Bruce Hutchison. Toronto, McClelland and Stuart Ltd., 1952. xiii + 272 (double column) pp.

3864. Oxford Dictionary of Quotations. 2nd ed. Oxford Univ. Press, 1953. xix + 1003 (double column) pp.—Original ed. 1941.

3865. Guerlac, Othon. Les citations françaises. Recueil de passages célèbres, phrases familières, mots historiques avec l'indication exacte de la source suivi d'un index alphabétique par auteurs et par sujets. Cinquième édition. Paris, Librairie Armand Colin, 1954. 458 pp.—Original ed. 1931.

3866. Kin, David. Dictionary of American Maxims. With an introduction by J. Donald Adams. New York, Philosophical Library, 1955. 597 pp.

3867. LeComte, Edward S. Dictionary of Last Words. New York, Philosophical Library, 1955. xxxi + 267 pp.

3868. Baron, Joseph L. A Treasury of Jewish Quotations. New York, Crown Publ'ers, 1956. xiv + 623 (double column) pp.

3869. Chapin, John. The Book of Catholic Quotations. Compiled from approved sources, ancient, medieval, and modern. New York, Farrar, Straus and Cudahy, 1956. xi + 932 (double column) + 933–1075 (triple column) pp.

3870. Zoozmann, Richard. Zitatenschatz der Weltliteratur. Eine Sammlung von Zitaten, Sentenzen, Aphorismen, Epigrammen, Sprichwörtern, Redensarten und Aussprüchen. Neunte, unveranderte Auflage. Vorwort zur achten und neunten Auflage von Otto A. Kielmeyer. Berlin, Verlag Praktisches Wissen, 1956. 922 (double column) pp.—Original ed. 1910.

3871. Vega, Vincente. Diccionario ilustrado de anécdotas. Barcelona, Editorial Gustavo Gili, 1957. xii + 1077 (double column) pp.

3872. Flesch, Rudolf. The Book of Unusual Quotations. London, Cassell and Co., 1959. x + 340 (double column) pp.

§158. ANONYMS AND PSEUDONYMS

3876. Hamst, Olphar. Handbook of Fictitious Names. Being a guide to authors, chiefly in the lighter literature of the nineteenth century, who have written under assumed names; and to literary forgers, imposters, plagiarists, and imitators. London, John Russell Smith, 1868. xv + 235 pp.

3877. Cushing, Wm. Initials and Pseudonyms. A dictionary of literary disguises. New York, Thomas Y. Crowell and Co., 1885. iv + 603 (double column) pp.—Also *Initials and Pseudonyms* . . . , Second series, New York, Thomas Y. Crowell and Co., 1888, [iii] + 314 (double column) pp.

3878. Weller, Emil O. Lexikon pseudonymorum. Wörterbuch der Pseudonymen aller Zeiten und Völker oder Verzeichnis jener Autoren, die sich falscher Namen bedienten. Zweite . . . Auflage. Regensburg, A. Coppenrath, 1886. x + 627 pp.

3879. Barbier, Antoine-Alexandre. Dictionnaire des ouvrages anonymes. Troisième édition revue et augmenté par Olivier Barbier, René et Paul Billard. . . . Suite de la second édition des Supercheries littéraires dévoilées par J. M. Quérard. . . . Paris, Féchoz et Letouzey, 1882. 4 vols.—Original ed. 1822–27; second ed. 1872–79. See also Gustave Brunet, Dictionnaire des ouvrages anonymes [de Barbier], suivi des Supercheries littéraires dévoilées [de Quérard]; supplément à la dernière édition de ces deux ouvrages . . . , Paris, Librairie de F.-J. Féchoz, 1889, iii pp. + 310 col. + cix pp. + 122 col. + xiv pp.

3880. Cushing, Wm. Anonyms. A dictionary of revealed authorship. Cambridge, Mass., published by the author, 1889. [iii] + 829 (double column) pp.

3881. Farrer, James A. Literary Forgeries. With an introduction by Andrew Lang. London, Longmans, Green and Co., 1907. xxvi + 282 pp.

3882. Stonehill, Chas. A., Jr., Block, Andrew, and Stonehill, H. Winthrop. Anonyma and Pseudonyma. Vol. I: A–E (1926); Vol. II: F–N (1926); Vol. III: O–T (1926); Vol. IV: U–Z, Addenda, Index (1927). London, C. A. Stonehill Jr., 1926–27. 4 vols.

3883. Holzmann, Michael, and Bohatta, Hanns. Deutsches Anonymenlexikon. Weimar, Gesellschaft der Bibliophilen, 1902–28. 7 vols.—See also Alfred Rosenbaum, "Beiträge zum deutschen Anonymenlexikon," *Zeitschrift zum Bücherfreunde*, Neue Folge, 15. Jahrg., Leipzig 1923, 77–88, 112–128.

3884. Marble, Annie Russell. Pen Names and Personalities. New York, D. Appleton and Co., 1930. [ix] + 256 pp.

3885. Taylor, Archer, and Mosher, Fredric J. The Bibliographical History of Anonyma and Pseudonyma. University of Chicago Press for the Newberry Library, 1951. ix + 289 pp.

3886. Kennedy, James, Smith, W[illiam] A., and Johnson, A[lfred] F., eds. Dictionary of Anonymous and Pseudonymous English Literature. (Samuel Halkett and John Laing.) New and enl. ed. Edinburgh, Oliver and Boyd, 1926–34. 7 (double column page) vols.—Also Dennis E. Rhodes and Anna E. P. Simoni, eds., *Dictionary of Anonymous and Pseudonymous English Literature 1900–1950*, Edinburgh, Oliver and Boyd, 1956, viii + 397 (double column) pp. Original ed. by Samuel Halkett and John Laing published Edinburgh, W. Patterson, 1882–88, 4 vols., as revised and edited by Catherine Laing.

§159. ABBREVIATIONS

3890. Rogers, Walter T. Dictionary of Abbreviations. Being citations of those terms used in the professions, sport, and trades. London, George Allen and Co., 1913. xi + 149 (double column) pp.

3891. Stephenson, Herbert John. Abbrevs. A dictionary of abbreviations. New York, Macmillan Co., 1943. ix + 126 (double column) pp.

3892. Shankle, Geo. Earlie. Current Abbreviations. New York, H. W. Wilson Co., 1945. 207 (double column) pp.

3893. [Allen, Edward Frank.] Allen's Dictionary of Abbreviations and Symbols. Over six thousand abbreviations and symbols commonly used in literature, science, art, education, business, politics, religion, engineering, industry, war. New York, Coward-McCann Inc., 1946. x + 189 pp.

3894. Matthews, Cecily C. A Dictionary of Abbreviations. Comprising all standard forms in commercial, social, legal, political, naval and military, and general use. London, George Routledge and Sons, 1947. viii + 232 (double column) pp.

§160. THE PROFESSIONAL WRITER

[See also §96. Library and Publisher Periodicals.]

3898. Literary Market Place. The business directory of American book publishing. New York, R. R. Bowker Co., 1940–date.—Annual.

3899. Writers' and Artists' Year Book. A directory for writers, artists, playwrights, writers for film, radio, and television, photographers and composers. London, Adam and Charles Black, 1902–date.

3900. Pitkin, Walter B. The Art and the Business of Story Writing. New York, Macmillan Co., 1912. xviii + 255 pp.

3901. Robinson, Mabel L. Juvenile Story Writing. New York, E. P. Dutton and Co., 1922. xv + 235 pp.

3902. Williams, Blanch C. A Handbook on Story Writing. Rev. and enl. ed. New York, Dodd, Mead and Co., 1930. xviii + 372 pp.—Original ed. 1917. "Bibliography," pp. 316–365.

3903. Marks, Percy. The Craft of Writing. New York, Harcourt, Brace and Co., 1932. viii + 231 pp.

3904. Woodford, Jack. Trial and Error. A dithyramb on the subject of writing and selling. New York, Carlyle House, 1933. xii + 13–298 pp.

3905. Mitchell, Edwin Valentine. The Art of Authorship. New York, Loring and Mussey, 1935. 128 pp.

3906. Weeks, Edward. This Trade of Writing. Boston, Little, Brown and Co., 1936. ix + 284 pp.

3907. Vestal, Stanley [pseud. William S. Campbell]. Writing Magazine Fiction. New York, Doubleday, Doran and Co., 1940. xii + 292 pp.—Bibliography, pp. 291–292.

3908. Vestal, Stanley [pseud. William S. Campbell]. Writing Non-Fiction. Boston, Writer Magazine, 1944. xiv + 321 pp.—Bibliography, pp. 314–316.

3909. Bailey, Robeson. Techniques in Article-Writing. New York, Appleton-Century-Crofts Inc., 1947. xi + 272 pp.

3910. Brickell, Herschel, ed. Writers on Writing. By the staff of the University of New Hampshire Writers' Conference. Garden City, N.Y., Doubleday and Co., 1949. x + 309 pp.—"Guide to Writers' Conferences," pp. 299–309.

3911. Cousins, Norman, ed. Writing for Love or Money. Thirty-five essays reprinted from The Saturday Review of Literature. New York, Longmans, Green and Co., 1949. ix + 278 pp.

3912. Harrison, W[illiam] R. Write for the Trade Journals. Boston, Writer Inc., [1949]. [xiii] + 183 pp.

3913. Vestal, Stanley [pseud. William S. Campbell]. Writing. Advice and devices. Garden City, N.Y., Doubleday, Doran and Co., 1950. xiii + 301 pp.—See also Vestal's *Professional Writing*, New York, Macmillan Co., 1938, vii + 338 pp.

3914. Garrison, Roger H. A Guide to Creative Writing. New York, Henry Holt and Co., 1951. xix + 221 pp.

3915. Munson, Gorham. The Writer's Workshop Companion. New York, Farrar, Straus and Young, 1951. x + 310 pp.

3916. Spring, Samuel. Risks and Rights in Publishing, Television, Radio, Motion Pictures, Advertising, and the Theater. New York, W. W. Norton and Co., 1952. xviii + 385 pp.

3917. Kearney, Paul W. Free-Lance Writing for a Living. New York, David McKay Co., 1953. vii +168 pp.

3918. Burack, Abraham S., ed. The Writer's Handbook. Boston, Writer Magazine, 1954. x + 650 pp.—Bibliography "Where to Sell," pp. 511–650.

3919. Nicholson, Margaret. A Manual of Copyright Practice for Writers, Publishers, and Agents. 2nd ed. New York, Oxford Univ. Press, 1956. x + 273 pp.—Original ed. 1945.

3920. Wincor, Richard. How to Secure Copyright. The law of literary property. 2nd ed. New York, Oceana Publications, 1957. 96 pp.—Number 21 in the Legal Almanac Series. Original ed. 1950.

3921. Gill, Robt. The Author Publisher Printer Complex. 3rd ed. Baltimore, Williams and Wilkins Co., 1958. xi + 134 pp.—Original ed. 1940; second ed. 1949. A discussion of how an author may remain on amicable terms with his publisher and printer.

3922. Farrar, Larston Dawn. Successful Writers and How They Work. London, Prentice-Hall, 1959. 285 pp.

3923. Jones, Ruth A., and Mathieu, Aron. Writer's Market. 17th ed. Cincinnati, Writer's Digest, 1959. 456 pp.—Original ed. 1930.

3924. McGraw, Eloise Jarvis. Techniques of Fiction Writing. Boston, Writer Inc., 1959. 209 pp.

3925. Niland, D'Arcy. Be Your Own Editor. Make your stories sell. New York, M. Barrows and Co., 1959. 128 pp.

3926. Writer. Boston, Mass., Writer Inc., 1887–date.—Monthly.

3927. Writer's Digest. Cincinnati, F. and W. Publ'ing Co., 1920–date.—Monthly.

CHAPTER XI

JOURNALISTIC ART, PERIODICAL AND NEWSPAPER BIBLIOGRAPHIES, AND PUBLICATION RIGHTS

[For lists of titles of periodicals and series publications of significance in the humanities see Chapter VI: Periodicals and Series.]

§161. PERIODICALS AND NEWSPAPERS: TITLE AND INFORMATION LISTS; PRESS DIRECTORIES

3931. Stephens, Ethel. American Popular Magazines. A bibliography. Boston, Boston Book Co., 1916. 32 pp.—Number 23 in the series Bulletin of Bibliography Pamphlets.

3932. Cannons, H[arry] G. T. Classified Guide to 1700 Annuals, Directories, Calendars, and Year Books. New York, H. W. Wilson Co., 1923. xxiv + 196 pp.

3933. Severance, Henry O. A Guide to the Current Periodicals and Serials of the United States and Canada. 5th ed. Ann Arbor, Mich., George Wahr, 1931. 432 pp.—Original ed. 1907.

3934. Stock, Leo F. A List of American Periodicals and Serial Publications in the Humanities and Social Sciences. Washington, D.C., American Council of Learned Societies, 1934. 130 pp.—Number 21 in the series Bulletins of the American Council of Learned Societies.

3935. Selected List of United States Newspapers Recommended for Preservation by the ALA Committee on Cooperative Microfilm Projects. Washington, D.C., Library of Congress, 1953. xvii + 92 (double column) pp.

3936. Brugghen, W van der. Library and Documentary Periodicals. Preliminary ed. The Hague, International Federation for Documentation, 1956. 36 pp.

3937. Die deutsche Presse 1956. Zeitungen und Zeitschriften. Berlin, Duncker und Humblot, 1956. 168 + 1026 pp.—Preparation by the Institut für Publizistik of the Freie Universität, Berlin.

3938. Farber, Evan Ira. Classified List of Periodicals for the College Library. 4th ed. Boston, F. W. Faxon Co., 1957. xi + 146 pp.—Number 86 in the Useful Reference Series. Original ed. 1934; second ed. 1938; third ed. 1946.

3939. MacMillan, Annabelle. American Journals in the Humanities. A guide to scope and editorial policy. PMLA, LXXII, 4, pt. 2 (Sept. 1957), 52–65.

3940. Byrd, Milton B., and Goldsmith, Arnold L. Publication Guide for Literary and Linguistic Scholars. Foreword by William R. Parker. Detroit, Mich., Wayne State Univ. Press, 1958. xiii + 149 pp.—Number 4 in the series Wayne State University Studies, Humanities.

3941. Deutsche Bibliographie. Zeitschriften 1945–1952. Bibliographie der in Deutschland erschienenden periodischen Veröffentlichungen sowie der deutschsprachigen Periodica Österreichs, der Schweiz, und anderer Länder. Vorwort von H. W. Eppelsheimer. Teil I: Systematisches Titelverzeichnis; Teil II: Register. Frankfurt a. M., Buchhandler-Vereinigung, 1954–58. 2 (continuously paged) vols., the first with double and the second with triple columns.

3942. Foreign Language Publications in the United States. Newspaper lists compiled February 1958. New York, Common Council for American Unity, 1958.—Unnumbered mimeographed leaves. Titles under 39 alphabetically arranged languages. Earlier ed. 1936.

3943. [Ulrich, Carolyn F.] Ulrich's Periodicals Directory. A classified guide to a selected list of current periodicals, foreign and domestic. Ninth ed. edited by Eileen C. Graves. New York, R. R. Bowker Co., 1959. xvi + 716 (double column) + 717–825 (chiefly triple column) pp.—Original ed. 1932, second ed. 1935, third ed. 1938, fourth ed. 1943, and fifth ed. 1947 by Carolyn F. Ulrich; sixth ed. 1951, seventh ed. 1953, and eighth ed. 1956 by Eileen C. Graves. The 4th ed. was an "Inter-American" one, covering North, Central, and South America. The 5th ed. included a list of clandestine periodical titles of World War II compiled by Adrienne F. Muzzy.

[For further titles dealing with publishers see §160. The Professional Writer.]

3948. American Book Trade Directory. Lists of publishers, booksellers, periodicals, trade organizations, book clubs, auctioneers, etc. New York, R. R. Bowker Co., 1915–date.—One issue every three years.

3949. Annuaire de la presse française et étrangère et du monde politique. Paris, Annuaire de la Presse, 1878–date.—Annual.

3950. [Ayer's Directory.] N. W. Ayer and Son's Directory of Newspapers and Periodicals. (Continuing American Newspaper Annual and Directory.) A guide to publications printed in the United States and its possessions, the Dominion of Canada, Bermuda, the Republics of Panama and the Philippines. . . . Philadelphia, N. W. Ayer and Son, 1880–date.—Annual.

3951. Catholic Press Directory. Official media reference guide to Catholic newspapers and magazines of the United States and Canada. New York, Catholic Press Association, 1923–date.—Annual.

3952. Gebbie Press House Magazine Directory. A public relations and free-lance guide to the nation's leading house magazines. New York, Gebbie Press, 1952–date.—Three-year issues. A guide to American house organs.

3953. Newspaper Press Directory and Advertiser's Guide. London, Benn Bros., 1846–date.—Annual. A newspaper and periodicals directory.

3954. Sperlings Zeitschriften- und Zeitungsaddressbuch. Leipzig, Börsenverein der Deutschen Buchhändler, 1859–date.—Annual.

3955. Willing's Press Guide. A comprehensive index and handbook of the press of the United Kingdom of Great Britain, Northern Ireland and the Irish Republic, together with the principal British Commonwealth, Dominion, Colonial, and foreign publications. London, Willing's Press Service Ltd., 1873–date.—Annual.

§162. PERIODICALS AND NEWSPAPERS: UNION LISTS; COLLECTION LISTS OF INSTITUTIONS; PERIOD LISTS

3960. Births and Deaths in the Periodical World. In Bulletin of Bibliography. Boston, F. W. Faxon Co., 1897–date.

3961. New Serial Titles. Washington, D.C., Library of Congress, 1953–date. —Monthly with annual cumulation. A development of *Serial Titles Newly Received* 1951–52.

3962. Griffin, A[ppleton] P. C. A Union List of Periodicals, Transactions, and Allied Publications Currently Received in the Principal Libraries of the District of Columbia. Washington, D.C., Library of Congress, 1901. v + 315 pp.

3963. Diesch, Carl. Bibliographie der germanistischen Zeitschriften. Leipzig, Verlag von Karl W. Hiersemann, 1927. xv + 441 (chiefly double column) pp.—Volume I in the series Bibliographical Publications: Germanic Section, Modern Language Association of America.

3964. Gesamt-Zeitschriften-Verzeichnis. Herausgegeben vom Auskunftsbureau der deutschen Bibliotheken. Berlin, Königliche Bibliothek, 1914. xviii + 355 pp.—Also *Gesamtverzeichnis der ausländischen Zeitschriften 1914–1924,* Berlin, Preussische Staatsbibliothek, 1929, xxiv + 785 pp. Together, the "GZV" and the "GAZ" make up Germany's union list of serials.

3965. Gregory, Winifred. American Newspapers 1821–1936. A union list of files available in the United States and Canada. New York, H. W. Wilson Co., 1937. [vi] + 791 (triple column) pp.

3966. Union Catalogue of the Periodical Publications in the University Libraries of the British Isles with Their Respective Holdings Excluding Titles in the World List of Scientific Periodicals. Edited by Marion G. Roupell. London, National Central Library, 1937. xii + 712 pp.

3967. McCoy, Helen. Union List of Serials of the San Francisco Bay Region. Compiled by the Special Libraries Association, San Francisco Bay Region Chapter. Stanford Univ. Press, 1939. 283 pp.

3968. Union List of Periodicals in Libraries of Southern California. 3rd ed. rev. and enl. Los Angeles, Public Library, 1941. viii + 582 pp.

3969. Postwar Foreign Newspapers. A union list. Washington, D.C., Library of Congress Reference Department, 1953. vi + 231 pp.—A finding list of foreign newspapers in the libraries of the U.S.

3970. Union List of Serials in Libraries of the United States and Canada. Second ed., edited by Winifred Gregory. New York, H. W. Wilson Co., 1943. [viii] + 3065 (triple column) pp.—Original ed. 1927 listed serials to 1924 and its supplements 1931 and 1933 brought coverage to 1932. Also *Union List of Serials . . .* [2nd ed.], Supplement January 1941–December 1943, edited by Gabrielle E. Malikoff, New York, H. W. Wilson Co., 1945, [*c.* xviii] + 1123 (double column) pp. Also

Union List of Serials . . . [2nd ed.], Second supplement January 1944–December 1949, edited by Marga Franck, New York, H. W. Wilson Co., 1953, [cxx] + 1365 (double column) pp. A third ed. of the *Union List of Serials* is to appear sometime in 1961; presumably it will be the final edition, since the monthly cumulative *New Serial Titles* will carry on from 1950. Abbr.: "ULS."

3971. Homer, Thos. J. A Guide to Serial Publications in the Libraries of Boston, Cambridge, and Vicinity. Boston, published by the cooperating committee, 1922–56. 779 pp.—Part VII: Ret–Z (xii + 613–779 pp.) compiled by Edith L. Shufelt.

3972. Union List of Little Magazines. Showing holdings of little magazines in the libraries of Indiana University, Northwestern University, Ohio State University, State University of Iowa, University of Chicago, and University of Illinois. Chicago, Midwest Inter-Library Center, 1956. 98 pp.

3973. British Union-Catalogue of Periodicals. A record of the periodicals of the world from the seventeenth century to the present day in British libraries. Edited by James D. Stewart, Muriel E. Hammond, and Erwin Saenger. London, Butterworths Scientific Publications, 1955–58. 4 (double column page) vols.—Abbr.: "BUCP."

3974. London Union List of Periodicals. Holdings of the municipal and county libraries of Greater London. Second ed., edited by Owen W. Keen and Kathleen Hancock. London, Library Association, 1958. [xvi] + 221 (double column) pp.—Original ed. 1951.

3975. New Serial Titles. A union list of serials commencing publication after December 31, 1949. Prepared under the sponsorship of the joint committee on the Union List of Serials. First series: 1955 cumulation. Preface by Andrew D. Osborn and L. Quincy Mumford. Washington, D.C., Library of Congress, 1956. [vii] + 667 (triple column) pp.—Also *New Serial Titles* . . . , Second series: 1958 cumulation, Washington, D.C., Library of Congress, 1959, vii + 1275 (triple column) pp.

3976. Schwegmann, Geo. A., Jr. Newspapers on Microfilms. A union checklist. 3rd ed. Washington, D.C., Library of Congress, 1957. viii + 202 (quadruple column) pp.—Original ed. 1949; second ed. 1953. Also Schwegmann's *Supplement I*, Washington, D.C., Library of Congress, 1959, iv + 37 (quadruple column) pp.

3980. Catalogue of Periodicals Contained in the Bodleian Library. Oxford Univ. Press, 1878. 2 vols.—Also *Current Foreign and Colonial Periodicals in the Bodleian and Other Oxford Libraries*, Oxford, Clarendon Press, 1925, iv + 135 pp.

3981. British Museum. Department of Printed Books. Catalogue of the Printed Books in the Library: Academies. London, W. Clowes and Sons, 1882. 1018 + 99 pp.

3982. British Museum. Department of Printed Books. Catalogue of Printed Books in the Library: Periodical Publications. Rev. ed. London, W. Clowes and Sons, 1899–1900. 6 parts and an index (1716 pp.).—Original ed. 1885–86. Inclusion of newspapers and society and institution publications only up to 1800. About 2500 titles. Volume XLI of the *British Museum Catalogue of Printed Books*, Ann Arbor reprint.

3983. Check List of American Newspapers in the Library of Congress. Compiled under the direction of A. B. Slauson. Washington, D.C., Library of Congress, 1901. 292 leaves.

3984. British Museum. Department of Printed Books. Catalogue of Printed Books. Supplement: Newspapers published in Great Britain and Ireland 1801–1900. London, W. Clowes and Sons, 1905. 532 columns.—Coverage of about 75000 titles arranged by place with title index.

3985. Catalogue of the Periodical Publications in the Library of the Royal Society of London. Oxford Univ. Press for the Royal Society, 1912. viii + 455 pp.

3986. List of Newspapers in the Yale University Library. New Haven, Yale Univ. Press, 1916. viii + 217 pp.—A world list.

3987. Parsons, Henry S. Check List of Foreign Newspapers in the Library of Congress. Washington, D.C., Library of Congress, 1929. v + 209 (double column) pp.

3988. Newspapers in Libraries of Chicago. A joint check list. University of Chicago Libraries, 1936. iv + 258 pp.

3989. Current Periodicals Available in the University Library and in Other Libraries Connected with the University. Cambridge, Eng., University Library, 1956. vii + 415 pp.

3993. Ford, Paul L. Check-List of American Magazines Printed in the Eighteenth Century. Brooklyn, published by the author, 1889. 12 numbered leaves.

3994. Ayer, Mary F. Check-List of Boston Newspapers 1704–1780 . . . with bibliographical notes by Albert Matthews. Boston, Colonial Society of Massachusetts, 1907. xvii + 527 pp.—Volume IX in the series Publications of the Colonial Society of Massachusetts.

3995. [Muddiman, Joseph George.] Tercentenary Handlist of English and Welsh Newspapers, Magazines, and Reviews [1620–1920]. Section I: London and Suburban; Section II: Provincial. London, The Times,

1920. 212 (double column) pp. + l pp. + 215–324 (double column) pp. + xxxv pp.—Additions and corrections Roland Austin, *Notes and Queries*, Twelfth Series, VIII (1921) and X (1922).

3996. Beer, Wm. Checklist of American Periodicals 1741–1800. Worcester, Mass., American Antiquarian Society, 1923. 18 pp.

3997. Crane, R[onald] S., and Kaye, F[rederick] B. A Census of British Newspapers and Periodicals 1620–1800. Chapel Hill, University of North Carolina Press, 1927. 205 pp.

3998. Gabler, Anthony J. Check List of English Newspapers and Periodicals . . . before 1800 in the Huntington Library [San Marino, Calif.]. Huntington Library Bulletin, No. 2 (1931), 1–66.

3999. Wallace, Wm. S. A Bibliography of Canadian Literary Periodicals 1789–1900. Edited by Dorothea D. Tod and Audrey Cordingley. Proceedings and Transactions of the Royal Society of Canada, Third Series, XXVI, 2 (1932), 87–96.

4000. Ingram, John Van N. A Check List of American Eighteenth Century Newspapers in the Library of Congress. New ed., rev. and enl. under the direction of Henry S. Parsons. Washington, D.C., Government Printing Office, 1936. vi + 401 pp.—Original ed. 1912.

4001. Milford, R[obert] T., and Sutherland, D[onald] M. A Catalogue of English Newspapers and Periodicals in the Bodleian Library 1622–1800. Oxford, Bibliographical Society, 1936. 184 pp.—Also in the Oxford Bibliographical Society Proceedings and Papers, Oxford 1936, IV, 2 (1935), 163–346.

4002. Wescott, Mary, and Ramage, Allene. A Checklist of United States Newspapers and Weeklies before 1900 in the General Library [of Duke University]. Durham, N.C., Duke University, 1932–37. 6 parts.—In the series Bibliographical Contributions of the Duke University Libraries.

4003. Collins, Douglas Cecil. A Handlist of News Pamphlets 1590–1610. London, South-West Essex Technical College, 1943. 129 pp.

4004. Brigham, Clarence S. History and Bibliography of American Newspapers 1690–1820. Worcester, Mass., American Antiquarian Society, 1947. 2 vols. (1508 pp.)

4005. Stewart, Powell. British Newspapers and Periodicals 1632–1800. A descriptive catalogue of a collection at the University of Texas. Austin, University of Texas, 1950. 172 pp.

4006. Dahl, Folke. A Bibliography of English Corantos and Periodical Newsbooks 1620–1642. London, Bibliographical Society, 1952. 283 pp.—See also Dahl's "Short Title Catalogue of English Corantos and Newsbooks," *The Library*, New Series, XIX (June 1938), 44–98. Locations indicated.

4007. Cranfield, Geoffrey A. A Handlist of English Provincial Newspapers and Periodicals 1700–1760. Cambridge, Bowes and Bowes, 1952. viii + 31 pp.—Number 2 in the series Cambridge Bibliographical Society Monographs. Locations indicated. Supplements in *Transactions of the Cambridge Bibliographical Society*, II, 3 (1956), 269–274, and 5 (1959), 385–389.

4008. Ward, Wm. S. Index and Finding List of Serials Published in the British Isles 1789–1832. Lexington, University of Kentucky Press, 1953. xv + 180 (double column) pp.—"Selected Bibliography," pp. 177–180.

§163. PERIODICALS AND NEWSPAPERS: OLDER INDEXES

4012. Coöperative Index to Periodicals. New York, American Library Association, 1884–92. 9 vols.—Actual coverage 1883–91.

4013. Cotgreave, A[lfred]. A Contents-Subject Index to General and Periodical Literature. London, E. Stock, 1900. xii + 743 pp.

4014. Index to the Periodicals. London, Review of Reviews, 1891–1903. 13 vols. in 10.

4015. Annual Literary Index. Including periodicals, American and English, essays, book-chapters, etc., with author index, bibliographies, necrology, and index to dates of principal events. New York, Publishers' Weekly, 1893–1905. 13 vols.—Actual coverage 1892–1904.

4016. Library Index to Periodicals and Current Events. New York, R. R. Bowker, 1905–07. 3 vols.

4017. New York Daily Tribune Index. New York, Tribune Association, 1876–1907. 31 vols.—Actual coverage 1875–1906.

4018. Poole, Wm. Frederick, and Fletcher, Wm. I. Index to Periodical Literature 1802–1881. Third ed. brought down to Jan. 1882. Part I: A–J; Part II: K–Z. Boston, Osgood and Co., 1882. xxvii + 1442 (double column) pp. bound in two parts.—Original ed. 1848; second ed. 1853; third ed. reprinted 1891. Also *Supplement 1882–1887*, by W. F. Poole and W. I. Fletcher; *Supplement 1887–1892*, by W. I. Fletcher; *Supplement 1892–1896*, by W. I. Fletcher and F. O. Poole; *Supplement 1897–1902*, by W. I. Fletcher and Mary Poole; *Supplement 1902–1907*, by W. I. Fletcher and Mary Poole. Reprint of main volumes and supplements New York, Peter Smith, 1938 and 1958. Also Thorwald Solberg, "Authors of Anonymous Articles in Poole," *Bulletin of Bibliography*, I, 6 (July 1898), 91–93. Also Marion V. Bell and Jean C. Bacon, *Poole's Index*, Date and volume key, Chicago, Association of College and Reference Libraries, 1957, 61 pp.

4019. Annual Library Index. Including periodicals, American and English, essays, book-chapters, etc. . . . New York, Publishers' Weekly, 1906–11. 6 vols.—Actual coverage 1905–11.

4020. [Palmer, Samuel.] Palmer's Index to the Times Newspaper. Corsham, Wiltshire, Eng., Samuel Palmer, 1868–1943. —Actual coverage 1790 to 1941 in quarterly vols.

4021. Nineteenth Century Readers' Guide to Periodical Literature 1890–1899. With supplement indexing 1900–1922. Edited by Helen Grant Cushing and Adah V. Morris. New York, H. W. Wilson Co., 1944. 2 (double column page) vols.

4022. Annual Magazine Subject Index [and (since 1910)] Drama Index. A subject index to American and English periodicals. Boston, F. W. Faxon Co., 1907–1952. 43 vols.

§164. PERIODICALS AND NEWSPAPERS: CURRENT INDEXES

4026. Godet, Marcel, and Vorstius, Joris. Index Bibliographicus. Weltliste laufender bibliographischer Zeitschriften. Zweite, neubearbeitete und stark vermehrte Auflage. Auf Grund der Bestände der Staatsbibliothek in Berlin und der Einsendungen von 37 Ländern. Berlin, Walther de Gruyter und Co., 1931. xxiii + 420 pp.—A development of Marcel Godet, *Index Bibliographicus*, International catalogue of sources of current bibliographical information, Geneva, League of Nations Committee on Intellectual Cooperation, 1925, xvi + 233 pp. Concentration on bibliographies in serial publications.

4027. Haskell, Daniel C. A Check-List of Cumulative Indexes to Individual Periodicals in the New York Public Library. New York, New York Public Library, 1942. 370 pp.

4028. Ireland, Norma O. An Index to Indexes. A subject bibliography of published indexes. Boston, F. W. Faxon Co., 1942. xvi + 107 pp.—Number 67 in the Useful Reference Series. An index to the indexes of periodicals, documents, and significant books.

4032. Clark, Alvan Witcombe. Checklist of Indexed Periodicals. New York, H. W. Wilson Co., 1917. 59 (double column) pp.—A list of periodicals and the abbreviations of the serial publications in which they are indexed.

4036. Art Index. A cumulative subject and author index to fine arts periodicals and museum bulletins covering archaeology, architecture, arts and crafts, ceramics, decorations and ornament, graphic arts, industrial design, interior decoration, landscape architecture, painting, sculpture. New York, H. W. Wilson Co., 1930–date.—Quarterly with annual and two-year cumulation.

4037. Bibliographic Index. New York, H. W. Wilson Co., 1938–date.—Two issues a year with annual cumulation.

4038. Canadian Index to Periodicals and Documentary Films. Ottawa, Canadian Library Association, 1948–date.—Monthly with six-month cumulation. Entries in French and English.

4039. Catholic Periodical Index. A cumulative author and subject index to a selected list of Catholic periodicals. Washington, D.C., Catholic Library Association, 1930–date.—Quarterly with annual and four-year cumulation.

4040. Education Index. New York, H. W. Wilson Co., 1932–date.—Monthly except June and August with annual and two-year cumulation. An index to books, monographs, and bulletins as well as to periodicals.

4041. Essay and General Literature Index. New York, H. W. Wilson Co., 1934–date.—Two issues a year with annual and five-year cumulation. An author and subject index with occasional titles to essays and composite works. Individual cumulations for 1900–33, 1934–40, 1941–47, and 1948–54.

4042. Index to Little Magazines. Denver, Col., Alan Swallow, 1948–date.—Annual 1948–52; three-year cumulation 1953–55; two-year cumulation 1956–57.

4043. Internationale Bibliographie der Zeitschriftenliteratur. Abteilung A: Bibliographie der deutschen Zeitschriftenliteratur mit Einschluss von Sammelwerken. Osnabrück, Verlag Felix Dietrich, 1896–date.—Six-month issues with no cumulation. An alphabetical subject index with six-month author index now covering about 3600 German language periodicals and 45 newspapers. Called "Dietrich" or "IBZ." The most extensive of all periodical indexes.

4044. Internationale Bibliographie der Zeitschriftenliteratur. Abteilung B: Bibliographie der fremdsprachigen Zeitschriftenliteratur. Osnabrück, Verlag Felix Dietrich, 1911–date.—Six-month issues with no cumulation. An alphabetical and since 1925 author index to periodicals in non-German languages now covering about 3200 titles from 30 countries in 20 languages. *Abteilung C:* Bibliographie der Rezensionen und Referate, 1900–43, 77 vols., indexed to 1911 only German reviews, but to 1943 indexed also reviews published in non-German languages.

4045. International Index to Periodicals. New York, H. W. Wilson Co., 1907–date.—Quarterly with annual and three-year cumulation.

4046. New York Times Index. New York, New York Times Co., 1913–date.—From 1913 to 1929 quarterly; from 1930 to 1947 monthly; from 1948 to date two issues a month; from 1930 annual cumulation. Available on microfilm is an earlier index issued in columnar form covering 1851–58, 1860, and 1863–1905.

4047. Official Index to the [London] Times. London, The Times, 1906–date. —Six issues a year. Monthly with annual cumulation to 1914; quarterly 1914–56.

4048. Readers' Guide to Periodical Literature. New York, H. W. Wilson Co., 1900–date.—Monthly to 1935; now two issues a month except July–August; annual and two-year cumulation. An author and subject index to over one hundred magazines. There is also an *Abridged Readers' Guide* which indexes around thirty-five magazines.

4049. Subject Index to Periodicals. London, Library Association, 1915–date. —Annual. Original title *Athenaeum Subject Index to Periodicals.*

4050. Vertical File Index. A subject and title index to selected pamphlet material. New York, H. W. Wilson Co., 1934–date.—Monthly September through July with annual cumulation.

4051. United Nations Documents Index. United Nations specialized agencies documents and publications. New York, United Nations, 1950–date.—Monthly.

§165. PERIODICALS AND NEWSPAPERS: HISTORIES AND STUDIES

[See also §36. Minor Prose: The Essay and Personal Letter.]

4054. Ditzion, Sidney. The History of Periodical Literature in the United States. A bibliography. Bulletin of Bibliography, XV, 6 (Jan.–April 1935), 110, and 7 (May–August 1935), 129–133.

4055. Ford, Edwin H. History of Journalism in the United States. A bibliography of books and annotated articles. Minneapolis, Burgess Publ'ing Co., 1938. 42 mimeographed pp.

4056. Weed, Katherine K., and Bond, Richmond P. Studies of British Newspapers and Periodicals from Their Beginnings to 1800. A bibliography. Chapel Hill, University of North Carolina, 1946. vi + 233 pp.—Number 2 in the series Studies in Philology: Extra Series.

4057. Andrews, Alexander. The History of British Journalism from the Foundation of the Newspaper Press in England to the Repeal of the Stamp Act in 1855. With sketches of press celebrities. London, R. Bentley, 1859. 2 vols.

4058. Madden, Richard Robt. The History of Irish Periodical Literature from the End of the Seventeenth to the Middle of the Nineteenth Century. London, T. C. Newby, 1867. 2 vols.

4059. Grant, James. The Newspaper Press. Its origin, progress, and present condition. London, Tinsley Bros., 1871–72. 3 vols.

4060. Hudson, Frederic. Journalism in the United States from 1690 to 1872. New York, Harper, 1873. xlviii + 789 pp.

4061. Bourne, H[enry] R. Fox. English Newspapers. Chapters in the history of journalism. London, Chatto and Windus, 1887. 2 vols.

4062. Williams, J. B. [pseud. of Joseph G. Muddiman]. A History of English Journalism from the Foundation of the Gazette. London, Longmans, Green and Co., 1908. 293 pp.

4063. Tassin, Algernon de V. The Magazine in America. New York, Dodd, Mead and Co., 1916. 374 pp.

4064. Lee, James M. History of American Journalism. Boston, Houghton Mifflin Co., 1917. x + 462 pp.

4065. Payne, Geo. History of Journalism in the United States. New York, D. Appleton and Co., 1920. xx + 453 pp.

4066. Salmon, Lucy Maynard. The Newspaper and the Historian. New York, Oxford Univ. Press, 1923. xliii + 566 pp.

4067. Graham, Walter. The Beginnings of English Literary Periodicals. A study of periodical literature 1665–1715. New York, Oxford Univ. Press, 1926. viii + 92 pp.

4068. Bleyer, Willard Grosvenor. Main Currents in the History of American Journalism. Boston, Houghton Mifflin Co., 1927. x + 464 pp.—"Readings in the History of Journalism," pp. 431–441.

4069. Shaaber, Matthias A. Some Forerunners of the Newspaper in England 1476–1622. Philadelphia, University of Pennsylvania, 1929. xi + 368 pp.

4070. Graham, Walter. English Literary Periodicals. New York, Thomas Nelson and Sons, 1930. 424 pp.—"Bibliography," pp. 394–402. Coverage of the eighteenth century.

4071. Gohdes, Clarence. The Periodicals of American Transcendentalism. Durham, N.C., Duke Univ. Press, 1931. vii + 264 pp.

4072. Richardson, Lyon N. A History of American Magazines 1741–1789. New York, Thomas Nelson and Sons, 1931. xi + 414 pp.

4073. Morison, Stanley. The English Newspaper. Some account of the physical development of journals printed in London between 1622 and the present day. New York, Macmillan Co., 1932. xii + 335 pp.

4074. Stutterheim, Kurt von. The Press in England. Translated by W. J. Johnston. London, George Allen and Unwin, 1934. 222 pp.—Original Ger. ed. 1933.

4075. Lee, Alfred M. The Daily Newspaper in America. New York, Macmillan Co., 1937. xiv + 765 pp.

4076. Carlson, C[arl] Lennart. The First Magazine. A history of the Gentleman's Magazine with an account of Dr. Johnson's editorial activity and of the notice given America in the magazine. Providence, R.I., Brown University, 1938. ix + 281 pp.—Bibliography, pp. 266–271.

4077. Mott, Frank L. American Journalism. A history of newspapers in the United States through 250 years 1690–1940. New York, Macmillan Co., 1941. x + 772 pp.—Reprint 1950.

4078. Hoffman, Frederick J., Allen, Chas., and Ulrich, Carolyn F. The Little Magazine. A history and a bibliography. Princeton, N.J., University Press, 1946. xiii + 440 pp.—"Bibliography," pp. 233–398. "A little magazine is a magazine designed to print artistic work which for reasons of commercial expediency is not acceptable to the money-minded periodicals or presses," p. 2.—For the titles of some little magazines, see §82. Humanistic Periodicals, §83. Belletristic Periodicals, and §84. Reviews.

4079. Jones, Robert W. Journalism in the United States. New York, E. P. Dutton and Co., 1947. xvi + 13–728 pp.—"Bibliography," pp. 705–716.

4080. The History of The Times. London, The Times, 1935–52. 4 vols. in 5. —Coverage 1785–1948.

4081. Varley, Frederick John, ed. Mercurius Aulicus. . . . The earliest regular English newspaper . . . 1643–1645. Oxford, Eng., Basil Blackwell, 1948. xiv + 108 pp.

4082. Brigham, Clarence S. Journals and Journeymen. A contribution to the history of early American newspapers. Philadelphia, University of Pennsylvania Press, 1950. xiv + 114 pp.—In the series Publications of the A. S. W. Rosenbach Fellowship in Bibliography.

4083. Berger, Meyer. The Story of the New York Times 1851–1951. New York, Simon and Schuster, 1951. xiv + 589 pp.

4084. Stewart, Kenneth, and Tebbel, John. Makers of Modern Journalism. New York, Prentice-Hall, 1952. 514 pp.—In the Prentice-Hall Journalism Series.

4085. Ewald, Wm. Bragg, Jr. The Newsmen of Queen Anne. Oxford, Eng., Basil Blackwell, 1956. xi + 243 pp.—"Descriptive List of Periodicals," pp. 219–236. American ed. title *Rogues, Royalty, and Reporters*, The age of Queen Anne through its newspapers, a collection of news items 1688–1714.

4086. Peterson, Theodore. Magazines in the Twentieth Century. Urbana, University of Illinois Press, 1956. xi + 457 pp.—"Bibliography," pp. 397–411.

4087. Watson, Melvin R. Magazine Serials and the Essay Tradition 1746–1820. Baton Rouge, Louisiana State Univ. Press, 1956. ix + 160 pp.—Number 6 in the Louisiana State University Studies Humanity Series. "Register of Essay Serials," pp. 107–151; "Checklist of Magazines Containing Essay Serials," pp. 152–155.

4088. Bond, Richmond P., ed. Studies in the Early English Periodical. Chapel Hill, University of North Carolina Press, 1957. [ix] + 206 pp.

4089. Mott, Frank L. A History of American Magazines. Vol. I: 1741–1850; Vol. II: 1850–1865; Vol. III: 1865–1885; Vol. IV: 1885–1905. Cambridge, Mass., Harvard Univ. Press, 1930–57. 4 vols.—Volume I 1930; volumes II and III 1938; volume IV 1957.

§166. THE ART AND PRACTICE OF JOURNALISM

[For the bases of prose composition see Chapter X: Methods, Style, and Basic Texts for Research and Writing *passim*; for free lance writing see §160. The Professional Writer.]

4093. Cannon, Carl L. Journalism. A bibliography. New York Public Library, 1924. vi + 360 pp.

4094. Desmond, Robert W. Newspaper Reference Methods. Foreword by John H. Finley. Minneapolis, University of Minnesota Press, 1933. xv + 229 pp.—"List of Books and Periodicals Valuable for Newspaper Libraries," pp. 139–196; "Bibliography on Newspaper Reference Libraries," pp. 207–221.

4095. Ford, Edwin H. A Bibliography of Literary Journalism in America. Minneapolis, Burgess Publ'ing Co., 1937. 68 numbered leaves.

4096. Nafziger, Ralph O. International News and the Press. Communications, organization of news-gathering, international affairs, and the foreign press. An annotated bibliography. New York, H. W. Wilson Co., 1940. xxix + 193 (double column) pp.

4097. Wolseley, Roland E. The Journalist's Bookshelf. An annotated and selected bibliography of United States journalism. 6th ed. Chicago, Quill and Scroll Foundation, 1955. 212 pp.—Original ed. 1939.

4098. Price, Warren C. The Literature of Journalism. An annotated bibliography. Oxford Univ. Press, 1959. xviii + 489 pp.

4099. Yost, Casper S. The Principles of Journalism. New York, D. Appleton and Co., 1924. ix + 170 pp.—A treatment *inter alia* of the Canons of Journalism of the American Society of Newspaper Editors.

4100. Olson, Kenneth E. Typography and Mechanics of the Newspaper. New York. D. Appleton and Co., 1930. xvi + 441 pp.

4101. Allen, John E. Newspaper Makeup. New York, Harper and Bros., 1936. x + 483 pp.—See also Allen's *The Modern Newspaper*, New York, Harper and Bros., 1940, ix + 234 pp. Emphasis in both works on typography.

4102. MacDougall, Curtis D. Covering the Courts. New York, Prentice-Hall, 1946. xvi + 713 pp.

4103. Allen, John E. Newspaper Designing. New York, Harper and Bros., 1947. x + 478 pp.

4104. Sutton, Albert A. Design and Makeup of the Newspaper. New York, Prentice-Hall, 1948. xiv + 483 pp.—Bibliography, pp. 468–470.

4105. Barnhart, Thos. F. Weekly Newspaper Makeup and Typography. Minneapolis, University of Minnesota Press, 1949. ix + 267 pp.

4106. Bush, Chilton R. Newspaper Reporting of Public Affairs. 3rd ed. New York, Appleton-Century-Crofts, 1951. xvi + 346 pp.—Original ed. 1929; second ed. 1940. Bibliography, pp. 339–340.

4107. Warren, Carl N. Modern News Reporting. Rev. ed. New York, Harper and Bros., 1951. xix + 498 pp.—Original ed. 1944.

4108. Brown, Chas. H. News Editing and Display. New York, Harper and Bros., 1952. 457 pp.

4109. Raus, Geoffrey. English Literary Magazines. Hudson Review, V (Spring 1952), 111–116.

4110. Bentley, Garth. Editing the Company Publication. Rev. ed. New York, Harper and Bros., 1953. 242 pp.—Original ed. 1944.

4111. Winkler, G P. Associated Press Style Book. New York, Associated Press, 1953. 64 pp.

4112. Bush, Chilton R. The Art of News Communication. A beginning textbook for classes in news writing. New York, Appleton-Century-Crofts, 1954. 246 pp.

4113. Facts of Journal Publishing. PMLA, LXIX, 5 (Dec. 1954), viii–ix.—A brief treatment of the limited distribution of the scholarly journal. See also "Facts of Journal Publishing II," *PMLA*, LXXII, 4, pt. 2 (Sept. 1957), vii–ix.

4114. Rucker, Frank W., and Williams, Herbert Lee. Newspaper Organization and Management. Ames, Iowa State College Press, 1955. 547 pp.

4115. Waldrop, Arthur G. Editor and Editorial Writer. Rev. ed. New York, Rinehart and Co., 1955. 511 pp.—Original ed. 1949.

4116. Wolseley, Roland E., ed. Writing for the Religious Market. New York, Association Press, 1956. 304 pp.

4117. Wyckoff, Edith Hay. Editing and Producing the Small Publication. Princeton, N.J., Van Nostrand, 1956. 289 pp.

4118. Heath, H[arry] E., and Gelfand, Lou. How to Cover, Write, and Edit Sports. Rev. ed. Ames, Iowa State College Press, 1957. 536 pp.—Original ed. 1951.

4119. Berry, T[homas] E. Journalism Today. Its development and practical applications. Philadelphia, Chilton Co., 1958. 501 pp.

4120. Ferguson, Rowena. Editing the Small Magazine. New York, Columbia Univ. Press, 1958. 271 pp.

4121. Mott, Geo. Fox, ed. New Survey of Journalism. With a foreword by Grant Milnor Hyde. 4th ed. New York, Barnes and Noble Inc., 1958. xxvii + 446 pp.—Number 15 in the College Outline Series. Copyrights 1937, 1940, 1950, 1953, 1957. Bibliographies, pp. 419–433.

4122. Sanderson, Arthur M. Iowa Newspaper Desk Book. 10th ed. Iowa City, State Univ. of Iowa, 1959. 40 pp.—Number 750 in the series State University of Iowa Bulletins. Original ed. 1917.

§167. CENSORSHIP AND THE LAW

[For works dealing with the laws of copyright see §160. The Professional Writer *passim.*]

4126. Reusch, Fr[anz] Heinrich. Der Index der verbotenen Bücher. Ein Beitrag zur Kirchen- und Literaturgeschichte. Bonn, Verlag von Max Cohen und Sohn, 1883–85. 2 vols. (Vol. I: 624 pp.; vol. II: 1266 pp.)

4127. Putnam, Geo. Haven. The Censorship of the Church of Rome and Its Influence upon the Production and Distribution of Literature. A study of the history of the prohibitory and expurgatory indexes, together with some consideration of the effects of Protestant censorship and of censorship by the state. New York, G. P. Putnam's Sons, 1906–07. 2 vols.

4128. Ernst, Morris L., and Seagle, Wm. To the Pure. A study of obscenity and the censor. New York, Viking Press, 1928. xv + 336 pp.—"Bibliography," pp. 311–321.

4129. Houben, H[einrich] H. Verbotene Literatur. Von der klassischen Zeit bis zur Gegenwart. Ein kritisch-historisches Lexikon über verbotene Bücher, Zeitschriften und Theaterstücke, Schriftsteller und Verleger. Berlin, Ernst Rowohlt Verlag, 1924–28. 2 vols.—A treatment chiefly of German works.

4130. Gillett, Chas. Ripley. Burned Books. Neglected chapters in British history and literature. New York, Columbia Univ. Press, 1932. 2 vols.—"List of Burned Books," pp. 665–682; "Books Cited or Mentioned," pp. 683–702, both lists being in vol. II.

4131. Clyde, Wm. M. The Struggle for the Freedom of the Press from Caxton to Cromwell. London, Oxford Univ. Press for St. Andrews University, 1934. xvi + 360 pp.

4132. Seldes, Geo. Freedom of the Press. Indianapolis, Bobbs-Merrill Co., [1935]. xv + 19–380 pp.—Bibliography, pp. 377–378. See also Seldes's *Lords of the Press,* New York, J. Messner Inc., [1938], viii + 408 pp.

4133. Craig, Alec. The Banned Books of England. With a foreword by E. M. Forster. London, George Allen and Unwin Ltd., 1937. 207 pp.—"Bibliography," pp. 187–195.

4134. Arthur, Wm. R., and Crosman, Ralph L. The Law of Newspapers. A text and case book for use in schools of journalism and a deskbook for newspaper workers. 2nd ed. New York, McGraw-Hill Book Co., 1940. xxxv + 615 pp.—Original ed. 1928.

4135. Betten, Francis S., S.J. The Roman Index of Forbidden Books Briefly Explained. 3rd ed. Chicago, Loyola Univ. Press, 1940. 48 pp.—Original ed. 1925; second ed. 1932.

4136. Craig, Alec. Above All Liberties. London, George Allen and Unwin Ltd., 1942. 205 pp.—"Bibliography," pp. 191–195.

4137. Ould, Hermon, ed. Freedom of Expression. A symposium based on the conference called by the London Centre of the International P.E.N. to commemorate the tercentenary of the publication of Milton's Areopagitica: 22–26th August 1944. London, Hutchinson International Authors Ltd., 1944. 184 pp.

4138. Williams, Francis. Press, Parliament, and People. London, William Heinemann Ltd., 1946. [v] + 254 pp.

4139. Hocking, Wm. Ernest. Freedom of the Press. A framework of principle. A report from the Commission on Freedom of the Press. University of Chicago Press, 1947. xi + 243 pp.

4140. Gerald, J[ames] Edward. The Press and the Constitution 1931–1947. Minneapolis, University of Minnesota Press, 1948. ix + 173 pp.—"A Selected Bibliography," pp. 166–169.

4141. Iversen, Max. Forbudte Bøger. To aarhundreders beslaglagte og konfiskerede vaerker. En annoteret bibliografi. Unter medvirken af bibliotekar Åse Henriksen. Copenhagen, Kirschbaum-Jørgensen Forlag, 1948. 199 pp.—A general European title list of censored works.

4142. Hughes, Frank. Prejudice and the Press. A restatement of the principle of freedom of the press with specific reference to the Hutchins-Luce Commission. Introduction by Kenneth E. Olson. New York, Devin-Adair Co., 1950. xi + 642 pp.

4143. Burke, Redmond A., C.S.V. What Is the Index? Milwaukee, Bruce Publ'ing Co., 1952. xi + 129 pp.—"Bibliography," pp. 117–123.

4144. Siebert, Fredrick Seaton. Freedom of the Press in England 1476–1776. The rise and decline of government controls. Urbana, University of Illinois Press, 1952. xiv + 411 pp.

4145. Cross, Harold L. The People's Right to Know. Legal access to public records and proceedings. New York, Columbia Univ. Press, 1953. xxiv + 405 pp.—"A report . . . to the American Society of Newspaper Editors."

4146. Inglis, Brian. The Freedom of the Press in Ireland 1784–1841. London, Faber and Faber Ltd., 1954. 256 pp.—Volume VI in the series Studies in Irish History. "Bibliography," pp. 236–248.

4147. Blanshard, Paul. The Right to Read. The battle against censorship. Boston, Beacon Press, 1955. [vii] + 339 pp.—"Bibliography," pp. 315–318.

4148. Chenery, Wm. L. Freedom of the Press. New York, Harcourt, Brace and Co., 1955. 256 pp.

4149. Haight, Anne Lyon. Banned Books. Informal notes on some books banned for various reasons at various times and in various places. Introduction by Morris L. Ernst. 2nd ed., rev. and enl. New York, R. R. Bowker Co., 1955. xix + 172 pp.—Original ed. 1935.

4150. Swindler, Wm. F. Problems of Law in Journalism. New York, Macmillan Co., 1955. 551 pp.

4151. Cooper, Kent. The Right to Know. An exposition of the evils of news suppression and propaganda. New York, Farrar, Straus and Cudahy, 1956. xiii + 335 pp.

4152. Gerald, J[ames] Edward. The British Press Under Government Economic Controls. Minneapolis, University of Minnesota Press, 1956. xiv + 235 pp.

4153. St. John-Stevas, Norman. Obscenity and the Law. With an introduction by Alan Herbert. London, Secker and Warburg Ltd., 1956. xxii + 289 pp.—"Bibliography," pp. 264–273.

4154. Thayer, Frank. Legal Control of the Press. Concerning those potential or actual controls that affect the press, particularly libel, privacy, contempt, regulation of advertising, and postal laws. 3rd ed. Brooklyn, N.Y., Foundation Press, 1956. 749 pp.—Original ed. 1944; second ed. 1950.

4155. Wiggins, James R. Freedom or Secrecy? New York, Oxford Univ. Press, 1956. 242 pp.

4156. McKeon, Richard, Merton, Robt. K., and Gellhorn, Walter. The Freedom to Read. Perspective and program. New York, R. R. Bowker Co. for the National Book Committee, 1957. xvii + 110 pp.

4157. Schramm, Wilbur L. Responsibility in Mass Communication. New York, Harper and Bros., 1957. xxiii + 391 pp.—Bibliography, pp. 370–374.

4158. Gardiner, Harold C., S.J. Catholic Viewpoint on Censorship. Garden City, N.Y., Hanover House, 1958. 192 pp.—Number 2 in the Catholic Viewpoint Series.

CHAPTER XII

PRINTING, THE BOOK TRADE, AND LIBRARY SCIENCE

§168. GLOSSARIES OF MODERN BIBLIOGRAPHICAL TERMS

[For printer's glossaries see nos. 4239–4241.]

4162. Medlicott, Mary. Abbreviations Used in Book Catalogues. Boston, Boston Book Co., 1906. 15 pp.—Number 15 in the series Bulletin of Bibliography Pamphlets.

4163. Walter, Frank Keller. Abbreviations and Technical Terms Used in Book Catalogues and in Bibliographies. Boston, F. W. Faxon Co., 1912. xi + 167 pp.—Number 5 in the Useful Reference Series. Reprint 1919. "This list was begun as an expansion of Miss Medlicott's Abbreviations in Book Catalogues . . . ," p. v.

4164. Moth, Axel. Glossary of Library Terms. English, Danish, Dutch, French, German, Italian, Spanish, Swedish. Boston, Boston Book Co., 1915. 58 pp.—Number 10 in the Useful Reference Series.

4165. Moth, Axel. Technical Terms Used in Bibliographies and by the Book and Printing Trades. Forming a supplement to F. K. Walter's Abbreviations and Technical Terms Used in Book Catalogs and Bibliographies. Boston, Boston Book Co., 1915. viii + 263 pp.

4166. Cowles, Barbara. Bibliographers' Glossary of Foreign Words and Phrases. An alphabet of terms in bibliographical and booktrade use compiled from twenty languages. New York, R. R. Bowker Co., 1933. [iv] + 82 (double column) pp. printed and numbered recto only.

4167. Thompson, Elizabeth H., ed. ALA Glossary of Library Terms. With a selection of terms in related fields. Prepared under the direction of the Committee on Library Terminology. Chicago, American Library Association, 1943. viii + 159 (double column) pp.

4168. Orne, Jerrold. The Language of the Foreign Book Trade. Abbreviations, terms, and phrases. Chicago, American Library Association, 1949. vii + 88 (double column) pp.

4169. Bookman's Glossary. 3rd ed. New York, R. R. Bowker Co., 1951. ix + 198 pp.—Original ed. 1925; second ed. 1931 edited by J. A. Holden. "Selected Reading List," pp. 192–198.

4170. Carter, John. ABC for Book-Collectors. New York, Alfred A. Knopf, [1951]. 191 pp.—A glossary of book terms.

4171. Lemaitre, Henri, and Thompson, Anthony. Vocabularium bibliothecarii. English / Anglais. French / Français. German / Allemand. Paris, Unesco, 1953. 296 pp.—Number 2 in the series Unesco Bibliographical Handbooks.

4172. The Bookman's Concise Dictionary. Preface by F. C. A[vis]. London, F. C. Avis, 1956. 325 (double column) pp.—Literary and linguistic as well as bibliographical terms.

4173. Hertzberger, Menno. Dictionary for the Antiquarian Booktrade in French, English, German, Swedish, Danish, Italian, Spanish, and Dutch. Paris, International League of Antiquarian Booksellers, 1956. 190 pp.

4174. Landau, Thos. Encyclopaedia of Librarianship. New York, Hafner Publ'ing Co., 1958. ix + 334 (double column) pp.

4175. Harrod, L[eonard] M. The Librarians' Glossary. Terms used in librarianship and the book crafts. 2nd ed. London, Grafton and Co., 1959. 332 pp.—Original ed. 1938.

§169. ALPHABET: HISTORIES AND STUDIES

4179. Taylor, Isaac. The History of the Alphabet. Vol. I: Semitic Alphabets; Vol. II: Aryan Alphabets. New ed. New York, Charles Scribner's Sons, 1899. 2 vols.—Original ed. 1883.

4180. Clodd, Edward. The Story of the Alphabet. New York, D. Appleton and Co., 1905. 209 pp.—Reprint 1915.

4181. Friesen, Otto von. Runes. Encyclopaedia Britannica. 14th ed. London, Encyclopaedia Britannica, 1929. XIX, pp. 659–664.

4182. Sprengling, Martin. The Alphabet. Its rise and development from the Sinai inscriptions. University of Chicago Press, [1931]. xi + 71 pp.—Number 12 in the series Oriental Institute Communications.

4183. Ogg, Oscar. The Twenty-Six Letters. New York, Thomas Y. Crowell Co., 1948. [xi] + 254 pp.—Reprint 1950. Semi-popular treatment.

4184. Diringer, David. The Alphabet. A key to the history of mankind. Foreword by Sir Ellis Minns. 2nd ed. New York, Philosophical Library, 1949. xii + 13–607 pp.—Original It. ed. 1937; second Eng. ed. reprinted with amendments 1953.

4185. Hayes, James. The Roman Letter. A study of notable graven and written forms from twenty centuries in which our Latin alphabet moved toward . . . the basic medium of printed communication. . . . Chicago, Lakeside Press, [1951]. 55 pp.

4186. Gelb, I[gnace] J. A Study of Writing. The foundations of grammatology. University of Chicago Press, 1952. xv + 295 pp.—Bibliography, pp. 254–264. A treatment of the major writing systems of the world, past and present.

4187. Moorhouse, A[lfred] C. The Triumph of the Alphabet. A history of writing. New York, Henry Schuman Inc., 1953. [xiv] + 223 pp.—Number 28 in the series Life of Science Library.

4188. Cohen, Marcel. La grande invention de l'écriture et son évolution. Paris, Imprimerie nationale, 1958. xii + 471 pp. + xcvi plates.—Also *Documentation et index,* Paris, Imprimerie nationale, 1958, 226 pp.

4189. Elliott, Ralph W. V. Runes. An introduction. Manchester, Eng., University Press, 1959. xvi + 124 pp. + xxiv plates.—"Select Bibliography," pp. 110–115.

§170. PRINTING: HISTORICAL ASPECTS

[See also §95. Periodicals Devoted Chiefly to Bibliographic Description and Historical Bibliography.]

4193. Bigmore, E[dward] C., and Wyman, C[harles] W. H. A Bibliography of Printing. London, Bernard Quaritch Ltd., 1880–86. 3 vols.—Reprint New York, P. C. Duschnes, 1945, 2 vols.

4194. Reed, Talbot B. A List of Books and Papers on Printers and Printing under the Countries and Towns to Which They Refer. Transactions of the Bibliographical Society, III (1895), 81–152.

4195. Besterman, Theodore. Early Printed Books to the End of the Sixteenth Century. A bibliography of bibliographies. London, Bernard Quaritch Ltd., 1940. 309 pp.—"This is not a bibliography of writings on printing, but only of bibliographies dealing . . . with the period to 1600/-1640," p. 5.

4196. McMurtrie, Douglas C. The Invention of Printing. A bibliography. Chicago, Chicago Club of Printing House Craftsmen, 1942.

4197. Ulrich, Carolyn F., and Küp, Karl. Books and Printing. A selected list of periodicals. New York Public Library, 1943. xi + 244 (double column) pp.

4198. Greenhood, David, and Gentry, Helen. Chronology of Books and Printing. Rev. ed. New York, Macmillan Co., 1936. ix + 186 pp.—Original ed. 1933. The annals of books and printing from 300 A.D. to 1935.

4199. Dibdin, Thos. Frognall. Typographical Antiquities. Or the history of printing in England, Scotland, and Ireland, containing memoirs of our ancient printers and a register of the books printed by them. Begun by the late Joseph Ames. . . . Considerably augmented by William Herbert . . . and now greatly enlarged with copious notes, and illustrated with appropriate engravings, comprehending the history of English literature, and a view of the progress of the art of engraving, in Great Britain. London, W. Miller, 1810–19. 4 vols.—Also Joseph Ames and William Herbert, *Index to Dibdin's Typographical Antiquities,* with a preface by Alfred W. Pollard, London, Blades, East and Blades, 1899, 77 pp.

4200. Thomas, Isaiah. The History of Printing in America. With a biography of printers and an account of newspapers. With the author's corrections and additions and a catalogue of American publications previous to the revolution of 1776. 2nd ed. Albany, N.Y., Joel Munsell, 1874. 2 vols. —Volumes IV and V in the series Archaeologia Americana: Transactions and Collections of the American Antiquarian Society. Original ed. 1810.

4201. DeVinne, Theo[dore] L. The Invention of Printing. A collection of facts and opinions descriptive of early prints and playing cards, the block books of the fifteenth century, the legend of Lourens Janszoon Coster of Haarlem, and the work of John Gutenberg and his associates. New York, Francis Hart and Co., 1876. 556 pp.

4202. Blades, Wm. The Biography and Typography of William Caxton, England's First Printer. 2nd ed. New York, Scribner and Welford, 1882. xii + 387 pp.—Original ed. 1877 based on Blades's earlier *The Life and Typography of William Caxton,* London, J. Lilly, 1861–63, 2 vols.

4203. Bouchot, Henri. The Book. Its printers, illustrators, and binders from Gutenberg to the present time. Revised and enl. by H. Grevel. London, H. Grevel and Co., 1890. xv + 383 pp.—Original Eng. ed. *The Printed Book,* Its history, illustration, and adornment from the days of Gutenberg to the present time, translated and enl. by Edward C. Bigmore, New York, Scribner and Welford, 1887, viii + 312 pp. Original Fr. ed. 1886.

4204. Dickson, Robt., and Edmond, John Philip. Annals of Scottish Printing from the Introduction of the Art in 1507 to the Beginning of the Seventeenth Century. Cambridge, Eng., Macmillan and Bowes, 1890. xv + 530 pp.

4205. Duff, E[dward] Gordon. Early Printed Books. London, Kegan Paul, Trench, Trübner and Co., 1893. xii + 219 pp.

4206. Proctor, Robt. The Printing of Greek in the Fifteenth Century. Oxford Univ. Press for the Bibliographical Society, 1900. [x] + 217 pp.—Number 8 in the series Illustrated Monographs Issued by the Bibliographical Society.

4207. Davenport, Cyril. The Book. Its history and development. New York, D. van Nostrand Co., 1908. vi + 258 pp.—Reprint New York, P. Smith, 1930.

4208. Plomer, Henry R. A Short History of English Printing 1476–1900. Editor's preface by A. W. Pollard. 2nd ed. New York, Empire State Book Co., 1915. xii + 276 pp.—In the series Books about Books. Original ed. 1900; second ed. reprinted 1927.

4209. Sperling, H[enry] Halliday. The Kelmscott Press and William Morris, Mastercraftsman. London, Macmillan Co., 1924. ix + 177 pp.

4210. Plomer, Henry R. William Caxton 1424–1491. London, Leonard Parsons, 1925. 195 pp.—In the Roadmaker Series. "Books Recommended," pp. 187–189.

4211. Plomer, Henry R. Wynkyn de Worde and His Contemporaries from the Death of Caxton to 1535. A chapter in English printing. London, Grafton and Co., 1925. 263 pp.—A study of Copland, the Faques, Lettou, de Maclinia, Notary, Pepwell, Pynson, the Rastells, Skot, and de Worde.

4212. Aurner, Nellie S. Caxton. Mirrour of fifteenth-century letters. A study of the literature of the first English press. Boston, Houghton Mifflin Co., 1926. xvi + 304 pp.—Appendices: Books about Caxton; Caxton's Books in Chronological Sequence; Editions and Reprints; Caxton's Prologues, Epilogues, and Interpolations.

4213. Some Account of the Oxford University Press 1468–1926. 2nd ed. Oxford Univ. Press, 1926. 133 pp.—Original ed. 1922.

4214. Peddie, R[obert] A., ed. Printing. A short history of the art. London, Grafton and Co., 1927. x + 390 pp.—Essays covering the growth of printing in Western Europe and written by specialists, such as Ernst Crous, Maurits Sabbe, Henry R. Plomer, and George P. Winship.

4215. Orcott, Wm. Dana. The Book in Italy during the Fifteenth and Sixteenth Centuries. Shown in facsimile reproductions from the most famous printed volumes. Introduction by Guido Biagi. New York, Harper and Bros., 1928. 221 pp.

4216. Oswald, John Clyde. A History of Printing. Its development through five hundred years. New York, D. Appleton and Co., 1928. xxi + 404 pp.—"Bibliography," pp. 389–391.

4217. Simpson, Percy. Proof-Reading in the Sixteenth, Seventeenth, and Eighteenth Centuries. Oxford Univ. Press, 1935. xii + 251 pp. + xvi facsimiles.

4218. Winterich, John T. Early American Books and Printing. Boston, Houghton Mifflin Co., 1935. viii + 253 pp.

4219. McMurtrie, Douglas C. A History of Printing in the United States. The story of the introduction of the press and of its history and influence during the pioneer period in each state of the Union. Vol. II: Middle and South Atlantic States. New York, R. R. Bowker Co., 1936. xxvii + 462 pp.—Volume I never issued.

4220. Oswald, John Clyde. Printing in the Americas. New York, Gregg Publ'ing Co., 1937. xii + 565 + xli pp.—A treatment that includes South America.

4221. Winship, Geo. P. William Caxton and His Work. Berkeley, Calif., Book Arts Club, 1937. xi + 55 pp.

4222. Barge, Hermann. Geschichte der Buchdruckerkunst von ihren Anfängen bis zur Gegenwart. Leipzig, Verlag Philipp Reclam jun., 1940. xvi + 520 pp.

4223. Blum, André. The Origins of Printing and Engraving. Translated from the French by Harry M. Lydenberg. New York, Charles Scribner's Sons, 1940. ix + 226 pp.—Original Fr. ed. 1935.

4224. Butler, Pierce. The Origin of Printing in Europe. University of Chicago Press, 1940. xv + 155 pp.

4225. Pottinger, David. Printers and Printing. Cambridge, Mass., Harvard Univ. Press, 1941. viii + 143 pp.

4226. McMurtrie, Douglas C. The Book. The story of printing and bookmaking. 3rd ed. New York, Oxford Univ. Press, 1943. xxx + 676 pp.—Original ed. 1937; second ed. 1938. The 3rd ed. is actually the 7th ed. of the author's *The Golden Book*, The story of fine books and bookmaking, past and present, Chicago, Pascal Covici, 1927, xiv + 406 pp. Bibliographies, pp. 603–646.

4227. Shipton, Clifford K. Isaiah Thomas. Printer, patriot, and philanthropist. Rochester, N.Y., Leo Hart, 1948. xii + 94 pp.

4228. Morison, Stanley. Four Centuries of Fine Printing. Two hundred and seventy-two examples of the work of presses established between 1465 and 1924. 2nd ed. New York, Farrar, Straus and Co., 1949. 342 pp.—Original ed. 1924.

4229. Lehmann-Haupt, Hellmut. Peter Schoeffer of Gernsheim and Mainz. With a list of his surviving books and broadsides. Rochester, N.Y., Leo Hart, 1950. xv + 146 pp.

4230. Aldis, Harry G. The Printed Book. Revised and brought up to date by John Carter and Brooke Crutchley. 3rd ed. Cambridge Univ. Press, 1951. vi + 142 pp.—Original ed. 1916; second ed. 1941. "Books for Further Reading," pp. 129–131.

4231. Carter, Thos. F. The Invention of Printing in China and Its Spread Westward. Second ed. rev. by L. Carrington Goodrich. New York, Ronald Press Co., 1955. xxiv + 293 pp.—Original ed. 1925; second ed. 1931.

4232. Mumby, F[rank] A., and Stallybrass, Frances H. S. From Swan Sonnenschein to George Allen and Unwin Ltd. With an introduction by John Murray. London, Allen and Unwin, 1955. 100 pp.

4233. Jennett, Seán. Pioneers in Printing. Johannes Gutenberg, William Caxton, William Caslon, John Baskerville, Alois Senefelder, Frederick Koenig, Ottmar Mergenthaler, Tolbert Lanston. London, Routledge and Kegan Paul, 1958. xi + 196 pp.

4234. Steinberg, S[igfrid] H. Five Hundred Years of Printing. With a foreword by Beatrice Ward. New ed. London, Faber and Faber Ltd., 1959. 286 pp.—Original ed. Harmondsworth, Eng., Penguin Books, 1955, 277 pp., number 343 in the series Pelican Books.

§171. PRINTING: TECHNICAL ASPECTS

4238. Lehmann-Haupt, Hellmut. One Hundred Books about Bookmaking. A guide to the study and appreciation of printing. 3rd ed. New York, Columbia Univ. Press, 1949. Unpaginated.—Original ed. 1933 *Fifty Books about Bookmaking*; second ed. 1941 *Seventy Books about Bookmaking.*

4239. Jacobi, Chas. T. The Printers' Vocabulary. A collection of some 2500 technical terms, phrases, abbreviations, and other expressions mostly relating to letterpress printing. . . . London, Chiswick Press, 1888. 164 pp.

4240. Collins, F[rederick] Howard. Authors' and Printers' Dictionary. 9th ed. Oxford Univ. Press, 1946. xvi + 428 (double column) pp.—Original ed. 1905; ninth ed. reprinted 1951.

4241. Hostettler, Rudolf. The Printer's Terms. London, Alvin Redman Ltd., 1949. 204 (double column) pp.—A list of printing and library terms with French, Italian, German, and Dutch equivalents beside each English term.

4242. Jacobi, Chas. T. Some Notes on Books and Printing. 4th ed. London, Charles Whittingham and Co., 1912. xi + 173 pp.—Original ed. 1891; second ed. 1892; third ed. 1902. Glossary, pp. 83–96.

4243. Ransom, Will. Private Presses and Their Books. New York, R. R. Bowker Co., 1929. 493 pp.—A treatment of presses stressing the aesthetic values of typography and design.

4244. Jackson, Holbrook. The Printing of Books. London, Cassell and Co., 1938. xiii + 285 pp.—Essays devoted to a study of the rapport necessary between author and printer.

4245. Tarr, John C. Printing To-Day. With an introduction by Francis Meynell and a note on modern typography by Bertram Evans. Rev. ed. Oxford Univ. Press, 1949. 184 pp.—Original ed. 1945.

4246. Jennett, Seán. The Making of Books. London, Faber and Faber, 1951. 474 pp.—"Selection of Books for Further Reading and Reference," pp. 455–460.

4247. Polk, Ralph W. The Practice of Printing. Rev. and enl. ed. Peoria, Ill., Charles A. Bennett Co., 1952. xii + 324 pp.—Original ed. 1926. "Bibliography," pp. 315–318. A shop manual for modern printers.

4248. Williamson, Hugh. Methods of Book Design. The practice of an industrial craft. Oxford Univ. Press, 1956. xv + 430 pp.—"Glossary," pp. 417–430.

4249. Karch, Robt. R. Graphic Arts Procedures. 2nd ed. Chicago, American Technical Society, 1957. xi + 384 pp.—Original ed. 1948.

4250. Davis, Herbert, and Carter, Harry, eds. Mechanick Exercises on the Whole Art of Printing (1683–4) by Joseph Moxon. Oxford Univ. Press, 1958. lxiii + 480 pp.

4251. Karch, Robt. Randolph. Printing and the Allied Trades. 4th ed. New York, Isaac Pitman, 1958. 318 pp.—Original ed. 1931; revised and enl. ed. 1939.

§172. PRINTING: TYPOGRAPHIC ASPECTS

4255. DeVinne, Theodore L. The Practice of Typography. A treatise on the processes of type-making, the point system, the names, sizes, styles, and prices of plain printing types. New York, Century Co., 1899. 403 pp.

4256. Johnson, A[lfred] F. Type Designs. Their history and development. London, Grafton and Co., 1934. viii + 232 pp.—"List of Authorities," pp. 216–228.

4257. Berry, W[illiam] Turner, and Johnson, A[lfred] F. Catalogue of Specimens of Printing Types by English and Scottish Printers and Founders 1665–1830. With an introduction by Stanley Morison. Oxford Univ. Press, 1935. liii + 98 pp. + xxvi plates.—In the series Oxford Books on Bibliography.

4258. Morison, Stanley. The Typographic Arts. Two lectures. London, Sylvan Press, 1949. 106 pp.

4259. Wroth, Lawrence C. Typographic Heritage. Selected essays. With an introduction by Carl P. Rollins. Portland, Me., Anthoensen Press, 1949. viii + 162 pp.—Number 20 in the Typophile Series of Chap Books.

4260. Bennett, Paul A., ed. Books and Printing. A treasury for typophiles. Cleveland, World Publ'ing Co., 1951. xv + 417 pp.

4261. Morison, Stanley. First Principles of Typography. Cambridge Univ. Press, 1951. 17 pp.—Number 1 in the series Cambridge Authors' and Printers' Guides.

4262. Updike, Daniel Berkeley. Printing Types. Their history, forms, and use. A study in survivals. 2nd ed. Cambridge, Mass., Harvard Univ. Press, 1951. 2 vols.—Original ed. 1922.

4263. Karch, R[obert] Randolph. How to Recognize Type Faces. Bloomington, Ill., McKnight and McKnight Publ'ing Co., 1952. 265 pp.

4264. Simon, Oliver. Introduction to Typography. Rev. ed. Harmondsworth, Eng., Penguin Books Ltd., 1954. ix + 117 pp.—Number 288 in the series Pelican Books. Original ed. Cambridge, Mass., Harvard Univ. Press, 1945, xi + 137 pp. "Glossary," pp. 102–113.

4265. Lewis, John. A Handbook of Type and Illustration. With notes on certain graphic processes and the production of illustrated books. Introduction by R. Geoffrey Smith. London, Faber and Faber, 1956. xi + 203 pp.

4266. Berry, W[illiam] Turner, Johnson, A[lfred] F., and Jaspert, W P. The Encyclopaedia of Type Faces. Rev. and enl. ed. London, Blandford Press, 1958. 358 pp.—Original ed. 1953.

§173. PRINTING: BINDINGS, ILLUSTRATIONS, DEVICES, BOOK PLATES, AND WATER MARKS

4270. Karch, R[obert] Randolph. Index to Graphic Art Periodical Literature Published during All or Some of the Years 1933–1940. Evanston, Ill., Education Commission, International Association of Printing House Craftsmen, 1941. 110 (double column) pp.—Also *Index . . . for the Year 1941*, Evanston, Ill., Educational Commission . . . , 1942, 50 (double column) pp.

4271. Castle, Egerton. English Book-Plates Ancient and Modern. New ed. London, George Bell and Sons, 1893. xx + 352 pp.—Original ed. 1892.

4272. Pollard, Alfred W. Early Illustrated Books. A history of the decoration and illustration of books in the fifteenth and sixteenth centuries. London, Kegan Paul, Trench, Trübner and Co., 1893. vii + 256 pp.

4273. Roberts, W[illiam]. Printers' Marks. A chapter in the history of typography. London, George Bell and Sons, 1893. xv + 261 pp.

4274. Horne, Herbert P. The Binding of Books. An essay in the history of gold-tooled bindings. London, Kegan Paul, Trench, Trübner and Co., 1894. xiii + 224 pp.

4275. Matthews, Brander. Bookbinding Old and New. Notes of a booklover. With an account of the Grolier Club of New York. New York, Macmillan Co., 1895. xiii + 342 pp.

4276. Hardy, W[illiam] J. Book-Plates. 2nd ed. London, Kegan Paul, Trench, Trübner and Co., 1897. xvi + 240 pp.—In the series Books about Books. Original ed. 1893.

4277. Kennard, Joseph Spencer. Some Early Printers and Their Colophons. Philadelphia, George W. Jacobs and Co., 1902. [iii] + 129 pp.

4278. McKerrow, Ronald B. Printers' and Publishers' Devices in England and Scotland 1485–1640. London, Bibliographical Society, 1913. liv + 216 pp.—Number 16 in the series Illustrated Monographs of the Bibliographical Society. Reprint 1949.

4279. Briquet, Chas. M. Les filigranes. Dictionnaire historique des marques du papier dès leur apparition vers 1282 jusqu'en 1600. 2e éd. Leipzig, K. W. Hiersemann, 1923. 4 (continuously paged) vols.—Original ed. 1907.

4280. McKerrow, R[onald] B., and Ferguson, F[rederic] S. Title-Page Borders Used in England and Scotland 1485–1640. Oxford Univ. Press for the Bibliographical Society, 1932. xlviii + 220 pp. + cccvi facsimiles + 221–234 pp.—Number 21 in the series Illustrated Monographs Issued by the Bibliographical Society.

4281. Johnson, Alfred Forbes. A Catalogue of Engraved and Etched English Title-Pages down to the death of William Faithorne 1691. Oxford Univ. Press for the Bibliographical Society, 1934. xi + 109 pp. + xciv leaves of facsimiles.—Number 4 in the series Facsimiles and Illustrations Issued by the Bibliographical Society.

4282. Churchill, W[illiam] A. Watermarks in Paper in Holland, England, France, etc., in the Seventeenth and Eighteenth Centuries and Their Interconnection. Amsterdam, M. Hertzberger and Co., 1935. 94 + cdxxxii pp.—Bibliography, pp. 93–94.

4283. Davies, Hugh Wm. Devices of the Early Printers 1457–1560. Their history and development with a chapter on portrait figures of printers. London, Grafton and Co., 1935. xi + 707 pp.

4284. French, Hannah D., Rogers, Joseph W., and Lehmann-Haupt, Hellmut. Bookbinding in America. Three essays. Portland, Me., Southworth-Anthoensen Press, 1941. xix + 293 pp.

4285. Diehl, Edith. Bookbinding. Its background and technique. Vol. I: Historical; Vol. II: Technical. New York, Rinehart and Co., 1946. 2 vols.

4286. Kepes, György, et al. Graphic Forms. The arts as related to the book. Cambridge, Mass., Harvard Univ. Press, 1949. 128 pp.

4287. Heawood, Edward. Watermarks Mainly of the Seventeenth and Eighteenth Centuries. Hilversum, Holland, Paper Publications Society, 1950. 154 pp.—Volume I in the series Monumenta chartae papyraceae historiam illustrantia; or Collections of works and documents illustrating the history of paper. Five hundred thirty-three plates.

4288. Ede, Chas., ed. The Art of the Book. Some record of work carried out in Europe and the U.S.A. 1939–1950. London, Studio Publications, 1951. xi + 214 pp.

4289. Jones, Louise S. The Human Side of Bookplates. [Los Angeles], Ward Ritchie Press, 1951. xiii + 158 pp.

4290. Town, Lawrence. Bookbinding by Hand for Students and Craftsmen. With a preface by E. E. Pullée. London, Faber and Faber, 1951. 281 pp.

4291. Loring, Rosamund B. Decorated Book Papers. Being an account of their designs and fashions. Second ed. edited by Philip Hofer. Cambridge, Mass., Harvard Univ. Press, 1952. xxxv + 171 pp.—Original ed. 1942.

4292. Rosner, Chas. The Growth of the Book Jacket. Cambridge, Mass., Harvard Univ. Press, 1954. xxxiv + 74 pp.

4293. Cockerell, Douglas. Bookbinding and the Care of Books. A textbook for bookbinders and librarians. 5th ed. London, Isaac Pitman and Sons, 1957. 345 pp.—Original ed. 1901.

4294. Banister, Manly M. Pictorial Manual of Bookbinding. Photography and drawings by the author. New York, Ronald Press Co., 1958. v + 40 pp.

4295. Bland, David. A History of Book Illustration. The illuminated manuscript and the printed book. London, Faber and Faber Ltd., 1958. 448 pp.—See also Bland's *The Illustration of Books,* London, Faber and Faber Ltd., 1951, 160 pp.

4296. Hamilton, Sinclair. Early American Book Illustrators and Wood Engravers 1670–1870. A catalogue of a collection of American books illustrated for the most part with woodcuts and wood engravings in the Princeton University Library. . . . With a foreword by Frank Weitenkampf. Princeton, N.J., University Press, 1958. xlviii + 265 (chiefly double column) pp.

4297. McLean, Ruari. Modern Book Design from William Morris to the Present Day. London, Faber and Faber Ltd., 1958. xii + 116 pp.

4298. Weitzmann, Kurt. Ancient Book Illumination. Cambridge, Mass., Harvard Univ. Press for Oberlin College, 1959. xv + 166 pp. + lxiv plates. —Volume XVI in the series Martin Classical Lectures.

§174. BOOK TRADE: HISTORICAL STUDIES

[See also §95. Periodicals Devoted Chiefly to Bibliographical Description and Historical Bibliography.]

4302. Growoll, Adolf. Book-Trade Bibliography in the United States in the Nineteenth Century. To which is added A Catalogue of All the Books Printed in the United States . . . , published by the booksellers in Boston, January 1804. New York, Kay Printing House for the Dibdin Club, 1898. lxxvii + 79 pp.—Reprint New York, E. B. Hackett, [1939].

4303. Growoll, A[dolf]. Three Centuries of English Booktrade Bibliography. An essay on the beginnings of booktrade bibliography since the introduction of printing and in England since 1595. Also a list of the catalogues, etc., published for the English booktrade from 1595–1902, by Wilberforce Eames. New York, M. L. Greenhalgh for the Dibdin Club, 1903. xv + 195 pp.

4304. Duff, E[dward] Gordon. A Century of the English Book Trade. Short notices of all printers, stationers, book-binders, and others connected with it from the issue of the first dated book in 1457 to the incorporation of the Company of Stationers in 1557. London, Bibliographical Society, 1905. xxxv + 200 pp.—Reprint 1948.

4305. Duff, E[dward] Gordon. The Printers, Stationers, and Bookbinders of Westminster and London from 1476 to 1535. Cambridge Univ. Press, 1906. 256 pp.—The Sanders Lectures 1899 and 1904.

4306. Plomer, Henry R. A Dictionary of the Booksellers and Printers Who Were at Work in England, Scotland, and Ireland from 1641 to 1667. London, Blades, East and Blades for the Bibliographical Society, 1907. xxiii + 199 pp.

4307. McKerrow, R[onald] B., et al. A Dictionary of Printers and Booksellers in England, Scotland, and Ireland and of Foreign Printers of English Books 1557–1640. London, Bibliographical Society, 1910. xxiii + 346 pp.—Number 13 in the series Monographs of the Bibliographical Society.

4308. Duff, E[dward] Gordon. The English Provincial Printers, Stationers, and Bookbinders to 1557. Cambridge Univ. Press, 1912. ix + 153 pp. —The Sanders Lectures 1911.

4309. Plomer, Henry R. A Dictionary of the Printers and Booksellers Who Were at Work from 1668 to 1725. With the help of H. G. Aldis, E. R. McC. Dix, G. J. Gray, and R. B. McKerrow. Edited by Arundell Esdaile. Oxford Univ. Press for the Bibliographical Society, 1922. xii + 342 pp.

4310. Plomer, H[enry] R., Bushnell, G[eorge] H., and Dix, E[rnest] R. McC. A Dictionary of the Printers and Booksellers Who Were at Work in England, Scotland, and Ireland from 1726 to 1775. . . . Oxford Univ. Press for the Bibliographical Society, 1932. xxi + 432 pp.

4314. Curwen, Henry. A History of Booksellers. The old and the new. London, Chatto and Windus, [1873]. viii + 483 pp.

4315. Roberts, Wm. The Earlier History of English Bookmaking. New ed. London, Sampson Low, Marston and Co., 1892. xii + 341 pp.—Original ed. 1889.

4316. Putnam, Geo. Haven. Books and Their Makers during the Middle Ages. A study of the conditions of the production and distribution of literature from the fall of the Roman Empire to the close of the seventeenth century. Vol. I: 476–1600; Vol. II: 1500–1709. New York, G. P. Putnam's Sons, 1896. 2 vols.

4317. Growoll, A[dolf]. American Book Clubs. Their beginnings and history and a bibliography of their publications. New York, Dodd, Mead and Co., 1897. xiv + 423 pp.

4318. Waldman, Milton. Americana. The literature of American history. New York, Henry Holt and Co., 1925. xviii + 271 pp.

4319. Plant, Marjorie. The English Book Trade. An economic history of the making and sale of books. London, George Allen and Unwin Ltd., 1939. 500 pp.—"References," pp. 451–480.

4320. Burlingame, Roger. Of Making Many Books. New York, Charles Scribner's Sons, 1946. xii + 347 pp.—An editorial history of Scribner's.

4321. Lehmann-Haupt, Hellmut. The Book in America. A history of the making and selling of books in the United States. In collaboration with Lawrence C. Wroth and Rollo G. Silver. 2nd ed. New York, R. R. Bowker Co., 1951. xiv + 493 pp.—Original ed. 1939. "Bibliography," by Janet Bogardus, pp. 422–466 (double column).

4322. Bennett, H[enry] S. English Books and Readers 1475 to 1557. Being a study in the history of the book trade from Caxton to the incorporation of the Stationers' Company. Cambridge Univ. Press, 1952. xiii + 336 pp.—"Handlist of Publications by Wynkyn de Worde 1492–1535," pp. 239–276; "Trial List of Translations into English Printed between 1475–1560," pp. 277–319; "Bibliography," pp. 320–322.

4323. Binns, Norman E. An Introduction to Historical Bibliography. With a preface by Arundell Esdaile. London, Association of Assistant Librarians, 1953. xii + 371 pp.—A treatment of both printing and the book trade.

4324. Mumby, Frank Arthur. Publishing and Bookselling. A history from the earliest times to the present day. 4th ed. London, Jonathan Cape, 1956. 442 pp.—Original ed. 1910 as *The Romance of Book Selling.* "Bibliography," by William Peet brought up to date by F. A. Mumby, pp. 373–415.

4325. Wiles, R[oy] McK. Serial Publication in England before 1750. Cambridge Univ. Press, 1957. xv + 391 pp.—"Short-Title Catalogue of Books Published in Fascicules before 1750," pp. 267–356; "A List of Booksellers, Printers, and Others," pp. 357–366.

§175. BOOK TRADE: CONTEMPORARY SCENE

[See also §96. Library and Publisher Periodicals; §160. The Professional Writer.]

4329. Tomkinson, G S. A Select Bibliography of the Principal Modern Presses Public and Private in Great Britain and Ireland. With an introduction by B. H. Newdigate. London, First Edition Club, 1928. xxv + 238 pp.

4330. Williams, Harold H. Book Clubs and Printing Societies of Great Britain and Ireland. London, First Edition Club, 1929. x + 126 pp.

4331. Growoll, A[dolf]. The Profession of Bookselling. A handbook of practical hints for the apprentice and bookseller. New York, Publishers' Weekly, 1893–1913. 3 (continuously paged) vols.

4332. Swinnerton, Frank. Authors and the Book Trade. With notes by Frederic Melcher. New York, A. A. Knopf, 1932. 146 pp.

4333. Harrison, Frederick. A Book about Books. London, John Murray, 1943. viii + 264 pp.—A semi-popular treatment of MSS, libraries, newspapers, printing, and modern book production.

4334. Adams, Scott. The O.P. Market. A subject directory to the specialties of the out-of-print book trade. With 1944 supplement. New York, R. R. Bowker, 1945. vii + 136 pp.

4335. Langdon-Davis, B[ernard] N. The Practice of Bookselling. With some opinions on its nature, status, and future. Foreword by Hubert N. Wilson. London, Phoenix House Ltd., 1951. xvi + 208 pp.

4336. Taubert, Sigfred. Grundriss des Buchhandels in aller Welt. Hamburg, Ernst Hauswedell und Co., 1953. 351 pp.—A treatment of the book trade in every country of the globe.

4337. Lehmann-Haupt, Hellmut. The Life of the Book. How the book is written, printed, sold, and read. Line drawings by Fritz Kredel. London, Abelard-Schuman Ltd., 1957. 240 pp.—"Suggested Books for Further Reading," pp. 227–230.

4338. Welter, Rush. Problems of Scholarly Publication in the Humanities and Social Sciences. New York, American Council of Learned Societies, 1959. 81 pp.

§176. BOOK COLLECTING

4343. Hart, Horace. Bibliotheca Typographica. In usum eorum qui libros amant. A list of books about books. With an introduction by George P. Winship. Rochester, N.Y., Leo Hart, 1933. xi + 142 pp.

4344. McKay, Geo. L. American Book Auction Catalogues 1713–1934. A union list. New York Public Library, 1937. xxxii + 540 pp.—For additions see 4886.

4345. Dibdin, T[homas] F. The Bibliographical Decameron. Or ten days pleasant discourse upon illuminated manuscripts and subjects connected with early engraving, typography, and bibliography. London, W. Bulmer and Co. for the author, 1817. 3 vols.

4346. Dibdin, Thos. F. The Library Companion. Or the young man's guide and the old man's comfort in the choice of a library. 2nd ed. London, Harding, Triphook and Lepard, 1825. 2 vols.—Original ed. 1824.

4347. Dibdin, Thos. Frognall. Reminiscences of a Literary Life. London, John Major, 1836. 2 parts (xxxv + 982 pp.)

4348. Dibdin, Thos. F. Bibliomania or Book Madness. A bibliographical romance. New and improved ed. [3rd ed.] London, H. G. Bohn, 1842. xviii + 618 + xxxiv pp.—Original ed. 1809; third ed. reprinted London, Bibliographical Society, 1903.

4349. Elton, Chas. I. and Mary A. The Great Book-Collectors. London, Kegan Paul, Trench, Trübner and Co., 1893. vi + 228 pp.—A study of Continental as well as English book collectors.

4350. Fletcher, Wm. Y. English Book Collectors. London, Kegan Paul, Trench, Trübner and Co., 1902. xviii + 448 pp.—A list of biographies in chronological order.

4351. Pollard, Alfred W. Fine Books. New York, G. P. Putnam's Sons, 1912. xv + 332 pp.

4352. Newton, A[lfred] Edward. The Amenities of Book-Collecting and Kindred Affections. Boston, Atlantic Monthly Press, 1918. xxi + 355 pp.—Reprint with new introduction New York, Modern Library, 1935, xix + 373 pp.

4353. De Ricci, Seymour. The Book Collector's Guide. A practical handbook of British and American bibliography. Philadelphia, Rosenbach Co., 1921. xviii + 649 pp.

4354. De Ricci, Seymour. English Collectors of Books and Manuscripts 1530–1930 and Their Marks of Ownership. Cambridge Univ. Press, 1930. ix + 203 pp.—The Sanders Lectures 1929–30. Reprint Bloomington, Indiana Univ. Press, 1960.

4355. Jackson, Holbrook. The Anatomy of Bibliomania. London, Soncino Press, 1930. 2 vols.—One-volume reprint London, Faber and Faber, 1950, 668 pp.

4356. Fabes, Gilbert H. Modern First Editions. Points and values. First, Second, and Third Series. London, W. and G. Foyle Ltd., 1929–31. 3 vols.—Second Series by Gilbert H. and William A. Fabes.

4357. Carter, John, ed. New Paths in Book Collecting. Essays by various hands. London, Constable and Co., 1934. v + 294 pp.

4358. Bennett, Whitman. A Practical Guide to American Book Collecting 1663–1940. New York, Bennett Book Studios Inc., 1941. 254 pp.

4359. Cannon, Carl L. American Book Collectors and Collecting from Colonial Times to the Present. New York, H. W. Wilson Co., 1941. xi + 391 pp.

4360. Muir, Percy H. Book-Collecting as a Hobby. In a series of letters to everyman. London, Gamol Publications Ltd., 1944. 101 pp.—Reprint New York, Alfred A. Knopf, 1947. Also *Book Collecting,* More letters to everyman, London, Cassell, 1949, 156 pp.

4361. Winterich, John T. A Primer of Book Collecting. Newly rev. and enl. ed. in collaboration with David A. Randall. New York, Greenberg Publ'er, 1946. xiii + 226 pp.—Original ed. 1926.

4362. Carter, John. Taste and Technique in Book-Collecting. A study of recent developments in Great Britain and the United States. New York, R. R. Bowker Co., 1948. xxiii + 203 pp.

4363. Evans, H[enry] H. A Guide to Rare Books. San Francisco, Porpoise Bookshop, 1948. 71 pp.—A list of rare Americana.

4364. Boutell, H[enry] S. First Editions of Today and How to Tell Them. American, British, and Irish. Third ed., rev. and enl. by Roger Boutell. Berkeley, University of California Press, 1949. ix + 209 pp.—Original ed. 1928; second ed. 1937. Publishers' statements as to whether they indicate their first editions.

4365. Horrox, Reginald. Book Handbook. An illustrated guide to old and rare books. Bracknell, Eng., Book Centre Ltd., 1951. iv + viii + 485 pp.

4366. Carter, John. Books and Book-Collectors. London, Rupert Hart-Davis, 1956. 196 pp.

4367. Collison, Robt. L. Book Collecting. An introduction to modern methods of literary and bibliographic detection. With a foreword by Andrew H. Horn. Fair Lawn, N.J., Essential Books, 1957. xvi + 17–244 pp.—"General Bibliography," pp. 189–193; "Glossary," pp. 194–203.

4368. Bradley, Van Allen. Gold in Your Attic. New York, Fleet Publ'ing Co., 1958. 277 pp.—A treatment of hunting up early Americana.

4369. Book Dealers in North America. A directory of dealers in secondhand and antiquarian books in Canada and the United States of America. London, Sheppard Press, 1951–date.—Annual.

4370. Directory of Dealers in Secondhand and Antiquarian Books in the British Isles. London, Sheppard Press, 1951–date.—Annual.

§177. LIBRARIES: HISTORICAL ASPECTS

4375. Gottlieb, Theodor. Ueber mittelalterliche Bibliotheken. Leipzig, Otto Harrassowitz, 1890. xi + 520 pp.

4376. Clark, John Willis. The Care of Books. An essay on the development of libraries and their fittings from the earliest times to the end of the eighteenth century. 2nd ed. Cambridge Univ. Press, 1902. xxvi + 352 pp.—Original ed. 1901.

4377. Savage, Ernest A. Old English Libraries. The making, collection, and use of books during the Middle Ages. London, Methuen and Co., [1911]. xv + 298 pp. + xxv plates.

4378. Streeter, Burnett Hillman. The Chained Library. A survey of four centuries in the evolution of the English library. London, Macmillan Co., 1931. xxi + 368 pp.

4379. Minto, John. A History of the Public Library Movement in Great Britain and Ireland. London, George Allen and Unwin Ltd., 1932. 366 pp.—Volume IV in the series Library Manuals of the Library Association.

4380. Norris, Dorothy M. A History of Cataloguing and Cataloguing Methods 1100–1850. With an introductory survey of ancient times. Foreword by H. M. Cashmore. London, Grafton and Co., 1939. ix + 246 pp.—Bibliography, pp. 235–240.

4381. Thompson, James Westfall. Ancient Libraries. Berkeley, University of California Press, 1940. 120 pp.—Bibliographical annotations, pp. 101–120.

4382. Thornton, John L. The Chronology of Librarianship. An introduction to the history of libraries and book-collecting. With an introduction by Ernest A. Savage. London, Grafton and Co., 1941. xi + 254 pp.—Bibliography, pp. 221–228.

4383. Taylor, Archer. Renaissance Guides to Books. An inventory and some conclusions. Berkeley, University of California Press, 1945. vi + 130 pp.

4384. Vorstius, Joris. Grundzüge der Bibliotheksgeschichte. 4. verbesserte Auflage. Leipzig, Otto Harrassowitz, 1948. vii + 114 pp.—Original ed. 1935.

4385. Hessel, Alfred. A History of Libraries. Translated with supplementary material by Reuben Peiss. Washington, D.C., Scarecrow Press, [1950]. v + 198 pp.—Original Ger. ed. 1925.

4386. Kenyon, Frederic G. Books and Readers in Ancient Greece and Rome. Oxford, Clarendon Press, 1951. vii + 136 pp.—Original ed. 1932.— See §75. The Author-Patron-Publisher-Audience Relationship.

4387. Munford, Wm. A. Penny Rate. Aspects of British public library history 1850–1950. London, Library Association, 1951. ix + 150 pp.

4388. Craster, Edmund. History of the Bodleian Library 1845–1945. Oxford, Clarendon Press, 1952. xi + 371 pp.

4389. Jayne, Sears Reynolds. Library Catalogues of the English Renaissance. Berkeley, University of California Press, 1956. 225 pp.

4390. Thompson, James Westfall. The Medieval Library. Reprinted with a supplement by Blanche B. Boyer. New York, Hafner Publ'ing Co., 1957. viii + 702 pp.—Original ed. 1939. The Supplement, a review which appeared in *Library Quarterly*, X, 3, July 1940, corrects errors and oversights.

4391. Irwin, Raymond. The Origins of the English Library. London, George Allen and Unwin Ltd., 1958. 255 pp.

4392. Oldman, C[ecil] B., Munford, W[illiam] A., and Nowell-Smith, Simon. English Libraries 1800–1850. London, H. K. Lewis and Co., 1958. 78 pp.

4393. Pinner, H L. The World of Books in Classical Antiquity. 2nd ed. Leiden, Holland, A. W. Sijthoff, 1958. 64 pp.—Original ed. 1948. "Source References," pp. 59–64.

4394. Wormald, Francis, and Wright, C[yril] E., eds. The English Library before 1700. Studies in its history. University of London Press, 1958. xi + 273 pp.

§178. LIBRARY SCIENCE

[See also §87. Periodicals That Are Primarily Review Organs; §96. Library and Publisher Periodicals.]

4397. Cannons, H[arry] G. T. Bibliography of Library Economy. A classified index to the professional periodical literature in the English language . . . from 1876 to 1920. Chicago, American Library Association, 1927. 680 (double column) pp.

4398. Burton, Margaret, and Vosburgh, Marion E. A Bibliography of Librarianship. Classified and annotated guide to library literature of the world (excluding Slavonic and Oriental languages). Introduction by Arundell Esdaile. London, Library Association, 1934. 151 (double column) + 152–176 (triple column) pp.

4399. Library Literature 1921–1932. A supplement to Cannon's Bibliography of Library Economy 1876–1920. Edited by Lucile M. Morsch. Chicago, American Library Association, 1934. x + 430 (double column) pp.

4400. Baker, Ernest A., ed. The Uses of Libraries. New and rev. ed. University of London Press, 1930. viii + 338 pp.—Original ed. 1927.

4401. Dingwall, Eric John. How to Use a Large Library. 2nd ed. Cambridge, Eng., Bowes and Bowes, 1933. 64 pp.—Original ed. also 1933.

4402. Joeckel, Carleton Bruns. The Government of the American Public Library. University of Chicago Press, 1935. xix + 393 pp.—"Selected Bibliography," pp. 356–366.

4403. Joeckel, Carleton, ed. Current Issues in Library Administration. University of Chicago Press, 1939. xii + 392 pp.—Papers presented before the Library Institute at the University of Chicago, August 1–12, 1938.

4404. Randall, Wm. M., ed. The Acquisition and Cataloging of Books. University of Chicago Press, 1940. x + 408 pp.—Papers presented before the Library Institute at the University of Chicago, July 29 to August 9, 1940.

4405. Hiss, Sophie K. ALA Rules for Filing Catalog Cards. Chicago, American Library Association, 1942. viii + 109 pp.

4406. Lydenberg, Harry M., and Archer, John. The Care and Repair of Books. 3rd ed. New York, R. R. Bowker Co., 1945. 123 pp.—Original ed. 1931; second ed. 1935. A list of references, pp. 96–116.

4407. Vorstius, Joris. Ergebnisse und Fortschritte der Bibliographie in Deutschland seit dem ersten Weltkrieg. Leipzig, Otto Harrassowitz, 1948. v + 172 pp.—Number 74 in the series of supplements to the *Zentralblatt für Bibliothekswesen.*

4408. Reece, Ernest J. The Task and Training of Librarians. New York, Columbia Univ. Press, 1949. [vii] + 91 pp.—"A report of a field investigation carried out in February to May 1947 to assist with curricular problems."

4409. Haines, Helen E. Living with Books. The art of book selection. 2nd ed. New York, Columbia Univ. Press, 1950. xxiii + 610 pp.—Number 2 in the series Columbia University Studies in Library Science. Original ed. 1935; second ed. reprinted 1952.

4410. Sayers, W[illiam] C. Berwick. An Introduction to Library Classification. Theoretical, historical, and practical with readings, exercises, and examination papers. 8th ed. London, Grafton and Co., 1950. xxiv + 314 pp.—"List of Authorities," pp. 301–307. Original ed. 1918.

4411. Schera, Jesse H., and Egan, Margaret E., eds. Bibliographic Organization. University of Chicago Press, 1951. xii + 275 pp.—Papers presented before the Fifteenth Annual Conference of the Graduate Library School July 24–29, 1950.

4412. Bradford, S[amuel] C. Documentation. With an introduction by Jesse H. Shera and Margaret E. Egan. 2nd ed. London, Crosby Lockwood and Son, 1953. 200 pp.—Original ed. 1948. A discussion of the Universal Decimal Classification.

4413. Larsen, Knud. National Bibliographical Services. Their creation and operation. Prepared in accordance with the recommendation of the International Advisory Committee on Bibliography. Paris, Unesco, 1953. x + 142 pp.—Number 1 in the series Unesco Bibliographical Handbooks.

4414. Williams, Edwin E. Farmington Plan Handbook. Bloomington, Ind., Association of Research Librarians, 1953. v + 170 pp.—A treatment of the plan whereby various libraries specialize in particular fields.

4415. Fussler, Herman H., ed. The Function of the Library in the Modern College. University of Chicago Graduate Library School, 1954. vii + 117 (double column) pp.—In the series University of Chicago Studies in Library Science. Papers presented before the Nineteenth Annual Conference of the Graduate Library School of the University of Chicago. Original publication in *Library Quarterly*, October 1954.

4416. Ireland, Norma Olin. The Pamphlet File in School, College, and Public Libraries. Rev. and enl. ed. Boston, F. W. Faxon Co., 1954. xi + 220 pp.—Number 84 in the Useful Reference Series. Original ed. 1937.

4417. McCrum, Blanch Prichard, and Jones, Helen Dudenbostel. Bibliographical Procedures and Style. A manual for bibliographers in the Library of Congress. Washington, D.C., Library of Congress, 1954. vi + 127 pp.

4418. Malclès, Louise-Noëlle. Bibliographical Services throughout the World. First and second annual reports (1 September–31 August 1951–52/-1952–53). Preface by Julian Cain. Prepared in accordance with the recommendations of the International Advisory Committee on Bibliography. Translated from the French. Paris, Unesco, 1955. 352 pp.—Number 4 in the series Unesco Bibliographical Handbooks.

4419. Osborn, Andrew D. Serial Publications. Their place and treatment in libraries. Chicago, American Library Association, 1955. xiv + 309 pp.

4420. Kirchner, Joachim. Lexikon des Buchwesens. Stuttgart, Hiersemann Verlag, 1952–56. 4 (double column page) vols., the last two being made up of illustrations.—A development of Joachim Kirchner and Karl Löffler, *Lexikon des gesamten Buchwesens*, Leipzig, Verlag Karl W. Hiersemann, 1935–37, 3 vols.

4421. McColvin, Lionel R. The Chance to Read. Public libraries in the world today. London, Phoenix House, 1956. 284 pp.—"Brief Bibliography," pp. 267–272.

4422. Asheim, Lester, ed. The Humanities and the Library. Problems in the interpretation, evaluation, and use of library materials. Chicago, American Library Association, 1957. xix + 278 pp.

4423. Metcalfe, John. Information Indexing and Subject Cataloging. Alphabetical : classified/coordinate : mechanical. New York, Scarecrow Press, 1957. 338 pp.

4424. [Dewey, Melvil.] Dewey Decimal Classification and Relative Index. Edited by Benjamin A. Custer. 16th ed. Vol. I: Tables; Vol. II: Index. Lake Placid, N.Y., Forest Press, 1958. 2 vols., Volume II having double column pages.—Original ed. 1876.

4425. Library Literature. An author and subject index to selected material on library science and librarianship, with occasional abstracts. New York, H. W. Wilson Co., 1936–date.—Quarterly (March, June, Sept., and Dec.) with annual and three-year cumulation. The first volume of 1936 covered the years 1933–35.

CHAPTER XIII

GENERAL BIBLIOGRAPHICAL GUIDES

§179. MANUSCRIPT COLLECTIONS: GUIDES AND CATALOGUE BIBLIOGRAPHIES

[An excellent treatment of literary Middle English MSS may be found in the initial fascicle of the *Middle English Dictionary* (no. 2772); further information on Middle English literary MSS may be found in nos. 1216 and 1217. See also §150. Old Records and Documents and Their Abbreviations; §151. Manuscript Hands and Manuscript Study.]

4429. Bernard, Edward. Catalogi librorum manuscriptorum Angliae et Hiberniae in unum collecti, cum indice alphabetico. Oxoniae, e theatro Sheldoniano, 1697. 2 vols. in 1.—Index by Humphrey Wanley.

4430. Wanley, Humphrey. Librorum vett. [i.e. veterum] septentrionalium, qui in angliae bibliothecis extant, nec non multorum vett. codd. septentrionalium alibi extantium catalogus historico-criticus cum sex indicibus. Volume II of George Hickes's Linguarum vett. septentrionalium thesaurus grammatico-criticus et archaeologicus, Oxoniae, e theatro Sheldoniano, 1705, 2 vols.

4431. Thorkelsson, Jón. Islandske Håndskrifter i England og Skotland. Arkiv för Nordisk Filologi, VIII, Ny följd, Fjärde bandet (1892), 199–237.

4432. Priebsch, Robt. Deutsche Handschriften in England. Vol. I: Ashburnham-Place, Cambridge, Cheltenham, Oxford, Wigan, mit einem Anhang ungedruckter Stücke; Vol. II: Das British Museum, mit einem Anhang über die Guildhall-Bibliothek. Erlangen, F. Junge, 1896–1901. 2 vols. in 1.

4433. Weinberger, Wilhelm. Wegweiser durch die Sammlung altphilologischer Handschriften. Vienna, Hölder-Pichler-Tempsky AG, 1930. 136 (chiefly double column) pp.—Number 209 in the series Sitzungsberichte der Akademie der Wissenschaften in Wien.

4434. Richardson, Ernest Cushing. A List of Printed Catalogues of Manuscript Books. New York, H. W. Wilson Co., 1935. v + 386.—Number 3 in the series Preliminary Studies in Method of a Union World Catalog of MS Books.

4435. A Guide to the Reports on Collections of Manuscripts of Private Families, Corporations, and Institutions in Great Britain and Ireland. London, H. M. Stationery Office for the Historical Manuscripts Commission, 1914–38. 2 vols. in 3.

4436. Ker, N[eil] R. Medieval Libraries of Great Britain. A list of surviving books. London, Royal Historical Society, 1941. xxiii + 169 pp.—Number 3 in the series Guides and Handbooks of the Royal Historical Society. A list of MSS and printed books which up to *circa* 1540 were known to be in various libraries and notations as to their present location if known.

4437. Griffin, Grace Gardiner. A Guide to Manuscripts Relating to American History in British Depositories Reproduced for the Division of Manuscripts of the Library of Congress. Washington, D.C., Library of Congress, 1946. xvi + 313 pp.

4438. Kristeller, Paul Oskar. Latin Manuscript Books before 1600. A bibliography of the printed catalogues of extant collections. Traditio, Studies in ancient and medieval history, thought, and religion, VI (1948), 227–317 (double column) pp.

4439. Ker, N[eil] R. Catalogue of Manuscripts Containing Anglo-Saxon. Oxford Univ. Press, 1957. lxiv + 567 pp. + viii plates.

§180. MANUSCRIPT COLLECTIONS: BRITISH MUSEUM

4443. Skeat, T C. The Catalogues of the British Museum. 2. Manuscripts. Journal of Documentation, VII, 1 (March 1951), 18–60.

4444. Planta, Joseph. Catalogue of the MSS in the Cottonian Library deposited in the British Museum. Printed by command of His Majesty King George III. . . . London, L. Hansard, Printer, for the Record Commission, 1802. xv + 618 + [75] pp.—For information on the Cottonian collection prior to the fire of 1731 the following is of occasional help: Thomas Smith, *Catalogus librorum manuscriptorum Bibliothecae cottonianae,* Oxonii, e theatro Sheldoniano, 1696.

4445. A Catalogue of the Harley MSS in the British Museum. London, G. Eyre and A. Strahan, 1808–12. 4 vols.

4446. Douce, Francis, and Ellis, Henry. A Catalogue of the Landsdowne MSS in the British Museum. London, R. and A. Taylor, 1819. 2 parts in 1 vol.

4447. Forshall, Josiah. Catalogue of MSS in the British Museum. Part I: The Arundel MSS; Part II: The Burney MSS; Part III: Index. London, printed by order of the Trustees, 1834–41. 3 vols.

4448. Catalogue of the Stowe MSS in the British Museum. London, printed by order of the Trustees, 1895–96. 2 vols.—Also *Catalogue of a Selection from the Stowe MSS Exhibited in the King's Library in the British Museum,* London, printed by order of the Trustees, 1883, iv + 83 pp. + xv facsimiles.

4449. Kenyon, Frederic G. Facsimiles of Biblical MSS in the British Museum. London, printed by order of the Trustees, 1900. vi + 50 pp. + xxv plates.

4450. Warner, Geo. F., and Gilson, Julius P. Catalogue of Western MSS in the Old Royal and King's Collections. London, printed for the Trustees, 1921. 4 vols.

4451. Catalogue of Additions to the MSS in the British Museum in the Years 1841–1845. Compiled by F[rederic] Madden. London, printed by order of the Trustees, 1850. 5 vols. plus an index vol.—The Additions catalogues have continued to the present; the years covered by and the year or years of publication of each of the additional volumes follow: 1846–1847 (1864); 1848–1853 (1868); 1854–1875 (1875–80), 2 vols. plus an index vol.; 1876–1881 (1882); 1882–1887 (1889); 1888–1893 (1894); 1894–1899 (1901); 1900–1905 (1907); 1906–1910 (1912); 1911–1915 (1925); 1916–1920 (1933); 1921–1925 (1950); 1926–1930 (1959).

§181. MANUSCRIPT COLLECTIONS: OXFORD UNIVERSITY

4455. Catalogue of the Printed Books and MSS Bequeathed by Francis Douce, Esq., to the Bodleian Library. Oxford Univ. Press, 1840. vi + 90 + 311 pp.

4456. Coxe, H[enry] O. Catalogus codicum MSS qui in collegiis aulisque Oxoniensibus hodie asservantur. Oxford, e typographeo academico, 1852. 2 vols.—Manuscripts listed by college.

4457. Black, Wm. H. A Descriptive, Analytical, and Critical Catalogue of the MSS Bequeathed unto the University of Oxford by Elias Ashmole. Oxford Univ. Press, 1845–66. 2 parts.

4458. Kitchin, G[eorge] W. Catalogus codicum MSS qui in bibliotheca aedis Christi apud Oxonienses adservantur. Oxonii, e typographeo Clarendoniano, 1867. 82 pp.

4459. Coxe, H[enry] O., Hackman, A[lfred], et al. Catalogi codicum manuscriptorum bibliothecae Bodleianae. Oxford, J. H. and J. Parker, et al., 1845–1918. 14 parts.—Inclusions, in part: Laud MSS (pt. 2, 1858–85); Tanner MSS (pt. 4, 1860); Rawlinson MSS (pt. 5, 1862–1900, 5 vols.); Digby MSS (pt. 9, 1883); and Ashmole MSS (pt. 10, 1845).

4460. Madan, Falconer. A Summary Catalogue of Western MSS in the Bodleian Library at Oxford, Which Have Not Hitherto Been Catalogued in the Quarto Series, with References to the Oriental and Other MSS. Oxford, Clarendon Press, 1895–1953. 7 vols.—See also H[erbert] H. E. Craster, *The Western MSS of the Bodleian Library*, London, S. P. C. K., 1921, 48 pp., number 43 in the series Helps for Students of History.

§182. MANUSCRIPT COLLECTIONS: CAMBRIDGE UNIVERSITY

4464. [Harwick, Chas., and Luard, Henry R.] A Catalogue of the MSS Preserved in the Library of the University of Cambridge. Cambridge Univ. Press, 1856–67. 5 vols.

4465. James, Montague Rhodes. A Descriptive Catalogue of the MSS in the Fitzwilliam Museum. With introduction and indices. Cambridge Univ. Press, 1895. l + 472 pp.

4466. James, Montague Rhodes. A Descriptive Catalogue of the MSS in the Library of Jesus College. Cambridge Univ. Press, 1895. viii + 122 pp.

4467. James, Montague Rhodes. A Descriptive Catalogue of the MSS Other Than the Oriental in the Library of King's College. Cambridge Univ. Press, 1895. x + 87 pp.

4468. James, Montague Rhodes. A Descriptive Catalogue of the MSS in the Library of Sidney Sussex College. Cambridge Univ. Press, 1895. viii + 132 pp.

4469. James, Montague Rhodes. A Descriptive Catalogue of the MSS in the Library of Peterhouse. With an essay on the history of the Library by J. W. Clark. Cambridge Univ. Press, 1899. xxxii + 389 pp.

4470. James, Montague Rhodes. The Western MSS in the Library of Emanuel College. A descriptive catalogue. Cambridge Univ. Press, 1904. xiv + 178 pp.

4471. James, Montague Rhodes. A Descriptive Catalogue of the Western MSS in the Library of Christ's College. Cambridge Univ. Press, 1905. vi + 36 pp.

4472. James, Montague Rhodes. A Descriptive Catalogue of the Western MSS in the Library of Clare College. Cambridge Univ. Press, 1905. viii + 51 pp.

4473. James, Montague Rhodes. A Descriptive Catalogue of the MSS in the Library of Pembroke College. With a handlist of the printed books to the year 1500 by Ellis H. Minns. Cambridge Univ. Press, 1905. xl + 314 pp.

4474. James, Montague Rhodes. A Descriptive Catalogue of the Western MSS in the Library of Queen's College. Cambridge Univ. Press, 1905. vi + 29 pp.

4475. James, Montague Rhodes. A Descriptive Catalogue of the MSS in the Library of Trinity Hall. Cambridge Univ. Press, 1907. viii + 46 pp.

4476. James, Montague Rhodes. A Descriptive Catalogue of the MSS in the College Library of Magdalene College. Cambridge Univ. Press, 1909. x + 59 pp.

4477. James, Montague Rhodes. A Descriptive Catalogue of the MSS in the Library of Corpus Christi College, Cambridge. Cambridge Univ. Press, 1909–12. 2 vols.

4478. James, Montague Rhodes. A Descriptive Catalogue of the MSS in the Library of St. John's College. Cambridge Univ. Press, 1913. xviii + 389 pp.

4479. James, Montague Rhodes. A Descriptive Catalogue of the MSS in the Library of Gonville and Caius College. Cambridge Univ. Press, 1907–08. 2 (continuously paged) vols.—Also James's *Supplement . . .*, Cambridge Univ. Press, 1914, xxiv + 56 pp.

4480. James, Montague Rhodes. A Descriptive Catalogue of the McClean Collection of Manuscripts in the Fitzwilliam Museum, Cambridge. Cambridge Univ. Press, 1912. xxxii + 410 pp.—See also Francis Wormald and P.M. Giles, "A Hand List of the Additional MSS in the Fitzwilliam Museum," *Transactions of the Cambridge Bibliographical Society*, 1951–54, 4 parts.

§183. MANUSCRIPT COLLECTIONS: BRITISH ISLES (EXCLUSIVE OF COLLECTIONS AT OXFORD AND CAMBRIDGE AND IN THE BRITISH MUSEUM)

4484. James, M[ontague] R. Descriptive Catalogue of the MSS in the Library of Eton College. Cambridge Univ. Press, 1895. xvi + 125 pp.

4485. Abbott, T[homas] K. Catalogue of the Manuscripts in the Library of Trinity College, Dublin. To which is added a list of the Fagel Collection of maps in the same library. Dublin, Hodges, Figgis and Co., 1900. xxvi + 606 pp.

4486. Floyer, John K., and Hamilton, Sidney G. Catalogue of MSS Preserved in the Chapter Library of Worcester Cathedral. Oxford, Eng., Parker and Co., 1906. 210 pp.—Compilation by Floyer, editing and revision by Hamilton.

4487. Young, John, and Aitken, P[atrick] H. A Catalogue of the MSS in the Library of the Hunterian Museum in the University of Glasgow. Glasgow, Maclehose and Sons, 1908. xi + 566 pp.

4488. Robinson, Joseph A., and James, M[ontague] R. The MSS of Westminster Abbey. Cambridge Univ. Press, 1909. 108 pp.—Number 1 in the series Notes and Documents of Westminster Abbey.

4489. Borland, Catherine R. A Descriptive Catalogue of the Western Mediaeval MSS in Edinburgh University Library. Edinburgh, Constable, 1916. xxxi + 359 pp. + xxiv facsimiles.

4490. Giuseppi, Montague S. A Guide to the Manuscripts Preserved in the Public Record Office. London, Joseph Causton and Sons for H. M. Stationery Office, 1923–24. 2 vols.—For background see V[ivian] A. Galbraith, *Studies in the Public Records*, London, Thomas Nelson, [1948], ix + 163 pp., The Ford Lectures 1941.

4491. Bannister, Arthur T. A Descriptive Catalogue of the MSS in the Hereford Cathedral Library. Hereford, Wilson and Phillips, 1927. viii + 190 pp.

4492. Woolley, Reginald M. Catalogue of the MSS of Lincoln Cathedral Chapter Library. Oxford Univ. Press, 1927. xxiv + 190 pp.

4493. James, M[ontague] R., and Jenkins, Claude. A Descriptive Catalogue of the MSS in the Library of Lambeth Palace. Cambridge Univ. Press, 1930–31. 2 vols.

4494. Durham Cathedral MSS to the End of the Twelfth Century. Introduction by R[oger] A. B. Mynors. Oxford Univ. Press for the Dean and Chapter, 1939. x + 91 pp.

4495. Tyson, Moses. Hand-List of the Collection of English MSS in the John Rylands Library 1928. Bulletin of the John Rylands Library, XIII (1929), 152–219.—Also Frank Taylor, *Supplementary Hand-List of Western MSS in the John Rylands Library,* Manchester Univ. Press, 1937, 49 pp. Also Taylor's "Hand-List of Additions to the Collection of English MSS in the John Rylands Library," *Bulletin of the John Rylands Library,* XXXIV (1951), 1–50.

§184. MANUSCRIPT COLLECTIONS: AMERICAN

4499. Manuscripts in Public and Private Collections in the United States. Washington, D.C., Government Printing Office for the Library of Congress Division of Manuscripts, 1924. ix + 98 pp.

4500. De Ricci, Seymour. Census of Medieval and Renaissance Manuscripts in the United States and Canada. With the assistance of W. J. Wilson. Introductory note by J. F. Jameson. New York, H. W. Wilson Co., 1935–37. 2 (consecutively paged) vols. 2343 pp.—*Volume III: Indices,* by Seymour De Ricci and W. J. Wilson, New York, H. W. Wilson Co., 1940, vii + 222 (double column) pp.

4501. Guide to Depositories of Manuscript Collections in the United States. One hundred sample entries. Preface by Luther H. Evans. Columbus, Ohio, Historical Records Survey, 1938. 134 leaves mimeographed recto only.—Lists of historically significant manuscripts arranged by state.

4502. [Shipman, Carolyn.] A Catalogue of MSS Forming a Portion of the Library of Robert Hoe. New York, privately printed, 1909. 230 pp.

4503. Turner, Van Arsdale B., et al. Handbook of MSS in the Library of Congress. Washington, D.C., Government Printing Office, 1918. xvi + 750 pp.

4504. De Ricci, Seymour. Medieval MSS in the New York Public Library. Bulletin of the New York Public Library, XXXIV (1930), 297–322.

4505. Garrison, Curtis Wiswell. List of MS Collections in the Library of Congress to July 1931. Annual Report of the American Historical Association for the year 1930. Vol. I Proceedings (Washington, D.C., Government Printing Office, 1931), 123–249.

4506. Butler, Ruth Lapham. Check-List of Manuscripts in the Edward E. Ayer Collection. Chicago, Newberry Library, 1937. viii + 295 pp.

4507. Guide to the Manuscript Collections in the Worcester Historical Society. Prepared by the Historical Records Survey, Division of Community Service Programs, Work Projects Administration. Boston, Historical Records Survey, 1941. iii + 54 pp.

4508. Schulz, Herbert C. American Literary Manuscripts in the Huntington Library. Huntington Library Quarterly, XXII, 3 (May 1959), 209–250.

§185. MANUSCRIPT COLLECTIONS: MISCELLANEOUS

4512. Bresslau, Harry. Handbuch der Urkundenlehre für Deutschland und Italien. 3. Aufl. Berlin, De Gruyter, 1958. 2 vols.—Original ed. 1888–89; second ed. 1912–31.

4513. Omont, Henri, Auvray, Lucien, et al. Bibliothèque nationale. Catalogue général des manuscrits français. Paris, E. Leroux, 1862–1902. 17 vols.

4514. Frank, Grace. English Manuscripts in the Vatican Library. PMLA, XL, 1 (March 1925), 98–102.

4515. Raynaud, Gaston. Catalogue des manuscrits anglais de la Bibliothèque nationale. Paris, H. Champion, 1884. 30 pp.—Also Max Förster, "Die altenglischen Texte der Pariser Nationalbibliothek," *Englische Studien,* LXII, 1/2 (Nov. 1927), 113–131.

4516. Frels, Wilhelm. Deutsche Dichterhandschriften von 1400 bis 1900. Gesamtkatalog der eigenhändigen Handschriften deutscher Dichter in den Bibliotheken und Archiven Deutschlands. Leipzig, K. W. Hiersemann, 1934. xiv + 382 pp.—Volume II in the series Bibliographical Publications: Germanic Section of the Modern Language Association of America.

4517. Catalogue des manuscrits de la Bibliothèque royale de Belgique. Brussels, H. Lamertin, 1901–09; Renaux, Des presses de J. Leherte Courtin, 1919–48. 13 vols.

§186. INCUNABULA AND EARLY PRINTED BOOKS: MAJOR CHECK AND FINDING LISTS WITH THEIR ADDENDA AND INDEXES, RECORDS AND REGISTERS OF THE STATIONERS' COMPANY, AND TERM CATALOGUES

[See also §170. Printing: Historical Aspects; §174. Book Trade: Historical Studies.]

4521. Arber, Edward. A Transcript of the Registers of the Company of Stationers of London 1554–1640. London, privately printed, 1875–77. 5 vols.—Reprints Birmingham, Eng., 1894 and New York, 1950.

4522. Aldis, Harry G. A List of Books Printed in Scotland before 1700. Including those printed furth of the realm for Scottish booksellers, with brief notes on printers and stationers. Edinburgh, Bibliographical Society, 1904. xvi + 153 pp.—Number 7 in the series Publications of the Edinburgh Bibliographical Society. For the present state of Scottish literary bibliography see W. R. Aitken, "The Bibliography of Scottish Literature," *Library Association Record*, LIX, 4 (April 1957), 121–126.

4523. Arber, Edward. The Term Catalogues 1668–1709. A contemporary bibliography of English literature in the reigns of Charles II, James II, William and Mary, and Anne. London, privately printed, 1903–06. 3 vols.

4524. De Ricci, Seymour. A Census of Caxtons. Oxford Univ. Press, 1909. xv pp. + xi leaves of reproductions + 196 pp.—Number 15 in the series Illustrated Monographs of the Bibliographical Society.

4525. Dix, Ernest R. M. Catalogue of Early Dublin-Printed Books 1601–1700. With an historical introduction and bibliographical notes by C. Winston Dugan. Dublin, T. G. O'Donoghue, 1898–1912. 5 parts in 1 vol.

4526. Duff, E[dward] Gordon, Greg, W[alter] W., McKerrow, R[onald] B., Plomer, H[enry] R., Pollard, A[lfred] W., and Proctor, R[obert]. Hand-Lists of Books Printed by London Printers 1501–1556. London, Blades, East and Blades for the Bibliographical Society, 1913. 4 parts in 1 vol.—Original issue *Hand-Lists of English Printers 1501–1556*, 1895–1913.

4527. Eyre, Geo. E. B. A Transcript of the Registers of the Worshipful Company of Stationers from 1640 to 1708 A.D. London, privately printed, 1913–14. 3 vols.—Reprint New York, 1950.

4528. Duff, E[dward] Gordon. Fifteenth Century English Books. A bibliography of books and documents printed in England and of books for the English market printed abroad. Oxford Univ. Press, 1917. ix + 119 (double column) + 120–136 (single column) pp. + liii leaves of reproductions following p. 124.

4529. Pollard, A[lfred] W., Redgrave, G[ilbert] R., et al. A Short-Title Catalogue of Books Printed in England, Scotland, and Ireland and of English Books Printed Abroad 1475–1640. London, Bibliographical Society, 1926. xvi + 609 (double column) pp.—A list of 26143 titles. Also Paul G. Morrison, *Index of Printers, Publishers, and Booksellers in A. W. Pollard and G. R. Redgrave A Short Title Catalogue . . .*, Charlottesville, Bibliographical Society of the University of Virginia, 1950, iii + 84 leaves printed recto only. Reprints 1946 and 1948 with a foreword by F. C. Francis. Known as the "*STC*" or "Pollard and Redgrave."

4530. Greg, W[alter] W., and Boswell, E[leanore]. Records of the Court of the Stationers' Company 1576 to 1602 from Register B. London, Bibliographical Society, 1930. lxxxi + 144 pp.

4531. Wing, Donald. Short-Title Catalogue of Books Printed in England, Scotland, Ireland, and Wales, and British America and of English Books Printed in Other Countries 1641–1700. Vol. I: A 1–E 2926; Vol. II: E 2927–O 1000; Vol. III; P 1–Z 28. New York, Columbia Univ. Press for the Index Society, 1945–51. 3 (double column page) vols.—Also Paul G. Morrison, *Index of Printers, Publishers, and Booksellers in Donald Wing's Short-Title Catalogue . . .*, Charlottesville, Bibliographical Society of the University of Virginia, 1955, 219 (triple column) pp.

4532. Alden, John. Bibliographica Hibernica. Additions and corrections to Wing. Charlottesville, Bibliographical Society of the University of Virginia, 1955. 39 pp.—Material of Irish origin omitted from or deserving of correction in Wing's *Short-Title Catalogue.*

4533. Allison, A[nthony] F., and Rogers, D[avid] M. A Catalogue of Catholic Books in English Printed Abroad or Secretly in England 1558–1640. Bangor Regis, Eng., Arundel Press, 1956. 2 (continuously paged) parts (xiii + 187 pp.).—Volume III, nos. 3 and 4, in the series Biographical Studies. A list of 930 titles with *STC* numbers given where possible.

4534. Hiscock, W[alter] G. The Christ Church Supplement to Wing's Short-Title Catalogue 1641–1700. Oxford, Eng., Holgwell Press for Christ Church, 1956. 47 (double column) pp.

4535. Jackson, Wm. A. Records of the Court of the Stationers' Company 1602 to 1640. London, Bibliographical Society, 1957. xxiii + 555 pp.

4536. Ramage, David, et al. A Finding-List of English Books to 1640 in Libraries in the British Isles Excluding the National Libraries and the

Libraries of Oxford and Cambridge. Based on the numbers in Pollard and Redgrave's Short Title Catalogue . . . 1475–1640. Durham, Eng., Council of the Durham Colleges, 1958. xvi + 92 (chiefly triple column) pp.

§187. INCUNABULA AND EARLY PRINTED BOOKS: MAJOR DESCRIPTIVE CATALOGUES OF EARLIEST PRINTED BOOKS

[When complete the British Museum catalogue of incunabula (no. 4564) will in many respects supersede all titles that follow. The universal bibliographies (nos. 4839 to 4844) often give excellent incidental information on incunabula. The national library catalogues (nos. 4627 to 4640) list incunabula where feasible. See also §149. Descriptive Bibliography.]

4540. Stillwell, Margaret Bingham. Incunabula and Americana 1450–1800. A key to bibliographical study. New York, Columbia Univ. Press, 1930. xviii + 483 pp.

4541. Lenhart, John M. Pre-Reformation Printed Books. A study in statistical and applied bibliography. New York, J. F. Wagner Inc., 1935. xiv + 197 pp.—Number 14 in the series Franciscan Studies.

4542. [Ohly, Kurt, Juchhoff, Rudolf, and Rath, Erich von.] Der Buchdruck des 15. Jahrhunderts. Eine bibliographische Übersicht. Berlin, Wiegendruck-Gesellschaft, 1929–36. xliv + 328 pp.

4543. Peddie, Robt. A. Conspectus Incunabulorum. An index catalogue of the fifteenth-century books, with reference to Hain's Repertorium, Copinger's Supplement, Proctor's Index, Pellechet's Catalogue, Campbell's Annales, and other bibliographies. London, Libraco Ltd., 1910–14. 2 vols.—Incomplete: Part I: A–B; Part II: C–G.

4544. Maittaire, Michael. Annales typographici ab artis inventae origine ad annum 1664. Hagae-Comitvm, apud Isaacum Vaillant, 1719–41. 5 vols. in 6.—Also Michael Denis, *Annalivm typographicorvm* . . . , Supplementum, Viennae, typis Josephi nobilis de Kurzbek, 1789, 2 vols.

4545. Panzer, Georg W. F. Annales typographici ab artis inventae origine ad annum 1536. Nuremberg, J. E. Zeh, 1793–1803. 11 vols.

4546. Hain, Ludwig. Repertorium bibliographicum. In quo libri omnes ab arte typographica inventa usque annum MD. Typis expressi, ordine alphabetico vel simpliciter enumerantur vel adcuratius recensentur. Stuttgart, J. G. Cotta, 1826–38. 2 vols. in two parts each.—Reprints Berlin, Altmann, 1948, and Milan, Gorlich, 1954. Also Konrad Burger, *Ludwig Hains Repertorium bibliographicum: Register*, Die Drucker des XV. Jahrhunderts, mit chronologischer Aufführung ihrer Werke, Leipzig, Otto Harrassowitz, 1891, vi + 428 pp.

4547. Copinger, Walter A. A Supplement to Hain's Repertorium bibliographicum. Or collections towards a new edition of that work. London, Southeran and Co., 1895–1902. 3 vols.—Also Konrad Burger, *The Printers and Publishers of the Fifteenth Century with Lists of Their Works*, Index to the supplement to Hain's Repertorium bibliographicum, London, Southeran and Co., 1902, xiii + 354 pp.

4548. Burger, Konrad. Supplement zu Hain und Panzer. Leipzig, K. W. Hiersemann, 1908. vii + 440 pp.

4549. Pellechet, M[arie] L. C. Catalogue général des incunables des bibliothèques publiques de France. Paris, Librairie Alphonse Picard, 1897–1909. 3 vols.—Coverage *Abano* to *Gregorius Magnus* only. Available on microfilm are vols. 4–14 (Gregorius to Zutphania) of the unpublished MS in the Bibliothèque Nationale, Paris.

4550. Reichling, Dietrich. Appendices ad Hainii-Copingeri Repertorium bibliographicum. Additiones et emendationes, etc. Munich, J. Rosenthal, 1905–11. 7 vols.—Supplement Münster, 1914, 109 + cxxxv pp.

4551. Polain, Louis. Catalogues des livres imprimés au quinzième siècle des bibliothèques de Belgique. Brussels, Société des Bibliophiles, 1932. 4 vols.

4552. Gesamtkatalog der Wiegendrucke. Herausgegeben von der Kommission für den Gesamtkatalog der Wiegendrucke. Leipzig, K. W. Hiersemann, 1925–40. 7 vols. (A to Eig) plus fascicule 1 of vol. 8 (Eike to Federicis).—Incomplete. Coverage continued by the British Museum *Catalogue of Books Printed in the Fifteenth Century.*

4553. Campbell, M[arinus]-F.-A.-G. Annales de la typographie néerlandaise au XVe siècle. The Hague, M. Nijhoff, 1874. xii + 629 pp.—Also four *Suppléments*, 1878–90. Also Robert Proctor, "Additions to Campbell's Annales . . . ," Tracts on Early Printing, III (London 1897), 79 pp. Also Maria Elizabeth Kronenberg, *Campbell's Annales . . .* , Contributions to a new edition, The Hague, M. Nijhoff, 1956, 167 pp.

4554. Nijhoff, Wouter, and Kronenberg, M[aria] E. Nederlandsche Bibliographie von 1500 tot 1540. The Hague, M. Nijhoff, 1923–58. 5 vols.

§188. INCUNABULA AND EARLY PRINTED BOOKS: BRITISH COLLECTIONS EXCLUSIVE OF THOSE IN UNIVERSITIES

4559. Catalogue of Books in the Library of the British Museum Printed in England, Scotland, and Ireland and of Books in English Printed Abroad to the Year 1640. London, British Museum, 1884. 3 vols.

4560. Duff, E[dward] G. Catalogue of Books in the John Rylands Library, [Manchester,] Printed in England, Scotland, and Ireland, and of Books in English Printed Abroad to the End of the Year 1640. Manchester, Cornish, 1895. iii + 147 pp.

4561. English Incunabula in the John Rylands Library. A catalogue of books printed in England and of English books printed abroad between the years 1475 and 1500. Edited by H. Guppy. Manchester, University Press, 1930. xvi + 102 pp. + 16 plates.

4562. The Britwell Handlist. Or a short-title catalogue of the principal volumes from the time of Caxton to the year 1800. Formerly in the library of Britwell Court, Buckinghamshire. London, Bernard Quaritch, 1933. 2 vols.

4563. Proctor, Robt. G. C. An Index to the Early Printed Books in the British Museum from the Invention of Printing to the Year 1500. With notes on those in the Bodleian Library. London, Kegan Paul, Trench, Trubner and Co., 1898–1938. 4 vols.—Also *Supplements* [for 1898–1902], London, Chiswick Press, 1900–03, 5 parts. Also *Register* [to the four supplements], by Konrad Burger, 1906, 15 pp. Reprint Oxford, Eng., Basil Blackwell, 1960.

4564. Catalogue of Books Printed in the Fifteenth Century Now in the British Museum. London, printed by order of the Trustees, 1908–48. 8 (chiefly double column page) parts.—Coverage to date xylographica, Germany, Italy, and French-speaking Switzerland. Excellent facsimiles. An extremely detailed and elaborate work with introductions by Alfred W. Pollard and Victor Scholderer. Arrangement by country, towns, and presses.

§189. INCUNABULA AND EARLY PRINTED BOOKS: BRITISH UNIVERSITY COLLECTIONS

4568. Hackman, Alfred, Clay, Henry, and Browne, Arthur. Catalogus librorum impressorum bibliothecae Bodleianae in Academia oxoniensi. . . . Oxonii, e typographeo academico, 1843–51. 4 vols.

4569. Sinker, Robt. A Catalogue of the English Books Printed before 1501 Now in the Library of Trinity College, Cambridge. Cambridge Univ. Press, 1885. 488 pp.

4570. Cambridge University Library. Early English Printed Books in the University Library 1475–1640. Vol. I: Caxton to F. Kingston; Vol. II: E. Mattes to R. Marriot and English Provincial Presses; Vol. III: Scottish, Irish, and Foreign Presses with Addenda; Vol. IV: Indexes. Cambridge Univ. Press, 1900–07. 4 vols.

4571. Wood, P[hilip] W., and Watts, G H. A Hand-List of English Books in the Library of Emanuel College, Cambridge, Printed before 1641. Cambridge Univ. Press for the Bibliographical Society, London, 1915. viii + 182 pp.—Volume II in the series Short Catalogues of English Books Printed before 1641.

4572. Gaselee, Stephen. The Early Printed Books in the Library of Corpus Christi College, Cambridge. Cambridge Univ. Press, 1921. 38 pp.

4573. A List of Fifteenth Century Books in the University of Aberdeen. [Aberdeen], printed for the University, 1925. vii + 85 pp.

4574. Schneider, G[ustavus] A. A Descriptive Catalogue of the Incunabula in the Library of Gonville and Caius College, Cambridge. Cambridge Univ. Press, 1928. iv + 45 pp.

4575. Powicke, Frederick M. The Medieval Books of Merton College, Oxford. Oxford, Clarendon Press, 1931. xii + 287 pp.

4576. Oates, J[ohn] C. T. A Catalogue of the Fifteenth-Century Printed Books in the University Library, Cambridge. Cambridge Univ. Press, 1954. xiii + 898 pp.

§190. INCUNABULA AND EARLY PRINTED BOOKS: AMERICAN COLLECTIONS

4581. Census of Fifteenth Century Books Owned in America. Compiled by a committee of the Bibliographical Society. Introduction by George Parker Winship. New York, [printed by the New York Public Library,] 1919. xxiv + 245 pp.—Reprint from the *Bulletin of the New York Public Library*, April/Dec. 1918 and August 1919.

4582. Stillwell, Margaret Bingham. Incunabula in American Libraries. A second census of fifteenth-century books owned in the United States, Mexico, and Canada. New York, Bibliographical Society of America, 1940. xlv + 619 (double column) pp.—Number 1 in the Bibliographical Society of America Monograph Series.

4583. Bishop, Wm. Warner. A Checklist of American Copies of Short-Title Catalogue Books. 2nd ed. Ann Arbor, University of Michigan Press, 1950. xi + 203 (chiefly triple column) pp.—Number 6 in the series University of Michigan General Library Publications. Original ed. 1944.

4584. A Contribution to a Union Catalog of Sixteenth Century Imprints in Certain New England Libraries. Providence, Brown Univ. Library, 1953. vii + 466 pp.—Photomechanical reproduction of a typed copy.

4585. [Wright, James O., and Shipman, Carolyn.] Catalogue of Books by English Authors Who Lived before the Year 1700 Forming a Part of the Library of Robert Hoe, New York. New York, G. H. Richmond and Son, 1904–05. 5 vols.—A collection now largely preserved in the Huntington Library.

4586. Pollard, Alfred W. Catalogue of Books Mostly from the Presses of the First Printers. . . . Collected by Rush C. Hawkins . . . and deposited in the Annmary Brown Memorial at Providence, Rhode Island. Oxford Univ. Press for Rush C. Hawkins, 1910. xxxv + 339 pp.

4587. Catalogue of the William Loring Andrews Collection of Early Books in the Library of Yale University. Preface by Addison Van Name. New Haven, Yale Univ. Press, 1913. 56 pp.

4588. Ashley, Frederick W. Catalogue of the John Boyd Thacher Collection of Incunabula. Washington, D.C., Government Printing Office for the Library of Congress, 1915. 329 pp.—A Library of Congress collection of 840 works.

4589. Stearns, Mae I. Check-List of Books Printed in English before 1641. Chicago, Newberry Library, 1923. ix + 198 pp.

4590. Haskell, Daniel C. Check-List of Early English Printing 1475–1640 in the New York Public Library. Bulletin of the New York Public Library, XXIX, 7 (1925), 484–512, and XXIX, 8 (1925), 545–578.

4591. Bartlett, Henrietta C. Catalogue of Early English Books Chiefly of the Elizabethan Period Collected by William Augustus White. New York, W. A. White, 1926. 170 pp.

4592. Catalogue of English Literature of the Seventeenth and Eighteenth Centuries. London, John W. Walker, 1926. 37 pp.—Catalogue 12 of John W. Walker. Most of the items are now in the Huntington Library.

4593. Butler, Pierce. A Check List of Fifteenth Century Books in the Newberry Library and Other Libraries of Chicago. Chicago, Newberry Library, 1933. xxiv + 362 pp.

4594. Waters, W[illard] O. American Imprints 1648–1797 in the Huntington Library. Huntington Library Bulletin, No. 3 (1933), 1–95.

4595. Haraszti, Zoltán. A Check-List of Incunabula in the Boston Public Library. Boston, Trustees of the Public Library, 1935. 12 pp.—Reprint from *More Books,* The Bulletin of the Boston Public Library, 1935.

4596. Mead, Herman R. Incunabula in the Huntington Library. San Marino, Calif., Huntington Library, 1937. xii + 386 pp.—Number 3 in the series Huntington Library Lists.

4597. Thurston, Ada, and Bühler, Curt F. Check List of Fifteenth Century Printing in the Pierpont Morgan Library. New York, Pierpont Morgan Library, 1939. xv + 348 pp.

4598. Woodward, Gertrude L. English Books and Books Printed in England before 1641 in the Newberry Library. A supplement to the record in the Short Title Catalogue. Chicago, Newberry Library, 1939. vii + 118 pp.

4599. Cook, Olan V. Incunabula in the Hanes Collection of the Library of the University of North Carolina. Chapel Hill, University of North Carolina, 1940. xviii + 125 pp.—Number 1 in the series Hanes Foundation Publications.

4600. Jackson, Wm. A. The Carl H. Pforzheimer Library, English Literature 1475–1700. New York, privately printed, 1940. 3 vols.

4601. A List of Books Printed in the Fifteenth Century in the John Carter Brown Library and the General Library of Brown University. Oxford Univ. Press for Brown University, 1910. 19 pp.—Also *Books Printed in the Sixteenth Century in the Brown University Library*, Providence, Brown University, 1946, 27 pp.

4602. Fay, C[hristopher] U. Fifteenth Century Printed Books at the University of Illinois. Foreword by Robert B. Downs. Urbana, University of Illinois Press, 1949. 160 pp.—Number 4 in the series Illinois Contributions to Librarianship.

§191. INCUNABULA AND EARLY PRINTED BOOKS: MISCELLANEOUS COLLECTIONS

4606. Pellechet, Marie. Catalogue des incunables et des livres imprimés de MD. à MDXX. Bibliothèque Publique: Versailles. Paris, A. Picard, 1889. viii + 302 pp.

4607. Beaulieux, Chas. Catalogue de la réserve XVIe siècle (1501–1540) de la Bibliothèque de l'Université de Paris. Paris, Librairie Ancienne Honoré Champion, 1910. [iii] + 324 pp.—Also *Supplément et suite (1541–1550)*, Paris, 1923, 216 pp.

4608. Short-Title Catalogue of Books Printed in France and of French Books Printed in Other Countries from 1470 to 1600 Now in the British Museum. London, British Museum Department of Printed Books, 1924. vii + 491 pp.

4609. A Catalogue of Books in English History and Literature from the Earliest Times to the End of the Seventeenth Century. London, Bernard Quaritch Ltd., 1930. 2 vols.—Essentially a bookseller's catalogue, but with good bibliographic descriptions.

4610. Pennink, R[enetta]. Catalogus der niet-nederlandse Drukken: 1500–1540 aanwezig in de koninklijke Bibliotheek 'S'Gravenhage. The Hague, Koninklijke Bibliotheek, 1955. xix + 267 (double column) pp.

4611. Deckert, H[elmut]. Katalog der Inkunabeln der sächsischen Landesbibliothek zu Dresden. Ein Bestandsverzeichnis nach den Kriegsverlusten des Jahres 1945. Leipzig, Otto Harrassowitz, 1957. 255 pp.—Number 80 in the series Zentralblatt für Bibliothekswesen: Beihefte.

§192. LISTS, CHIEFLY RETROSPECTIVE, OF EARLIER AMERICAN BOOKS

[See also Blanck's *Bibliography*, no. 508.]

4615. Wemyss, Stanley. The General Guide to Rare Americana with Auction Records and Prices. A hand book and guide to rare and notable books relating to America. Philadelphia, Stanley Wemyss, 1950. 323 pp.—Original ed. 1944. Bibliography, pp. 11–13.

4616. Stevens, Henry. Catalogue of the American Books in the Library of the British Museum at Christmas MDCCCLVI. London, C. Whittingham at the Chiswick Press for H. Stevens, 1866. 4 parts in 1 vol.

4617. Paine, Nathaniel. A List of Early American Imprints 1640–1700 Belonging to the Library of the American Antiquarian Society. Worcester, Mass., Charles Hamilton, 1896. vi + 80 pp.—Reprinted from *Proceedings of the American Antiquarian Society*, Oct. 1895.

4618. [Staton, Frances M.] Books and Pamphlets Published in Canada up to 1837 Copies of Which Are in the Public Reference Library, Toronto. Toronto Public Library, 1916. 76 pp.—Two *Supplements*, 1919–26.

4619. Evans, Chas. American Bibliography. . . . A chronological dictionary of all books, pamphlets, and periodical publications printed in the United States from . . . 1639 down to and including the year 1820. With bibliographical and biographical notes. Chicago, privately printed, 1903–34. 12 vols.—Unfinished (Vol. XII: 1798–99). A finding list. Supplement for the years 1648–1797 in the *Huntington Library Bulletin*, No. 3 (1933), 1–95.

4620. Sabin, Joseph, Eames, Wilberforce, et al. Bibliotheca Americana. A dictionary of books relating to America from its discovery to the present time. Completed by R. W. Vail. New York, Bibliographic Society of America, 1868–1936. 29 vols.—A descriptive and finding list. Title varies.

4621. Tod, Dorothea D., and Cordingley, Audrey. A Check-List of Canadian Imprints 1900–1925. Ottawa, Canadian Bibliographic Centre, Public Archives, 1950. iv pp. + 370 leaves.

4622. Tremaine, Marie. A Bibliography of Canadian Imprints 1751–1800. University of Toronto Press, 1952. xxvii + 705 pp.

4623. Shaw, Robt. R., and Shoemaker, Richard H. American Bibliography. [A preliminary checklist for 1801 to 1805.] New York, Scarecrow Press, 1958. 5 vols.—One volume for each year. Items (1 to 9785) are numbered consecutively from the first to the last volume.

§193. NATIONAL LIBRARY CATALOGUES: AMERICAN; BRITISH; FRENCH; GERMAN

4627. A Catalog of Books Represented by Library of Congress Printed Cards. Ann Arbor, Mich., Edwards Brothers Inc., 1942–46. 167 (triple column page) vols.—Coverage August 1898 through July 1942. Also *Supplement,* Ann Arbor, Mich., J. W. Edwards Inc., 1948, 42 (triple column page) vols., coverage August 1942 through December 1947. Continuation as *Library of Congress Author Catalog 1948–1952,* Ann Arbor, Mich., J. W. Edwards Inc., 1953, 24 (triple column page) vols. (vol. 24 a film list), and *The National Union Catalog,* A cumulative author list 1953–1957, Ann Arbor, Mich., J. W. Edwards Inc., 1958, 28 (triple column page) vols. (vol. 27 *Music and Phonorecords* and vol. 28 *Motion Pictures and Filmstrips*). For the subject index see no. 4834.

4631. Catalogue of the Printed Books in the Library of the British Museum. London, William Clowes and Sons, 1881–1900. 95 vols.—Also *Supplement,* London, William Clowes and Sons, 1900–05, 15 vols., covering titles added 1882–99. Reprint of *Catalogue* 1946 in 58 vols. and *Supplement* 1950 in 10 vols., Ann Arbor, Mich., J. W. Edwards. Partial replacement by *General Catalogue of Printed Books,* London, British Museum 1931–54, 51 vols., A–Dez., which has been left incomplete. A new *General Catalogue of Printed Books,* of which first issues, reproduced by photo-offset lithography, are to appear in 1960, will be completed in *circa* five years in 250 to 300 vols. For the numerous special catalogues issued by the Museum see F. C. Francis, "The Catalogues of the British Museum. 1. Printed Books," *Journal of Documentation*, IV, 1 (June 1948), 14–40.

4635. Catalogue général des livres imprimés de la Bibliothèque Nationale: Auteurs. Paris, Imprimerie Nationale, 1897–date. 184 vols.—Incomplete; by 1959 carried into the letter *t*: Tome CLXXXIV Tendlau–Texier-Westmuller.

4639. Berliner Titeldrucke. Fünfjahrs Katalog 1930–1934. Berlin, Staatsbibliothek, 1935. 8 vols.

4640. Gesamtkatalog der preussischen Bibliotheken. Mit Nachweis des deutschen Besitzes der bayerischen Staatsbibliothek in München und der Nationalbibliothek in Wien. Herausgegeben von der preussischen Staatsbibliothek. Berlin, Preussische Druckerei- und Verlags-Aktiengesellschaft, 1931–39. 14 vols.—Coverage only "A" to "Beethordnung." From 1936 to 1939 title *Deutscher Gesamtkatalog*.

§194. DIRECTORIES OF SPECIAL COLLECTIONS AND RESOURCES IN BRITISH AND AMERICAN LIBRARIES

[See also §177. Libraries: Historical Aspects; §178. Library Science.]

4644. Check List of Collections of Personal Papers in Historical Societies, University and Public Libraries, and Other Learned Institutions in the United States. Prefatory note by J. C. Fitzpatrick. Washington, D.C., Government Printing Office, 1918. 87 pp.

4645. Richardson, Ernest C. An Index Directory to Special Collections in North American Libraries. Provisional ed., unedited. Yardley, Penn., F. S. Cook and Son, 1927. x + 168 pp.

4646. Winchell, Constance M. Locating Books for Interlibrary Loan. With a bibliography of printed aids which show location of books in American libraries. New York, H. W. Wilson, 1930. 170 pp.—See also *General Interlibrary Loan Code 1952,* Revised ed., Chicago, American Library Association, 1956, 10 pp.

4647. Downs, Robt. B. Resources of Southern Libraries. Chicago, American Library Association, 1938. xii + 370 pp.

4648. Carlson, Wm. H. Scandinavian Collections in the Libraries of the United States. Scandinavian Studies, XV, 7 (Aug. 1939), 217–238.—Also Carlson's "Some Further Notes on Scandinavian Collections in Libraries of the United States," *Scandinavian Studies,* XVI, 8 (Nov. 1941), 291–303.

4649. Downs, Robt. B. Resources of New York City Libraries. A survey of facilities for advanced study and research. Chicago, American Library Association, 1942. xiii + 442 pp.

4650. Van Male, John. Resources of Pacific Northwest Libraries. A survey of facilities for study and research. Seattle, Wash., Pacific Northwest Library Association, 1943. xv + 404 pp.

4651. Besterman, Theodore, et al. British Sources of Reference and Information. A guide to societies, works of reference, and libraries. London, Aslib for the British Council, 1947. vii + 56 pp.

4652. Ireland, Norma O. Local Indexes in American Libraries. A union list of unpublished indexes. Boston, F. W. Faxon Co., 1947. xxxv + 221 (double column) pp.—Number 73 in the Useful Reference Series. A list of card files in various U.S. libraries that index special subjects.

4653. Special Library Resources. Vol. I: United States and Canada; Vol. II: Alabama–Montana; Vol. III: Nebraska–Wyoming and Canada; Vol. IV: Cumulated Indexes to Vols. I–III. New York, Special Libraries Association, 1941–47. 4 vols.—Volumes I and II edited by Rose L. Vormelker; volumes III and IV edited by Isabel L. Towner.

4654. Guide to the Records in National Archives. Washington, D.C., Government Printing Office, 1948. xvi + 684 pp.

4655. Philip, Axel J. Index to Special Collections in Libraries, Museums, and Art Galleries (Public, Private, and Official) in Great Britain and Ireland. London, F. G. Brown for the author, [1949]. viii + 190 pp.

4656. Downs, Robt. B. American Library Resources. Chicago, American Library Association, 1951. 428 (double column) pp.

4657. Towner, Isabel L. Directory of Special Libraries. Preface by Elizabeth Ferguson. New York, Special Libraries Association, 1953. 297 (double column) pp.

4658. American Library Directory. A classified list of 14260 libraries with names of librarians and statistical data compiled triennially. 21st ed. New York, R. R. Bowker Co., 1957. xiii + 957 (chiefly double column) pp.—Original ed. 1908.

4659. Aslib Directory. A guide to sources of information in Great Britain and Ireland. Edited by Miriam Alman. Vol. I: Indexes and Appendixes; Vol. II: Directory of Libraries and Information Services [and] Regional Index. [New ed.] London, Aslib, 1957. 2 vols.—Original ed. 1928 in 1 vol.

4660. Ash, Lee. Subject Collections. A guide to special book collections and subject emphasis as reported by university, college, public and special libraries in the United States, the Territories, and Canada. New York, R. R. Bowker Co., 1958. xv + 476 (double column) pp.

§195. LIBRARY SURVEYS BY INSTITUTION, CITY, OR AREA

[See also §177. Libraries: Historical Aspects; §178. Library Science.]

4664. Botfield, Beriah. Notes on the Cathedral Libraries of England. London, no publisher, 1849. xvi + 527 pp.

4665. Macray, Wm. D. Annals of the Bodleian Library. With a notice of the earlier library of the University. Second ed., enl. and continued from 1868 to 1880. Oxford, Clarendon Press, 1890. x + 545 pp.—Original ed. 1868.

4666. Newcombe, Luxmoore. The University and College Libraries of Great Britain and Ireland. A guide to the material available to the research student. London, J. and E. Bumpus, 1927. 220 pp.

4667. Rye, Reginald Arthur. The Students' Guide to the Libraries of London. 3rd ed. University of London Press, 1927. xxv + 580 pp.—Original ed. 1908; second ed. 1910.

4668. [Potter, Alfred Claghorn.] The Library of Harvard University. Descriptive and historical notes. 4th ed. Cambridge, Mass., Harvard Univ. Press, 1934. 186 pp.—Volume VI in the series Library of Harvard University Special Publications. Original ed. 1903. Also the series *Guides to the Harvard Libraries*: No. 1 "Economics and Business," by Arthur H. Cole, 1947, x + 64 pp.; no. 2 "Fine Arts," by E. Louise Lucas, 1949, ix + 54 pp.; no. 3 "The Research Services of the Harvard College Library," by David C. Weber, 1956, viii + 40 pp.; no. 4 "The Harvard University Archives," 1957, 10 pp.; no. 5 "A Guide to the Baker Library," 1957, 8 pp.; no. 6 "Harvard Law School Library," 1957, [11] pp.; no. 7 "Guide to Lamont Library," 1958, 18 pp.

4669. Hill, David Spence. The Libraries of Washington. A study of the governmental and non-governmental libraries in the District of Columbia in relation to the units of government and other organizations which they serve. Chicago, American Library Association, 1936. xvi + 296 pp.

4670. Burton, Margaret. Famous Libraries of the World. Their history, collections, and administrations. Introduction by Arundell Esdaile. London, Grafton and Co., 1937. xix + 458 pp. + xxxi plates.

4671. Davies, W[illiam] L. The National Library of Wales. A survey of its history, its contents, and its activities. Aberystwyth, National Library of Wales, 1937. xxiv + 212 pp.

4672. Leroy, Émile. Guide pratique des bibliothèques de Paris. Préface de Julien Cain. Paris, Éditions des Bibliothèques Nationales, 1937. viii + 283 pp.

4673. Adams, Joseph Q. The Folger Shakespeare Memorial Library. A report on progress 1931–1941. Amherst, Mass., Trustees of Amherst College, 1942. 61 pp.—See Giles E. Dawson, "The Resources and Policies of the Folger Shakespeare Library," *Library Quarterly*, XIX, 3 (July 1949), 178–185, and James G. McManaway, "The Folger Shakespeare Library," *Shakespeare Survey*, Cambridge, Eng., 1948, vol. I, pp. 57–78. The Folger Library, in addition to Shakespeareana, contains medieval MSS, incunabula, and early printed books.

4674. Rivera, Rodolfo O. Preliminary List of Libraries in the Other American Republics. Washington, D.C., Government Printing Office, 1942. ix + 181 (double column) pp.—Number 5 in the series Studies of the A.L.A. Committee on Library Cooperation with Latin America.

4675. Esdaile, Arundell. The British Museum Library. A short history and survey. Introduction by Sir Frederic G. Kenyon. London, G. Allen and Unwin Ltd., [1946]. 388 pp.

4676. Führer durch die schweizerische Dokumentation / Guide de la documentation en Suisse. Herausgegeben von der schweizerischen Vereinigung für Dokumentation unter Mitarbeit der schweizerischen Landesbibliothek. 2. verm. Aufl. Zürich, [Bühler-Buchdruck], 1946. 80 pp.—Original ed. 1942.

4677. Hove, Julien van. Répertoire des organismes de documentation en Belgique. Centres de documentation, bibliothèques, dépôts d'archives, musées, etc. Brussels, Éditions de la Librairie Encyclopédique, 1947. 335 pp.

4678. Directory of Special Libraries in Boston, Vicinity, and Member Libraries in New England. Fifth ed. compiled by the Boston Chapter of the Special Libraries Association. Boston, [Special Libraries Association,] 1948. 70 pp.—Also Ralph Lester, *Boston's Special Libraries*, New York, Prentice-Hall Inc., 1917, 138 pp.

4679. Hoffman, C   and Milan, C[arl] H. Libraries in the United States. Chicago, American Library Association, 1948. 214–231 pp.—"Reprinted from Actes du Comité international des bibliothèques, 1947 meeting."

4680. Irwin, Raymond, ed. The Libraries of London. London, Library Association, 1949. iv + 234 pp.—Seventeen lectures delivered at the University of London School of Librarianship in April 1948. Bibliography, pp. 219–224.

4681. Adressenverzeichnis deutscher Bibliotheken. Herausgegeben von der Auskunftsabteilung der öffentlichen wissenschaftlichen Bibliothek, Berlin. Leipzig, Verlag des Börsenvereins der deutschen Buchhändler, 1950. 248 pp.

4682. Répertoire des bibliothèques de France. [Vol. I:] Bibliothèques de Paris; [Vol. II:] Bibliothèques des départments; [Vol. III:] Centres et services de documentation. Paris, Bibliothèque Nationale, 1950–51. 3 vols.

4683. A Guide to Government Libraries. London, Her Majesty's Stationery Office, 1952. viii + 139 pp.—Reprints 1958, 1959.

4684. Dokumentation in Österreich. Verzeichnis der Dokumentationsstellen und der periodischen erscheinenden Bibliographien. Herausgegeben von der österreichischen Gesellschaft für Dokumentation und Bibliographie. Vienna, Verlag Brüder Hollinek, 1953. viii + 63 pp.—Volume II in the series Biblos-Schriften.

4685. James, Geraldine R. Directory of Libraries and Information Sources in the Philadelphia Area. 9th ed. Philadelphia, Special Libraries Council of Philadelphia and Vicinity, 1956. 132 pp.—Original ed. 1920.

4686. Esdaile, Arundell. National Libraries of the World. Their history, administration, and public services. Second ed. completely rev. by F[rancis] J. Hill. London, Library Association, 1957. xv + 413 pp.—Original ed. 1934.

4687. Horecky, Paul L. Libraries and Bibliographic Centers in the Soviet Union. [Washington, D.C., Council on Library Resources Inc., 1959.] xviii + 275 pp.—Volume XVI in the Indiana University Publications: Slavic and East European Series.

4688. Munby, A[lan] N. L. Cambridge College Libraries. Aids for research students. Cambridge, Eng., W. Heffer and Sons, [1960]. xv + 55 pp.—An excellent survey of the research materials available at the Cambridge college libraries with notations of collection catalogues.

§196. INDIVIDUAL LIBRARY COLLECTIONS: AMERICAN

4692. Catalogue of the Library of the Boston Athenaeum 1807–71. Boston, no publisher, 1874–82. 5 vols.—Original ed. 1827 (356 pp.).

4693. [Cogswell, Joseph Green.] Catalogue or Alphabetical Index of the Astor Library. Part I: Authors and Books. New York, R. Craighead, Printer, 1857–61. 4 vols.—A "Part II" was not issued; the index of subjects appears in *Supplement to the Astor Library Catalogue,* With an alphabetical index of subjects in all the volumes, New York, R. Craighead, 1866, 605 pp. Accessions to 1880 were listed 1886–88 in 4 vols. Since 1895 part of the New York Public Library.

4694. Catalogue of the Library of the Peabody Institute of the City of Baltimore. Baltimore, I. Friedewald, 1883–1905. 13 vols.

4695. [Shipman, Carolyn.] A Catalogue of Books in English Later Than 1700 Forming a Portion of the Library of Robert Hoe. New York, privately printed, 1905. 3 vols.—Also Shipman's *Catalogue of Books in Foreign Languages Published after the Year 1600 Forming a Portion of the Library of Robert Hoe,* New York, privately printed, 1909, 4 vols.

4696. Cole, Geo. W. A Catalogue of Books Relating to the Discovery and Early History of North and South America Forming a Part of the Library of E. D. Church. New York, Dodd, Mead and Co., 1907. 5 vols. —Also Cole's *A Catalogue of Books Consisting of English Literature and Miscellanies . . . Forming a Part of the Library of E. D. Church,* New York, Dodd, Mead and Co., 1909, 2 vols. Both collections are now in the Huntington Library.

4697. Rosenbach, A[braham] S. W. Catalogue of the Books and Manuscripts of Harry Elkins Widener. Philadelphia, privately printed, 1918. 2 vols. —A collection now in the Harvard University Library.

4698. Wrenn, Harold B. A Catalogue of the Library of the Late John Henry Wrenn. Edited by Thomas J. Wise. Austin, University of Texas, 1920. 5 vols.—A University of Texas collection of eighteenth century English literature and Americana.

4699. A Classified Catalogue of the Carnegie Library of Pittsburgh. Pittsburgh, Carnegie Library, 1907–26. 11 vols.—First Series 1907 in 3 vols.; Second Series 1908 in 2 vols.; Third Series 1914 in 3 vols.; Fourth Series 1920–26 in 3 vols.

4700. The Robert B. Adam Library Relating to Dr. Samuel Johnson and His Era. Oxford Univ. Press for Robert B. Adam, 1929. 3 vols.—A collection now in the library of the University of Rochester, N.Y.

4701. Cowan, Robt. A. The Library of William Andrews Clark Jr. Index to authors and titles. San Francisco, John Henry Nash, 1922–30. 2 vols. —A collection, now at the University of California, Los Angeles, of seventeenth century and later works.

4702. Gillett, Chas. Ripley. Catalogue of the McAlpin Collection of British History and Theology. New York, Union Theological Seminary, 1927–30. 5 vols.—A collection in the Library of the Union Theological Seminary, New York, covering the religious and political history of England especially of the seventeenth and eighteenth centuries.

4703. Ashley, Frederick W. The Collection of John Boyd Thacher in the Library of Congress. Washington, D.C., Government Printing Office, 1931. 3 vols.—Volume I was originally issued in 1915 with the title *Catalogue of the John Boyd Thacher Collection of Incunabula* (329 pp.) and lists 840 works.

4704. Bibliotheca Americana. Catalogue of the John Carter Brown Library in Brown University, Providence, R.I. Providence, Brown University, 1919–31. 3 vols. in 5.

4705. Osborne, Lucy Eugenia. The Chapin Library, Williams College. A short-title list. Portland, Me., Southworth-Anthoensen, 1939. viii + 595 pp.—A collection which includes incunabula and Americana.

4706. Walter, Frank K., and Doneghy, Virginia. Jesuit Relations and Other Americana in the Library of James F. Bell. Minneapolis, University of Minnesota Press, 1950. xiv + 419 pp.

4707. McNiff, Philip J. Catalogue of Lamont Library, Harvard University. Cambridge, Mass., Harvard Univ. Press, 1953. ix + 562 (double column) pp.—A list of books designed to fulfill the needs of a large modern undergraduate college library.

4708. Carnegie Institution. Catalogues of Publications and Depositions of the Institution. Washington, D.C., Carnegie Institution of Washington, 1954. vii + 397 pp.

§197. INDIVIDUAL LIBRARY COLLECTIONS: BRITISH

4712. Catalogue of the Printed Books in the Library of the Faculty of Advocates. Edinburgh, Blackwood and Sons, 1867–79. 6 vols. plus supplementary vol.

4713. Duff, E[dward] G. Catalogue of Printed Books and MSS in the John Rylands Library, Manchester. Manchester, Eng., Rylands Library, 1899. 3 vols.

4714. De Ricci, Seymour. A Handlist of a Collection of Books and Manuscripts Belonging to the Right Hon. Lord Amherst of Hackney. . . . Cambridge Univ. Press, 1906. 433 pp. printed recto only.

4715. Leigh, Chas. W. E. Catalogue of the Christie Collection. Comprising the printed books and MSS bequeathed to the Library of the University of Manchester by the late Richard Copley Christie. London, Longmans, Green and Co. for the Manchester Univ. Press, 1915. xvi + 536 pp.

4716. Catalogue of the Bradshaw Collection of Irish Books in the University Library, Cambridge. London, Bernard Quaritch, 1916. 3 vols.

4717. Catalogue of the Famous Huth Library of Printed Books, Illuminated MSS, Autograph Letters, and Engravings. Collected by Henry Huth and since maintained and augmented by his son Alfred H. Huth. The printed books and illustrated MSS . . . sold by Messrs. Sotheby, Wilkinson, and Hodge. London, Dryden Press, 1911–20. 9 parts in 3 vols. —Also *The Huth Library,* Catalogue of books unsold and returned . . . , London, Dryden Press, 1922, 54 pp. Original catalogue: William C. Hazlitt and Frederick S. Ellis, *The Huth Library,* A catalogue of the printed books, MSS, autograph letters, and engravings collected by Henry Huth, with collations and bibliographical descriptions, London, Ellis and White, 1880, 5 vols.

4718. Catalogue of the Printed Books in the Library of the University of Edinburgh. Edinburgh, T. and A. Constable for the University of Edinburgh, 1918–23. 3 vols.

4719. Wise, Thos. J. The Ashley Library. A catalogue of the printed books, MSS, and autograph letters collected by Thomas James Wise. London, printed for private circulation only, 1936. 11 vols.—A collection, now in the British Museum, rich in first editions.

4720. [Tanner, Joseph R., Duff, Edward G., et al.] Bibliotheca Pepysiana. A descriptive catalogue of the library of Samuel Pepys [in Magdalene College]. London, Sidgwick and Jackson, 1914–40. 4 vols.

4721. Wright, C[harles] T. H., and Purnell, C[hristopher] J. Catalogue of the London Library, St. James Square, London. 2nd ed. London, no publisher, 1913–14. 2 vols.—Original ed. 1847; revised and enl. ed. 1903. Also *Supplement 1913–20,* 1920; *Supplement 1920–28,* 1929; *Supplement 1928–50,* 1953.

§198. CUMULATIVE CATALOGUES: COMPLETED—AMERICAN; BRITISH; FRENCH; GERMAN

4726. Peddie, Robt. A. National Bibliographies. A descriptive catalogue of the works which register the books published in each country. London, Grafton and Co., 1912. vi + 34 pp.

4727. Berthold, Arthur. Union Catalogues. A selective bibliography. With an introduction by Ernest Cushing Richardson. Philadelphia, Union Library Catalogue of the Philadelphia Metropolitan Area, 1936. xii + 70 leaves.—A list of articles and portions of books dealing with national union catalogues. See also William Warner Bishop, "Union Catalogs," *Library Quarterly*, VII, 1 (Jan. 1937), 36–49.

4728. Downs, Robt. B., ed. Union Catalogs in the United States. Chicago, American Library Association, 1942. xxii + 409 pp.—On pp. 229–263 is George A. Schwegmann Jr.'s "The National Union Catalog in the Library of Congress."

4729. Pinto, Olga. Le Bibliografie Nazionali. Florence, Leo S. Olschki Editore, 1951. 94 pp.—Volume XX in the series Biblioteca di Bibliografia Italiana. A list of titles of national bibliographies of over seventy countries.

4730. Conover, Helen F. Current National Bibliographies. Washington, D.C., Library of Congress, 1955. v + 132 pp.

4731. Linder, Le Roy Harold. The Rise of Current Complete National Bibliography. New York, Scarecrow Press, 1959. viii + 9–290 pp.

[See also §192. Lists, Chiefly Retrospective, of Earlier American Books.]

4732. The American Catalogue of Books. Or English guide to American literature, giving the full title of original works published in the United States since the year 1800. With especial reference to works of interest to Great Britain. With the prices at which they may be obtained in London. London, S. Low, Son and Co., 1856. vii + 190 pp.

4733. Trübner, Nikolaus. Trübner's Bibliographical Guide to American Literature. A classified list of books published in the United States of America during the last forty years. London, Trübner and Co., 1859. 149 + 554 pp.

4734. Roorbach, O[rville] A. Bibliotheca Americana. Catalogue of American publications including reprints and original works from 1820 to 1852 inclusive. Together with a list of periodicals published in the United States. New York, O. A. Roorbach, 1849–52. xi + 652 pp.—Supplement 1852–55 (1855), vii + 220 pp. Supplement 1855–58 (1858), vii + 256 pp. Supplement 1858–61 (1861), vii + 162 pp. All four volumes reprinted New York, Peter Smith, 1939.

4735. Morgan, Henry James. Bibliotheca canadensis. Or, A manual of Canadian literature. Ottawa, G. E. Desbarats, 1867. 411 pp.—See also Watters's *A Check List of Canadian Literature*, no. 8.

4736. Kelly, James. The American Catalogue of Books (Original and Reprints) Published in the United States from Jan. 1861 to Jan. 1866. New York, J. Wiley and Sons, 1866. 303 pp.—Also *Volume II*, New York, J. Wiley and Sons, 1871, 488 pp., which covers the period Jan. 1866 to Jan. 1871. Both volumes contain a "Supplement" listing names of learned societies and other literary associations together with their publications. Both volumes reprinted New York, Peter Smith, 1938.

4737. Haight, W[illet] R. Canadian Catalogue of Books 1791–1897. Toronto, Haight and Co., 1896–1904. 3 vols.—Reprint London, Pordes, 1958, 130 + 48 + 57 pp.

4738. [Leypoldt, F(rederick), Jones, L(ynds) E., et al.] The American Catalogue of Books in Print and for Sale . . . 1876–1910. New York, Publishers' Weekly Office, 1880–1911. 21 vols. in 15. —Reprint New York, Peter Smith, 1941, 9 vols. in 15. Also *Annual American Catalogue 1886–1910,* New York, Publishers' Weekly Office, 1887–1911, 25 vols.

4739. United States Catalog. Books in print January 1, 1928. Edited by Mary Burnham, Carol Hurd, et al. 4th ed. New York, H. W. Wilson Co., 1928. [vii] + 3164 (triple column) pp.—Original ed. 1900; second ed. 1903; third ed. 1912.

4740. Cumulative Book Index. A world list of books in the English language 1928–1932. Supplementing the United States Catalog Fourth Edition. Edited by Mary Burnham, Carol Hurd, et al. New York, H. W. Wilson Co., 1933. [vii] + 2298 (triple column) pp.—Also *Cumulative Book Index.. . . 1933–1937,* edited by Mary Burnham, Carol Hurd, et al., New York, H. W. Wilson Co., 1938, [vii] + 2680 (triple column) pp. Also *Cumulative Book Index . . . 1938–1942,* edited by Mary Burnham, Regina Goldman, et al., New York, H. W. Wilson Co., 1945, [vii] + 2722 (triple column) pp. Also *Cumulative Book Index . . . 1943–1948,* edited by Regina Goldman Grossman, Nina R. Thompson, et al.,

New York, H. W. Wilson Co., 1950, [vii] + 2566 (triple column) pp. Also *Cumulative Book Index . . . 1949–1952*, edited by Nina R. Thompson, Regina Grossman, et al., New York, H. W. Wilson Co., 1953, [vii] + 2123 (triple column) pp. A cumulation for the period 1953–1956 is in process.

4741. United States Quarterly Book Review. Washington, D.C., Library of Congress, 1945–56. 12 (double column page) vols.—Brief reviews of major works in all major fields. Title to 1951 *United States Quarterly Book List.*

[The sequence and proprietorship of the cumulative catalogues of the British book trade are here given in abbreviated form; the most complete list in chronological order from Maunsell's *Catalogue* (1595) to the still current *English Catalogue* is in Adolf Growoll's *Three Centuries of the English Book Trade,* New York, 1903, pp. 107–160.]

4745. Maunsell, Andrew. The First Part of the Catalogue of English Printed Books. Which concerneth such matters of divinitie as have bin either written in our owne tongue or translated out of anie other language and have bin published. London, printed by John Windet, 1595. [viii] + 123 pp.—Also *The Seconde Parte . . . ,* London, James Roberts, 1595, [vi] + 27 pp., which deals with the sciences. A third part, dealing with the humanities, was planned, but never issued.

4746. [London, Wm.] A Catalogue of the Most Vendible Books in England Orderly and Alphabetically Digested. London, Edward Brewster, 1658. Unpaged. [236 pp.]—Also *A Supplement of New Books Come Forth since August the First 1657 till June the First 1658,* London, 1658, [8] pp. Also *A Catalogue of New Books by Way of Supplement to the Former,* Being such as have been printed from that time till Easter-term 1660, London, printed by A. M., sold by L. Fawn and F. Tyton, 1660, [22] pp.

4747. [Clavel, Robt.] A Catalogue of Books Printed in England since the Dreadful Fire of London in 1666. To the end of Michaelmas term 1695. . . . 4th ed. London, printed for R. Clavel and B. Tooke, 1696. 127 pp.—Original ed. 1673; second ed. 1675; third ed. 1680–81.

4748. The London Catalogue of Books in All Languages . . . since 1700. London, W. Bent, 1773. vi + 144 pp.—Reissues with additions London, W. Bent, 1786, 1791, and 1799.

4749. The London Catalogue of Books. . . . Corrected to August 1811. London, W. Bent, 1811. 239 pp.—Reissues with additions London, W. Bent, 1814, 1822, and 1827, and London, Longman, Rees, et al., 1831, 1835–37, and 1839. Also supplement London, W. Bent, 1844.

4750. [Hodgson, Thos.] The London Catalogue of Books Published in Great Britain. With their sizes, prices, and publishers' names. From 1814 to 1846. London, Thomas Hodgson, 1846. viii + 542 pp.—Reissues with additions London, Thomas Hodgson, 1851 and 1855.

4751. [Low, Sampson.] The British Catalogue of Books Published from October 1837 to December 1852. Containing the date of publication, size, price, publisher's name, and edition. London, S. Low and Son, 1853. 408 + 57 + 64 + 62 pp.—Also *Index to the British Catalogue of Books Published during the Years 1837 to 1857 Inclusive,* London, S. Low, Son and Co., 1858, 292 + xxix + xlviii + 297–341 pp.

4752. Peddie, Robt. Alexander, and Waddington, Quintin. The English Catalogue of Books (Including the Original London Catalogue). Giving in one alphabet, under author, title, and subject, the size, price, month, and year of publication, and publisher of books issued in the United Kingdom of Great Britain and Ireland 1801–1836. London, Low, Marston and Co. for Publishers' Circular, 1914. 655 pp.—A retrospective list compiled from the trade catalogues which preceded *The Publishers' Circular* and from the *London Catalogues* 1800–1839 published by W. Bent and others.

4753. The English Catalogue of Books Published 1801–1951. London, Publishers' Circular Ltd., 1864–1952. 16 vols.—Also *Index,* London, Publishers' Circular Ltd., 1858–93, 4 vols.

4757. Quérard, J[oseph]-M[arie]. La littérature française contemporaine. XIXe siècle. . . . Le tout accompagné de notes biographiques et littéraires. Paris, Daguin frères, et al., 1842–57. 6 vols.

4758. Chéron, Paul. Catalogue général de la librairie française au XIXe siècle, indiquant, par ordre alphabétique de noms d'auteurs les ouvrages publiés en France 1800–1855. Paris, Courrier de la Librairie, 1856–59. 3 vols.—Completion only through *D.*

4759. Quérard, J[oseph]-M[arie]. La France littéraire. Ou, Dictionnaire bibliographique des savants, historiens, et gens de lettres de la France, ainsi que des littérateurs étrangers qui ont écrit en français, plus particulièrement pendant les XVIIIe et XIXe siècles. Paris, Firmin Didot, 1827–64. 12 vols.

4760. Le Soudier, Henri. Bibliographie française. Recueil de catalogues des éditeurs français, accompagné d'une table alphabétique par noms d'auteurs et d'un table systématique. Deuxième éd. Paris, H. Le Soudier, 1900. 10 vols.—Original ed. 1896. Also *Deuxième série,* 1908–11, 2 vols. in 3.

4761. Catalogue mensuel de la librairie française. Paris, Agence Générale de Librairie et de Publications, et al., 1878–1929. 51 vols.—Coverage 1877–1929.

4762. [Lorenz, Otto Henri, et al.] Catalogue général de la librairie française. Paris, Lorenz, et al., 1867–1945. 34 vols.—Coverage 1840–1925. Usually called "Lorenz."

4763. La librairie française. Catalogue général des ouvrages en vente au 1er janvier 1930. Paris, Cercle de la Librairie, 1931–34. 4 vols.—Also *Catalogue général des ouvrages parus du 1er janvier 1933 au 1er janvier 1946*, Paris, Cercle de la Librairie, 1946, 2 vols. plus title index vol.

4767. Thelert, Gustav. Supplement zu Heinsius, Hinrichs, und Kaysers Bücherlexicon. Grossenhain, Baumert und Ronge, 1893. 405 pp.

4768. Buch- und Kunst-Katalog. Gesamt-Verlags-Katalog des deutschen Buchhandels. Ein Bild deutscher Geistesarbeit und Kultur. Münster, A. Russels Verlag, 1881–94. 17 vols.

4769. Heinsius, Wilhelm. Allgemeines Bücherlexikon. Oder, vollständiges alphabetisches Verzeichnis der von 1700 bis zu Ende [1892] erschienenen Bücher. Leipzig, F. A. Brockhaus, 1812–94. 19 vols. in 26.

4770. Systematisches Verzeichnis gebundener Bücher, Atlanten, Karten, Bilder . . . zu beziehen durch F. A. Brockhaus. Leipzig, F. A. Brockhaus, 1905–08. 3 vols.

4771. Kayser, Christian G. Vollständiges Bücherlexicon. Enthaltend alle von 1750 bis zu Ende des Jahres [1910] in Deutschland und in den angrenzenden Ländern gedruckten Bücher. Leipzig, Tauchnitz, 1834–1911. 36 vols.—Also *Register 1896–1912*, 5 vols.

4772. Georg, Carl, and Ost, Leopold. Schlagwort-Katalog. Verzeichnis der im deutschen Buchhandel erschienenen Bücher und Landkarten in sachlicher Anordnung. Leipzig, Volckmar, et al., 1889–1913. 7 vols.

4773. Hinrichs' Fünfjahrskatalog der . . . im deutschen Buchhandel erschienenen Bücher, Zeitschriften, Etc. Leipzig, J. C. Hinrichs, 1851–1913. 13 vols.

4774. Deutsches Bücherverzeichnis der Jahre 1911–40. Eine Zusammenstellung der im deutschen Buchhandel erschienenen Bücher, Zeitschriften und Landkarten, mit einem Stich-und Schlagwortregister. Leipzig, Börsenverein der deutschen Buchhändler, 1915–43. 22 vols.

4775. Deutsche Bibliographie 1945–1950. Bücher und Karten. Frankfurt a. M., Buchhändler-Vereinigung GmbH, 1953–57. 4 vols.

4776. Deutsches Bücherverzeichnis 1941–1950. Verzeichnis der in Deutschland, Oesterreich, der Schweiz und im übrigen Ausland herausgegebenen deutschsprachigen Verlagsschriften sowie der wichtigsten Veröffentlichungen ausserhalb des Buchhandels. Leipzig, Börsenverein der deutschen Buchhändler, 1952–date. 6 vols.—By 1959 complete except the final of the two index volumes. Chiefly an author catalogue. Five-year cumulations are planned.

§199. CUMULATIVE CATALOGUES: CURRENT—AMERICAN; BRITISH; FRENCH; GERMAN

4780. Books in Print. An author-title-series index to the Publishers' Trade List Annual. New York, R. R. Bowker Co., 1948–date.—Annual. Usually kept near the *Publishers' Trade List Annual.* The 1958 edition, edited by Sarah L. Prakken, contains xxxi + 1798 (double column) pp.

4781. Canadiana. Publications of Canadian interest noted by the National Library. Ottawa, National Library of Canada, 1951–date.—Monthly with annual cumulation. A development of *The Canadian Catalogue of Books Published in Canada, about Canada, as well as Those Written by Canadians,* Toronto Public Libraries, 1923–50, with coverage 1921–49.

4782. Cumulative Book Index. New York, H. W. Wilson Co., 1898–date.—"A monthly author, title, and subject catalog of new books published in English in all countries. All entries are in one alphabet. . . . The *Index* is published monthly, except August, and is cumulated frequently. . . ." H. W. Wilson Co. As a rule there are semi-annual, annual, two-year, and four-year cumulations. Cf. 4740.

4783. Paperbound Books in Print. New York, R. R. Bowker Co., 1955–date.—Quarterly with six-month cumulation, but two issues a year 1955–59.

4784. Publishers' Trade List Annual. New York, R. R. Bowker Co., 1873–date.—Current issues in two volumes. A gathering of publishers' catalogues in alphabetical order. Equivalent to the English *Reference Catalogue.* The editor of the 1958 issue was Muriel Pollock.

4785. Subject Guide to Books in Print. An index to the Publishers' Trade List Annual. New York, R. R. Bowker Co., 1957–date.—Annual. Usually kept near the *Publishers' Trade List Annual.* The 1958 edition, edited by Sarah L. Prakken, contains xxxi + 1452 (double column) pp.

4789. British National Bibliography. London, British Museum, Council of the British National Bibliography Ltd., 1950–date.—Weekly and quarterly with annual cumulation.

4790. Directory of Directories, Annuals, and Reference Books. London, Business Publications Ltd., 1950–date.—Annual to five-year issues.

4791. English Catalogue of Books. Giving in one alphabet, under author and title, the size, price, month of publication and publisher of books issued in the United Kingdom. London, Publishers' Circular Ltd., 1837–date.—Quarterly with six-month, nine-month, annual, and four-year cumulation.

4792. Reference Catalogue of Current Literature. Containing the full titles of books now in print and on sale. London, J. Whitaker and Sons, 1874–date.—Issues at intervals of a few years. From 1874 to 1932 a collection of publishers' catalogues, now with author and title-catchword sequences.

4793. Whitaker's Cumulative Book List. A classified list of publications together with an index to authors and titles. London, J. Whitaker and Sons, 1924–date.—Quarterly with annual cumulation.

4797. Biblio. Catalogue des ouvrages parus en langue française dans le monde entier. Paris, Service Bibliographique des Messageries Hachette, 1933–date.—Ten issues a year with annual cumulation. A publication designed to be used by the trade and listing works in French wherever published.

4798. Bibliographie de la France. Ou, Journal général de l'imprimerie et de la librairie. Paris, Cercle de la Librairie, 1811–date.—Weekly. Three parts: *Bibliographie* (full descriptions from the Bibliothèque Nationale for each work); *Chronique* (bibliographical news); *Annonces* (a collection of publishers' circulars). There are also various supplements which appear irregularly. The entries in the *Annonces* are cumulated eight times a year in *Livres de la semaine,* in April and October in *Livres du trimestre,* and in June in *Livres du semestre.* The annual volume is *La librairie française,* Les livres de l'année, catalogue général des ouvrages parus en langue française (1930–date), in which entries are arranged in eleven major categories. There are also two- and three-year cumulations.

4802. Deutsche Bibliothek. Deutsche Bibliographie. Verzeichnis aller in Deutschland erschienenen Veröffentlichungen und der in Oesterreich und der Schweiz im Buchhandel erschienenen deutschsprachigen Publikationen sowie der deutschsprachigen Veröffentlichungen anderer Länder. Frankfurt a. M., Buchhändler-Vereinigung, 1947–date—Weekly: *Wöchentliches Verzeichnis,* 1947–date; monthly: *Verfasser- und Sachregister,* 1953–date; half-yearly: *Halbjahres-Verzeichnis,* 1951–date; yearly: *Jahresregister,* 1954–date; and quintennial: *Fünfjahres-Verzeichnis,* 1957–date. Initial issues of the weekly (1947–1953) were entitled *Bibliographie der deutschen Bibliothek.*

4803. Das deutsche Buch. Neuerscheinunger der deutschen Verlage. Frankfurt a. M., Buchhändler-Vereinigung, 1950–date.—Two issues a month. A selected list of new publications for the book trade abroad.

4804. Deutsche Nationalbibliographie. Gesamtverzeichnis des in Deutschland erschienenen Schrifttums und der deutschsprachigen Schriften des Auslands. Leipzig, Deutsche Bücherei und Börsenverein der deutschen Buchhändler, 1931–date.—Weekly ("Reihe A"), bi-monthly ("Reihe B"), and annual ("Jahresverzeichnis des deutschen Schrifttums," 1945/-46–date). A development of the *Wöchentliches Verzeichnis* begun in 1842, the *Jahresverzeichnis* being the successor of *Hinrichs' Halbjahrskatalog,* Leipzig, Börsenverein der deutschen Buchhändler, 1798–1944.

4805. Gesamtdeutscher KAWE–Katalog. Berlin, KAWE Kommissionsbuchhandlung GmbH, 1956–date.—Annual. Each issue contains an author catalogue and a subject catalogue. East and West German publications are listed.

§200. BIBLIOGRAPHIES OF BIBLIOGRAPHIES

4809. Petzholdt, Julius. Bibliotheca Bibliographica. Kritisches Verzeichnis der das Gesammtgebiet der Bibliographie betreffenden Literatur des In- und Auslandes in systematischer Ordnung. Leipzig, Engelmann, 1866. xii + 939 pp.

4810. Porter, G[eorge] W. List of Bibliographical Works in the Reading Room of the British Museum. Second ed. rev. by G. K. Fortescue. London, printed by order of the Trustees, 1889. xi + 103 pp.—Original ed. 1880.

4811. Stein, Henri. Manuel de bibliographie générale (Bibliotheca bibliographica nova). Paris, Alphonse Picard et Fils, 1897. xx + 895 pp.—Number 2 in the series Manuels de bibliographie historique.

4812. Langlois, Chas. V. Manuel de bibliographie historique. 2ᵉ éd. Paris, Librairie Hachette et Cie., 1901–04. 2 vols.—Original ed. 1896. A bibliography of bibliographies and also of universal and national bibliographies and bibliographies of history.

4813. Courtney, Wm. P. A Register of National Bibliography. With a selection of the chief bibliographical books and articles printed in other countries. London, Archibald Constable and Co., 1905–12. 3 (double column page) vols.

4814. Besterman, Theodore. Index Bibliographicus. Directory of current periodical abstracts and bibliographies. Vol. I: Science and Technology; Vol. II: Social Sciences, Education, Humanistic Studies. 3rd ed. Paris, United Nations Educational, Scientific, and Cultural Organization, 1952. 2 (double column page) vols.—Original ed. 1925; second ed. 1931.

4815. Smith, F Seymour. Pamphlet Bibliographies. Cambridge Univ. Press for the National Book League, 1948. 24 pp.—A bibliography of booklets giving bibliographies on general subjects.

4816. Bohatta, Hans, and Hodes, Franz. Internationale Bibliographie der Bibliographien. Ein Nachschlagewerk. Unter Mitwirkung von Walter Funke. Frankfurt a. M., Vittorio Klostermann, 1950. 538 (double column) + 539–652 (triple column) pp.

4817. Collison, Robt. L. Bibliographies. Subject and national. A guide to their contents, arrangement, and use. Foreword by Lawrence Clark Powell. New York, Hafner Publ'ing Co., 1951. xii + 172 pp.—An annotated list of major bibliographies for most major fields of knowledge.

4818. Fisher, John H. Serial Bibliographies in the Modern Languages and Literatures. PMLA, LXVI, 3 (June 1951), 138–156.

4819. Widmann, Hans. Bibliographien zum deutschen Schrifttum der Jahre 1939–1950. Tübingen, Max Niemeyer Verlag, 1951. xii + 284 pp.—Bibliographies mostly of German, but often of English origin, some of which impinge on English literature.

4820. Besterman, Theodore. A World Bibliography of Bibliographies and of Bibliographical Catalogues, Calendars, Abstracts, Digests, Indexes, and the Like. 3rd ed. Geneva, Societas Bibliographicà, 1955–56. 4 (double column page) vols.—Original ed. 1939–40; second ed. 1947–49.

4821. Bibliographie der versteckten Bibliographien aus deutschsprachigen Büchern und Zeitschriften der Jahre 1930–1953. Leipzig, Verlag für

Buch- und Bibliothekswesen, 1956. 371 (double column) pp.—Number 3 in the series Sonderbibliographien der Deutschen Bücherei.

4822. Bibliographic Index. A cumulative bibliography of bibliographies. New York, H. W. Wilson Co., 1945–date.—Quarterly with annual cumulation. Vol. I: 1937–42; Vol. II: 1943–46; Vol. III: 1947–50; Vol. IV: 1951–55; Vol. V: 1956; Vol. VI: 1957; Vol. VII: 1958.

4823. Bibliographie der deutschen Bibliographien. Jahresverzeichnis der selbständig erschienenen und der in deutschsprachigen Büchern und Zeitschriften enthaltenen versteckten Bibliographien. Bearbeitet von der Deutschen Bücherei. Leipzig, VEB Verlag für Buch- und Bibliothekswesen, 1957–date.—Annual. Jahrgang 1 / Berichtzeit 1954 appeared 1957; Jahrgang 2 / Berichtzeit 1955 appeared 1958.

4824. Bibliographische Beihefte der Zeitschrift für Bibliothekswesen und Bibliographie. Frankfurt a. M., Verlag Vittorio Klostermann, 1957–date.—Quarterly.

4825. Bulletin of Bibliography and Magazine Notes. Boston, F. W. Faxon Co., 1897–date.—Three issues a year. Each issue contains articles, checklists, and especially bibliographies and also a record of new and changed periodical titles. Former title *Bulletin of Bibliography and Dramatic Index.*

§201. SUBJECT INDEXES

[See also the trade publication *Subject Guide to Books in Print,* no. 4785.]

4829. Sonnenschein, Wm. Swan. The Best Books. A reader's guide and literary reference book. Being a contribution towards systematic bibliography. 3rd ed. Part I: A. Theology, B. Mythology and folklore, C. Philosophy (1910); Part II: D. Society, E. Geography (1912); Part III: F. History and historical biography, G. Archaeology and historical collaterals (1923); Part IV: H. Natural Science, H*. Medicine and surgery, I. Arts and trades (1926); Part V: K. Literature and philology (1931); Part VI: Index (1935). London, George Routledge and Sons, 1910–35. 6 vols.—Original ed. 1887; second ed. 1891. Supplement to 2nd ed. *Reader's Guide,* 1895.

4830. Peddie, R[obert] A. Subject Index of Books Published before 1880. A–Z. London, Grafton and Co., 1933. xv + 745 (double column) pp. —Also Peddie's *Subject Index of Books Published up to and Including 1880,* Second series A–Z, London, Grafton and Co., 1935, xv + 857 (double column) pp. Also Peddie's *Subject Index of Books Published up to and Including 1880,* Third series A–Z, London, Grafton and Co., 1939, xv + 945 (double column) pp. Also Peddie's *Subject Index of Books Published up to and Including 1880,* New series A–Z, London, Grafton and Co., 1948, vii + 872 (double column) pp.

4831. Subject Index of the Modern Works Added to the Library of the British Museum in the Years 1881–1900. Edited by G[eorge] K. Fortescue. London, printed by order of the Trustees, 1902–03. 3 (double column page) vols.—Supplements to "Fortescue" now bear the title *Subject Index of Modern Books Acquired*; they have appeared as follows: 1901–05 (1906); 1906–10 (1911); 1911–15 (1918); 1916–20 (1922); 1921–25 (1927); 1926–30 (1933); 1931–35 (1937), 2 vols.; 1936–40 (1944), 2 vols.; 1941–45 (1953).

4832. Wright, C[harles] T. Hagberg. Subject Index of the London Library, St. James Square, London. London, Williams and Norgate, 1909. xxvii + 1254 (triple column) pp.—Also C. T. H. Wright and C[hristopher] J. Purnell, *Subject Index . . . ,* Additions 1909–22, London, 1923, xviii + 1083 (triple column) pp. Also C. T. H. Wright and C. J. Purnell, *Subject Index . . . ,* Additions 1923–38, London, 1938, xiv + 1045 (triple column) pp. Also *Subject Index 1938–1953,* London, 1955, x + 801 (triple column) pp.

4833. Hoffman, Hester R. Bookman's Manual. A guide to literature. 8th ed. New York, R. R. Bowker Co., 1958. xv + 987 pp.—Original ed. 1921, second ed. 1924, third ed. 1928, fourth ed. 1934, and fifth ed. 1941 by Bessie Graham; sixth ed. 1948 and seventh ed. 1954 by Hester R. Hoffman.

4834. Library of Congress Catalog. Books: Subjects 1950–1954. Ann Arbor, Mich., J. W. Edwards Inc., 1955. 20 (triple column page) vols.—Now annual supplements, the publications for 1955, 1956, 1957, and 1958 being three-volume works. For the basic work see no. 4627.

4835. Malclès, L[ouise]-N[oëlle]. Les sources du travail bibliographique. Préface de Julien Cain. Tome I: Bibliographies générales; Tome II: *Bibliographies spécialisées (sciences humaines), **Bibliographies spécialisées (sciences humaines); Tome III: Bibliographies specialisées (sciences exactes et techniques) avec la collaboration de G. Garnier, P.-M. Guelpa, G. Koest, M.-G. Madier, J. Miet. Geneva, Libraire E. Droz, 1950–58. 3 vols., the second in two parts.—An international list of major works in all scientific, social, and humanistic fields.

§202. UNIVERSAL BIBLIOGRAPHIES

[The term "universal bibliography" is often restricted to the following works compiled by bibliographers who apparently intended to list, often with auction prices, all humanistic works either of their own country or of a number of countries. Their feature of giving numerous annotations concerning lives of authors and sequences of editions distinguishes them sharply from cumulative book catalogues.]

4839. Georgi, Theophil. [i.e., Gottlieb Baur.] Allgemeines europäisches Bücherlexicon. . . . Vor dem Anfange des xvi. seculi bis 1739 . . . in vier Theile abgetheilet. Leipzig, T. Georgi, 1742. 4 parts in 1 vol.—Also *Fünffter Theil* . . . , In welchem die französischen auctores und Bücher von allen Disciplinen . . . in alphabetischer Ordnung zu finden . . . , Leipzig, 1753. Also *Erstes bis drittes Supplement 1739–57*, Leipzig, Schönemarck, 1750–58.

4840. Watt, Robt. Bibliotheca Britannica. Or a general index to British and foreign literature. Vols. I and II: Authors; Vols. III and IV: Subjects. Edinburgh, Archibald Constable and Co., et al., 1824. 4 (double column page) vols.—S. A. Allibone's *Critical Dictionary of English Literature* (no. 19) is based in large part on Watt.

4841. Graesse, Jean George Théodore. Trésor de livres rares et précieux ou nouveau dictionnaire bibliographique. . . . Dresden, Kuntze, 1859–69. 7 (double column page) vols.—Reprints Berlin, 1922, and Milan, 1950–51.

4842. Brunet, Jacques Charles. Manuel du libraire et de l'amateur de livres. Paris, Librairie de Firmin Didot Frères, 1860–64. 6 (double column page) vols.—Supplement 1878–80 in 2 vols.

4843. Lowndes, Wm. Thos. The Bibliographer's Manual of English Literature. Containing an account of rare, curious, and useful books published in or relating to Great Britain and Ireland from the invention of printing, with bibliographical and critical notices, collations of rarer articles, and the prices at which they have been sold in the present century. New ed., rev., corrected, and enl. by Henry G. Bohn. London, Henry G. Bohn, 1885–89. 5 vols. in 10 separately bound parts plus an additional appendix vol. (chiefly double column pages).—Original ed.

1834 in 4 vols. The appendix vol. by Henry G. Bohn (vii + 336 pp.) gives *inter alia* lists of titles in learned society serial publications. Bohn's revision was printed repeatedly by Bell and Daldy and later by George Bell and Sons up to 1914, a fact that accounts for the different imprints found on the title pages of various sets. See George Watson Cole, "Do You Know Your Lowndes? A bibliographical essay on William Thomas Lowndes and incidentally on Robert Watt and Henry G. Bohn," *Papers of the Bibliographical Society of America*, XXXIII (1939), 1–22.

4844. Vapereau, Gustav. Dictionnaire universel des littératures. Contenant 1, des notices sur les écrivains de tous les temps et tous les pays . . . 2, la théorie et l'historique des différents genres de poésie et de prose . . . 3, la bibliographie générale et particulière. 6th ed. Paris, Hachette et Cie., 1893. xvi + 2096 + 25 pp.—Original ed. 1876.

4845. Vicaire, Georges. Manuel de l'amateur de livres du XIXe siècle 1801–1893. Paris, Rouguette, 1894–1920. 8 vols.

§203. STANDARD CATALOGUES OF MODERN BOOKS

4849. Fletcher, Wm. I. The A.L.A. Index. An index to general literature, biographical, historical, and literary essays and sketches, reports, etc. 2nd ed. Boston, Houghton Mifflin Co., 1901. iv + 679 pp.—Original ed. 1893. Also *Supplement 1900–1910,* Chicago, American Library Association, 1914, iv + 223 pp.

4850. Shaw, Chas. B. A List of Books for College Libraries. Approximately 14000 titles selected on the recommendation of 200 college teachers, librarians, and other advisers. Second preliminary ed. Chicago, American Library Association, 1931. xii + 696 (double column) + 697–810 (triple column) pp.—Also supplement *A List of Books for College Libraries 1931–38,* Chicago, American Library Association, 1940, ix + 284 (chiefly double column) pp.

4851. Smith, F Seymour. An English Library. An annotated list of classics and standard works. With a foreword by Edmund Blunden. 4th ed. Cambridge Univ. Press for the National Book League, 1950. 198 pp.—Original ed. 1943; second ed. 1943; third ed. 1944. A list of books by major categories which omits works belonging to the natural and social sciences and which enters the approximate price for each volume currently available.

4852. Cooper, Isabella M. A.L.A. Catalog 1926. An annotated basic list of 10000 books. Chicago, American Library Association, 1926. 915 (double column) + 916–1295 (triple column) pp.—*A.L.A. Catalog 1926–1931*, by Marion Horton, Chicago, American Library Association, 1933, viii + 225 (double column) + 226–330 (triple column) pp. *A.L.A. Catalog 1932–1936*, by Marion Horton, Chicago, American Library Association, 1938, viii + 272 (double column) + 273–357 (triple column) pp. *A.L.A. Catalog 1937–1941*, by Marion Horton, Chicago, American Library Association, 1943, vi + 221 (double column) + 222–306 (triple column) pp. *A.L.A. Catalog 1942–1949*, by Florence Boochever and Minna H. Breuer, Chicago, American Library Association, 1952, x + 372 (double column) + 373–448 (triple column) pp.

4853. Dickinson, Asa D. The World's Best Books. Homer to Hemingway. 3000 books of 3000 years, 1050 B.C. to 1950 A.D. . . . New York, H. W. Wilson Co., 1953. xi + 484 pp.

4854. Orton, Robt. M. Catalog of Reprints in Series. 18th ed. New York, H. W. Wilson Co., 1958. 342 (double column) pp.—Original ed. 1940. A list of works which are again printed from the original type or from reset type; hence, paperback reprint titles are present.

4855. West, Dorothy Herbert, and Fidell, Estelle A. Standard Catalog for Public Libraries. 4th ed. New York, H. W. Wilson Co., 1959. 1349 (double column) pp.—Original ed. 1934; second ed. 1940; third ed. 1950.

§204. THESES: GUIDES, BIBLIOGRAPHIES, AND CURRENT LISTS

[For a list of German dissertations 1885–1950 on English language and literature see no. 3; for a list of dissertations 1891–1955 on American literature see no. 509.]

4859. Palfrey, Thos. R., and Colman, Henry E., Jr. Guide to Bibliographies of Theses, United States and Canada. 2nd ed. Chicago, American Library Association, 1940. 48 pp. planographed.—Original ed. 1936. See also Robert P. Rosenberg, "Bibliographies of Theses in America," *Bulletin of Bibliography*, XVIII, 8 (Sept./Dec. 1945), 181–182, and 9 (Jan./April 1946), 201–203.

4860. Record, P D. A Survey of Thesis Literature in British Libraries. London, Library Association, 1950. 21 pp.

4861. Varnhagen, Hermann. Systematisches Verzeichnis der Programmabhandlungen, Dissertationen und Habilitationsschriften aus dem Gebiete der romanischen und englischen Philologie. Zweite Auflage von Johannes Martin herausgegeben. Leipzig, C. A. Koch, 1893. xv + 296 pp.

4862. Maire, Albert. Répertoire alphabétique des thèses de doctorat ès lettres des universités françaises 1810–1900. Avec table chronologique par universités et table détaillée des matières. Paris, A. Picard et Fils, 1903. vi + 226 pp.

4863. Klussmann, Rudolf. Systematisches Verzeichnis der Abhandlungen, welche in den Schulschriften sämtlicher an dem Programmtausche teilnehmenden Lehranstalten erschienen sind, nebst zwei Registern. Leipzig, Teubner, 1889–1916. 5 vols.—Coverage 1876–1910.

4864. List of American Doctoral Dissertations Printed 1912–38. Washington, Government Printing Office for the Library of Congress Catalog Division, 1913–40. 26 vols.

4865. Canadian Graduate Theses in the Humanities and Social Sciences 1921–1946. Ottawa, Canadian Bibliographic Centre, 1951. 194 pp.

4866. Catalogue des thèses et écrits académiques . . . . Paris, Ministère de l'éducation nationale, 1884–date.—Annual.

4867. Dissertation Abstracts. A guide to dissertations and monographs available in microfilm. Ann Arbor, Mich., University Microfilms, 1938–date. —Monthly. Title 1938–51 *Microfilm Abstracts.*

4868. Doctoral Dissertations Accepted by American Universities. New York, H. W. Wilson Co., 1934–date.—Annual. "List of Periodic University Publications Abstracting Dissertations," Number 5 (1938)–date.

4869. Index to Theses Accepted for Higher Degrees in the Universities of Great Britain and Ireland. London, Aslib, 1953–date.—Annual.

4870. Jahresverzeichnis der deutschen Hochschulschriften. Leipzig, Deutsche Bücherei, 1887–date.—Annual.

§205. GOVERNMENT PUBLICATIONS

4874. Schmeckebier, Lawrence F. Government Publications and Their Use. Foreword by Alton P. Tisdel. Washington, D.C., Brookings Institution, 1936. xiii + 446 pp.—Number 33 in the series Studies in Administration. "List of Depository Libraries," pp. 407–417.

4875. Childs, James B. Government Document Bibliography in the United States and Elsewhere. 3rd ed. Washington, D.C., Library of Congress Division of Documents, 1942. xviii + 78 pp.—Original ed. 1927; second ed. 1930. A bibliography of government publications bibliographies.

4876. Hirshberg, Herbert S., and Melinat, Carl H. Subject Guide to United States Government Publications. Chicago, American Library Association, 1947. ix + 230 (double column) pp.

4877. Boyd, Anne Morris. United States Government Publications. Third ed. rev. by Rae Elizabeth Rips. New York, H. W. Wilson Co., 1949. xx + 627 pp.

4878. Leidy, W[illiam] Philip. A Popular Guide to Government Publications. New York, Columbia Univ. Press, 1953. xxii + 296 pp.

4879. Powell, J[ohn] H. The Books of a New Nation. United States Government Publications 1774–1814. Philadelphia, University of Pennsylvania Paris, 1957. 170 pp.—In the series Publications of the A. S. W. Rosenbach Fellowship in Bibliography.

4880. Meyriat, Jean. Études des bibliographies courantes des publications officielles nationales / A Study of Current Bibliographies of National Official Publications. Guide sommaire et inventaire / Short guide and inventory. Paris, Unesco, 1958. 260 pp.

§206. AUCTION CATALOGUES

[See also §174. Book Trade: Historical Studies; §175. Book Trade: Contemporary Scene.]

4884. Livingston, Luther Samuel. Auction Prices of Books . . . . New York, Dodd, Mead and Co., 1905. 4 vols.—Coverage 1886–1904.

4885. List of Catalogues of English Book Sales 1676–1900. Now in the British Museum. London, printed by order of the Trustees, 1915. xv + 523 pp. —"The compilation was begun by Harold Mattingly, continued by I. A. K. Burnett, and completed by A. W. Pollard," Preface.

4886. McKay, Geo. L. American Book Auction Catalogues 1713–1934. A union list. With an introduction by Clarence S. Brigham. New York Public Library, 1937. xxxii + 540 pp.—Original printing *New York Public Library Bulletin,* 1935–36. Bibliography, pp. xv–xvi; list of American auction houses, pp. xvii–xxxii. See also McKay's two articles, both entitled "American Book Auction Catalogues 1713–1934: Additions," in the *Bulletin of the New York Public Library,* L, 3 (1946), 177–184, and LII, 8 (1948), 401–412.

4887. Jahrbuch der Bücherpreise 1906–38. Leipzig, Otto Harrassowitz, 1907–39. 33 vols.

§207. MICROFILMS

[For a list of dissertations available on microfilm see the various issues of *Dissertation Abstracts,* no. 4867.]

4891. Raymond, Jurgen G. Directory of Microfilm Services in the United States and Canada. Rev. ed. New York, Special Libraries Association, 1947. xv + 30 (double column) pp.—Original ed. 1946.

4892. Reproductions of MSS and Rare Printed Books. Short title list. PMLA, LXV, 3 (April 1950), 289–338 (double column).—A list of rotographs and microfilms placed on deposit at the Library of Congress by the Modern Language Association of America and available through interlibrary loan.

4893. Born, Lester K. British Manuscripts Project. A checklist of the microfilms prepared in England and Wales for the American Council of Learned Societies 1941–1945. Washington, D.C., Library of Congress, 1955. xvii + 179 pp.

4894. Union List of Microfilms. Philadelphia Bibliographical Center and Union Library Catalogue. Revised, enl. and cumulated ed. Ann Arbor, Mich., J. W. Edwards, 1951. xvi + 1961 columns.—Original ed. 1942. *Supplement 1949–1952,* Ann Arbor, Mich., J. W. Edwards, 1953, vi + 995 columns. *Supplement 1952–1955,* Ann Arbor, Mich., J. W. Edwards, 1957, vii + 1019 columns. The 1951 ed. lists newspapers, but the supplements do not, since they are listed in *Newspapers on Microfilm.*

4895. Tilton, Eva Maude. A Union List of Publications in Opaque Microfilms. New York, Scarecrow Press, 1959. 346 pp.

§208. MISCELLANEOUS LISTS

4899. Martin, John. Bibliographical Catalogue of Privately Printed Books. 2nd ed. London, J. Van Voort for the author, 1854. 593 pp.—Original ed. 1834.

4900. Rowlands, Wm. Cambrian Bibliography. Containing an account of the books printed in the Welsh language or relating to Wales from the year 1546 to the end of the eighteenth century, with biographical notices. Edited and enl. by Daniel Evans. Llanidloes, J. Pryse, 1869. xxii + 762 pp.

4901. [Quaritch, Bernard.] A General Catalogue of Books Offered to the Public at Affixed Prices. London, [G. Norman and Son], 1887–92. 7 vols.—Also ten *Supplements,* London, B. Quaritch, 1888–97.

4902. Ballinger, John, and Jones, James Ifano. Catalogue of Printed Literature in the Welsh Department. Cardiff, Free Libraries Committee, 1898. 559 pp.—The major catalogue of Welsh literature to the end of the nineteenth century.

4903. Lemonnyer, J[ules] [pseud. of Jules Gay]. Bibliographie des ouvrages relatifs à l'amour, aux femmes, au marriage et des livres facétieux, pantagruéliques, scatologiques, satyriques, etc. Quatrième édition . . . . Paris, C. Gilliet, Libraire, 1894–1900. 4 (double column page) vols.—French and occasional English and German titles. Not a list of erotica.

4904. Faxon, Frederick W. Ephemeral Bibelots. A bibliography of the modern chap-books and their imitators. Boston, Boston Book Co., 1903. 26 pp.—Number 11 in the series Bulletin of Bibliography Pamphlets.

4905. Dobell, Bertram. Catalogue of Books Printed for Private Circulation . . . Described and Annotated. London, printed by the author, 1906. 238 pp.

4906. Corns, Albert R., and Sparke, Archibald. A Bibliography of Unfinished Books in the English Language. With annotations. London, Bernard Quaritch, 1915. xvi + 255 pp.

4907. Borchling, Conrad, and Claussen, Bruno. Niederdeutsche Bibliographie. Gesamtverzeichnis der niederdeutschen Drucke bis zum Jahre 1800 . . . . Neumünster, Karl Wachholst, 1931–36. 2 vols.

4908. Weiss, Harry B. A Catalogue of the Chapbooks in the New York Public Library. New York Public Library, 1936. 90 (double column) pp.—Reprint with revisions and corrections from the *Bulletin of the New York Public Library*, 1935. "Bibliography," pp. 8–9. Coverage 1510 to 1850.

4909. Krieg, Michael O. Mehr nicht erschienen. Ein Verzeichnis unvollendet gebliebener Druckwerke. Vienna, Walter Krieg Verlag, 1954–58. 2 vols. —Volume II, part 1, in the series Bibliotheca bibliographica. A catalogue of works left incomplete.

CHAPTER XIV

GENERAL REFERENCE

§209. REFERENCE WORK GUIDES

[See also §200. Bibliographies of Bibliographies; §201. Subject Indexes.]

4913. Index to Reference Lists Published in Library Bulletins from October 1901 to December 1906 Inclusive. Compiled by the Providence (R.I.) Public Library. Boston, Boston Book Co., 1907. 31 pp.—Number 16 in the series Bulletin of Bibliography Pamphlets.

4914. Minto, John. Reference Books. A classified and annotated guide to the principal works of reference. London, Library Association, 1929. vii + 295 (double column) + 296–356 (triple column) pp.—Also *Supplement*, London, Library Association, 1931, vii + 120 (double column) + 121–140 (triple column) pp.

4915. Hirshberg, Herbert S. Subject Guide to Reference Books. Chicago, American Library Association, 1942. xvi + 238 (double column) + 239–259 (triple column) pp.—An alphabetical subject guide to books needed for answering reference questions.

4916. Calot, Frantz, and Thomas, Georges. Guide pratique de bibliographie. 2e ed., refondue avec le concours de Clément Duval. Paris, Delagrave, 1950. 278 pp.—In the series Bibliothèque des chercheurs et des curieux. Original ed. 1936.

4917. Roberts, Arthur D. Introduction to Reference Works. 2nd ed. London, Library Association, 1951. ix + 214 pp.—Original ed. 1948. An explanation of the significance of each of the major English language reference works.

4918. Shores, Louis. Basic Reference Sources. An introduction to materials and methods. With a chapter on science reference sources by Helen Focke. Chicago, American Library Association, 1954. ix + 378 pp.—A development of Shores's *Basic Reference Books,* An introduction to the evaluation, study, and use of reference materials with special emphasis on some 300 titles, 2nd ed., Chicago, American Library Association, 1939, xiii + 472 pp., original ed. 1937.

4919. Totok, Wilhelm, and Weitzel, Rolf. Handbuch der bibliographischen Nachschlagewerke. Frankfurt a. M., Vittorio Klostermann, 1954. xxiii + 258 pp.—A bibliography of reference works in the various Western European languages.

4920. Winchell, Constance M. Guide to Reference Works. Seventh ed. based on the Guide to Reference Books, 6th ed., by Isadore Gilbert Mudge. Chicago, American Library Association, 1951. xvii + 517 (double column) + 518–645 (triple column) pp.—Original ed. 1902 by Alice B. Kroeger; second ed. 1908 also by Kroeger; third ed. 1917, fourth ed. 1923, fifth ed. 1929, and sixth ed. 1936 by Mudge. *Supplement 1950–1952*, by Constance M. Winchell and Olive A. Johnson, Chicago, American Library Association, 1954, 89 (double column) + 90–117 (triple column) pp. *Supplement 1953–1955*, by Constance M. Winchell, Chicago, American Library Association, 1956, 102 (double column) + 103–134 (triple column) pp.

4921. Sabor, Josefa E. Manual de Fuentes de Información. Obras de referencia: enciclopedias, diccionarios, bibliografías, biografías, etc. Buenos Aires, Argentina, Editorial Kapelusz, 1957. xiv + 335 pp.—Number 2 in the series Contribuciones Bibliotecológicas. A reference work bibliography useful in Spanish-American studies.

4922. Murphey, Robt. W. How and Where to Look It Up. A guide to standard sources of information. Consultant Mabel S. Johnson. Foreword by Louis Shores. New York, McGraw-Hill Book Co., 1958. xiv + 649 (double column) + 650–721 (triple column) pp.

4923. Barton, Mary Neill. Reference Books. A brief guide for students and other users of the library. 4th ed. Baltimore, Enoch Pratt Free Library, 1959. 117 pp.—Original ed. 1938.

4924. Walford, A[rthur] J. Guide to Reference Material. With assistance of L. M. Payne. London, Library Association, 1959. viii + 543 (double column) pp.—The successor to Minto and the British equivalent of Winchell.

4925. Zischka, Gert A. Index Lexicorum. Bibliographie der lexikalischen Nachschlagewerke. Vienna, Verlag Brüder Hollinek, 1959. xliv + 290 (chiefly double column) pp.

4926. List of Books Forming the Reference Library in the Reading Room of the British Museum. 4th ed. London, printed for the Trustees, 1910. 2 vols.—Original ed. 1859; second ed. 1871; third ed. 1889.

4927. Brown, Karl. A Guide to the Reference Collections in the New York Public Library. New York Public Library, 1941. xiv + 416 pp.

§210. ENCYCLOPEDIAS

4931. New International Encyclopaedia. 2nd ed. New York, Dodd, Mead and Co., 1914–16. 23 (double column page) vols.—Original ed. 1894 in 15 vols. Reissue of 2nd ed. 1922. Supplement vols. XXIV–XXV in 1925; supplement vols. XXVI–XXVII in 1930.

4932. Chambers's Encyclopaedia. New ed. Oxford Univ. Press, 1950. 15 (double column page) vols.—Original ed. 1850–68. Maps by John Bartholomew and Sons.

4933. Encyclopaedia Britannica. A new survey of universal knowledge. Published with the editorial advice and consultation of the faculties of the University of Chicago and . . . Oxford, Cambridge, and London Universities. Chicago, Encyclopaedia Britannica Inc., 1954. 24 (double column page) vols.—Original ed. 1768–71 in 3 vols.; ninth ed. (best of the "monographic editions") 1875–89 in 25 vols.; eleventh ed. (the "popularized edition") 1911 in 29 vols.; fourteenth ed. 1929 in 24 vols. Since 1929 the *Britannica* has been printed annually so that revision is given the twenty-five per cent of the material presumably needing revision. Volume XXIV of the current printings contains an index, atlas, and atlas index. See Herman Kogan, *The Great EB,* The story of the Encyclopaedia Britannica, University of Chicago Press, 1958, vii + 339 pp., bibliography pp. 317–321.

4934. Columbia Encyclopedia. Second ed. with supplement of illustrations and a record of events 1950–56. Edited by William Bridgwater and Elizabeth J. Sherwood. New York, Columbia Univ. Press, 1956. [viii] + 2203 (triple column) + 32 (chiefly triple column) pp. + 63 plates.—Original ed. 1935; second ed. 1950. Twelfth printing 1956.

4935. Encyclopedia Americana. The international reference work. New York, Americana Corporation, 1956. 30 (double column page) vols.—A "continuous revision" encyclopedia, repeatedly copyrighted since 1936, with the bulk of its material based on the 1918–20 revision of the 22 vol. ed. of 1912, itself based on the 1st ed. of 1903–04.

§211. ART

4939. Lucas, Edna L. The Harvard List of Books on Art. Cambridge, Mass., Harvard Univ. Press, 1952. vi + 163 pp.

4940. Chamberlin, Mary W. Guide to Art Reference Books. Chicago, American Library Association, 1959. 418 pp.

4941. Catalogue of Political and Personal Satires. London, British Museum Department of Prints and Drawings, 1870–1954. 11 vols.—Coverage: Vol. I: 1320–1689 (1870); Vol. II: 1689–1733; Vol. III (1): 1734–1750, (2) 1751–1760 (1877); Vol. IV: 1761–1770 (1883); Vol. V: 1771–1783 (1935); Vol. VI: 1784–1792 (1938); Vol. VII: 1793–1800 (1942); Vol. VIII: 1801–1810 (1947); Vol. IX: 1811–1819 (1949); Vol. X: 1820–1827 (1952); Vol. XI: 1828–1832 (1954).

4942. Anderson, Mary D. Misericords. Medieval life in English woodcarvings. Harmondsworth, Eng., Penguin Books Ltd., 1954. 30 pp. + xlviii plates.—Number 72 in the series King Penguin Books.

4943. Baltrušaitis Jurgis. Le moyen âge fantastique. Antiquités et exotismes dans l'art gothique. Paris, Armand Colin, 1955. 299 pp.—In the series Collection Henri Focillon.

4944. Who's Who in Art. Biographies of leading men and women in the world of art to-day—artists, designers, craftsmen, critics, writers, teachers, collectors, and curators. With appendices of signatures. 8th ed. London, Art Trade Press, 1956. xv + 882 pp.—Original ed. 1927.

4945. Bénézit, Emmanuel, ed. Dictionnaire critique et documentaire des peintres, sculpteurs, dessinateurs et graveurs de tout les temps et de tout les pays . . . . Nouvelle éd. Paris, Librairie Gründ, 1948–57. 8 (double column page) vols.—Original ed. 1911–13 in 3 vols.

4946. Oxford History of English Art. Edited by T[homas] S. R. Boase. Oxford, Clarendon Press, 1949–date. 11 vols. (projected).—Already issued are volumes covering the years 871–1100, by D. Talbot Rice (1952); 1100–1216, by T. S. R. Boase (1953); 1216–1307, by Peter Brieger (1957); 1307–1461, by Joan Evans (1949); 1625–1714, by Margaret Whinney and Oliver Millar (1957); and 1800–1870, by T. S. R. Boase (1959).

4947. Art Index. A cumulative subject and author index to a selected list of fine arts periodicals and museum bulletins. New York, H. W. Wilson Co., 1929–date.—Quarterly with annual and three-year cumulation.

§212. BIOGRAPHICAL REFERENCE: GENERAL

[See also §2. Biographical Reference: Writers; §33. Minor Prose: Biography and Autobiography Including Diaries.]

4951. [Ungherini, Aglauro.] Manuel de bibliographie biographique et d'iconographie des femmes célèbres. . . . Turin, L. Roux et C., 1892. xi + 896 (double column) pp.—Also *Supplément*, 1900, x + 634 pp.; *Second et dernier supplément*, xiii + 758 pp., the latter containing an index.

4952. Arnim, Max von. Internationale Personalbibliographie 1800–1943. Zweite verbesserte und vermehrte Auflage. Stuttgart, Hiersemann, 1944–52. 2 vols.—Original ed. 1936 with coverage 1850–1935. An international index to bibliographies of individual authors.

4953. Riches, Phyllis M. An Analytical Bibliography of Universal Collected Biography. Comprising books published in the English tongue in Great Britain and Ireland, America, and the British Dominions. New York, H. W. Wilson Co., 1934. ix + 709 pp.

4954. Thomson, Theodore R. A Catalogue of British Family Histories. With an introduction by Lord Farrar. London, J. Murray, 1935. 202 pp.—Original ed. 1928.

4955. Hyamson, Albert M. A Dictionary of Universal Biography of All Ages and of All Peoples. 2nd ed. London, Routledge, 1951. xii + 680 pp.—Original ed. 1916. An international index to biographies in major biographical works.

4956. Dargan, Marion. Guide to American Biography. Foreword by Dumas Malone. Albuquerque, University of New Mexico Press, 1949–52. 2 vols. in 1.—Coverage of vol. I: 1607–1815 and of vol. II: 1815–1933.

4957. Michaud, Joseph F. and Louis G., eds. Biographie universelle, ancienne et moderne . . . . Nouv. éd. Paris, Mme. C. Desplaces, 1843–65. 45 vols.—Original ed. 1811–62 in 84 vols.

4958. Hoefer, Jean C. F., ed. Nouvelle biographie générale . . . . Paris, Firmin Didot Frères, 1852–66. 46 vols.

4959. Foster, John, ed. Alumni oxonienses. The members of the University of Oxford 1500–1886. Oxford Univ. Press, 1887–92. 8 vols.

4960. Musgrave, Wm. Obituary Prior to 1800 as far as Relates to England, Scotland, and Ireland . . . . Edited by George T. Armytage. London, Harleian Society, 1899–1901. 6 vols.—Volumes XLIV–XLIX in the series Publications of the Harleian Society.

4961. Allgemeine deutsche Biographie. Herausgegeben durch die historische Commission bei der Königlichen Akademie der Wissenschaften. Leipzig, Dunker und Humblot, 1875–1912. 56 vols.

4962. Boase, Frederic. Modern English Biography. Containing many thousand concise memoirs of persons who have died since the year 1850 . . . . Truro, Eng., Netherton and Worth for the author, 1892–1901. 3 vols.—Also *Supplement,* Truro, 1908–12, 3 vols.

4963. Wallace, W[illiam] Stewart. The Dictionary of Canadian Biography. Toronto, Macmillan Co., 1926. iv + 433 pp.—"No living person . . . included," Preface.

4964. Stuart, Margaret. Scottish Family History. A guide to works of reference on the history and genealogy of Scottish families. To which is affixed an essay on how to write the history of a family by James Balfour Paul. Edinburgh, Oliver and Boyd, 1930. vii + 386 pp.—Bibliography, pp. 385–386.

4965. Burtchaell, Geo. D., and Sadleir, Thos. U. Alumni dublinenses. A register of the students, graduates, professors, and provosts of Trinity College . . . . New ed. . . . Dublin, A. Thom and Co., 1935. xix + 905 pp.—Original ed. 1924.

4966. Dictionary of National Biography. Founded in 1882 by George Smith. The concise dictionary. Oxford Univ. Press, [1939]. viii + 1456 (double column) + 184 (double column) pp. See 4974.

4967. Webster's Biographical Dictionary. First edition. A dictionary of names of noteworthy persons with pronunciations and concise biographies. Edited by William Allan Neilson, John P. Bethel, Lucius H. Holt, et al. Springfield, Mass., G. and C. Merriam Co., 1953. xxxvi + 1697 (double column) pp.—Original copyright 1943.

4968. Neue deutsche Biographie. Herausgegeben von der historische Kommission bei der Bayerischen Akademie der Wissenschaften. Berlin, Dunker und Humblot, 1953–date. 3 vols.—Coverage to date: A–Ditmar.

4969. Venn, John and J[ohn] A. Alumni cantabrigienses. A biographical list of all known students, graduates, and holders of office at the University of Cambridge from the earliest times to 1900. Cambridge Univ. Press, 1922–54. 10 vols.

4970. Coulson, John. The Saints. A concise biographical dictionary. With an introduction by C. C. Martindale, S.J. New York, Hawthorn Books, 1958. 496 (chiefly double column) pp.—"For Further Reading," pp. 489–496.

4971. Johnson, Allen [1925–31], and Malone, Dumas [1931–36], eds. Dictionary of American Biography. New York, Charles Scribner's Sons, 1928–37. 20 vols. plus index (all double column page).—Also *Supplement One*, edited by Harris E. Starr, 1944, 718 pp. Also *Supplement Two*, edited by Robert L. Schuyler and Edward T. James, 1958, ix + 745 pp.

4972. Emden, A[lfred] B. A Biographical Register of the University of Oxford to A.D. 1500. Oxford, Clarendon Press, 1957–59. 3 vols.

4973. Lloyd, John Edward, et al., eds. Dictionary of Welsh Biography down to 1940. Cardiff, William Lewis for the Honourable Society of Cymmrodorion, 1959. lviii + 1157 (double column) pp.

4974. Stephen, Leslie, and Lee, Sidney, eds. Dictionary of National Biography. Founded in 1882 by George Smith. London, Smith, Elder and Co., 1885–1901. 66 vols.—Reprints 1908–09, 1921–22, and 1937–38 in 22 (double column page) vols. Beginning with the 1921–22 reprint, issued by Oxford Univ. Press. The last volume of the 22 vol. issue is the first supplement. Second supplement 1913, third 1921, fourth 1930, fifth 1949, and sixth 1959.

4975. Biography Index. A quarterly index to biographical material in books and magazines. New York, H. W. Wilson Co., 1946–date—Annual cumulation.

4976. Current Biography. Who's news and why. New York, H. W. Wilson Co., 1940–date.—Monthly September through July with annual cumulation.

4977. Who's Who. An annual biographical dictionary with which is incorporated Men and Women of the Time. London, A. and C. Black, 1849–date.

4978. Who's Who in America. A biographical dictionary of notable living men and women of the United States. Chicago, A. N. Marquis, 1900–date.—One issue every two years. There are three supplementary volumes *Who Was Who in America,* 1897–1942, 1943–1950, and 1951–1960. See Cedric A. Larson, *Who,* Sixty years of American eminence, the story of Who's Who in America, New York, McDowell, Obolensky Inc., 1958, xvi + 390 pp.

§213. COSTUME

4982. Colas, René. Bibliographie générale du costume et de la mode. Paris, R. Colas, 1933. 2 vols. in 1.

4983. Munro, Isabel, and Cook, Dorothy E. Costume Index. A subject index to plates and to illustrated text. New York, H. W. Wilson Co., 1937. x + 338 (double column) pp.—Also *Supplement,* by Isabel Stevenson Munro and Kate M. Munro, New York, H. W. Wilson Co., 1957, x + 210 (double column) pp.

4984. Hiler, Hilaire and Meyer. Bibliography of Costume. A dictionary catalog of about eight thousand books and periodicals. Edited by Helen Grant Cushing. New York, H. W. Wilson Co., 1939. xxxix + 911 (double column) pp.—An author and occasionally title index.

4985. Racinet, A[lbert]. Le costume historique. Cinq cents planches, trois cents en couleurs, or et argent, deux cents en camaieu . . . . Paris, Firmin Didot et Cie., 1888. 6 vols.

4986. Calthorp, Dion Clayton. English Costume from William I to George IV 1066–1830. London, A. and C. Black, 1906. 4 vols.—Reprint 1907 in one vol.; one-volume ed. frequently reprinted, as in 1937.

4987. Withington, Robt. English Pageantry. An historical outline. Cambridge, Mass., Harvard Univ. Press, 1918–20. 2 vols.

4988. Brooke, Iris, and Laver, James. English Costume from the Fourteenth through the Nineteenth Century. New York, Macmillan Co., 1937. 427 pp.

4989. McClellan, Elisabeth. History of American Costume 1607–1870. With an introductory chapter on dress in the Spanish and French settlements in Florida and Louisiana. Illustrations by Sophie B. Steel and Cecil W. Trout. New ed. New York, Tudor Publ'ing Co., 1937. 661 pp.—Original ed. 1904. "Glossary," pp. 615–640.

4990. Houston, Mary G. Medieval Costume in England and France. The thirteenth, fourteenth, and fifteenth centuries. London, Adam and

Charles Black, 1939. xi + 228 pp.—Volume III in the series A Technical History of Costume. "Glossary," pp. 219–226; "Bibliography," pp. 227–228.

4991. Norris, Herbert. Costume and Fashion. Illustrated in color and black and white by the author. London, J. M. Dent and Sons, 1924–40. 6 vols.

4992. Leloir, Maurice. Dictionnaire du costume et de ses accessoires, des armes et des étoffes, des origines à nos jours. Achevé et réalisé sous la direction de André Dupuis. Préface de Georges G.-Toudouze. Paris, Librairie Gründ, 1951. xi + 435 (double column) pp.

4993. Cunnington, C[ecil] Willett. English Women's Clothing in the Present Century. London, Faber and Faber, 1952. 312 pp.

4994. Cunnington, C[ecil] Willett and Phillis. Handbook of English Mediaeval Costume. With illustrations by Barbara Phillipson. Philadelphia, Albert Saifer, 1952. 192 pp.—"Glossary," pp. 169–175; "Bibliography," pp. 176–178.

4995. Cunnington, C[ecil] Willett and Phillis. Handbook of English Costume in the Sixteenth Century. With illustrations by Barbara Phillipson. London, Faber and Faber Ltd., 1954. 224 pp.—"Glossary of Materials," pp. 190–205; "Sources," pp. 206–209.

4996. Cunnington, C[ecil] Willett and Phillis. Handbook of English Costume in the Seventeenth Century. With illustrations by Barbara Phillipson and Phillis Cunnington. London, Faber and Faber Ltd., 1955. 222 pp. —"Glossary," pp. 194–200; "Sources," pp. 201–206.

4997. Cunnington, C[ecil] Willett and Phillis. Handbook of English Costume in the Eighteenth Century. With illustrations by Barbara Phillipson and Phillis Cunnington. London, Faber and Faber Ltd., 1957. 443 pp. —"Sources," pp. 416–421.

4998. Bradfield, Nancy. Historical Costumes of England from the Eleventh to the Twentieth Century. Foreword by James Laver. New ed. New York, Barnes and Noble Inc., 1958. 184 pp.—Original ed. 1938.

4999. Brooke, Iris. Dress and Undress. The Restoration and eighteenth century. London, Methuen and Co., 1958. xi + 161 pp.

5000. Cunnington, C[ecil] Willett and Phillis. Handbook of English Costume in the Nineteenth Century. Philadelphia, Dufour, 1959. 606 pp.

§214. HISTORY: CHRONOLOGICAL TABLES; MAJOR BRITISH AND EUROPEAN MANUALS, GUIDES, AND BIBLIOGRAPHIES; MAJOR BRITISH AND EUROPEAN SURVEYS AND STUDIES

5003. Keller, Helen R. The Dictionary of Dates. New York, Macmillan Co., 1934. 2 vols.

5004. Powicke, F[rederick] M. Handbook of British Chronology. With the assistance of Charles Johnson . . . and W. J. Harte. London, Offices of the Royal Historical Society, 1939. xii + 424 pp.—Number 2 in the series Royal Historical Society Guides and Handbooks.

5005. Steinberg, Sigfrid H. Historical Tables. Foreword by G. P. Gooch. London, Macmillan Co., 1939. x + 256 pp.

5006. Cheney, Christopher R. Handbook of Dates for Students of English History. London, Offices of the Royal Historical Society, 1945. xvii + 164 pp.—Number 4 in the series Royal Historical Society Guides and Handbooks.

5007. Mayer, Alfred. Annals of European Civilization 1501–1900. Foreword by G. P. Gooch. London, Cassell, [1949]. xxii + 457 pp.

5012. [Macray, William Dunn.] Manual of British Historians to A.D. 1600. Containing a chronological account of the early chroniclers . . . their printed works and unpublished MSS. London, William Pickering, 1845. xxiii + 110 pp.

5013. Hardy, Thos. Duffus. Descriptive Catalogue of Materials Relating to the History of Great Britain and Ireland to the End of the Reign of Henry VII. Vol. I: From the Roman period to the Norman invasion; Vol. II: From A.D. 1066 to A.D. 1200; Vol. III: From A.D. 1200 to A.D. 1327. London, Longman, Green, Longman and Roberts, 1862–71. 3 vols.—Number 26 in the series Rerum britannicarum medii aevi scriptores.

5014. Potthast, August. Bibliotheca historica medii aevi. Wegweiser durch die Geschichtswerke des europäischen Mittelalters bis 1500. Vollständiges Inhaltsverzeichnis zu Acta sanctorum Boll., Bouquet, Migne, Monum. germ. hist., Muratori, Rerum britann. scriptores, etc. 2. Aufl. Berlin, Weber, 1896. 2 vols.—Original ed. 1862. Frequent reprints, as in 1959. Part I indexes the collected *scriptores* of each country; Part II is an author list.

5015. Langlois, Ch[arles] V. Manuel de bibliographie historique. Paris, Hachette, 1901–04. 2 vols.—Part I, 2nd ed. 1901; original ed. of Part I 1896.

5016. Molinier, Auguste E. L. M., et al. Les sources de l'histoire de France des origines aux guerres d'Italie 1494. Paris, A. Picard et Fils, 1901–06. 6 vols.

5017. Gross, Chas. Sources and Literature of English History from the Earliest Times to about 1485. 2nd ed. rev. and enl. London, Longmans, Green and Co., 1915. xxiii + 820 pp.—Original ed. 1900. A list of over 3234 titles.

5018. Humphreys, Arthur L. A Handbook to County Bibliography. Being a bibliography of bibliographies relating to counties and towns of Great Britain and Ireland. London, Strangeways and Sons, 1917. x + 501 pp.

5019. Kerner, Robt. Joseph. Slavic Europe. A selected bibliography in the Western European languages, comprising history, languages, and literature. Oxford Univ. Press, 1918. xxiv + 402 pp.

5020. Daremberg, Chas. V., and Saglio, Edmund. Dictionnaire des antiquités grecques et romaines, d'après les textes et les monuments, contenant l'explication des termes qui se rapportent aux moeurs, aux institutions, à la religion . . . et en général à la vie publique et privée des anciens. Paris, Hachette, 1873–1919. 5 vols. plus index vol.

5021. Dutcher, Geo. M., et al. Guide to Historical Literature. New York, Macmillan Co., 1931. xxviii + 1222 pp.

5022. Paetow, Louis John. A Guide to the Study of Medieval History. Rev. ed. New York, F. S. Crofts and Co., 1931. xix + 643 pp.—Original ed. 1917. Revised ed. prepared under the auspices of the Mediaeval Academy of America.

5023. Pirenne, Henri. Bibliographie de l'histoire de Belgique. Catalogue méthodique et chronologique des sources et des ouvrages principaux relatifs à l'histoire de tous les Pays-Bas jusqu'en 1598 et à l'histoire de Belgique jusqu'en 1914. 3e éd. rev. et complétée avec la collaboration de Henri Nowé . . . et Henri Obreen. Brussels, M. Lamertin, 1931. viii + 440 pp.—Original ed. 1893; second ed. 1901.

5024. Dahlmann, Friedrich C., and Waitz, Georg. Quellenkunde der deutschen Geschichte. 9. Aufl. unter Mitwirkung von Ernst Baasch, Max von Bahrfeldt, u. a. . . . herausgegeben von Herman Haering. Leipzig, K. F. Koehler, 1931. 2 parts in 1 vol.

5025. Coulter, Edith M., and Gerstenfeld, Melanie. Historical Bibliographies. A systematic and annotated guide. Berkeley, University of California Press, 1935. xii + 206 pp.

5026. Caron, Pierre, and Jaryc, Marc. World List of Historical Periodicals and Bibliographies. Oxford Univ. Press, 1939. xiv + 391 pp.

5027. [Ploetz, Karl J.] An Encyclopedia of World History, Ancient, Medieval, and Modern, Chronologically Arranged. A revised and modernized version of Ploetz's Epitome compiled and edited by William L. Langer. Boston, Houghton Mifflin Co., 1940. xxviii + 1155 pp.—Original Ger. ed. 1880. The current Ger. ed.: *Auszug aus der Geschichte*, 24. Aufl., Bielefeld, Ploetz, [1951], xvi + 1104 pp.

5028. Schottenloher, Karl. Bibliographie zur deutschen Geschichte im Zeitalter der Glaubensspaltung 1517–1585. Im Auftrag der Kommission zur Erforschung der Geschichte der Reformation und Gegenreformation. Leipzig, K. W. Hiersemann, 1933–40. 6 vols.

5029. Frewer, Louis B. Bibliography of Historical Writings Published in Great Britain and the Empire 1940–1945. Oxford, Eng., Basil Blackwell, 1947. xx + 346 pp.

5030. Strakhovsky, Leonid I. A Handbook of Slavic Studies. Cambridge, Mass., Harvard Univ. Press, 1949. xxi + 753 pp.—"Bibliography" [chiefly of works in English and other western European languages exclusive of Russian on all social and political phases of Russian life], pp. 649–672.

5031. Franz, Günther. Bücherkunde zur deutschen Geschichte. München, R. Oldenbourg, 1951. 279 pp.

5032. Williams, Harry Franklin. An Index of Medieval Studies Published in Festschriften 1865–1946. With special reference to Romanic material. Berkeley, University of California Press, 1951. x + 165 pp.

5033. Halphen, Louis. Initiation aux études d'histoire du moyen âge. 3e éd. rev., augm. et mise à jour par Y. Renouard. Paris, Presses universitaires de France, 1952. xv + 205 pp.—Original ed. 1940.

5034. Langer, Wm. L. An Encyclopedia of World History, Ancient, Medieval, and Modern. Revised ed. with the assistance of Hans W. Gatzke. Boston, Houghton Mifflin Co., 1956. xl + 1243 + lxxxix pp.—Original ed. 1940 (see no. 5027); second ed. 1948.

5035. Lancaster, J[oan] C. Bibliography of Historical Works Issued in the United Kingdom 1946–56. Compiled for the Sixth Anglo-American Conference of Historians. London, Institute of Historical Research, 1957. xxii + 388 pp.

5039. Ker, W[illiam] P. The Dark Ages. Edinburgh, William Blackwood, 1904. 361 pp.—Volume X in the series Periods of European Literature. Reprint with a foreword by B. Ifor Evans, London, Thomas Nelson, 1955.

5040. Traill, Henry D., and Mann, J[ames] S., eds. Social England. A record of the progress of the people in religion, laws, learning, arts, industry, commerce, science, literature, and manners from the earliest times to the present day. New illustrated ed. London, Cassell and Co., 1901–04. 6 vols.—Original ed. 1894–98.

5041. Brown, P[eter] Hume. History of Scotland. Cambridge Univ. Press, 1899–1909. 3 vols.—Reprint 1911.

5042. Oman, Chas. The Dark Ages 476–918. 6th ed. London, Rivingtons, 1919. x + 532 pp.—Volume I in the series Periods of European History. Original ed. 1901. "Bibliographical Note," pp. ix–x.

5043. Oman, Chas. A History of the Art of War in the Middle Ages. 2nd ed. Vol. I: A.D. 378–1278; Vol. II: 1278–1485. London, Methuen and Co., [1924]. 2 vols.—Original ed. 1898 in 1 vol. Reprint New York, Burt Franklin, [1959], 2 vols. Also the condensation *The Art of War in the Middle Ages A.D. 378–1515,* revised and ed. by J. H. Beeler, Ithaca, N.Y., Cornell Univ. Press, [1953], xviii + 176 pp. See also Oman's continuation *History of the Art of War in the Sixteenth Century,* New York, E. P. Dutton and Co., [1937], xv + 784 pp.

5044. Gwatkin, H[enry] M., Whitney, J[ames] P., et al., eds. The Cambridge Medieval History. Planned by J. B. Bury. Cambridge Univ. Press, 1911–36. 8 vols.—Bibliographies at the end of each volume.

5045. Lawrence, Margaret. The School of Femininity. A book for and about women as they are interpreted through feminine writers of yesterday and today. New York, Frederick A. Stokes Co., 1936. xii + 382 pp.

5046. Bury, J[ohn] B., et al. The Cambridge Ancient History. Cambridge Univ. Press, 1923–39. 12 vols.

5047. Curtis, Edmund, and McDowell, R[obert] B., eds. Irish Historical Documents 1172–1922 . London, Methuen and Co., 1943. 331 pp.

5048. Curtis, Edmund. A History of Ireland. 6th ed. London, Methuen and Co., 1950. xi + 434 pp.—Original ed. 1936.

5049. Quirin, Heinz. Einführung in das Studium der mittelalterlichen Geschichte. Mit einem Vorwort von Hermann Heimpel. Braunschweig, G. Westermann, [1950]. 142 pp.—"Literaturverzeichnis," pp. 118–120.

5050. Cazamian, Louis. The Development of English Humor. Part I: From the Early Times to the Renaissance; Part II: The Renaissance. Durham, N.C., Duke Univ. Press, 1952. ix + 421 pp.—Part I originally published New York, Macmillan Co., 1930, xi + 160 pp.

5051. Previté-Orton, Chas. W. The Shorter Cambridge Medieval History. Cambridge Univ. Press, 1952. 2 vols.

5052. Trevelyan, G[eorge] M. Illustrated Social History of England. Illustrations chosen by Ruth C. Wright. London, Longmans, Green and Co., 1949–52. 4 vols.—Original ed. of text 1942; one-volume reprint of illustrated ed. 1956.

5053. Rait, Robt., and Pryde, Geo. S. Scotland. Second ed. rev. throughout by George S. Pryde. New York, Praeger, 1955. 356 pp.—Original ed. 1934.

5054. [Pauly, August F.] Pauly's Realencyclopädie der classischen Altertumswissenschaft. Neue Bearbeitung begonnen von Georg Wissowa, fortgeführt von Wilhelm Kroll und Karl Mittelhaus, unter Mitwirkung zahlreicher Fachgenossen. Herausgegeben von Karl Ziegler. Stuttgart, J. B. Metzler, 1893–date. Reihe I: vols. 1–22 (Aal–Priscianus); Reihe II: vols. 1–8 (Ra–Vergillius).—Also *Supplementbände* 8 vols. (1903–56). Usually called "Pauly-Wissowa."

5055. Rougemont, Denis de. Love in the Western World. Translated by M. Belgion. Rev. ed. New York, Pantheon Press, 1956. 336 pp.—Original Fr. ed. 1939; original Eng. ed. 1940. Original Eng. ed. published in England as *Passion and Society.*

5056. Lunt, Wm. Edward. History of England. 4th ed. New York, Harper, 1957. 980 pp.—Original ed. 1928.

5057. Stenton, Doris Mary. The English Woman in History. London, George Allen and Unwin Ltd., 1957. xi + 363 pp.

5058. Bark, Wm. Carroll. Origins of the Medieval World. Stanford Univ. Press, 1958. xiii + 162 pp. Reprint New York, Doubleday and Co., 1960, in the series Anchor Books.

5059. Singer, Chas., Holmyard, E[ric] J., Hall, A[lfred] R., and Williams, Trevor I., eds. A History of Technology. Vol. I: From Early Times to Fall of Ancient Empires; Vol. II: The Mediterranean Civilization and the Middle Ages c. 700 B.C. to c. A.D. 1500; Vol. III: From the Renaissance to the Industrial Revolution c. 1500–c. 1750; Vol. IV: The Industrial Revolution c. 1750 to c. 1850; Vol. V: The Late Nineteenth Century, c. 1850 to c. 1900. Oxford, Clarendon Press, 1954–58. 5 vols.

5060. English Historical Documents. Edited by David C. Douglas. London, Eyre and Spottiswoode, 1953–date. 12 vols.—The coverage of each volume: Vol. I: *c.* 500–1042; Vol. II: 1042–1189; Vol. III: 1189–1327; Vol. IV: 1327–1485; Vol. V: 1485–1558; Vol. VI: 1558–1603; Vol. VII: 1603–1660; Vol. VIII: 1660–1714; Vol. IX: American Colonial Documents to 1776; Vol. X: 1714–1783; Vol. XI: 1783–1832; Vol. XII (1): 1833–1874; Vol. XII (2): 1874–1914. To date have appeared: Vol. I (1955); Vol. II (1953); Vol. VIII (1953); Vol. IX (1955); Vol. X (1957); Vol. XI (1959); Vol. XII (1) (1956).

5061. Rose, J[ohn] Holland, et al., eds. The Cambridge History of the British Empire. Cambridge Univ. Press, 1929–date. 8 vols. (projected).—To date have appeared: Vol. I: *The Old Empire from the Beginning to 1783*; Vol. II: *Growth of the New Empire 1783–1870*; Vol. IV: *British India 1497–1858*; Vol. V: *Indian Empire 1858–1918*; Vol. VI: *Canada and Newfoundland*; Vol. VII: Pt. 1 *Australia,* Pt. 2 *New Zealand*; Vol. VIII: *South Africa, Rhodesia, and the Protectorates.*

5062. New Cambridge Modern History. Advisory Committee G[eorge] N. Clark, et al. Cambridge Univ. Press, 1957–date. 14 vols. (projected).

—To date: Vol. I: 1493–1520 (1957); Vol. II: 1520–1559 (1958); Vol. VII: 1713–1763 (1957); Vol. XII: 1898–1945 (1960). Successor to the *Cambridge Modern History,* Planned by Lord Acton, Edited by A[dolphus] W. Ward, et al., Cambridge Univ. Press, 1902–12, 13 vols. plus atlas.

5063. Oxford History of England. General ed. G[eorge] N. Clark. Oxford, Clarendon Press, 1936–date. 14 vols. (projected).—The chronological sequence of volumes: Vol. I: *Roman Britain and the English Settlements,* by R. G. Collingwood and J. N. L. Myres, 2nd ed., 1937; Vol. II: *Anglo-Saxon England,* by F. M. Stenton, 2nd ed., 1947; Vol. III: *From Domesday Book to Magna Carta 1087–1216,* by A. L. Poole, 2nd ed., 1955; Vol. IV: *The Thirteenth Century 1216–1307,* by F. M. Powicke, 1953; Vol. V: *The Fourteenth Century 1307–1399,* by May McKisack, 1959; Vol. VI: *The Fifteenth Century 1399–1485,* by E. F. Jacob, in progress; Vol. VII: *The Earlier Tudors 1485–1558,* by J. D. Mackie, 1952; Vol. VIII: *The Reign of Elizabeth 1558–1603,* by J. B. Black, 1936; Vol. IX: *The Early Stuarts 1603–1660,* by Godfrey Davies, 2nd ed. 1959; Vol. X: *The Later Stuarts 1660–1714,* by G. N. Clark, 2nd ed., 1956; Vol. XI: *The Whig Supremacy 1714–1760,* by Basil Williams, 1939; Vol. XII: *The Reign of George III 1760–1815,* by J. S. Watson, 1959; Vol. XIII: *The Age of Reform 1815–1870,* by E. L. Woodward, 1938; Vol. XIV: *England 1870–1914,* by R. C. K. Ensor, 1936.

§215. HISTORY: EARLY BRITAIN AND NORTHERN CIVILIZATION

[For a bibliography of the period see Wilfred Bonser's *An Anglo-Saxon and Celtic Bibliography,* no. 146. See also §38. Minor Prose: Historiography Including Reprints of Early Annals and Chronicles.]

5068. Du Chaillu, Paul B. The Viking Age. The early history, manners, and customs of the ancestors of the English-speaking nations illustrated from the antiquities discovered in mounds, cairns, and bogs as well as from the ancient sagas and eddas. New York, Charles Scribner's Sons, 1889. 2 vols.

5069. Stevenson, Wm. Henry, ed. Asser's Life of King Alfred. Together with the Annals of Saint Neots erroneously ascribed to Asser. Edited with introduction and commentary. Oxford Univ. Press, 1904. cxxxii + 386 pp.

5070. Cook, Albert S. Asser's Life of King Alfred. Translated from the text of Stevenson's edition. Boston, Ginn and Co., 1906. xii + 83 pp.

5071. Bede. The Ecclesiastical History of the English Nation. With an introduction by Vida D. Scudder. London, J. M. Dent and Sons, 1910. xxxiv + 370 pp.—Number 479 in the series Everyman's Library. Frequent reprints, as in 1930.

5072. Williams, Mary Wilhelmine. Social Scandinavia in the Viking Age. New York, Macmillan Co., 1920. xiv + 451 pp.—"Bibliography," pp. 431–44.

5073. Haverfield, F[rancis J.] The Roman Occupation of Britain. Oxford Univ. Press, 1924. 304 pp.—Six Ford Lectures revised by George MacDonald.

5074. Foord, Edward. The Last Age of Roman Britain. London, George G. Harrap and Co., 1925. 294 pp.—"Bibliography," pp. 281–284.

5075. Jane, L[ionel] C., ed. Asser's Life of King Alfred. Translated with introduction and notes. London, Chatto and Windus, 1926. lx + 163 pp.—In the series Medieval Library.

5076. Grönbeck, Vilhelm. The Culture of the Teutons. Oxford Univ. Press, 1931. 2 vols.—Original Danish ed. 1909–12.

5077. Thompson, A[lexander] Hamilton, ed. Bede. His life, times, and writings. Essays in commemoration of the twelfth centenary of his death. With an introduction by the Lord Bishop of Durham. Oxford Univ. Press, 1935. xvi + 277 pp.—"Select Bibliography," pp. ix–xii.

5078. Collingwood, R[obin] G., and Myres, J[ohn] N. L. Roman Britain and the English Settlements. 2nd ed. Oxford Univ. Press, 1937. xxvi + 515 pp.—In the series Oxford History of England. Original ed. 1936.

5079. Schetelig, Haakon, and Falk, Hjalmar. Scandinavian Archaeology. Preface by Magnus Olsen. Translated by E. V. Gordon. Oxford Univ. Press, 1937. xx + 458 pp.

5080. Levison, Wilhelm. England and the Continent in the Eighth Century. Oxford Univ. Press, 1946. xii + 347 pp.—The Ford Lectures, Oxford University, 1943.

5081. Martin-Clarke, D[aisy] Elizabeth. Culture in Early Anglo-Saxon England. A study with illustrations. Baltimore, Johns Hopkins Press, 1947. xi + 100 pp. + xxviii plates.

5082. Hodgkin, R[obert] H. A History of the Anglo-Saxons. 3rd ed. Oxford Univ. Press, 1952. 2 vols.—Original ed. 1935; second ed. 1939. The 3rd ed. contains "The Sutton Hoo Ship-Burial," II, pp. 696–734.

5083. Oman, Chas. England before the Norman Conquest. Being a history of the Celtic, Roman, and Anglo-Saxon periods down to the year A.D. 1066. 9th ed. London, Methuen and Co., [1949]. xiv + 679 pp.—Volume I of Oman's *A History of England.* Original ed. 1910.

5084. Duckett, Eleanor Shipley. Alcuin, Friend of Charlemagne. New York, Macmillan Co., 1951. xii + 337 pp.

5085. Turville-Petre, G[abriel]. The Heroic Age of Scandinavia. London, Hutchinson House, 1951. viii + 9–196 pp.—In the series Hutchinson's University Library.

5086. Whitelock, Dorothy. The Beginnings of English Society. Harmondsworth, Eng., Penguin Books Ltd., 1952. 256 pp.—Number 2 in the series Pelican History of England. A245 in the series Pelican Books. Reprint 1956. "Select Bibliography," pp. 244–248.

5087. Jackson, Kenneth. Language and History in Early Britain. A chronological survey of the Brittonic languages first to twelfth century. Cambridge, Mass., Harvard Univ. Press, 1953. xxvi + 752 pp.

5088. Richmond, I[an] A. Roman Britain. Harmondsworth, Eng., Penguin Books Ltd., 1955. 240 pp.—Number 1 in the series Pelican History of England. A315 in the series Pelican Books. Reprint 1958. "Bibliography," pp. 215–227.

5089. Blair, Peter Hunter. An Introduction to Anglo-Saxon England. Cambridge Univ. Press, 1956. xvi + 382 pp.

5090. Duckett, Eleanor Shipley. Alfred the Great. University of Chicago Press, 1956. x + 221 pp.

5091. Robertson, Agnes J., ed. Anglo-Saxon Charters. With translation and notes. Cambridge Univ. Press, 1956. xxv + 555 pp.—In the series Cambridge Studies in English Legal History.

5092. Hawkes, Jacquetta and Christopher. Prehistoric Britain. Rev. ed. Harmondsworth, Eng., Penguin Books Ltd., 1958. 176 pp.—Number A115 in the series Pelican Books. Original ed. 1944. "Bibliography," pp. 166–171.

§216. HISTORY: MEDIEVAL AND RENAISSANCE BRITAIN

[See also §38. Minor Prose: Historiography Including Reprints of Early Annals and Chronicles.]

5096. Thomason, Geo. Catalogue of the Pamphlets, Books, Newspapers, and Manuscripts Relating to the Civil War, the Commonwealth, and Restoration. London, British Museum Department of Printed Books, 1908. 2 vols.

5097. Davies, Godfrey, ed. Bibliography of British History. Stuart Period 1603–1714. Oxford, Clarendon Press, 1928. x + 459 pp.—"Literature, Ballads, and Journalism," pp. 226–248. Supplement in the bibliography, pp. 417–443, of Davies' *The Early Stuarts*, 2nd ed., Oxford, Clarendon Press, 1959, xxiii + 458 pp.

5098. Read, Conyers, ed. Bibliography of British History. Tudor Period 1485–1603. Introduction by Edward P. Cheyney. 2nd ed. Oxford, Clarendon Press, 1959. xxiv + 624 pp.—Original ed. 1933. "Literature," pp. 308–320.

5099. Doran, [John]. The History of Court Fools. London, R. Bentley, 1858. 389 pp.—Reprint Boston, Francis A. Niccolls, [ ], [x] + 463 pp.

5100. Einstein, Lewis D. The Italian Renaissance in England. New York, Columbia Univ. Press, 1902. xvii + 420 pp.—In the series Columbia University Studies in Comparative Literature. Bibliography, pp. 391–409.

5101. Stubbs, Wm. Historical Introductions to the Rolls Series. Collected and edited by Arthur Hassall. London, Longmans, Green and Co., 1902. vii + 534 pp.

5102. Lee, Sidney. Great Englishmen of the Sixteenth Century. New York, Charles Scribner's Sons, 1904. xxiii + 337 pp.

5103. Schofield, Wm. Henry. Chivalry in English Literature. Chaucer, Malory, Spenser, and Shakespeare. Cambridge, Mass., Harvard Univ. Press, 1912. x + 294 pp.—Volume II in the series Harvard Studies in Comparative Literature.

5104. Allen, P[ercy] S. The Age of Erasmus. Oxford Univ. Press, 1914. 303 pp.—Lectures delivered in the Universities of Oxford and London.

5105. Coulton, G[eorge] G. Social Life in Britain. From the Conquest to the Reformation. Cambridge Univ. Press, 1918. xvi + 540 pp.

5106. Taylor, Henry Osborn. Thought and Expression in the Sixteenth Century. New York, Macmillan Co., 1920. 2 vols.

5107. Einstein, Lewis D. Tudor Ideals. New York, Harcourt, Brace and Co., 1921. xiii + 366 pp.

5108. Jusserand, J[ean] J. English Wayfaring Life in the Middle Ages (Fourteenth Century). Translated by Lucy Toulmin Smith. London, Ernest Benn Ltd., 1925. 464 pp.—Original Fr. ed. 1884; original Eng. ed. 1889; second Eng. ed. 1920; third Eng. ed. reprinted 1931.

5109. Taylor, Henry Osborn. The Mediaeval Mind. A history of the development of thought and emotion in the Middle Ages. 4th ed. Cambridge,

Mass., Harvard Univ. Press, 1925. 2 vols.—Original ed. 1911; second ed. 1914; third ed. 1919; fourth ed. reprinted 1949.

5110. Salzman, L[ouis] F. English Life in the Middle Ages. Oxford Univ. Press, 1926. 287 pp.—Frequent reprints, as in 1937.

5111. Kelso, Ruth. The Doctrine of the English Gentleman in the Sixteenth Century. With a bibliographical list of treatises on the gentleman and related subjects published in Europe to 1625. Urbana, University of Illinois Press, 1929. 288 pp.—Volume XIV, nos. 1–2, in the series University of Illinois Studies in Language and Literature.

5112. Mead, Wm. Edward. The English Medieval Feast. London, George Allen and Unwin Ltd., 1931. 272 pp.—"Bibliographical Note," pp. 260–265.

5113. Swain, Barbara. Fools and Folly during the Middle Ages and Renaissance. New York, Columbia Univ. Press, 1932. 234 pp.

5114. Wright, Louis B. Middle-Class Culture in Elizabethan England. Chapel Hill, University of North Carolina Press, 1935. xiii + 733 pp.—In the series Huntington Library Publications. "Bibliography," pp. 661–677.

5115. Bennett, Henry Stanley. Life on the English Manor. A study of peasant conditions 1150–1400. Cambridge Univ. Press, 1937. xviii + 364 pp. —In the series Cambridge Studies in Medieval Life and Thought. "Authorities," pp. 341–351.

5116. Coulton, G[eorge] G. Medieval Panorama. The English scene from Conquest to Reformation. Cambridge Univ. Press, 1938. xiv + 801 pp.

5117. Lewis, C[live] S. The Allegory of Love. A study in medieval tradition. Corrected ed. Oxford Univ. Press, 1938. ix + 378 pp.—Original ed. 1936; corrected ed. frequently reprinted, as in 1958 by Oxford as no. 17 in the series Galaxy Books.

5118. Ferguson, Wallace K. The Renaissance in Historical Thought. Five centuries of interpretation. Boston, Houghton Mifflin Co., 1948. xiii + 429 pp.—"Bibliography," pp. 398–407.

5119. Salusbury, G[oronwy] T. Street Life in Medieval England. 2nd ed. Oxford, Eng., Pen-in-Hand Publ'ing Co., 1948. 213 pp.—Original ed. 1939.

5120. Bennett, H[enry] S. The Pastons and Their England. Studies in an age of transition. 2nd ed. Cambridge Univ. Press, 1951. xx + 289 pp.—In the series Cambridge Studies in Medieval Life and Thought. Original ed. 1922.

5121. Bethell, S[amuel] L. The Cultural Revolution of the Seventeenth Century. New York, Roy Publ'ers, 1951. 161 pp.

5122. Chrimes, S[tanley] B. An Introduction to the Administrative History of Mediaeval England. Oxford, Eng., Basil Blackwell, 1952. xv + 277 pp.—Number 7 in the series Studies in Mediaeval History.

5123. Holmes, Urban Tigner, Jr. Daily Living in the Twelfth Century. Based on the observations of Alexander Neckam of London and Paris. Madison, University of Wisconsin Press, 1952. xiv + 337 pp.

5124. Stenton, Doris Mary. English Society in the Early Middle Ages 1066–1307. 2nd ed. Harmondsworth, Eng., Penguin Books Ltd., 1952. 303 pp.—Number 3 in the series Pelican History of England. A252 in the series Pelican Books. Original ed. 1951; second ed. reprinted 1955.

5125. Caspari, Fritz. Humanism and the Social Order in Tudor England. University of Chicago Press, 1954. ix + 293 pp.

5126. Myers, A[lec] R. England in the Late Middle Ages 1307–1536. [Rev. ed.] Harmondsworth, Eng., Penguin Books Ltd., 1956. xvi + 264 pp. —Number 4 in the series Pelican History of England. A234 in the series Pelican Books. Original ed. 1952. "Book List," pp. 245–248.

5127. Pearson, Lu Emily. Elizabethans at Home. Stanford University Press, 1957. 630 pp.

§217. HISTORY: BRITAIN FROM THE EIGHTEENTH CENTURY TO MODERN TIMES

5131. Williams, Judith Blow. A Guide to the Printed Materials for English Social and Economic History 1750–1850. New York, Columbia Univ. Press, 1926. 2 vols.—In the series Records of Civilization: Sources and Studies.

5132. Grose, Clyde LeClare. A Select Bibliography of British History 1660–1760. University of Chicago Press, 1939. xxv + 400 (regular) + 401–507 (double column) pp.

5133. Morgan, Wm. T. and Chloe S. A Bibliography of British History 1700–1715. With special reference to the reign of Queen Anne. Bloomington, Indiana University Press, 1934–42. 5 vols.—Volumes XVIII–XIX, XXIII–XXIV, and XXVI, nos. 94–95, 114–118, and 123–124 in the series Indiana University Studies.

5134. Pargellis, Stanley, and Medley, D[udley] J., eds. Bibliography of British History. The eighteenth century 1714–1789. Oxford, Clarendon Press, 1951. xxvi + 642 pp.—"Literature," by Louis L. and Edwine M. Martz, pp. 275–306.

5135. Robinson, Edward Forbes. The Early History of Coffee Houses in England. With some account of the first use of coffee and a bibliography of the subject. London, Kegan Paul, Trench, Trübner and Co., 1893. xviii + 240 pp.

5136. Patton, Julia. The English Village 1750–1850. New York, Macmillan Co., 1919. xi + 236 pp.

5137. Jackson, Holbrook. The Eighteen Nineties. A review of art and ideas at the close of the century. New ed. London, Jonathan Cape, 1927. 304 pp.—Original ed. 1913.

5138. Turberville, A[rthur] S. English Men and Manners in the Eighteenth Century. An illustrated narrative. 2nd ed. Oxford, Clarendon Press, 1929. xxiii 539 pp.—Original ed. 1926; second ed. reprinted 1932.

5139. Allen, Robt. J. The Clubs of Augustan London. Cambridge, Mass., Harvard Univ. Press, 1933. xi + 305 pp.—Volume VII in the series Harvard Studies in English.

5140. Turberville, A[rthur] S., ed. Johnson's England. An account of the life and manners of his age. Oxford, Clarendon Press, 1933. 2 vols.—A sociological coverage 1730–1790.

5141. Young, G[eorge] M., ed. Early Victorian England 1830–65. Oxford Univ. Press, 1934. 2 vols.

5142. Brinton, Crane. The Political Ideas of the English Romanticists. Oxford Univ. Press, 1936. [viii] + 242 pp.

5143. Mead, Geo. H. Movements of Thought in the Nineteenth Century. Edited by Merritt H. Moore. University of Chicago Press, 1936. xxxix + 519 pp.

5144. Routh, H[arold] V. Towards the Twentieth Century. Essays in the spiritual history of the nineteenth. New York, Macmillan Co., 1937. x + 392 pp.

5145. Marchand, Leslie A. The Athenaeum. A mirror of Victorian culture. Chapel Hill, University of North Carolina Press, 1941. xvi + 411 pp.

5146. Quinlan, Maurice J. Victorian Prelude. A history of English manners 1700–1830. New York, Columbia Univ. Press, 1941. 301 pp.—Number 155 in the series Columbia University Studies in English and Comparative Literature.

5147. Lochhead, Marion. The Scots Household in the Eighteenth Century. A century of Scottish domestic and social life. Edinburgh, Moray Press, 1948. 410 pp.

5148. Brinton, Crane. English Political Thought in the Nineteenth Century. 2nd ed. London, Ernest Benn Ltd., 1949. vii + 312 pp.—Original ed. 1933.

5149. Ellis, Aytown. The Penny Universities. A history of the coffee-houses. London, Secker and Warburg, 1956. xvii + 290 pp.—"Bibliography," pp. 240–243.

5150. Marshall, Dorothy. English People in the Eighteenth Century. London, Longmans, Green and Co., 1956. xvi + 288 pp.

5151. Houghton, Walter E. The Victorian Frame of Mind 1830–1870. New Haven, Yale Univ. Press for Wellesley College, 1957. xvii + 467 pp.—"Bibliography," pp. 431–444.

5152. Lochhead, Marion. Young Victorians. London, John Murray Ltd., 1959. xii + 240 pp.—"Bibliography," pp. 235–238.

5153. Moers, Ellen. The Dandy. Brummell to Beerbohm. London, Secker and Warburg, 1960. 372 pp.—Bibliographical notes, pp. 336–363.

5154. Wood, Anthony. Nineteenth Century Britain 1815–1914. London, Longmans, 1960. xiii + 476 pp.—"Further Reading," pp. 458–462.

§218. HISTORY: AMERICAN CIVILIZATION

[See also §§17–21. American Literature.]

5158. [Harrisse, Henry.] Bibliotheca americana vetustissima. A description of works relating to America published between the years 1492 and 1551. New York, George P. Philes Publ'er, 1866. liv + 519 pp.—Also *Additions*, Paris, Libraire Tross, 1872, xl + 199 pp. Reprint of both volumes Paris, Maisonneuve, 1922. Also Carlos Sanz, *Henry Harrisse 1829–1910*, Principe de los Americanistas, su vida, su obra, con nuevas adiciones a la Bibliotheca americana vetustissima, Madrid, Suarez, 1958, 286 pp.

5159. Larned, J[osephus] N. The Literature of American History. A bibliographical guide. Boston, American Library Association, 1902. 596 pp. —Also *Supplement for 1900–01*, American Library Association, 1902, v + 37 pp.

5160. Baxter, Chas. N., and Dearborn, James M. Confederate Literature. A list of books and newspapers, maps, music, and miscellaneous matter printed in the South during the Confederacy, now in the Boston Athenaeum. With an introduction by James Ford Rhodes. Boston Athenaeum, 1917. x + 213 pp.—Volume V in the series Publications of the Robert Charles Billings Fund.

5161. Beers, Henry Putney. Bibliographies in American History. Guide to materials for research. Rev. ed. New York, H. W. Wilson Co., 1942. xv + 487 pp.—Original ed. 1938.

5162. Guides to Manuscript Materials for the History of the United States. Washington, D.C., Carnegie Institution, 1906–43. 23 vols.

5163. McMurtrie, Douglas Crawford. Locating the Printed Source Materials for United States History. With a bibliography of lists of regional imprints. Mississippi Valley Historical Review, XXXI (Dec. 1944), 369–406.

5164. Billington, Ray Allen. Guides to American History Manuscript Collections in Libraries of the United States. Mississippi Valley Historical Review, XXXVIII (Dec. 1951), 467–496.

5165. Greene, Evarts B., and Morris, Richard B. A Guide to the Principal Sources for Early American History 1600–1800 in the City of New York. Second ed. rev. by Richard B. Morris. New York, Columbia Univ. Press, 1953. xxxvi + 400 pp.—Original ed. 1929.

5166. Handlin, Oscar, Schlesinger, Arthur Meier, Morison, Samuel Eliot, Merk, Frederick, Schlesinger, Arthur Meier, Jr., and Buck, Paul Herman. Harvard Guide to American History. Cambridge, Mass., Harvard Univ. Press, 1954. xxiv + 689 pp.

5167. Weimer, D[avid] R., ed. Bibliography of American Culture 1493–1875. Ann Arbor, Mich., University Microfilms, 1957. xvi + 228 pp.

5168. [Staton, Frances M., and Tremaine, Marie.] A Bibliography of Canadiana. Being items in the Public Library of Toronto, Canada, Relating to the Early History and Development of Canada. Introduction by George H. Lock. Toronto Public Library, 1934. 828 pp.—Also *Supplement* by G. M. Boyle and M. Colbeck, Toronto Public Library, 1959.

5169. Thwaites, Reuben Gold, ed. The Jesuit Relations and Allied Documents. The travels and explorations of the Jesuit missionaries in New France 1610–1791. Cleveland, Burrows Bros., 1896–1901. 73 vols.—Reprint New York, Pageant Book Co., 1960, 36 vols.

5170. Winship, Geo. Parker, ed. Sailors' Narratives of Voyages along the New England Coast 1524–1624. With notes. Boston, Houghton Mifflin Co., 1905. 292 pp.

5171. Thwaites, Reuben Gold, ed. Early Western Travels 1748–1846. A series of annotated reprints of some of the best and rarest contemporary volumes of travel, descriptive of the aborigines and social and economic conditions in the middle and far West during the period of early American settlement. Cleveland, A. H. Clark Co., 1904–07. 32 vols.

5172. Allen, Frederick Lewis. Only Yesterday. An informal history of the nineteen-twenties. New York, Harper and Bros., 1931. xiv + 370 pp. —Reprint New York, Harper and Bros., 1957. See also Allen's *Since Yesterday,* The nineteen-thirties . . . , New York, Harper and Bros., 1940, xiv + 362 pp., and *The Big Change,* America transforms itself 1900–1950, New York, Harper and Bros., 1952, xi + 308 pp.

5173. Chitwood, Oliver Perry. A History of Colonial America. New York, Harper and Bros., 1931. xiii + 811 pp.—Bibliography, pp. 708–790.

5174. Sullivan, Mark. Our Times. The United States 1900–1925. New York, Charles Scribner's Sons, 1926–35. 6 vols.

5175. Adams, Samuel Hopkins. Incredible Era. The life and times of Warren Gamaliel Harding. Boston, Houghton Mifflin Co., 1939. vii + 456 pp.

5176. Hansen, Marcus L. The Atlantic Migration 1607–1860. A history of the continuing settlement of the United States. Edited with a foreword by Arthur M. Schlesinger. Cambridge, Mass., Harvard Univ. Press, 1940. xvii + 391 pp.

5177. Cargill, Oscar. Intellectual America. New York, Macmillan Co., 1941. xxiii + 777 pp.

5178. Adams, James Truslow, and Coleman, R[oy] V. Dictionary of American History. 2nd ed. New York, Charles Scribner's Sons, 1942. 5 vols. plus index vol.—Original ed. 1940.

5179. Beard, Chas. A. and Mary R. The Rise of American Civilization. New ed., rev. and enl. New York, Macmillan Co., 1947. 2 vols. in 1.—Original ed. 1927–39.

5180. Schlesinger, Arthur M., and Fox, Dixon R., eds. A History of American Life. New York, Macmillan Co., 1927–48. 13 vols.

5181. Billington, Ray Allen. Westward Expansion. A history of the American frontier. With the collaboration of James Blaine Hedges. New York, Macmillan Co., 1949. xiii + 873 pp.—Bibliography, pp. 757–834.

5182. Commager, Henry Steele. The American Mind. An interpretation of American thought and character since the 1880's. New Haven, Yale Univ. Press, 1950. xii + 476 pp.

5183. Morison, Samuel Eliot, and Commager, Henry Steele. The Growth of the American Republic. 4th ed., rev. and enl. New York, Oxford Univ. Press, 1950. 2 vols.—Original ed. 1930; second ed. 1937; third ed. 1942; fourth ed. reprinted 1956.

5184. Riesman, David. The Lonely Crowd. A study of the changing American character. With Nathan Glazer and Reuel Denney. New Haven, Yale Univ. Press, 1950. xvii + 386 pp.—Number 3 in the series Studies in National Policy. Frequent reprints, as in 1958.

5185. Smith, Henry Nash. Virgin Land. The American West as symbol and myth. Cambridge, Mass., Harvard Univ. Press, 1950. xiv + 305 pp.—Bibliographical notes, pp. 261–298.

5186. Schlesinger, Arthur Meier. The Rise of Modern America 1865–1951. 4th ed. New York, Macmillan Co., [1951]. xvii + 607 pp.—Original ed. 1925.

5187. Morris, Richard B. Encyclopedia of American History. New York, Harper and Bros., 1953. 776 pp.

5188. Billington, Ray Allen. The Far Western Frontier 1830–1860. New York, Harper and Bros., 1956. 324 pp.

5189. Gurko, Leo. The Angry Decade. New York, Dodd, Mead and Co., 1947. viii + 306 pp.—See also Gurko's *Heroes, Highbrows, and the Popular Mind,* Indianapolis, Bobbs-Merrill, 1953, 319 pp., and *Crisis of the American Mind,* London, Rider, 1956, xiii + 222 pp.

5190. Bode, Carl. The Anatomy of American Popular Culture 1840–1861. Berkeley, University of California Press, 1959. xx + 292 pp.

5191. Flexner, Eleanor. Century of Struggle. The woman's rights movement in the United States. Cambridge, Mass., Harvard Univ. Press, 1959. xiv + 384 pp.

§219. MAPS AND MAPMAKING

[See also §39. Minor Prose: Travel and Descriptive Geography; §92. Periodicals Devoted to the Study of Names; §121. Place Names.]

5195. Anderson, John P. The Book of British Topography. A classified catalogue of the topographical works in the library of the British Museum relating to Great Britain and Ireland. London, Satchell and Co., 1881. xvi + 472 pp.

5196. Phillips, Philip Lee, ed. Check List of Large Scale Maps Published by Foreign Governments (Great Britain Excepted) in the Library of Congress. Washington, D.C., Library of Congress, 1904. 58 leaves.

5197. Daniell, Walter V., and Nield, Frederick J. Manual of British Topography. A catalogue of county and local histories, pamphlets, views, drawings, maps, etc., connected with and illustrating the principal localities in the United Kingdom. London, W. V. Daniell, 1909. 284 pp.

5198. Hawley, Edith J. R. Literary Geography. A bibliography. Boston, Boston Book Co., 1917. 28 pp.—Number 25 in the series Bulletin of Bibliography Pamphlets.

5199. Wright, John Kirtland. Aids to Geographical Research. Bibliographies and periodicals. New York, American Geographical Society, 1923. xiii + 243 pp. (65–229 printed recto only).—Number 10 in the American Geographical Society Research Series. Rev. ed. New York, Columbia Univ. Press, 1947.

5200. Le Gear, Clara E. United States Atlases. A list of national, state, county, city, and regional atlases in the Library of Congress. Washington, D.C., Library of Congress, 1950–53. 2 vols.

5201. Ristow, W[alter] W., and Le Gear, C[lara] E. A Guide to Historical Cartography. A selected, annotated list of references on the history of maps and map making. Washington, D.C., Government Printing Office, 1954. 14 pp.

5202. Library of Congress Catalog: Maps and Atlases. Ann Arbor, Mich., J. W. Edwards Inc., 1953–55. 3 (triple column page) volumes.

5203. Dictionnaire de géographie ancienne et moderne à l'usage du libraire et de l'amateur de livres. Par un bibliophile [i.e. Pierre Deschamps]. Paris, Librairie Firmin Didot Frères, 1870. viii + 1592 columns (two per page).—A supplement of Brunet's *Manuel du libraire . . .* [Volume IX]. Contains a list of modern place names with Latin equivalents.

5204. Poole, Reginald Lane. Historical Atlas of Modern Europe from the Decline of the Roman Empire. Comprising also maps of parts of Asia, Africa, and the New World connected with European history. Oxford, Clarendon Press, 1902. viii + 328 pp. + xc maps.

5205. Fox, Dixon R. Harper's Atlas of American History Selected from the American Nation Series with Map Studies. New York, Harper and Bros., 1920. 180 pp.

5206. Goode, Clement Tyson, and Shannon, Edgar Finley. An Atlas of English Literature. New York, Century Co., 1925. [ix] + 136 pp.

5207. Bartholomew, J[ohn] G. Literary and Historical Atlas of Europe. Rev. ed. London, J. M. Dent and Sons, 1930. xiv + 254 pp.—Original ed. 1910; revised ed. reprinted 1940.

5208. Briscoe, John d'Auby, Sharp, Robt. Lathop, and Borish, Murray Eugene. A Mapbook of English Literature. New York, Henry Holt and Co., 1936. 47 pp.

5209. Brown, Lloyd A. The Story of Maps. Boston, Little, Brown and Co., 1949. xix + 397 pp.—"Bibliography," pp. 341–373.

5210. Webster's Geographical Dictionary. A dictionary of names of places with geographical and historical information and pronunciations. Edited by John B. Bethel, et al. Springfield, Mass., G. and C. Merriam Co., 1949. xxxi + 1293 (double column) pp. + xxvi maps.

5211. Ristow, Walter W. Services and Collections of the Map Division. Washington, D.C., Library of Congress, 1951. 22 pp.

5212. Everyman's Atlas of Ancient and Classical Geography. London, J. M. Dent and Sons, 1952. xiii + 256 pp.—In the series Everyman's Reference Library. Original ed. 1907.

5213. Seltzer, Leon E., ed. Columbia Lippincott Gazetteer of the World. New York, Columbia Univ. Press, 1952. x + 2148 (double column) pp.—Prior Lippincott gazetteer 1905.

5214. American Guide Series. Washington, D.C., Work Projects Administration, 1937–54. 48 vols.—All volumes, now in the process of being reprinted, contain information on literature, folklore, and libraries. See *Catalogue,* WPA Writers' Program Publications, The American Guide Series / The American Life Series, foreword by Florence Kerr, Washington, D.C., Work Projects Administration, 1941, 54 pp.

5215. Le Gear, C[lara] E. Maps. Their care, repair, and preservation in libraries. Rev. ed. Washington, D.C., Library of Congress, 1956. ix + 75 pp.—Original ed. 1949. Bibliography, pp. 56–75.

5216. Swayne, J[ohn] C. A Concise Glossary of Geographical Names. London, George Philip and Sons, 1956. 164 pp.

5217. Meer, F[rederik] van der, and Mohrmann, Christine. Atlas of the Early Christian World. Translated and edited by Mary F. Hedlund and H. H. Rowley. London, Nelson, 1958. 216 pp.—Original Dutch ed. 1958.

5218. Skelton, Raleigh A. Explorers' Maps. Chapters in the cartographic record of geographical discovery. New York, Frederick A. Praeger, 1958. xi + 337 pp.

§220. MUSIC

[See also §142. Ballad and Folksong Studies; §143. Old World Songs and Ballads; §144. New World Songs and Ballads.]

5221. Sears, Minnie E., and Crawford, Phyllis. Song Index. An index to more than 12000 songs in 177 song collections comprising 262 volumes.

New York, H. W. Wilson Co., 1926. xxxii + 650 (double column) pp. —Also *Supplement,* An index to more than 7000 songs in 104 song collections comprising 124 volumes, New York, H. W. Wilson Co., 1934, xxxix + 367 pp.

5222. Cushing, Helen Grant. Children's Song Index. An index to more than 22000 songs in 189 collections comprising 222 volumes. New York, H. W. Wilson Co., 1936. xlii + 798 (double column) pp.

5223. Oxford History of Music. Edited by W[illiam] H. Hadow. 2nd ed. Oxford Univ. Press, 1929–34. 7 vols.—Original ed. 1901 in 6 vols.

5224. Reese, Gustave. Music in the Middle Ages. With an introduction on the music of ancient times. New York, W. W. Norton and Co., 1940. xvii + 502 pp.—"Bibliography," pp. 425–463.

5225. Bukofzer, Manfred F. Music in the Baroque Era. From Monteverdi to Bach. New York, W. W. Norton and Co., 1947. xv + 489 pp.—"Check-list of Baroque Books on Music," pp. 417–431; "Bibliography," pp. 433–459.

5226. Barlow, Harold, and Morgenstern, Sam. A Dictionary of Vocal Themes. New York, Crown Publ'ers, 1950. vi + 547 pp.—Themes and their words under alphabetically arranged composers' names.

5227. [Grove, Geo., ed.] Grove's Dictionary of Music and Musicians. Fifth ed. edited by Eric Blom. London, Macmillan Co., 1954. 9 (double column page) vols.—Original ed. 1878–89 in 4 vols.

5228. Scholes, Percy A. Oxford Companion to Music. Self-indexed and with a pronouncing glossary. 9th ed. Oxford Univ. Press, 1955. lx + 1195 (chiefly double column) pp.—Original ed. 1938; ninth ed. reprinted with corrections 1956.

5229. New Oxford History of Music. Edited by J[ack] A. Westrup. Oxford Univ. Press, 1954–date. 11 vols. (projected).—Already issued are: Vol. I: *Ancient and Oriental Music,* by Egon Wellesz (1957) and *Early Medieval Music up to 1300,* by Dom Anselm Hughes (1954).

§221. PHILOSOPHY, PSYCHOLOGY, AND RELIGION

[See also §37. Minor Prose: Hagiography, Homiletics, and Devotional Literature; §69. Basic Principles of Criticism; §70. Aristotle and Other Ancient Authorities; §77. Religion and Literature; §78. Science, Psychology, and Literature; §133. Mythology and Myth: Studies.]

5233. Case, Shirley J., et al. A Bibliographical Guide to the History of Christianity. University of Chicago Press, 1931. 265 pp.

5234. Parsons, Wilfred, S.J. Early Catholic Americana. A list of books and other works by Catholic authors in the United States 1729–1830. New York, Macmillan Co., 1939. xxv + 282 pp.

5235. Ellis, John Tracy. A Select Bibliography of the History of the Catholic Church in America. New York, Declan X. McMullen, [1947]. 96 pp.

5236. Dudley, Fred A., et al. The Relations of Literature and Science. A selected bibliography 1930–1949. Pullman, Department of English of the State College of Washington, 1949. 59 pp.

5237. Barrow, John Graves. A Bibliography of Bibliographies in Religion. [Ann Arbor, Mich., Edwards Bros., 1955.] xi + 489 pp.

5238. Diehl, Katherine Smith. Religions, Mythologies, Folklore. An annotated bibliography. New Brunswick, N.J., Scarecrow Press, 1956. 315 pp.—Emphasis primarily on religion.

5239. Stephen, Leslie. The English Utilitarians. Vol. I: Jeremy Bentham; Vol. II: James Mill; Vol. III: John Stuart Mill. London, Duckworth and Co., 1900. 3 vols.

5240. Stephen, Leslie. History of English Thought in the Eighteenth Century. 3rd ed. London, G. P. Putnam's Sons, 1902. 2 vols.—Original ed. 1876; second ed. 1881; third ed. reprinted 1927.

5241. Henson, H[erbert] Hensley. Studies in English Religion in the Seventeenth Century. London, John Murray, 1903. xix + 265 pp.—The Saint Margaret's Lectures 1903.

5242. Patrologiae cursus completus seu bibliotheca universalis. . . . Omnium S.S. patrum, doctorum, scriptorumque ecclesiasticorum, sive latinorum, sive graecorum, qui ad aevo apostolico ad . . . concilii florentini tempora (ann. 1439) pro graecis floruerunt. Edited by Jacques P. Migne. Paris, Garnier Frères, 1844–1904. 382 vols.—Latin series 1844–1903 in 221 vols.; Greek series 1857–1904 in 161 vols. Usually called "Migne."

5243. Baldwin, James M. Dictionary of Philosophy and Psychology. Including many of the principal conceptions of ethics, logic, aesthetics, philosophy of religion, etc. New York, Macmillan Co., 1901–05. 3 vols. in 4.

5244. Benn, Alfred Wm. The History of English Rationalism in the Nineteenth Century. London, Longmans, Green and Co., 1906. 2 vols.

5245. [Schaff, Philip, ed.] New Schaff-Herzog Encyclopedia of Religious Knowledge. Edited by Samuel M. Jackson, et al. Index by George W. Gilmore. New York, Funk and Wagnalls Co., [1908–14]. 12 vols. plus index vol.—Reprint Grand Rapids, Mich., Baker Book House, 1949–50, 13 vols. The English version goes back to the *Realencyclopädie für protestantische Theologie,* begründet von Johann J. Herzog und herausgegeben von Albert Hauch, 3. Aufl., Leipzig, J. C. Hinrichs, 1896–1913, 24 vols., original ed. 1877–88. *Schaff-Herzog* is supplemented by the *Twentieth-Century Encyclopedia of Religious Knowledge,* An extension of the New Schaff-Herzog Encyclopedia of Religious Knowledge, edited by L. A. Loetscher, Grand Rapids, Mich., Baker Book House, 1953–55, 2 vols.

5246. The Jewish Encyclopedia. A descriptive record of the history, religion, literature, and customs of the Jewish people from the earliest times to the present day. Edited by Cyrus Adler, et al. New York, Funk and Wagnalls Co., 1901–16. 12 vols.

5247. Bury, J[ohn] B. The Idea of Progress. An inquiry into its origin and growth. London, Macmillan Co., 1920. xv + 377 pp.—Reprint with introduction by Charles A. Beard, New York, Dover Publications, 1955, xli + 357 pp.

5248. Sorley, W[illiam] R. A History of English Philosophy. Cambridge Univ. Press, 1920. xvi + 380 pp.—Reprint 1937. "Comparative Chronological Table," pp. 303–321; "Bibliography," pp. 322–373.

5249. The Catholic Encyclopedia. An international work of reference on the constitution, doctrine, discipline, and history of the Catholic Church. Edited by Charles G. Herbermann, Edward A. Pace, et al. New York, Robert Appleton, 1907–22. 17 vols. plus index vol.

5250. Rogers, Arthur Kenyon. English and American Philosophy since 1800. A critical survey. New York, Macmillan Co., 1922. xv + 468 pp.

5251. Hertzler, Joyce O. The History of Utopian Thought. London, George Allen and Unwin, 1923. xxii + 321 pp.

5252. [Ueberweg, Friedrich.] Ueberwegs Grundriss der Geschichte der Philosophie. 12 Aufl. Berlin, E. S. Mittler und Sohn, 1923–28. 5 vols.—Original ed. 1863–66 in 3 vols. Volume II is actually an 11th ed.

5253. Hastings, James, et al. Encyclopedia of Religion and Ethics. New York, C. Scribner's Sons, 1920–30. 12 vols. plus index vol.

5254. Burtt, Edwin Arthur. The Metaphysical Foundations of Modern Physical Science. Rev. ed. London, Routledge and Kegan Paul Ltd., 1932. xi + 343 pp.—In the series International Library of Psychology, Philosophy, and Scientific Method. Original ed. 1924; revised ed. reprinted 1949. "Bibliography," pp. 325–338.

5255. Seligman, Edwin R. A., and Johnson, Alvin, eds. Encyclopaedia of the Social Sciences. New York, Macmillan Co., 1930–35. 15 vols.—Reissue 1937 in 8 vols.

5256. Billington, Ray Allen. The Protestant Crusade 1800–1860. A study of the true origins of American nativism. New York, Macmillan Co., 1938. viii + 514 pp.—"Bibliography," pp. 445–504.

5257. Somervell, D[avid] C. English Thought in the Nineteenth Century. 6th ed. London, Methuen and Co., 1950. xi + 241 pp.—Original ed. 1929.

5258. Hinsie, Leland E., and Shatzky, Jacob. Psychiatric Dictionary. With encyclopedic treatment of modern terms. 2nd ed. with supplement. New York, Oxford Univ. Press, 1953. [xvi] + 781 (double column) pp.—Original ed. 1940.

5259. Gilson, Étienne Henry. History of Christian Philosophy in the Middle Ages. New York, Random House, [1955]. 829 pp.

5260. Cross, F[rank] L. Oxford Dictionary of the Christian Church. Second corrected impression. Oxford Univ. Press, 1958. xix + 1492 (double column) pp.—Original impression 1957.

5261. Leff, Gordon. Medieval Thought. St. Augustine to Ockham. Harmondsworth, Eng., Penguin Books Ltd., 1958. 317 pp.—Number A424 in the series Pelican Books. "Select Bibliography," pp. 305–307.

5262. Watts, Harold H. The Modern Reader's Guide to the Bible. New York, Harper and Bros., 1959. xiii + 544 pp.

5263. Altaner, Berthold. Patrology. Translated by Hildo C. Graef. Freiburg, Herder, [1960]. xxiv + 659 pp.—Original Ger. ed. 1938; current Ger. ed.: *Patrologie*, Leben, Schriften und Lehre der Kirchenväter, 5. Aufl., Freiburg, Herder, 1958, xxvii + 507 pp.

5264. Frankel, Chas., ed. The Golden Age in American Philosophy. Selected and edited with an introduction and notes. New York, George Braziller Inc., 1960. viii + 535 pp.—Orienting selections from Chauncey Wright, Charles Peirce, William James, Josiah Royce, George Santayana, John Dewey, R. B. Perry, C. I. Lewis, and Morris Cohen.

5265. Gilson, Étienne Henry. Elements of Christian Philosophy. Garden City, N.Y., Doubleday and Co., 1960. 358 pp.—"Bibliography," pp. 339–343.

§222. WORLD LITERATURE: HANDBOOKS

[See also §1. Outlines, Annals, and Literary Lexicons.]

5269. Swan, Helena. Who's Who in Fiction? A dictionary of noted names in novels, tales, romances, poetry, and drama. London, George Routledge, 1907. 308 pp.

5270. Brewer, E[benezer] C. The Reader's Handbook of Famous Names in Fiction, Allusions, etc. New ed. rev. London, Chatto and Windus, 1911. viii + 1243 pp.—Original ed. 1885; new ed. rev. reprinted 1925.

5271. Van Tieghem, Paul. Outline of the Literary History of Europe since the Renaissance. Translated from the French by Aimée L. McKenzie. New York, Century Co., 1930. 361 pp.—Original Fr. ed. 1925.

5272. Sharp, R[obert] Farquharson. A Short Biographical Dictionary of Foreign Literature. London, J. M. Dent and Co., 1933. vii + 302 pp.—Number 900 in the series Everyman's Library.

5273. Shipley, Joseph T. Encyclopedia of Literature. New York, Philosophical Library, 1942. 2 (double column page) vols.—Monographic treatments of English and Continental literary figures and literatures.

5274. Brown, Alan W., et al., eds. Classics of the Western World. With a foreword by John Erskine. 3rd ed. Chicago, American Library Association, 1943. 145 pp.—Original ed. 1927. A check list of authors and their works.

5275. Oberholzer, Otto. Kleines Lexikon der Weltliteratur. Bern, A. Franke AG, 1946. 371 pp.—Volume I in the series Kleines literarisches Lexikon in drei Teilen.

5276. Smith, Horatio, ed. Columbia Dictionary of Modern European Literature. New York, Columbia Univ. Press, 1947. xiv + 899 (double column) pp.

5277. Eppelsheimer, Hanns W. Handbuch der Weltliteratur. Erster Band: Von den Anfängen bis zum Ende des achtzehnten Jahrhunderts; Zweiter Band: Neunzehntes und zwanzigstes Jahrhundert. Frankfurt a. M., Vittorio Klostermann, 1947–50. 2 vols.

5278. Spemann, Adolf. Vergleichende Zeittafel der Weltliteratur vom Mittelalter bis zur Neuzeit 1150–1939. Stuttgart, Engelhornverlag, 1951. 160 (double column) pp.

5279. Steinberg, S[igfrid] H., ed. Cassell's Encyclopaedia of World Literature. New York, Funk and Wagnalls Co., 1953. 2 (double column page) vols.—In three parts: histories and literatures of the world and general literary subjects; biographies of authors who died before 1 August 1914; and biographies of authors who were living on 1 August 1914 or who were born after that date.

5280. Barnhart, Clarence L., ed. New Century Cyclopedia of Names. New York, Appleton-Century-Crofts Inc., 1954. 3 (double column page) vols.—Original ed. 1911 as vol. XI of the *Century Dictionary and Cyclopedia.*

5281. Dictionnaire des oeuvres de tous les temps et de tous les pays. Littérature, philosophie, musique, sciences. Paris, Laffont-Bompiani, 1952–55. 4 (double column page) vols. plus a (double column page) index vol.

5282. Romig, Walter. The Guide to Catholic Literature. An author-subject-title index in one straight alphabet of books and booklets in all languages on all subjects by Catholics or of particular Catholic interest. . . . Vol. I: 1888–1940; Vol. II: 1940–1944; Vol. III: 1944–1948; Vol. IV: 1948–1951; Vol. V: 1952–1955. Vols. I–II: Detroit, Walter Romig and Co.; Vols. III–V: Grosse Pointe, Mich., Walter Romig and Co., 1940–55. 5 vols.

5283. Magill, Frank N., and Kohler, Dayton. Masterplots Cyclopedia of World Authors. Vol. I: A–Kao; Vol. II: Kay–Z. New York, Salem Press, 1958. 2 (double column page) vols.—See also Magill and Kohler's earlier *Masterplots,* 510 plots in story form from the world's fine literature, New York, Salem Press, 1949, 2 vols.

§223. WORLD LITERATURE: SURVEYS

5287. Farrar, Clarissa P., and Evans, Austin P. Bibliography of English Translations from Medieval Sources. New York, Columbia Univ. Press, 1946. xiii + 534 pp.—Number 39 in the series Records of Civilization: Sources and Studies.

5288. Baldensperger, Fernand, and Friederich, Werner P. Bibliography of Comparative Literature. Chapel Hill, University of North Carolina, 1950. xxiv + 701 (double column) pp.—Volume I in the series University of North Carolina Studies in Modern Languages and Literatures: III Studies in Comparative Literature.

5289. Hopper, Vincent F., and Grebanier, Bernard D. N. Bibliography of European Literature. Companion to Essentials of European Literature. Great Neck, N.Y., Barron's Educational Series Inc., 1954. xiii + 158 pp.—A list of English translations of European classics.

5290. Tucker, T[homas] G. The Foreign Debt of English Literature. London, George Bell and Sons, 1907. vii + 270 pp.

5291. Croce, Benedetto. European Literature in the Nineteenth Century. Translated from the Italian with introduction by Douglas Ainslee. New York, Alfred Knopf, 1925. 373 pp.—Original It. ed. 1923.

5292. Magnus, Laurie. English Literature in Its Foreign Relations 1300 to 1800. London, Kegan Paul, Trench, Trubner and Co., 1927. xi + 291 pp.

5293. Knowlton, Edgar C. An Outline of World Literature from Homer to the Present Day. New York, Thomas Nelson and Sons, 1929. 391 pp. —Reprint 1937.

5294. Chandler, Frank W. Modern Continental Playwrights. New York, Harper and Bros., 1931. xiii + 711 pp.—"Bibliography," pp. 596–680.

5295. Chadwick, H[ector] Munro and N[ora] Kershaw. The Growth of Literature. Vol. I: The Ancient Literatures of Europe; Vol. II: Russian, Yugoslav, East Indian, Early Hebrew; Vol. III: The Tartars, Polynesia, the Sea Dyaks, African Peoples, and a General Survey. New York, Macmillan Co., 1932–40. 3 vols.

5296. Guérard, Albert L. A Preface to World Literature. New York, Henry Holt and Co., 1940. 458 pp.

5297. Brewster, Dorothy, and Burrell, John Angus. Modern World Fiction. Ames, Iowa, Littlefield, Adams and Co., 1951. [iv] + 220 pp.—Number 18 in the series Littlefield College Outlines. See also Brewster and Burrell's *Modern Fiction,* New York, Columbia Univ. Press, 1934, vii + 442 pp.

5298. Häusermann, H[ans] W. The Genevese Background. Studies of Shelley, Francis Danby, Maria Edgeworth, Ruskin, Meredith, and Joseph Conrad in Geneva, with hitherto unpublished letters. London, Routledge and Kegan Paul Ltd., 1952. x + 224 pp.

5299. Hopper, Vincent F., and Grebanier, Bernard D. N. Essentials of European Literature. A guide to great books. Vol. I: Early Middle Ages to Romantic Movement; Vol. II: Romantic Movement to Present. Great Neck, N.Y., Barron's Educational Series Inc., 1952. 2 vols.

5300. Hutchins, Robt. M., and Adler, Mortimer J. Great Books of the Western World. Chicago, Encyclopaedia Britannica in collaboration with the

Univ. of Chicago, 1952. 54 vols.—Volume I is a discussion of the great books idea; volumes II and III make up the "Syntopicon," an index of 102 great ideas.

5301. Lamm, Martin. Modern Drama. Translated by Karin Elliott. Oxford, Eng., Basil Blackwell, 1952. xx + 359 pp.—Original Swedish ed. 1948.

5302. Auerbach, Erich. Mimesis. The representation of reality in Western literature. Translated from the German by Willard R. Trask. Princeton, N.J., University Press, 1953. [vii] + 563 pp.—"Written in Istambul between May 1942 and April 1945. First published in Bern, Switzerland, 1946, by A. Francke Ltd, Co.," p. [iv].

5303. Curtius, Ernst Robt. European Literature and the Latin Middle Ages. Translated from the German by Willard R. Trask. New York, Pantheon Books Inc., 1953. xviii + 662 pp.—Volume XXXVI in the Bollingen Series. Original Ger. ed. 1948.

5304. Brett-James, Antony. The Triple Stream. Four centuries of English, French, and German literature 1531–1930. Philadelphia, Dufour Editions, 1954. x + 178 pp.—A listing in four chronological columns of literary highlights.

5305. Heiney, Donald W. Essentials of Contemporary Literature. Great Neck, N.Y., Barron's Educational Series Inc., 1954. xviii + 555 pp.—"Bibliography," pp. 505–540.

5306. Horton, Rod W., and Hopper, Vincent F. Backgrounds of European Literature. The political, social, and intellectual development behind the great books of Western civilization. New York, Appleton-Century-Crofts Inc., 1954. xv + 462 pp.—In the series Appleton-Century Handbooks of Literature.

5307. Trawick, Buckner B. World Literature. Vol. I: Greek, Roman, Oriental, and Medieval Classics; Vol. II: Italian, French, Spanish, German, and Russian Literature since 1300. New York, Barnes and Noble Inc., 1953–55. 2 vols.—Numbers 88 and 93 in the series College Outline Series. Reprint 1958.

5308. Priestley, J[ohn] B. Literature and Western Man. New York, Harper and Bros., 1960. xi + 512 pp.

5309. Index translationum. Répertoire international des traductions / International bibliography of translations. New series. Paris, Unesco, 1949–date.—Annual. A development of *Index translationum,* International bibliography of translations, Paris, International Institute of Intellectual Cooperation, 1932–40, quarterly, 7 vols. Arranged by country. Over 65 countries currently represented.

§224. WORLD LITERATURE: GREEK AND ROMAN

[See also §4. English Literature: Classical Influences; §5. Latin Literature Chiefly Medieval: Anglo-Latin and Some General European Titles; §70. Aristotle and Other Ancient Authorities; §132. Mythology and Myth: Handbooks; §133. Mythology and Myth: Studies.]

5313. Palmer, Henrietta R. List of English Editions and Translations of Greek and Latin Classics Printed before 1641. With an introduction by Victor Scholderer. London, Blades, East and Blades, 1911. xxxii + 119 pp.—In the series Bibliographical Society Publications.

5314. Smith, F   Seymour. The Classics in Translation. An annotated guide to the best translations of the Greek and Latin classics into English. Preface by Henry Bartlett Van Hoesen. London, Charles Scribner's Sons, 1930. 307 pp.

5315. Sellar, W[illiam] Y. The Roman Poets of the Republic. 3rd ed. Oxford Univ. Press, 1889. xv + 474 pp.—Original ed. 1863; second ed. 1881; third ed. reissued 1932.

5316. Haigh, A[rthur] E. The Attic Theatre. A description of the stage and theatre of the Athenians and of the dramatic performances at Athens. 2nd ed. Oxford, Clarendon Press, 1898. xv + 420 pp.—Original ed. 1889.

5317. Browne, Henry, S.J. Handbook of Homeric Study. New York, Longmans, Green and Co., 1905. xvi + 333 pp.

5318. Cornford, Francis MacDonald. The Origin of Attic Comedy. London, Edward Arnold, 1914. xii + 252 pp.—Reprint Cambridge Univ. Press, 1934.

5319. D'Alton, J[ohn] F. Horace and His Age. A study in historical background. London, Longmans, Green and Co., 1917. x + 296 pp.

5320. Sikes, E[dward] E. Roman Poetry. London, Methuen and Co., 1923. vii + 280 pp.

5321. Allen, James T. Stage Antiquities of the Greeks and Romans and Their Influence. New York, Longmans, Green and Co., 1927. xii + 206 pp.

5322. Whibley, Leonard. A Companion to Greek Studies. 4th ed. Cambridge Univ. Press, 1931. xxxviii + 790 pp.—Original ed. 1905.

5323. Wright, F[rederick] A., and Sinclair, T[homas] A. A History of Later Latin Literature. From the middle of the fourth to the end of the seventeenth century. London, George Routledge and Sons, 1931. vii + 418 pp.—"Select Bibliography," pp. 401–408.

5324. Sinclair, T[homas] A. A History of Classic Greek Literature. From Homer to Aristotle. London, George Routledge and Sons, 1934. viii + 421 pp.

5325. Flickinger, Roy C. The Greek Theater and Its Drama. 4th ed. University of Chicago Press, 1936. xxviii + 385 pp.—Original ed. 1918; second ed. 1922; third ed. 1926.

5326. Harvey, Paul. Oxford Companion to Classical Literature. Oxford, Clarendon Press, 1937. xv + 468 (double column) pp. + 14 pp. of plates. —Reprint 1955.

5327. Cary, M[ax], Nock, A[rthur] D., et al., eds. Oxford Classical Dictionary. Oxford, Clarendon Press, 1949. xx + 971 (double column) pp.

5328. Rose, H[erbert] J. A Handbook of Latin Literature from the Earliest Times to the Death of St. Augustine. 2nd ed. London, Methuen and Co., 1949. ix + 557 pp.—Original ed. 1934.

5329. Wright, F[rederick] A. Lemprière's Classical Dictionary of Proper Names Mentioned in Ancient Authors. With a chronological table. A new edition, revised with additions, and a short notice of Dr. J[ohn] Lemprière. New York, E. P. Dutton and Co., 1949. xxviii + 675 (double column) pp.—Lemprière's original ed. *Bibliotheca Classica* 1788; reprint of Wright's ed. 1951.

5330. Rose, H[erbert] J. A Handbook of Greek Literature from Homer to the Age of Lucian. 4th ed. London, Methuen and Co., 1950. ix + 454 pp.—Original ed. 1934.

5331. Havelock, E[ric] A. The Crucifixion of Intellectual Man. Incorporating a fresh translation into English verse of the Prometheus Bound of Aeschuylus. Boston, Beacon Press, 1951. ix + 218 pp.—The initial pages are devoted to drama.

5332. Hadas, Moses. A History of Latin Literature. New York, Columbia Univ. Press, 1952. viii + 474 pp.—"Bibliographical Notes," pp. 447–459.

5333. Duff, J[ohn] Wight. A Literary History of Rome. From the origins to the close of the golden age. 3rd ed. New York, Barnes and Noble Inc., 1953. xvi + 535 pp.—Original ed. 1909. "Supplementary Bibliography," pp. 488–512.

5334. Beare, W[illiam]. The Roman Stage. A short history of Latin drama in the time of the Republic. London, Methuen and Co., 1955. xiv + 365 pp.

5335. Arnott, Peter D. An Introduction to the Greek Theatre. With a foreword by H. D. F. Kitto. London, Macmillan Co., 1959. xvi + 240 pp.

§225. WORLD LITERATURE: NORTHERN EUROPEAN

[Belgian literature is grouped in this category.]

5339. Morgan, Bayard Quincy. A Critical Bibliography of German Literature in English Translation 1481–1927. With supplement embracing the years 1928–1935. 2nd ed. Stanford Univ. Press, 1938. xiii + 773 pp. —Original ed. 1922.

5340. Crawford, John Martin. The Kalevala. The epic poem of Finland [translated] into English. New York, John A. Berry and Co., 1888. 2 vols.

5341. Seyn, Eugène de. Dictionnaire des écrivains belges. Bio-bibliographie. Bruges, Excelsior, 1930–31. 2 vols.

5342. Comparetti, Domenico. The Traditional Poetry of the Finns. Translated by Isabella M. Anderton. With an introduction by Andrew Lang. London, Longmans, Green and Co., 1898. xxvii + 359 pp.—Original It. ed. 1891.

5343. Downs, Brian W. Anglo-Dutch Literary Relations 1867–1900. Some notes and tentative inferences. Modern Language Review, XXXI, 3 (July 1936), 289–346.

5344. Tielrooy, Johannes B. Panorama de la littérature hollandaise contemporaine. Paris, Édition du Sagittaire, [1938]. 186 pp.

5345. Hechtle, Martha. Die flämische Dichtung von 1830 bis zur Gegenwart. Jena, E. Diederichs, [1942]. 94 pp.

5346. Closset, François. Aspects et figures de la littérature flamande. 2e éd. Brussels, Office de Publicité, 1944. 110 pp.—Number 26 in the series Collection nationale, 3e série. Original ed. 1943.

5347. Closset, François. La littérature flamande au moyen âge. Brussels, Office de publicité, 1946. 87 pp.—Number 70 in the series Collection nationale, 6e série.

5348. Goris, Jan Albert. Belgian Letters. A short survey of creative writing in the French and Dutch languages in Belgium. 2nd ed. New York, Belgian Government Information Service, 1948. 48 pp.—Number 4 in the series Art, Life, and Science in Belgium. Original ed. 1946.

5349. Bresdorff, Elias, Mortensen, Brita, and Popperwell, Ronald. An Introduction to Scandinavian Literature. Copenhagen, Einar Munksgaard, 1951. 245 pp.

5350. Price, Lawrence M. English Literature in Germany. Berkeley, University of California Press, 1953. viii + 548 pp.—Volume XXXVII in the series University of California Publications in Modern Philology. A development of *The Reception of English Literature in Germany*, Berkeley, University of California Press, 1932, x + 356 pp.

5351. Bithell, Jethro. Germany. A companion to German studies. 5th ed. London, Methuen and Co., 1953. xii + 559 pp.—Original ed. 1932.

5352. Bostock, J[ohn] Knight. A Handbook of Old High German Literature. Oxford Univ. Press, 1955. ix + 257 pp.

5353. Einarsson, Stefán. A History of Icelandic Literature. New York, Johns Hopkins Press for the American-Scandinavian Foundation, 1957. xii + 409 pp.—"Bibliography," pp. 355–362.

5354. Kosch, Wilhelm. Deutsches Literaturlexikon. Biographisches und bibliographisches Handbuch. 2. Aufl. Bern, A. Francke, 1944–58. 4 vols.—Original ed. 1927–30 in 2 vols.

5355. Robertson, J[ohn] G. A History of German Literature. Third ed., rev. and enl. by Edna Purdie with the assistance of W. I. Lucas and M. O'C. Walsche. Edinburgh, William Blackwood and Sons, 1959. xvi + 700 pp.—Original ed. 1902; second ed. 1931.

5356. Weevers, Theodoor. Poetry of the Netherlands in Its European Context 1170–1930. Illustrated with poems in original and translation. University of London, 1960. xiv + 376 pp.—"Select Bibliography," p. 364.

§226. WORLD LITERATURE: ROMANCE

[See also §6. British Literature: Anglo-Norman. For Belgian literature see §225. World Literature: Northern European.]

5360. Bell, Aubrey F. G. Portuguese Bibliography. Oxford Univ. Press, 1922. 381 pp.—Number 1 in the Hispanic Notes and Monographs: Bibliography Series.

5361. Fitzmaurice-Kelly, James. Spanish Bibliography. Oxford Univ. Press, 1925. 389 pp.—In the Hispanic Notes and Monographs: Bibliography Series.

5362. Thieme, Hugo P. Bibliographie de la littérature française de 1800 à 1930. Paris, E. Droz, 1933. 3 vols.—Continuations: S. Dreher and M. Rolli, *Bibliographie de la littérature française, 1930–1939,* Geneva, Droz, 1948–49, xviii + 439 pp., and Marguerite L. Drevet, *Bibliographie de la littérature française 1940–1949,* Geneva, Droz, 1955, xvi + 644 pp.

5363. Palfrey, Thos. R., Fucilla, Joseph G., and Holbrook, Wm. C. A Bibliographical Guide to the Romance Languages and Literatures. Evanston, Ill., Chandler's Inc., 1946. ix + 84 leaves.—Original ed. 1939; second ed. 1940.

5364. Rochedieu, Chas. A. E. Bibliography of French Translations of English Works 1700–1800. Introduction by Donald F. Bond. University of Chicago Press, [1948]. xiii + 387 pp.

5365. Cabeen, David C., ed. A Critical Bibliography of French Literature. Syracuse, N.Y., University Press, 1947–date. 7 vols. (projected).—To date have appeared: Vol. I: *The Medieval Period,* edited by U. T. Holmes, Jr., 1947; Vol. II: *The Sixteenth Century,* edited by A. H. Schutz, 1956; Vol. IV: *The Eighteenth Century,* edited by G. R. Havens and D. F. Bond, 1951.

5366. Loiseau, Arthur. Histoire de la littérature portugaise depuis ses origines jusqu'à nos jours. Paris, E. Thorin, 1886. viii + 404 pp.—"Sources" [French and Portuguese], pp. 401–404.

5367. Hume, Martin. Spanish Influence on English Literature. London, Eveleigh Nash, 1905. xviii + 322 pp.

5368. Post, Chandler Rathfon. Mediaeval Spanish Allegory. Cambridge, Mass., Harvard Univ. Press, 1915. xii + 331 pp.—Volume IV in the series Harvard Studies in Comparative Literature.

5369. Goldberg, Isaac. Brazilian Literature. With a foreword by J. D. M. Ford. New York, Alfred A. Knopf, 1922. xiv + 303 pp.—"Selective Critical Bibliography" [of studies in French, Portuguese, and English], pp. 293–297.

5370. Voretzsch, Carl. Introduction to the Study of Old French Literature. Authorized translation of the third and last German edition by Francis M. DuMont . . . . New York, G. E. Stechert and Co., 1931. xii + 532 pp.—Original Ger. ed. 1905; second Ger. ed. 1913; third Ger. ed. 1925.

5371. Bell, Aubrey F. G. Contemporary Spanish Literature. Rev. ed. New York, A. A. Knopf, 1933. 315 pp.—Original ed. 1925. Bibliography, pp. 289–310.

5372. Waddell, Helen. The Wandering Scholars. 7th ed. London, Constable and Co., 1934. xxviii + 302 pp.—Original ed. 1927. "Bibliography," pp. 275–296. On medieval Latin poets, especially the Goliards.

5373. Riedel, F[rederick] Carl. Crime and Punishment in the Old French Romances. New York, Columbia Univ. Press, 1938. viii + 197 pp.—Number 135 in the series Columbia University Studies in English and Comparative Literature. "Bibliography," pp. 179–186.

5374. Fisher, Fay. Narrative Art in Medieval Romances. Cleveland, Western Reserve Univ. Press, 1939. [vi] + 122 pp.—Concentration on Old French romance.

5375. Torres-Rioseco, Arturo. The Epic of Latin American Literature. New York, Oxford Univ. Press, 1942. vii + 279 pp.

5376. Peña, Carlos González. History of Mexican Literature. Rev. ed. Translated by Gusta Barfield Nance and Florene Johnson Dunstan. Introduction by Angel Flores. Dallas, Texas, Southern Methodist Univ. Press, 1943. xii + 398 pp.—In the series Inter-American Publications. Original ed. 1928. "Author's Bibliography," pp. 385–386; "Mexican Works in English," pp. 387–388.

5377. Putnam, Samuel. Marvelous Journey. A survey of four centuries of Brazilian writing. New York, Alfred A. Knopf, 1948. xvi + 269 + xii pp.—"Bibliography" [of studies in Portuguese, French, and English], pp. 260–269.

5378. Torres-Rioseco, Arturo. New World Literature. Tradition and revolt in Latin America. Berkeley, University of California Press, 1949. [vii] + 250 pp.

5379. Bacon, Leonard. The Lusiads of Luiz de Camões. With an introduction and notes. New York, Hispanic Society of America, 1950. xxxv + 435 pp.

5380. Pauphilet, Albert. Le legs du moyen âge. Études de littérature médiévale. Melun, Librairie d'Argences, 1950. 249 pp.—In the series Bibliothèque elzévirienne / nouvelle série: études et documents.

5381. Mazzoni, Guido. Avviamento allo studio critico delle lettere italiane. 4. ed. riveduta e aggiornata per cura di Carmine Jannacó . . . . Florence, Sansoni, 1951. xvi + 238 pp.—Volume III in the series Manuali di filologia e storia, ser. 2. Original ed. 1892.

5382. Turnell, Martin. The Novel in France. Mme. de la Fayette, Laclos, Constant, Stendhal, Balzac, Flaubert, Proust. New York, New Directions, [1951]. xv + 432 pp.—Reprint New York, Vintage Books, 1958, xiv + 447 + vii pp., number K62 in the series Vintage Books.

5383. Lanson, Gustave. Histoire de la littérature française. Remaniée et complétée pour la période 1850–1950 par Paul Tuffrau. Paris, Hachette, [1952]. xviii + 1441 pp.

5384. Frank, Grace. The Medieval French Drama. Oxford Univ. Press, 1954. x + 296 pp.—"List of Books," pp. 273–288.

5385. Hale, J[ohn] R. England and the Italian Renaissance. The growth of interest in its history and art. London, Faber and Faber Ltd., 1954. 216 pp.

5386. Fusco, Enrico M. Scrittori e idee. Dizionario critico della letteratura italiana. Turin, Società Editrice Internazionale, 1956. xii + 626 pp.

5387. Braun, Sidney. Dictionary of French Literature. New York, Philosophical Library, 1958. xv + 362 pp.

5388. Donovan, Richard B., C.S.B. The Liturgical Drama in Medieval Spain. Toronto, Pontifical Institute of Mediaeval Studies, 1958. [vii] + 229 pp.—Number 4 in the series Studies and Texts of the Pontifical Institute of Mediaeval Studies. "Bibliography," pp. 200–222.

5389. Harvey, Paul, and Heseltine, J[anet] E., eds. Oxford Companion to French Literature. Oxford, Clarendon Press, 1959. x + 775 (double column) pp.

§227. WORLD LITERATURE: EASTERN EUROPEAN

5393. Harkins, Wm. E. Bibliography of Slavic Folk Literature. New York, King's Crown Press, 1953. 28 pp.—In the series Columbia Slavic Studies.

5394. Morfill, W[illiam] R. Slavonic Literature. London, S.P.C.K., 1883. viii + 264 pp.—In the series Dawn of European Literature.

5395. Wilson, C[harles] T. Russian Lyrics in English Verse. London, Trübner and Co., 1887. xvi + 244 pp.—Biographical sketches of each poet.

5396. Francis, Count Lützow. [Franz Heinrich Hieronymus Valentin, Graf von Lützow.] A history of Bohemian Literature. New York, D. Appleton and Co., 1899. ix + 425 pp.—In the series Literatures of the World.

5397. Horváth, C[yrill], Kardos, A[lbert], and Endrödi, A. [i.e. Sandor]. Histoire de la littérature hongroise. Ouvrage adapté du Hongrois par I. Kont. Avec une préface de M. Gaston Boissier. Budapest, "Athenaeum" Soc. Anon., 1900. xii + 420 pp.

5398. Brückner, A[lexander]. Geschichte der polnischen Literatur. Leipzig, C. F. Amelangs Verlag, 1901. vii + 628 pp.—In the series Literatur des Ostens in Einzeldarstellungen.

5399. Wiener, Leo. Anthology of Russian Literature. From the earliest period to the present time. Vol. I: From the tenth century to the close of the eighteenth century; Vol. II: The nineteenth century. New York, G. P. Putnam's Sons, 1902–03. 2 vols.

5400. Riedl, Frederick. A History of Hungarian Literature. Preface by C. Hagberg Wright. New York, D. Appleton and Co., 1906. ix + 293 pp. —In the series Short Histories of the Literatures of the World.

5401. Jelinek, H[anuš]. La Littérature tchèque contemporaine. Avec une préface de Ernest Denis. Paris, Mercure de France, 1912. 366 pp.— "Cours professé à la Sorbonne en 1910." "Bibliographie" [in French, English, and German], pp. 361–364.

5402. Noyes, Geo. Rapall, and Bacon, Leonard. Heroic Ballads of Servia. Translated into English verse. Boston, Sherman, French and Co., 1913. [vii] + 275 pp.

5403. Dyboski, Roman. Periods of Polish Literary History. Oxford Univ. Press, 1923. 163 pp.—The Ilchester Lectures 1923.

5404. Chudoba, F[rantišek]. A Short Survey of Czech Literature. London, Kegan Paul, Trench, Trübner and Co., 1924. vii + 280 pp.—"Bibliography" [of studies in English], pp. 273–276.

5405. Dyboski, Roman. Modern Polish Literature. Oxford Univ. Press, 1924. 131 pp.—A course of lectures delivered in the School of Slavonic Studies, King's College, University of London.

5406. Wiener, Leo. The Contemporary Drama of Russia. Boston, Little, Brown and Co., 1924. ix + 276 pp.—In the Contemporary Drama Series. "Authors and Plays," pp. 191–242; "Book List," pp. 242–260.

5407. Selver, Paul. An Anthology of Czechoslovak Literature. Selected and translated with an introduction. London, Kegan Paul, Trench, Trubner and Co., 1929. xv + 302 pp.

5408. Simmons, Ernest J. English Literature and Culture in Russia 1553–1840. Cambridge, Mass., Harvard Univ. Press, 1935. xi + 357 pp.—Volume XII in the series Harvard Studies in Comparative Literature.

5409. Mirsky, D[mitrii] S. A History of Russian Literature. Comprising A History of Russian Literature and Contemporary Russian Literature. Edited and abridged by Francis J. Whitfield. New York, Alfred A. Knopf, 1949. xi + 518 + xxiv (double column) pp.—"Short English Bibliography," pp. 517–518. See also Mirsky's *A History of Russian Literature from Its Beginnings to 1900,* New York, Alfred A. Knopf, 1958, x + 383, xviii, number K67 in the series Vintage Books.

5410. Borland, Harriet. Soviet Literary Theory and Practice during the First Five Year Plan 1928–32. New York, King's Crown Press, 1950. xii + 256 pp.—"Bibliography" [chiefly of studies in English], pp. 229–242.

5411. Struve, Gleb. Soviet Russian Literature 1917–50. Norman, University of Oklahoma Press, 1951. xvii + 414 pp.—"Bibliography" [chiefly of studies in English], pp. 373–400.

5412. Lavrin, Janko. Russian Writers. Their lives and literature. New York, D. Van Nostrand Co., 1954. v + 363 pp.—"Short Bibliography of Works in English and French," pp. 351–358.

5413. Kridl, Manfred. A Survey of Polish Literature and Culture. Translated from the Polish by Olga Scherer-Virski. New York, Columbia Univ. Press, 1956. xi + 525 pp.—In the series Columbia Slavic Studies.

5414. Harkins, Wm. E. Dictionary of Russian Literature. London, Allen and Unwin, 1957. vi + 439 pp.—In the series Midcentury Reference Library.

5415. Slonim, Marc. An Outline of Russian Literature. Oxford Univ. Press, 1958. [v] + 253 pp.—Number 236 in the series Home University Library of Modern Knowledge. "Bibliographical Notes," pp. 241–248.

5416. Zavalishin, Vyacheslav. Early Soviet Writers. New York, Frederick A. Praeger Publ'ers, 1958. ix + 394 pp.—Number 20 in the series Studies of the Research Program on the U.S.S.R. and no. 66 in the series Praeger Publications in Russian History and World Communism.

5417. Poggioli, Renato. The Poets of Russia 1890–1930. Cambridge, Mass., Harvard Univ. Press, 1960. xxi + 383 pp.—"General Bibliography" (English and Russian titles), pp. 345–367.

§228. WORLD LITERATURE: JEWISH, ARABIC, AND ORIENTAL

5421. Chauvin, Victor C. Bibliographie des ouvrages arabes ou relatifs aux Arabes publiés dans l'Europe chrétienne de 1810 à 1885. Liége, H. Vaillant-Carmanne, 1892–1922. 12 parts in 7 vols.

5422. Storey, C[harles] A. Persian Literature. A bio-bibliographical survey. London, Luzac and Co., 1927–53. 1443 pp.

5423. Aston, W[illiam] G. A History of Japanese Literature. New York, D. Appleton and Co., 1899. xi + 408 pp.—Reprint 1933.

5424. Giles, Herbert A. A History of Chinese Literature. London, W. Heinemann, 1901. viii + 448 pp.—Reprint New York, Grove Press, 1958. "Bibliographical Note," pp. 441–442.

5425. Smith, Geo. Adam. The Early Poetry of Israel in Its Physical and Social Origins. Oxford Univ. Press for the British Academy, 1912. xi + 102 pp.—The Schweich Lectures. Reprint 1927.

5426. Sencourt, Robt. India in English Literature. London, Simpkin, Marshall, Hamilton, Kent and Co., [1923]. xvi + 468 pp.

5427. Browne, Edward G. A Literary History of Persia. London, T. Fisher Unwin, 1906–24. 4 vols.—Reprint Cambridge Univ. Press, 1928.

5428. Keith, A[rthur] Berriedale. The Sanskrit Drama in Its Origin, Theory, and Practice. Oxford, Clarendon Press, 1924. 405 pp.

5429. Keith, A[rthur] Berriedale. A History of Sanskrit Literature. Oxford, Clarendon Press, 1928. xxxvi + 575 pp.

5430. Nicholson, Reynold A. A Literary History of the Arabs. 2nd ed. Cambridge Univ. Press, 1930. xxxi + 506 pp.—Original ed. 1907; second ed. reprinted 1953.

5431. Petrov, D[mitrii] K., ed. A Book Containing the Risāla, Known as the Dove's Neckring, about Love and Lovers, Composed by Abū Muhammad 'Alī ibn Hazm al-Andalusi. Translated from the unique manuscript in the University of Leiden . . . by Alois Richard Nykl. Paris, P. Geuthner, 1931. cxxiv + 244 pp.—See also Nykl's *Hispano-Arabic Poetry*, no. 1238.

5432. Winternitz, Moriz. A History of Indian Literature. Translated by Mrs. S. Ketkar. Calcutta, University Press, 1927–33. 2 vols.—Original Ger. ed. 1908–22 in 3 vols. Coverage of Vedic literature.

5433. Leftwich, Joseph. The Golden Peacock. An anthology of Yiddish poetry. Cambridge, Mass., Sci-Art Publ'ers, 1939. lviii + 910 pp.

5434. Waxman, Meyer. A History of Jewish Literature. From the close of the Bible to our own days. Vol. I: From the Close of the Canon to the

End of the Twelfth Century, 2nd ed. rev. and enl.; Vol. II: From the Twelfth Century to the Middle of the Eighteenth Century; Vol. III: From the Middle of the Eighteenth Century to the Year Eighteen-Eighty; Vol. IV: From Eighteen-Eighty to Nineteen-Thirty-Five. New York, Block Publ'ing Co., 1938–41. 4 vols.—Original ed. 1930 of vol. I. Each volume concludes with a bibliography.

5435. Kokusai, Bunka Shinkokai, ed. Introduction to Classic Japanese Literature. Tokyo, Kokusai Bunka Shinkokai (The Society for International Cultural Relations), 1948. xxi + 443 pp.—Reprint 1956. An anthology of synopses.

5436. Gaster, Theodor H. Thespis. Ritual, myth, and drama in the ancient Near East. Foreword by Gilbert Murray. New York, Henry Schuman, 1950. xv + 498 pp.

5437. Ringgren, Helmer. Fatalism in Persian Epics. Uppsala, Lundequistska Bokhandeln, [1952]. 133 pp.

5438. Arberry, Arthur John. Classical Persian Literature. New York, Macmillan Co., [1958]. 464 pp.

INDEX OF AUTHORS, EDITORS, Etc.

[References are to individual entries by number, not by page. For subject index see p. 465]

579

SUBJECT INDEX

[Numbers are section numbers.]